Proceedings of the Twelfth International CODATA Conference

Data for Discovery

15–19 July 1990
Columbus, Ohio, U.S.A.

Edited by

Phyllis Sloane Glaeser

Executive Secretary
Committee on Data for Science and Technology (CODATA)
Paris

begell house

DATA FOR DISCOVERY

Library of Congress Cataloging-in-Publication Data

International CODATA Conference (12th: 1990: Columbus, Ohio)
Data for Discovery: proceedings of the Twelfth International CODATA Conference, 15–19 July 1990, Columbus, Ohio, U.S.A. / edited by Phyllis Sloane Glaeser.
p. cm.
Includes bibliographical references and index.
ISBN 1-56700-002-9: $110.00
1. Data base management—Congresses. 2. Science—Data bases—Congresses. 3. Technology—Data bases—Congresses. I. Glaeser, Phyllis S. II. Title.
QA76.9.D31553 1990
502′.85′574—dc20

92-34429
CIP

TABLE OF CONTENTS

PREFACE

Since 1968 the ICSU Committee on Data for Science and Technology has held a conference every two years to bring together individuals concerned with the evaluation, storage, and dissemination of scientific and technical data. These conferences have provided an opportunity for those concerned with data in various disciplines of science, as well as specialists in information technology, to exchange ideas and report on recent developments. The conferences have formed one of the key mechanisms by which CODATA carries out its mission to improve the quality, reliability, management, and accessibility of data of importance to all fields of science and technology.

The Twelfth International CODATA Conference was held in Columbus, Ohio, July 15-19, 1990, and was attended by over 300 scientists from 26 countries. This volume contains selected papers of long-term value prepared by some of the speakers at the Conference.

A major theme of the Conference was the data requirements for the rapidly growing studies of man's impact in the biosphere and geosphere. Research on global change is data-intensive; observations of the earth's surface from satellites, geological studies of long-term climate changes, and monitoring of the constituents of the atmosphere and oceans generate enormous quantities of data. Other data from the physical and biological sciences are needed as input to models for predicting environmental changes. The first section of this volume contains papers dealing with plans and programs for the quality control, storage, generation, dissemination, and use of the data involved in major aspects of global change.

The second section of the book contains papers on generic aspects of data handling, including expert systems, storage and retrieval strategies, and knowledge tools. New developments in information technology which may have application to various types of scientific data management are discussed. Subsequent sections deal with database developments in specific scientific fields, particularly in materials science, chemistry and chemical engineering, and molecular biology. Finally, there are several papers reviewing CODATA's role in international data management programs.

We are greatly indebted the Scientific Program Committee, the Local Organizing Committee in Columbus, and the numerous sponsors who made this Conference possible. We hope that the broader scientific community will find the papers in this volume both interesting and useful.

David R. Lide
President of CODATA, 1986-1990

EDITOR'S NOTE

This volume which contains only 50 of the 110 papers presented at the 12th International CODATA Conference, nonetheless gives a flavor of the stimulation that took place in Columbus in July 1990 and details some of the highlights.

Thanks in great part to the contagious enthusiasm and energy of Dr. Margaret Courain as International Scientific Program Chairman, the program of this Conference reflected the importance of scientific data within a broadened scientific context and the first section of the book brings this out on a global scale.

The Closing Session of the Conference found at the end of the book is of special interest in giving a perspective of data, past, present and future and it was a special pleasure to have been able to include the wonderful *History of Data* by Jack Westbrook which we have reprinted in its entirety.

I would like to take this opportunity to thank the local Organizing Committee in Ohio for their excellent facilities and help during the Conference, especially Mr. George Minot, who quietly and efficiently ensured that the CODATA Secretariat worked under optimum conditions, as well as Gerard Platau, Chip Brenner and Emmett Crawley.

In editing this book, I was fortunate to have had the careful and diligent proofreading of Dr. E.R. Cohen, the assistance of Dr. David Lide and Edgar F. Westrum, Jr., and typing assistance from Jordan Berger and Jessica Cashdan.

I hope the readers will not hesitate to contact the authors for additional information and refer back to *CODATA Bulletins* for complete abstracts and additional papers from the Conference.

Lastly, I express my thanks to the authors who delivered the papers and the session chairmen who animated the discussions.

Phyllis Sloane Glaeser
Editor

Paris, June 1992

INTERNATIONAL SCIENTIFIC PROGRAM COMMITTEE

Chairman:	
Dr. Majorie E. Courain	United States of America
Members:	
Prof. D. Abir	Israel
Prof. S. Alexander	United States of America
Dr. H. Behrens	Federal Republic of Germany
Prof. J.-E. Dubois	France
Dr. M.I. Krichevsky	United States of America
Prof. F.A. Kuznetsov	U.S.S.R.
Prof. A. Tsugita	Japan
Dr. J.R.G. Townshend	United Kingdom

LOCAL ORGANIZING COMMITTEE

Dr. G.O. Platau, Chairman
Chemical Abstracts Service
Mr. G.M. Minot, Business Agent
Applied Information Technologies Research Center
Mr. H. Mindlin
Battelle Memorial Institute
Dr. M. Muller
The Ohio State University
Dr. J.A. Price
Ashland Chemical, Inc.
Mr. R.P. Root
CompuServe Incorporated
Mr. D.L. Trotier
OCLC Online Computer Library Center, Inc.

CODATA EXECUTIVE COMMITTEE

Officers:

Dr. D.R. Lide, Jr., President
Prof. A. Bylicki, Vice-President
Prof. L.V. Gurvich, Vice-President
Prof. A.E. Bussard, Secretary General
Mr. J. Crease, Treasurer

Elected Members:

Prof. D. Abir (Israel)
Prof. C.B. Alcock (Canada)
Dr. H. Behrens (F.R.G.)
Prof. J.-E. Dubois (France)
Prof. I.L. Khodakovsky (U.S.S.R.)
Prof. R.J. Simpson (Australia)
Prof. R. Sinding-Larsen (I.U.G.S.)
Prof. A. Tsugita (Japan)

Secretariat:
Mrs. P. Glaeser, Executive Secretary

ACKNOWLEDGEMENTS

CODATA gratefully acknowledges support for the Conference from:

- Applied Information Technologies Research Center
- Ashland Chemical, Inc.
- Battelle Memorial Institute
- Bricker & Eckler
- Central Ohio Transit Authority (COTA)
- Chemical Abstracts Service
- City of Columbus, Ohio
- Columbia Gas of Ohio Inc.
- The Columbus Area Chamber of Commerce
- CompuServe Incorporated
- Committee on Earth and Environment Sciences Working Group on Global Change
- Coopers & Lybrand
- CRC Press
- Dialog Information Services, Inc.
- EBSCO Industries Inc.•
- E.I. Du Pont de Nemours & Co.
- Foster Wheeler Development Corporation
- Huntington National Bank
- Information Dimensions, Inc.
- International Plastics Selector
- McElroy-Minister Company
- National Institute of Standards and Technology (U.S.) Office of Standard Reference Data
- National Library of Medicine (U.S.)
- National Science Foundation
- OCLC Online Computer Library Center, Inc.
- Officescapes
- The Ohio State University
- Ohio's Thomas Edison Program
- Springer-Verlag New York, Inc.
- STN International
- TRW Inc.
- U.S. Department of Energy Office of Scientific and Technical Information (OSTI)
- XEROX Corporation
- XEROX Corporation, Mid-Ohio District

LIST OF PARTICIPANTS

(addresses corrected in June 1992)

Abel, Dr. David J., Center for Spatial Information Systems, CSIRO Division of Information Technology, GPO Box 664, Canberra ACT. 2601, Australia

Abir, Prof. David, Faculty of Engineering, Tel Aviv University, Ramat Aviv, Tel Aviv 69978, Israel

Agena, Joey Albert, AIBA/SEARCA, 4031 College, Laguna 3720, France

Alcock, Prof. C.B., Center for Sensor Materials, University of Notre Dame, 114 Cushing Hall, Notre Dame, IN 46556, U.S.A.

Alemasov, Prof. Viatcheslav, Presidiem, Kazan Aviation Institute, Russian Academy of Science, Karl Marx Street, 420084 Kazan, Russia

Alexander, Dr. S., College of Earth and Mineral Sciences, Department of Geosciences, 503 Deike Building, University Park, PA 16802, U.S.A.

Alexandrov, Prof. A.A., Institute of Molecular Genetics, Russian Academy of Sciences, Kurchatov Sqv., Moscow 123182, Russia

Allan, Ferne C., Sandia National Laboratories, Org. 3144, P.O. Box 5800, Albuquerque, NM 87185-5800, U.S.A.

Andrick, Barb, Onlinc Computer Library Center, 6565 Frantz Road, Dublin, OH 43017, U.S.A.

Aoto, Kazumi, Materials Development Section, Power Reaction & Nuclear Fuel Development Corporation, 4002 Narita, Oarai-machi, Higashi-Ibaraki-gun, Ibaraki 311-13, Japan

Areskoug, Magnus, Swedish Materials Information, P.O. Box 5506, 114 85 Stockholm, Sweden

Arora, Dr. J.R., Director, Bioinformatics Division, Department of Biotechnology, Ministry of Science & Technology, Block 2, 7th Floor, C.G.O. Complex, Lodi Road, New Delhi 110003, India

Bale, Prof. Chris W., Co-Directeur, Centre de Recherche en Calcul Thermochimique, Ecole Polytechnique de Montréal, C.P. 6079, Succursale "A", Montréal, Québec, H3C 3A7, Canada

Bardinet, Dr. Claude, Ecole Normale Supérieure, 45, rue d'Ulm, Paris 75230 Cédex 05, France

Barker, Dr. Winona C., National Biomedical Research Foundation, Georgetown University Medical Center, 3900 Reservoir Road N.W., Washington, D.C. 20007, U.S.A.

Barrett, Dr. A.J., Information Development International, P.O. Box 166, Chalfont Street Giles, Bucks HP8 4JG, United Kingdom

Barth, Dr. Andreas, STN International/Fachinformationszentrum Karlsruhe, D-7514 Eggenstein-Leopoldshafen 2, Germany

Baumgardner, Prof. Marion F., Professor of Agronomy, Lilly Life Sciences, Purdue University, West Lafayette, IN 47907-7899, U.S.A.

Begell, Dr. William, Begell House, Inc., 79 Madison Avenue, New York, NY 10016, U.S.A.

Behrens, Dr. Heinrich, Fachinformationszentrum Karlsruhe, D-7514 Eggenstein-Leopoldshafen 2, Germany

Beiter, P. William, Owens-Corning Fiberglass, 2790 Columbus Road, Route 16, Granville, OH 43023-1200, U.S.A.

Bengtson, Ulf, Bergsskolan I Filipstad, Box 173, S-682 01 Filipstad, Sweden

Benjamin, Bruce, Chemical Abstracts Service, Box 301, Columbus, OH 43210, U.S.A.

Bergerhoff, Dr. Geunter, Institute for Inorganic Chemistry, Gerhard-Domagk-Str. 1, D-5300 Bonn 1, Germany

Bernstein, Amira, Chemical Abstracts Service, 2540 Olentangy Road, Columbus, OH 43210, U.S.A.

Bestougeff, Prof. H., U.F.R. d'Informatique, Université de Paris VII, 2 place Jussieu, 75251 Paris Cédex 05, France

Bisby, Dr. Frank A., Department of Biology, School of Biological Sciences, University of Southampton, Bassett Crescent East, Southampton, SO9 3TU, United Kingdom

Blaine, Lois, Hybridoma Data Bank, American Type Culture Collection, 12301 Parklawn Drive, Rockville, MD 20852-1776, U.S.A.

Blower, Paul E., Chemical Abstracts Service, 2540 Olentangy Road, Columbus, OH 43210, U.S.A.

Boden, Thomas A., Carbon Dioxide Information Analysis Center, Environmental Science Division, Oak Ridge National Laboratory, Oak Ridge, TN 37831-6335, U.S.A.

Borhidi, Prof. Attila Lajos, Janus Pannonius University, Faculty of Human & Natural Sciences, Dean, H-7624 Pécs, Ifjusag u. 6., Hungary

Brandstätter, Dipl.-Ing. Anni, Gesellschaft für Mathematik & Datenverarbeitung mbH (GMD), Projektträger Fachinformation (PTF), Dolivostr. 15, D-6100 Darmstadt, Germany

Brenner, Chip, Chemical Abstracts Service, 2540 Olentangy Road, Columbus, OH 43210, U.S.A.

Brody, James K., Executive Editor, CRC Press, 2000 Corporate Boulevard N.W., Boca Raton, FL 33431, U.S.A.

Broff, Nancy, Battelle Memorial Institute, 505 King Avenue, Columbus, OH 43201, U.S.A.

Bros, Prof. Jean Pierre, Université de Provence, Marseille, France

Buckel, Walter, FIZ Karlsruhe, P.O. Box 2465, 75 Karlsruhe 1, Germany

Burgeson, Nancy, International Plastics Selector, 8977 Activity Road, PO Box 26875, San Diego, CA 92126, U.S.A.

Bussard, Prof. Alain E., CERDIC-HDB, c/o C.I.C.A., 2229 route des Crêtes, Sophia Antipolis, 06560 Valbonne, France

Butrum, Dr. Rita, 4082 Norbeck Square Drive, Rockville, MA 20853, U.S.A.

Büyükkoca, Dr. Edip, Department of Chemical Engineering, Yildiz University, Abide i Hürriyet Cad., Sisli, Istanbul, Turkey

Buzahkalova, Natalie, Hemisphere Publishing Corporation, 79 Madison Avenue, New York, NY 10016, U.S.A.

Bylicki, Prof. Andrzej, Institute of Physical Chemistry, Polish Academy of Sciences, ul. Kasprzaka 44/52, 01224 Warsaw, Poland

Caliste, Jean-Pierre, Laboratoire National D'Essais, 1, rue Gaston Boissier, 75015 Paris, France

Campbell, Peter A., Argonne National Laboratory/EID, 9700 S. Cass Avenue, Building 362/3F, Argonne, IL 60439, U.S.A.

Carter, Judi Ann, Department of Motor Vehicles, Commonwealth of Virginia, P.O. Box 27412, Richmond, VA 23269-0001, U.S.A.

Carter, Dr. G.C. "Cynthia", U.S. Department of Energy, Division of Advanced Energy Projects, ER-16, GTN, Washington, D.C. 20585, U.S.A.

Chandrasekaran, Prof. B., Laboratory for Artificial Intelligence Research, Department of Computer & Information Science, The Ohio State University, 216 Bolz Hall, 2036 Neil Avenue Mall, Columbus, OH 43210-1277, U.S.A.

Chase, Dr. Malcolm W., National Institute of Standards & Technology, Standard Reference Data Program, Physics Building, Room A323, Gaithersburg, MD 20899, U.S.A.

Chiang, Katherine Shen, Computer Files Librarian, Albert R. Mann Library, Cornell University, Ithaca, NY 14853-4301, U.S.A.

Chihara, Dr. Hideaki, Japan Association for International Chemical Information (JAICI), Gakkai Center Building, 2-4-16 Yayoi, Bunkyo-ku, Tokyo 113, Japan

Chinnery, Dr. Michael A., National Oceanographic & Atmospheric Administraton (NOAA E/GC), 325 Broadway, Boulder, CO 80303, U.S.A.

Clor, Mary , National Materials Property Data Network, Inc., (c/o Chemical Abstracts Service) 2540 Olentange River Road, P.O. Box 02224, Columbus, OH 43202, U.S.A.

Cohen, Dr. E. Richard, Rockwell International Science Center, P.O. Box 1085, 1049 Camino Dos Rios, Thousand Oaks, CA 91360, U.S.A.

Cosmides, Dr. George J., Specialized Information Services, National Library of Medicine, 8600 Rockville Pike, Bethesda, MD 20894, U.S.A.

Courain, Dr. M.E., 420 Harding Drive, South Orange, NJ 07079, U.S.A.

Crawley, Emmett L., Chemical Abstracts Service, 2540 Olentangy Road, Columbus, OH 43210, U.S.A.

Crease, James, College of Marine Studies, University of Delaware, 700 Pilottown Road, Lewes, Deleware 19958-1298, U.S.A.

Cross, Kevin P., Chemical Abstracts Service, 2540 Olentangy Road, Columbus, OH 43210, U.S.A.

Cverna, Fran, ASM International, Route 87, Materials Park, OH 44073, U.S.A.

De Maeyer, Prof. Leo C.M., Max-Planck-Institute für Biophysikalische Chemie, Am Fassberg, Postfach 2841, 3450 Göttingen-Nikolausberg, Germany

Delcroix, Prof. J.-L., Laboratoire Physique des Plasmas, Bâtiment 212, 91405 Orsay, France

Derrendjeau, Prof. Borris, Institute of Inorganic Chemistry, Russian Academy of Sciences, Lavrent'ev Avenue 3, 630090 Novosibirsk, Russia

Dierk, Sig. F., Online Computer Library Center, 6565 Frantz Road, Dublin, OH 43107, U.S.A.

Dodson, Ann T., Online Computer Library Center, 6565 Frantz Road, Dublin, OH 43107, U.S.A.

Domokos, Dr. Laszlo, Beilstein Institut, Varrentrappstr 40-42, 6 Frankfurt/M, Germany

Dong, Qian, Guest Scientist, NIST, Building 222, Room A158, Gaithersburg, MD 20899, U.S.A.

Doucet, Prof. J.P., Institut de Topologie et de Dynamique des Systèmes, Associé au CNRS, Université Paris VII, 1 rue Guy de la Brosse, 75005 Paris, France

Doyle, Dr. Alan, ECACC, PHLS-CAMR, Porton Down, Salisbury, Wilts, United Kingdom

Drăgan, Dr. George, 2061 Serra Drive, Sterling Heights, MI 48310, U.S.A.

Dredup, Judy, Compuserve, Inc., 5000 Arlington Center Boulevard, Columbus, OH 43220, U.S.A.

Dubois, Prof. Jacques-Emile, ITODYS, Université de Paris VII - CNRS, 1 rue Guy de la Brosse, 75005 Paris, France

Majumder, Prof. D.D., Indian Statistical Institute, 203 Barrackpole Trunk Road, Calcutta, 700035 India

Eckermann, Dr. R., DECHEMA, Postfach 970146, Theodor-Heuss Allée 25, 6000 Frankfurt/Main 97, Germany

El-Sharawy, Hoda A., Science & Technology Information Center (SCITIC), Tabir Street, National Research Center Building, DOKKI, Cairo, Egypt

Fagan, Phoebe, Standard Reference Data, Physics Building, Room A323, Gaithersburg, MD 20899, U.S.A.

Farmer, Dr. Nick A., Chemical Abstracts Service, P.O. Box 3012, 2540 Olentangy River Road, Columbus, OH 43210, U.S.A.

Feilden, Dr. G.B.R., Feilden Associates Ltd., Verlands, Painswick, Gloucesterchire, GL6 6XP, United Kingdom

Fernandez, Dr. R. Noberto, LARS/Purdue University, 214 ENTM, West Lafayette, IN 47907, U.S.A.

Ferrell, Wanda R., Office of Scientific & Technological Information, U.S. Department of Energy, Box 62, Oak Ridge, TN 37831, U.S.A.

Fluck, Dr. Ekkehard, Gmelin-Institute, Postfach 90 04 67, D-6000 Frankfurt(Main) 90, Germany

Friedrichs, Prof. Hans Adolf, Lehrstuhl für Theoretische Hüttenkunde und Metallurgie der Kernbrennstoffe, RWTH, Aachen, Hackhausen 1, 5650 Solingen II, Germany

Fujiwara, Prof. Yuzuru, University of Tsukuba, Institute of Electronics and Information Science, Tsukuba-shi, Ibaraki 305, Japan

Furste, Wesley L., Biochemistry Department, Chemical Abstracts Service, 2540 Olentangy Road, Columbus, OH 43210, U.S.A.

Garrow, Clyde, Chairman, National Committee for Scientific Information, Australian Academy of Science, c/o CSIRO, Information Services Branch, P.O. Box 89, East Melbourne, VIC 3002, Australia

Gaune-Escard, Dr. Marcelle, Université d'Aix-Marseille I, Centre de Saint Jérome, rue Henri Poincaré, 13397 Marseille Cédex 4, France

George, Dr. David G., Protein Identification Resource, National Biomedical Research Foundation, Georgetown University Medical Center, 3900 Reservoir Road, N.W., Washington DC 20007, U.S.A.

Gibson, John K., ECMWF, Shinfield Park, Reading, RG2 9AX, United Kingdom

Glaeser, Phyllis Sloane, Executive Secretary, CODATA Secretariat, 51 Boulevard de Montmorency, 75016 Paris, France

Glasser, Frederick D., Product Development, Chemical Abstracts Service, 2540 Olentangy Road, Columbus, OH 43210, U.S.A.

Golashvili, Tengis, Central Research Institute of Management, Economics and Information (Atominform) of the Department of Nuclear Power and Industry (MAPI), 127434 AD/1-271, Moscow, Russia

Gordon, Dr. William E., Rice University, Department of Space Physics, Weiss School of Natural Sciences, P.O. Box 1892, Houston, TX 77251, U.S.A.

Gough, S. Roger, NRC Canada, Montreal Road (M-55), Ottawa, Ontario, K1A 0S2, Canada

Granot, Dr. Reuven, Interdisciplinary Center for Technical Analysis & Forecasting, Tel Aviv University, Ramat Aviv, 69978 Tel Aviv, Israel

Green, Dr. Mildred R., Technical Database Services, Inc., 10 Columbus Circle, Suite 2300, New York, NY 10019, U.S.A.

Gruebel, Bob, STN International, (c/o Chemical Abstracts Service) 2540 Olentange River Road, P.O. Box 02224, Columbus, OH 43202, U.S.A.

Guigo, Dr. Roderic, Dana-Farber Cancer Institute, MBCRR-Galleria, 44 Binney Street, Boston, MA 02115, U.S.A.

Gurke, Sasha I., MPD Networks, 2540 Olentangy Road, Columbus, OH 43210, U.S.A.

Gurvich, Prof. Lev V., Data Center of Russia, Academy of Sciences on Thermodynamic Properties of Individual Substances (THERMOCENTER), Institute for High Temperatures, Izorskaye Street 13/19, Moscow 127412, Russia

Hall, Dr. John Kendrick, Geological Survey of Israel, 30 Malchei Israel Street, Jerusalem, 95501, Israel

Haller, Huddy B., Defense Technical Information Center, Cameron Station 5A204, Alexandria, VA, U.S.A.

Han, Qunli, UNESCO, SC/ECO, 7, place de Fontenoy, 75700 Paris, France

Hara, Osamu, JAICI, 787 Brittingham Ct., Columbus, OH 43214, U.S.A.

Hart, Pembroke J., National Academy of Sciences, 2101 Constitution Avenue N.W., Washington, D.C. 20418, U.S.A.

Hayamizu, Dr. Kikuko, National Chemical Laboratory for Industry, Tsukuba Research Center, Tsukuba, Ibaraki 305, Japan

Hellner, Prof. Erwin Emil, Institute for Minerology, Phillips University, D-3550 Marburg, Germany

Hendricks, Thomas C., U.S. Food & Drug Administration, Center for Food Safety & Applied Nutrition, 200 C Street S.W., Room 6820 (HFF-8), Washington, D.C. 20204, U.S.A.

Herner, Albert, USDA:ARS:BA:NRI:SRL, Building 011A, Room 165-B, BARC-WEST, Beltsville, MD 20705, U.S.A.

Hitt, Jim, American Ceramic Society, 757 Brooksedge Plaza Drive, Westerville, OH 43081, U.S.A.

Hogan, Jacqueline L., The Ohio State University, 120 W. 18th Avenue, Columbus, OH 43210, U.S.A.

Hufford, Stephen, Information Management & Services Division, Office of Information Resource Management, U.S. Environmental Protection Agency, 401 M Street, S.W., Washington, D.C. 20460, U.S.A.

Ikcheol, Kim, Korea Standards Research Institute, P.O. Box 3, Taejon Science Town, Taejon, Korea

Ilten, Dr. David F., DECHEMA, Theodor-Heuss-Allée 25, D-6000 Frankfurt/Main 97, Germany

Iwata, Prof. Shuichi, Faculty of Engineering, University of Tokyo, 7-3-1 Hongo, Bunkyo-ku, Tokyo 113, Japan

Janicki, Prof. Bernard W., Director for Research, Dana-Farber Cancer Institute, 44 Binney Street, Room 1826, Boston, MA 02115, U.S.A.

Jenkins, Robert, Science, The Nature Conservervancy, 1815 N. Lynn Street, Arlington, VA, U.S.A.

Julien, Paula, Online Computer Library Center, 6565 Frantz Road, Dublin, OH 43017, U.S.A.

Kaaret, Dave R., Copper Development Association, 51 Weaver Street, P.O. Box 1840, Greenwich, CT 03836, U.S.A.

Kanafarski, Lilianna, Royal Institute of Technology, Valhallavagen 81, S-10044 Stockholm, Sweden

Karim, Touati, Ecole Centrale de Paris, 92295 Chatenay-Malabry Cédex, France

Karnes, Sandi, Compuserve, 5000 Arlington Centre Boulevard, Columbus, OH 43220, U.S.A.

Kaufman, J. Gilbert, National Materials Property Data Network, Inc., (c/o Chemical Abstracts Service) 2540 Olentange River Road, P.O. Box 02224, Columbus, OH 43202, U.S.A.

Kaye, Barry, Compuserve, 5000 Arlington Centre Boulevard, Columbus, OH 43220, U.S.A.

Kelly, Maureen C., BIOSIS, 2100 Arch Street, Philadelphia, PA 19103, U.S.A.

Kezer, Barb, Compuserve, 5000 Arlington Centre Boulevard, Columbus, OH 43220, U.S.A.

King, Edmund T., Chemical Abstracts Service, P.O. Box 3012, Columbus, OH 43220, U.S.A.

Koetzle, Dr. Thomas F., Chemistry Department, Brookhaven National Laboratory, Associated Universities, Inc., Upton, NY 11973, U.S.A.

Kolaskar, Prof. A.S., Bioinformatics, DIC, Department of Zoology, University of Poona, Ganeshkhind, Pune 411007, India

Kozlov, Prof. Alexander D., Director, All-Union Research Center on Materials Problems, Gosstandart, 21 Kalyaevskaya, Moscow 103006, Russia

Krichevsky, Dr. Micah I., Microbial Systematics Section, National Institute of Dental Research (NIDR), National Institute of Health (NIH), Park 5 Building, Room 451, Bethesda, MD 20892, U.S.A.

Kunisawa, Dr. Takashi, Research Institute for Biosciences, Science University of Tokyo, 2669 Yamazaki, Noda, Chiba 278, Japan

Kuznetsov, Prof. F.A., Institute of Inorganic Chemistry, Russian Academy of Sciences, Lavrent'ev Avenue 3, 630090 Novosibirsk, Russia

Lal, Dr. Krishan, FNA Deputy Director, National Physical Laboratory, Hillside Road, New Delhi 110 012, India

Lalieu, Dr. M.L. Henri, Library & Information Center of the Royal Netherlands Academy of Arts & Sciences, P.O. Box 41950, 1009 DD Amsterdam, The Netherlands

Langer, Isolde, Springer-Verlag, 175 Fifth Avenue, New York, NY, U.S.A.

Lee, Ke Yup, KRDA, Seodoondong, Suwon, Korea

Lempe, Prof. Dieter A., Technische Huchschule "Carl Schorlemmer", Leuna-Merseburg, Otto-Nuschke-Strasse, Merseburg, 4200, Germany

Levavasseur, Sarah, CODATA, 51, boulevard de Montmorency, 75016 Paris, France

Li, Prof. Senliang, Scientific Database Center, Academia Sinica, Box 2745, Beijing 100080, China

Liang, Bo, Department of Geological Sciences, University of British Columbia, 6339 Stores Road, Vancouver, B.C. V6T 2B4, Canada

Lide, Dr. B.B., National Institute of Standards & Technology, Building 225, Room B110, Gaithersburg, MD 20899, U.S.A.

Lide, Jr., Dr. David R., Office of Standard Reference Data, National Institute of Standards & Technology, Gaithersburg, MD 20899, U.S.A.

Loening, Dr. Kurt L., Topterm, North American Division, P.O. Box 21213, Columbus, OH 43221, U.S.A.

Ludwig, Dr. George H., NASA, CODE SE, Washington, D.C., U.S.A.

Luo, Prof. Baichang, Computing Center, Academia Sinica, P.O. Box 2719, Zhongguancun, Beijing 100080, China

Lynch, Steven Day, Department of Agricultural Engineering, University of Natal, P.O. Box 375, Pietermaritzburg, 3201, Republic of South Africa

Malone, Thomas, St. Joseph's College, West Hartford, CT 06117, U.S.A.

Manosky, Bob, STN International, (c/o Chemical Abstracts Service) 2540 Olentange River Road, P.O. Box 02224, Columbus, OH 43202, U.S.A.

Marsh, Dr. Kenneth N., Thermodynamics Research Center, Texas A&M University System, College Station, TX 77843-3111, U.S.A.

Mason, Dr. David C., NERC Unit for Thematic Information Systems, Department of Geography, Reading University, Whiteknights, Box 227, Reading RG6 2AB, Berks, United Kingdom

McGillivray, George, Division of Information Services, CSIR, P.O. Box 395, 0001 Pretoria, South Africa

McGillivray, Rosemary, Division of Information Services, CSIR, P.O. Box 395, 0001 Pretoria, South Africa

Melton, Dr. Ronald B., Battelle Northwest, P.O. Box 999, Richland, WA 99342, U.S.A.

Menot, George M., Applied Information Technologies Institute, 1880 MacKenzic Drive, Suite 111, Columbus, OH 43220, U.S.A.

Metanomski, Dr. W. Val, Chemical Abstracts Service, 2540 Olentangy Road, Columbus, OH 43210, U.S.A.

Metzler, Heribert, Boehringer Mannheim GMBH, Biochemica Werk Tutzing, Postfach 12 63/64, Tutzing D-8132, Germany

Mindlin, Harold, Battelle Memorial Institute, 505 King Avenue, Columbus, OH 43201, U.S.A.

Moesl, Franz G., UBM Consulting, Kirchwaldstr 1, D-8000 Mueuclen 21, Germany

Moline, Sandra, IT Libraries, 117 Pleasant Street S.E., Minneapolis, MN 55455, U.S.A.

Morrison, Jool L., U.S.G.S., 519 National Center, Reston, VA, U.S.A.

Muller, Dr. Mervin E., Department of Computer and Information Science, The Ohio State University, 2036 Neil Avenue Mall, Columbus, OH 43210, U.S.A.

Naborov, Dr. Ivan Valery, Intermechanic JV, 1 Mitchurinsky Prospect, Moscow 117192, Russia

Naik, Prashant S., Department of Zoology, University of Poona, Ganeshkhind, Pune 411 007, Maharashtra, India

Newton, Crystal H., Materials Science Corporation, 930 Harvest Drive, Blue Bell, PA 19422, U.S.A.

Ni, Jianhua, Commission Integrated Survey Natura, The Chinese Academy of Sciences, P.O. Box 767, Beijing, China

Okamura, Fujio P., National Institute for Research in Inorganic Materials, Namiki 1-1, Tsukuba, Ibaraki 305, Japan

Östberg, Prof. G., University of Lund, Engineering Materials, Box 118, 22100 Lund, Sweden

Owens, Barrie, International Plastics Selector, 8977 Activity Road, PO Box 26875, San Diego, CA 92126, U.S.A.

Padgett, Florence, Associate Publisher, Hemisphere Publishing Corporation, 79 Madison Avenue, New York, NY 10016, U.S.A.

Panaye, Prof. A., Institut de Topologie et de Dynamique des Systèmes, Associé au CNRS, Université Paris VII, 1 rue Guy de la Brosse, 75005 Paris, France

Papitashvili, Dr. Natasha, Soviet Geophysical Committee, Molodezhnaya 3, Moscow 117293, Russia

Pfeiffer, Jr., Edward J., Chemical Abstracts Service, 2540 Olentangy Road, Columbus, OH 43210, U.S.A.

Plateau, Dr. Gerard O., Chemical Abstracts Service, 2540 Olentangy Road, Columbus, OH 43210, U.S.A.

Poleshaev, Prof. V.I., Institute for Problems in Mechanics, Russian Academy of Sciences, Prospect Vernadskogo 101, Moscow 117526, Russia

Pollack, Dr. J.V., Laboratory for Artificial Intelligence Research, Department of Computer and Information Science, The Ohio State University, 2036 Neil Avenue Mall, Columbus, OH 43210-1277, U.S.A.

Poole, David W., Central Research, Mead Corporation, 8th and Hickory Streets, Chillicothe, OH 45601, U.S.A.

Popp, Dr. Heribert, Institute for Phyical and Theoretical Chemistry, Waldgasse 3, 8414 Maxhutte-Haidof, Germany

Popp, Dr. Karlheinz Josef, FIZ Chemie Berlin, Steinplatz 2, 1000 Berlin 12, Germany

Posson, Douglas, U.S. Geological Survey, 12201 Sunrise Valley Drive, MS801, Reston, VA 22092, U.S.A.

Price, Dr. John A., Ashland Chemical, Inc., 5200 Blazer Parkway, Dublin, OH 43017, U.S.A.

Raj, Dr. P.C. Ashok, Bio-Informatics Centre, Indian Agricultural Research Institute, New Delhi, 110067, India

Rasool, Dr. S.I., IGBP-DIS, Université de Paris VI, Tour 26, 4ème étage, Aile 2606, 4 Place de Jussieu,75230 Paris Cédex 05, France

Ratliff, Priscilla, Ashland Chemical, Inc., 5200 Blazer Parkway, Dublin, OH 43017, U.S.A.

Rauch, Laura, Compuserve, 5000 Arlington Centre Boulevard, Columbus, OH 43220, U.S.A.

Réchaussat, Dr. Louis, CERDIC-HBD, c/o C.I.C.A., 2229 routes des Crêtes, Sophia Antipolis, 06560 Valbonne, France

Reynard, Keith W., Wilkinson Consultancy Services, Stable Cottage, Broad Lane, Newdigate, Surrey RH5 5AT, United Kingdom

Rhem, Prof. Dieter, Institut für Organische Chemie, Johann Wolfgang Goethe-Universität, Niederurseler Hang, D-6000 Frankfurt/Main 50, Germany

Ritter, Dr. Edward R., New Jersey Institute of Technology, Chemistry Engineering & Chemistry Department, University Heights, Newark, NJ 07102, U.S.A.

Robins, April, Bureau of the Census, Washington, D.C. 22204, U.S.A.

Root, Robert, Compuserve, Inc., 5000 Arlington Centre Boulevard, Columbus, OH 43220, U.S.A.

Rose, John Brandt, UNESCO, 7, place de Fontenoy, 75700 Paris, France

Rosenblatt, Dr. Gerd M., Lawrence Berkeley Laboratory, Materials Sciences Division, Building 62, Room 205, University of California, Berkeley, CA 94720 U.S.A.

Royer, Dr. Jean-Jacques, Centre de Recherches Pétrographiques et Géochimiques, CNRS, B.P. 20, 15, rue Notre-Dame des Pauvres, 54501 Vandoeuvre-les-Nancy Cédex, France

Rumble, Jr., Dr. John, National Institute of Standards & Technology, A323 Physics Building, Gaithersburg, MD 20899, U.S.A.

Rybakov, Mikhail Anatoly, Intermechanics JV, 1 Mitchurinsky Prospect, Moscow 117192, Russia

Sanduleak, Barbara, Materials Information, ASM International, Materials Park, OH 44073, U.S.A.

Sargent, Dr. Philip Michael, EDRC, Carnegie-Mellon University, Pittsburgh, PA, U.S.A.

Sasabe, Dr. Hiroyuki, Frontier Research Program, RIKEN (The Institute of Physical & Chemical Research), 2-1 Hirosawa, Wako-shi, Saitama 351-01, Japan

Sasaki, Prof. Shin-ichi, Toyohashi University of Technology, Tempaku-cho, Toyohashi 440, Japan

Schenck, Roger J., Chemical Abstracts Service, 2540 Olentangy Road, Columbus, OH 43210, U.S.A.

Schnitzer, Christine, American Ceramic Society, 757 Brooksedge Plaza Drive, Westerville, OH 43081, U.S.A.

Schönholzer, Dr. Peter O., Stuketen Street 6, CH-8332 Rumlikon, Switzerland

Schwarzwalder, Robert N., Engineering Libraries, University of Michigan, 308 Undergraduate Library, Ann Arbor, MI 48109-1185, U.S.A.

Scurr, Erica M., Chemical Abstracts Service, 2540 Olentangy Road, Columbus, OH 43210, U.S.A.

Seals, James V., Chemical Abstracts Service, 2540 Olentangy Road, Columbus, OH 43210, U.S.A.

Seamons, Kent, Graduate Student, University of Illinois, Urbana, IL, U.S.A.

Seavey, Beverly Robin, BioMagResBank (NMR Database), Biochemistry Department, 420 Henry Mall, University of Wisconsin, Madison, WI 53706-1569, U.S.A.

Selover, Jr., Theodore B., Design Institute for Physical Property Data, 3575 Traver Road, Shaker Heights, OH 44122, U.S.A.

Shanbrom, Eileen Marie, Chemical Abstracts Service, 2540 Olentangy Road, Columbus, OH 43210, U.S.A.

Shao, Dr. Kwang-Tsao, Institute of Zoology, Academia Sinica, Nankang, Taipei, Taiwan

Shoemaker, Polly, Battelle Memorial Institute, 505 King Avenue, Columbus, OH 43201, U.S.A.

Silberring, Dr. Ludwig, Silberring Engineering Ltd., Wipkingerplatz 7, P.O.Box 368, CH-8037 Zurich, Switzerland

Sinding-Larsen, Prof. Richard, The Norwegian Institute of Technology, Department of Geology, Hogskoleringen 6, N-7034, Trondheim-NTH, Norway

Sirotyuk, Dr. Vladislav A., MINK 'GEOS', VNII Geoinformsystem, Varshavskoye sh., 8, Moscow 113105, Russia

Skevington, Joe, Chemical Abstracts Service, P.O. Box 3012, Columbus, OH 43210, U.S.A.

Smith, Prof. F.J., Computer Science Department, The Queen's University, Belfast, Ireland BT7 1NN

Smith, Ken, University of Illinois, 502 W. Main Street, #319, Urbana, IL, U.S.A.

Songstad, Virginia H., Chemical Abstracts Service, P.O. Box 3012, Columbus, OH 43210, U.S.A.

Srivastava, Sudhir, National Cancer Institute, 9000 Rockville Pike, Bethesda, MD 20853, U.S.A.

Stein, Dimitri R., Scientific Information Service, Inc., 7 Woodland Avenue, Larchmont, NY 10538, U.S.A.

Steiner, John, STN International, (c/o Chemical Abstracts Service) 2540 Olentange River Road, P.O. Box 02224, Columbus, OH 43202, U.S.A.

Stemne, Lennart David, Bergaskolan I Filipstad, Box 173, S-682 01 Filipstad, Sweden

Stokke, Per R., VISTA, Drammensvelen 78, 0271, Oslo 2, Norway

Sugawara, Dr. Hideaki, WDC/RIKEN, 2-1 Hirosawa, Wako-shi, Saitama 351-01, Japan

Sun, Prof. Jiulin, Commission Integrated Survey Natura, The Chinese Academy of Sciences, P.O. Box 767, Beijing, China

Swindells, Dr. Norman, Touchstone International, 14 Mere Farm Road, UK-Meryside, L43 9TT, United Kingdom

Takeyama, Shozo, Okayama College of Commerce, 2-10-1, Tsushihakyomachi, Okayama-shi, Japan

Thacher, Dr. Peter, World Resources Institute, 54 Gold Street, Stonington, CT 06378, U.S.A.

Thieman, James Richard, National Centers for Earth & Space Science Data, Code 936, NASA, Goddard Space Flight Center, Greenbelt, MD 20771, U.S.A.

Thomas, Bob, Database Coordinator & Exhibits Manager, Communications Department, Battelle Colombus Laboratories, Battelle Memorial Institute, 505 King Avenue, Columbus, OH 43201, U.S.A.

Tichler, Joyce L., Brookhaven National Laboratory, Building 051, Upton, NY 11973, U.S.A.

Trinity, Philip M., Chemical Abstracts Service, 2540 Olentangy River Road, Columbus, OH 43210, U.S.A.

Tscherning, Prof. Carl Chr., Geophysical Institute, University of Copenhagen, Haraldsgade 6, DK-2200, Copenhagen N, Denmark

Tsugita, Prof. Akira, Research Institute Biosciences, Science University of Tokyo, 2669 Yamazaki, Noda, Chiba 278, Japan

Tucker, Michael J., Unix World, Boston, Massachusetts, U.S.A.

Tusscher, Dr. Ben C.J.M., Library KNAW, Box 41950, 1009 DD Amsterdam, The Netherlands

Underwood, Daniel E., Chemical Abstracts Service, 2540 Olentangy River Road, Columbus, OH 43210, U.S.A.

Valkonen, Aki E., Helsinki University of Technology, 02150 ESPOO, Finland

Vaughan, Fred R., Chemical Abstracts Service, P.O. Box 3012, Columbus, OH 43210, U.S.A.

Venkataraghavan, Dr. Babu, Medical Research Division, American Cyanamid Company, Pearl River, NY 10965, U.S.A.

Vinard, Daniel R., Saint-Gobain Recherche, 39 Quai Lucien Lefranc, BP 135, 93303 Aubervilliers, Cédex, France

Walczak, Cynthia A., NIOR/NIH, Parks Building-Room 451, Bethesda, MD, U.S.A.

Wallace, Craig, 5000 Arlington Centre Boulevard, Columbus, OH 43220, U.S.A.

Walters, Phyllis, Battelle Memorial Institute, 505 King Avenue, Columbus, OH 43201, U.S.A.

Webster, Prof. Ferris, College of Marine Studies, University of Deleware, Lewes, DE 19958, U.S.A.

Wehe, Richard R., Richard Wehe Associates, 11117 Woodmont Drive, Raleigh, NC 27613, U.S.A.

Weida, Bill, National Materials Property Data Network, Inc., (c/o Chemical Abstracts Service) 2540 Olentange River Road, P.O. Box 02224, Columbus, OH 43202, U.S.A.

Weisgerber, Dr. David W., Chemical Abstracts Service, 2540 Olentangy River Road, Columbus, OH 43210, U.S.A.

West, Catherine, ATCC, 12301 Parklawn Drive, Rockville, MD 20852, U.S.A.

Westbrook, Dr. Jack H., Brookline Technologies, 5 Brookline Road, Ballston Spa, NY 12302, U.S.A.

Westrum, Jr., Prof. Edgar F., Department of Chemistry, University of Michigan, Ann Arbor, MI 48109, U.S.A.

Wiersma, Dr. Bruce, Dean, College of Forest Resources, University of Maine,206 Nutting Road, Orono, ME 04469, U.S.A.

Wigington, Dr. Ronald L., Director of Information Technology, American Chemical Society, P.O. Box 3337, Columbus, OH 43210, U.S.A.

Wilhoit, Randolph C., Thermodynamics Research Center, Texas A&M University, College Station, TX 77843-3111, U.S.A.

Wilson, Dr. Kenneth G., The Ohio State University, 174 W. 18th Avenue, Columbus, OH 43210, U.S.A.

Wilson, Patricia S., Special Assistant for Database Development, Chemical Abstracts Service, 2540 Olentangy River Road, Columbus, OH 43210, U.S.A.

Withee, Gregory N., National Oceanographic Data Center, 1835 Connecticut Avenue N.W., Washington, D.C. 20235, U.S.A.

Wodak, Prof. Shoshana, Université Libre de Bruxelles, Unité Conformation des Macromolécules Biologique, avenue Paul Héger, CP160, Brussels B-1050, Belgium

Wood, Dr. Gordon H., National Research Council, Montreal Road, Ottawa, Ontario, K1A OS2, Canada

Wu, Dr. Jen-Leih, Institute of Zoology, Academia Sinica, Nankang, Taipei, 11529, Taiwan, China

Xu, Prof. Zhihong, Director, Institute of Chemical Metallurgy, Academia Sinica, P.O. Box 353, Beijing, 100080, China

Yang, Dr. Young Kyu, 12 Research Group, KIST/SERI, P.O. Box 1, Yoosung, Daejeon, Republic of Korea,

Yoder, Lori, Online Computer Library Center, 6565 Frantz Road, Dublin, OH 43017, U.S.A.

Zemankova, Dr. Maria, National Science Foundation, 1800 G. Street, N.W., Room 310, Washington, D.C., U.S.A.

Zhang, Shizhen, CODATA Chinese National Committee, Box 2745, Zhongguancun, Beijing, China

Zhang, Xianoyang, CODATA Chinese National Committee, Box 2747, Zhongguancun, Beijing, China

Zhu, Prof. Jinning, Deputy Director, Bureau of International Cooperation, Chinese Academy of Sciences, 54 Sanlihe Road, Beijing 100864, China

Zupan, Dr. Maria D., Chemical Abstracts Service, 2540 Olentangy River Road, Columbus, OH 43210, U.S.A.

SOCIAL IMPERATIVES FOR GLOBAL CHANGE STUDIES

Peter S. Thacher
World Resources Institute
1709 New York Avenue NW
Washington, D.C. 20006, U.S.A.

Kenneth Wilson's charge to this conference is challenging and sets the right course for the week. But I believe the problem is even more difficult and more demanding than he described. We live in what some have called an "exponential age," and since much of this century is characterized by exponential, explosive growth, I question his view that the next 400 years will resemble the past 400 years. Some of his "retrospective views" may be heard in only 40 years -- rather than 400.

For ours has been a century of exponential and explosive growth. In 90 years world population has tripled; the global economy has grown twenty-fold; and fossil fuel use tenfold. The world economy reached $600 billion in 1900, but it now grows by more than this sum every two years. The population curve is equally daunting. It took all of history for human numbers to grow to 2.5 billion in 1950 but world population doubled since the 1950s -- in only 37 years -- and is now over 5 billion and still climbing [1]. We're now adding roughly a billion people a decade, and with this comes a consequential need to increase the economy of the planet by something like 7- or 8-fold just to maintain the present, inadequate provision of goods and services for the human race.

From a background of handling global environmental problems since the UN Conference on the Human Environment in 1972, I would like to turn your attention to the next big event at the international level: the UN Conference on Environment and Development in Brazil in June 1992. Already governments are asking for data about the changes that have taken place even in that short time, not yet 20 years since Stockholm, with concern for what's coming next in that catchall phrase, "global change."

René Dubos and Barbara Ward summed up the view in 1972 in their book for the Stockholm Conference, *Only One Earth*:

> "Our sudden, vast accelerations -- in numbers, in the use of energy and new materials, in urbanization, in consumptive ideas, in consequent pollution -- have set technological man on a course which could alter dangerously and perhaps irreversibly, the natural systems of his planet upon which his biological survival depends."

Thanks in large part to international data collection programs encouraged since then by UNEP (the UN Environment Program) today we see how right they were. Many local and regional problems are now better understood, and are being addressed. What's new since 1972 is the clarity with which distant global threats, then seen on the horizon, have now come into focus. Some of these, like climate warming, may still be subject to such uncertainty which results in a delay in precautionary actions. Others, like demographic growth rates and the effect of rising energy consumption, are in sharper focus, but also not being acted upon.

One such global issue that is being addressed is stratospheric ozone depletion. In 1972 it was seen as a distant risk from second-generation supersonics flying slightly higher and ejecting nitrous oxides directly into the stratosphere. This did not come to pass, but the publication in 1974 of the paper by Rowland and Molina on a stratospheric sink for chlorofluoromethanes [2] accelerated work in UNEP's "Earthwatch" program which, only two weeks ago, led governments to agree in London that the Montreal Protocol -- itself only signed in September 1987 -- would be further strengthened to reduce a global risk that is now well-defined.

What's new then -- and the theme of my remarks on the subject I was asked to address, "societal imperatives for global change studies" -- is the need to close the gap between knowledge and action; to connect and make meaningful improved scientific understanding to the *human* actors who are, for the first time ever, recognized as driving the process we call "global change".

****

Many times during the design of UNEP's activities, particularly in GEMS -- the Global Environment Monitoring System -- we were faced with choices about the accuracy requirements for data for science, as against the needs of the policy-maker who is not a scientist.

Looking at methylmercury in tuna fish in the Mediterranean, for example, we didn't really need to know levels in terms of parts per billion, or for every tuna fish caught in any one place. At best we needed weekly or monthly averages and we wanted, above all, to distribute the data collection and analysis capabilities in such a way that local institutions would be empowered by the sort of help we could provide through the use of UNEP's voluntary fund; AAS's and other instruments that many qualified labs might not otherwise be able to afford. Our purpose was to stimulate the generation of new understanding and insight in such a way that it would be credible to the national planner and decision-maker; rarely a scientist, more often a finance minister or CEO or a municipal leader, and to help those in positions of responsibility to take account of new insights that science made possible.

And so we sometimes compromised between excellence and relevance. I don't mean to suggest that anything less than high-quality science will help to build a good understanding of the sort that can help to prod policy. But I do believe traditional, top-down science, driven by big, well-financed laboratories, is giving way -- not quite as fast as I think it should -- to the need to strengthen local capabilities to receive, and more importantly, to measure and generate data that is relevant to local decision-making. UNEP's role was largely this, as well as connecting data in networks to cooperatively attack common problems. Today, 15 years later, more than 100 laboratories collectively pursue a common research agenda their governments support, and they are tied together in networks that enable them to communicate, even when their governments cannot.

What are the implications of such an approach to global issues like climate change?

There is no way to confirm the Villach findings in 1985 which suggests the likelihood of an equivalent to a doubling of CO_2 by the 2030s, and consequent increase of global mean equilibrium surface temperature of 1.5 - 4.5 degrees Celsius [3]. But there is no doubt about the growth of heat-trapping constituents in the atmosphere, specifically CO_2, methane, nitrous oxide, and chlorofluorocarbons, and most would agree that these increases arise from a variety of human actions that are elevating their levels beyond natural processes.

A "Greenhouse Index" prepared at WRI [4] based on net annual emissions of three major greenhouse gases converted into equivalent CO_2 heat-trapping effects. When combined with estimates on national emissions for 1987, it shows that some developing countries, specifically China, Brazil, India, Mexico, and Indonesia, are already in the "top 10" in terms of their contributions to greenhouse heat-trapping emissions.

These calculations include rough estimates of biotic contributions of CO_2 -- itself a matter of study in the ICSU "Global Change" program -- and reflect high rates of deforestation rather than industrialization in tropical countries. Another "greenhouse" gas, methane, can similarly be correlated with population, and cattle growth, as well as termites.

Looking to the future one can reasonably expect industrialized countries to reduce emissions of the principle gas of concern, CO_2. Presumably the OECD countries will continue to improve their energy efficiency, getting more useful energy per unit of CO_2 . Regardless of the greenhouse, there are compelling reasons for the United States to improve its energy efficiency, at least up to France's current ability to produce twice the GDP per unit of energy as the US today. Though it calls for much more optimism, one can hope that Eastern Europe and the Soviet Union also achieve comparable energy efficiencies.

But the point I want to make pertains to the rest of the world, the so-called "developing countries" where demographic growth alone, even with no change in energy-per-capita, will soon commit this planet to CO_2 equivalent emissions exceeding current levels from the industrialized nations.

I suggest this calls for much more effort to connect science to policy in both East-West and North-South terms. The opportunity to do this is now, while preparing for the 1992 Conference in Brazil; and its agenda includes many headings in which CODATA is already active: atmosphere, fresh water, biodiversity, desertification, urbanization, and so on.

A possible occasion to consider targeting during the preparations for "Eco-92" -- as the Brazil Conference is becoming known -- is described in material recently circulated by the ICSU secretariat in Paris reporting the results of the Conference on Sustainable Development, Science and Policy organized in Bergen by some 30 scientific policy and other groups. One of their recommendations was for a global science conference some six months before the June 1992 UN conference.

CODATA and other multidisciplinary ICSU mechanisms such as yours will play vital roles in resolving uncertainties about global change. To translate new insights from global to local scales, I suggest you look for opportunities to expand cooperation with the UN system and its many components. Existing areas of cooperation are reflected in abstracts of papers you will be discussing this week, from which I see that UNESCO is well engaged in your agenda, along with my old organization, UNEP, and many other agencies and programs of the UN system as well. I believe growing collaboration between ICSU and the UN system is to everyone's benefit, even though it is little recognized, and under-funded, by governments.

Looking beyond Brazil in 1992 one sees a whole new cast of actors tackling the issues of "global change." States are no longer the exclusive, dominant actor at the international level they were when they wrote the UN Charter. Increasingly, *non*-governmental organizations play important roles, especially in providing early warning and credible advice to governments nationally, and internationally. And the private sector and international movement of capital is another obvious and growing human spur to global change.

I therefore urge you to look for opportunities to expand cooperation with non-scientific actors as you contemplate global change. For if multidisciplinary, "hard-science" groups such as this cannot make your findings comprehensible and relevant to the needs of institutions whose decisions are driving the process of global change, then your early-warning signals will go unheeded, unwelcomed, and unfunded, and the ability of the planet to feed and clothe a doubled population within the lifetime of some of you in this room will be severely compromised.

As to possible tools for this purpose, my own bias is for geographic information systems as a way of integrating different layers of data and presenting the composite in a fashion that is useful to scientists, and persuasive to local decision-makers. Since retiring I have been associated with UNEP's GRID (Global Resources Information Database) that is known to many of you. I think the economists have let down the policy-makers; simply put, there is no way in conventional economics to place value on a standing tree. No countries' GNP calculation would change if all the trees in a country were removed; they are simply not taken into account in the System of National Accounts. "Externalities" and intangibles are therefore serious obstacles to coping with many aspects of global change. Without waiting for the economists to sort out their problems, I think those who can count trees or measure arable land, and are capable of showing change over time, should get on with it. Even this is a lot tougher to do than we realized in 1972.

I find it disturbing that a U.S. Senator can seize an audience's attention by snapping his fingers every second in front of a microphone, warning that in that interval a plot of Amazonian forest the size of a "football field" has disappeared. That's bad enough, but what should bother this audience is that a Brazilian spokesman could claim that only a ping-pong table plot has disappeared, and -- here's the problem, NOBODY KNOWS WHO'S RIGHT!

In the mid 1970s, UNEP and FAO (Food and Agriculture Organization) put together a global study of rates of deforestation in the tropics [5]. It's still the best work that has been done, but it was flawed when we published it, and it is certainly out-of-date now. Techniques by which to measure changes in forest cover have advanced in recent years [6] but resources with which to do an up-to-date enumeration of changes in the size of forest cover have not yet been applied and no better analysis is available except for those concerning local conditions.

Agreement at the Houston Summit last week to make a real effort to monitor the world's forests may open the door to progress. But some of the best data, from Landsat and the French SPOT system, is far from complete (because under the ground rules of commercialization, imaging devices are only turned on when there's a prospective "market", and no such market exists for this kind of information), and commercialization immediately put the price of this kind of "invaluable" data beyond the reach of non-profit researchers.

Hopefully, the Houston Summit states will provide the means to map changes in forest cover, helping IGBP pin down the biotic contributions and sinks for CO_2, while stimulating reforestation efforts for sustainable development, if not reducing greenhouse risks. But I also hope this effort will be launched with a view to producing results that are useful for researchers and, as well, to the humans who are driving the process of deforestation. This calls for strengthening local capabilities on the ground in those areas where forest destruction is the greatest: tropical, developing countries.

Otherwise a disconnect is likely between the picture emerging at the global scale -- about changes in the natural resource system on which life depends on this planet -- and, on the other hand, the actions of consumers and decision-makers who are driving the process of deforestation. Many of us sitting in this room like grass-fed beef for our hamburgers, but we want them cheap and prefer not to grow it in North America. So we encouraged our banks in the 1970s to "recycle petroleum dollars" by making loans to Central America where forest cover could be cleared for "profitable" cattle ranching schemes. This "Hamburger Connection" is well-known in conservation circles [7].

****

To finish, let me briefly touch on some of the characteristics suggested by the new "societal imperatives":

- Multidisciplinary. The nature of global change issues demands multidisciplinary approaches. Climate change issues cannot be tackled by atmospheric science alone.

- Independent expert assessment. Independent of government instruction. Governments set policy and priorities at the international level, but they need uninstructed expert assessments on which to base their judgement of what the traffic will bear, economically and politically. Some of you know from personal experience that scientists sometimes come under instruction, even when asked to give *expert* personal opinion or testimony. Let's face it, possible climate change is not the only global change issue carrying difficult economic and political implications. The role of internationally-recruited scientific expert advisers is one of growing importance. Hard economic and policy choices must be based on objective advice.

  We've seen this at the international level for many decades, notably in the field of radiation, where ICRP (the International Commission on Radiological Protection) and UNSCEAR (the UN Scientific Committee on the Effects of Atomic Radiation) played key roles in the 1950s leading up to the Partial Test Ban Treaty in 1963.

  In the field of marine pollution there's growing recognition of the work of GESAMP (the Group of Experts on Effects of Marine Pollution) experts appointed by international organizations with the right mix of disciplines and nationalities. The point is that these experts, even when they come from government labs, are not responsive to governmental instruction; they call the shots as they see them.

  ICSU and its constituent unions and multidisciplinary committees should gear up to be able to contribute independent expert assessments in all main parameters of global change. To the degree that it depends on governmental financing, this may be difficult; their support for IGBP has been generous up to now, but governmental willingness to support uninstructed expert advice in the future will be put to the test at the Second World Climate Conference this fall in Geneva.

- Transparency. Glasnost must prevail. There's no way for your work to be meaningful to the men and women in the street who, in Dr. Wilson's literate society, will put enlightened pressure on the politicians, unless that information is available, and, almost as important, unless it can be presented in a way that is intelligible to a non-scientific audience. I commend to your attention in this regard the project of your sister committee, ICSU/SCOPE, on "Use of Scientific Information for Sustainable Development." [8] Issues of cost-recovery and commercialization pose real dilemmas.

- Common formatting and Common definitions are, of course, increasingly important for exchanging info. UNEP's International Registry of Potentially Toxic Compounds (IRPTC) is a good example of what can be done. Yet even without agreement on any one of three competing soil classification systems in 1972, useful work was started at Stockholm to measure, and even to quantify *risks* of soil erosion due to specific causes. Practical results can be achieved despite inherent difficulties in classification schemes.

- Scales. The scales that are feasible for IGBP with the constraint of present data processing capabilities make it difficult to think in terms of useful map products at a local scale of, say, 1:250 000, yet that's what might be needed for national decisions on whether or not to open up forest lands for agricultural production.

- Networking is something you increasingly practice, but it should also be thought of in terms of connections with non-scientific communities. Let me use UNEP's GRID to illustrate. Thanks to the generosity of IBM/UK, UNEP this year found it possible to install 15 PS/2 Model 80s in their Nairobi training program for African teams. Each team goes home with a machine, and the software, and a national GIS database that has been a part of the training exercise. Thereafter, the task is to get help from the UN Development Programme, the World Bank and other sources to care and feed that national capability by providing additional equipment, software, training, and the rest of it.

  I think such a distributed system is entirely feasible on a global scale. While GRID today is run from UNEP Headquarters in Nairobi, the main data processing facility is in Geneva, where training has been under way for several years. A regional office is operational in Bangkok and training there will be replicated as soon as possible. Mexico City has been designated as a regional node in this Hemisphere, and there are a number of national nodes -- one in Norway, and others on the drawing board. The World Bank has a growing GIS capability. One can foresee a distributed system at the global scale in which GIS databases will be freely exchanged with those who need them, whether for analyzing Global Change, or for mapping local changes in the resource base and planning sustainable national development.

- Flexibility. Changing levels of uncertainty require flexibility so as to adjust to new insights. But the process involves feeding new insights back into a negotiating process. Again, stratospheric ozone depletion is a good example. In 1987 it seemed adequate to call for a 50 percent reduction of chlorofluorocarbon production by the year 1998. One year later new evidence showed this to be inadequate; two weeks ago contracting parties agreed in London on a complete cessation of production of controlled chemicals, and the addition of other chemicals under the control system accompanied by, for the first time, the creation of a new fund to assist those developing countries who will need help and who merit help if they are to contribute to reducing global risk. This didn't "just happen", the feedback mechanisms were developed under the 1977 "Action Plan to Protect Stratospheric Ozone" and incorporated in the treaties which followed in 1983 (Vienna) and 1987 (Montreal).

- This brings up my final characteristic, perhaps the most important, support. Part of the problem in London was that the tropical countries are more dependent on refrigeration than are the temperate parts of the planet. CFC substitutes will cost them more and require new valves and new compressors to handle the changed characteristics of the substitutes. It's not reasonable to expect tropical, developing countries to sacrifice national development imperatives to cover the extra costs of switching over to CFC substitutes, especially when some of them were poised to manufacture CFCs themselves; besides, they didn't cause the problem we are now asking them to help reduce.

  Therefore the donor countries agreed at London to put together an additional fund of a couple of hundred million dollars as an inducement to use CFC substitutes and thereby reduce their future contributions to a global problem. (If local scientific capabilities had been able to show how increased UVb would damage their crops and ecosystems, perhaps the pricetag in London would have been smaller.)

  This highlights an important, but less expensive aspect of support -- the need to strengthen human and institutional capabilities, not only to receive and process data about global change, but to produce it with sufficient quality and relevance to serve both the scientific community and local decision-making for national, sustainable development strategies. When you look at demographic projections and energy consumption patterns, it is clear that national development strategies in the third world may be soon the dominant causal factors in global change.

I therefore hope that as you address the papers before you this week, you will look for opportunities to try to attack that literacy problem that Kenneth Wilson put before us. I particularly hope you can find ways to present findings about global change in ways that not only improve understanding of global change, but also have beneficial influence on human actions that drive that process. Thank you.

REFERENCES

[1] Based on remarks by Gus Speth, President of World Resources Institute, on 27 June to the "Science-Technology and Global Environment Conference" in Japan.

[2] "Stratospheric sink for chlorofluoromethanes: chlorine atom-catalyzed destruction of ozone", M. Molina and F.S. Rowland, *Nature*, 249, 1974.

[3] "An Assessment of the Role of Carbon Dioxide and of Other Greenhouse Gases in Climate Variations and Associated Impacts", sponsored by UNEP, WMO, ICSU, printed by WMO Geneva, 1985.

[4] See *World Resources - 1990-1991*, Part II, "Climate Change: A Global Concern."

[5] The "Lanly Report" based on the FAO/UNEP Tropical Forests Resources Assessment Project was published by FAO Rome in 1981 and is currently being updated.

[6] See for example, the ICSU/SCOPE Report, "The Role of Terrestrial Vegetation in the Global Carbon Cycle: Measurement by Remote Sensing", *SCOPE 23*, 1984.

[7] See *The Primary Source: Tropical Forests and Our Future* by Norman Myers, 1984.

[8] See the SCOPE note describing the results of a Scientific Advisory Committee meeting 6-8 November 1989 at SCOPE, Paris.

A NATIONAL GLOBAL CHANGE INFORMATION MANAGEMENT STRATEGY

Ferris Webster
College of Marine Studies
University of Delaware
Lewes, Delaware, U.S.A.

Successful management of data and information is critical to the success of the U.S. Global Change Research Program. The existing environmental data management components in this country have served reasonably well the purposes for which they were set up. However, to meet the data and information challenge of the U.S. Global Change Research Program, many necessary components are inadequate or wholly lacking.

The Committee on Geophysical Data of the U.S. National Research Council is reviewing this issue. The Committee, made up of scientists representing a number of geophysical disciplines, is working to define a strategy for a global change data and information system.
The principal elements of that strategy are:

A. Priorities for investment in data and information management should be visibly driven by and accountable to the scientific objectives of global change research.
B. Data and information management must be adequately supported to ensure success of the U.S. Global Change Research program. Existing national data centers are generally not adequately supported to service present users, much less the expanded user community and data needs the global program will involve.
C. The existing system, of national data centers and academic and project data units provides a useful starting point for a distributed Global Change data and information management system.
D. A global change data and information system should provide for an evolving data management system and an expanding user base.
E. The system that is created should ensure that a scientist, decades hence,

can use the datasets effectively.

F. The preparation of products and analyses is a needed and valuable function that should be an integral part of an effective data and information management system.

I. INTRODUCTION

As its national program to understand global change, the United States has initiated the U.S. Global Change Research Program. It aims to elucidate the causes and effects of natural and human-induced global change. Responding to the challenge of global change, the program is unprecedented in several ways:

A. The amount of environmental information it will generate.
B. The U.S. Government's priority for the creation and implementation of the program.
C. The recognition in the program plans (Earth Sciences Committee, 1990) of the critical importance of data and information management.
D. The coordination by the federal agencies involved in the program of data and information management needs—the Interagency Working Group on Data Management for Global Change (IWG).
E. The opportunity for the scientific community to participate in the definition and creation of the kind of data and information management system that such a program calls for.

The U.S. Global Change Research Program is starting off with strong support: the fiscal year 1991 budget for this program is proposed to be $1034 million and further growth is foreseen (Earth Sciences Committee, 1990). Of that total, $129 million is labelled data management, a proposed 98 percent increase over the previous budget year.

Seeking input from the scientific community, the IWG turned to the Committee on Geophysical Data (CGD) of the National Research Council for guidance and advice. What scientific strategy should be followed in developing a U.S. system to manage data and information for global change research?

In response to the IWG's request, the CGD has prepared a report that addresses a strategy for data and information management for the U.S. Global Change Research Program. What are the global change data system requirements? What are the functions of a data and information system? What principles should be followed in creating a new system?

Part of the CGD activity involves seeking input from a variety of involved sources. Though the report is now in final review, I, or other members of the CGD (listed at the end of this paper) would be most happy to receive advice or comments from participants at this CODATA Conference as they relate to global change data systems.

II. GLOBAL CHANGE RESEARCH OBJECTIVES

Heightened public awareness of potential global warming-climate change-from increasing atmospheric CO_2 concentrations and other greenhouse gases has focussed scientific attention on this and other global issues. At the heart of global change research will be the need to acquire and analyze large amounts of information. This information should allow researchers to address the four core questions of the U.S. Global Change Research Program (Global Change Committee, 1989). They are:

A. What forces initiate global change?
B. How does the Earth system respond to changes in forcing functions?
C. How has the Earth's environment changed in the past?
D. How well can global change be predicted?

A data and information system to support a global change research cannot be a simple extension of existing systems. Global issues by their nature have common and demanding properties. For example, they have larger spatial and longer temporal scales than usually addressed by traditional research. They are truly global in scale and scope (*e.g.*, climate, atmospheric chemistry, and global carbon and nitrogen cycles). They can be local or regional issues with important feedbacks to global systems (*e.g.*, deforestation). They require multidisciplinary approaches to analysis. They require national and international understanding and agreement before solutions can be realized.

A data and information system for global change research must foster the process to identify global change, evaluate its impact on human activities, and set a course of action to mitigate harmful effects. Consequently, the U.S. Global Change Research Program will make unprecedented demands for the assembly and dissemination of large volumes of diverse and interdisciplinary data and information.

III. DATA SYSTEM REQUIREMENTS

Data requirements for global change fall into five categories of activity:

IV. Collection, processing, and analyses of past and existing global

measurements to:
1. establish the relative mean state of the Earth system
2. obtain measures of system variability
3. detect change
4. understand large-scale interactive processes

A. Sustained (future) global measurements to monitor and document change, and to supply essential state variables for Earth system models
B. Process studies to understand particular phenomena and relate smaller-scale processes with the large-scale variables of the global system
C. Analysis of past records, both instrumental and proxy, to:
   1. obtain long-term reference states of the global system
   2. document and understand secular fluctuations in the Earth system and their relationship to shorter-time-scale processes
   3. provide a basis for testing models
D. Production of data fields (with known or uniform requirements) from assimilation and/or simulation models.

Measurements acquired on regional and world-wide scales must be merged with other, often dissimilar, data to produce analyses and products. Subsets of these data must be quality assured, documented, distributed, and archived. Contemporary and future researchers must be able to acquire and use these data in their analyses of global change phenomena.

The efficient acquisition, quality assurance, documentation, distribution, and preservation of relevant datasets of all types is crucial to the success of the U.S. Global Change Research Program. The existing system must improve. There must be a new way of handling research data for global issues. The Geophysical Data Committee's report on *Geophysical Data: Policy Issues* (1988) dealt primarily with geophysical data, but its conclusion applies to all disciplines concerned with global change:

> "The quantity of geophysical data obtained ... has increased dramatically in the past few decades. Collected often at enormous expense, these data represent a national resource that must be managed carefully to ensure that they are preserved and available when needed. However, because of a substantial increase in the amount and complexity of geophysical data being collected and in the demands for them, *the management policies and procedures that have been developed are no longer adequate.*"

V. KINDS OF DATA NEEDED

Data needed for broad global change research run the gamut from site-specific to truly global datasets. The Committee on Geophysical Data has found the report by the Earth System Sciences Committee (1988) to be a valuable reference to data type needs. Disciplines involved include the geosciences, ecology, biology, and socio-economics. Many datasets will cross disciplines, and will need multiple talents to assemble. Time series data of all types are prominent in global change research to detect past and present trends. Proxy data are necessary when direct measurements are impossible. The need for accuracy is important, as some of the predicted changes will be small and take place over long periods of time. Often datasets will be enormous, due to the resolution and spatial scale needed to address global issues. The datasets must be accessible and useable by future generations. Detecting global change is a long-term process.

VI. FUNCTIONS OF A DATA AND INFORMATION SYSTEM

The prime function of a data and information management system is the stewardship of the data and information, with all its ramifications. Such information is costly to acquire. Its safekeeping must not be left to chance.

Functions may vary depending on programmatic goals, attributes of the thematic data or programmatic issues, and researcher needs. Most components of a data management system will have these elements. The functions of the system include, but may not be limited to:

A. *Data preservation.* The long-term stewardship of research data must be assured.
B. *Data distribution.* Data must be easily accessible by the world research community with as few restrictions (including cost) as possible.
C. *Data integration and product production.* The system must be able to integrate data within and across disciplines to create data products for use by the research community and policy makers.
D. *Assuring data quality.* High standards of data quality assurance must be used to maximize the application of data to answer global change questions.
E. *Providing data documentation.* Datasets must be fully documented (documentation is often termed "metadata") to insure their complete understanding today and their useability in the future.
F. *Data identification and acquisition.* An active role must be taken with scientists to identify datasets useful for global change research.
G. *Providing a programmatic focus for data management.* The flow of information necessary must be focussed to conduct global change research.
H. *Selective data retrieval.* It must be possible to retrieve selectively data

relevant to a user's needs.

I. *Standardization of procedures.* Standards for quality assurance, documentation, and distribution must be similar among system components.

Global change studies are interdisciplinary and long-term. Many requests to the data management system will be for derived products such as analyses or edited data collections in association with descriptive text or graphical material, rather than raw observational data. Thus, the system must provide information as well as data. It must keep the raw data as well, to provide the material for future reanalyses. It must play an active role in the generation, acquisition, quality control, dissemination, and retention of value-added products.

VII. WILL AND COMMITMENT

The biggest single challenge facing the U.S. Global Change Research Program is the need to develop the collective will and commitment to managing data properly. The critical problems of setting up a data and information system are often perceived as being technical. They generally are not, they are policy problems. There are indeed some important technical problems to be overcome to create the system. However, these are not as serious as the policy issues.

The support of data management is inadequate. Federal agencies need to support data management with adequate funds. The scientific community must support data management by being part of its development and operation. The funds allocated by the agencies for data storage and dissemination often represent the weakest part of a research budget. The enthusiasm of scientists for the data management part of research programs is generally tepid. The budget tells the story: it is inadequate.

Factors contributing to budget inadequacies include the frequent need to cover cost over-runs in other parts of a project, unrealistically low estimates of data management costs in order to sell a project, or ignorance or apathy about resources needed for data archival and preservation. Most scientists would rather see budgets directed to their perceived "real research" than to data management. Thus federal managers who inadequately fund data management are not often called to account. Data management is "everyone's second priority". Data management must show that it gives value for money.

Partly because of the lack of a policy for the handling of scientific data, the broad range of data facilities in the federal government has suffered a general decline of funding. The result is decreased efficiency of data processing and decreased data availability. Some centers are technologically decades behind. (For this reason, large volumes of satellite and hard-copy data have been effectively lost during the past several decades).

Funding inadequacies are especially serious. Existing centers offer potentially unique combinations of long-term continuity, general accessibility, data-management expertise, and the service orientation required to broaden the use of the data. The data management system for global change must build upon existing national centers. Thus the present underfunding of data centers in particular and data management in general must be remedied.

VIII. CREATING A NEW SYSTEM

A new system for data and information management begins with the establishment of objectives. What datasets are needed to describe global change? What are the highest priorities? Setting objectives and priorities goes beyond data management. The fundamental scientific design of the U.S. Global Change Research Program should include setting objectives for the data and information that will be needed. These objectives must be set with a data-management input into the scientific process.

Data centers should be created for those disciplines important to global change research that are not included in the network of national data centers. This can be through the establishment of new centers or by expanding the purview and resources of existing centers. A network of discipline-oriented data centers is an important and necessary component of the system to support global change research. However, because of the extraordinary information requirements that the global change program will make on existing data management elements, a new mechanism to handle these data will be necessary to augment the existing system.

IX. BUILD A STRONG SYSTEM ON EXISTING ELEMENTS

To accomplish all this, a data management infrastructure must exist. One does exist today, but it is incomplete, inadequate, and poorly supported. It must be strengthened. If the U.S. Global Change Research Program is to be a success, a strong data management system must exist to support it. Existing U.S. environmental data management units must be improved, restructured, or replaced. New components must be created. Some existing institutions can serve as models. Above all, data and information management must be adequately supported.

A new system should build upon itself. Though new elements will be needed, we must make sure that the existing components work. Then we can move on to create the more complex system. This represents a challenge: can we make the existing elements work? Making them work is not a technical challenge, but one of will and resources.

Agencies must shoulder the responsibility of providing for the stewardship of the data they generate. Data management should be considered at the outset of every project, explicitly defined, and adequately budgeted for the life of the project. Arrangements should be made for the long-term archiving of the data.

A new system should demonstrate success through practical prototypes. Confidence will be built by proving accuracy, by showing that things can be done right, and by producing some early products of value. This can be done by beginning feasible pilot projects of high importance.

The Master Directory project sponsored by the Interagency Working Group on Data Management for Global Change (the IWG) is an excellent example. This project is creating a high-level directory of datasets held by many agencies and institutions related to global change. Its success depends on information standards between centers and on operational computer network links.

X. ENSURE SCIENTIFIC INVOLVEMENT

If we look at existing data and information management activities we find that often successful data systems and centers combine data management with scientific use. Successful data centers not only work *with* scientists but have their active support. Users support the development of the data system and provide feedback. This leads to the conclusion that a successful system must involve the scientific user community at all stages of development and operation. Without that support and involvement, the data system is unlikely to meet the needs of the program (Data Management and Computation Committee, 1982).

Achieving effective scientific involvement will not be easy. Unfortunately, much of the scientific community is not aware of the need to be involved in any unified global change data and information management approach. This attitude is part of a pattern: data management has long been considered a secondary aspect of research. Since data will be such a critical element in global change research, a change of attitude is essential. Fortunately, there are many signs that this change is taking place, both by research scientists and sponsoring agencies.

For example, an elaborate system is being devised to handle the data which will be generated by NASA's Earth Observing System (EOS) program. The EOS Data and Information System (EOSDIS) is being planned in parallel with the EOS program in an attempt to ensure that the scientists will be involved in not only the analysis, but the storage and archiving of data from EOS.

Active researchers must be participants in the process. They should define needs and create the framework for a data and information system to meet those needs. They should help establish procedures and data centers. It will not be enough for them simply to assent to what a group of data technologists are creating. They must be involved.

There must be incentives for researchers to be involved. The system must respond to scientists' needs. It must be perceived as the optimal way to do research with data. A simple feedback process will have a beneficial effect. For example, data centers should involve researchers working with the datasets in the development of the data system. When advice is sought and heeded, there is an incentive for involvement.

Not only should incentives be created, but existing disincentives should be removed. User fees above a minimal cost for reproduction for scientific use of data constitute an existing disincentive. The nature of global problems requires access to large datasets. If their cost makes this prohibitive, then exploratory research will be obstructed. For example, Landsat data are currently so expensive that the data are generally beyond the reach of the research community. The global change data system should have the lowest possible user fee structure. Data should be free wherever possible.

There may be innovative ways to recognize data contributions. The Committee on Geophysical Data has discussed the possibility of creating a CD-ROM "journal," or of refereeing and referencing dataset contributions as is done with scientific contributions. However, there is a strong community reluctance to recognizing the preparation of a scientific dataset as being equivalent to the preparation of a scientific paper. This attitude must change.

There are encouraging signs: the *Journal of Geophysical Research (Space Physics)* has begun soliciting "brief data reports"' of datasets that have been submitted to national data centers. Referees are asked to use the protocol to access the data and to comment on the data's relevance and quality.

XI. DATA DIRECTORIES

Many scientists face major obstacles in finding out what pertinent data are available; in some situations, obtaining the data may be a practical impossibility. In other cases, inadequate documentation makes personal contact with the primary user imperative.

There is a need for all centers holding data acquired through federal funding to provide well documented information about the extent of their holdings and the accessibility of the data. Furthermore, data interchange between agencies will become a major issue as global change programs require data from ever-wider sources. The lack of interoperability between data directories is a serious deficiency of the current system. It must be addressed if the U.S. Global Change Research Program is to draw upon existing and future data holdings.

Location of data, both nationally and internationally, will be helped by the establishment of a centralized data directory. This directory will have information about information. It will be created by a joint effort, initially of the national data centers, with eventual expansion to include international sources of data. The data directory should be accessible electronically and user friendly. It should provide as much information about datasets as possible, including location, access policies and procedures, and information about the data's completeness, accuracy, general usefulness, documentation, and limitations. It should be free to use.

XII. DATA SUBMISSION

The scientific research community participates unevenly in data management. This creates the many-sided problem of accessibility. There are valuable datasets that remain in the custody of individual research groups or even individual investigators, with the consequent acceptance by them of the data-handling task. Some of these datasets are widely known and accessible; others are not.

There are many reasons for the failure of individual scientists to provide data to the data centers. Among these are a desire for exclusive access to data, the reluctance to divert time and effort away from research in order to clean up a messy research dataset, and unawareness of the existence of appropriate repositories or of the importance of depositing data in such centers.

In general, the research community is not sufficiently aware of the importance of ensuring the availability of environmental data. Until this changes, potentially valuable datasets will continue to be lost as primary users retire, relocate, or move on to other projects.

There also remains the question of data ownership: how long should recently collected data remain under the exclusive control of the scientist(s) who collected the data? This issue is being addressed by the federal agencies involved in the global change program.

XIII. QUALITY ASSURANCE AND DOCUMENTATION

Many data centers provide little or no quality assurance of their data holdings. The assumption is that the individual researcher has applied adequate attention to assuring the accuracy of the data. This is often not the case.

Data are frequently separated from information about the data. This is an unfortunate byproduct of the explosion over recent decades of digital data and techniques for handling them. Information about the algorithms used for a derived product, quality control procedures, comparisons with independent measurements, reviews by outside experts, etc., permit the user to judge the reliability or value of the product for a particular application, and therefore should be an inseparable part of the data. The same is true for original data in terms of calibration, quality control flags, station histories, and so on.

The quality assurance and documentation standards of datasets important to global change research must be upgraded. Quality assurance and documentation should be at the heart of a data management system supporting the global change program. Only after extensive testing by independent reviewers should important global research datasets be considered accurate. Depending on the data involved, the effort can be extensive and often can be the single most expensive step in processing a dataset for distribution. This process, analogous to independent peer review of a journal article, maximizes the integrity of the information. It is necessary for the U.S. Global Change Research Program. Future research and policy decisions will rest in part on these important datasets.

Data documentation must pass the '20-year test'. That is, can someone 20 years from now, not familiar with the data or how they were obtained, be able to understand fully and use the data solely with the aid of the documentation archived with the dataset? This is a tough test, yet one that must be passed for many of the data collections if long-term, global environmental programs are to be successful.

Documentation must do more than describe the values represented in each field and the format information to read the data tape. It must fully document the dataset from all possible points of view. Complete data documentation is a crucial portion of data processing and, along with quality assurance, will be the heart of successful data management activities for global change.

XIV. COOPERATION AND SHARING

For most global change studies, regional and global data and information will be required. No one nation, agency, or institution will be able to gather the appropriate data without cooperation from other nations, agencies, and institutions. In the United States this means that any one agency will often need the cooperation of others to produce datasets for global change. Internationally, the Global Change Research Program will require cooperation and data exchange with many countries and international institutions.

The U.S. Global Change Research Program will depend on scientists sharing their data with each other. The timely submission of data to national centers requires a policy to ensure it. The policy must recognize the needs of principal investigators to protect their intellectual investment and to encourage their continued efforts to collect useful global change data.

XV. CONCLUSIONS

Global change research is a scientific challenge. Creating a data and information management system to serve it also presents a challenge. Many in the scientific and engineering community are excited by the challenge and are being stimulated to respond to it and support it. However, we must be careful not to lose sight of the objective. A global change data and information management system must provide the means for gaining an understanding of global change processes. No matter how technically advanced or powerful the data and information system might be, if it does not support the research, it will have failed.

ACKNOWLEDGEMENTS

Current members of the Committee on Geophysical Data of the National

Research Council are Shelton Alexander, Peter Cornillon, Murray Dryer, Glenn Flierl, Robert Gold, Dorothy Hall, William Hinze, Roy Jenne, Ken Jezek, Clifford Mass, Robert McPherron, Joseph Siscoe, and Ferris Webster. The CGD Staff Officer is Pembroke Hart. Others who have participated actively in preparing the study are Francis Bretherton, Will Harrison, John Walsh, and Victor Zlotnicki.

REFERENCES

[1] Data Management and Computation Committee, National Research Council, *Data Management and Computation, Volume 1: Issues and Recommendations*, National Academy Press, Washington, DC, 1982, 167 pp. (The "CODMAC Report".)

[2] Earth Sciences Committee, *Our Changing Planet: The FY 1991 U.S. Global Change Research Program*. Committee on Earth Sciences, Federal Coordinating Council for Science, Engineering, and Technology, Washington, DC, 1990, 60 pp.

[3] Earth System Sciences Committee, NASA Advisory Council, *Earth System Science, A Closer View*, University Corporation for Atmospheric Research, Boulder, CO, 1988, 208pp.

[4] Geophysical Data Committee, National Research Council, *Geophysical Data: Policy Issues*. National Academy Press, Washington, DC, 1988, 40 pp.

[5] Global Change Committee, National Research Council, *Toward an Understanding of Global Change*, National Academy Press, Washington, DC, 1989, 213 pp.

[6] Interagency Working Group on Data Management for Global Change, *Recommendations from an Interdisciplinary Forum on Data Management for Global Change*. Office for Interdisciplinary Earth Studies, UCAR, Boulder CO, 1990, 75 pp.

TECHNOLOGY RECONCILIATION [1] IN THE REMOTE-SENSING ERA OF U.S. CIVILIAN WEATHER FORECASTING 1957-1987.

Margaret Eileen Courain, Ph.D.
Rutgers University
New Brunswick, NJ 08903, U.S.A.

INTRODUCTION

Any scientific or technical database has problems assimilating data collected by instruments from a new technology. The larger the database, the greater the problems encountered. Very large national databases (*e.g.,* weather forecasting), with global data collection and requirements for processing and output within minutes to hours of observation, might appear to be fruitful places to find all the reasons why assimilation of data from a new technology (*e.g.,* remote-sensing) cannot be accomplished. There have been several studies describing the problems involved. This study - the subject of my Ph.D. dissertation research at Rutgers University - acknowledges but does not focus on the problems. It focuses on the management of technological change as one aspect of scientific management, investigating the changes in production and initial (real-time) use of information for weather forecasting from new remote-sensing observations over a thirty year period (1957-1987). It includes U.S. weather data collection from space platforms (satellites) and earth platforms (radar).

THE 1957-1987 REMOTE-SENSING ERA IN WEATHER FORECASTING

In 1957, radar made it possible to detect hurricanes and tornadoes over land within a range of 250 miles. That was the beginning of a new remote-sensing era for the U.S. Weather Bureau. Three years later, meteorological satellites provided a totally new perspective on the earth's weather over the entire globe and new kinds of data to analyze. Enabled by the ability of computers to accept and analyze enormous quantities of weather observations, these new remote-sensing methods brought major changes to meteorology. Where meteorologists had previously complained that the accuracy of their weather forecasts were limited by insufficient observations and unreliable instrumentation, they were now overwhelmed with more data than they knew what to do with. The U.S. civilian weather service had no precedent to draw on to help it assimilate the flood of satellite images of cloud cover and other new data forms into its weather forecasts. Managing the process of "technology reconciliation" was vital to improving weather forecasting.

RESEARCH TO ANSWER AN IMPORTANT QUESTION

We know we have more remote-sensing weather observations in the last 30 years than we had from direct weather observations in the previous 100 years (see Figure 1). The real question is what has it (remote-sensing) done for us in improving weather forecasting? To answer this broad question, it was necessary to ask four specific questions:

1. What were the new data products derived from the remote-sensing weather observations during the period 1957-1987?

2. How did the use of these derived data products improve our weather forecasting?

3. Who were the individuals or groups responsible for reconciling the remote-sensing data products with traditional operational weather forecasting products?

4. How were the reconciliations accomplished?

METHODOLOGY USED

There was no single, accepted methodology for a data management inquiry in an observational science. It was necessary to make a mosaic of four techniques from different disciplines appropriate for a broad study with a disciplinary focus; a history of science perspective on this era, a meteorological data systems analysis, an extended management case study, and a history of remote-sensing technology.

Developing a historical framework for the remote-sensing era revealed 3 progressive, technology-driven expansions in direct (*in situ*) weather observations prior to 1957. In Era 1 [5th Century B.C. to 1845], we had individual weather watchers, then (after 1700 A.D.) individual weather observers taking direct surface observations with thermometers and barometers and recording them in their almanacs and diaries. In Era 2

[1845-1900], *in situ*, simultaneous surface observations from a nationwide network of weather observers were telegraphed to Washington, D.C. and cumulated into the first U.S. weather forecasts. In Era 3 [1900-1957], *in situ* observations from the atmosphere using kites, balloons, airplanes, and radiosondes were added to surface observations. This resulted in improved weather forecasts.

A Data Accountability and Review Technique (DART) was developed by the author which included:

- Developing 13 appropriate research questions to collect the facts, explanations, and evidence to document the development and use of remote-sensing data products
- Developing a general process structure from the 13 questions (see Figure 2) in order to select 43 primary data sources to be interviewed and to organize the data and information collected.

DART made it possible to look at the application of one technology (remote-sensing) as a data-flow-chart which included the individuals (technology reconciliators) as well as the traditional linear sequence of observational instruments and systems - to find out how one technology worked from the inside, both as a technical system and as a social system.

DEVELOPMENT OF REMOTE-SENSING NETWORKS

Development of both radar and satellite remote-sensing networks are chronicled in the study. Between 1957 and 1987, there were two upgrades of the WSR-57 radar instrument, replicated into a national and local network of 128 radar instruments on stationary 70-foot towers across the country. Seventy-one remote-sensing weather data collection instruments were flown on 40 satellites - 62 instruments on 31 polar satellites and 9 instruments on 9 geostationary satellites. It is important to remember that the scale of space-based remote-sensing observations was *global*, in contrast to the previous *national* limit from surface observations. The scale of earth-based remote-sensing observations (radar) was *mesoscale* (less than 250 miles), providing a closer and more intense look at severe storm development than had ever been available for analysis and forecasting. Temperatures of the upper air, originally recorded only by radiosondes, were now extended from a specific height to a sounding stretching from the altitude of a polar satellite (400-850 miles) to the earth. Television pictures and radiometric images captured the cloud formations and measured the speed of their movements over the earth from satellites positioned in geostationary orbit. Images were animated to replay the daily weather or the formation of a hurricane.

NEW REMOTE-SENSING DATA PRODUCTS

In this era, 25 new data products were derived from remote-sensing observations (see Table 1). Seven of them were from radar data, ten from polar satellite data, and thirteen from geostationary satellite data. Five products were derived from both polar and geostationary satellite data.

USE AND EVALUATION IN FORECASTING

There was documentation for use of 16 remote-sensing data products by the National Weather Service, use of snow and ice cover by NOAA/NAVY Ice Center, sea surface temperatures by Marine Fisheries Service, radar-coded storm detection messages by the Federal Aviation Administration and the airline industry, and a vegetation index used by the U.S. Department of Agriculture.

Use of these data products brought about 18 long-term improvements in weather forecasting (the process) and 15 improvements in weather forecasts (the products). Their use contributed to the evolution in the science of U.S. weather forecasting, rather than a revolution in science described by Thomas Kuhn [2]. It was an evolution in the length (from a reliable 1-day to reliable 5-day forecast). It was also an evolution in improved accuracy, especially in severe storm forecasts (tornado forecasts improved 40-50%, and there was a dramatic improvement in false alarm ratios).

The original proposals to use space remote-sensing (satellite instruments) to collect weather data did not promise any specific, quantitative improvements in forecasting [3]. Therefore, no program was set up by the National Weather Service to gather data separate from all other data collected during this period, in order to evaluate the contribution of remote-sensing observations alone.

TECHNOLOGY RECONCILIATORS

People are the most important elements in the success of our technology-driven scientific systems. As individuals or teams, they make new systems work. They manage changes in technologies by reconciling new data products [4].

Looking backward, it was quite easy to identify individuals and teams who served as "technology reconciliators" in the remote-sensing era of U.S. weather forecasting. They themselves agreed that the term described their unexpected, undefined responsibilities. Their reflections on their roles in the process of technology reconciliation, obtained through a series of interviews with 43 scientists and science managers, are the primary sources for this study. I also drew on my own years as "participant-observer," as Manager of Research Information Systems at Merck & Co., Inc., in Rahway, NJ, and as Deputy Assistant Administrator of National Environmental Satellite, Data and Information Service at NOAA (National Oceanic and Atmospheric Administration) in Washington, D.C.

Sixteen of the 43 primary data sources interviewed (none self-selected) were identified as technology reconciliators (See Table 2). They represented four levels of titles (from member of a unit to assistant administrator). Although they did not all work for the same line office or single agency, they all shared the same expressed mission or goal: to have remote-sensing data used in operational weather forecasting. None had the title of technology reconciliator. "Technology Reconciliator" is a newly defined role; differing from Thomas Allen's technological gatekeepers [5] and Everett Rogers' change agents [6]. These technology reconciliators seem to bear a remarkable resemblance to our keynote speaker Dr. Kenneth Wilson's "members of a missing profession - thoroughly versed in scientific discipline and focused on the information issues." [7] It was possible to identify many of their contributions to the evolution of U.S. weather forecasting from remote-sensing technology 1957-1987.

TECHNOLOGY RECONCILIATION TEAMS AND PROCESSES

Stories of the sixteen technology reconciliators working as members of five teams are told in a case study synthesized from 43 interviews. Members of the five teams identified in Table 2 explored different, but not conflicting, methods to use remote-sensing data products in operational weather forecasting. TEAM 1 used satellite imagery in civilian weather forecasting. TEAM 2 coordinated civilian/military use of satellite imagery. TEAM 3 reconciled satellite soundings with the computer-based models in the National Meteorological Center. TEAM 4 used radar data products for severe weather forecasting. TEAM 5 developed interactive data management and analysis systems for forecasters to access and use both remote-sensing and direct weather observations in the same system.

Common to all the teams were 3 stages found in their technology reconciliation processes: (1) conception/interpretation, (2) automation for improved access, and (3) integration of data sets. The speed of reconciliation varied among the teams from 2 weeks to 10 years: 2 weeks for radar summary maps to be used by the forecasters (Team 4); 1 year for temperature sounding to be input into the National Meteorological Center computer (Team 3); more than 10 years for satellite imagery to be used routinely by operational forecasters (Team 1).

Factors affecting the speed with which each stage in the technology reconciliation process advanced depended upon: creativity of the technology reconciliator(s), sufficient management and financial support, adequate training and education in interpretation and integration of new data products, competition with direct observational technology, data collection meeting the requirements of operations, enthusiasm of operational forecasters for the change, and outside support from the National Aeronautics and Space Administration (NASA) and the World Meteorological Organization (WMO).

Education and training in the interpretation of the remote-sensing data products were vital elements in accomplishing remote-sensing reconciliation. Three types of vehicles were used: training programs for users (forecasters), establishment of Satellite Field Service Station organizational units, and specific application projects carried out through technology reconciliation teams.

The speed of reconciliation increased when new data products were introduced into operational weather forecasting using non-competitive data representations, which allowed an enhanced product to evolve. The speed of reconciliation decreased when new data products were introduced into operational weather forecasting using competitive data representations or where there was any other unresolved, perceived competition between remote-sensing technology and direct observational technology (*e.g.*, radiosondes) for technical or monetary resources.

SUMMARY

As a data history of a new technology, the present study is a unique contribution to the history of meteorology and the National Weather Service. The Data Accountability and Review Technique (DART) developed by the author made it possible to trace the 1957-1987 evolution in U.S. weather forecasting through a review of data collection, output, use, and evaluation of remote-sensing data products. Building on the information obtained through the interviews, attention is focused on the process of managing new technological data products. A model of technology reconciliation is proposed. The model and methods developed in the study can be applied to understanding the contemporary history of other sciences, and beyond the sciences to the management of technological change. Scientists, engineers, R & D managers, or science/technology policy-makers may find the case study, the methodology, and the generalized model helpful as it guides one through the complex process of interpreting new data from new technology.

REFERENCES

[1] As defined by the author, technology reconciliation is the function or process by which data products and information from a new technology are made consistent or congruent with the existing data representations of a science in order to be used effectively.

[2] Kuhn, Thomas S. 1970. *The Structure of Scientific Revolutions.* 2nd. ed. Chicago: University of Chicago Press.

[3] Verner E. Suomi, interview with author, Madison, WI, 25 July 1989.

[4] Data products are results derived form the processing of original scientific observations into more useful formats such as images, graphs, profiles, displays, indices, analyses, interpretation, analyses, or quantitative numeric measurements (corresponding to NASA Levels 2-5 data).

[5] Allen, Thomas J. 1966. "The Differential Performance of Information Channels in the Transfer of Technology." *MIT Conference on Human Factors in the Transfer of Technology.* Cambridge, MA.

[6] Rogers, Everett M. 1983. *Communication of Invention.* 3rd. ed. New York: The Free Press.

[7] Wilson, Kenneth G. 16 July 1990. "Future Directions of Science and Large-Scale Scientific Computing." 12th International CODATA Conference, Columbus, OH.

TABLE 1

NEW DATA PRODUCTS DERIVED FROM REMOTE-SENSING OBSERVATIONS FOR U.S. WEATHER FORECASTING 1957-1987

NDP No.	New Data Product
1.	Nephanalysis
2.	APT Imagery
3.	Cloud motion
4.	Cloud top temperature
5.	Imagery; cloud cover, day and night over Western Hemisphere imagery
6.	Wind field from cloud motion (cloud tracer winds)
7.	Wind speed over land
8.	Snow/ice cover (land/water boundaries)
9.	Image animation
10.	Atmospheric water vapor profile
11.	Sea surface temperature
12.	Vertical temperature profile of the atmosphere
13.	Temperature profile of the atmosphere in the presence of clouds
14.	Temperature profile of the stratosphere
15.	Temperature and moisture profile of the atmosphere
16.	National Radar Composite, National Radar summary chart
17.	Radar scope imagery
18.	Digitized Radar/Interactive Computerized Radar display (ICRAD)
19.	Vertically Integrated Liquid-water content of storm (VIL)
20.	Satellite Interpretive Message for national distribution (SIM)
21.	Summary Radar Interpretive Messages for national distribution (SD-I)
22.	Centralized Storm Information System (CSIS) display of radar and satellite data
23.	VAS Data Utilization Center (VDUC) display
24.	Vegetation Index
25.	Quantitative precipitation estimate; Interactive Flash Flood-Analysis (IFFA)

TABLE 2
THE TECHNOLOGY RECONCILIATION TEAMS

Team 1.	**Satellite Imagery Reconciliation Team**
Leader:	David S. Johnson
Members:	Lee M. Mace
	Vincent J. Oliver
	Edward W. Ferguson
	Ralph K. Anderson
	Donald C. Gaby
Team 2.	**Civilian/Military Interagency Coordination Team**
Leaders:	Col. James Jones, USAF
	Vincent Oliver, NESS
Team 3.	**Satellite Soundings Reconciliation Team**
Leader:	(Richard E. Hallgren)
Members:	William D. Bonner
	Christopher M. Hayden
Team 4.	**Radar Technology Reconciliation Team**
Leaders:	1957-1976 Harold Foster
	1976-1989 Paul Hexter
Members:	David Higginbotham
	Frederick Zbar
Team 5.	**Interactive Data Management and Analysis Systems Reconciliation Team**
Leaders:	1960-70 Charles Bristor
	1970-87 Verner E. Suomi
Members:	Frederick R. Mosher
	Frederick S. Zbar

Note: This table was compiled by the author from information collected for this study

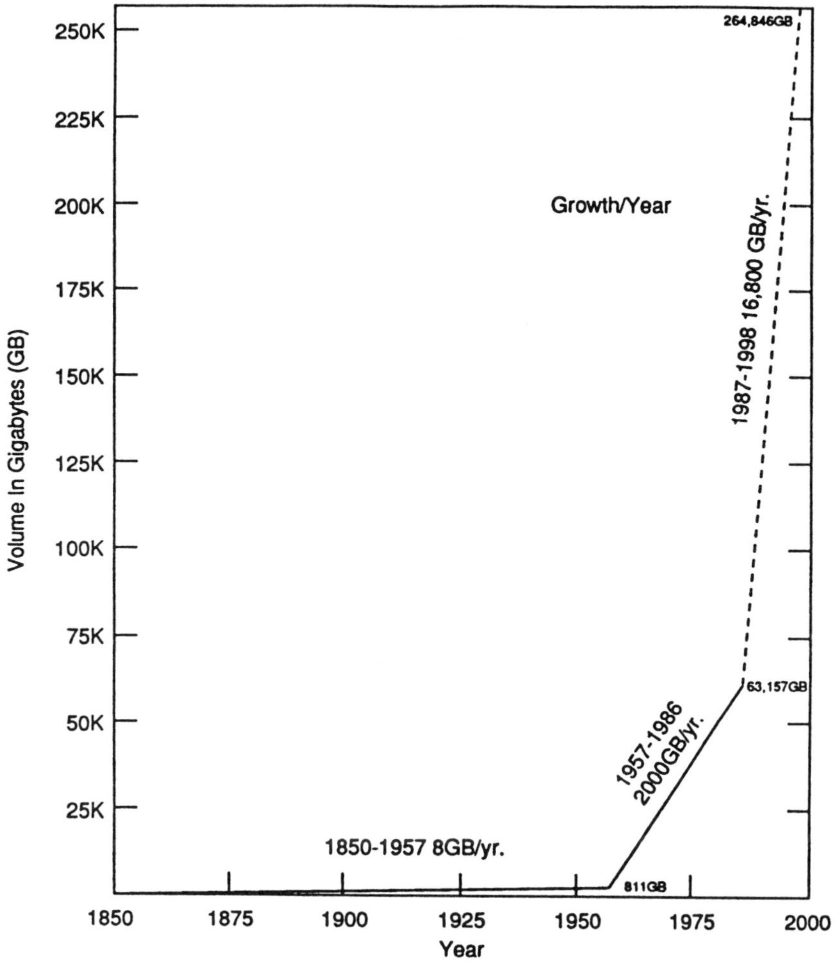

FIGURE 1
Exponential Increases in Remote-Sensing Meteorological Data Since 1957.

Figure 1 shows growth in volume of digital data in NESDIS database as of August, 1986. The projected growth through 1998 was derived from the NOAANET Requirements Report (U.S. Department of Commerce, 1986). Meteorological data from satellites account for 98% of the totals after 1960.

Overall management source for organizational development and perspective		*	Management
	1. Date of First Measurement or Observation	A	Input
	2. Platform		
	3. Instrument (Technique or Measurement of Observation)		
	4. Variable Measured or Observed		
	5. Time Period Over Which Observations Were Made		
ERSO	6. Volume of Raw Data Collected	B	Summation
SRSO	6. Volume of Raw (Level 0) Data Collected		
	Processing Assumed		
ERSO	7. Data Products Derived from Raw Data	C	Output
SRSO	7. Data (Levels 2-5) Products Derived from Raw (level 0) Data		
	Production Of Data Products Assumed		
	8. Use of Data Product in Operational Forecasting & Guidance	D	Use
	9. Date of First Use		
	10. Improvement in Weather Forecasting?	E	Evaluation
	11. How was Improvement Validated?		
	12. Who Did the Technology Reconciliation?	F	Technology Reconciliation
	13. How Did They Do It?		
	14. a) From Interview (Primary Source Name)	G	Source of Facts
	b) From Literature (Secondary Source)		

FIGURE 2
General System Perspective on Data Collection Form: Weather Forecasting Improvements from Both Earth Remote-Sensing Observations (ERSO) and Space Remote-Sensing Observations (SRSO)

1957 - 1987. N = 199

THE GLOBAL CHANGE DATABASE PROJECT: A PILOT DISKETTE PROJECT FOR AFRICA

Michael A. Chinnery, John J. Kineman, David A. Hastings,
and Herbert Meyers
NOAA National Geophysical Data Center
Boulder, Colorado, U.S.A.

INTRODUCTION

Global environmental modeling typically involves supercomputers running complex mathematical simulations which may require days of iterative processing. Because of the complexity of these models, and thus the amount of computer time required for them to run, only rather coarse-scale gridded data (from 1 to 5 degree cell sizes) can be considered. Yet these models need to be linked to other modeling activities at finer scales, and even to resource analysis using high-resolution satellite imagery. Medium scale (from 1/6 to 1 degree) data and analysis are thus required to provide a test base for coarser scale theoretical models, and perhaps to serve as a link between the two scale extremes.

The National Geophysical Data Center in Boulder, Colorado is working with a wide variety of scientists and other U.S. Federal Agencies to bring global, medium scale, modern observational data and environmental analysis capabilities to much smaller laboratories around the world. It does this using personal computers or small UNIX work stations and low cost or public domain software.

The Global Change Diskette Project for Africa [1-6] was an experimental project which initiated an ambitious program within participating organizations to integrate a comprehensive set of global databases together with Geographic Information Systems (GIS) software for the global change research community. Africa was chosen as a regional test case in answer to a request from the IGBP to support the involvement of developing country scientists in the use of Global Change data.

The project developed cooperatively, involving many different organizations. The principal participants in the Africa pilot project are listed below:

- ICSU/IGBP Working Group on Data and Information Systems
- ICSU Panel on World Data Centers
- NOAA National Geophysical Data Center and World Data Center - A, Boulder, CO
- NOAA National Climatic Data Center, Asheville, NC
- Clark University, Worcester, MA
- UNEP/GEMS Global Resources Information Database, Nairobi & Geneva
- UN Institute for Training and Research, Paris
- National Center for Geographic Information Analysis, Santa Barbara, CA

In addition, various in-kind contributions were provided by:

- Environmental Systems Research Institute, Redlands, CA
- International Business Machines Corporation, Boulder, CO
- USGS EROS Data Center, Sioux Falls, SD

Many individual laboratories and scientists that contributed data sets...

Funding for the Africa pilot project has been provided by the ICSU Panel on World Data Centers, the Interagency Working Group on Data Management for Global Change, the United Nations Environment Programme, the NOAA Climate and Global Change Program, and the National Geophysical Data Center. Data compilation and documentation were carried out at the National Geophysical Data Center; the software was developed at Clark University; and training materials were developed by these organizations plus the National Center for Geographic Information Analysis.

The project consisted of:

1. Collecting appropriate data sets.
2. Evaluating received data.
3. Integrating the data into a coordinated database.
4. Compiling and editing documentation of the data, and producing a documentation manual.
5. Reviewing capabilities of the GIS software used in the project and

interacting with the software developers to improve the software.
6. Developing training materials, including an exercise workbook.
7. Developing demonstrations of the use of the data.
8. Establishing a network of research/test facilities for evaluation.
9. Conducting two training workshops in Africa.
10. Evaluating comments from data producers, software producers, workshop participants, and others.

PURPOSE OF THE PROJECT

Increasing interest in the Earth as a complex system is fueling the development of many global data sets. These pioneering data sets often involve exhaustive compilations from the scientific literature, contacts with colleagues, ground observations, and analyses of satellite data. Nevertheless, at this early stage of their development, the data can greatly benefit from increased exposure to scientists worldwide. They also can benefit from careful integration with other scientific data sets for multivariate study and quality assessment.

Sophisticated GISs allow one to analyze spatial data sets individually or in combinations with other data. One can theoretically model the vigor of vegetation with combinations of data on soils, ecosystems, vegetation classes, climate, weather, and perhaps other data. One can theoretically compare these with models made from satellite data. Such comparisons can be used to assess the accuracy of the satellite measurements, the ground-based data, and the modeling process itself. GIS provides a toolbox for interactive explorations of the data and development of derivation models, which require much less programming and computer power than theoretical simulation modeling. The GIS technique thus complements the global circulation modeling activities, provides observational analysis capabilities, and is accessible to a greater number of scientists worldwide.

In addition, providing integrated data and software on small computers should allow many new scientists to review the individual data sets themselves. The editorial comments and improvements that should come from such review will benefit the pioneering developers of the data sets as well as scientific users.

The end result from this activity should be improved data, improved software, improved understanding of the modeling process, improved models, and an enlarged global change analytical community.

The Global Change Diskette Project was a pilot test of this philosophy which has now grown into an ongoing database development effort with a multi-stage quality assurance program. With developers of scientific data sets contributing data to a laboratory specializing in the integration and distribution of the data and software, benefits from division of labor are occurring.

THE CONTRIBUTION OF DATA INTEGRATION

The initial task of a multivariate study of spatial data involves selection and assembly of the database. For most laboratories this is an unattractive task. The result may be a hasty assembly of the data, hoping to get to the more rewarding analysis - at the cost of detailed investigation of possible artifacts in the assembled data set.

However, the artifacts contained in virtually every one of these new data sets can propagate throughout the analysis, with sometimes unseen but unfortunate results. The Diskette Project, through the NGDC/WDC database development efforts, attempted to overcome some of these problems with an initial effort at integration accompanied with a widespread public review of the data.

Tasks of data integration included:

1. Assessing and correcting registration to the pixel (and sometimes the sub-pixel) level.
2. Finding possible errors in data transmission, such as corruptions of files.
3. Analyzing artifacts in the data. Continuing review of the data to attempt to reduce such artifacts, and to document remaining characteristics of the data.
4. Assessing and improving documentation (generally considered to be inadequate for multivariate study).
5. Correction of problems found in steps 1-4 above, informing data contributors and others of the progress of the integration effort.

The in-house integration exercise took about 18 months, and was completed in September, 1990. At the end of this period, "Beta-test" copies of the data, software, and documentation were distributed to several dozen pre-selected test sites on all six continents. Comments are now being received from these test sites.

DATABASES ASSEMBLED FOR THE PROJECT

Besides easy exchange of the data via floppy diskettes, the Diskette Project required easy use of the integrated data. This meant providing the data in a GIS structure, registering the data to a uniform grid and projection, and making the pilot database readily usable on IBM-compatible personal computers with standard configurations of VGA graphics and hard disk.

The project decided to use the latitude-longitude projection. This projection is the reference from which most projection programs convert to any other projection, and many data come in this format. A 10-minute latitude-longitude grid was chosen for full-screen VGA display of Africa, and to give a common ground to representation of data that had primarily been gridded at about 10-minutes and up to 1-degree grids.

The following data sets were integrated for the continent of Africa. These consisted of:

1. Global data sets contributed by their authors or designated distribution centers, data held at NGDC and the National Climatic Data Center, and reference data such as World Data Bank II, from which the data for Africa were extracted.
2. Data sets for Africa that were provided by the United Nations Environment Programme from its offices in Nairobi, Kenya, and Geneva, Switzerland.

Global databases contributed to the project, or provided by NGDC included:

1. NOAA normalized vegetation index, monthly 10 minute gridded composites, April 1985 through December 1988
2. Olson World Ecosystems database, decadal composite of characteristic ecosystem classes, 0.5 degree grid with 10 minute updates for Africa, prepared by Jerry S. Olsen
3. Holdridge Life Zones, characteristic classes, 0.5 degree grid, prepared by R. Leemans
4. Matthews Vegetation, Land-Use and Seasonal Albedo, characteristic classes, 1.0 degree grid, prepared by E. Matthews
5. Wilson and Henderson-Sellers Soil and Vegetation database, characteristic classes, 1.0 degree grid, prepared by M. F. Wilson and A. Henderson-Sellers
6. Zobler Soil Type, Soil Texture Surface Slope and Other Properties, characteristic classes, 1.0 degree grid, prepared by L. Zobler
7. FAO Soil Units, characteristic classes, 2 minute (re-sampled to 10

minute) grid, prepared by Environmental Systems Research Institute under contract to UNESCO/FAO
8. Legates and Willmott Average Monthly Air Temperature and Precipitation, 0.5 degree grid, compiled from multiple sources by D. Legates and C. Willmott
9. Revised FNOC Elevation, Terrain and Surface Characteristics, 10 minute grid, digitized from available maps and reprocessed by L. Clark, D. Joseph and J. Kineman
10. Integrated Elevation and Bathymetry, 10 minute grid, integrated by NGDC staff from a variety of 5 and 10 minute digital compilations
11. Micro-World Data Bank II: Coastlines, Country Boundaries, Islands, Lakes and Rivers, 1:3 000 000 scale vector lines, compiled from unclassified CIA and US Air Force data, with contributions from F. Pospeschil
12. World Data Bank II: Country Regions and Rivers, 1:1 000 000 vector lines and polygons, compiled by CIA, reprocessed by EROS Data Center, USGS

Databases for Africa supplied by the UNEP/FAO Global Resources Information Database (GRID) consisted of 1:5 000 000 scale vector points, lines and polygons which were rasterized to a 10 minute grid. The databases provided were:

1. Cropland
2. Rainfall in mm
3. Major Soil Classes
4. Vegetation
5. Wind Speed in m/sec
6. Desertification
7. Nairobi January Temperatures in degrees K - 100

As database development efforts progress beyond this initial test phase, improved versions of both the Africa and Global databases are being developed.

COMPUTER HARDWARE

The above databases were assembled onto a set of ten IBM/AT-compatible high density (5.25 inch, 1.2 Mbyte; or 3.5 inch, 1.44 Mbyte) floppy diskettes. IBM/AT compatibility was chosen since IBM compatible personal computers are the most common type to be found in African nations. VGA graphics capability is recommended for the display of the data, though other video standards allow more limited display capabilities.

COMPUTER SOFTWARE

A complete PC-based software package named IDRISI has been prepared by J. Ronald Eastman and others at Clark University, Worcester, Massachusetts. This package provides a powerful GIS display and processing capability. Special permission was granted by Clark University to distribute this package to African users as part of the Global Change Diskette Project package.

IDRISI is a grid-based geographic analysis system specially designed for personal computers. It utilizes a raster display with vector plotting and overlay capabilities. It has analytical capabilities useful at local, regional and global scales. It is relatively inexpensive and functionally substantial, and has been chosen as the PC-based GIS system of choice for training purposes by both UNEP and UNITAR.

CONCLUSION

Current computer technology allows the scientific community greater access to global environmental modeling. Personal computers and work stations provide the hardware, and low-cost public domain GIS and related programs comprise the software. Database development is still at an embryonic stage, but one embryo, provided by the Global Change Diskette Project has brought us new knowledge about integrating data, activities, and interests to improve the data and observational analysis capabilities for an enlarged and richer scientific community. Continued advances in hardware, software, and data appear to offer us an exciting time ahead.

REFERENCES

[1] Clark, D.M., and Kineman, J.J., Global databases: A NOAA experience, in Mounsey, H. and Tomlinson, R., Eds., *Building Databases for Global Science*. London: Taylor and Francis, 1988, pp. 216-223.

[2] Hastings, D.A., Kineman, J.J., and Clark, D.M., Increased access to global environmental modeling data and tools: The Global Change Database Program, *International Journal of Geographical Information Systems*, V.5 (1991, in press).

[3] IGBP Special Committee, *The International Geosphere-Biosphere Program: a study of Global Change - A Plan for Action*. Report #4, Stockholm, Sweden: International Geosphere-Biosphere Programme Secretariat, 1988.

[4] IGBP Special Committee, *Pilot Studies for Remote Sensing and Data Management*. Report #8, Stockholm, Sweden: International Geosphere-

-Biosphere Programme Secretariat, 1989.
[5] Kineman, J.J., Clark, D.M., and Croze, H., Data integration and modeling for global change: an international experiment. *Proceedings of the International Conference and Workshop on Global Natural Resource Monitoring and Assessments: Preparing for the 21st Century*, September, 1989, Venice, Italy. Rockville, Maryland: American Society of Photogrammetry and Remote Sensing, pp. 660-669
[6] Ruttenberg, S., Kineman, J., and R. Eastman, The global change database project (GCDP): A data project for the IGBP. *Science International*, ICSU Newsletter 41, 1990, Paris, pp. 46-48

OVERVIEW OF THE U. S. DEPARTMENT OF ENERGY'S <u>ARM</u> PROGRAM*

Gerald M. Stokes
Global Studies Program
Pacific Northwest Laboratory
Richland, WA 99352 U.S.A.

Joyce L. Tichler
Department of Applied Science
Brookhaven National Laboratory
Upton, NY 11973 U.S.A.

1. INTRODUCTION

The Department of Energy (DOE) is initiating a major atmospheric research effort, the Atmospheric Radiation Measurement Program (ARM). The program is a key component of DOE's research strategy to address global climate change and is a direct continuation of DOE's decade-long effort to improve the ability of General Circulation Models (GCMs) to provide reliable simulations of regional and long-term climate change in response to increasing greenhouse gases. The effort is multi-disciplinary and multi-agency, involving universities, private research organizations and more than a dozen government laboratories.

The objective of the ARM Program is to provide an experimental testbed for the study of important atmospheric effects, particularly cloud and radiative processes, and to test parameterizations of these processes for use in atmospheric models. This effort will support the continued and rapid improvement of GCM predictive capability.

* This research was performed under the auspices of the United States Department of Energy under Contract No. DE-AC02-76CH00016.

Over the past ten years, the research programs of DOE and other agencies have made significant progress toward understanding the potential for global climate change and the resulting consequences. Models of the global climate system have advanced to include realistic geography, the annual cycle of the seasons, and varying cloud cover. Very recently, models have begun to include coupling of the ocean-atmosphere system. Results of climate models suggest that projected greenhouse gas emission patterns may lead to a global climate warming of 1.5 to 4.5 degrees Celsius and to significant changes in water availability during the next century.

However, this decade of research has also revealed that considerable uncertainties in model estimates remain. For example, although the 1980s have been especially warm, the extent of global warming over the past century may have been two to three times less than that estimated by current models. Further, when the results of different models are compared, there are substantial differences among their estimates of temperature and precipitation changes in response to doubled CO_2. We therefore do not know with sufficient accuracy how large the climatic changes will be, how rapidly the changes will occur, or how the changes will be distributed over the globe.

The ARM Program consists of three components. Initial members of the Science Team will be selected this summer based on accepted peer reviewed research proposals. This group will set the scientific direction of the program and will be the primary recipient of the experimental data. The Clouds and Radiation Testbed (CART) team provides the experimental testbed for the program. An Instrument Development Program will provide for further development of new instrumentation in response to programmatic needs. Initial participants in the Instrument Development Program are also to be selected this summer based on accepted peer reviewed proposals. Activities are coordinated and directed through the ARM program office and the Atmospheric and Climate Research Division of DOE.

2. ARM SCIENTIFIC PROGRAM REQUIREMENTS

The following scientific requirements emerge as the most critical for a program designed to remedy key weaknesses of current models:

A quantitative description of the spectral radiative energy balance profile under a wide range of meteorological conditions must be developed. Such descriptions must come from field measurements and must be quantified at a level consistent with climatologically significant energy flows of 1 to 2 W m^{-2}.

The processes controlling the radiative balance must be identified and investigated. Validation of our understanding of these processes must come from a direct and comprehensive comparison of field observations with detailed calculations of the radiation field and associated cloud and aerosol interactions.

The knowledge necessary to improve parameterizations of radiative properties of the atmosphere for use in GCMs must be developed. This requires intensive measurements at a variety of temporal and physical scales. A major emphasis must be placed on the role of clouds, including their distribution and microphysical properties.

Within this framework, the goals of ARM are two-fold. First, it will attempt to improve the treatment of radiative transport in GCMs for the clear sky, general overcast, and broken cloud cases. Second, it will provide a testbed for cloud parameterization models used in GCMs. The measures of the quality of the models will include their ability to reproduce observed wavelength and direction-dependent fluxes of longwave and shortwave radiation and the time-varying distribution of cloud type and amount.

3. EXPERIMENTAL APPROACH

ARM is an observational program driven by theoretical and modeling requirements. The ARM Program must provide data that can improve and test the GCM parameterizations of clouds and their microphysical composition. The smallest domain explicitly represented in a GCM is the single grid cell. A GCM cell is orders of magnitude larger than the scale associated with important cloud characteristics. It is possible that over the next decade model resolution will increase substantially so that single grid cells will have dimensions of a few tens of kilometers (comparable to an ERBE pixel). Even so, since clouds can have dimensions less than a kilometer, subgrid parameterization will remain necessary.

Of all the subgrid-scale characteristics that may affect radiation, cloud inhomogeneities and surface albedo variations are most important. Uncertainties in climate models will be reduced substantially when a reliable cloud parameterization is developed that will consistently apply under important mean climate conditions. Data that characterizes the statistics of clouds on a subgrid-scale is necessary for the development of improved cloud models.

The ARM experiment will consist of coordinated sets of instruments at each of four to six permanent base sites. These sites are the primary experimental resource of CART. Each ARM site will have three closely associated components. Each component is briefly described here:

3.1 The Central Facility

A critical experimental task of ARM is to make intensive measurements of the radiation field and the physical conditions that control the radiative transfer. Therefore, ARM will field two classes of equipment at the central facility: those for measuring the radiation field directly and those intended to characterize the local radiative circumstances, such as surface and cloud properties. The focus of the observations at the central facility will be the detailed characterization of the atmospheric column above the facility and high spectral resolution radiometric instruments.

3.2 The Three-Dimensional Mapping Network

A series of auxiliary stations will surround the central facility within a 20-km radius (this radius was derived from consideration of the scale height of the atmosphere). These stations will contain instrumentation designed to measure the three-dimensional structure of the atmosphere near the base site and will make use of fundamental profiling equipment, as well as basic radiometric and meteorological equipment. A focus of the specialized stations will be the reconstruction of the cloud geometry surrounding the base site using state-of-the-art photogrammetric methods. This cloud "visualization system" will be supplemented with a system of wind profilers capable of measuring large-scale vertical velocities.

3.3 Extended Observing Network

Surrounding the central facility and the mapping network will be 16 to 25 extended observing stations. These stations will support the development and study of methods used to generalize detailed atmospheric models for use in GCMs and related models through the process of parameterization. The extended observing area of a base site will include a region of the order of magnitude expected for GCM grid cells in the near future, approximately 200 x 200 km. The instruments at the extended stations will be designed to collect the basic radiometric information and conventional meteorological data needed to characterize the radiative transfer throughout the extended area. Only limited vertical information will be collected, with the more extensive and demanding profiling equipment reserved for the base sites and mapping stations. Wind profilers will, however, be employed on this scale as well to observe the general vertical motions associated with mesoscale phenomena.

3.4 The Mobile Observing System and Campaign Studies

In addition to the permanently placed equipment at the base and extended sites, ARM will maintain a mobile version of the basic experimental equipment found at the central facility and additional instrumentation for use in directed campaign studies. The ARM Program will take several approaches to planning campaigns which will supplement the more operational and continuous observations at the base sites. First there will be a series of short-term operations aimed at the exploration of specific physical mechanisms and processes. An example might be the deployment of the mobile system to support an intensive field experiment in conjunction with another program. The second approach will be through longer-term operation and data acquisition at a site chosen to reveal experimental or climatological anomalies at the base sites. Another approach might deploy equipment at a location chosen to verify models for conditions intermediate to those of the base sites.

A campaign may also involve the addition of instruments to the basic instrument site at a permanent site in order to achieve a specific scientific or technical objective. Examples might include a comprehensive calibration experiment on a highly specialized prototype or an intensive set of observations aimed at understanding an extraordinary transient climate condition.

3.5 Aircraft and Satellite Observations

Despite all of the advances in remote sensing technology in the past two decades, ground-based instrumentation alone will not meet all of the observational requirements of ARM. As a result both aircraft and satellite observations will play an important role in the experimental strategy. Aircraft will be involved in two ways. First, some aircraft observations will be used on a regular basis to support, for example, calibration of remote sensing systems and to profile the radiation field as a function of altitude. Next, aircraft will be used for direct sampling of key atmospheric constituents in support of intensive campaign periods.

Satellite observations offer critical data for ARM. Top of the atmosphere radiative fluxes and profiling atmospheric conditions in regions beyond the range of sondes and ground based sensors will be crucial. Alternatively, ARM sites will themselves offer extraordinary opportunities for providing ground-truth for satellite sensors. The ARM data system will be designed to support what appears to be a highly synergistic relationship.

4. MEASUREMENT STRATEGY AND INSTRUMENT SELECTION

In order to meet the goals of ARM, the instrument selection must support:

- the measurement of key aspects of the radiation field under a range of climatologically significant meteorological conditions sufficient to constrain detailed radiative calculations;

- detailed studies of atmospheric trace gas, aerosol, and water-vapor distributions;

- detailed studies of meteorological variables, including cloud type and distribution, wind field, temperature, etc.;

- measurement of large-scale vertical velocities; and

- measurement of critical microphysical properties of clouds.

To support these measurements, it will be necessary to have a support infrastructure with: near real-time processing of data and execution of model state-of-the-art calibration methods, including on-site calibration at facilities explicitly designed to support the measurement systems and redundant measurement sites providing near real-time evaluation of instrument performance.

The intent of the measurements in ARM is to test the predictive power of the models. The instrumentation will be improved continuously. Specialized research instruments, either developed through this program or by others, may be brought to an operational state and then added to the complement of instruments. Observing protocols may also be changed to increase the quality of the tests. All critical measurements will be systematically replicated. The Science Team will have a critical role in the selection of instruments and their evolution at particular sites. The instrument complement for a specific site may be tailored to individual site characteristics.

5. SITE SELECTION

In response to the nature of the problem of studying subgrid phenomena, the experimental equipment will be deployed at a series of field sites. These sites will be chosen on the basis of their climatological significance and ability to support a systematic exploration of the performance of radiation cloud parameterization and cloud formation models under a wide range of climatologically significant conditions.

The site-selection process for ARM will be complicated. The choices must incorporate the optimal combination of characteristics in several areas. The general groupings of the criteria are: climatic significance, appropriate climatic sampling, synergistic potential with other programs, scientific viability, and logistical viability.

6. COLLABORATION WITH OTHER PROGRAMS

During the ARM Program, DOE will collaborate extensively with existing programs at other agencies, such as the National Oceanic and Atmospheric Administration (NOAA), the National Science Foundation (NSF), and the National Aeronautics and Space Administration (NASA) as well as programs outside of the United States. The collaborations will include joint participation in campaigns, the exchange of data, and direct involvement in experimental design and instrument development. ARM's objectives make it necessary to acquire data generated by other agencies and programs and ARM intends to provide access to the data sets it will generate to other scientific investigators.

7. SUMMARY AND STATUS

The ARM Program is a highly focused observational and analytical research effort that will compare observations with model calculations in the interest of accelerating improvements in both observational methodology and GCMs.

The initial program plan (DOE 1990) for ARM outlined the classes of observational tools which are capable of meeting the observational requirements discussed in section 4. The instrumentation is currently undergoing extensive review in light of the detailed experimental requirements of the individual ARM investigators. This review will include pilot observational programs in late 1990 and early 1991. These observational campaigns will be supported by sensitivity studies of models conducted during the same period. The data system for ARM is in the design phase and the conceptual design will be reviewed twice during the summer of 1990.

The Science Team for the Program will convene for the first time in November 1990. Current plans call for initial occupation of the first ARM site in 1992.

Other programs interested in suggesting potential sites, providing or receiving data, or participating in campaigns should contact Dr. Gerald M. Stokes, Technical Director, ARM Program Office, Pacific Northwest Laboratories, Battelle Boulevard, Richland, WA 99352, USA.

The ARM scientific program requirements as well as details on the logistics of the program are discussed in a paper by Patrinos et. al., which is soon to be published.

8. REFERENCES

[1] Department of Energy, Atmospheric Radiation Measurement Program Plan, DOE/ER-0441, U.S. Department of Energy, Washington D.C. (1990).

[2] Patrinos, A., R. G. Ellingson, G. M. Stokes and D. Sowle, The Department of Energy Initiative on Atmospheric Radiation Measurements: A Study of Radiation Forcing and Feedbacks. to appear in Bulletin of the American Meteorological Society issue on the Seventh Conference on Atmospheric Radiation, July 23 - 27, 1990.

ECO-ENVIRONMENT CHANGE MONITORING IN CHINA

Wang Changyao
Institute of Remote Sensing Application
Chinese Academy of Sciences
P.O. Box 775
Beijing, China

INTRODUCTION

Human activities and exploitation of natural resources on a broad scale lead to great global eco-environment change. China is suffering from some serious eco-environment problems, such as a decrease in farmland and forest, soil erosion, desertification, water shortage, pollution, drought, floods, etc.

In order to grasp eco-environment change and its course, and to provide prior warning and thus allow for advanced planning, we have recently monitored some fast-changing eco-environment events. These include a land use change survey in the Beijing area, desertification research in Yu Lin, Shannxi, Yellow River Delta growth detection, and forest fire monitoring in the Da Xing An Ling Range. We used remote sensing technology and a geographical information system.

DESERTIFICATION AND LAND USE CHANGE SURVEY

Food and pollution is a big problem about which we have been extremely concerned in our country. As the population increases, correspondingly the average farmland area of each person decreases. Environmental change and human activities also cause a reduction in cultivated land. Nowadays, the desertification area is about 328 000 km^2. It is 3.4% of the total area of our country [1]. Sixteen and seven tenths percent of our territory is suffering from soil erosion; the total area is about 1 603 000 km^2. Cultivated land is seriously damaged by industrial pollution.

In order to investigate desertification change, we selected Yu Lin county as a study area. Remote Sensing data include Landsat TM acquired in August 1987 and a panchromatic aerial photo taken in July 1960. First of all, Landsat TM was classified with the likelihood algorithm method. The classification criterion was based on Table 1.

class	type	vegetation cover (%)
1	latent desertification	> 50
2	desertification	35 - 50
3	intense desertification	15 - 30
4	critical desertification	5 - 15
5	desert	< 5

Table 1. Criterion of Desertification Classification

For each type classification we selected 2-3 training areas, which was checked by field work. After all of the image pixel had been calculated, five types of desertification were classified.

Meanwhile, the desertification map at a 1:100 000 scale was made through the interpretation of the panchromatic aerial photo in 1960.

For the realization of desertification monitoring, ARC/INFO, a GIS was used for overlapping the desertification map (1960) and Landsat TM classification result. The overlap criterion is that, overlap (A,B,C,D)

where:
A --- coverage 1960
B --- coverage 1987
C --- definite change type
D --- corresponding color

this means:

overlay (A, B, C, 1): -A=C, B=C, !
overlay (A, B, C, 2): -not(A=C), B=C, !
overlay (A, B, C, 3): -not(B=C), A=C, !

overlay (-, -, -, 4): -!

With only two years of remote sensing, we obtained data for the purposes of comparison in this area. The regional regression model has been established for desertification change analysis. The outcome indicates that the desertification area in Qin He Township of Yu Lin Country was reduced by 5% from 1960-1987 as a result of planting trees and grass.

As for the urban area growth monitoring of Beijing city, normalized difference, ratio and principal components methods were applied to the different images process. The results show that these methods are useful for extract of land use change dynamic.

WATER CHANGE DICTATION

As the population increases and industry develops, a shortage of water is also a crucial problem in our country. The water area in the northern part of China tends to shrink continuously and some lakes have been drying up even more rapidly in recent time, lakes such as Tarozuo in Tibet, Manas, Lubupo in Xinjiang, etc.

For the research of long period water area change in the North China Plain, the method comparing Landsat data with historical records was adopted. The result shows that the area of big lakes and low-lying water bodies in this region was 12 000 km^2 before the Tang and Song Dynasties, and that now the area of the remaining 37 lakes and low-lying water bodies is only 5000 km^2.

Computer matching analysis of multi-temporal remote sensing data from the area of interest was made to study quantitatively their recent dynamic changes. Take Baiyangdian Lake as an example, which is one of the biggest lakes in the North China Plain, the ratio N_1, N_2 and N_3 were obtained by applying data from SIR-A (Sa), Landsat Mss 7 (M_7) and TM 4 (T_4) in following formulas and color transformation was then made with the ratio N_1, N_2 and N_3 to enhance the difference in dynamic changes of this lake.

$$N_1 = \frac{S_a \times S_a}{S_a + M_7 + T_4} \qquad N_2 = \frac{S_a \times M_7}{S_a + M_7 + T_4} \qquad N_3 = \frac{S_a \times T_4}{S_a + M_7 + T_4}$$

We also chose five years remote sensing data of this lake for correlative matrix analysis of the factors affecting the change in the water area of Baiyangdian Lake from 1961 to 1984. (Table 2.)

The result proved that the expansion of cultivated land and residential area is negatively correlated to the water area in this region. This means that the

Table 2. Result of Correlative Matrix Analysis

Y: water surface (acre)	X_1: cultivated land (acre)	X_2: residen-tial area (acre)	X_3: water entering (million m^3)	X_4: annual average rainfall (mm)
108 098.0	89 286.0	4912.0	769.62	684.2
18 117.0	181 105.0	7088.0	314.49	558.2
1 363.0	191 743.0	8875.0	92.32	357.0
17 391.0	188 905.0	10 101.0	174.99	779.8
1 685.0	198 558.0	10 606.0	92.32	330.0
Correlation	R x 1	R x 2	R x 3	R x 4
Coefficient	-0.997	-0.859	0.968	0.496

increase of water consumption by industry and the expansion of irrigation are important factors for the drying up of low-lying water bodies in dry seasons.

The Huanghe River underwent a great change from north to south in the North China Plain. It carried more than one billion tons of silt annually to build the massive delta and caused the coastline in this region to move rapidly seaward [2].

Through the matching analysis of 14-temporal Landsat images of the outlet area of Huanghe River Delta has extended seaward nearly 100 km, the Delta increase 3080 km^2 of land at an average of 23.7 km^2/per year in 130 years from 1855-1985.

VEGETATION DYNAMIC CHANGE MONITORING

Forest cover is a crucial factor in our geo-ecosystem and an important sign representing the earth's health. The most worrisome thing is that the forest area is decreasing at an astonishing speed all over the world.

The main reason for the decrease in forest area is overfelling. Another reason is natural disasters such as forest fires, insects, pests, etc.

For the sake of monitoring the vegetation dynamic changes on a large scale, NOAA AVHRR data has been used. We have compared for two years AVHRR data in the North China Plain by using an image processing system. Each has been processed with a normalized difference Vegetation Index formula.

$$NDVI = \frac{CH_2 - CH_1}{CH_2 + CH_1}$$

After the two NDVI data matched together, we can clearly seen the "green wave change" in different years in this area.

However, the most successful application example of NOAA AVHRR data is in monitoring the biggest forest fire in the Da Xing An Ling Range of China, which took place from May 6 to June 2, 1987. NOAA data was not only used to monitor the whole process of the forest fire, but also the eco-environment recovery.

Based on Wien's law,

$$\lambda_m \times T = 2897.8 \ \mu m \cdot K$$

Where λ_m is the wave-length at the blackbody maximum emission at temperature T.

The AVHRR channel 3 (13.35—3.39 μm) is the optimum band for detecting the forest fire. The forest fire color image was composed with AVHRR channel 1 (0.56—0.68 μm), channel 2 (0.725—1.1 μm) and channel 3. In the evening, channel 4 (10.5—11.5 μm), channel 5 (11.5—12.5 μm) and channel 3 have been used to composite the forest fire images.

At the first stage of the forest fire, the initial two fire points can be clearly seen in the image of May 6, 1987. The Xilin area where the fire passed (left) is about 1300 hectares, the Pangu area where the fire passed (right) is about 1900 hectares, its smoke reaching 80 km in length [3].

The stage of the forest fire developing and joining was from May 9 to 22. In the AVHRR image acquired on May 13, it can easily be found that the

Xilin and Gulian fire points were joined together and formed the western fire place, the fire passed area is about 550 000 hectares, the Pangu area where the fire passed grew to 290 000 hectares.

At the last stage, the western and eastern fire places joined together and formed a big fire area. The outline of the whole forest fire area of Da Xing An Ling Range is very clear in the Landsat TM or AVHRR image obtained on June 13.

During the time the forest fire took place, more than 100 AVHRR data were received. These data played an important role in putting out this big forest fire.

CONCLUSION

Global eco-environment and renewable resources changes have aroused the attention of many countries. Obviously, remote sensing technology has an advantage, owing to its large and fast coverage and multispectral data. In short, Landsat TM and SPOT are fitted to county level land use change survey. Landsat MSS is suitable for province level eco-environment change dictation, and NOAA AVHRR data are suited to the monitoring of large events of frequent occurrence. Furthermore, a geographical information system is useful for analyzing the changed factors and predicting future tendencies.

BIBLIOGRAPHY

[1] Zhu Zhengda, 1984. *Criterion and Method for Desertification Mapping Desert in China*, Vol. 1.

[2] Qian Ning, 1965. *The Evolution of Riverbed in the Lower Reaches of Yellow River*. Science Press.

[3] Chen Weiying, 1988. *Monitoring the Forest Fire in Da Xing An Ling Range with NOAA AVHRR Data*.

GENERATION OF A SPATIAL DATABASE OF CLIMATIC VARIABLES IN A DEVELOPING REGION

S.D. Lynch and R.E. Schulze
Department of Agricultural Engineering
University of Natal, P.O. Box 375
Pietermaritzburg, 3200
Republic of South Africa

M.C. Dent
Computing Centre for Water Research
University of Natal, P.O. Box 375
Pietermaritzburg, 3200
Republic of South Africa

INTRODUCTION

The three basic climatic variables of rainfall, temperature and evaporation place important constraints on ecological systems, hydrological response as well as on agricultural and other activities of man. It goes without saying that these variables are included in many important planning exercises in a developing region like southern Africa which covers the Republic of South Africa, the Kingdom of Lesotho, the so-called National Independent States, and part of the Kingdom of Swaziland.

Rainfall, temperature and evaporation are measured and recorded daily at approximately 10 000, 1200 and 600 stations respectively in southern Africa. To place these figures in perspective with regard to spatial coverage it is pertinent to consider that 440 000 grid points cover this area on a 1′ by 1′ grid. The distance between successive minutes of arc is approximately 1.6 km. Thus it is evident that a large amount of spatial climatic information needs to be generated, in addition to the observed data, to provide a useful spatial coverage.

This paper describes a series of studies which have been completed successfully and which generated a number of spatial information sets of climatic variables. These information sets were produced at a spatial resolution of 1′ by 1′ and include mean annual precipitation (MAP), 80th and 20th percentile of annual precipitation, mean and median monthly precipitation, 80th and 20th percentile of monthly precipitation, monthly means of daily maximum, minimum and average temperature and mean monthly evaporation.

PHYSIOGRAPHIC DATA AND INFORMATION SETS

The fluctuations in climatic variables induced by topographic complexities dictate that complex functions are required to estimate climatic variables at ungauged sites. Polynomial spline, multi-quadric surfaces, Thiessen polygons and the subjective interpolation of isohyets rely on a fundamental assumption of the juxtaposition of similar values of the climatic variable. The use of the above techniques are therefore generally confined to flatter areas where gradients of the climatic variable being mapped and particularly rainfall gradients are not marked (Mandeville and Rodda, 1970). Regions of similar topography in southern Africa were also found, by Lynch and Dent (1985), to be well suited to the mapping of climate variables using such techniques. In the mountainous areas of southern Africa where the climate network is often sparse in relation to the complex nature of the climate it is more suitable to undertake the mapping of climatic variables using techniques which are able to reflect these complexities. The influence of physiography on the spatial distribution of mean annual precipitation and on temperature, for example, has been well documented and it is therefore logical that physiographic variables should be used as a basis in mapping these climatic variables. Southern African studies by *inter alia,* de Villiers (1962), Whitmore (1968), Torrance (1973), Schulze (1976; 1979; 1981; 1983), Tyson, Preston-Whyte and Schulze (1976), de Jager and Schulze (1977), Buys, Fabricius, van den Bergh and Klopper (1979) and Dent, Lynch and Schulze (1988) support the above assertion for generation of long term average rainfall and temperature surfaces in this region.

BASIC CLIMATIC AND PHYSIOGRAPHIC DATA

The nature of the mapping studies described in this paper dictate that they be founded on what should be the most comprehensive climatic data sets readily available in southern Africa at the time of this study. Numerous organisations and individuals contributed most generously to these climatic data sets. Substantial contributions were received from the South African Weather Bureau, State Departments of Agriculture and Water Supply, and of Water Affairs, South African Sugar Association, Natal Parks Board, Natal Tanning Extract Company, organized agriculture, municipalities and private individuals. Many of the stations for which data were supplied have daily records which were processed to yield monthly and annual means as well as other statistics.

In view of the aforementioned evidence in respect of the influence of physiography on climate it was evident that an appropriate physiographic information set should be established for southern Africa. The exact location and altitude of each rainfall, temperature and pan evaporation station in the region was established from the 1:50 000 topographic map series. The altitude data were derived in the following manner. A grid of 1 arcminute was overlain on the 1:50 000 topographic map and the altitude at each grid intersection point was noted. No attempt was made to average altitudes for a 1 minute square or to find a "representative" altitude. It is entirely possible therefore that small topographical features will not be reflected by this digital image of 440 000 altitude values which in many areas is adequate but in other areas may not be detailed enough to depict all the features of a complex topography.

GENERATED CLIMATIC AND PHYSIOGRAPHIC INFORMATION

The annual rainfall sequences were too short, in many cases, to achieve the desired reliability and had therefore to be extended by synthetic means. Lynch and Dent (1987) found that a minimum rainfall sequence of between 15 and 35 years was sufficient to use in the generation of a spatial mean annual precipitation information set for southern Africa. As many of the rainfall station records were less than the desired length of record it was preferable to use some synthetic rainfall data in order to increase the record length rather than to estimate the long term mean by using too short a record (Matalas and Jacobs, 1964). After taking due cognizance of these and other research findings it was decided to synthesize monthly rainfall where necessary in order to increase the rainfall data record length of stations with short records where stations were located critically. The so-called Model 5 of Zucchini and Hiemstra (1984) was selected to perform this synthesis. Other techniques which were considered were linear and multiple regression, other models proposed by Zucchini and Hiemstra (1984), Gandin's method described by Creutin and Obled (1982) and Universal Kriging. The generated monthly rainfall values were flagged appropriately. The above research of extending rainfall record lengths to a critical minimum is described in detail by Dent, Lynch and Schulze (1988).

The altitude data formed the primary input to a set of techniques which produced other physiographic indices at each grid point. These indices were exposure, surface roughness, aspect with respect to rainbearing weather systems and a continentality index using distance from the sea was also calculated for every grid point within 300 km of the sea as was a valley topographic index used as an indicator of temperature inversion influences on minimum temperatures. These indices were then used as predictors in the regression analysis of mean annual precipitation (MAP), temperature and pan evaporation equivalents.

AUTOMATED MANAGEMENT OF THE RAINFALL AND TEMPERATURE DATA SETS

A system of computer programs and files was developed in order to manage these recorded rainfall and temperature data. This system consists of three main data files, namely an index file, a monthly direct access data file and the daily records which are kept in a VSAM indexed sequential data file. The monthly data file contains all the monthly and annual data as well as selected attributes of each station and a statistical summary of each station's data (Dent and Wills, 1986).

REGRESSION OF MEAN ANNUAL PRECIPITATION AND TEMPERATURE ON PHYSIOGRAPHIC VARIABLES

The large volumes of data, numbers of variables and possible regression models made it imperative to develop techniques to automate the management of the procedures leading up to and including the regression procedure for relating MAP, temperature and pan evaporation to physiographic variables. An intricate system involving numerous major procedural steps and incorporating 27 programs in FORTRAN and SAS languages was developed to perform the abovementioned functions. Throughout the system there were points at which human intervention and checking was required.

Southern Africa was divided into 34 and 11 regions for the purposes of the MAP and temperature/evaporation regression mapping respectively. All these regions overlapped by 30 arcminutes with neighbouring regions to ensure continuity of the isohyet, isotherm and isoevap surfaces at these regional boundaries.

The process of achieving the best regression expression for the rainfall, temperature and evaporation surface was an iterative one in the sense that maps of residuals from regression at the station points were produced and then studied before accepting, rejecting or modifying the regression expression. Outliers, anomalies and hyper- or insensitivity of the surfaces were thus detected and could be corrected.

TECHNIQUES OF MAPPING CLIMATIC VARIABLES

The techniques of mapping rainfall, temperature and evaporation fall into two broad categories, viz. trend surface analysis based on multiple regression and direct interpolation. The merits of trend surface analysis and direct interpolation were investigated. A combination of the regression surface and the surface generated by interpolating between the residuals was considered to be the most pragmatic solution for rainfall mapping.

The surface of MAP provided the foundation for the mapping of mean monthly rainfall and the variability of monthly and annual rainfall. The amount of work involved in producing separate regression expressions for each of the monthly surfaces and for each of the abovementioned statistics was prohibitive. An alternative technique which established the ratio between the mean monthly rainfall and MAP at station points was therefore employed. These ratios were interpolated onto a regular grid and then multiplied by the MAP image. The resulting image was one of mean monthly rainfall which fitted the observed data exactly at station points and followed the general shape of the MAP surface in areas between stations. Similar techniques were employed to produce spatial information sets of monthly and annual variability of rainfall.

Multiple regression techniques using latitude, longitude, continentality and a topographic inversion index as predictors were used to determine the monthly means of daily minimum, maximum and average temperature surfaces for southern Africa. The 1′ by 1′ surfaces of monthly maximum temperature, altitude and daylength indices were used to generate the monthly pan evaporation surfaces for southern Africa.

DISCUSSION AND CONCLUSIONS

The climatic and physiographic information procedures discussed in this paper provide a most valuable base for a range of present and future studies and plans. These information sets have already found many uses in *inter alia* agricultural, civil and communications engineering, agriculture, forestry, town and regional planning and in satellite and other remote sensing applications.

ACKNOWLEDGEMENTS

The research described in this paper was funded by the Water Research Commission and their support is acknowledged gratefully. All computations were performed at the Computing Centre for Water Research at the

University of Natal in Pietermaritzburg.

REFERENCES

[1] Buys, M.E.L., Fabricius, A.F., van den Bergh, P. and Klopper, A.P.J. (1979): Analysis of rainfall in South Africa. Expectancy of monthly rainfall. Dept. Agric. Tech. Services, Pretoria. Tech. Comm. No. 148, pp 33.

[2] Creutin, J.D. and Obled, C. (1982): Objective analysis and comparison. Water Resour. Res., 18: 413-431.

[3] De Jager, J.M. and Schulze, R.E. (1977): The broad geographic distribution in Natal of climatological factors important to agricultural planning. Agrochemophysica., 9: 81-91.

[4] Dent, M.C. and Wills, H.M.M. (1986): On-line data base management system for monthly rainfall in southern Africa. Integrated Design of Hydrological Networks. Proceedings Budapest Symposium. IAHS Publ. 158: 381-387.

[5] Dent, M.C., Lynch, S.D. and Schulze, R.E. (1988): Mapping mean annual and other rainfall statistics over southern Africa. Dept. Agricultural Engineering, University of Natal, Pietermaritzburg. ACRU Report 27. Water Research Commission, Pretoria, Report No. 109/1/89.

[6] De Villiers, J.M. (1962): A study of soil formation in Natal. Unpubl. Ph.D. Thesis, University of Natal, Pietermaritzburg.

[7] Lynch, S.D. and Dent, M.C. (1985): A comparison between two techniques for the spatial estimation of mean annual precipitation. Proc. Hydrological Sciences Symposium, Univ. of Natal, Pietermaritzburg.

[8] Lynch, S.D. and Dent, M.C. (1987): Appropriate record lengths for the estimation of mean annual and mean monthly precipitation in South Africa. Proc. Hydrological Sciences Symposium, Grahamstown.

[9] Mandeville, A.N. and Rodda, J.C. (1970): A contribution to the objective assessment of areal rainfall amounts. J. Hydrol. N.Z., 9: 281-291.

[10] Matalas, N.C. and Jacobs, B. (1964): A correlation procedure for augmenting hydrologic data. Statistical studies in hydrology. Geological Survey Professional paper 434-E. United States Govt. Printing Office, Washington, D.C.

[11] Schulze, R.E. (1976): On the application of trend surfaces of precipitation to mountainous areas. Water SA, 2: 110-118.

[12] Schulze, R.E. (1979): Hydrology and water resources of the Drakensberg. Dept. of Agricultural Engineering, University of Natal, Pietermaritzburg, ACRU Report 6. Natal Town and Regional Planning

Commission, Pietermaritzburg. pp 179.

[13] Schulze, R.E. (1981): Mean monthly temperature distributions for Natal. Dept. Agricultural Engineering, University of Natal, Pietermaritzburg, ACRU Report 11. pp 27.

[14] Schulze, R.E. (1983): Agrohydrology and -climatology of Natal, Dept. Agricultural Engineering, University of Natal, Pietermaritzburg, ACRU Report 14. Water Research Commission, Pretoria, pp 138.

[15] Torrance, J.D. (1973): The variation of meteorological elements with increasing altitude in the eastern border mountains of Rhodesia. Rhod. J. Agric. Res., 11: 181-189.

[16] Tyson, P.D., Preston-Whyte, R.A. and Schulze, R.E. (1976): The climate of the Drakensberg. Natal Town and Regional Planning Commission, Pietermaritzburg, pp 79.

[17] Whitmore, J.S. (1968): The relationship between mean annual rainfall and locality and site factors. S. Afr. Jour. Sci., 64: 423-427.

[18] Zucchini, W. and Hiemstra, L.A.V. (1984): Part 1: Augmenting hydrological records. Water Research Commission, Pretoria. Report No. 91/3/84.

OPERATIONAL DATA MANAGEMENT AT THE EUROPEAN CENTRE FOR MEDIUM-RANGE WEATHER FORECASTS (ECMWF)

J. K. Gibson
Head, Meteorological Applications Section
European Centre for Medium-Range Weather Forecasts
Shinfield Park
Reading, Berkshire RG2 9AX
United Kingdom

1. DEFINITION

Management is the act, art, or manner of managing or controlling (Collins Concise English Dictionary, 1978). It follows that Data Management is the act, art, or manner of controlling, as opposed by being controlled by, data.

On first joining ECMWF in 1976, the then Head of Research (now Director) Lennart Bengtsson advised me to "get the data right, and you will get the rest right as well!". The pertinence of that advice is that, by and large, people do *not* get the data right. All too often data are written on an "as is" basis, then archived that way for posterity. The result:

* diversity of data representation
* applications interfacing to specific formats
* difficulty in locating suitable data
* difficulty in using data once located, without transformation
* anarchy rather than control

Data are not confined to end results; computer programmes and applications too are data, and must be controlled. The management of source code has been addressed by many (*e.g.,* Dijkstra, 1976); indeed, structured programming is far more widely accepted than structured data representation.

Data management is the framework which supports and integrates:

* systems design
* programming methodology

* data representation
* the generation, processing, exchange, archive and retrieval of data
* systems review, testing, integration and reliability
* systems implementation, regeneration, and maintenance
* optimisation and efficiency.

The art of bringing order to chaos is centred on the identification of simplicity amongst complexity; simplification is often the key to successful data management. The science of data management is to apply this art to produce solutions which:

* maximise reliability and maintainability
* generalise user interfaces
* minimise the human resources required
* balance efficiency against simplicity
* ensure timely production of correct results suitably represented.

2. ECMWF'S METEOROLOGICAL OPERATIONAL SYSTEM - A DATA MANAGEMENT PROBLEM

ECMWF provides numerical medium range forecast products for 18 Member States, and, via the World Meteorological Organisation's Global Telecommunications System (WMO/GTS) to the world. Data in support of these activities are acquired from the WMO/GTS, augmented by special arrangements to receive additional high resolution satellite data. The operational system (EMOS) includes comprehensive facilities for the pre-processing and assimilation of the observational data to produce initial conditions for global forecast models, post-processing of the forecast and analysis output, generation and dissemination of products, and the maintenance of a comprehensive global archive of reports and products from the First Global Geophysical Experiment (FGGE) beginning December 1978.

The growing role of ECMWF's archived data as a unique vehicle for scientific investigation has required the development of a fully supported set of data services made available in support of international projects such as the World Climate Research Programme (WCRP), and Tropical Ocean Global Atmosphere (TOGA).

Figure 2.1 illustrates the sub-systems (simplified) outlined above, as they would appear if treated as a set of linked applications. In addition a large number of graphical, statistical and analytical applications need access to the raw bulletins, the decoded reports, the global fields, and the archive data. Dissemination products may need to be repeated or examined.

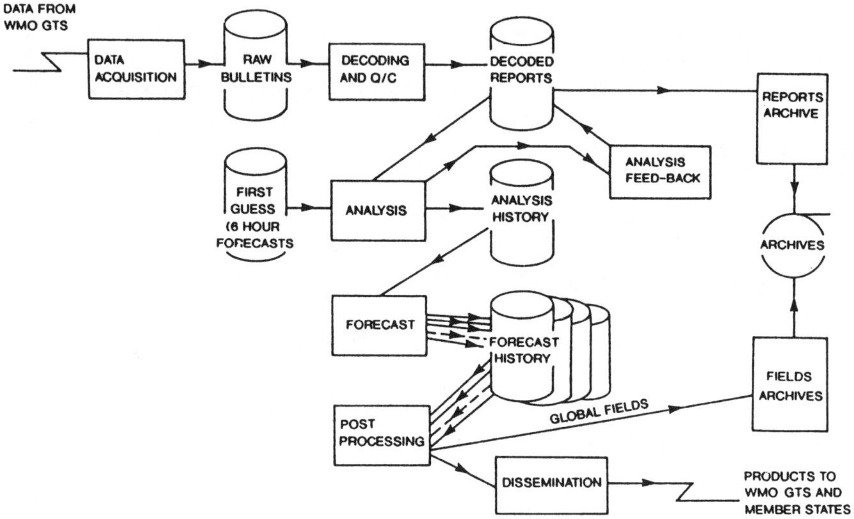

FIGURE 2.1 EMOS sub-systems

Results must be produced to schedule. The operational cycle involves some 200 batch jobs, many of which may be run 40 times in a day. Jobs must run according to dependencies, and in suitable mixes. This requires not only careful scheduling, but also full facilities for monitoring progress and status, and for manual supervision and intervention where necessary.

The applications comprise code written by many people, maintained not necessarily by the authors. They run over a range of computer hardware. Requests for modifications, coming from many quarters, occasionally may be sufficiently radical to require the complete replacement of a sub-system.

Substantial volumes of data are produced. If archive policy were to store all the raw data, it would be necessary to archive over 5 gigabytes daily. Successful data management requires full consideration of the requirements to access and use the data both immediately after its initial production, and for many years to come.

3. ECMWF'S METEOROLOGICAL OPERATIONAL SYSTEM - DATA MANAGEMENT APPLICATION

3.1 Background and History

The original EMOS system was designed as a modular collection of quasi-independent sub-systems, with clearly defined data interfaces. This approach enabled replacements sub-systems to be tested in parallel, then substituted when ready into the daily operations. Attention to many aspects of data management practice have been a contributing feature to the ability of EMOS to support the migration of improved forecast and analysis techniques into operations, with a minimum delay from the verification of their worth in research mode.

In 1985 comprehensive plans were formulated for an integrated approach to the data management of the complete operational system; the feasibility of the extension of these principles to the management of research experiments and their resulting data was also envisaged. To establish a methodology for control, standards were defined (Gibson, 1986) for source code structure and style, applications design, development, implementation and maintenance, with attention being given to simple review procedures, testing and verification. Emphasis was given to source code style, using a system called "Doctor" (Gibson, 1982), based on the Olympus system (Roberts, 1974) used in a number of European scientific establishments. This approach has resulted in the many source codes taking on a similar appearance; this helps maintenance analysts to understand codes inherited from elsewhere; the fact that the code looks familiar adds to the analysts' comfort - they can concentrate on its logic without being confronted with an alien, off-putting style.

3.2 A Second Generation EMOS - Analysis and Planning.

The application of data management was approached first by analyzing the data flow through the system; this established the need for common interfaces, revealing those areas of data concentration where simple file interfaces are not sufficient, necessitating some organisation of the data. The structures required for this organisation are termed "databases"; this does not imply the use of commercial database managements systems (DBMS), but rather specialised structures, supported by home grown software packages, designed to meet specific needs. Figure 3.1 illustrates the re-arrangement of the components after attention has been given to data flow.

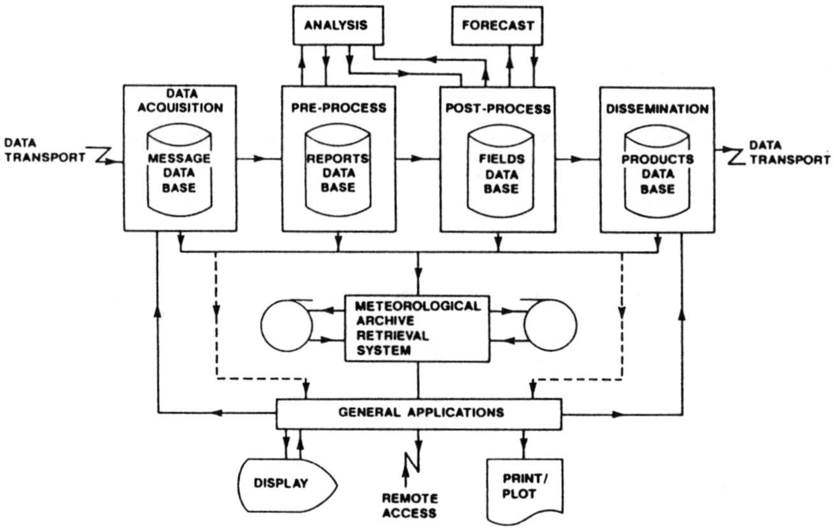

FIGURE 3.1 EMOS sub-systems with attention to data flow

From the beginning, ECMWF had tried to "get the data right". Forecast and analysis systems had been configured to be general with respect to resolution; their initial data had been augmented with sufficient data description so that no additional information would be required to define resolution parameters. The self defining data principles applied to forecast and analysis history data were used as examples in the construction of other data sets. Nevertheless, inspection of the data representation forms in use revealed:

* three complimentary forms for the representation of decoded observational data

* three different forms for the representation of fields of analysis and forecast results

* two forms of data packing, both based on the formula

$V = R + SP$ where V = unpacked value
R = reference value
S = scale factor
P = packed binary value

* the volume of forecast and analysis data used by applications and subsequently archived was 50 times the volume of the decoded observational data

* the volume of raw forecast and analysis results was 10 times that of the data selected for archive; nevertheless, the archive data fully represented the scientific content of the results - the reduction in volume being the result of applying sound principles to represent the data in a packed form.

Data representation obviously would have an important part to play in the second generation system. Limitation of binary data representation to three forms, one for the representation of all decoded observational data, one for the fields of forecast and analysis results, and the Computer Graphics Metafile (CGM) standard for graphical output, became the fundamental data management principle.

The following basic principles were laid down for the new system:

* the recommended standards for software development and maintenance be followed as far as is reasonable

* agreed standard forms of data representation be used for interfacing to the applications, and for archival storage

* data concentrations be organised, and relevant data retained in on-line databases for an appropriate period of time

* the analysis and forecast be configured to run from the packed data stored within the databases and archives; this would enable operational cases to be repeated exactly in research mode without the necessity to retain the unpacked data

* data be transferred between computers of different types to utilise the machine independence of the standard binary forms

* archive data be retained in an hierarchical file system, under the management of the Los Alamos "Common File System" (CFS), using the facilities of an IBM 3090 150E

* a Meteorological archive/retrieval system (MARS) be provided such that users request data in meteorological terms, and MARS delivers the data either from the CFS system or the on-line databases, as

appropriate

* standard representation forms be introduced for all forms of data delivery

* continued use be made of a programmable supervisor-monitor-scheduler (SMS) to manage the process control of all the system components

* an expert system be tried as a means of documenting and making available suitable material to operators and analysts to recover from system problems.

3.3 A Second Generation EMOS - Data Representation.

The second generation EMOS required that data representation be rationalised. Benefits were foreseen if internationally accepted data representation standards could be developed and adopted within the system.

3.3.1 FM92 GRIB

At this time, the WMO and ICAO were endeavouring to establish a standard binary representation for forecast and analysis products. The ECMWF Bit Code, together with the American H code, were both considered at a WMO Expert meeting. Some of the principles of each, together with initial proposals for the description of grids were combined to form the basis of the new representation form - but what should it be called? The Russian expert came up with GRIB (GRId in Binary), reasoning that in his dialect it means "mushroom", and that is what he expected it to do!

3.3.2 FM94 BUFR

Having standardised GRIB, the WMO moved towards addressing the binary representation of the more irregular observational data. Considering the scope of this task, the development process has been astonishingly swift.

There exist 30 to 40 different character codes for observational data. Even before the advent of binary representation, the problem of the proliferation of these character codes had been addressed: people with vision had attempted to advance the concept of a single, universal code, but without success. This concept was resurrected in what began as BIOB (BInary OBservations), but which later blossomed into BUFR (Binary Universal

Form for the Representation of data).

The BUFR concepts may be summarised as:

* table driven data description
* data in binary, presented as defined by that description

The concept of table driven data description has steadily evolved into a powerful data description language. It contains three principle elements:

* data descriptors (*i.e.*, numeric table reference values)
* operators (*e.g.*, replication, table content modification, etc.)
* references to pre-defined lists of data descriptors and operators.

The main table contains a definition, for each element, of the element name, the units used, a reference value (to give positive coded values), a scale factor, and the binary data width in bits. Virtually all Meteorological and Oceanographic data can be represented using the current tables; data relating to other branches of science could be accommodated, provided alternative tables were assembled.

3.4 A Second Generation EMOS - Implementation

The approach adopted with EMOS was modular, to renew subsystems one at a time, while simultaneously planning and preparing work on other subsystems.

First to be addressed was the archive of forecast and analysis results. These data represent by far the largest in volume of any data owned and retained by ECMWF. When sufficient software had been developed, parallel archiving began using MARS, the IBM system, and data represented in GRIB. Next followed support for the planned retrieval facilities, concentrating on access from the Cray X-MP initially, where most users wished to use the data. Software was added to perform data processing using the IBM 3090's vector facility, in preparation for the widening of the MARS user interface to embrace other networked computers.

Next, the fields database (FDB) software enabling access to randomly addressable fields of data on the Cray was developed and implemented. Naming conventions which related closely to those used in the MARS system were adopted to simplify the construction of the MARS-FDB interface. With the FDB software in place, the products generation and dissemination software, (previously run on a CDC NOS/BE system), were migrated to the Cray and were introduced into daily operations after parallel check-out.

It was then possible to adapt the interfaces to the analysis and forecast to use data from the FDB, rather than the full precision write-up data previously used. Users of the on-line data and archives soon became familiar with GRIB, which rapidly became the basic interface to all applications requiring analysis and forecast results. GRIB was then introduced into the dissemination. Progress towards acceptance here is less rapid, as some Member States will require some time to adapt; nevertheless, all have accepted the principle, and eventually will convert.

Meanwhile the BUFR representation form was taking shape. ECMWF's pre-processing, previously a batch system run 8 to 10 times a day, was considered unsatisfactory first because of the delay awaiting its completion before the subsequent analysis could be run, and second because of the need to obtain the earliest possible warning of problematic observational data. Thus it was configured as a set of real time processes and migrated to a VAX system. This included development of database structures for the incoming messages, and for the (BUFR) decoded reports.

Data services were designed, with selected data sets being assembled under the MARS system. Descriptive documentation together with carefully constructed application forms were published. Retrieval software was prepared to enable the information from these forms to be entered in full screen mode.

System integration was completed by the introduction of a new version of SMS for the process control of all system components.

4. CONCLUSIONS

In the Meteorological world more attention is being paid to data management than ever before; the WMO Commission for Basic Systems has set up a special working group which held its first meeting last March. This is rightly so; without control of data through management the anarchy which develops leads to extensive waste of valuable resources, to over complex applications, and to unnecessary barriers to progress.

The strategy outlined above is valid not unique. The use of standards, especially with respect to data representation, cannot be over-stated. Methodology is also important, together with analysis aimed at simplification wherever possible.

Centralised process control, supervision and monitoring provide an invaluable management tool. The effectiveness of SMS is perhaps best illustrated by the record of more than 10 years of ECMWF operational forecasts without loss.

Data management is still a learning process; nevertheless it has proved, and will continue to prove increasingly effective as the learning process continues.

REFERENCES

[1] Collins, 1976, *Collins Concise English Dictionary.*

[2] Dijkstra, E., 1976, *Structured Programming, Software Engineering Techniques*, Petrocelli/Charter.

[3] Gibson, J. K., 1986, *Standards for Software Development and Maintenance*, ECMWF Technical Memorandum No. 120.

[4] Gibson, J. K., 1982, *The Doctor System - A DOCumenTart ORientated Programming System*, ECMWF Technical Memorandum No. 52.

[5] Roberts, K. V., 1974, The Olympus Programming System, *Computer Physics Communications*, 7, 237-240.

RECOMMENDED ADDITIONAL READING

[1] Martin, J., and McClure, C., 1983, *Software Maintenance: The Problem and its Solutions*, Prentice-Hall.

[2] Rock-Evans, Rosemary, 1989, *A Simple Introduction to Data and Activity Analysis*, Computer Weekly Publications.

A SPATIAL DATABASE FOR AN IMAGE UNDERSTANDING SYSTEM

D.C. Mason, C. Angelikaki, S.B.M. Bell, M. Illingworth, and E. Pearson
Natural Environment Research Council Unit
for Thematic Information Systems (NUTIS)
Department of Geography
University of Reading
Whiteknights, Reading, United Kingdom

C. Oddy, K. Preedy, and A.J. Rye
GEC Marconi Research Centre (MRC)
Space and Defence Research Laboratory
West Hanningfield Road
Great Baddow, Chelmsford, Essex
United Kingdom

INTRODUCTION

This paper discusses the design of a spatial database management system for an image understanding system for multi-source image processing (MuSIP).

MuSIP is being developed within a European ESPRIT II project involving a multinational collaboration. A main aim of the MuSIP project is to develop a generic knowledge-based architecture providing a basic environment for combining possibly multi-temporal image information from different sensors and other spatial information such as maps, in order to provide a unified description of an imaged scene. A demonstrator will be developed illustrating the application of image understanding techniques to fused data sets in the two disparate fields of remote sensing and medical image processing.

Figure 1 illustrates the major structural components of the MuSIP system. MuSIP will employ a decoupled message-passing architecture. The system supervisor controls the system by issuing commands which include the initiation of algorithms. When an algorithm has completed its task, the new image data is placed in the database and a summary of the salient features of the image placed on the blackboard. The knowledge bases are used by the supervisor to plan a sequence of algorithms to satisfy a particular operator goal. Details of the overall architecture are given in [1].

REQUIREMENTS OF A PICTURE UNDERSTANDING DATABASE MANAGEMENT SYSTEM

A picture understanding database management system (PUDBMS) is a special form of pictorial database management system (see *e.g.*, [2]). It tends to be biased towards the use of raster data, because one of the data sets being operated on is always an input image. The requirements of PUDBMS may be summarized as follows.

(1) They must be able to handle a variety of spatial data models, including not only raster data and topologically-structured vector data with associated attribute information, but also models for compressed raw raster, generalized raster (*e.g.*, hierarchical data models), and possibly specialized models such as triangulated irregular networks.

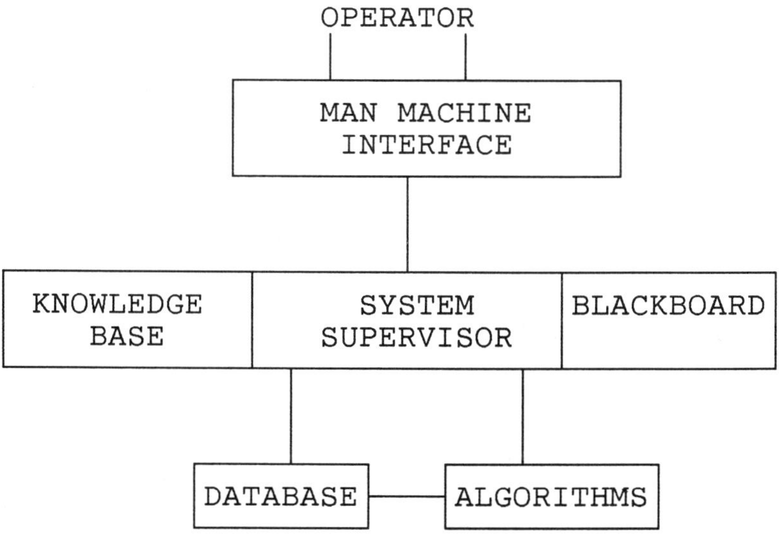

FIGURE 1. Simplified MuSIP Diagram

(2) To cope with the remote sensing case, they must be able to handle very large images within the restrictions of limited computer memory and disc space, and with minimum disc input/output.

(3) They are required to cope with the majority of functions handled by general spatial information systems. However they must be particularly efficient at performing local search operations and database updating. As they are generally accessed by image processing modules, facilities for user interaction (*e.g.,* spatial query languages) may be of less importance.

(4) There are difficulties in adapting conventional database models for use with image databases, due mainly to the characteristics of spatial data. A number of PDBMS have been developed based on the relational model. However, this has a number of drawbacks for handling spatial data, including the fact that access times for spatial information tend to be slow. There are also difficulties in using the network model, which is rather inflexible. However, it is more suited to handling spatial data as the system of pointers permits fast access and retrieval.

THE VECTOR DATABASE

The basis of the spatial database for MuSIP is Marconi Research Centre's PUD (Picture Understanding Database) database [3]. PUD is an object-oriented database designed to store vector information derived from segmenting images, and map information. The database is basically a tree structure, with additional pointers between branches to make certain access paths more efficient (Figure 2). The information stored in PUD is essentially 2-dimensional. Each of the three spatial data types handled (regions, lines and points) is a top-level index in the hierarchy and for each there is also a top-level attribute index and classification index. These index types are described below.

(i) Region index

The region index contains identifiers for all the regions in the image. For each region, information is stored on its bounding rectangle, boundary, adjacent regions, holes, and attributes (*e.g.,* perimeter). In addition, the facility for storing sub-regions and super-regions is available.

The region attribute index gives access to information about all attributes which have been calculated for the region. In contrast, the attribute region index gives the regions for which a particular attribute has been calculated. An occurrence index allows PUD to contain more than one computation of a given attribute (*e.g.*, obtained using different algorithms).

A separate region classification index allows access to a list of possible classification categories, such as wheat, field, urban, etc. A probability may be associated with each possible classification. There is also a classification occurrence index. The meanings of attribute and classification identifiers are stored in a dictionary to allow controlled expansion.

The boundary segment index contains the indices of the line segments making up a region's boundary. Boundaries are defined as being in the 'cracks' between regions and are coded as a 4-way Freeman 'crack' code.

The region line index lists those lines which pass through the region (but not region boundaries). Similarly the point index lists the identifiers of points contained within the region.

(ii) **Line index**

The line index is used for storing region boundaries, as well as other lines. Attributes may be associated with lines (*e.g.*, edge strength) using the line attribute index. There is also a separate line classification index. A line may be represented in a number of possible forms, including Freeman code, by storing its description as a line attribute. Left and right region identifiers are also stored.

(iii) **Point index**

The point index stores the location, attributes and classification of point features, together with the containing region identifier.

The database is able to process images which are too large to fit into the available memory. The database is split into a number of rectangular tiles, each of which contains all the information on the regions, points and lines within the tile boundary. As most processing is local, only the current and neighboring tiles need be present in memory at any one time. Tiles are created at the time of image segmentation, and tile boundaries are defined by the user. A region is placed in the tile containing its frame centre. A line is placed in the tile containing its start point. A point is assigned to the tile containing it.

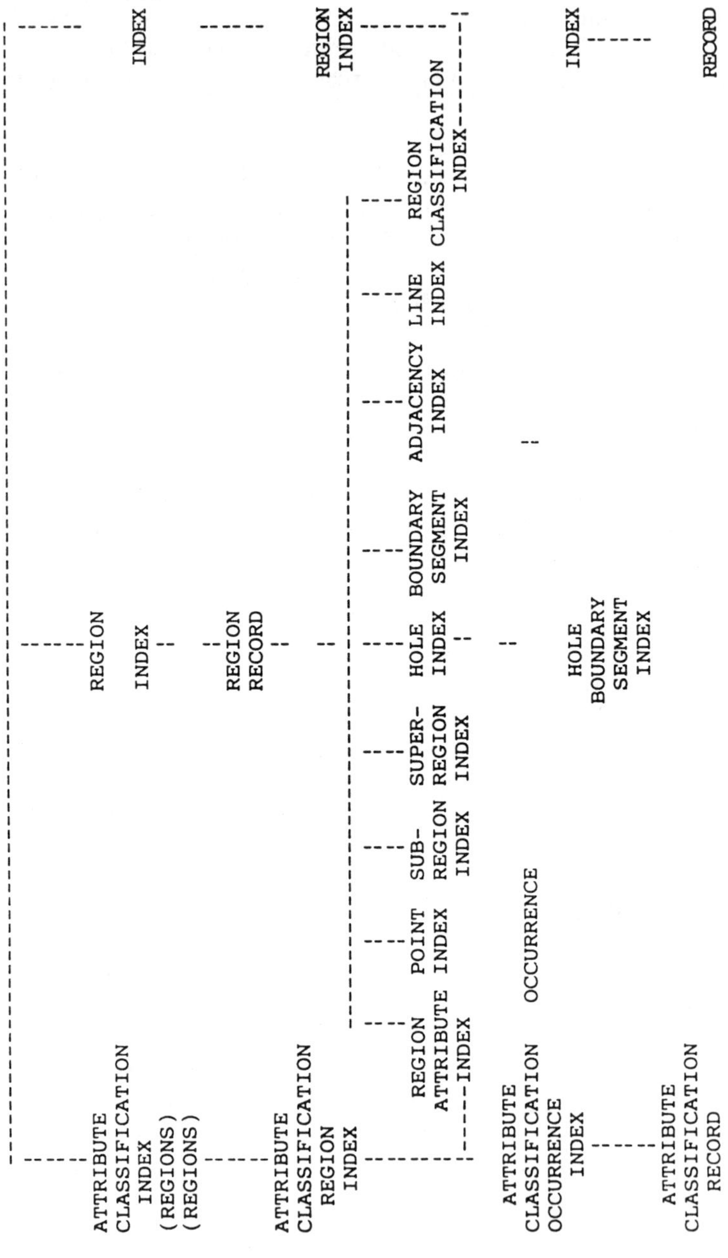

FIGURE 2
Vector Database Schema

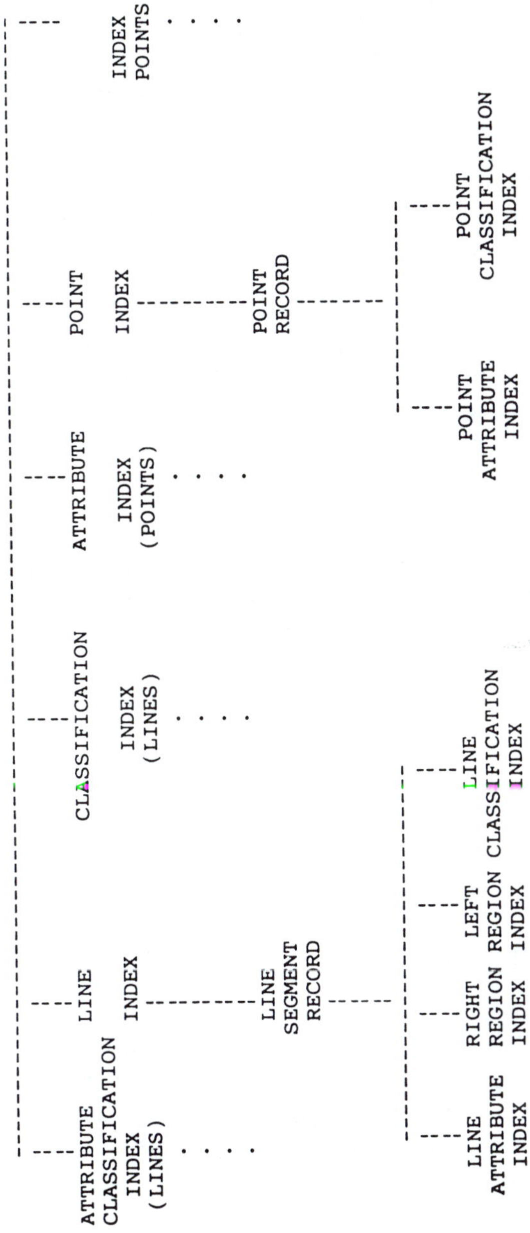

FIGURE 2 - continued

In order to make tiling efficient it is desirable to make all the tiles from an image approximately the same size in terms of memory buffer storage. Adjacent tiles are therefore merged together when the data contained in them falls below a certain amount. Conversely, if the data in a single tile become too large, then the tile may be split into two.

The database consists of one file for each tile in the database plus a master file holding information on the filing structure, all of which are held in a common directory. More than one input database (image), together with a single output image, may be operated on simultaneously within a program.

There is a separate related header file to hold ancillary data describing the database (*e.g.*, image frame, image sample spacing, etc). This header file is in free format so that it can easily be read by a user, but it is also compilable for machine interpretation. A dictionary of known keywords is used to assemble the compiled header. The header file also holds information on the processing history of the image.

In order to use PUD for the MuSIP database, it has been extended in a number of ways. These are discussed below. The resulting database for MuSIP is called MuSID (Multi-Source Image Database).

4. THE RASTER DATABASE

The ability to handle multi-band raster image data is an important extension. To match the tiling of the vector data, the image data must also be tiled. To create the tiled vector structure, the raster image is scanned in a non-raster ('tiled-raster') scan order, by performing a raster scan within each image tile and examining the tiles themselves in a raster fashion. One important consequence of this scan-order is that special routines for image processing are needed, *e.g.*, for connected component labelling; it is necessary to transmit partially detected objects across tile boundaries (see below).

The file structure of a raw raster image is such that it is suitable for processing in a tiled-raster fashion. The raw data is reformatted, and held as a single file in a form which is tile-sequential and band-sequential within each tile. This means tiles may either be read as 1-band or n-band and in either case tile I/O is as fast as possible.

Raster data may also be held in compressed form on disc. Raw raster imagery can be subjected to 'error-free' compression, by coding the differences between adjacent pixels' grey values in each band of each tile line. It is possible to achieve compressions of up to a factor of 3.5 by such methods. The enormous sizes of the raw imagery means that a large reduction in disc storage can be achieved even for modest compressions. Raster data which have been generalized may be compressed by storing them in run-length-encoded form. For both these compressed raster types, image tiles are of variable length on disc, and each tile is held as a separate file.

5. RELATING RASTER AND VECTOR DATA

It is necessary to relate raster and vector data easily and efficiently *e.g.*, when partially segmented regions have been produced and it is necessary to measure region parameters using the raw image. A number of complementary facilities are provided.

(1) The usual way of relating raster and vector data is to use a region map *i.e.*, an image containing the covering region label at each pixel. Given a particular position, this allows the covering region identifier to be determined. The region map is stored on disc in runcoded form.

(2) An important requirement is to be able to perform a raster scan of the region domain, for example to calculate some feature of the region (*e.g.*, mean intensity). Whilst the shape of the region is encoded in the region map and the region boundary, neither of these data structures is particularly suitable for a raster scan of the region. An alternative data structure which is suitable is an 'intervals list', a form of 1-D run-encoding [4]. An interval in a line is defined by two x-positions xb_i and xe_i, marking the start and end positions of a connected segment of the region in that line. For each line the region may have a number of such intervals (xb_1,xe_1), (xb_2,xe_2), ... Traversing the intervals of a region in order allows a raster traversal of the region. Algorithms exist for performing most image processing operations using intervals lists. The intervals list is stored as a region attribute.

The intervals list also identifies the grey levels in the raster image with which it is associated, because it is possible to calculate the grey level file offset given position (x,y). In this case, the description of a region domain based on its intervals list is linked dynamically with a description of its grey values within a single C structure. All the relevant information relating to this region can then be accessed via the single address of the structure [4]. For image data, the interval can be regarded as the logical interface between the database and the user.

(3) It is also possible to store the grey values associated with a region directly with the region as an attribute.

6. IMAGE SETS

It is necessary to cope with sets of related images *e.g.,* image sequences or images of the same place taken with different sensors. This necessitates matching one region with another in a different image and using the information to provide a fuller unified description. The image set database (Figure 3) has been designed to use the vector database low level routines, but to allow maximum flexibility in relating different images. Three new types are used, set-entities, attributes and relations. A set-entity is a point, line, region, or super-region from a particular image in a vector database. Two set-entities from different images may have a relation between them. The relation is qualified by attributes. Examples of relation attributes might be: match, no match, is different from, encloses, is enclosed by. A relation may have numeric information held on it, for example a confidence level. No restriction is made on the number of set-entities participating in a single relation, and n to m as well as 1 to 1 relations are possible. The image set database may be accessed on set-entity, attribute, or relation. The key for a set-entity is the same as the vector database key for that entity, but qualified by the particular image from which it comes. From this key the relations in which the set-entity participates, and the attributes of these relations, can be found (Figure 3). The other set-entities in the relation can be found, and traced to their original vector database representations if desired.

7. DATABASE INTERFACES

The database interfaces with the rest of the system consist mainly of C functions, a number of which may also be called by the supervisor module (Figure 4). The functions are summarized below.

1) File connection routines for image file I/O initialization and termination.
2) Raster database functions for reading/writing intervals of raster data.
3) PUD functions for read/write/edit/delete of region/line/point data. Higher-level functions for merging adjacent regions and splitting regions are also provided, together with Lisp interfaces.
4) Functions for operating on image sets.
5) Image headerfile manipulation functions.
6) Interrogation functions for user operations on images, including image deletion, image and map input from tape, image output, sub-image extraction and printing, and vector database interrogation.

7) Display utilities for image display, zoom, contrast stretch, and cursor manipulation
8) A number of programs for performing common tasks (discussed below), including -
   a) a data flow control module
   b) raster to vector conversion
   c) vector to raster conversion.

8. COMMON DATA-HANDLING UTILITIES

The database subsystem encompasses certain low level image processing utilities which make extensive use of the database. These cope with tiled images. Of particular interest are the data flow control module and connected component finder.

(a) Data Flow Control Module

Many low level algorithms have a common form and are best supported by a Data Flow Control Module which provides data input/output facilities to a class of algorithms. The simplest area where this is required is in the area of local operations *i.e.*, those algorithms which operate on a window of pixels which scans the image. These local operations include: convolutions, smoothing, filters, edge detection (*e.g.*, Sobel), edge thinning, thresholding and others. Local operations are often chained together to form algorithm sequences of up to say 10 algorithms. For example, an image may be smoothed iteratively five times using the same algorithm, edge detected, thinned and thresholded, edge linked, and so on.

A Data Flow Control Module has the advantage that it allows algorithm pipelining, thereby saving disc I/O and disc storage requirements since intermediate results do not need to be saved to disc. It also permits rapid algorithm prototyping and evaluation.

The module performs a local parallel transform modifying the value of pixels in a specified domain. The domain may be a complete tiled-raster image or an individual region. The new value is a function of the input pixel values in a rectangular window centered on the current pixel. The modification is performed by a user-supplied function called for each current pixel. If a complete tiled image is being processed, each input tile is subjected to all pipeline stages to produce an output tile before proceeding to the next input tile.

(b) Connected Component Finder

The connected component finder operates over a domain which may either be a complete tiled-raster image, or an individual region in a PUD. At the same time as finding connected components, the algorithm also finds certain features of each connected region in the domain, including its intervals and boundary lists, and its area, frame centre and perimeter. In the input image, pixels in the interior of regions must be marked with '0', and pixels having edges along their S, W, or S and W sides marked with 1, 2, 3 respectively (*i.e.*, edges lie in the 'cracks' between pixels); 4-connectivity is used to demarcate regions.

If the domain is a tiled-raster image, this is processed in tiled-raster scan order. In the first stage, for each line of the current tile, horizontal strips of '0' pixels are run-coded into intervals. An interval begins either with a '2' or '3' pixel and ends with the last '0' before the next '2' or '3' pixel or the end of line. The algorithm given in [5] is then used to build up connected regions by searching for touching intervals in the current and previous lines.

The next stage puts all the regions completely contained within the current raster tile into the corresponding PUD tile, and puts any 'unfinished' regions touching the tile boundaries onto a stack for further consideration.

The final stage 'stitches' unfinished objects straddling the W and S tile boundaries together as far as possible for this tile. Each set of n unfinished touching regions in the current tile and previous tiles to the W and S is merged to a single region. If the resulting region is now complete (*i.e.*, if it does not continue into unprocessed tiles to the N or E), it is put into the vector tile containing the centre of its frame.

9. CONCLUSION

A spatial database satisfying the system requirements of the MuSIP project has been designed. The database is currently being implemented on a SUN workstation prior to integration with the rest of the system. This will then be evaluated against the diverse applications of change detection in forests, and the identification of anatomical structures using multiparametric NMR data.

10. ACKNOWLEDGMENTS

The authors would like to thank the other Consortium members for their assistance, namely M. Bishop and I. Jones-Parry (Marconi Space Systems

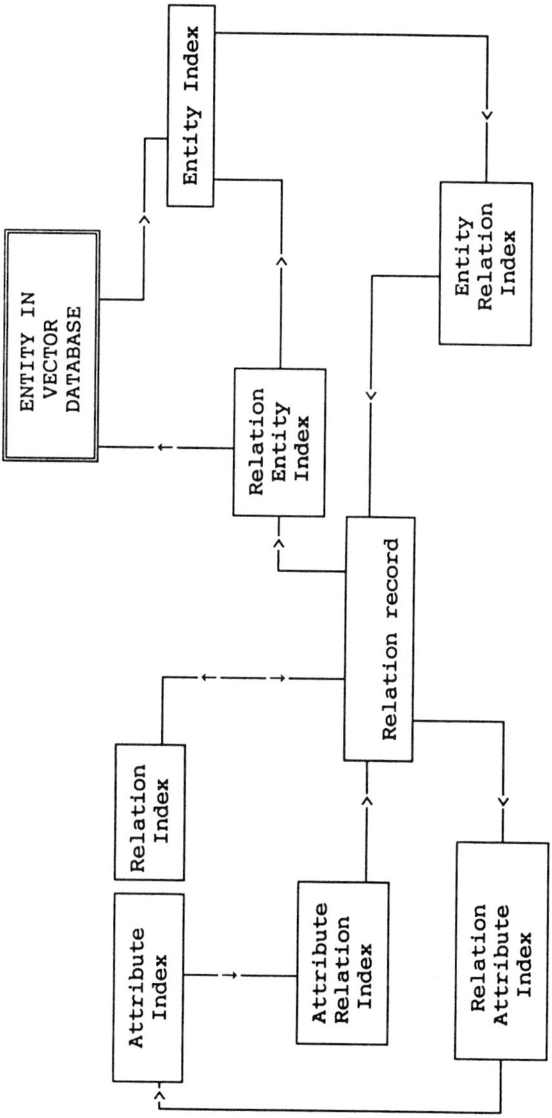

FIGURE 3. Image set database schema.

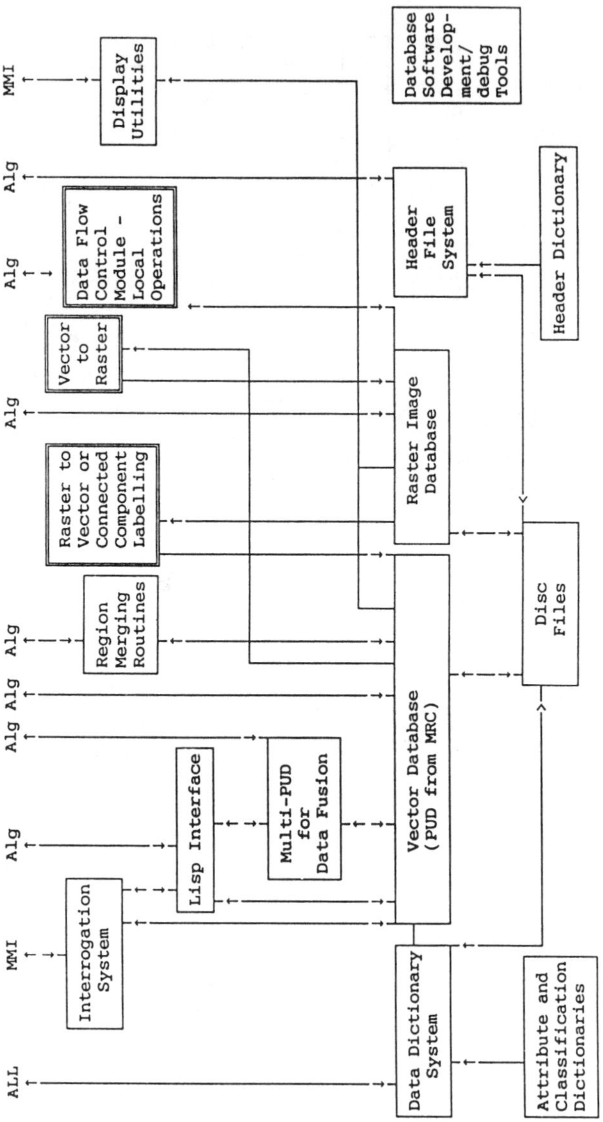

FIGURE 4. Database Subsystem Diagram.

(prime contractor)), N. Hindley and J. Fullwood (Marconi Command and Control Systems), C. Boeswetter, T. Pike and A. de Salabert (Messerschmitt-Bolkow-Blohm), J-Y. Catros, S. Latrous and P. Pressigout (Thompson CSF), M. Barr and A. Wielogorski (Huntings Technical Services), S. Dellapiane, S. Serpico and G. Vernazza (University of Genoa). The ESPRIT II Project (P2316) is partly funded by The European Commission.

11. REFERENCES

[1] Bishop M. and I Jones-Parry (1989). MuSIP - Multisensor image processing: ESPRIT Project No. 2316. *Proc ESPRIT 1989 Conference*. 6 pages.

[2] Levine M. and Shaheen S. (1981). A modular computer vision system for picture segmentation and interpretation. *IEEE Trans. Pattern Anal. Mach. Intell.* Vol 3 No 5

[3] Oddy C.J. (1988). Picture Understanding Database - PUD system specification. Marconi Research Centre Report PALS/WN/108.

[4] Piper J. and Rutovitz D. (1985). Data structures for image processing in a C language and Unix environment. *Pattern Recognition Letters* 3, pp 119-129.

[5] Rosenfeld A., Kak A.C. (1982). *Digital picture processing*. Academic Press. p. 243.

INTEGRATION OF VECTOR AND RASTER DATA AND MODULES

David J. Abel and Murray A. Wilson
Centre for Spatial Information Systems,
CSIRO Division of Information Technology,
Canberra, Australia.

Murray A. Wilson
CSIRO Division of Wildlife and Ecology,
Lyneham, Australia

1. INTRODUCTION

Researchers and decision-makers in areas such as natural resources management typically find it necessary to draw together data from many sources in performing an analysis of a geographic region. Some of the problems of integrating data have now been alleviated. At a technical level, most Spatial Information Systems (SIS) software packages, for example, now cater for several layers or themes within a database. At an organisational level, national catalogues of data sets are beginning to become available (*e.g.*, Johnson et al, 1989). An outstanding issue is the integration of data available in raster or vector form. To a researcher, the raster-vector distinction is most evident as the distinction between remotely-sensed data (such as satellite imagery) and data digitised from traditional maps. This distinction, however, is also carried through in the software systems which allow manipulation and display of data in one form or the other, even if some systems include vector- and raster-subsystems. Arguably this reflects the origins of currently-available software as systems for the raster-oriented Image Processing or for the predominantly vector-oriented Geographic Information Systems (GIS) market sectors. More certainly it reflects the different algorithms required for the two representations for core spatial analysis operations such as overlay and interrogation.

Integration of raster and vector data remains a cumbersome task. One solution is to have vector and raster systems share the same display device, so that vector information (for example, a road network and cadastral boundaries) can be drawn over a raster display (for example, a LANDSAT image interpreted to show forest communities). Another is to convert a vector representation of a set of objects to a raster representation or vice versa so that analysis and display can proceed within a single software system. Neither approach is fully satisfactory. The shared-display solution provides weak support for analyses combining data in the two representations while conversion is slow and maintains the distinction in the analytical functions available at any time to the user.

There has been a considerable research effort to discover alternative representations which would deliver the combined strengths of vector and raster data processing. While forms such as the quadtree (Samet, 1984) have been shown to be promising, it will clearly be several years before systems based on novel representations will provide the full functionality of existing systems.

Another path to integration is through the system architecture. Here the user is provided with a high-level view of data sets and operations which shield the user from the representations used for the data sets. Support for such a logical view is principally delivered by a directory module which maps the user's model of the database (his logical view) to the internal database model. The directory module also provides support for configuring the user interface to his normal problem-solving methodology.

This paper discusses the design of such a system. The CSIRO Division of Information Technology, Centre for Spatial Information Systems is developing a system architecture and a set of tool-kits (collectively called SIRO-SIS) together providing a system framework for Spatial Information Systems. The major themes of the project are the generation of systems configured to applications and the integration of raster, vector and tabular data in a workstation environment. Experience with a prototype system IBGIS (Image-Based GIS) developed for a modeling agricultural and pastoral production from NOAA Normalised Difference of Vegetation Index imagery is discussed.

2. SYSTEM OVERVIEW

SIRO-SIS is a set of tools for building applications systems in the broad area of Spatial Information Systems. More broadly SIRO-SIS is an architecture which exploits the new styles of problem-solving made possible by graphic work stations and advanced data management facilities. These new styles particularly include highly-interactive forms of interrogation, display and analysis, and the use of several visualisations of a geographic region to enhance perception of underlying structure in the problem.

The outline architecture of SIRO-SIS has four major sets of components: a user interface, an executive and a directory of data sets and operations, functional modules and the data management facilities.

3. USER INTERFACE

The user interface (*i.e.,* the command-and-control screens, graphic windows and text panels seen by the end-user) are implemented by a User Interface Management System (UIMS) specification language such as Open Dialog. The sophisticated facilities of UIMS offer powerful support in implementing the interface as sets of pull-down menus, icons, panels and windows. The typical separation of application and UIMS, however, calls for exploration of new forms of expression of commands from the interface to the other modules.

A particular target of SIRO-SIS is the ability to provide a user with several simultaneous visualisations of a region to enhance perception and to support the graphic expression of complex queries, simultaneously (*i.e.,* in several windows on the workstation screen) several visualisations of a region or set of objects to enhance user perception and to support graphical rather than textual specification of complex queries. For example, in an investigation to determine underlying factors in farm productivity, a researcher would find it helpful to identify farms which are unusually productive for their size (by examining a scattergram of farm size against production), to choose farms by circling data points on the scattergram and then seeing their geographic location shown on a map at the same time as a tabular report of other known attributes.

4. THE EXECUTIVE AND THE DIRECTORY

The Executive and the Directory together provide the mapping from the logical view of operations and data sets to their physical forms. The Executive traps commands (typically as fragments of commands) passed from the user interface, determines the best way in which the requested action can be performed and passes a sequence of commands to the functional modules. It also maintains a common data area in RAM for communication between the functional modules.

The Directory essentially provides the information necessary to map the user's model of his information base and tasks to the actual database and the functional modules available. The Directory database extends the usual data dictionary of database management and GIS in several ways (Abel, in press):

- the data sets are described in terms of their content (*e.g.*, the themes included), their coverage (the geographic region mapped), their lineage (how the data sets were captured or derived), the representations used and their current location. This information supports selection of data sets by a user directly or by the executive by, for example, content and coverage. It might ultimately allow determination of the limits of valid interpretation of derived data sets;

- it includes descriptions of the functional modules in terms of permissible inputs, the transformation processes and the forms of outputs. Some functional modules are specified as macros (sets of commands) which synthesize a task as a set of operations by available functional modules;

- the directory stores descriptions of standard forms of displays and of standard graphics representations of objects by class and standard names for data sets.

5. DATA MANAGEMENT FACILITIES

The design includes a spatial database management system and data management facilities native to functional modules. To a certain extent this is a pragmatic design decision necessary to allow incorporation of off-the--shelf systems. The spatial database management system is implemented with SIRO-DBMS (Abel, 1989), a spatial database tool-kit implemented as a shell for relational database management systems. It offers a high-level view of vector data sets through an extended form of the relational data model and provides fast retrieval of objects satisfying mixed qualifications on attributes of objects and spatial relationships.

Experiments to extend SIRO-DBMS to raster data have been very encouraging. Under this representation, an image is stored as runs of pixels of pixel values so that the raster representation for a specified geographic region (such as the coverage of an object or a set of objects) can be rapidly retrieved for analysis and display. This region might be a small portion of an existing image or might lie astride the edges of two or more images.

6. FUNCTIONAL MODULES

The functional modules provide transformation and visualisation operations. 'Transformation' includes any operations which derive or modify data sets. Transformations include such operations as derivation of statistics, reclassification of pixel intensities and overlaying of thematic maps in addition to conversion between representations.

7. IBGIS

A prototype system IBGIS (Wilson, 1989) was developed to support a CSIRO Division of Wildlife and Ecology project to investigate the use of NOAA Normalised Difference of Vegetation Index (NDVI) imagery to predict agricultural and pastoral production. The NDVI images provide a measure of vegetation health continent-wide. The project had available monthly images for a 5-year period. Australian Bureau of Statistics data sets (in a tabular form) provided yearly production as a set of 121 items for each of some 1000 Statistical Local Areas (SLAs). Boundaries of the SLAs were acquired in vector form. Other supporting data included a set of 230 000 locational references (to enable specification of localities of interest) and soils and major river basins as possibly significant predictive variables.

The design of IBGIS, implemented on a SUN workstation, followed the SIRO-SIS architecture. The user interface was implemented with SUNView user interface management system. Context restriction was applied through a facility for a user to designate a sub-set of data sets and a geographic region of interest, with only those data sets appearing in pull-down menus and operations restricted to the region of interest.

Image data management used modules of the DISIMP image processing system developed by CSIRO. The SIRO-DBMS spatial database tool-kit (Abel, 1989) was ultimately used in conjunction with the ORACLE relational database management system for the SLA boundaries and other vector data. ORACLE was used for the tabular production data.

Graphics and analysis facilities were provided by a mix of DISIMP and purpose-written modules. Operations included generation of displays of production and greenness for specified periods, aggregation (with reporting in tabular and graphic forms) and cross-tabulation.

The system proved effective as a 'browsing' facility and a means of generating cross-tabulations of production against NDVI values aggregated by SLA. Successor systems are under development at the Division of

Wildlife and Ecology in a number of projects broadly combining remotely--sensed data with cadastral and other data to assist, for example, the summary reporting on individual agricultural and pastoral properties.

8. CONCLUSIONS

A single-system approach has considerable potential as a means of integrating vector and raster data through allowing the user to adopt a high-level view of his databases and operations. A directory of data sets and of functional modules is a key element of the system architecture in separating the user's conceptualization of the database and manipulations on it, the system-internal database organization and the elemental operations available. Introducing this separation offers many research opportunities for development of hybrid systems blending existing techniques and novel approaches.

9. BIBLIOGRAPHY

[1] Abel, D.J., SIRO-DBMS: a database tool-kit for geographical information systems, *Int. J. Geographical Information Systems*, 3(2), 1989, pp. 103-116.

[2] Abel, D.J., A Model for Data Set Management in Large Spatial Information Systems, *Int. J. Geographical Information Systems*, in press.

[3] Johnson, B.D., Mott, J.J. and Robey, T., Providing effective access to resource information- progress towards a national directory of Australian resource data, *Proceedings of URPIS 17*, Perth, Australia, 22nd-24th November 1989, pp. 187-260.

[4] Samet, H., The quadtree and related hierarchical data structures, *Association for Computing Machinery Surveys 16*, 1984, pp. 187-260.

[5] Wilson, M.A., The integration of Image-based Processing within a Geographic Analysis System, *Proceedings of Ausgraph '89*, Melbourne, 10th-14th July 1989, pp. 141-145.

KNOWLEDGE BASED PATTERN RECOGNITION: APPLICATION TO LANDSAT AND SPOT/STEREO DIGITAL DATA ON CHINA

Claude Bardinet
Ecole Normale Supérieure (G-SAT)
Paris, France

Wei Luo, F. Martel, H. Maître, F. Perlant, and Yi Feng Wu
Télécom (Image)
Paris, France

Zheng Yu
Université de Nice
Nice, France

INTRODUCTION

This paper describes two complementary approaches of knowledge pattern recognition in geomorphology applied on physical landscape in China. Part 1 concerns automatic detection of contours and lineaments and Part 2 concerns stereo digital analysis and digital terrain model (DTM).

These two complementary approaches are in relation to the need of synthetic image analysis in earth sciences, as a result of data processing using complex geographical databases including multisatellite data. At least the final DTM image will combine stereo DTM and synthetic image of the landscape, that means classification of physical structures, physical units and land use units.

1. AUTOMATIC DETECTION OF CONTOURS AND LINEAMENTS IN THE AREA OF LIN CHENG DAM (HEBEÏ)

This part 1 is illustrated by Figure 1.1 "Object detection: data flow diagram"

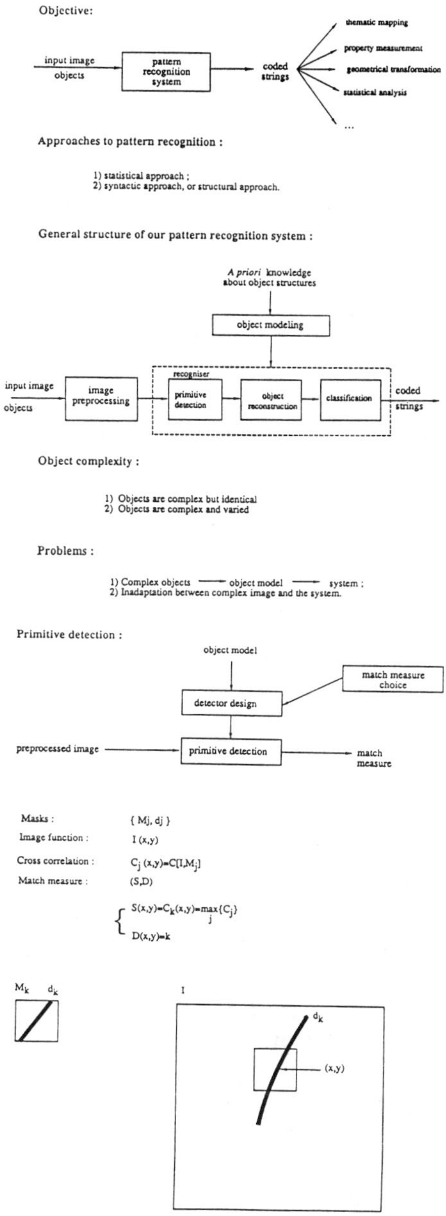

FIGURE 1.1 - Object detection: data flow diagram

and Figure 1.2 "Digital Landscape Units of the Test Site of Lin Cheng Dam (Hebeï) using Landsat MSS7 (May 6 1975). In 1986, we proposed a method [1-3] for the infographic selection of structural information contained in the multisatellite data, as a contribution to the automatic construction of geophysics database. The image processing described here thins and enhances lines, and cleans the other undesirable non-line information. Images thus preprocessed are more suitable for the linear feature detection.

1.1 Objectives of automatic detection of lineaments

An image pattern recognition system is presented [2-11]. Particular effort has been made to improve the system's flexibility, *i.e.,* to reduce its dependence on the physical shape of the input objects which have to be recognized. New architecture has therefore been introduced for the system design: a recognizer, an image preprocessor (which works as an adaptor between objects and the recognizor) and a data model which interacts with users, providing information about input images and contained objects, and transferring it to the reasoning processor at the recognize phase. In building a dictionary of forms, we have to use primitives to describe objects and lineaments.

The objective was to design a general image pattern recognition system for applications of remote sensing analysis [2-8]. Given a digital image, aerial or from satellite, the system must be able to identify in the image, objects that have significance in application areas such as geology, geography, geophysics, oceanography, ecology,.... Some simple examples of such objects are roads, rivers, valleys, sea coast line and more complex ones are hydrographic nets, tectonic faults and lineaments, lithogical units and landscapes units. The recognition outputs are coded strings, each expressing an identified object in a more compact and concise way, suitable for the object classification and easy to manipulate in further processing: thematic mapping, property measurement, geometrical transformation and statistical analysis.

1.2 Problem of pattern recognition

Many pattern recognition techniques have been proposed in the past [9-11]. These techniques can be divided into two principal categories:

- the statistical approach [11];
- the syntactic, or more generally, structural approach [3-6].

We focused on the structural approach for the major reason that it uses the structure of the objects for their description.

One basic idea [3] is that a complex pattern can be described in terms of simpler patterns, called primitives; then the recognition problem of complex objects becomes one of finding these primitives, and with them, reconstructing the objects for their classification. Here is the general structure of our system (Figure 1.1).

Initially, we establish a mathematical model of the objects using *a priori* knowledge about their structures. This model contains descriptions of the object primitives and rules which specify how to reconstruct the objects with these primitives. Under the guidance of the model, we detect the primitives in the input image and then assemble them to form the objects for their classification. For the system's reliability, the model would be required to be complete and accurate, to match with the actual objects; however, for the system design, the simplicity of the model would be preferred. The best is to have a model with a few standard primitives and explicit reconstruction rules. In practice, this simplicity is not always guaranteed, especially with complex objects. There we distinguish two levels of complexity (Figure 1.1):

- objects are complex but identical;
- objects are complex and varied.

In general, the second ones bring more difficulties to the system than the first's, usually having various primitives of a great number and complicated reconstruction rules. It is for this reason that many pattern recognition systems are specialized in one application for well defined objects.

Besides object complexity, image quality may also pose serious problems to the system. Intricate image background with noise, microtexture may distort recognition result, even cause the system to fail.

In our case, images come from Landsat MSS data, are rich in textures, and objects are varied both in geometrical form and in gray level shape. Therefore we need a flexible system, capable of adapting itself to image and object complexities.

To have such a system, the first problem to solve is to pass from the complex model to the system. The second is to overcome the inadequacy between complex image and the system. Of course one could always do something to improve the system so as to make is more powerful and more intelligent for recognizing complex objects in "unclean" images. But that would be more difficult and less efficient than acting directly on the input image "the source of the problem" through an image preprocessing.

This method allows for the infographic selection of structural information contained in multisatellite data and will contribute to the combination of geophysics multisources databases and DTM.

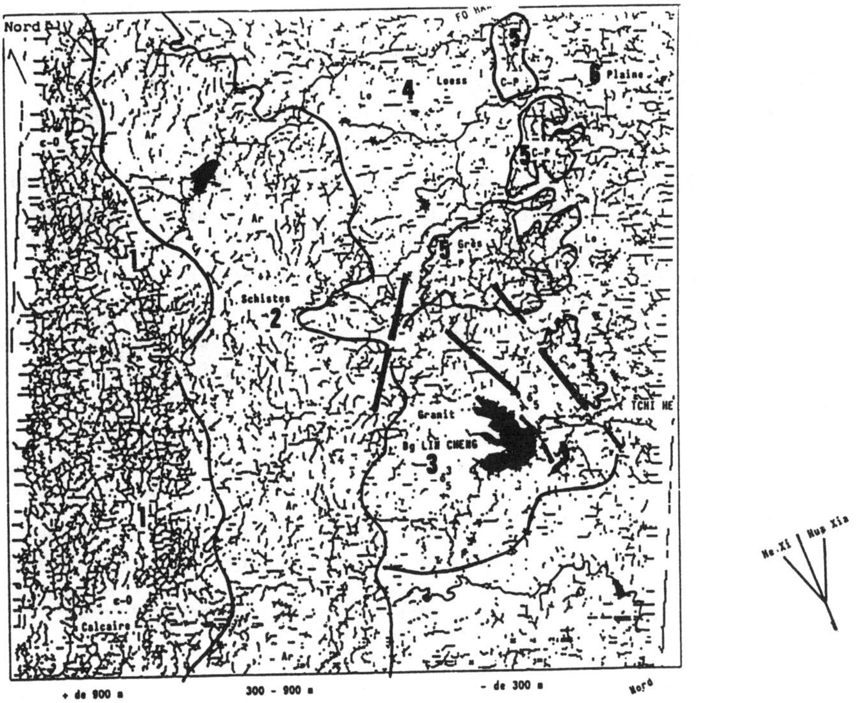

FIGURE 1.2
Digital Landscape Units of the Test Site of Lin Cheng Dam (Hebeï) using Landsat MSS7 (6 May 1975)

Legend Figure 1.2: Digital Landscape Unit of the Test Site of Lin Cheng Dam (Hebeï). The method used the ternary detection of local structures (3 x 3 matrix) in order to detect the density and orientation of lineaments. The landscape units resulting from the classification are:

I	= Limestone (altitude more than 900 m)
II	= Schists (300-900 m)
III	= Granite (less than 300 m)
IV	= Loess (less than 300 m)
V	= Sandstone (less than 300 m)
VI	= Alluvial Plain (Fo Hang He)

The structural lineaments (He Xi NNW and Hua Xia NNE) are detected in relation to the site of the Lin Cheng Dam.

1.3 Application on the MSS image of Lin Cheng Dam (Hebeï)

The Landsat MSS data has been processed on a HP-21MX [2] in 1984-1986 at the Ecole Nationale Supérieure des Mines de Paris (CTAMN Sophia Antipolis and CTT Nice University) as a contribution to the CODATA Program [1] on multisatellite thematic mapping.

The applications presented here [3,8] concern the area of the Lin Cheng Dam (Figure 1.2) in the Taihang Shan (Hebeï), located in the district of Xingtaï, Hebeï Province (China). On Figure 1.2., we present the geographical units, as a result of the classification of the density of lineaments in the MSS image. We have mapped the contour of structural units, in relation to the location of the Lin Cheng Dam, and the geomorphological units of the landscape in relation to the bedrock and to the density of detected lineaments.

2. STEREO DIGITAL ANALYSIS AND DTM IN THE LOESS PLATEAU (CHINA)

In this part 2, the DTM procedure applied to Spot imagery is detailed and resumed in a dataflow diagram (Figure 2.1), and is applied to Spot imagery of the Loess Plateau of Shaanxi (Figure 2.2).

Satellite images are full of useful information from which one can extract many important data for interpretation. Spot imagery provides a larger pixel to ground ratio than other civil satellite such as Landsat. One interesting realization is to generate (DTM) from stereo images. Spot's unique facility is the ability to tilt its sensors during consecutive orbits, providing off-nadir imagery for stereorestitution applications.

Rectification of images, plane transformations and DTM realizations are the subjects discussed. The geometry as well as the stereoscopic aspects of stereorestituting an image are presented. The model procedure is detailed and resumed in dataflow diagram format (Figure 2.1).

The complete approach to rectifying the DTM is described and presented [12-18]. This procedure is applied to Spot imagery and the results produced (Figure 2.2) are discussed.

We have used the panchromatic Spot data which represent the information captured between 0.51-0.73 μm and have a ground to pixel resolution of 10 meters. The scene covers an area of 80 x 60 km (8000 pixels by 6000 lines) and concerns the area of Yan'an in the province of Shaanxi (4800 km- on 48 Megabytes).

The 2 registrations of Spot (right and left image) are identified as follows:

- first date: SPOT1 HRV1, 01775277T K268/J276, Dec. 27 1986 (L)
- second date: SPOT1 HRV1, 0177682G K268/J276, Jan. 8 1987 (R)

Geographically, the area of Yan'an in Shaanxi is located in the Yellow River basin, where soil types are Loess and main geomorphological characteristics are eroded badlands. At these dates, small cultivated areas appear in and about the valleys. We are in the central part of the Loess plateau. The lowest valley is approximately 1025 meters above sea level and the highest peak is 1410 meters. The average denivelation is therefore only about 385 meters high and during this period, in winter, the terrain is mostly deprived of vegetation and locally, on ridges, covered by snow.

Ideally, the left and the right images are taken at very small time intervals. However, in our case, the only cloudless images available were taken 10 days apart. The left image was taken at an angle of +20.9 degrees off-nadir, 27 December 1986, and the right image was taken at an angle of -27 degrees off-nadir, 8 January 1987. The spectral differences between the two images are therefore quite numerous and are due to temperature (ice on lake) and precipitation factors (snow).

The preprocessing applied to this imagery by Spot Image was of radiometric and geometric nature (1B level).

2.1 Stereoscopy

The procedure used in reconstituting a three dimensional impression of depth is called stereoscopy. One of the oldest system of the sort is the human eye. Stereoscopy consists mainly in viewing one object from different directions, producing two slightly different views (images) of the object. Through the human eyes, the brain recognizes the two views as originating from the same object and calculates the spatial position of the object.

From this model, we can retain the basic and most important steps to stereorestitution, that means:

1) the object to be recognized is photographed or radiometrically recorded from two (the minimum number views) different viewing angles;

2) the views, recognized as originating from the same object, are transposed into a single viewing plane. This is called the rectification step. Rectification is usually done in a geometry adapted to the problem, that is epipolar geometry. This step is often performed by interactively selecting ground control points (GCP) in each left and right images;
3) for each easily recognizable point in the left image, a corresponding point in the right image is determined. This is the correspondence step and processing of these data produces a disparity image;
4) each pixel in the image, has a corresponding disparity level. According to this level, altitude can be determined, providing a DTM;
5) the original right image (8 January 1987) is mapped onto the altitude model (DTM), creating an impression of depth throughout the image, and a contour map.

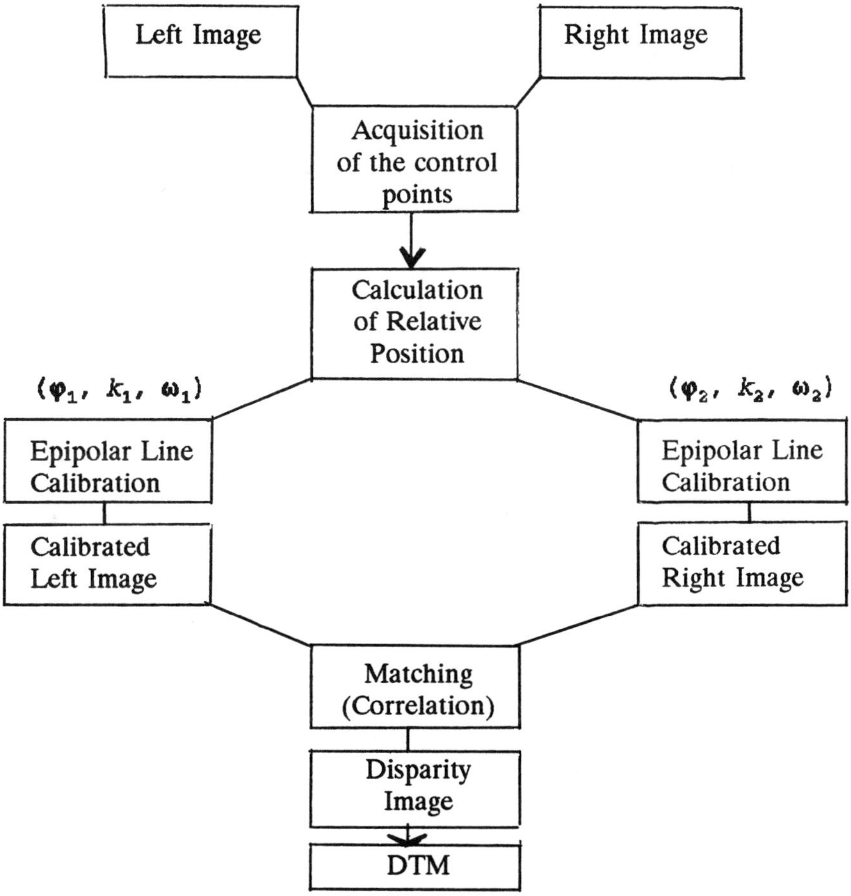

FIGURE 2.1 - Data Flow Diagram of a 3-D DTM

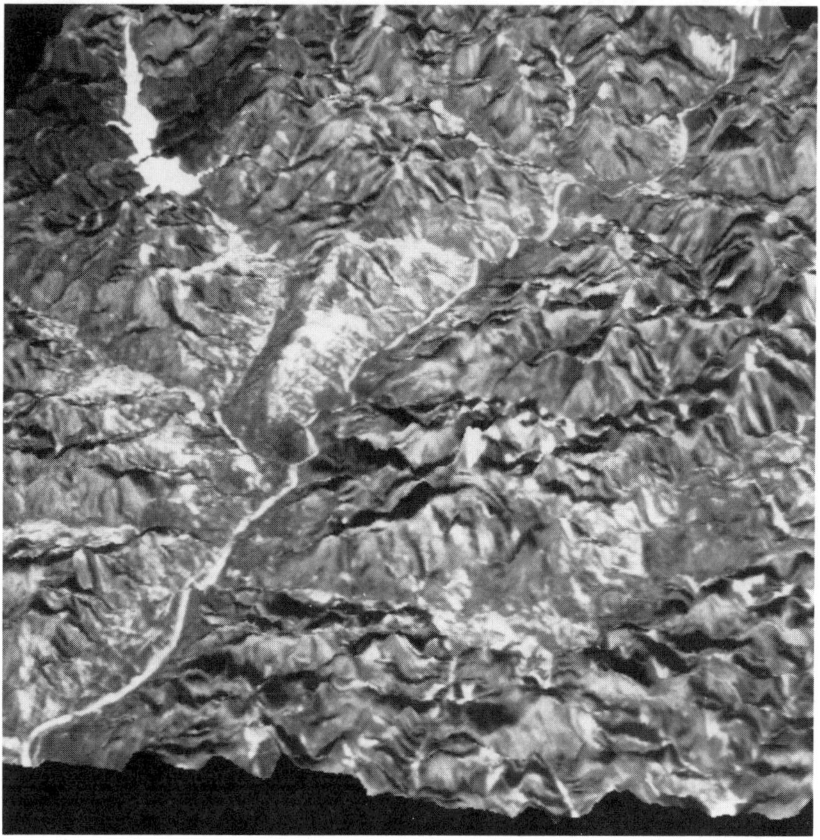

FIGURE 2.2
Digital terrain model using Stereo Spot data combined with Spot panchromatic albedo (8 January 1987), area of Pan-long Dam, North-east of Yan'an (Shaanxi, China).

2.2 Matching method

The more difficult step in stereovision is to find correspondences, point by point, between two images. As explained above, the two images have been taken about 10 days apart, so that the photometric differences are very important. It is found that, the only use of classical cross-correlation technique is not sufficient, so we adopt here a hierarchical method.

The original images are represented as a pyramid, and at each level are reduced by a certain factor. By this way, at the top of the pyramid, the original images are zoomed to very small images, in which all of noises and details are smoothed, and finally only the distinguished features remain.

Of course, at this level, the correlation method can easily work; it may give us an accurate matching result in a very short time. However, the results obtained in this low resolution level are not sufficient for us. The next step is to project these results to a higher resolution level, which are then used as constraints to guide the corresponding search in this level. It is worth noting that using the constraints coming from the low resolution level is decisive; it can largely reduce the matching error as well as the computation's time. This procedure is repeated until the full resolution.

In our case, the original images selected have a size of 1500 x 1500 pixels, and after the calibration step, a square area of 1024 x 1024 is taken into account. At the first step, the original images are reduced by a factor of 8, so we obtain two images of 128 x 128, and the correlation is made between these two images. Then the results are projected to the higher resolution (256 x 256), and the correlation here is constrained by the results coming from the lower level. This procedure is repeated until the initial image size (1024 x 1024) is reached.

At a different level, the correlation functions are calculated with a same size window (8 x 8) and we find that the result thus obtained is very satisfactory (Figure 2.2.).

Technique for the construction of a DTM using Spot stereo image pair are presented [12-17]. The most important steps to stereorestitution are:

- the recognition of similarities between the two views of one object (corresponding GCP are selected in each image of the pair);
- the rectification of the views in an epipolar geometry;
- the computation of a disparity image (for each point in the left image, determination of a corresponding point in the right image);

- for each pixel in the image, computation of the corresponding disparity level and determination of the altitude.

Three main decisions have to be taken in order to build a digital stereorestitution algorithm:

- choice of the primitives which are candidates for pairing;
- choice of the criterion to decide whether a pairing is good or not;
- strategy allowing to exhibit the best pairing for each primitive.

If latitude, longitude and elevation are available for a specific number of ground control points (GCP) in the Spot image, a relatively accurate DTM could be produced for each pixel in the image. During the field work in the Loess Plateau in the area of Yan'an, we tested this importance of a control of the location of the GCP, in relation with the dislevelment in a 10 x 10m pixel (satellite ground resolution).

The question of automatic selection of GCP in the images in relation to the cartographic database has to be studied if we consider the difficulties resulting from the variation of the attitude of the satellite from one date to an other and the consecutive variation of the location of the pixel on the ground surface.

Some of the results are presented in Figure 2.2 as a computer aided map of a digital terrain model in the Loess Plateau using Stereo Spot data combined with Spot panchromatic albedo (8 January 1987, area of Pan-long Dam, North-east of Yan'an, Shaanxi, China).

CONCLUSION

The knowledge based pattern recognition system in Earth sciences described here concerns automatic methods and applications to Landsat and Spot/Stereo digital data on China. The object reconstruction has as its goal to thin the primitive magnitudes, to link these primitives, and finally, to code them into strings for automated classification of lineaments. The stereo image processing (3-D) has as its goal to produce a digital terrain model (DTM) on which it will be possible to project detected geographical objects and thematic classifications. Multisatellite Landsat and Spot data are the fundamentals of databases for Geographical Information System (GIS) devised as a tool for the study of "Global Change Multiscale Evaluation".

ACKNOWLEDGMENT:

The authors wish to thank for their help in the field all the colleagues of IRSA (Beijing) and mainly Yang Shi-ren, Wan Zheng-ming, Wang Chang-yao and Mm Zhou Liya, and from North-West university (Xi'an) Wang Yong-yan and Yuan Kan-shen. They wish also to acknowlege for their aid and financial support Phyllis Glaeser and Sarah Levavasseur, D.R. Lide Jr., A.E. Bussard, J. Crease, G. Gabert and R. Sinding-Larsen, all from CODATA, V. Sibrava and R. Missotten from Unesco, J.M. Monget from CTAMN, and C. Jung from Spot Image.

REFERENCES

[1] Bardinet, C., Chen, Y.Y., Gabert, G., Wan, Z.M., Yang, S.R., Chinese Mapping Project Using Satellites, *Scientific and Technical Data in a New Era, Proceedings 11th International CODATA Conference, Karlsruhe, F.R.G.*, ed. P. Glaeser, Hemisphere, 1990, pp 213-218.

[2] Bardinet, C., Monget, J.M., Gabert, G., Yu, Z., Methodology for multisatellite thematic mapping: a report of the CODATA Task Group on multisatellite thematic mapping. Ph. Glaeser ed., *CODATA Bulletin 62*, 1986, pp. 1-86, Pergamon Press.

[3] Yu, Z., Reconnaissance automatique des formes appliquée à la géologie structurale. Ph.D Thesis, April 1987, Nice University, France.

[4] Yu, Z., Bardinet, C., Image preprocessing for line detection based on local structure analysis. *CODATA Bulletin 62*, 1986, pp. 9-26, Pergamon Press.

[5] Yu, Z., A structural approach to image pattern recognition. Seminar organized by British Medical Research Council, Edinburgh, Great Britain, June, 1987.

[6] Bardinet, C., Yu, Z., Modélisation assistée en géomorphologie numérique: application aux paysages de Tanzanie et de Chine, *Bul. Soc. Languedocienne de Géog.* (1-2) 1988, pp. 97-121, Montpellier, France.

[7] Bardinet, C., Gabert, G., Monget, J.M., Yu, Z., Application of multisatellite data to thematic mapping. *Geol. Jb.* (B67) 1988, pp. 3-74, Hannover, Germany.

[8] Bardinet, C., Télédétection, environnement et urbanisation: de l'image globale aux objets géographiques, applications à l'impact de l'urbanisation sur les paysages en Afrique et en Chine (vol. 2 et 2, vol. annexes, cartes infographiques), Thèse d'Etat, 1987, Paris, ISBN 2-9504465-0-7, ISSN 0294-1767.

[9] Paton, K., Line detection by local methods, *Computer Graphics and image processing* (9) 1979, pp. 316-332.

[10] Prager, J.M., Extraction and labelling boundary segments in natural

scenes, *IEEE Trans. Patt. Anal. Mach. Intell.*, vol. PAMI-2 (1) 1980, pp. 16-27.

[11] Ikonomopoules, A., An approach to edge detection based on the direction of edge elements, *Computer graphics and image processing* (19) 1982, pp. 179-195.

[12] Bénard, M., Boutaler, A.K., Kolbl, O., Penis, C., Automatic stereo photogrammetry: implementation and comparison of classified correlation methods and dynamic programming based techniques. *ISPRS Comm.III*, 1986, Rovaniemi, Finland.

[13] Maître, H., Bardinet, C., Digital stereo relief reconstruction of Tanzania (Karema region) using aerial imagery, In "The Unesco/IUGS GARS Program in Africa", J. Lavreau and C. Bardinet eds., Musée Royal Afrique Centrale, *An. Série Sc. Géol.* 96, 1988, pp. 131-138, Tervuren, Belgium.

[14] Perlant, F., Luo, W., Maître, H., Bardinet, C., Stéréorestitution sur imagerie Spot d'une zone du Burundi, *Bul. Sc. Languedocienne Géogr.* (1-2) 1988, 111e année, pp. 77-95, Montpellier, France.
Maître, H. and Wu Y.F., Improving Dynamic Programming to Solve Image Registration, *Pattern Recognition*, Vol-20, No.4, 1987, pp. 443-462.

[15] Maître, H., and Wu, Y.F., A Dynamic Programming Algorithm for Elastic Registration of Distorted Pictures Based on Autoregressive Model, *IEEE Trans. ASSP*, Vol.37, No.2, February 1989, pp. 288-297.

[16] Wu, Y.F., Application de la programmation dynamique au recalage d'images. Thèse doctorat ENST-Paris, 1987.

[17] Martel, F., Stereorestitution of Spot imagery in Shaanxi (China). *Co-operative Education Work Term Report*, Telecom Paris, 1988, pp. 1-48.

[18] Bardinet, C., Maître. H., Martel, F., Wang, C.Y., Wu, Y.F., Stéréoradiométrie et modèle numérique de terrain par Spot: application à la région de Yan'an dans le Plateau des loess, Shaanxi, *Chine. Proc. CEGET-Table ronde intern. CNRS*, Oct. 1989, in Télédétection et Tiers-Monde. *Ed. CNRS*, CEGET, 1991, pp. 283-318, Bordeaux, France.

DATA: Part.1: Landsat 2 MSS data, E 2104-021193 6 May 1975 (Center N-36.57° and E-114.57°)

Part.2: first date: SPOT1 HRV1, 01775277T K268/J276, 27 December 1986, 3H50'54", mode P, correction 1B, left, quality E, gain 5, angle E18.04°Right; orbite incidence angle +L20.9°, scene orientation +13.0°. Dkm/GRS=W3; coordinates N-36.51.28°/E-109.27.44; Az:+166.6, El-site:+28.5, Cloud 0000 (<10%), 6013 lines, 7096 pixels;

second date: SPOT1 HRV1, 0177682G K268/J276, 8 January 1987, 3H17'55", mode P, correction 1B, right, quality E, gain 5, angle W25.03°Left; orbite incidence angle -R29.0°, scene orientation +7.0°, Dkm/GRS=W4; coordinates N-36.51.28°/E-109.27.26; Az:+156.8, El-site:+27.4, Cloud 0000 (<10%), 5977 lines, 8016 pixels.

COMPUTERIZED SYSTEM FOR GEOINFORMATION COLLECTION AND PROCESSING (Project)

A.S. Alekseev, O.L. Kuznetsov and V.A. Sirotyuk
MNTK "GEOS"
8 Varshavskoe sh.
Moscow 113105, Russia

The computerized system for collection, storage and processing of geological, geophysical and geochemical investigation data ("GEOSISTEMA") is now under development with the aim of increasing the efficiency and raising the level of investigation of the earth's structure and evolution, as well as the human activities in the field of geo-utilization.

The goals of the GEOSISTEMA are to be achieved through the creation of computerized technologies intended to solve problems of geological exploration work, monitoring the process of exploration of mineral resources and the environmental geological medium.

From the standpoint of general science, the GEOSISTEMA project is aimed at providing for a unified methodical approach in our investigation of the Earth's structure and geological processes therein; in practice, it is to ensure a support for making decisions in the field of geo-utilization.

The integrated analysis method for the analysis of geoinformation constitutes the basis of the GEOSISTEMA project.

Hereinbelow, the notation of "integrated analysis" will imply a complex process of multilevel and various geoinformation processing and interpretation (*i.e.*, information obtained at all levels of sounding and a combination of geological, geophysical and geochemical methods of investigation) on the basis of the systems analysis method.

Let us emphasize that the integrated analysis method is aimed at investigation of the following aspects:

- general principles of structural division of the geological, geophysical and geochemical space;
- spatial, power and time hierarchy of geoprocesses including investigation of four-dimensional dynamic and non-linear phenomena;
- general and basic features of the lithosphere and new processes occurring in the Earth;
- new fundamental features of the lithosphere and new processes occurring in the Earth;
- physical and chemical memory properties of the rocks.

The integrated analysis will result, on the one hand, in obtaining volumetric physical-and-geological models of geo-objects, essentially new knowledge of the geosphere properties and, on the other hand, information indispensable in selecting the most reasonable solution at any stage of the geological prospecting work or process.

The development work aimed at working out computer- processing technologies of optimized projecting and planning, as well as organization of the process of geological prospecting work with respect to the kinds of mineral resources, has been underway within the framework of the subsystems "OIL & GAS", "ORE", "UNDERGROUND HYDROSPHERE" - predication, prospecting, exploration.

Geological and economical estimates of mineral deposits, calculation of geological resources and extraction coefficients, as well as construction of multi-factor physical-and-geological, geochemical and hydrodynamic models - are problems that are being solved with respect to stages of the geological prospecting process.

Realization of the computerized technologies contemplated by the project and intended for solving problems of geological prospecting and exploration work is carried out through implementation of regional subsystems to be created by taking into consideration the organizational structure of the branch of the industry, its mineral-and-material complex resources and the specific features of the territorial geological zoning.

The conception of the GEOSISTEMA organization provides for creation of a multi-level hierarchical information-and-computer medium on the basis of computer networks. Provided at every organizational level will be reference information-and-computer centers. Constituting the basis of the system are databases, technologies of specialized data processing with the use of specialized work-stations, interactive graphics and telecommunication means.

Digital and analogue models of geofields are located from four levels of the lithosphere sounding: the space- air- earth- borehole. The information-and- -measuring systems of this level are used for execution of the function of controlling the processes of measurement and registration, monitoring the quality testing results, mapping the geophysical and geochemical fields and geological space, and separating (in a plan view and section view) the required object with the pre-determined properties of the parameter to be mapped. The development work has been going on through the establishment of field computer centers based on microcomputer and specialized (mono-method) computerized work-stations adequate to function for many users according to a constant technology. The databases of the lower levels contain information on some types of geological-and-geophysical investigations and levels testing; these databases are of a file structure. With the aim of providing for a most effective and complex performance of geological prospecting work in the region, as well as supplying the territorial business entities with required information on the mineral resources, and engineering-and-geological and geo-ecological situation (figures), special interdepartmental regional data banks are now under formation.

Aimed at supplying governmental bodies with required information, a number of branch and interdepartmental databases are now being established. These databases will include information on mineral and raw-material resources of the country and world oceans. In addition, databases in regional exploration work, depth structure and prospecting geo-physics are also under development.

Geo-information available on the network of the interdepartmental and branch data banks constitutes an integral information resource about the Earth. These data banks are intended to provide a great number of specialists of various branches and departments with required information indispensable in solving fundamental and applied problems relating to Earth sciences, as well as to provide an information support to governmental bodies on various aspects of geo-ecology, forecasting catastrophic natural phenomena, and protection of mineral wealth.

The distributed access method and means ensure the following advantages for the users: obtaining information on availability and volume of data in the GEOSISTEMA on the territory, geological object, some natural mineral resource; interrogation on the structure and content of the database; operation of using the database in a query mode; formation of local databases for solving applied problems. These means have been developed for users in the form of unified technologies for data organization. Such unified technologies for applied problem programmers, are in fact a multi-purpose interface with data providing for operation of applied programs with a standard "call" language of a high level and the use of database control systems; a functional interface for operation with databases of hierarchical, network and relational structure; a dialogue language for interrogation close to the natural language of the specific subject field; means for operation by using the computer graphics in an interactive mode; means for multiple access to the data.

At every hierarchical level, the distributed technology of data processing is embodied in the firm of parametric train of specialized work-stations (CWS-GEO in English which implies computerized work-station).

Specialization in solving problems with CWS-GEO is ensured by a system of functional and applied programs to solve problems of various object fields of geological prospecting.

The major problem in the way of computerization of geological prospecting work is the poor formalization of its knowledge base. A special apparatus is required to process such knowledge. Recently, claiming rather successfully to be such an apparatus are the expert systems (ES). They are developed specially for solving problems with a poorly expressed structure. In the course problem solving, expert systems use various heuristic methods and some other professional knowledge of the expert-specialist. Combination of this knowledge will determine the efficiency of the use of expert systems *per se*.

As a rule, expert systems only make it possible to obtain some qualitative solution to a problem. Used for finding more accurate, *i.e.,* quantitative evaluation figures are systems of some other type based on formalized theories and models. Such systems, as opposed to the expert systems, are called theoretical systems.

Probably a constructive unification of these theoretical systems (integration) will take place in the near future. In so doing, the expert methods will be reasonably used for elimination of uncertainties in the initial formulation of the problem (namely: structurization of the space of objects, formation of images, monitoring the completeness and reliability of data, grounding the criteria and limitations, etc.), *i.e.,* for posing a problem formally, while the theoretical part of the operation will be used for construction of an algorithm for its solution and realization of this algorithm.

Integrated systems essentially offer new possibilities for modeling objects and processes of geological prospecting work by means of computers. The sphere of utilization of these systems will cover such aspects of work as: complex interpretation of geological and geophysical data (constructing models of geological bodies on the basis of data obtained by various types of survey systems); prediction of occurrence of mineral deposits; geological and economical evaluation of mineral deposits; planning of actions, *i.e.,* determination of sequence of geological prospecting and exploration work, systems and networks of survey, processing graphs, etc.; projecting complicated technological objects (project sections of boreholes, open pits, useful minerals recovery schemes and so on); determination of regularities in occurrence of geological bodies; and formulation of prospecting hypotheses and criteria.

It should be stressed that incorporation of integrated systems into the content of CWS-GEO software will make it possible to have all the links of the normative chain of the mathematic modeling classical scheme (including a mathematician and programmer) "transparent". It is realistic, of course, on condition that the problem of communication of geologists with the computer in a language that is habitual for the users, has been solved.

Relative to the basic directions of research and projected work required for the creation of specialized computerized CWS-GEO work-stations are the following tasks: organization of machine databases to cover various aspects of geology; construction of expert systems and decision-support systems for various staging of geological prospecting work; development of languages and means for maintenance of the "geologist-computer" dialogue; creation of a system for modeling geological prospecting objects and processes as well as development of information-and-computer networks (both local and regional); and reorganization of geological funds.

A personal base of knowledge (PBK), that reflects the sphere of the professional activities of every concrete user of a CWS-GEO work-station, constitutes the kernel of the CWS-GEO professional activities support sub-system. The sphere of activities of a specialist-geologist can be described in terms of correlation of two sets: a complex of geological prospecting tasks (GPT) and a complex of geological prospecting objects (GO). A spatial grid GPT/GO conforms to the concrete data of the two sets, and it determines the structure of any respective PBK. Let us note that the notion of PBK relates to the computerized work-station as a whole, *i.e.,* to a "human-to-machine" system but not to some independent components thereof. The main function of the professional activities support sub-system consists in organization and formation of knowledge on geological objects and geological prospecting tasks and utilization of the PBK in practical activities.

The organization and formation of knowledge on geological objects is comprised of the following tasks: determination of hierarchy of the objects; division of the objects of every hierarchical level (classification of objects) into classes (kinds, types); construction of typical generalized descriptions of objects of the classes (image formation); determination (description) of preconditions (factors) which are indispensable and comprehensive for relating every particular object to a particular class (kind or type); description of theoretical provisions, hypotheses, heuristics and prospecting criteria reflecting the spatial and cause-and-effect regularities location and formation of objects relating to different classes (kinds, types); description of methods (techniques, processes, procedures) to be used for determination of the values of factors that are essential for classification and localization of objects; and creation and maintenance of factor (data) base, *i.e.,* formation of models of concrete objects as they are being investigated. For every fact being input into the factor (data) base, the method of obtaining this fact and the degree of reliability thereof shall be registered.

For the realization of the functions and tasks cited above, the CWS-GEO work-station shall be supplemented with special means, namely, a sub-system for formation of geological objects.

Three inter-connected layers of description (tasks, operations, procedures) constitute the basis of the knowledge base for the solution of geological prospecting tasks. The structure of the layer of tasks reflects the division of the geological prospecting tasks into classes and determines the correlations between the classes of tasks. For every class, a typical description is constructed that determines a list of initial data and results of the task solution.

The next layer determines a set of operations to be used (fully or partially) for solving the problems. It is expedient to distinguish three types of operations, namely: (a) routine operations intended for determination of the values of various characteristics of concrete or specific objects; (b) logical operations to be used for evaluation of the degree of reliability (reality) of certain conditions, hypotheses or regularities; and (c) modeling operations used for simulation of natural processes or results of certain activity (non-activity) of the human society.

The sequence of operations that ensures a solution of a given problem is called a "problem solution scenario" (PSS). In principle, several PSSs can be adequate for one problem. Let us note here that since all the operations have been formalized (*i.e.*, all of them have an unambiguous interpretation), the notion of a PSS becomes equivalent to the traditional notion of "algorithm".

The third layer comprises descriptions of procedures used for performing operations of the computer. Correlating with every particular operation can require a great number of procedures distinguished by the programming language, calculation schema, data representation, time of performance, volume of storage, etc. Respective characteristics are reflected in the procedure description. The procedures *per se* can be constructed independently and then stored in a procedures library.

The knowledge stored in the personal base of knowledge is used mainly for information service or for solving various problems. Solution of problems can be performed both by way of a direct readout or in the modeling mode. In case a ready scenario for solving a given problem is not available in the personal knowledge base, a required scenario is constructed by a planner which is a special component of the solution sub-system. Depending on the nature of the data, models and operations involved, a decision will be realized either according to the traditional schema (procedure generator) or according to the technology of expert systems (operation interpreter). Any operation can be commented by the explanation block.

The organization offered in the present paper will make it possible to unite the advantages of the traditional and expert system with the aim of providing for effective modeling of the objects and processes of geological prospecting work.

A sub-system for the assessment of functioning and self-organization has a considerable and important role in improving the organization of the personal knowledge base, as well as the whole CWS-GEO work-station operation. This sub-system performs the functions of accumulation, systematization and analysis of the parameters characterizing the efficiency and quality of functioning of the CWS-GEO work-station components and work out recommendations on their improvement. Communication between the user and the computer in the course of the CWS-GEO work-station operation, will be effected in a language habitual for the user. Such a possibility will be maintained by the dialogue system.

The possibility of a multiple-access operation of the CWS-GEO work-station will be provided for by the communication medium of the GEOSISTEMA information-and-computer network.

ADVANCES IN DATA STORAGE, RETRIEVAL, AND ANALYSIS

OBJECT-ORIENTED KNOWLEDGE BASE SYSTEMS

F.J. Smith and S.R. Tripathy
Department of Computer Science
The Queen's University of Belfast
Northern Ireland

1. INTRODUCTION

Object-oriented design has recently become a fashionable subject amongst computer scientists as it offers a different approach to traditional software and, it is claimed [1], that it leads to more efficient programming, particularly because object-oriented code is more readily reusable than conventional code. Object-oriented databases are also the subject of a great deal of research for one additional reason: they enable us to store, as objects, much more complex representations of the real world than is possible with the other models, Relational, Network or Hierarchical. However, the object-oriented approach is likely to have a larger impact on knowledge base systems than on database systems, because it can store code as well as data in its knowledge base.

Most current database systems in engineering store information only in the form of data, *e.g.,* as sets of numbers and alpha-numeric characters. Usually an engineer is able to retrieve such data quickly and easily, but always in the same form as it has been entered. Thus an engineer can retrieve data on the strength of a material which might be used to design a special bolt, but not obtain a selection of optimum designs of the bolt, thickness, length, material, cost, etc. For this, we need efficient representation and flexible manipulation of the complex physical laws which, in engineering databases, govern many of the relationships between the data objects and the attributes; for example, laws on how the strength of a bolt of a particular size and a particular material varies with high temperature. An object-oriented design appears to provide an ideal method of achieving these objectives since it provides mechanisms for handling the many complex interrelationships, and inference-based selection rules which can be stored explicitly in the knowledge base.

It is unlikely at the present time that an object oriented system would be used for technical data, except for research purposes; the subject is not yet sufficiently developed. However, within a few years, these types of databases and knowledge bases will probably become important, particularly in such subjects as computer aided design where the nature of the data which have to be stored and retrieved is more complex than most other data.

To explain object oriented databases and knowledge bases further, we need first to describe the principles of object oriented programming.

2. OBJECT ORIENTED PROGRAMMING

The term *object oriented programming* has been appearing frequently in the computer literature recently; but the term *object*, as a computer representation of some entity in the real world is appearing with much greater frequency, and is becoming universal. Any data item, such as a record, can be viewed as an object. Sometimes a collection of records, or a whole file is referred to an object. However, normally in object oriented literature the definition of an object goes further than representing information as data in a program because they include not only the attributes of the entity but also the actions or processes associated with the entity. For example, if an object is an atom in an atomic physics database, then amongst the properties might be name, atomic number and atomic mass. The traditional model of an atom might also include multiple occurrences of energy and cross section. However an "object" goes further and may include processes in its model, including for example:

- the printing of the name and attributes of an atom,
- changing the units in the cross sections from MKS to CGS units,
- the computation of a rate coefficient by integrating the cross sections over a Maxwellian distribution of energies for a particular temperature.

These possible actions, called "methods" in object-oriented terminology, would be stored along with the other data representing the object in the computer system and would become part of the object. This is illustrated in Figure 1.

2.1 Classes

The language describing object oriented systems is slightly different from traditional systems. The *class* of an object is equivalent to the object type and is defined as a series of *members*, similar to fields which can have two forms:

(a) **Instance variables** - these are the equivalent of property fields and contain the properties or attributes of objects;

(b) **Methods** - As explained above, this is the terminology for action fields and they include the commands to execute actions on the object. In the example above the methods would be "print", "change units" and "compute rate data".

Class is similar to a type and all objects of the same class have the same instance variables (attributes) and methods (processes). The attribute names, units, constants, ranges of values and methods need only be stored once for a whole class.

The **instance** of a class is a particular object in the class, *i.e.*, the equivalent to a tuple in a relation. One fundamental aspect of object oriented programming is that when an action has to be performed, such as print, the program need only send a message to the object to execute the command, nothing else, because the object has built into its class, the methods needed to execute the actions which can be performed on it. Thus the same method applied to two different classes of objects may have different outcomes. For example, the printing of two (attributes) will result in different types of print-outs, *i.e.*, different headings and numbers of columns.

2.2 Inheritance

An important feature of all object oriented programming systems is **inheritance.** In the real world objects are seldom atomistic, but are made up of combinations of other existing objects; for example an airplane is a general concept which has a limited number of attributes, such as number of engines, type of engine, weight, range, etc. This will represent one class of object; we can then define new classes (known as derived classes or sub-classes) which are defined by inheriting all of the instance variables and methods of the original class and adding additional properties or actions. For example, in the case of our planes, illustrated in Figure 2, we might classify the planes according to their use or according to the company of manufacture. If we use company of manufacture, then we would add as additional instance variables the name of the company, its address, the factory where the entity was built, the airplane types, and so on. There might be a further sub-division into different classes of airplanes, built by that one company, *e.g.,* Boeing 747, 737, 727 and so on. In this way a structure is defined for classes, with their associated properties and actions.

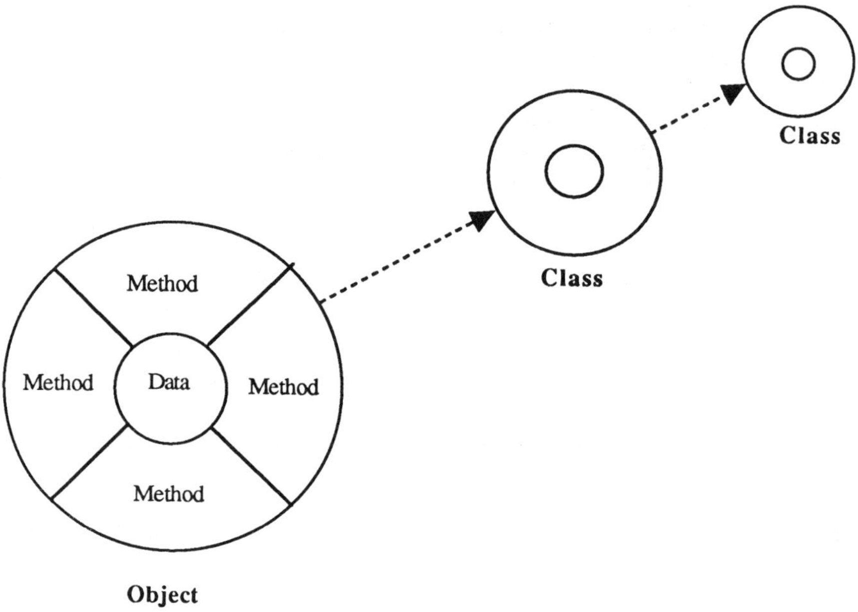

FIGURE 1
Example of an object consisting of data surrounded by methods (actions or processes) and inheriting data and methods from a succession of higher classes.

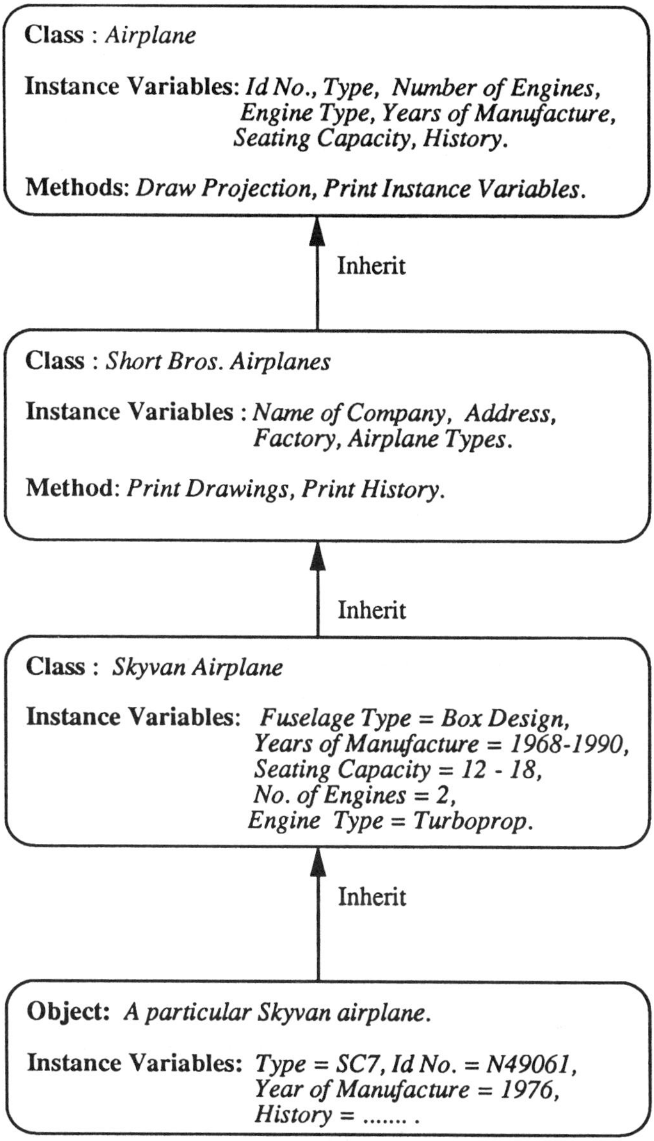

FIGURE 2

Example in an object oriented system of classes (similar to types), each inheriting above classes and each with its own instance variables (similar to fields). The actions which can be performed on each object are called "methods" in the figure and are part of the class. The History member in an airplane object is a relation of parts replaced, no. of hours flying, dates, etc.

2.3 Language

There are several languages available for object oriented programming. The main languages available on a wide range of computers are (i) SMALLTALK, the first object-oriented language and the one which has effectively started the subject of object-oriented systems, (ii) EIFFLE, an advanced language from France, (iii) Objective-C and (iv) the more common C++ which are both upwards compatible with C. For the scientist and engineer, any of these languages can be used; however C++ is probably the most convenient as it is available on a wide range of computers, including a VAX and is becoming almost a standard for object oriented programming in engineering. A good and readable introduction to object oriented programming has been written by Cox [1]. Rumble and Smith have described the concepts in the context of science and engineering [2].

2.4 Modularity

Possibly the greatest advantage of object oriented programming is that it makes programmers write more modular code than other language methodologies. By storing the methods (processes) with the data representing some entity, it makes it easier to think of the whole data and code together as one single object, complete in itself. Programmers automatically tend to do this and the result is better designed software and more reusable code.

However, there is still a danger that the improvement in software productivity is really due to the enthusiasm of the elite few who have begun to use the method. Unfortunately it has a long learning curve: it will take a month before you can be proficient in C++ after learning C. So it is not widely used as yet.

Whatever the eventual outcome on *software* productivity, the object-oriented approach is still likely to be important for *databases* and *knowledge bases* in science and technology, as we explain in the following sections.

3. OBJECT ORIENTED DATABASES

Object oriented databases view all data as objects. These objects may be any data model of the entities described by the databases; if the objects are all tuples of relations, the database would then be equivalent to a relational database. But generally we mean by an object oriented database system, one which stores more complex objects, usually one including processes, and one which includes inheritance as a fundamental part of its structure.

The data model may also include operators which can operate on complex objects. For example, a single operation might be sufficient to activate a method of the airplane object which can draw an aeroplane from a particular angle; it would automatically invoke the operators to draw the parts: body, wings, engines etc.

The above description of object oriented databases is brief and is meant only to give the reader a general idea of the subject. For further reading we recommend the book by Cox [1] already mentioned and the reports on the International Workshops on Object Oriented Database Systems [3,4].

4. KNOWLEDGE BASE SYSTEMS

A database system is a system for the storage and retrieval of data. A user may search the database for data to solve some problem, but the database system does not solve the problem. All it can do is retrieve data for the user and at most manipulate the data (such as change units) to help the user solve the problem. On the other hand, a knowledge base system stores rules and laws as well as data, but its purpose is not to provide a system to retrieve the rules and facts, a relatively easy task, but rather to use the rules and data together to find a solution or solutions to the problem posed by the user.

4.1 Expert systems

In the simpler form of a knowledge base system, called an expert system, the rules are based on the experience of an expert, and the system attempts to emulate the expert's ability to solve problems - more complex than that of a database system. It normally operates in a precise and very limited domain, *i.e.*, on a knowledge base of only a few hundred facts and rules (or at most a few thousand), whereas a database system has no difficulty in dealing with tens of thousands of records. Unfortunately expert systems normally only deal with logical rules which can be expressed in the form -

If antecedent A is true then consequence C has probability P of being true.

Although these logical rules are sufficient for many purposes, particularly for modelling the "know-how" of an expert, they are not sufficient for a wide range of problems in science and engineering.

4.2 Combined databases and expert systems

It is not uncommon for a combined database and expert system to be used

[5]. For example, for computer aided design, an engineering company may already have a database of drawings of items designed by the company along with many modifications; it may also have a database of components and materials. However, the experience of an expert designer may be crucial in the selection of an old design as the basis of a new one or in the selection of materials or components.

So one possibility is to combine an expert system with a database system by passing data from one to the other, for example to use the DBMS, Oracle, and the expert system, Expertease together, by executing one then the other. However, this process is slow and since moving from one system to the other may be very frequent during the interrogation of the whole system by a user, the process is unacceptably slow.

An alternative is either to build suitable database structures onto an expert system shell or to add some reasoning capabilities to the user interface of a database system. This second approach we think is the more promising of the two and it has been demonstrated that it is not difficult to build a PROLOG written reasoning capability on top of a database system such as Oracle. However, for some problems the first approach, a modified expert system will be more appropriate.

Such combined systems are still new and the subject of research [6]. So it is still early to give advice on them. When an expert systems is extended to widen the types of data and processing possible, the software system (or shell) is called a knowledge based management system (KBMS) [7]. But all such systems are still experimental and are still the subject of debate by specialists in computer science and artificial intelligence.

An object-oriented approach, discussed next, is designed as a total system, rather than combining two systems which were originally designed for another purpose; it is likely to widen the range of applications while producing a more efficient system.

4.3 Object oriented knowledge base systems

Object oriented knowledge base systems are also the subject of a great deal of research and discussion at present. A traditional expert system stores facts and logical rules only. But this is not sufficient in many real situations, unless they are simple ones. Most larger expert systems need special software written into the system to deal with special cases and to model processes which cannot be modelled by our simple logical rules. So the storage of facts and rules alone is not sufficient in practice and each expert system has substantial special implicit code built into the software to model additional processes and without which it would not be effective. So every expert system is, in a sense, a once-off system.

A more general system would permit the explicit storage of the processes in the knowledge base in a more flexible form, *i.e.,* as code in the form of modules, or routines or whole programs. To do this we need a system which can store and process a richer variety of objects than, for example, a relational database system can handle. Object oriented database systems are ideal structures for this purpose.

In an object-oriented system, as we have explained, the objects include data and the methods (*i.e.,* processes) operating on the data. These methods, represented by explicit code stored with the data, may include the equivalent of the logical rules found in a traditional expert system, but in addition, because any code, any module, any program can be included as part of an object (or inherited by an object) the range of methods which can be implemented is as wide as the knowledge base permits. For example, objects may include methods which include the relevant laws of Physics and Chemistry, search through large knowledge bases, carry out substantial numeric processing, process images, analyze language and so on. So the object oriented approach is a suitable wide vehicle for the storage and implementation of a very flexible knowledge base system. In this approach, complex objects, including processes and relationships between objects, replace the facts and rules of an expert system. Within a decade such systems may be common place tools in the armory of the knowledge engineer.

In the next section we discuss how the data may be structured in an object oriented system for two simple examples.

5. ENGINEERING EXAMPLE

5.1 Materials

Our two examples, slightly contrived for simplicity, concern the problem of the design of a cable to carry a particular current between two pylons and the design of a polymer panel on an aircraft. We need to build object oriented data structures for the entities in these examples. In the first the entities are the cable and the steel from which it is made and in the second it is the panel and the polymer. These entities have several relevant properties such as tensile strength, resistivity and weight. Some of these properties can be inherited from higher classes as illustrated in Figures 3 and 4.

In the first example, in Figure 3, the object "cellulose acetate" inherits many of its properties from "polymers" which inherits the basic data members from the super-class "Materials". In the second, more complex example, the possible steels from which the cable is made belong to the class "steels" and inherit all of their properties. Amongst these properties are methods which enables the knowledge base system to compute the tensile strength from a formula and the resistivity from a table for a range of temperatures.

The class "steels" inherits some properties from "alloys" such as the fuzzy concept of "high tensile strength", if the temperature is above the melting point. Note that this property is not only fuzzy, it also includes a logical rule. The class "alloys" inherits many data members from the superior class "materials" including all of the property names or attributes such as density, resistivity, conductivity, tensile strength, etc. This also includes the units of these properties.

5.2 Solids

The other two entities are "cable" and "panel". These can both be represented as instances of the class "solid", *i.e.,* objects which belong to this class and inherit from this class many properties including such data members as volume, weight, heat capacity, etc, and their units. It would also include the instance variable that the solid is made of some material, and methods such as the simple formula

$$W = dV$$

i.e., that the weight equals the density times the volume. The attribute density is inherited from the class "material".

A subclass of "solid" is the class "cylinder" which has as an instant variable the object "cable". The "cylinder" class includes the method that its volume equals

$$V = \pi r^2 L$$

where r and L are its radius and length. It will also include the simple formula that

$$R = \rho L/\pi r^2$$

where R is the resistance of the cable and ρ is the resistivity of the steel. A method for its tensile strength in terms of its length and cross section would also be included. This enables an engineer to examine the possible choice of materials for a cable in terms of its strength, cost and resistance properties.

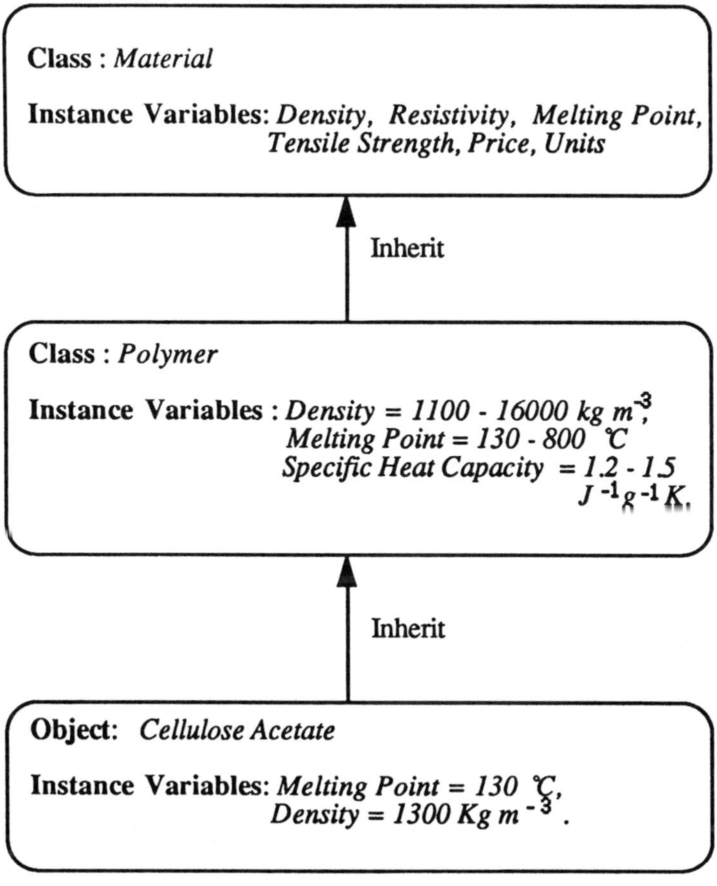

FIGURE 3
Example of the object cellulose acetate which includes properties and methods from the classes "Polymers" and "Material". Since there is no heat capacity included in the object, it can use the range of values from the class "polymer".

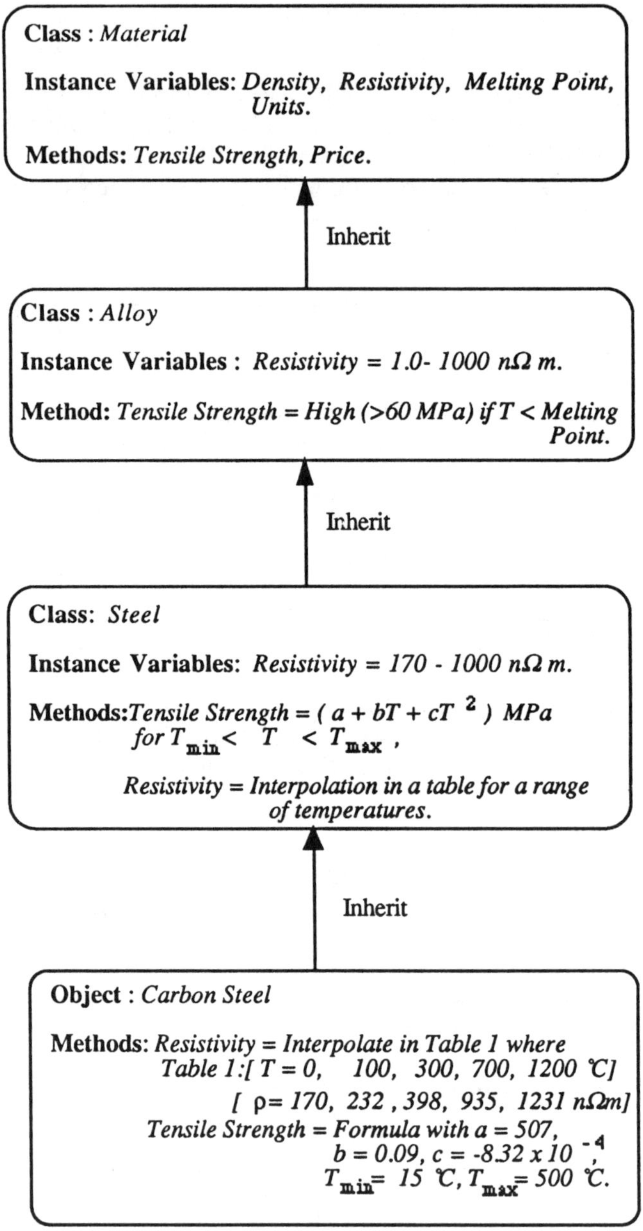

FIGURE 4
Example of the object carbon steel and a few methods defined in associated classes.

The object panel in its simplest form would be part of a class of rectangular solids as in Figure 5. However in practice it is likely to be a more complicated solid, needing a method for surface fitting (which can be stored as a separate object on its own), and a method made up of programs to compute the strength of the panel from its shape, thickness and materials under different conditions.

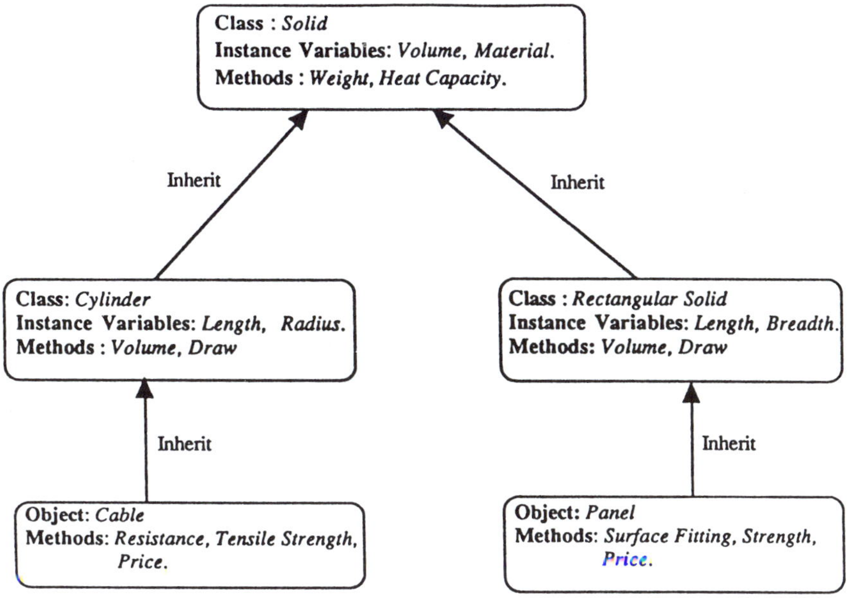

FIGURE 5
Example of objects cable and panel which are instances of the classes above. They also inherit properties such as resistivity from the class "material" needed to compute the resistance. Units (not shown) must be included.

REFERENCES

[1] B J Cox, *Object Oriented Programming*, Addison-Wesley, Reading, Mass, p274, 1986.

[2] J R Rumble and F J Smith, *Database Systems in Sciences and Technology*, Adam Hilger, Bristol, p278, 1990.

[3] K R Dittrich and U Doyal, Eds, *International Workshop on Object Oriented Database Systems*, IEEE Comp Soc Press, Washington DC, p237, 1986.

[4] K R Dittrich, *2nd International Workshop on Object Oriented Database Systems*, Springer-Verlag, New York, p373, 1988.

[5] G Wiederhold, Knowledge versus data, in M L Brodie and J Mylopoulos, *On Knowledge Based Management Systems*, Springer-Verlag, New York, pp 77-82, 1986.

[6] U Dayal and J M Smith, PROBE : A knowledge-oriented database management system in Ed M L Brodie and J Mylopoulos, *On Knowledge Base Management Systems*, Springer-Verlag, pp 227-257, 1986.

[7] J Mylopoulos, *On Knowledge Base Management Systems*, Ibid, pp 3-8. 1986.

KNOWLEDGE-BASED SYSTEMS AND DEDUCTIVE DATABASES

Hélène Bestougeff
Université de Paris VII
2 place Jussieu
75251 Paris Cédex 05, France

INTRODUCTION

A standard relational system is defined as a collection of relation schemes together with a set of integrity constraints.

To retrieve the data from the stored relations, a language is defined (for instance the relation algebra using set operations such as projection, selection, join, etc.), and efficient management secondary storage is available [1]. The stored relations can be seen as sets of facts and are therefore called "Extensional Database" (EDB).

In a deductive database, in addition to sets of facts, there are sets of rules which describe new facts to be derived through some kind of reasoning. These new facts constitute the "Intentional Database" (IDB). Deductive databases are one way to achieve what is now called knowledge-based systems and are seen as an important future tool in scientific data management [2]. The need for such a system is clearly stated, for instance, in the Genome Project [3].

Theoretical interest in deductive databases began rather early and solid foundations are now available [1]. The logic-based approach and the development of the PROLOG language led first to some practical implementation coupling PROLOG systems and relational databases, but the real challenge is to build a fully integrated system that would combine efficient inference procedures with efficient data management.

BASIC CONCEPTS

A deductive database can be defined as:

- a collection of rules of the form

(i) $C \longleftarrow A_1,A_2,...,A_m$ with $m > 0$, C denoting an atomic formula and A_i's denoting litterals (positive and negative atomic formulas). C is called the head of a rule and A_i's are subgoals of the body of the rule. (i) is read as "C if A_1 and A_2 and ... A_n."

An atomic formula has the following form $p_i(t_1,...,t_k)$ where p_i is a predicate symbol and t_i's are terms. The only terms that are considered in this paper are constraints and variables. We therefore limit ourselves to what are commonly called DATALOG rules [4]. Moreover all variables are assumed to be universally quantified.

- a collection of integrity constraints given as a set of closed, well-formed formulas. Constraints are conditions that a database must satisfy when updates are performed; generally they can be defined on extensional and intentional predicates. If there is a violation of integrity constraints, the update is rejected or the set of integrity constraints must be modified.

The general format of (i) must however be examined more closely to understand the different problems raised by deductive databases.

- If $m=0$ then a rule is just a fact C.
- If all A_i's are positive atoms, rules are Horn clauses as in PROLOG where negated subgoals are not allowed.

At first sight, rules with the same head can be seen as defining *a view* as in relational databases where defined relations, which are not physically stored, can be queried as if they were. The main difference is that, in a deductive database, rules are in general *recursive*, *i.e.,* the dependency graph of the set of rules has one or more cycles. This situation appears typically in applications where structures are defined recursively in terms of some basic structures as in computer aided design or pattern recognition databases, for instance the string of proteins that make up a gene.

To illustrate this point we shall describe an example of an arbitrary pattern. Let us decide that a pattern is a chain of elements of different colors. Each element is defined by three attributes:

- its color (red, blue, white, etc.)
- its left coupling position
- its right coupling position

For instance, we can have the following facts:

- element (blue, 1, 3)
- element (blue, 3, 5)
- element (red, 1, 4)
- element (black, 2, 3)

These facts define an EDB relation ELEMENT (COL, POS 1, POS 2).

A chain is defined by the color and position of its end elements, and is constructed by adding either an element to the left or to the right of a chain. Moreover an element added to the

- left of a chain must be of the same color as the left end elements of the chain,
- right of a chain must not be of the same color as the right end of the chain.

The new relation chain can therefore be defined using the following recursive rules:

chain (C, Lp, C, Rp) ⟵ element (C, Lp, Rp)
chain (C1, Lp, C2, Rp) ⟵ element (C1, Lp, X), chain (C1, X, C2, Rp)
chain (C1, Lp, C2, Rp) ⟵ element (C2, X, Rp), chain (C1, Lp, C0, X), C0 C2

These three rules allow us to compute the IDB relation: CHAIN (COL1, POS1, COL2, POS2)

Different types of queries involving the chain predicate can be asked, for instance: "List all the chains which have a blue left end and a red right end":

chain (blue, X, red, Y)

Typically a deductive database will have several "EDB predicates" (corresponding to basic relations) occurring only in the body of the rules and several "IDB predicates" occurring in the head and body of the rules. How can a query be answered in this setting?

QUERY EVALUATION

The well-known Prolog strategy for query evaluation is a tuple at a time, top down, depth first, with a backtracking approach. But other strategies can be devised that are more adequate for database applications. One important point is that for databases, in general the whole answer relation is needed and not just a tuple satisfying the logical query. Moreover in database applications there are generally a large number of facts compared to the number of rules, and therefore facts must be stored in the secondary stage.

For instance the answer to the query: chain (black, X, C, Y) using the above definitions must return the relation: {<black, 2, black, 3>,<black, 2, blue, 5>}.

Difficulty in query evaluation depends on whether the rules are recursive or not and whether negation is involved.

- Negation introduces the idea of the "complement of a relation," which is not always a well-defined concept. Different solutions can be proposed besides the negation by finite failure used in PROLOG. In [5], J.C. Shepherdson gives a survey of different treatments of negation in logic programming.

- Recursive Horn clauses are however the major problem. F. Bancilhon and R. Ramakrishnan [6] analyze several methods and compare their theoretical performances. They propose the following criteria to compare different strategies:

- Size of the application domain
- Performance of the strategy
- Ease of implementation

For each strategy three main characteristics are given:

- Top down or bottom up
- Compiled or interpreted
- Iterative or recursive

(a) Top down strategies start from the query (head of a rule) and try all the ways in which the proof of the goal can succeed. Bottom up strategy starts from the base relations and constructs derived relations.
(b) In a compiled strategy there is a preliminary phase in the process in

which only the intentional database is accessed and some "object program" is generated.

(c) Recursive methods are those which involve a stack as control mechanism.

Finally three factors are considered as having a great influence on performance:

- Duplication of work, for instance repeating the same computation when intermediate results are not stored.
- Relevant facts: knowing in advance which facts are relevant to the processed query and which are not; this can avoid accessing the whole extensional database.
- The size (number and parity) of intermediate relations.

Part of the proposed methods have not yet been implemented, let alone integrated in a real size system. However, the analysis shows clearly the problems to be solved.

OPTIMIZATION

In deductive databases, optimization can be seen at different levels:

- Optimization of the rules to make evaluation more efficient.
- Optimization of the deductive component.
- Optimization of the data management component (storage and retrieval).

The first level covers all programs (set of rules) transformations. Compiled evaluation methods mentioned in the previous section are one of these. Some other methods use the integrity constraints to perform, for instance, rule transformations [7].

The next two levels depend on the practical implementation of the deductive database. Right now there are mainly three kinds of approaches:

- Loose coupling with PROLOG
- Tight coupling with PROLOG
- Integrated systems

In the first case the Database management system (DBMS) and PROLOG system communicate through an interface, *i.e.,* the DBMS is called by the PROLOG interpreter, it sends relational queries to the DBMS and the corresponding answers are treated as ground clauses by the interpreter. Several commercial systems have been proposed; B. Knifes and E. Herkimer present an evaluation of these products [8].

In the second case the PROLOG interpreter is modified in such a way that the DBMS is transparent to the user, for instance PROLOG can directly access the DBMS primitives such as relation management in secondary storage and relation access through indexed, or sophisticated algorithms for recursive queries can be implemented.

The last case covers all experimental systems that are now developed in laboratories, and which correspond to the next generation DBMS. For instance the NAIL system at Stanford University [1] or the LDL system at MCC [11].

Another way to improve the deductive component is to use parallel processing. Parallelism in logic programs using top down evaluation are generally classified into three classes [12]:

- AND parallelism: subgoals in the same rule body are processed in parallel.
- OR parallelism: different rules that unify with a query goal are evaluated in parallel.
- Stream parallelism: one subgoal waits for an attribute value being constructed by another subgoal.

Much work has been devoted to this subject in logic programming. The relevance for deductive databases has not yet been evaluated.

CONCLUSION

Deductive databases have the power to process general recursive queries, but some researchers have questioned the usefulness of such generality, arguing that for most applications only transitive closures are sufficient. Moreover the interfacing of PROLOG with DBMS does not seem to be a promising road for future knowledge systems because of the operational semantics of PROLOG where the choice in the order of rules and goals determines not only the efficiency, but the correctness and termination of the program. Today, even if the need to integrate AI and databases is well recognized, commercial systems are yet to come [13].

REFERENCES

[1] J.D. Ullman, "Principles of Database and Knowledge-base Systems," Volume 1, 2. Computer Science Press, 1989.

[2] H. Bestougeff, "Applications of Database and Knowledge-base Systems to Scientific Data," Computer Handling and Dissemination of Data, P. Glaeser (Ed.), Elsevier Science Publishers B.V. (North Holland), 1987.

[3] S.C. Loken, "Data Management Support for Human Genome," New Perspectives in Scientific Complex Data Management," CODATA Bulletin Vol. 22, No. 4, 1990.

[4] S. Ceri, G. Gottlob, L. Tanca, "What You Always Wanted to Know About DATALOG (and never dared to ask)," IEE Transactions on Knowledge and Data Engineering, Vol. 1, No. 1, pp.146-166.

[5] J.C. Shepherdson, "Negation in Logic Programming," Deductive Databases and Logic Programming, J. Minker (ed.), Morgan Kaufmann Publishers, 1988, pp.19-88.

[6] F. Bancilhon and R. Ramakrishnan, "Performance Evaluation of Data Intensive Logic," Deductive Databases and Logic Programming," J. Minker (ed.), Morgan Kaufmann Publishers, 1988, pp.439-518.

[7] U.S. Chakravarthy, J. Grant, J. Minker, "Foundations of Semantic Query Optimization for Deductive DataBases," Deductive Databases and Logic Programming, J. Minker (ed.), Morgan Kaufmann Publishers, 1988, pp.243-274.

[8] B. Knifes and D. Herkimer, "A Look at Loosely-coupled PROLOG Database Systems," Expert Database Systems: Proceedings from the Second International Workshop. L. Kerschberg (ed.), 1988, pp.257-271.

[9] K. Rothermel, "An Effective Method for Storing and Retrieving PROLOG Clauses from a Relational Database," in Proceedings, Third International Conference on Data and Knowledge Bases, Israel, 1988, Morgan Kaufmann Publishers.

[10] A. Lefebvre and L. Vieille, "On Deductive Query Evaluation in the DedGin System," Proceedings, 1st International Conference on Deductive and Object Oriented Databases, Kyoto 1989.

[11] C. Zaniolo, "Deductive Databases - Theory Meets Practice," Advances in Database Technology, LNCS N-416 Springer Verlag 1990, pp.1-15.

[12] J.S. Conery, "Parallel Execution of Logic Programs," Kluwer Academic Publishers, Boston, 1987.

[13] M.L. Brodie, "Future Intelligent Information Systems: AI and Database Technologies Working Together," in Readings in Artificial Intelligence and Databases, J. Mylopoulos, M.L. Brodie, Morgan Kaufmann, 1989, pp.623-644.

NEW NUMERIC DATA RETRIEVAL SYSTEMS

Andreas Barth
Fachinformationszentrum Karlsruhe
D-7514 Eggenstein-Leopoldshafen 2
Germany

INTRODUCTION

In the last decade the interest in numeric databases has significantly increased and this is reflected in the number of new released databases and in the development of the corresponding numeric retrieval systems. These databases cover business and social sciences as well as natural sciences and technology. According to the different subjects covered in these files the characteristics of the numeric data and their retrieval vary strongly and require different capabilities. In this paper the main focus is lying on databases and retrieval systems for natural sciences, *i.e.,* chemistry, material sciences, mathematics and physics.

STORAGE AND RETRIEVAL OF NUMERIC DATA

Numeric entities are not simply represented by numbers. Physical properties for example are quantities which are recorded with an associated uncertainty and are given in a certain physical unit. In some cases it is only known whether a property is above or below a certain limit, *e.g.,* the life time of a proton. The properties depend on other quantities (parameters), *i.e.,* if one or more parameters are changed the value of the property changes, too. The property may be specific for a given material or it may depend on the preparation process or the macroscopic structure.

STN International has provided a capability to retrieve fuzzy numeric property data. The retrieval of this data is described in detail elsewhere [1]. In the following, a short overview on this topic is presented. Numeric entities which are recorded as single values, *e.g.*, chemical element counts for molecules or publication years, are stored as numbers but the retrieval works similar to text data. A search for these values can be formulated using the well-known numeric relation operators like '<', '=', or '<='. Physical properties could be recorded as a range or a value plus/minus an uncertainty. Both representations are equivalent and in the following the notations 'range' or 'interval' will be used to refer to this concept. It is important to obtain a complete retrieval of fuzzy numeric data which means that a search for a numeric range must retrieve all intervals overlapping with the query range. An example for such a search of a physical property is given in Figure 1. Numeric range searches can be specified either as a range or as a value plus/minus a tolerance corresponding to the two different notations for recording the data. Again, both forms are completely equivalent. The answer set comprises all intervals overlapping with the query range which is represented by the rectangle between the dotted lines are valid lines.

```
 Query Range:          10-20 /MP

                  5         10        15        20        25
              ..--+---------+---------+---------+---------+..
                            :                   :
8  - 25                  <--:-------------------:---------->
 7 - 9                <-->  :                   :
12 - 16                     :<-------->         :
15                          :       X           :
20 - 25                     :                   <--------->
≥ 8                      <-----------------------------------
```

FIGURE 1. Schematic representation of a numeric range search

The value of a physical property like the Entropy depends on other entities and the retrieval language must provide a mechanism for such parameter-dependent searches. Fortunately, the proximity operators allow for such a 'coupling' between several entities (fields). STN International has used the (P)-proximity to combine physical entities to a parameter-dependent search. An example is given in Figure 2 where a range of boiling points is searched at a specific pressure.

SEARCH 100 - 140 /BP (P) BP.P = 760

FIGURE 2. Example for a parameter-dependent search

The knowledge about the physical properties of materials and substances is not homogeneously distributed, *i.e.,* for most compounds only a few properties are known. Even in the most systematic handbooks or databases like Beilstein there are big holes of data and the problem arises how it can be achieved to search and retrieve these data gaps. There are essentially two solutions: in the first case a flag is stored for each property that is not recorded in the file and these flags are searched directly. This solution may require a lot of additional disk space and cannot be applied to large numeric files like Beilstein. In the other case, missing values are not stored and they are searched indirectly by subtracting the set of compounds for which the property is recorded from the complete file.

CONVERSION OF PHYSICAL UNITS

As stated above, physical properties are recorded in a specific unit. Despite the fact that much effort has been spent to standardize the physical units which are in common use there are still different systems in use in the scientific community. It is therefore of great importance for a numeric data retrieval system to provide the online users with a capability for a unit conversion. This capability must enable the user to use the original units, to overwrite single units as well as the complete unit system, and to set all units globally and store them permanently. Several database systems possess such a capability for a restricted subject area like thermodynamics or materials properties. A global unit conversion capability has been developed by STN International to support all numeric databases independent of the subject coverage.

TABLE MANAGEMENT

The storage and display/print of tables is an essential feature of a numeric data retrieval system. For a relational database management system tables are the basic objects, however, most numeric retrieval systems have been developed at universities or research laboratories for specific applications and they are not based on the relational calculus as defined by Codd [2]. Also the large online retrieval systems which are built for general utilization do not make use of this concept, mainly due to performance reasons. The capability for table management must supply more functionality than just the retrieval of data in formatted form. The following is a list of functions which must be a part of such a table manager:

- storage of the tables in a cellular form, not as rows or text
- use of common spreadsheet functions
- appearance of several titles, column headers, references, and footnotes

- random access of the individual cells of the table or of blocks of a column or a row
- application of the relational calculus as defined by Codd
- display or print of the complete table or of arbitrary parts of it
- user-defined tables
- sorting of tables by columns (and rows)
- generation of graphs from the table.

In the current numeric data retrieval systems only a part of this functionality is available.

GRAPHICS MANAGEMENT

A graphical display or print is an intrinsic function of several retrieval systems. The display and offline print of chemical structures has been available for many years, however, a general sophisticated capability for a graphical output of complex objects is still outstanding. A database of patent drawings (PATGRAPH) is online available on STN International but the capability is still rather basic. Several stand-alone numeric retrieval systems like C13NMR/IR are capable of sending graphical information, *e.g.*, line spectra, to a screen. A general graphics manager for retrieval systems is required providing the following functionality:

- full screen control with mouse support
- fast display of complete screens
- interfaces to existing graphical workstation software
- support of the most important operation systems like UNIX or OS/2
- display of shadings and colors
- display of graphical objects of various complexity, like chemical structures including 3-D structures, mathematical equations with graphical symbols, spectra, two- and three-dimensional drawings, patent images, and photographs amongst other things
- graphical search capabilities for more complex graphical objects than chemical structures
- Integration of text, tables and graphics (hypertext).

ONLINE NUMERIC DATABASE DIRECTORY

An important question for an online user is where to find the answers to his problems. For numeric databases the situation is worse than for bibliographic databases because there are many small files with a rather limited subject coverage and the files are distributed among many small hosts some of which are not even professional online hosts. Recently, a numeric database directory has been released on STN International, called NUMERI-GUIDE, which combines a thesaurus file with a data directory. The idea of this file is to provide online information about the content of the numeric files on STN via a search of property names and their corresponding synonyms. The answer is a table of databases together with the preferred property names, the names used in the particular database, the corresponding field qualifiers and the physical units in which the entity is stored in the file. The queries can be crossed over to a numeric file where they may be used for further searches. It would be nice to have such an online guide with these search and retrieval capabilities containing all available numeric databases and the corresponding hosts.

SPECIAL SOFTWARE PACKAGES

In general, numeric databases require more than pure retrieval functions like a SEARCH and DISPLAY command. However, most of these additional capabilities depend strongly upon the subject and the application. These functions are often integrated in the database system because the system has evolved from a prototype developed in a research laboratory. Therefore, it is rather complicated to get access to these systems and work with them. An online host, on the other hand, has to provide the numeric databases

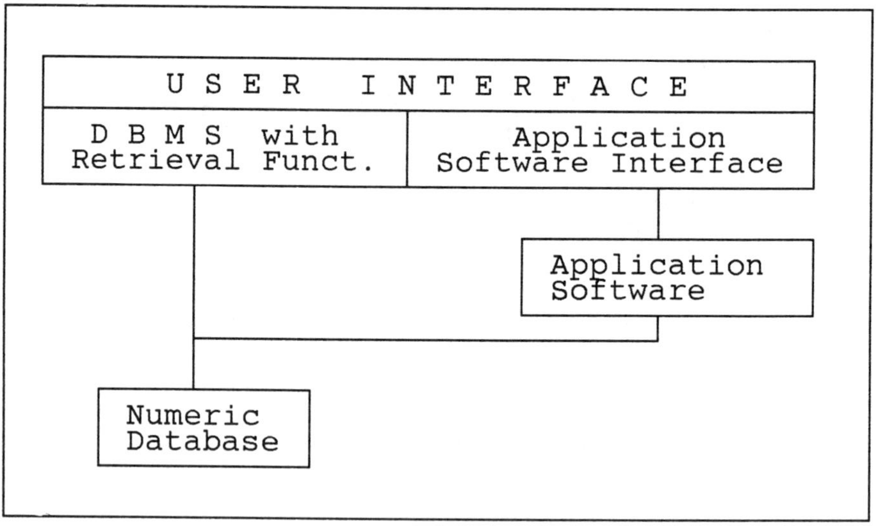

FIGURE 3
Conceptual scheme for an application software integrated in an online retrieval system

together with the specific application software, especially if this software-needs access to the database. This requires an interface to the online retrieval software which allows an execution of the 'external' application software packages (see Figure 3).

Examples for application software which could become an integrated part of an online retrieval system as shown in Figure 3 are:

- statistic packages
- calculation of numeric data, *e.g.,* solution of physical equations
- spectral data generation, interpretation of spectra, simulation of spectra from a chemical structure, and spectra manipulation
- software for the determination of quantitative structure-activity relationships (QSAR).

SPECINFO (formerly C13NMR/IR), a complex spectral data information system, developed at BASF in Germany contains several numeric tools which enable the user to estimate the various kinds of spectra from the chemical structures based on the spectra of other substances stored in the database. The DETHERM system from DECHEMA and FIZ CHEMIE in Germany comprises a numeric data retrieval system and a package of software to generate thermodynamic properties for pure substances and mixtures in both the gas and liquid phase. On the host NUMERICA (TDS) there are several small and very specific numeric database systems available with the corresponding application software.

DOWNLOADING AND UPLOADING OF DATA

An important element of numeric data retrieval systems is the development of a downloading and an uploading capability which enables the user to pre- and post-process numeric data. For text data like in bibliographic files it is often sufficient if the online user captures the data using his communication software. Numeric data, on the other hand, is often produced by an experiment and it should be possible to use this data as a starting-point for an online search. This requires an uploading capability from a standard data format. The postprocessing of numeric data from a search result on a local computer demands a function for downloading information from the host computer. Obviously, the data have to be exchanged in an internationally accepted standard exchange format, *e.g.,* the JCAMP format from the Joint Committee for Atomic and Molecular Properties.

ADAPTABLE USER INTERFACES

Retrieval systems generally interact with the online user through a line-oriented command language. More 'intelligent' systems offer two different dialogue modes: a command language and a menu interface. Generally, the user has to specify the dialogue mode of his choice in advance and cannot change it within a command or within the whole session. The two dialogue modes address users with different levels of knowledge of the system and are rather rigid to manipulate. A command language is designed for expert users who know the language and have some experience with online searching, a menu interface is more appropriate for novice users who have to be guided through the system. For users who are neither experts nor novices there is no adequate dialogue mode available. Recently, an 'Adaptable User Interface' has been proposed by Kantorowitz and Sudarsky [3] which they defined as an interface with the following characteristics:

- support of different dialogue modes (there could be more than two)
- possibility to switch between the modes at any time, even in the middle of a command.

This enables the user of the system to change smoothly between the command language and the menu interface. It is easy to become familiar with the system, one can always work with his appropriate level of knowledge and switch to the menu mode if necessary. It should be added that the system must have a full screen control and a graphic support including a mouse device.

For the retrieval of numeric data there are many applications where such an interface would be very helpful. A search for a property with a given range could be entered as a line command; the field name, the corresponding field qualifier and the associated physical units could be specified in a menu.

NUMERIC TOOLBOX: DATA MANIPULATION AND GENERATION

The results from a numeric data search could be used as input data for postprocessing programs. Some of these programs are an integrated part of the retrieval system, others could be delivered to the online users as a software package for their workstation. In addition to these packages, a high language programming toolbox for numeric applications is very desirable. Mathematical scratch-pads enable us to compute complex mathematical expressions in a very compact and efficient way and some of them can also perform symbolic calculations like differentiation. However, they do not interface directly with online retrieval systems and they do not provide any standard physical tools. Examples are the calculation of the vapor pressure of a mixture, the solution of an *eigenvalue* problem, or a statistical analysis.

APPLICATIONS OF ARTIFICIAL INTELLIGENCE

In addition to the computational toolbox there should also be more support from the conceptual or methodological point of view. One element is a more intelligent information retrieval system with a good thesaurus support. This should enable the user to perform searches with any property name or synonym as in NUMERIGUIDE. A rule base could provide both axiomatic and heuristic knowledge to aid the user in the process of finding a more precise question to a rather diffuse verbal description of a concept. However, it is not very probable that a general expert system for online users of numeric retrieval systems will be developed in the near future. It can be imagined that expert systems for very special applications are developed, *e.g.*, a system for spectroscopic analysts or for chemical engineers. However, I cannot believe that these systems could be handled by anybody but experts.

NEW HARDWARE TECHNOLOGIES

A detailed discussion of new hardware developments for numeric retrieval systems is not within the scope of this paper. Parallel and vector processors, however, may have a direct impact on the architecture of retrieval systems. For small numeric databases parallel processing is of minor importance. A large file like Beilstein where some fields contain millions of entries could benefit from a distributed architecture. A vector processor, on the other hand, is more important for computationally intensive processes where a few instructions are applied to a vector of data. The latter could become more useful when application software is available which performs such CPU-intensive calculations.

CONCLUSIONS

In this paper, only a few topics on numeric data retrieval systems could be outlined providing a rather personal view of the requirements and developments of these systems. More general developments in database theory like expendability of database systems or object bases have not been mentioned at all. Although, these issues are of importance for numeric data retrieval they could not be discussed in this paper.

There is a clear tendency from bibliographic and textual files towards factual and numeric databases. The number of databases will continue to increase, especially the number of small databases for special applications. Online retrieval systems must provide capabilities to work with these databases effectively. A comfortable numeric data retrieval system is not yet available. Some of the requirements for such a system have been discussed in this paper.

ACKNOWLEDGEMENT

The author would like to acknowledge the financial support of the Federal German Ministry for Research and Technology (BMFT).

REFERENCES

[1] Barth, A., Physical Property Data in the Beilstein Database, in *The Beilstein Online Database*, by Heller, S.R. (Ed.), to be published in spring 1990

[2] Codd, E.F., A relational model of data for large shared data bases, *Commun. ACM* 13, 1970, pp. 377-387

[3] Kantorowitz, E. and Sudarsky, O., The adaptable User Interface, *Commun. ACM* 32, November 1989, pp. 1352-1358

STN INTERNATIONAL: STRATEGIES FOR DISCOVERY ASSISTANCE

Nick Farmer
Chemical Abstracts Service
Columbus, Ohio, U.S.A.

INTRODUCTION

The correlation of data has long been a major component of the scientific discovery process. The importance of data correlation increases as discovery is more and more concerned with cross discipline activities, specifically as the concern for health, safety, and environmental issues strengthens, and as international cooperation/competition increases in importance. While significant new capabilities have been developed during the eighties to help in the discovery process, much remains to be done.

This paper will focus on how STN International® has approached this issue. It will describe what has been done over the last ten years to aid the discovery process, and will give some ideas of items planned for the future.

The major part of the paper describes the different data types important in any scientific discovery process, and describes how these data types have been addressed by STN International. The different data types include chemical or molecular structures, numeric data, text, and graphics.

MOLECULAR STRUCTURE

Many problems in chemistry and physics relate to the molecular structure of a physical entity, and a variety of sophisticated techniques have been developed by STN for searching and manipulating molecular structures. Some questions are very specific, relating to a single molecule, while others are very general, relating to a broad class of molecules. Some questions can be related to the molecule or class of molecules in isolation, while others relate to how molecules react with each other.

Data on a specific molecule can be located using the trade name or identifier of that molecule (*e.g.*, the CAS Registry Number®) if it is known, or by a systematic name or molecular structure diagram which fully describes the molecular entity. Classes of molecules can be identified using names or name fragments, partial structures, or molecular formulae. Newer techniques being investigated by STN will allow classes of molecules to be identified by a variety of similarity measures, in addition to the techniques described above.

Several different levels of geometric based searching are available in STN, depending on the level of detail present in a particular molecular database. At the lowest level, using only the molecular formula, no geometric information is used in the search process. This might be considered one dimensional information, and is available in most retrieval systems, including STN. The most common level currently used for searching the databases on STN describes the two-dimensional relationship between the atoms in a molecule. However, with increasing frequency the stereochemical detail of the molecule is of interest, where the atoms are noted as being either above, below, or in the plane of the molecule. This is sometimes referred to as 2.5-dimensional information. This capability is available in some retrieval systems, and is being added to STN. The increasing use of molecular modeling techniques, especially for drug design, requires the use of the full three-dimensional coordinates of each atom in a molecule, as well as some description of the size of each atom. This three-dimensional information is created either from x-ray crystallographic studies, or by calculations using molecular orbital computations. While STN has the ability to display three-dimensional information, it is not yet possible to search this information.

NUMERIC DATA

Data of interest in the discovery process are often numeric. Numeric data are common in many business applications, but they are typically stored either in integer or decimal form. STN handles floating point numbers, which provide the precision and range required in scientific applications. STN also provides a full set of numeric operations: greater than, less than, equal to, greater than or equal to, and less than or equal to.

Within STN all data points are stored with a defined precision, and the system allows searches to be done with a user defined tolerance. For instance, a scientist searching for a molecule with a boiling point equal to 112 °C can retrieve a molecule with a boiling point stored at 111.82 °C, plus or minus (.20) degrees. Numeric data are often reported as a range. For example, a boiling point might be represented as a range of 100-105 °C. STN stores this range, and it is retrieved as an answer in all of the following searches: 100=BP; 102.345=BP; 105=BP; 98<BP<101; 98<BP<109; 101<BP<103; 103<BP<110.

In order to make the system easier to use, STN provides for automatic unit conversion. Data are stored in the database using system-wide standards, but users can ask for data using any unit, and the system converts the input data to the standard form for searching, and converts any retrieved data to the user defined unit prior to display of the answer. During this conversion process proper attention is paid to maintaining the precision and tolerance of the data.

Another interesting problem that often occurs with numeric data is that of determining what action should be taken when a required data item is not present. For instance, suppose a scientist is interested in all molecules with a particular structural component, a boiling point greater than x, a melting point less that y, and a viscosity equal to z. Clearly any substance on the database that meets all of these criteria is of interest. What is not always so clear is whether or not the record for a particular molecule should be retrieved if only three of the four criteria are satisfied, and the fourth data point is not in the record. STN provides this capability to retrieve these records, although the search process is quite complex.

TEXT

Most databases contain a considerable amount of textual information. Molecular structure databases may contain the names of molecules stored as text strings. Numeric databases may contain descriptive information stored as text strings. Secondary or reference databases contain many text fields, such as author names, location of work, abstracts, and key words. And of course, full-text databases are composed primarily of textual information.

As with molecular structures and numeric data, there are a number of levels of specificity possible in a search request. At the most specific level a fully defined text string can be specified for matching. In some cases it is desirable to specify only the root of the item for which a search is being made, leaving either the prefix or the suffix or both unspecified. It should also be possible to search for partial text strings, where certain positions in the string are left unspecified. These are often called "wild cards". Positional operators should be present to allow for retrieval of two or more strings within a specific proximity of each other. STN provides all of these capabilities.

An interesting specific case of text searching occurs when searching for large molecules of proteins or nucleic acids. These molecules are defined by a series of one or three letter codes, and a typical search is to retrieve all molecules whose representations contain a string of these codes "similar" to the query string. This type of searching is often called homology searching, and is being investigated as a possible extension to STN.

GRAPHICS

Perhaps the most complex data type used in the scientific discovery process is graphics. There are two general types of graphical information that can be handled by computers: line art, or image data. Line art is composed of characters, lines, arcs, circles, etc. These basic components are then combined in some way to represent a complex data object. In some cases line art is simply stored by itself as a pictograph, while in other cases, such as chemical structure diagrams, metadata describing the scientific meaning of the pictograph are associated with the line art. Images are comprised of picture elements, or pixels, with a resolution of anywhere from 10 000 pixels per square inch, to over 1 000 000 pixels per square inch. Each of the pixels represents a minute portion of the image. Complex recognition algorithms are required in order to search and manipulate image data. STN provides the ability to retrieve and display or print image data, but does not yet provide any searching of image data.

THE DISCOVERY PROCESS

The first step in the discovery process is for an individual or organization to take the responsibility to collect a variety of information of different data types, to analyze it, process it, and assemble it into a database. The next step is to have several of these independent databases suitably processed for loading into a search and retrieval system. Finally, it is important to have search and retrieval software with the features noted above for handling all of the complex data types important in the scientific discovery process. Once all of this has been done, the most difficult portion of the discovery process begins: the actual search, retrieval, and correlation of the subset of data appropriate to the scientific problem at hand.

The first problem encountered in this complex process is knowing which database might contain the data appropriate to this particular question. While many databases may be present on a particular system, it will usually be necessary to use several systems to find the desired data. Even within a single database it may not be obvious how the data are identified, in what field they are stored, what units have been used, and what search techniques are appropriate.

Another problem has to do with the ambiguity present in those databases. Within different molecular databases different structuring conventions might have been used to represent the same molecule. For text databases different terms (*i.e.*, synonyms) might be used to represent the same concept. For numeric databases different levels of precision might be used to represent the same numeric value.

The final and most difficult problem is that the desired data are typically not present in a single database. Rather they are spread over several databases, and the user must "navigate" through this ocean of data to locate and bring together the required information. This is only possible if different databases are "linked" together with common data. If a particular data element is present in every database, then the navigation process is fairly straightforward. Otherwise, the user must find the proper sequence to navigate through the set of databases, and each step must have a piece of data in common with the next step. The user goes from database to database until all of the appropriate information has been collected.

STRATEGIES FOR DISCOVERY ASSISTANCE

Fortunately there are a number of techniques available to help overcome the problems inherent in the discovery process noted above. Many of these techniques are already available in STN International, and most of the remaining ones are in some stage of research or development.

The problem of locating the appropriate databases to be searched can be addressed by providing a data directory. The directory lists a wide variety of possible data types, and shows which databases contain that particular data type. Thus, a user can specify the data type(s) wanted, and the data directory can provide a list of the databases that contain that type of data. An example of such a data directory is the NumeriGuide directory available on STN.

The problem of ambiguity of text terms can be partially addressed through the use of a thesaurus. The thesaurus can provide synonyms, or related terms, that the user can use to augment the concept term that he or she has used in the query specification. A thesaurus can also provide for broader or narrower terms, as an aid in expanding or restricting the search strategy if too few or too many potential answers are found at any point in the search. A multilingual thesaurus can provide some assistance to users not familiar with the language of a particular database, by accepting an input term in the source language and supplying the equivalent term in the target language. The Messenger software used within STN provides a thesaurus capability, and several of the databases on STN provide a thesaurus as part of the database offering.

The problem of different units can be handled through the use of automatic units conversion. "STN provides for automatic conversion for all numeric fields in the STN numeric files. Any unit that is dimensionally correct for the specific field is accepted".

KNOWLEDGE-BASED SYSTEMS

While many of the strategies for discovery assistance noted above have been implemented by STN to assist scientists in the process of retrieving information, the overall process is still quite complex. Thus, STN is researching knowledge-based systems that will provide considerably more support for the intellectual process involved in finding and retrieving pertinent information. These knowledge-based systems often contain three types of knowledge bases: world knowledge, discipline specific knowledge, and knowledge of search and retrieval techniques.

Knowledge bases that contain world knowledge address the most general type of knowledge. This includes knowledge about such subjects as nature, geography, and geopolitical divisions. For example, if a user is interested in the absorption of mercury by fish in North America, the system would be able to search for information on mercury in different species of fish, in both salt water and fresh water, in Canada, the United States and Mexico. Perhaps the user could even be referred to papers that discuss the absorption of mercury by fish in particular bodies of water in particular regions or states.

Knowledge bases that are discipline specific will provide more detailed support in a particular discipline or subdiscipline, such as chemistry, physics, electrical engineering, or automotive engineering. These knowledge bases would begin to capture the knowledge learned during a postsecondary education. Following the previous example, a discipline-specific knowledge-based system would be able to distinguish an interest in mercury as a chemical from an interest in the planet Mercury. It would also be able to suggest to a user, if no information were found on the specific question asked, that the question might be broadened to look into other heavy metals in addition to mercury.

Knowledge-based systems at the search and retrieval level would contain information on all of the features of potential interest in the different search systems, such as logical operators, truncation, proximity, molecular structuring convention rules, precision/tolerance, and units in numeric data. This knowledge-based system would automatically convert the question from a vague, ambiguous, or imprecise one into a more focused, effective question that could be handled by one or more search systems. This would be achieved through effective use of the system specific features previously listed, and through use of a data directory as a map for navigating through the various databases to collect the desired information.

While each of these areas is being investigated by STN, it is likely to be a number of years before a practical capability is realized.

CONCLUSION

For centuries scientists have depended on personal knowledge, contact with colleagues, and collections of printed material as sources of the data that are the basis for scientific discovery. Each of these sources will continue to be of value in the future. However, over the last 20 years computer databases have emerged as a major new source of data. There are hundreds of these computer databases available today and many more being created every year. Over 75 databases are available through STN.

As the number of databases containing scientific information has increased, the search and retrieval systems supporting them have become more sophisticated. While many systems still support only text databases, the more sophisticated systems, such as STN, support molecular structure, numeric and graphic data types, as well as text. Improved capabilities for finding and correlating data have also been developed.

This resulting environment, while very powerful, is also very complex. A very sophisticated knowledge-based system that would offer the potential of reducing the intellectual burden currently required to effectively use existing computer based systems is being investigated by STN.

The economic considerations of this situation are daunting. It is very expensive to assemble properly evaluated data into a computer database. It is also costly to take these data and incorporate them into one or more search and retrieval systems. It is very expensive to develop the computer software and the knowledge-based systems required to effectively access this data. And, because of the complexity involved, the computational resources required for the search process are also fairly expensive.

While it is relatively easy to determine the costs to develop a system with all of the capabilities described above, it is much more difficult to establish the value of the resulting system, if it can be realized at all. However, the value must be very substantial. There are hundreds of thousands of scientists and engineers throughout the world, and even a small improvement in their productivity would have enormous value. Of even more value, and even harder to estimate, is the lost opportunity from discoveries not made, or from mistakes made (*e.g.*, in the design of a nuclear power plant), due to the ineffective use of existing data. A major challenge of the next decade will be to secure the funding necessary to complete the building of the systems noted above, and to achieve the potential value that will result when existing data can be effectively marshaled in the scientific discovery process.

THE USE OF OPTIMAL ESTIMATION FOR GROSS ERROR DETECTION IN DATABASES OF SPATIALLY CORRELATED DATA

C.C. Tscherning
Geophysical Institute
University of Copenhagen
Haraldsgade 6
Dk-2200 Copenhagen N., Denmark

INTRODUCTION

When establishing a (scientific) database it is important to eliminate or at least flag gross errors. The size of many modern databases now makes it virtually impossible to check and correct a suspected error. A remeasurement of quantities obtained e.g. by a satellite 10 years ago will in most cases be impossible due to the costs involved.

Databases seems to obey the same law as computer programs: there is always an error left. Unfortunately, many data sets, in the Earth sciences at least, seems to contain up to 1 % erroneous data, see e.g. Tscherning (1990), Remmer (1984). Despite these errors, excellent scientific results are generally obtained because one single data entity is not used alone, but together with other entities. A simple example is from surveying, where one always will try to observe all three angles in a triangle, even if two are sufficient when determining the shape of the triangle. The databases will therefore contain redundant data, even if this generally is one of the characteristics used to describe a file system which is not a database. An important requirement for databases in many fields of earth sciences is therefore that the data contained are redundant. This is then used when applying least-squares procedures for the determination of associated parameters like the positions of the vertices of a triangle. Even if data are not as clearly redundant as in the case of the triangle, data may be strongly correlated, simply because they are associated with points spatially close to each other. The gravity in two points a few meters apart will be only slightly different, because the attracting masses, as seen from the points, will be nearly identical.

This spatial correlation may be used to detect gross-errors, in the same manner as it is done for time series. If a value differs more than usual from its neighboring values, it may be a gross-error.

For time series, the similarity of two values $x(t_1)$, $x(t_2)$ is expressed through the auto-covariance function, $C(t)$, which for stationary time series is a function of time difference $(t_1 - t_2)$ only. For spatially distributed data, the correlation may be expressed through a covariance function generally only dependent on the distance and the altitude of two points. We will explain this in section 2.

When a covariance function is given, we may qualitatively express what we mean by stating that a value differ more than usual from other values. This is expressed by a comparison of the observed value with the value obtained by optimal prediction (interpolating or extrapolation) from the neighboring values. In section 3 we give the necessary algorithms.

The method is routinely used to detect gross errors in databases containing gravity field related data, and in section 4 two examples illustrate this.

2. COVARIANCE FUNCTION FOR SPATIALLY DISTRIBUTED DATA

We will in the following discuss spatially distributed data. These data may also vary as a function of time, but we will here keep the time fixed.

For such data the (horizontal) distance plays (or as we shall see may be forced to play) the role time difference does for a time series. The directional (azimuthal) dependence is often small or may be removed, but (as with gravity data) the altitude does play a role, which should not be disregarded.

For a time series, we generally have many repetitions of the same phenomena. This has been used to justify the description of the signal as a stochastic process or random function. For repeated occurrences the covariance may be computed in the usual manner as the mean value of products of observations, observed at the same time by two observers. If only one observer is "active", the products are formed for observations, observed with a constant time difference. The time series is supposed to be stationary.

For spatially distributed data, especially data observed on or outside the surface of the Earth, we have no possibility to have repeated occurrences. We only have one Earth! But as with time-series, repetitions may be introduced artificially. The Earth (or a planet) rotated around its center, is regarded as a new Earth. (It may be enough to rotate around a certain axis, but we will not discuss this here). Data located in the same altitude may therefore be used when estimating the covariance, as a function of the (spherical) distance between pairs of points where observations have taken place.

The estimation of the covariance C, as a function of distance d, is in practice simply done by grouping pairs of data in classes according to distance intervals, and then forming the mean of the products of the pairs,

$$C(d_k) = \langle \sum_{i=1}^{n} X(P_i) X(Q_i) \rangle / n \tag{1}$$

Here P_i and Q_i are points with distance d_i,

$$d_k - \tfrac{1}{2}v \leq d_i < d_k + \tfrac{1}{2}v,$$

where v is the magnitude of the interval within which the products are sampled, and d_k the k'th interval midpoints. We have in eq (1) supposed that the mean value has been subtracted.

An example of a gravity autocovariance function is given in Figure 1, computed using data in a local areas (Ohio). Note that the function has both positive and negative values.

The applied procedure is statistically correct, if we may regard the physical phenomena as an isotropic random function (see e.g. Sanso (1986)). But even if it is not correct, we are able to evaluate numerically eq. (1) and obtain a sample of values $C(d_k)$, $k = 1, \ldots m$C(d_k), k = 1, ... m. If data are distributed globally, the covariance function may be expressed as the sum of a Legendre series,

$$C(d) = \sum_{i=1}^{\infty} \sigma_i P_i(\cos d) \tag{2}$$

where d is the distance in radians, P_i are the Legendre-polynomials and σ_i are positive constants called degree-variances. The σ_i express the variation

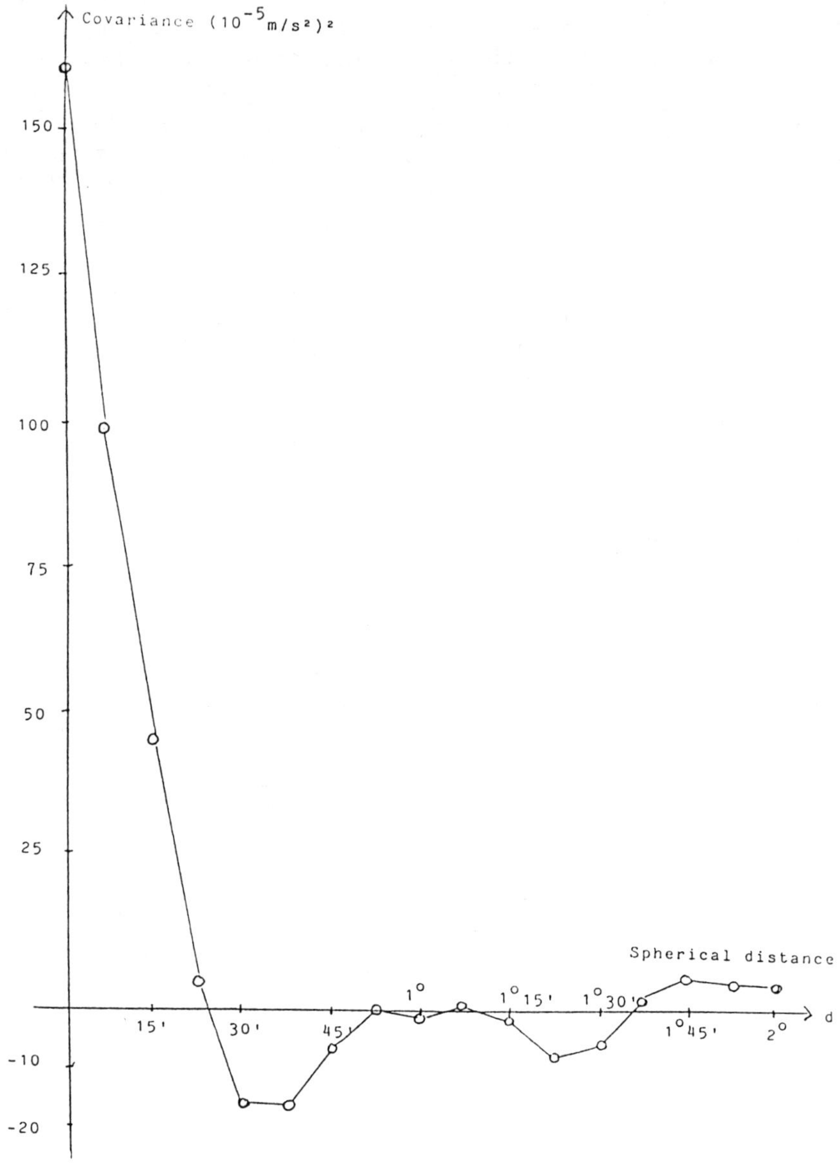

FIGURE 1
Empirically determined gravity covariances for the state of Ohio, U.S.A.

per spherical harmonic degree of the observed quantity. These quantities will not be known, but their values may be expressed as simple functions of the degree. For gravity values simple exponential "rules" have been found, see e.g. Kaula (1959), Rapp (1990). Some of these rules makes it possible to express C(d) by a closed formula. If data are given only in a limited area, a Fourier analysis may be used to obtain the coefficients of the Fourier series. The square of the coefficients (the power-spectrum) are then the coefficients in the planar auto-covariance function similar to eq. (2).

3. GROSS-ERROR DETECTION FOR SPATIALLY DISTRIBUTED DATA

Simple statistical tools, such as the formation of a histogram, are extremely useful when trying to detect gross-errors. Here it may be useful to first low-pass filter the data (trend removal), and then inspect the histogram of the filtered data. For globally distributed data, a spherical harmonic analysis, will produce a function representing the global trend. For regional or local data, the first coefficients in a Fourier expansion or a low degree polynomial in plane coordinates (x, y) will represent the trend.

The filtered data may then be contoured, and gross-errors may then show up as "chimneys" or volcanos on a contour map, see Figure 2. However, a contour map may show several chimneys, and it may be very difficult to judge which are important, and which are "normal".

Here the method of optimal linear prediction (Krigging, least-squares collocation) has been used with success, as will be described in the next section. The idea is to interpolate or extrapolate (predict) an observed value from neighboring values, and then compare the predicted and the observed value. If the difference is larger than for example 3 times the error of the prediction, then the observative is flagged as a suspected gross-error.

Let us denote the observation to be analyzed by y, and the surrounding observations by x_i, $i = 1, \ldots, n$. Then linear prediction determines an estimate $\tilde{y}$ by

$$\tilde{y} = \sum_{i=1}^{n} a_i x_i \qquad (3)$$

where a_i are unknown constants. We may decide to determine $\tilde{y}$ so the mean square error is as small as possible, where the mean is take over all point configurations, which may be created on a sphere by rotations of the observation points Q, P_i, $i = 1, \ldots, n$ associated with y_{obs}, x_i, $i = 1, \ldots, n$, respectively. Then it is easily shown (Moritz, 1980) that

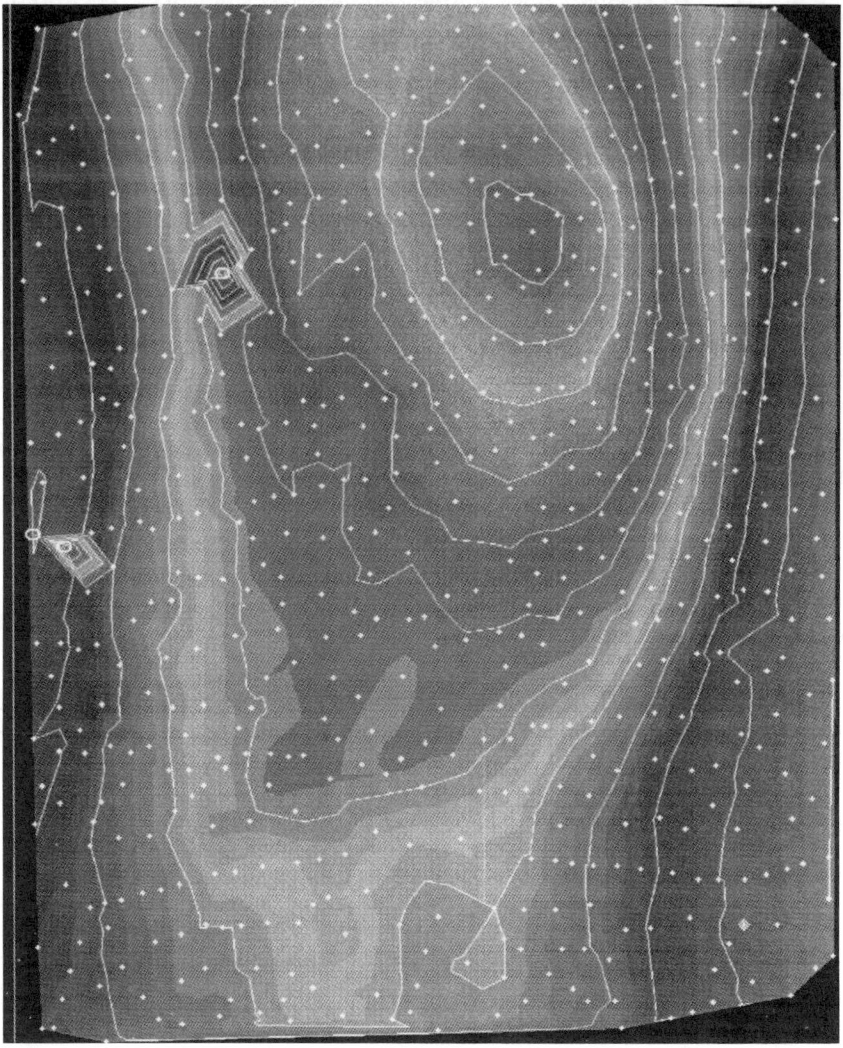

FIGURE 2
Gravity map with six measurements predicted as suspected gross- errors using collocation (map realized by D. Toustou with soft and hardware of BGI and C. Poitevin with gravimetric data from the Observatoire Royal de Belgique - from BGI, 1989, p. 120)

$$\{a_i\} = \{C_{Qi}\}^T \{\overline{C}_{ij}\}^{-1} \qquad (4)$$
$$\overline{C}_{ij} = C_{ij} + D_{ij}$$

where C_{Qi} is the covariance between y and x_i, C_{ij} is the covariance of the observations and D_{ij} the covariance of the observation error associated with x_i and x_j. The mean square error of $\tilde{y}$ will be

$$\sigma^2(y-\tilde{y}) = C_o - \{C_{Qi}\}^T \overline{C}^{-1} \{C_{Qj}\}, \qquad (5)$$

where C_o is the variance of y. If this quantity and the observation error of $\tilde{y}$, σ_y, are both χ^2 - distributed, then

$$\sigma^2(y_{obs} - \tilde{y}) = \sigma_y^2 + \sigma^2(y - \tilde{y}) \qquad (6)$$

If the actual difference

$$| y_{obs} - \tilde{y} | > k \cdot \sigma(y_{obs} - \tilde{y}) \qquad (7)$$

then we may decide to regard y as a possible gross-error.

The success of this procedure depends on the statistical homogeneity of the data. A good (and actual example) is the situation where data consist of two subsets each associated with a separate unknown linear parameter: satellite observations, from two different time periods from the same area, affected by different satellite orbit errors, may form two such sets. The above described linear estimation method may be extended to take account of this. Also data do not need to be of the same type, as long as a cross-covariance function is also known, see Moritz (1980).

Other inhomogeneities may have physical causes, such as varying geology or topography. These physical causes may be taken into account (removed), see Forsberg (1986).

The above described procedure is not without pitfalls. A gross-error may "contaminate" neighboring values. So an iterative procedure is recommended, where the largest suspected gross-errors are removed, and the prediction is repeated for smaller suspected errors.

4. GROSS-ERROR DETECTION IN GRAVITY FIELD DATA

A database with global gravity coverage is managed by Bureau Gravimetrique International (BGI) in Toulouse, France. Here several million data are stored. Data originate from both scientific and commercial sources, and date 100 years back. Many national institutions also administrate gravity databases.

Gravity is the modulus of the gradient of the gravity potential. The Mean sea-level coincides with a surface where the potential is constant called the geoid. The height of this surface above a reference ellipsoid, plus height variations due to tides, currents etc. may be observed by measuring the distance from a satellite to the sea surface by a radar altimeter. Such data has been collected by several satellites at a rate of 1 per second, and new satellites will be launched in the coming years (ERS-1, Topex-Poseidon).

So, huge gravity field data sets are and will be collected, which are spatially correlated. But the data contain many errors, which must be eliminated or flagged. At BGI, optimal linear prediction is used to mark suspected gross-errors on a CRT (see Figure 3), which is used to display a contour map of the data. Interactively the suspected errors may be removed, and if smooth contour lines occur after the removal, then the observation is flagged as an error. An experienced analyst can validate 5000-7000 points per day under optimal conditions, (BGI, 1989, p. 110).

The method is also used when analyzing gravity and satellite radar altimeter data [8]. Here the possibility of also removing biases were used.

The method of least-squares collocation is not restricted to be used with only one data type. The combined use of altimeter and gravity data improved the power of the method, so that 0.3% further gross errors were detected in addition to the 0.7% error detected using the altimeter data alone.

5. CONCLUSION

Spatially distributed data are often spatially correlated. A covariance function which primarily is a function of distance may be estimated by forming mean values of products of data having the same spherical distance. Using optimal linear prediction, the values may be computed from neighboring values and compared with the observed value, thereby indicating an error if the difference is larger than a factor k times the prediction error.

The use of the method requires that the observations are "homogenized", by low-pass filtering, and removal of anisotropies, if possible. It has been used with success for gravity field data, but it should be possible to use the method for many other types of spatial data.

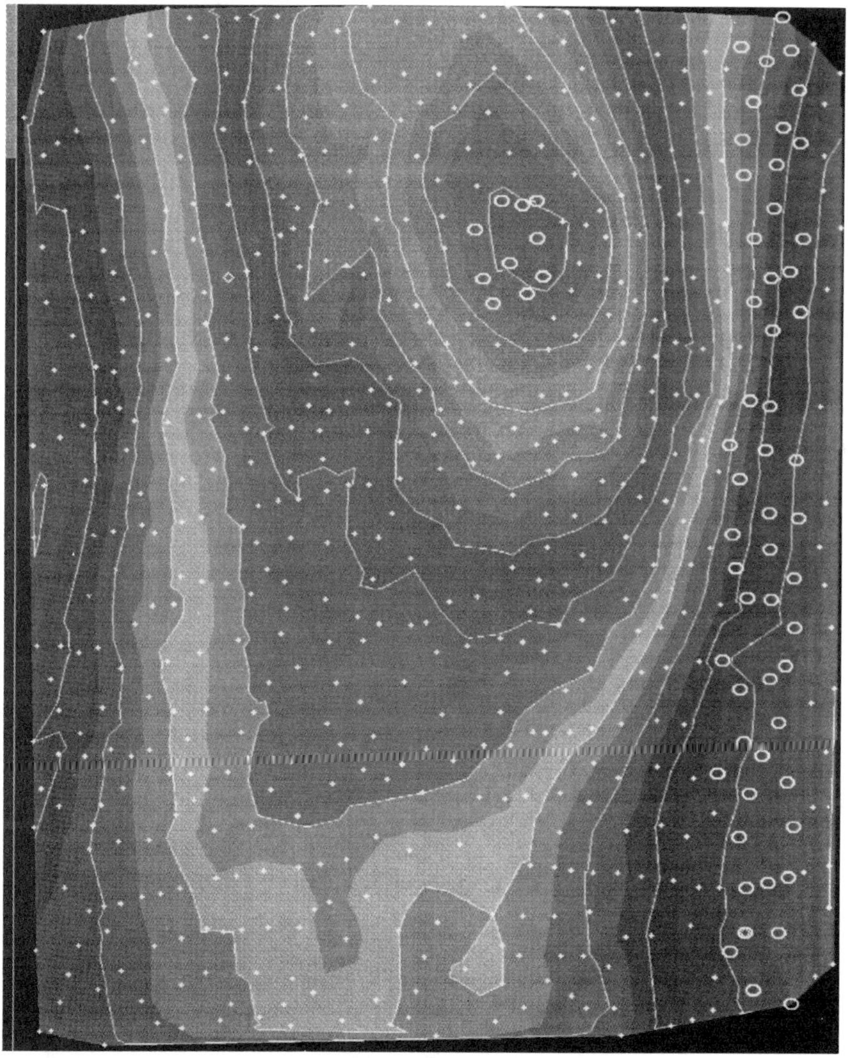

FIGURE 3
Gravity map, same as Figure 2, but with two largest errors removed (map realized by D. Toustou with soft and hardware of BGI and C. Poitevin with gravimetric data from the Observatoire Royal de Belgique - from BGI, 1989, p. 121)

REFERENCES

[1] Bureau Gravimetrique International: Workshop on Gravity Data Validation (Review), October 17-19, 1989. Bulletin d'Information, No. 65, pp. 89-142, 1989.

[2] Forsberg, R.: Spectral Properties of the Gravity Field in the Nordic Countries. Boll. Geodesia e Sc. Aff., Vol. XLV, pp. 361-384, 1986.

[3] Moritz, H.: Advanced Physical Geodesy. H. Wichmann Verlag, Karlsruhe, 1980.

[4] Rapp, R.H.: The decay of the spectrum of the gravitational potential and the topography for the Earth. Geophys. J. Int., Vol. 99, pp. 449-455, 1989.

[5] Remmer, O.: Modelling errors in geometric levelling. Proceedings Control Survey Networks, Meeting of (FIG) Study Group 5B, 7-9 July, 1982, Aalborg University Center, pp. 355-372, Hochschule der Bundeswehr Muenchen, 1982.

[6] Remmer, O.: New Error Parameters in Levelling. Report of SSG 1.53 at the IAG General Assembly, Hamburg, August 15-26, 1983. Travaux de l'Association Internationale de Geodesie, Tome 27, pp. 116-122, 1984.

[7] Sanso', F.: Statistical methods in physical geodesy. In: Suenkel, H.: Mathematical and Numerical Techniques in Physical Geodesy. Lecture Notes in Earth Sciences, Vol. 7, pp. 49-155, Springer-Verlag, 1986.

[8] Tscherning, C.C.: A strategy for gross error detection in satellite altimeter data applied in the Baltic-Sea area for enhanced geoid and gravity determination. Presented Nordic geodetic Commission XI meeting, Copenhagen, May, 1990b.

THE CREATION AND DEVELOPMENT OF THE SCIENTIFIC DATABASE SYSTEM AT THE CHINESE ACADEMY OF SCIENCES

Luo Baichang
Scientific Databases
The Chinese Academy of Sciences
Beijing 100080, China

The Scientific Database System (SDBS) of the Chinese Academy of Sciences started in 1986 as the key project in the National Five Year Plan for 1986-1990 and followed the establishment of a chemistry database, one of the important projects placed in the National Programmer for Basic Sciences Development earlier in the period from 1978 to 1985. The growth of non-bibliographic and bibliographic databases implemented in the Academia Sinica has been fairly rapid over the past ten years. This paper describes briefly the project's current major activities, database products and their management system.

1. INTRODUCTION

The Chinese Academy of Sciences, a uniquely multidisciplinary institution in China with more than 120 research institutes, is China's largest comprehensive research center in the natural sciences.

Scientific data and information are vital for the research activity of the Academy. The need for developing an effective system for information acquisition, handling, storage and retrieval have become more and more essential. The Chinese government and the Chinese Academy of Sciences decided to establish the "Scientific Database and Information System of the Chinese Academy of Sciences," (SDBS) and make it one of the national key projects during the period from 1986 to 1990. SDBS offers scientists, engineers, managers, professors and students detailed information in the fields of chemistry, biology, astronomy, and optics, as well as the national resources for energy, economic plants, microbiology, etc., through the various bibliographic and non-bibliographic factual databases and retrieval files.

These databases are produced by the research institutes of the Chinese Academy of Sciences. For example, the Institute of Chemical Metallurgy, the Shanghai Institute of Organic Chemistry, the Institute of Microbiology, the Astronomical Observatory, the Institute of Computer Science and Technology, the Center for Ecology and the Environment, etc.

Discipline-oriented and problem-oriented databases will be supported by specially developed software packages.

More than 250 people from 30 institutes of the Academy are involved in the creation and maintenance of these databases. An appropriate computer network facility is provided.

2. A BRIEF REVIEW OF SDBS

At present the SDBS of the Chinese Academy of Sciences contains more than twenty databases covering various subject fields (Table 1). Some of them are in service and some of them are in progress. It is expected that the number of databases will increase to sixty or more by 1995.

Many of the products of chemistry databases implemented nationally are characterized by their close relationship to research work and engineering requirements. An integrated and comprehensive Chemical Information System and problem-oriented programming package will be realized in the coming year. In these databases we used data from both foreign and domestic sources. As for the databases of natural resources of China, which are necessary for the planning of regional and national development and reconstruction, we have to collect all the necessary information through our own efforts, in collaboration with different organizations of related ministries. In addition there are many other useful databases being created.

2.1 The Engineering Chemistry Database System

The creation of an Engineering Chemistry Database (ECDB) is based on the needs of industry, which require not only data retrieval functions but also software packages involving essential formulas, laws and mathematical models. There are several subdatabases produced by the Institute of Chemical Metallurgy: the ITDB (Inorganic Thermochemistry Database), with 3500 thermochemical and thermodynamic property data for more than 2000 inorganic compounds, provides users with a software package with sixteen functions, such as computing the thermodynamic data of a chemical reaction and predicting thermochemical properties; the NEDB (Vapor-liquid Equilibrium Non-Electrolytes Database) is composed of 750 organic compounds, 1996 activity coefficient model parameters, 189 242 vapor-liquid equilibrium experimental data, and 1296 functional group parameters, as well as 21 activity coefficient models and 14 retrieving and calculating functions. The ATDB (Aqueous Solution Thermodynamic Database) contains fundamental thermodynamic data for 879 ions and 287 molecules in solution.

2.2 The Chemical Structural Elucidation Database System

There are several spectrographic databases including Mass Spectra (73 000 spectra); infrared spectra (55 000 spectra); and Carbon-13 NMR spectra (20 000 spectra) which have been developed by our chemists in the Institute of Organic Chemistry and the Institute of Applied Chemistry. The correlation of substructure-property has also been studied. All these databases can be linked through the structure database, the core of the system. Inorganic and Organic CRYDB (Crystal Database) are based upon the crystal data provided by the NBS (USA) and Cambridge University (England) and further developed by our chemists.

TABLE 1. The 25 Databases of the Scientific Database System

No.	Database	Current Status
1	Engineering Chemistry	in service
2	Mass Spectra	in service
3	C-13 NMR Spectra	in service
4	IR Spectra	in service
5	Toxicity of Chemical Compounds	in service
6	Crystallographic Compounds	in service
7	Nomenclature & Structure of Chemical Compounds	in service
8	Rare-Earth	in progress
9	Nucleic Acid Sequences	in progress
10	Protein Sequences	in progress

11	National Energy Resources	in progress
12	Optical & Electronic Technology	in progress
13	Natural Resources	in progress
14	Chinese Biological Resources	in progress
15	Chinese Chemical Abstract	in service
16	Computer and Automation Abstract	in service
17	Chinese Optical Abstract	in progress
18	China's Natural Resources Abstract	in progress
19	Chinese Biology Abstract	in progress
20	Scientists & Technicians in the Chinese Academy of Sciences	in progress
21	Astronomy	in progress
22	Microbial Resources	in progress
23	Chinese Medicinal Herbs	in progress
24	Corrosion	in progress
25	Economic Plants Resources	in progress

2.3 Numerical Databases Concerning National Resources

For scientific research work and economic use, the databases created include:

1) *Natural resources including land, climate, water, biology, minerals, energy and tourism.* For example, the Energy Database of China (ENDC) is concerned with the energy science, technology, and energy economics of China. Historical data with two million items from 1949 to 1980 and current data with 200 000 items per year after 1980 have been collected. Sixteen kinds of energy carriers such as coal, petroleum, natural gas, hydropower, etc., and ten stages according to the energy flow chart such as resources, production, processing, conversion, consumption and conservation, etc., are included in the ENDC.

2) *Microbial resources consisting of microbial classification, toxicology and ecology.* Microbial Resources Databases of China (MRDC) is a database system with five sub-databases concerned with microbiology: a database for microbial characters data; a database for microbial taxonomy and ecology; a database for methods useful in the exploitation of microbial resources; a database for examined and approved terms and names used in microbiology in China; and a database for markets of microbial products.

3) Economic plants, which contain the data of medicinal plants, timber plants, oil plants, fibre plants, ornamental plants, starch plants, aromatic plants, rare and endangered plants as well as the botanical data of morphology, geography, cytology, ecology and chemical constituents, etc.

2.4 Some Other Numerical Databases

CRDC stands for the "Corrosion Database of China." It contains the experimental monitored corrosion data of metallic and non-metallic materials buried and exposed in various corrosive media and environments such as soil, atmosphere, sea water, etc., in different locations in China. It will be able to provide information for the design of engineering construction and be helpful to engineers for predicting service life and selecting specific materials. China is rich in Rare Earth resources. REDB is a comprehensive database system consisting of subdatabases of extraction, physical and chemical properties, spectra data, materials and the natural resources of Rare Earths. Several subsystems are going to be set up in 1990. One interesting function of the subsystem for physical and chemical properties is the utilization of the pattern recognition method for classifying compounds and predicting new compounds.

2.5 Bibliographic Database

CCDOC is a bibliographic database produced by chemists from sixteen Chemistry-related institutes of the Chinese Academy of Sciences. It covers original research papers, reviews, patents, conference proceedings, dissertations and new books in all areas of chemistry and chemical engineering in China. It is a bilingual, Chinese-English bibliographic database containing 50 000 citations from 1983 to date. CBDOC (Chinese Biological Document Database), CREDOC (Chinese Rare Earths Document Database), CODOC (Chinese Optical Document Database) and CADOC (Chinese Astronomical Document Database) are also retrieval database systems at the Chinese Academy of Sciences.

3. MANAGEMENT OF SDBS

The main objectives and responsibilities of the Management Board of SDBS are as follows:

1) To promote and coordinate database creation and other related R & D projects at the different institutes of the Academy.
2) To educate all users of effective use of different forms of information services and provide them with easy access to SDBS.
3) To ensure the availability and improvement of the computer-network facility.
4) To maintain and extend cooperative relationships with foreign and other Chinese information centers.

Most of the research institutes of the Chinese Academy of Sciences are equipped with mini-computers and personal computers. The main frame machines of the SDBS are installed in the building of the Computing Center of the Academy.

Since the databases of the SDBS are produced on computers of different types and from different vendors, several software packages have been implemented for their data management.

The distributed scientific database library (SLIB) is a comprehensive and integrated system composed of diverse databases on different subjects in science, with the general design purpose of sharing and offering joint on-line services through all of the separate databases. SLIB is set up for managing all kinds of scientific databases and their application software. SLIB is available for VAX machines and a similar package for IBM (mainframe) machines is under development. These computers are scattered throughout five cities in China. There is a public data communication network of the Ministry of Posts and Telecommunications which can be used for transmitting data between most big cities of China. A local area network is expected to be implemented within the Academy in Beijing, which will offer a more convenient and effective working environment to users. Special financial support for this network has been approved by the government.

The overseas data links with large foreign databases are undoubtedly very helpful to the activities of the Scientific Database System of the Chinese Academy of Sciences. For the time being we have a data link with Europe only. The situation will be changed for the better during the period of the next five year plan.

MOLECULAR SHAPE REPRESENTATION AND CODES

A. Panaye
Institut de Topologie et de Dynamique des Systèmes
Associé au CNRS, Université de Paris VII
Paris, France.

The 3D representation of a given molecule can be attained through various means: X-ray coordinates give the actual location of atoms. On the other hand, using standard values of bond lengths and valence angles leads to a guess geometry which is subsequently refined by energy minimization. Intermediately, assembling realistic fragments provides an efficient way to get this representation either directly or via energy minimization. Using such structural primitives offers various advantages:

- starting from adapted parameters saves some iteration steps; the potential energy minimum is more quickly attained. Furthermore, if the starting geometry is not too far from the true minimum, the risk to fall down into a local minimum decreases.

- one can even avoid energy minimization in accepting only approached geometries in which local environment effects are already taken into account. From these geometries, even without optimization, some parameters are fairly well reproduced: surface and volume.

After presenting the basic principles of our molecular builder, we discuss the choice of the structural fragments and the determination of their geometrical parameters.

THE ED-3D MODEL BUILDER

To build molecular representations we have chosen to associate structural primitives which can be atoms or groups. Atoms are surrounded by their immediate links; this expresses their hybridization. Among the environment of a group, a bond is distinguished to be the anchoring point for the next step.

Assembling two fragments is carried out via two links: one hanging on the current moiety, one active on the added fragment (Figure 1). These two links are aligned and checked to verify chemical consistency. Then the length is calculated according to the type of the bond and the dihedral angle is evaluated. Treatment by fragments offers the capability to use non standard parameters.

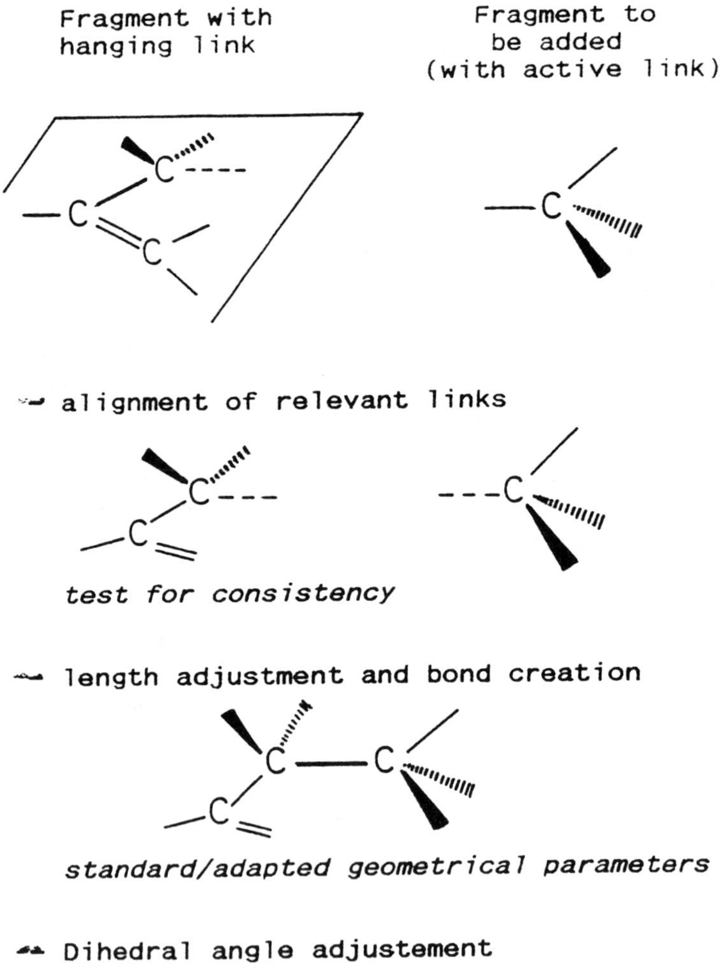

FIGURE 1: Assembling fragments in the ED-3D model builder.

The scheme of the total system exhibits two different parts: the model builder itself which runs on a PC, and a transfer module which allows for running heavier modelling programs on a minicomputer and which monitors this process.

The user builds interactively the skeleton of the target structure. At the end the skeleton is completed by adding hydrogen atoms on the remaining hanging bonds. The molecule can be directly displayed or stored in a file for further refinements on a minicomputer. This display can be interactively improved by local assistance programs (geometrical transformations, rendering, etc.).

One of the main problems is the choice of the parameters intervening in the templates. Some statistical results from the Cambridge Crystallographic Database precise the range and the mean values of the diverse bond lengths according mainly to the number of substituents and the ring size [1]. The immediate environment is nevertheless insufficient and more precision is required to express information as conjugation or large steric hindrance. For this, two ranks of atoms around the current link are necessary. But this leads to a combinatorial problem.

With nine substituents linked by a single bond to the starting atoms one can build 45 different duples and 149 triples. The association of these tuples to constitute the environment of double or single bonds leads to very high numbers, respectively 1035 and 11 175. All of these do not exist with the same probability; we have paid great attention to select sets of relevant substructures.

ABOUT THE CHOICE OF THE FRAGMENTS: STATISTICAL ANALYSIS.

Statistical analysis carried out on the CAS file (about 9.4 million structures in June 90) provides frequencies of more occurrent atoms and rings [2]. Previous works gave some insights on bonds and augmented atoms [3,4]. But we lack information about concentric fragments, the structural primitives which constitute the core of our system.

The DARC concentric substructures called FRELs (Fragment Reduced to an Environment that is Limited) can be focused on an atom or a bond [5]. A FREL is composed of concentric layers of atoms and bonds distributed around the focus. A letter (A,B,C...) designates the depth of the environment, that is the number of ranks considered (Figure 2).

At first, we determined the frequency of the saturated carbon FRELs

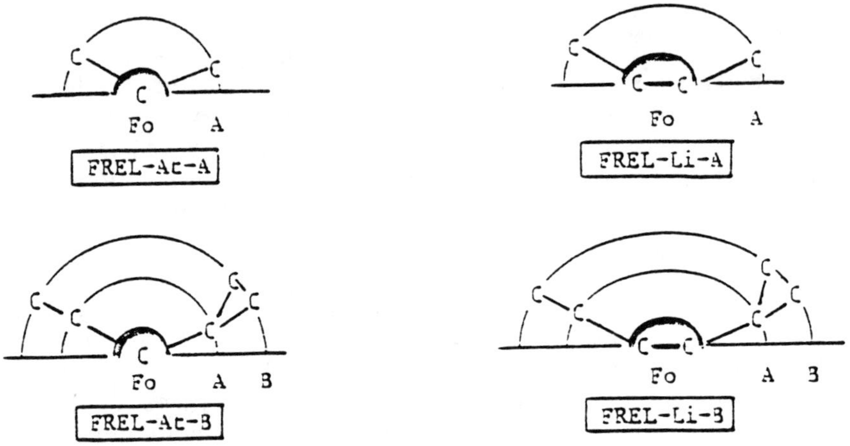

FIGURE 2: DARC Concentric Substructures.

centered on an atom and with two ranks of atoms as environment [6]. This set ranges from the simplest (C) to the most highly substituted (C(tBu)4) and includes the seventy basic saturated carbon skeletons that are possible. The distribution frequencies were sorted by carbon number and subsorted by focus hindrance. Frequency decreases as the carbon number or the focus hindrance increases. Over twelve atoms, the retrievals are always less than 1000. This influence of the steric hindrance was expected but this global view contains some more complex and sometimes contradictory local phenomena (Figure 3).

If the carbon number is an important factor we, however, observe tremendous differences of frequency within some isomeric levels. Furthermore, surprisingly, adding a carbon raises the occurrence. These abnormal behaviors have been identified and analyzed. For this we introduced a new parameter: the cyclic or acyclic nature of bonds. The previous indicated frequencies are obtained in summing up the frequencies of acyclic and cyclic isotopologous FRELs.

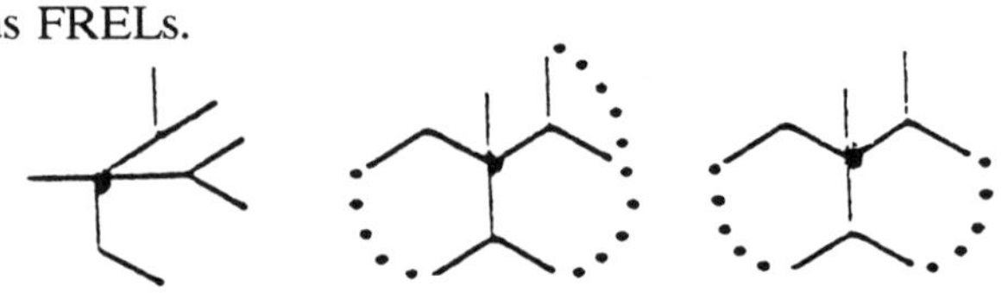

50 74 100 46 100

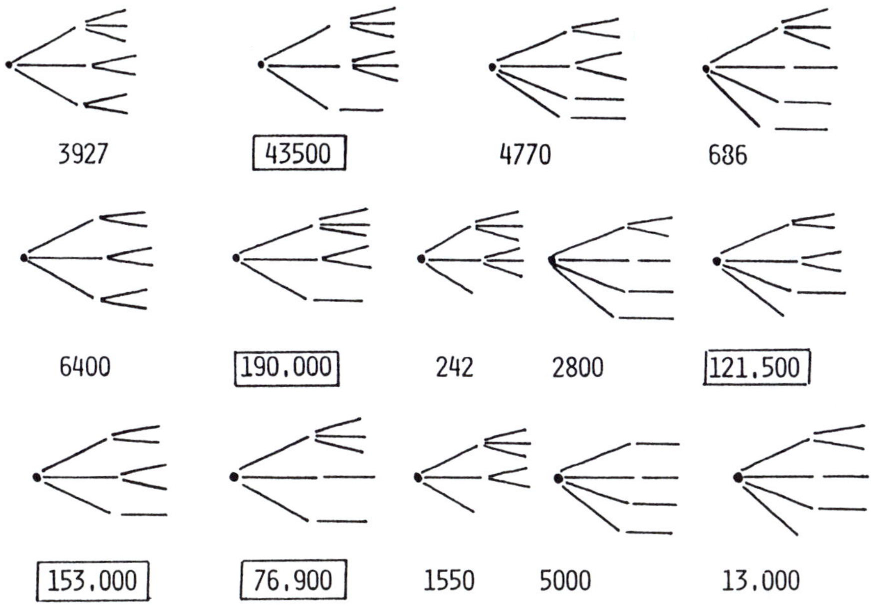

FIGURE 3: FREL occurrence and saturated carbon Environment.

Acyclic FRELs follow regular rules but some cyclic FRELs lead to high abnormal frequencies. These curious FRELs can be related to some particular chemical families as steroids, terpenes, etc. These results have been used to study FRELs centered on a link. A FREL-Li can be formally considered as the association of two FRELs-At. So analogous behavior is observed.

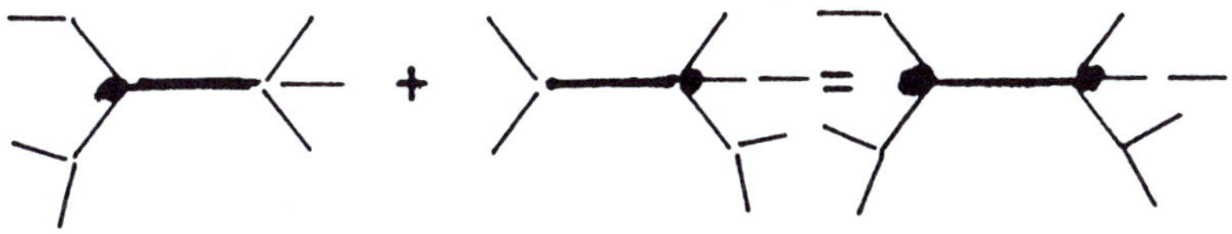

The introduction of a double bond is a constraint which lessens the occurrence. Within a given topology, a double bond can be located differently, but some locations are preferred: the more frequent is on an isopropyl group between the ranks A and B, then on an ethyl group between the focus and the rank A. Globally, topology remains the main factor since the representative curves of saturated or unsaturated FRELs evolve concurrently (Figure 4).

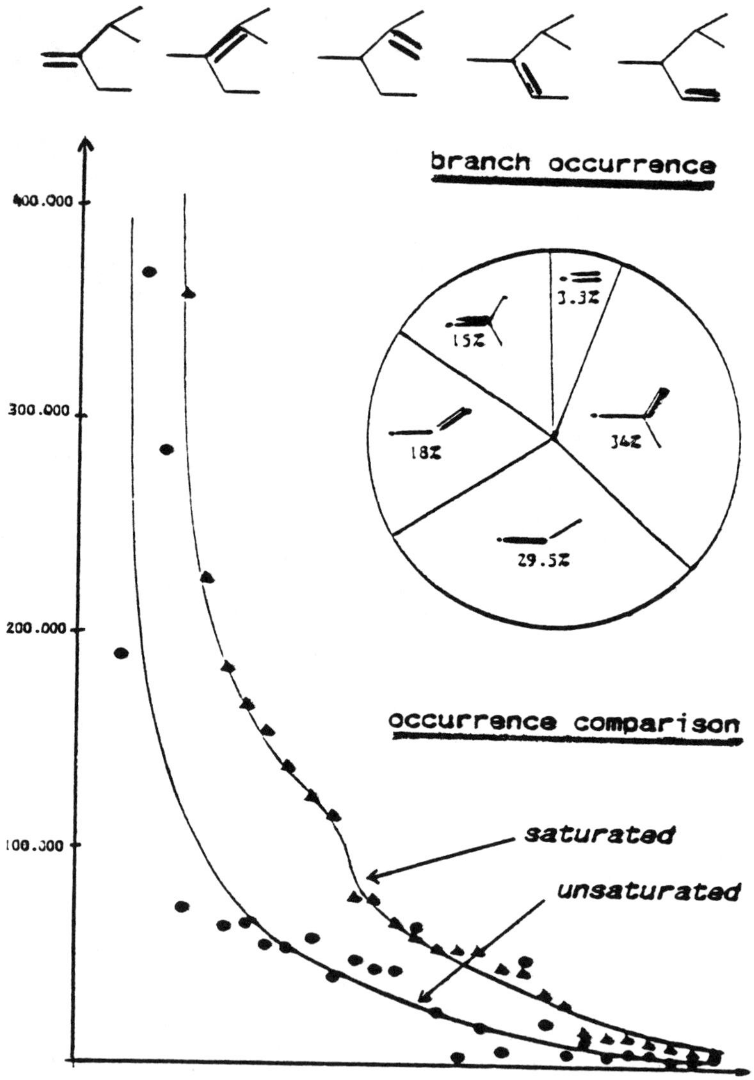

FIGURE 4: Carbon FRELs with a double Bond.

A more precise analysis points out the distribution of frequency vs. the number of substituents of the double bond. The more frequent olefins are the disubstituted ones (cis + trans: 38.7%), then the trisubstituted ones (33.0%). The three remaining subsets (mono-, gem-, and tetra -substituted) are nearly equivalent. On the other hand, the cyclic part increases as the number of substituents. Nearly 48.5% of double bonds are acyclic, 44% are cyclic; the remainder corresponds to the exocyclic bonds.

DETERMINING GEOMETRICAL PARAMETERS

As an example, we analyzed the various geometrical parameters around the C=C double bond. Three main motions can affect the reference geometry of ethylene:

- angle bending when two geminal substituents go nearer to or farther from each other or when the double bond is included in a cycle,
- twisting the plane of the double bond, frequently to avoid interactions between substituents in cis position,
- pyramidalizing the olefinic carbons in strained molecules, more often in folded structures.

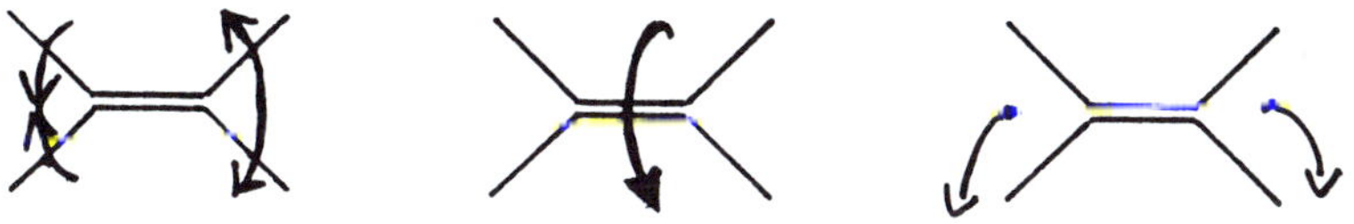

bending twisting pyramidalizing

To analyze the various olefinic parameters we must share double bonds into diverse categories: the constraints are different according to the aliphatic exocyclic or cyclic state of the bond. This cannot avoid special cases where an overcrowded environment leads the double bond very far from the reference.

Aliphatic series: for these olefins the first terms adopt an eclipsed conformation; the carbons are added successively far from the double bond and at last towards it. This conformational filiation is broken down when two isopropyl groups are geminal or when two tertButyl groups are in cis position. For all olefins with low and medium hindered environments it is possible to define averaged models for each subset (mono-, di-,tri-, tetra- substituted).

In taking ethylene as a reference, the valence angles are modified: in monosubstituted series, the values depend on the nature (H or C) of the atom towards the double bond. With a trans substituted, no more models are needed: it is sufficient to duplicate monosubstitution. With two cis substituents, two carbons cannot be located towards each other. Three gem models have been evaluated. The trisubstituted olefins are well approached by summing up gem and cis deviations. At last, for tetrasubstituted olefins all the diverse interactions must be taken into account. All these models can be gathered in a single scheme.

Cyclic series: The first terms have been calculated and some of them experimentally determined by microwave spectroscopy or electron diffraction. It results that the main factor determining the parameters is the ring size; the bond angle varies from 65° for cyclopropene to 124° for cyclohexene. After, for cycloheptene and upper terms, the variation is lesser. We have checked these results with X-ray values from the crystallographic database of Cambridge [8]. The number of available compounds is greater when the cyclic constraint is lesser. The two sources are in relatively good agreement.

When we precise for each cycle the number of authorized substituents the values are more accurate. We found for instance in the acyclic series that the bond length increases with the number of substituents. As to angles, some mean values can be extracted. For example, with cyclohexene, the internal angle is about 123.5 - 124.5° when the olefinic carbon is not substituted, or about 122 - 123° when it is. Whereas the external angle between the substituent and the double bond is about 121-123.5°. The twist angle remains close to zero (Figure 5). These averages have also been carried out for cyclopentene.

	Nb	d	θ_1	θ_2	θ_3	θ_4	Φ
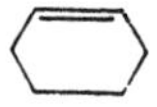	22	1.320	123.5	123.4			0.1
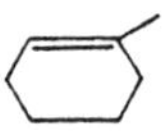	36	1.328	124.7	122.1	121.3		0.6
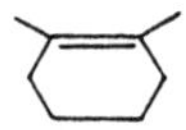	17	1.341	123.3	122.1	120.8	123.7	0.5
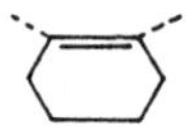	75	1.328	123.4	123.2	121.1	123.7	0.3

FIGURE 5
Geometrical parameters. Influence of connectivity on a given ring size.

Are these values transferable when these basic cycles are embedded into a polycyclic system? We gathered the results for cyclohexene (the more frequent unsaturated cycle). These indicate clearly that the values are very close: the nature of the polycyclic ring system has no influence on the mean geometrical parameters of the double bond in cyclohexene. More refinements are attained by sharing hydrogen and authorized substituents (carbon or heteroelements). The average model of monosubstituted cyclohexene illustrates that for a given cycle the connectivity is more important than the nature of the polycyclic ring system. No change exceeds one degree or one picometer.

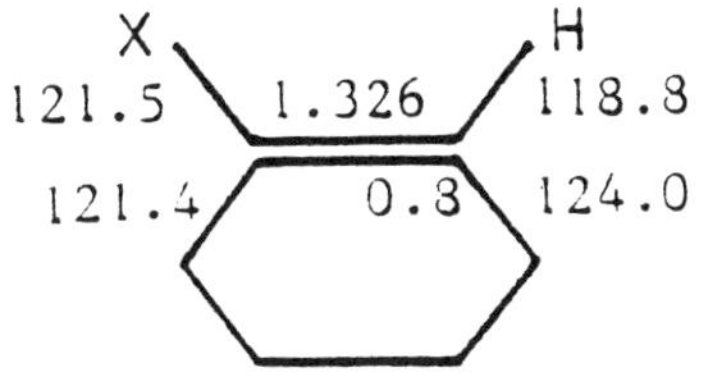

These mean values must not hide the fact that individual values may vary over a wider range from one compound to another. So, the twist angle can take values up to 13°.

CONCLUSION

Our first results demonstrate the capability of our ED-3D model builder to offer structural representations of varying precision and indicates the next goals. By allowing to accommodate realistic fragments and to interactively modify their characteristics, our system provides an efficient and flexible tool. The determination of the geometrical parameters will be sought for by exploring the Cambridge Crystallographic Database or via usual energy minimization programs.

ACKNOWLEDGMENTS

The assistance of the following co-workers is greatfully acknowledged: Eric Feuilleaubois is in charge of the molecular builder, Gerard Carrier carried out the statistical analysis of the DARC fragments, and Veronique Fabart takes care of X-ray data treatment.

REFERENCES

[1] Allen, F.H., Kennard, O., Waston D.G., Brammer, L., Orpen, A.G. and Taylor, R., J.Chem.Soc., Perkin Trans II, S1-S19, 1987.

[2] Stobaught, R.E., "Chemical Abstract Service Chemical Registry System. 11. Substance-Related Statistics: Update and Additions" J. Chem. Inf.

Comput. Sci., 28, 180-187, 1988.

[3] Crowe, J.E., Lynch, M.F. and Town, W.G. "Analysis of Structural Characteristics of Chemical Compounds in a Large Computer-Based File. Part 1. Noncyclic Fragments", J. Chem. Soc. (C), 990-996, 1970.

[4] Adamson, G.W., Lynch, M.F. and Town, W.G., "Analysis of Structural Characteristics of Chemical Compound in a Lare Computer-Based File, Part II., Atom-Centered Fragments", J. Chem. Soc. (C), 3702-3706, 1971.

[5] Attias, R. "Darc Substructure Search System: A New Approach to Chemical Information", J. Chem. Inf. Comput. Sci., 23, 102-108, 1983. Dubois, J.E., Panaye, A. and Attias, R., "Darc System: Notion of Defined and Generic Substructures. Filiation and Coding of Frel Substructure (SS) Classes", J. Chem. Inf. Comput. Sci., 27, 74-82, 1987.

[6] Carrier, G., Panaye, A. and Dubois, J.E., Topological Structural Information in the CAS File: Statistical Occurrences of DARC Concentric Fragments. 1. Basic Carbon Substructures, J. Chem. Inf. Comput. Sci., Vol. 30, 110-121, 1990.

[7] Doucet, J.P., in this volume, p 195.

[8] Allen, F., Kennard, O. and Taylor, R., Systematic Analysis of Structural Data as a Research Technique in Organic Chemistry, Acc. Chem. Res.,16, 146-153, 1983.

TOPOLOGY AND TOPOGRAPHY CONCEPTS IN CONFORMATION ELUCIDATION

J.P. Doucet and V. Sabart
Institut de Topologie et de Dynamique des Systèmes
Associé au CNRS, Université de Paris VII
Paris, France.

Topology (formal proximity) and Topography (geometrical proximity) concepts are directly involved in solving individual molecules through 2D-NMR experiments since some pulse sequences depend on links between atoms and others on spatial distances. In a somewhat different concern we analyze how these concepts intervene in treating data sets through structure/property relationships and how they can awaken dormant information embedded in the raw data.

Relationships between a molecular structure and its related properties (physicochemical, spectroscopic, pharmacological, etc.) can be sought for through holistic models treating each molecule as a whole quite independently from the other molecules of the set (as for example in quantum chemistry applications). However, more frequently one uses structural descriptors to encode the molecular features. Properties depend on the actual spatial location of atoms. So, structural descriptors had to be topographical. Nevertheless, because of easiness, topological descriptors (precising only the nature of atoms and bonds) are very widely used. We examine here three main points: how to build true topographical correlations, why topological correlations can be valid and what geometrical information can they provide?

Correlation strategies depend on molecular flexibility. For frozen systems atomic positions are well defined and their influence on properties is easily characterized. Similarly when a few conformers are largely predominant, the changes observed in the properties can also be attributed to spatially well identified atom positions within these favored species. So, true topographical correlations can be readily proposed. On the other hand, for molecules existing as a mixture of conformers, one would have to evaluate the properties for each conformer and carry out conformational weighting. Conversely, in a global view one can use raw topological descriptors which implicitly weight geometrical features.

TOPOGRAPHICAL CORRELATIONS

Within the framework of the DARC system, structure/property relationships have been approached through topo-information correlations which rely on two key concepts [1]:

- **filiation**: within a set, each molecule is considered as formally generated by successive additions of sites on a given root (the focus). This progressive generation pathway defines filiation relating structures deriving one from the others.

- **Site perturbation**: the variation of property observed between one structure and the following one in the generation series is considered as a perturbation and conventionally attributed to the new site introduced.

In topological models, we consider a formal adjunction of ordered sites whereas topographical models deal with actual atom location in the 3D space.

As a first example, we examine geometrical distorsions on aliphatic alkenes. We consider here only one conformer, the most stable one (calculated or determined experimentally). For these compounds the following conformational filiation is observed: the most stable conformer corresponds to a C=C bond eclipsed by a C–H bond for the Methyl, Ethyl, isoPropyl groups or a C–C bond for the tertButyl group. For more crowded alkenes (with two isoPropyl in geminal position or two tertButyl in cis) a new filiation appears with a bisected C=C bond.

These successive branchings induce small but definite geometrical variations. They can be readily rationalized, with an accuracy of about one degree in the following topographical correlation (Figure 1) which individualizes the influence of each position of the environment of the double bond. The values indicated on the graph represent the perturbations induced on the valence angle by introducing a carbon atom in place of an hydrogen in the relevant position. So, starting from ethylene, the first substitution enlarges the adjacent angle by *ca.* 3° whereas the effect is nearly 0° if the carbon is

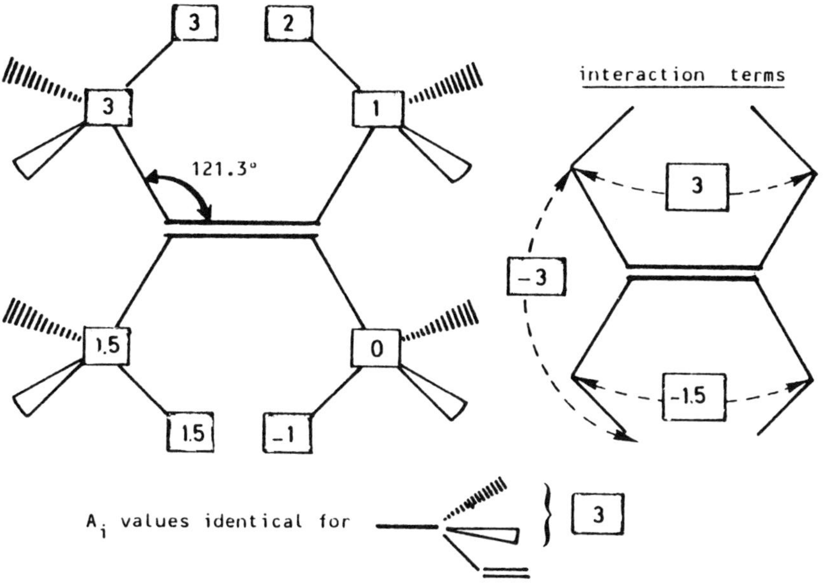

FIGURE 1
Topographical correlation for the valence angle distorsions in aliphatic alkenes (site values in degrees by reference to ethylene).

introduced in trans. For polysubstituted systems perturbations are additive. However, some interaction terms are necessary to express dampening or exaltation effects (cooperative effects) when two substituents are simultaneously present (cis compounds for instance) (Figure 2). The same set of parameters is fortunately valid for more crowded alkenes where the double bond is bisected.

The same topographical approach may also be proposed when only one (or a few) conformer is present, so that conformational filiation can still be defined. The following example corresponds to the carbonyl stretching vibration in the infrared spectra of aliphatic ketones. Starting with a learning population of 19 compounds, the preferred conformations of which were known via molecular mechanics, we define a self-consistent set for the perturbations induced on **nu** CO according to the spatial position of the new atom introduced (Figure 3). For the first terms, the preferred structures have a carbonyl group eclipsed by a C–C bond as in ethyl methyl ketone whereas for more branched terms a bisected geometry is favored (dihedral angles of 180° and 60°) [2].

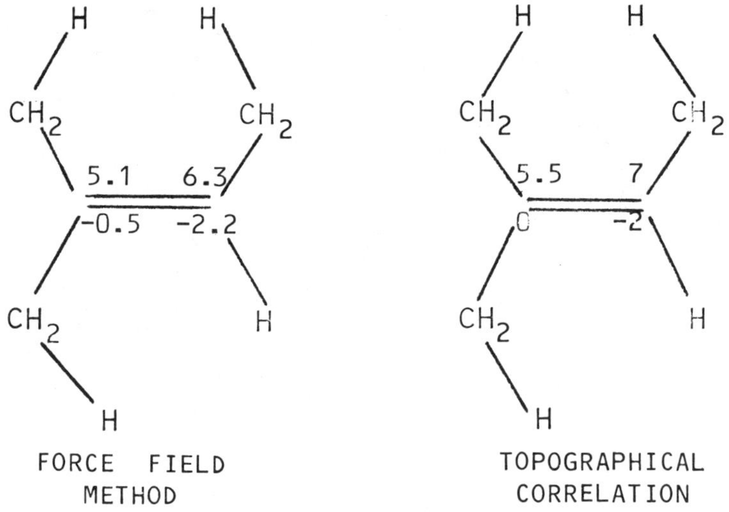

FIGURE 2: Angular distorsions in trimethyl ethylene.

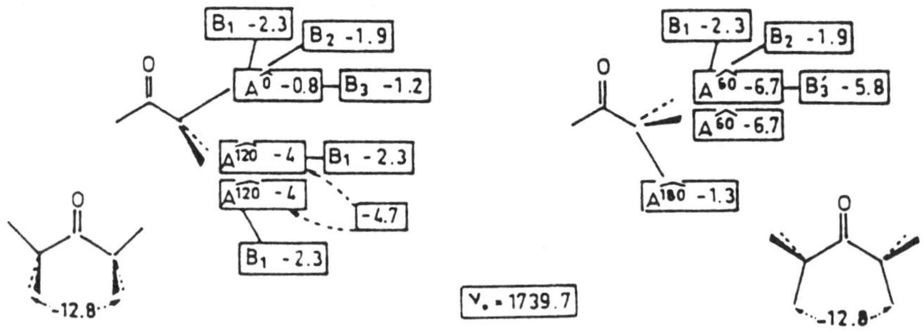

FIGURE 3
Topographical correlation for the carbonyl stretching frequency of aliphatic ketones (gas phase); site values: cm^{-1}.

This model has been successfully applied to 61 compounds where it allows for interpreting the shifts observed. It can also definitely be used to predict the more likely conformation. On this basis, the **nu** CO splitting of neoPentyl ketones is interpreted as resulting from the mixture of two conformations: the higher frequency band corresponds to a tertButyl group eclipsing the carbonyl, the low frequency band being attributed to a bisected conformer.

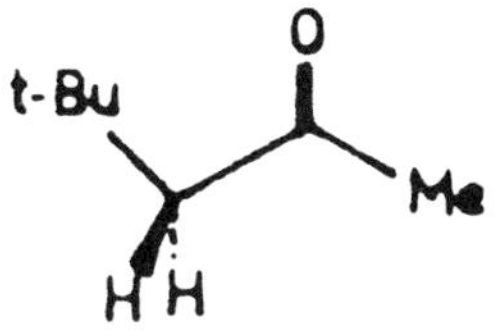

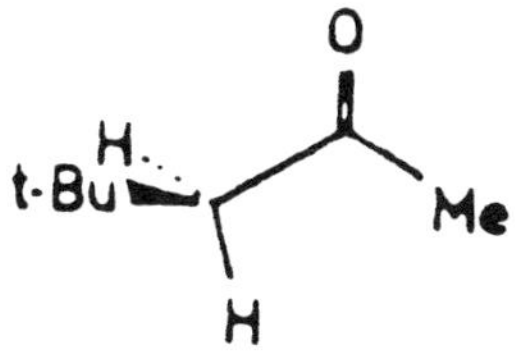

ν_{cal}	1733,5	1723,0
ν_{exp}	1733,0	1723,0

The situation is more puzzling for systems existing as a mixture of conformers. Indeed topological correlations, which take only into account the nature of the atoms and the existence of bonds between them, work well in very diverse areas. But one may challenge the validity of this approach since properties depend on the actual spatial organization *i.e.*, on the molecular topography.

VALIDITY OF TOPOLOGICAL CORRELATIONS

The validity domain of a topological correlation can be efficiently estimated by determining domains of homogeneous geometrical evolvement and identifying the sites acting on the property.

Regularity domain

Writing a topological filiation assumes that each compound is deduced from the preceding one by adjunction of a topological site. Are these filiations maintained in the 3D space? In other words, is the most probable conformation of a compound deduced from the most probable conformation of the anterior one in the series or does the conformational mixture drastically change from one compound to the following one?

To precise the interrelations between topological and topographical filiations we chose alkanes as a typical example of the common molecular framework. We performed a simplified conformational analysis using the force field of Beierbeck and Saunders [3], mainly lying on gauche and delta interactions. From energy calculations we evaluated the weight of each conformer and the statistical occupation of individualized atom positions [4]. For example, passing from 2-methyl Butane to 2,3-dimethyl Butane is described in ordered topological description as occupation the B12 site around a CH3–C focus. This cannot be assigned to a given geometrical position but rather corresponds to a large increase in the population of the gauche position (Figure 4).

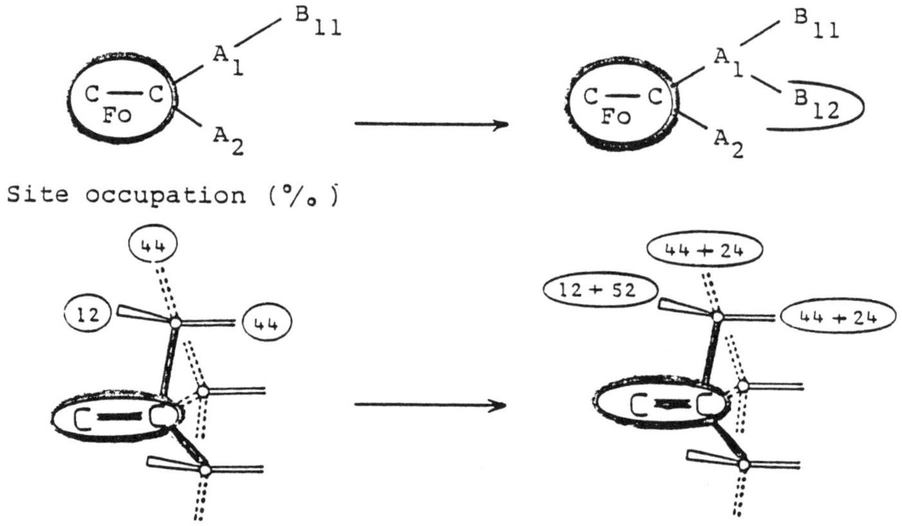

FIGURE 4. Topological Adjunction and Topographical Adjunction.

Such an analysis enables us to define structural homogeneous areas corresponding to regularity domains where the conformational percentages remain nearly constant.

Active environment

At a first level, some information about the active sites on a property can be gained by global comparison between rigid cyclic and flexible acrylic structures [5]. The example treated here refers to α-substituent shifts in ^{13}C-NMR (*i.e.,* shifts induced when introducing a group on the resonating carbon). Usual models generally evaluate these shifts by assuming additivity of characteristic constant increments, clearly, against obviousness. Indeed these α-shifts largely vary and even change sign according to the skeleton where the substituent is introduced.

We rationalize a large set of data (10 substituents on 25 substrates) in a factor analysis treatment. For this representation in the plane of the first two factors, proximity between points means behavior analogy for the carbon substrates (Figure 5). (2,2,2) Bicyclooctyl or adamantyl skeletons look more likely as trimethyl than triethyl group. Cyclohexyl behaves like diethyl for an axial incoming group but as dimethyl for an equatorial one.

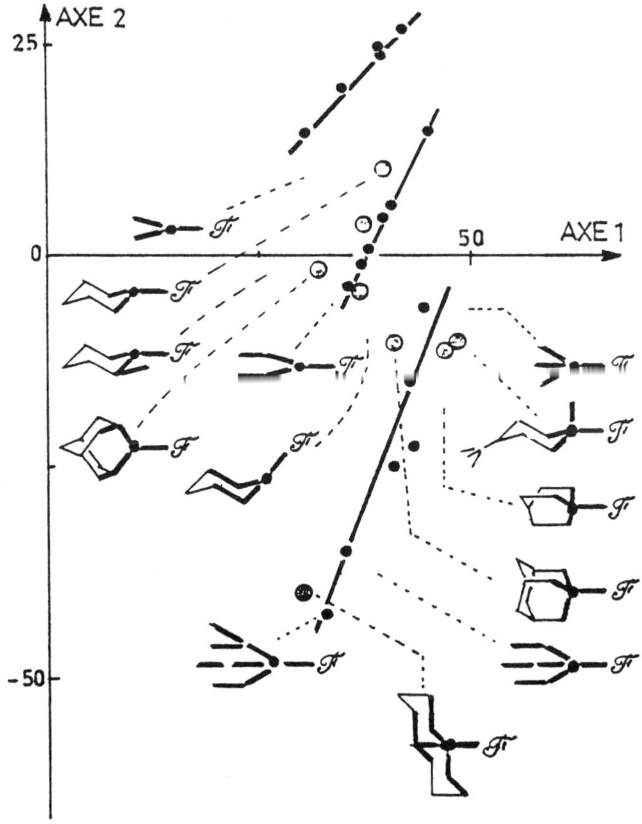

FIGURE 5

Factor analysis of α substituent shifts in ^{13}C NMR. Equivalent cyclic and acyclic active environments. Points refer to carbon skeletons.

So we can express that the topographically active environment encompasses the sites "seen" by the ^{13}C focus: A positions and B gauche bonds. *A contrario*, B anti bonds have no influence. A similar behavior was already detected for steric effect constants (hindrance to an incoming reagent).

Simplified model

Remaining in ^{13}C spectroscopy, we will work now on the chemical shifts of alkanes. Among the various solutions proposed to evaluate the shifts, the model of Beierbeck and Saunders is very attractive since it takes into account conformational averaging. This model uses additive terms for interactions involving H or C on Cß carbons and δ syn axial terms. However it did not reflect the influence of Cß connectivity. Derived from it, we refine and adapt this model into a topographical site correlation [4]. The perturbations in the ^{13}C environment are individualized in terms of occupied A positions and B bonds gauche, syn or anti by respect to the bonds starting from the resonating carbon.

Assuming some site equivalence, this topographical correlation can be expressed by the following equations:

$$\boxed{\delta = \delta_{FO + A} + a\ Bg + b\ B_{syn}}$$

FO = Me, Et, iPr
a = -4.0   b = 1.0

FO = tBu
a = +1.0

This simplified DARC model is very efficient since it reproduces the chemical shifts with a mean error less than 1 ppm.

Such a treatment requires however the cumbersome calculations of the conformers. But, surprisingly, it is not so far from a simple topological description. Indeed we established that the number of B gauche and syn positions (intervening in our simplified expression) and the total number of B occupied positions are very simply related through linear correlations.

We can conclude that the efficiency of topological models in very large and diverse areas is due to the fact that:

TOPOLOGY implicitly encodes TOPOGRAPHY

GEOMETRICAL INFORMATION FROM TOPOLOGICAL CORRELATIONS

If a more refined treatment has to consider explicitly all the individual conformers, topo-information relationships may also give some help in this field.

Not only topology encodes topography within structurally homogeneous areas, but it also gives specific information on borderline cases where conformational filiation breaks down or sudden distorsions appear. This is detected in topological correlations by unusual site values or by interaction terms (no additivity of perturbation terms).

When looking at the ^{13}C spectra of ketones, it appears that successive carbon introduction from propanone to branched alkyl ketones shifts as expected the carbonyl signal downfield but for the sixth substitution (from tBu–CO-iPr to tBu-CO-tBu), the shift is reverse (upfield). This behavior is easily pointed out on the corresponding topological correlation which establishes that such a reverse effect is characteristic of hexasubstituted ketones [6].

This GEM-6 effect [7], corroborated by various other physico chemical parameters, is readily interpreted in terms of geometrical distorsions: opening the valence angle of nearly 5° as estimated by molecular mechanics calculations.

EXTRACTION OF 3D COMMON SUBSTRUCTURES

Since topological descriptors somewhat encode geometrical information, they can be of some help for identifying topographical features. Some previous algorithms have been proposed to recognize a given 3D fragment within a molecular structure or to determine the greatest fragment common to a set of molecules. But all these methods rely directly on interatomic distances. The original OCTANG method [8] we developed uses a topological description on which topographical information is superimposed but without metrics (Figure 6). **Local Environment** is perceived through the direction of the bonds stemming from the current atom towards 8 regions sharing the space about it. The **global description** of a molecule encompasses chromatic, connectivity and direction tables. Identifying a substructure is carried out through a pathway representation of overlapping fragments. The concept of elementary equivalent fragments allows one to cope with a change in the reference axes.

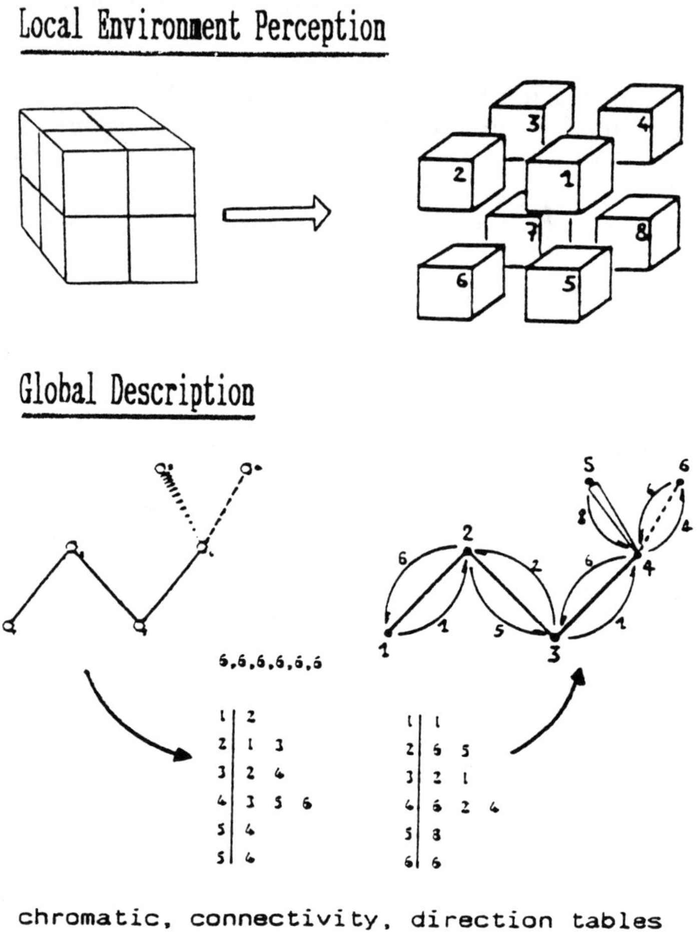

FIGURE 6. OCTANG description.

CONCLUDING REMARKS

For a few years, we gradually passed from 2D descriptors and topological models to 3D fragments and true topographical correlations. But, they still remain limited to geometrical parameters. Next steps would presumably be to incorporate in such treatments structural features not directly linked to the molecular skeleton such as elements of molecular surfaces, location of electron orbitals or areas of high electrostatic potentials given by 3D modelling programs.

REFERENCES

[1] Dubois, J.E., Laurent, D. and Aranda, A., *J. Chim. Phys.*, 70, pp. 1608 and 1616, 1973.
[2] Massat, A., Thesis University Paris 7, 1987.
[3] Beierbeck, H. et Saunders, J.K., *Canad. J. Chem.*, 55, p. 771, 1977; 58, p. 1258, 1980.
[4] Dubois, J.E., Doucet, J.P. and Panaye, A., *Bull. Soc. Chim. Belg.*, Vol. 98, pp. 31-44, 1989.
[5] Doucet, J.P., Panaye, A., Yuan, S.G. and Dubois, J.E., *J. Chim. Phys.*, 82, 6, pp. 607-611, 1985.
[6] Panaye, A., Doucet, J.P. and Dubois, J.E., *Tetrahedron Letters*, Vol. 22, n° 13, pp. 1235-1238, 1981.
[7] Dubois, J.E. and Cossé-Barbi, A., *J. Am. Chem. Soc.*, Vol. 110, n° 4, pp. 1220-1228, 1988.
[8] Delance, E., Doucet, J.P. and Dubois, J.E., *Stud. Phys. Theo. Chem.*, Elsevier Science Publishers B.V., Amsterdam, Vol. 71, pp. 755-761, 1990.

RECENT ADVANCES IN THE AUTOMATED STRUCTURE ELUCIDATION SYSTEM - CHEMICS

Shin-ichi Sasaki and Kimito Funatsu
Toyohashi University of Technology
Tempaku, Toyohashi 440, Japan

1. INTRODUCTION

The CHEMICS system, developed by the authors, is a computer-assisted structure elucidation system for organic compounds, which depends on a structure generation method; that is, the most probable structure is generated by the automated analysis of data (for instance, chemical spectra) of an unknown using empirical and theoretical rules [1]. The principle of the system is that all possible structures, which are known to exist or which might exist on chemical grounds, are stored in a computer. The number of the structures in a particular case is then narrowed down by successively entering information from spectroscopic measurements. CHEMICS is designed to store all the substructures (called 'components') necessary for building any likely structures. At present, CHEMICS contains 630 components for the structure elucidation of organic compounds consisting of C, H, O, N, S and halogen atoms (Table 1). To store such a set of components in a computer is synonymous with storing all the complete structures which could be present.

2. BASIC FUNCTIONS OF CHEMICS

The CHEMICS system is basically composed of the following three functional modules (within the dotted lines in Figure 1): a) Data analysis, b) Structure generation, c) Entering of macrocomponents (partial structures).

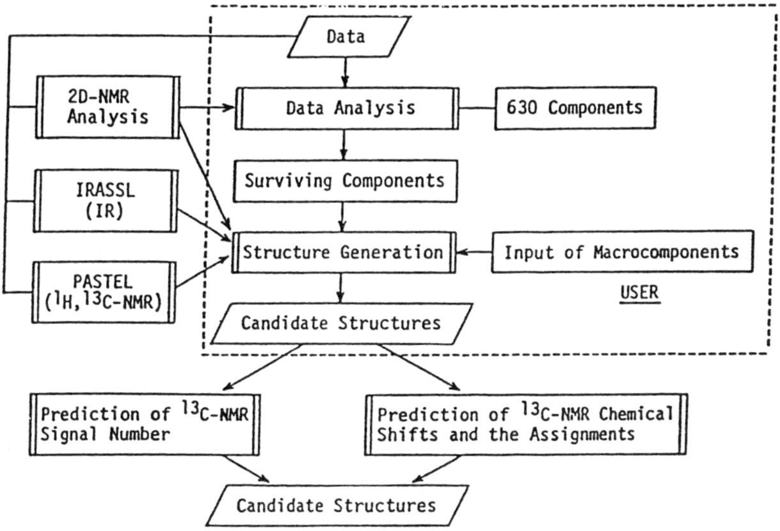

FIGURE 1. The current CHEMICS.

TABLE 1
Component set for structure elucidation of organic compounds containing C, H, O, N, S, and halogens

#	COMPONENT		#	COMPONENT	
1	tert-BU-	(S)	372		(I)
2		(ND)	373	>C-	(Br)
⋮			374		(Cl)
51		(CD)	⋮		
52	CH3-CH2-	(CT)	403	>N→O	(Y)
53		(CS)	404	>S→O	(Y)
⋮			⋮		
185	O↑	(O)	547		(CD)
186	CH3-S- ↓O	(Y)	548	-OH	(CT)
⋮			549		(CS)
351		(F)	⋮		
352	>C=NH	(S)	626	-F	
353		(ND)	627	-Cl	
⋮			628	-Br	
			629	-I	
			630	-D-	

a) **Data analysis**: Some of the components which have survived because they are consistent with the molecular formula can be subsequently discharged because they are inconsistent with ^{1}H and ^{13}C-NMR chemical shift values, or IR data. In the selection of components by CHEMICS these spectral data measured on the sample are compared by computer with those in component/chemical shift or component/wave number correlation table shown in Table 2. The next step is to make component sets by using the components which have been selected as being non-contradictory to the molecular formula and spectral data.

TABLE 2

Correlation Tables for ^{1}H- and ^{13}C-NMR Analyses

		^{1}H-NMR(PPM)			^{13}C-NMR(PPM)		
No.	Component	L	H	L	H	L	H
1	TERT-BU-(S)	1.81	.31	40.75	1.97	90.00	20.00
2	TERT-BU-(ND)	1.81	.31	40.75	1.97	90.00	30.00
3	TERT-BU-(N)	1.81	.31	40.75	1.97	71.97	41.20
:							
34	(CH3)2N-(CD)	4.56	1.33	50.19	20.04		
35	(CH3)2N-(CT)	4.56	1.44	50.19	20.04		
36	(CH3)2N-(CS)	4.56	1.44	50.19	20.04		
:							
192	CH2:(CL)	6.22	3.09	56.67	39.46		
193	CH2:(F)	5.32	4.23	90.00	70.00		
:							
246	-C#N (S)			119.00	109.00		
247	-C#N (ND)			123.00	103.00		
248	-C#N (N)			123.00	103.00		
:							
292	O=CH-(S)	12.39	5.99	200.00	180.00		
293	O=CH-(ND)	12.39	5.99	180.00	140.00		
:							
351	NH=C:(F)	12.59	3.35	190.00	130.00		
352	NH=C:(S)	12.59	3.35	190.00	130.00		

b) **Structure generation**: This step generates structures from the individual component combinations. The generation is carried out taking all possibilities into account, in due consideration of the principle that most of the components can only be linked to a limited number of species. Using specially designed logic, connectivity stack [2], when the system functions properly it does not reproduce the same structure nor does it fail to generate any structure which can justifiably be built.

c) **Entering of macrocomponents (partial structures)**: The chemist often has some information about the structure of a sample. This may be obtained from the past record of the sample or from laboratory tests.

When the partial structure is entered by the user, the constitutional information is broken down into its components, which are then compared with the components that the system has selected. The system will adopt the information entered only when all the components derived from the partial structure inserted have already been selected by CHEMICS. This means that the components which the system has selected with a full safety factor will take precedence over the additional information which has been entered manually.

As obvious from the above explanation, the fragments for making up structures and carriers of spectral information are just components. The unit of examining the reasonable allocation of each component to NMR signals, is also a component in relation to the correlation table. Essentially, the analytical ability of 'data analysis' in CHEMICS never exceeds what is provided by component units. Thus, the correspondence of candidate structures with input data is said to become ambiguous in some cases. The number of candidates increases in proportion to the ambiguity. According to the principle of never missing a correct solution, this result is said to be unavoidable. One of the ideas developed to cope with this situation, CHEMICS-F, has a file retrieval function [3], and the modules for predicting the number of ^{13}C-NMR signals [4] and judging probability on the basis of strain energy calculation [5], have also been provided. These functions play an effective role after generation of whole structures.

On the other hand, the introduction of partial structures selected by the user has enhanced the correctness and practicality of structure elucidation by our system. Ideally however, the partial structures entered should be determined both by computer deduction and by the user's judgement. In order to realize about this situation an analytical way different from that in 'data analysis' of the above, CHEMICS is required. In this sense, as a new approach to automated partial structure elucidation, an interdependent analytical method based on the relationships between ^{1}H- and ^{13}C-NMR chemical shifts for each atomic group with specified neighboring groups, has been developed [6]. According to this method, relatively large-sized partial structures can be generated automatically. This is most helpful in reducing the number of candidates. Furthermore, the introduction of ^{13}C–^{13}C, ^{13}C–^{1}H, and ^{1}H–^{1}H (vicinal) signal connectivity information provided by two-dimensional NMR measurement into CHEMICS has been accomplished so that the connectivity of carbons in the skeletal structure of an unknown and the carbon-proton relationship are automatically analyzed and elucidated at both steps of 'data analysis' and 'structure generation' in generating whole candidate structures [7]. This also results in fewer candidates.

3. CURRENT STATUS OF CHEMICS

So far I have referred to the system within the dotted lines in Figure 1. Using this basic system, large numbers of candidates may be sometimes outputted. For example, the basic system would provide 21 candidate structures for the input data shown in Figure 2. To cope with this, we have composed an optional program (IRASSL) to make a more detailed analysis of IR-analysis is based on the technique of symbolic logic [8]. Figure 2 shows two substructures (carbonyl and vinyl groups) predicted by this program. The substructures are added to the components provided by the fundamental approach and these are all used for structure generation. Thus, the present approach has provided only two answers (Figure 2), either of which is the right answer.

If the spectra of the two structures in Figure 2 could be predicted the one on the right might be selected with more confidence, by comparing each of the predicted spectra with the one observed from the sample substance. However, since it is not easy to predict the whole spectrum from a structure, only the prediction of the number of ^{13}C-NMR spectral signals will be carried out [9]. The algorithm for the prediction is not based on symmetrical equivalence of each carbon atom, but on environmental equivalence. The position of each signal is shifted according to the difference of the environment for each carbon atom. Therefore, our task is to examine which carbon belongs to which environment and to count the number of different environments. This approach is applicable to any other structures. Readers will note many complicated structures in Figure 3. The left-hand column indicates the observed number of signals for each of the structures, and the right-hand column indicates the predicted number. Both numbers are in excellent agreement. A complete agreement has been confirmed between the predicted and observed values for other samples beyond a hundred.

This approach was applied to the two structures shown in Figure 2. It predicts five and six signals for the lower and upper candidates, respectively. Since the observed number of signals is six for this substance, as shown in Figure 2, the upper structure in Figure 2 is concluded to be the right answer.

As already mentioned, the key point of our system is to use various means to help to arrive quickly at the single right answer.

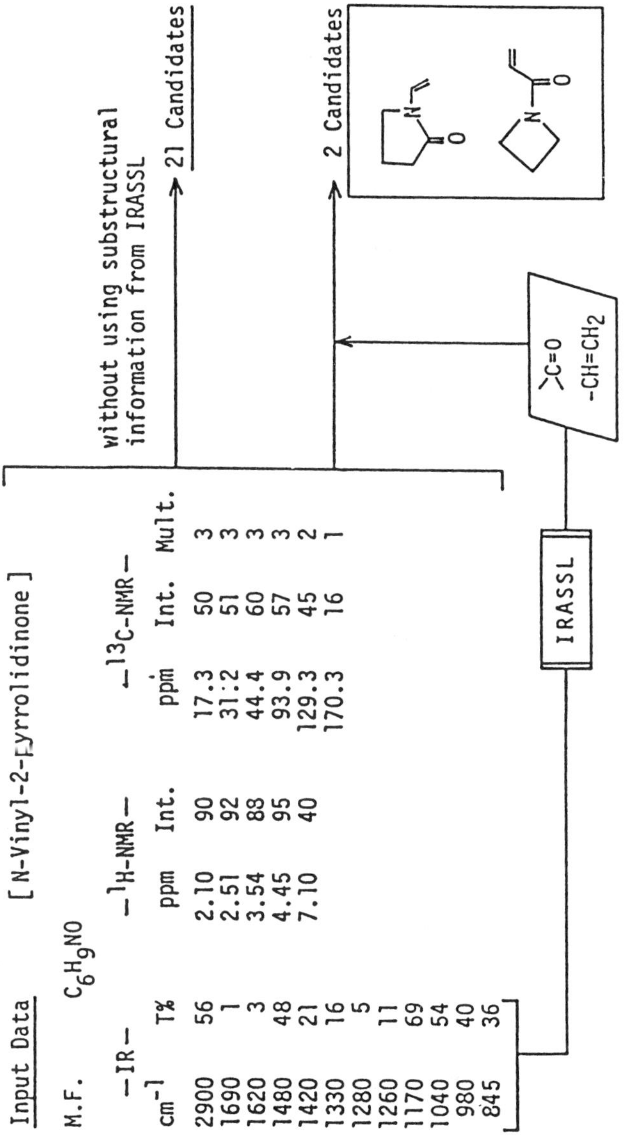

FIGURE 2
Input data and execution results of CHEMICS with and without using IRASSL.

	Sample	Observed	Predicted
(1)	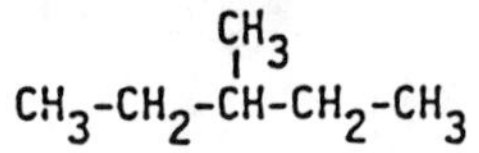	4	4
(2)	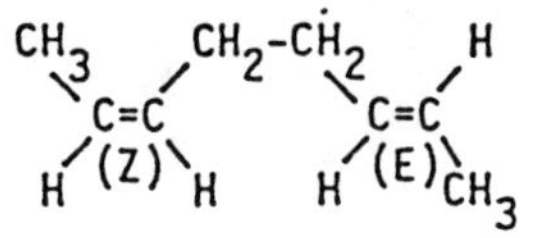	8	8
(3)	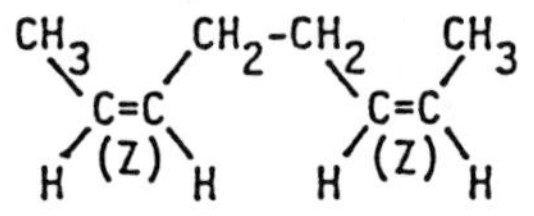	4	4
(4)	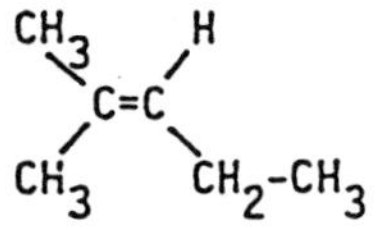	6	6
(5)	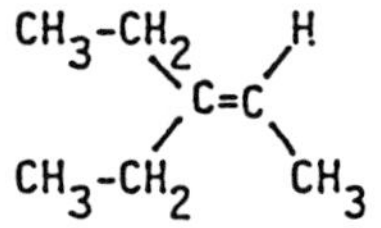	7	7
(6)	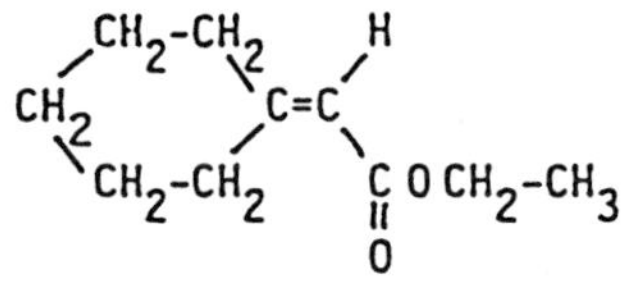	10	10
(7)	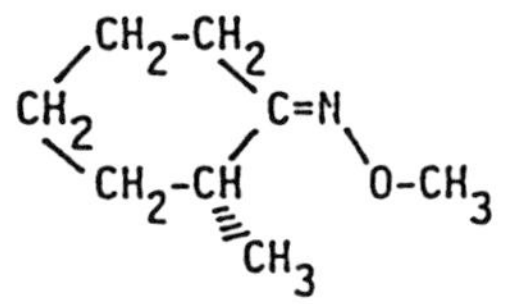	9	9
(8)		11	11

FIGURE 3. Results of ^{13}C NMR signal number prediction.

The next example of the elucidation process of an unknown compound (actually, nicotine) is serially illustrated in Figure 4. Chemical data of the unknown, molecular formula and spectroscopic data of IR, ^{1}H- and ^{13}C-NMR, are compared with 630 components at the step of 'data analysis'

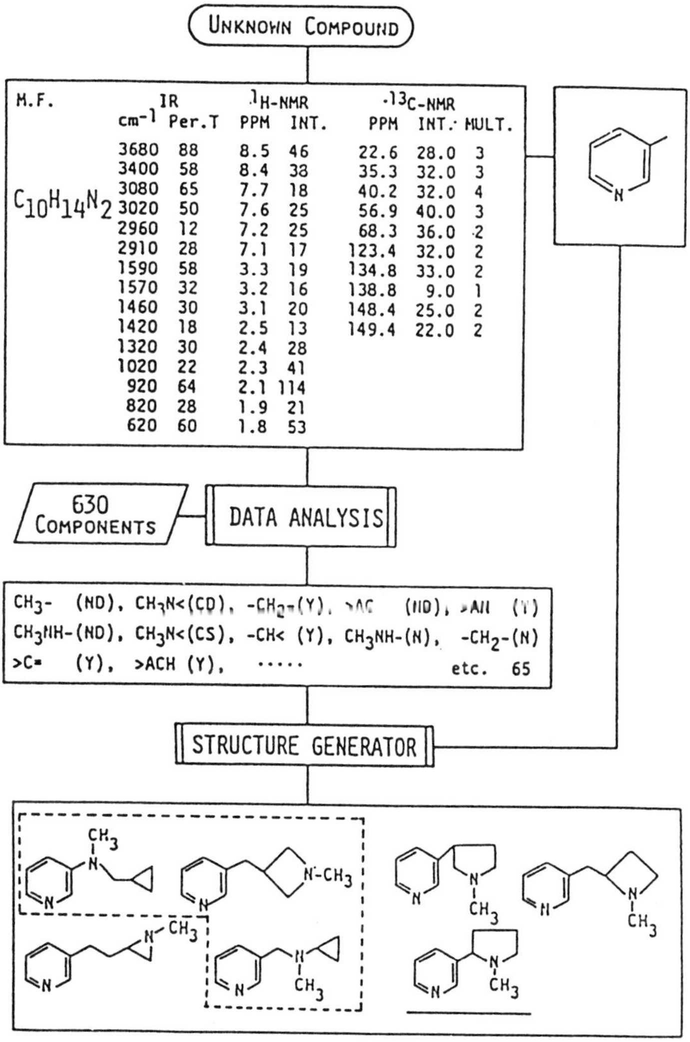

FIGURE 4
A practical example of structure elucidation using interdependent analysis of ^{1}H and ^{13}C NMR.

to give rise to 65 components. The number of candidates will amount to more than ten thousand if all the possible structures are constructed on the basis of the 65 components. In this example, the interdependent analytical method based on the relationships between ^{1}H and ^{13}C-NMR chemical shifts to suggest automatically the presence of '3-substituted pyridyl group' as a possible substructure in the unknown structure so that the number of candidates drastically diminishes to only seven structures in which the underlined correct solution is involved [6]. Incidentally, in this case, three candidates within the dotted lines are removed by ^{13}C-NMR signal number prediction mentioned above.

The next is application of our system to the structure elucidation of a natural product by using two-dimensional NMR data [7]. CHEMICS can analyze three types of 2D NMR data, that is, complete and partial ^{13}C–^{13}C signal connectivity information, ^{13}C–^{1}H, and ^{1}H–^{1}H (vicinal) signal connectivity information. Each of the 2D NMR data types is used in CHEMICS independently or in their combinations. Several examples are shown in the following.

The first example is application of ^{13}C–^{13}C signal connectivity information. Generally, it may be expected that the introduction of complete ^{13}C–^{13}C signal connectivity information into the system should provide only one candidate structure. However, in spite of using this kind of information, three candidate structures were generated with the reasonable ^{13}C-NMR signal assignments, as shown in Figure 6. It is emphasized that this fact just indicates one of the most important points concerning the implementation of 2D NMR data analysis on CHEMICS. These three candidates are objectively reasonable and probable if we have no information more than these spectral data. More information in the field of natural product chemistry, for instance, isoprene rule etc., would be necessary for further discrimination of the candidates. In next example, H–H COSY data is handled together with C–H COSY data and partial ^{13}C–^{13}C signal connectivity information (Figure 6). H–H COSY data is presented as pairs of proton signal numbers between vicinal protons. H–H COSY data is automatically converted into the corresponding partial ^{13}C–^{13}C signal connectivity information using C–H COSY data. Of course, independent analysis of H–H COSY is possible in the system. And in this example, α, β-unsaturated carbonyl group is proposed as macrocomponent by the IR data processing module, IRASSL, mentioned before. Furthermore, since assignment of the ^{13}C-NMR signal to the macrocomponent by the user is relatively easy, the macrocomponent with the assignment information is entered into CHEMICS. Thus, in this case, pseudo-2D NMR data, that is, ^{13}C–^{13}C signal connectivity information can be obtained automatically from

$C_{15}H_{22}O_3$ 11,13-Dihydroparthenolide

	^{13}C-NMR PPM	MULT.	C-C SIGNAL CONNECTIVITY	
1.	125.00	2	1	2
2.	24.00	3	1	10
3.	36.60	3	2	3
4.	61.30	1	3	4
5.	66.60	2	4	5
6.	82.00	2	4	15
7.	51.80	2	5	6
8.	29.70	3	6	7
9.	41.00	3	7	8
10.	134.40	1	7	11
11.	42.30	2	8	9
12.	177.20	1	9	10
13.	13.10	4	10	14
14.	16.70	4	11	12
15.	17.00	4	11	13

(F.J. Parodi et al., SPECTROSCOPY LETTERS, 20(1987)445)

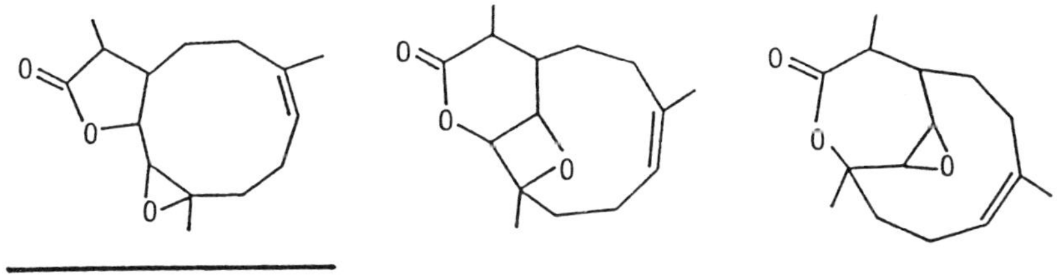

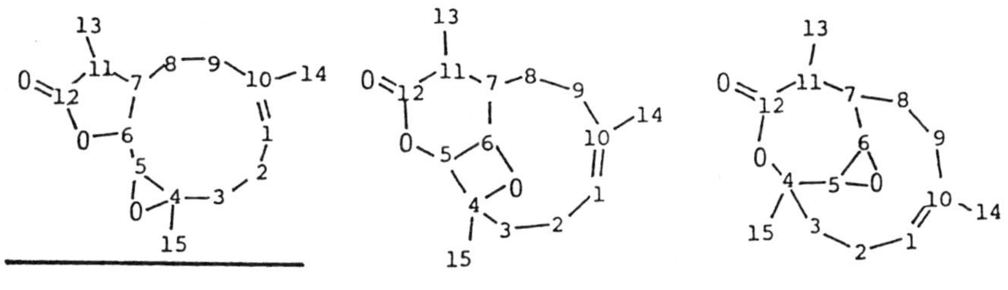

FIGURE 5
Data of 11,13-Dihydroparthenolide and result of elucidation by CHEMICS

<Input Data (underlined)>

MF = $C_{13}H_{20}O$ (β-Ionone)

^{13}C-NMR

NO.	PPM	INT.	MULT.
1	197.6	10	1
2	142.3	10	2
3	135.7	10	1
4	135.2	10	1
5	131.2	10	2
6	39.4	10	3
7	33.7	10	1
8	33.1	10	3
9	28.3	20	4
10	26.8	10	4
11	21.3	10	4
12	18.3	10	3

^{13}C-^{13}C signal connectivity derived from path 2 long-range C-H COSY (by user)

1	10
4	11
7	9

^{13}C-^{13}C signal connectivity

6	12
12	8
2	5

C-H COSY

H	C
1	9
2	6
3	12
4	11
5	8
6	10
7	2
8	5

H-H COSY (Vicinal)

2	3
3	5
7	8

automatically derived

^{1}H-NMR

NO.	PPM	INT.
1	1.10	24
2	1.15	8
3	1.70	8
4	1.80	12
5	2.10	8
6	2.30	12
7	6.20	4
8	7.30	4

Macrocomponent

α,β-unsturated carbonyl group
(with ^{13}C-NMR signal assignments)

FIGURE 6. Input data of β-Ionone for CHEMICS.

the assignments and utilized during the structure generation procedure with usual macrocomponent processing. Using all the underlined data in Figure 6, CHEMICS generates 6 candidate structures with the corresponding NMR assignments (Figure 7). Some results of CHEMICS executions with 2D NMR data are summarized in Figure 8. The numbers in the left column [(A)Basic version] indicate results by basic CHEMICS without 2D NMR data. On the other hand, the numbers in the right column [(B)2D version] are the results with 2D NMR data and the support of other functions.

The following example deals with an unknown compound a part of which is already identified from chemical or instrumental analysis made by the chemist [10]. The remaining part is generated automatically and connected to the known part to form the whole structure. Let's assume an unknown compound which has the molecular formula $C_{17}H_{17}O_6Cl$ and comprises a

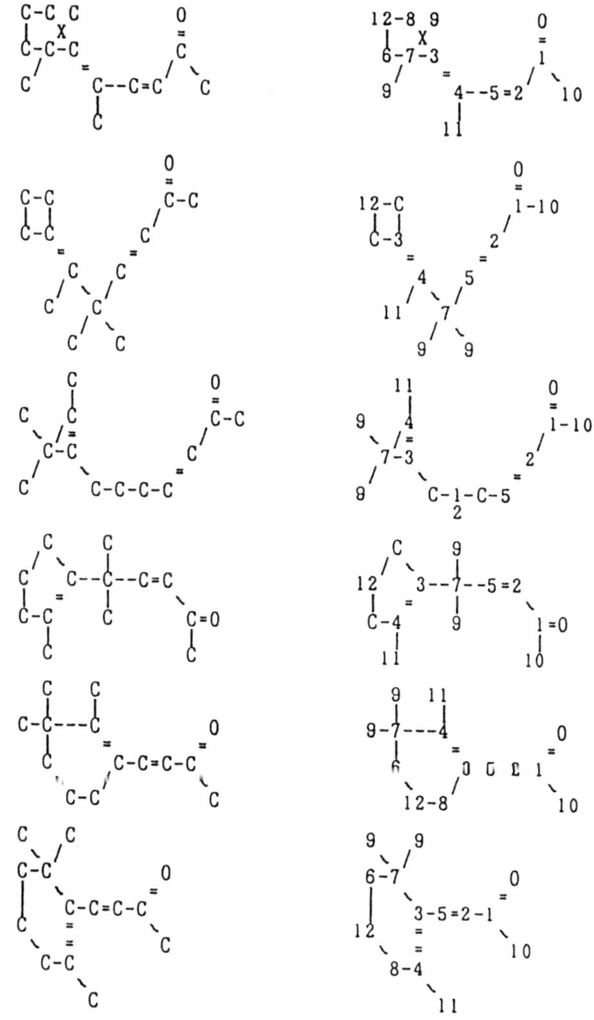

CMR CHEMICAL SHIFT		NO.	PMR CHEMICAL SHIFT -- 90 MHz
197.60	(C)	1	
142.30	(CH)	2	6.20 -(1H)
135.70	(C)	3	
135.20	(C)	4	
131.20	(CH)	5	7.30 -(1H)
39.40	(CH2)	6	1.50 -(2H)
33.70	(C)	7	
33.10	(CH2)	8	2.10 -(2H)
28.30	(CH3)	9	1.10 -(6H)
26.80	(CH3)	10	2.30 -(3H)
21.30	(CH3)	11	1.80 -(3H)
18.30	(CH2)	12	1.70 -(2H)

FIGURE 7. Analytical result of data in Figure 6 by CHEMICS.

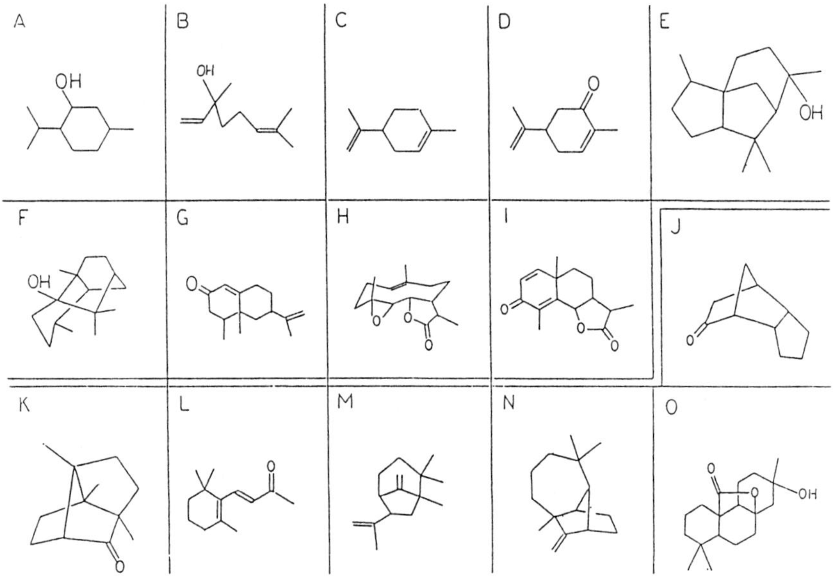

	MOLECULAR FORMULA	NO. OF CANDIDATE STRUCTURES (A) Basic ver.	(B) 2D ver.	KINDS OF NMR SIGNAL PAIR
A	C10 H20 O	219 →→	1	ALL C-C, C-H
B	C10 H18 O	48 →→	1	ALL C-C
C	C10 H16	151 →→	1	ALL C-C
D	C10 H14 O	1,673 →→	1	ALL C-C
E	C15 H26 O	115,870 →→	1	ALL C-C
F	C15 H26 O	297,162 →→	1	ALL C-C
G	C15 H22 O	2,969,100 →→	1	ALL C-C
H	C15 H22 O3	> 692 →	3	ALL C-C
I	C15 H18 O3	> 25,814 →	1	ALL C-C
J	C10 H14 O	440 →→	12 → 8	PART C-C, C-H
K	C12 H18 O	3,953 →→	4	PART C-C
L	C13 H20 O	1,417 →→	36 → 6	PART C-C & H-H, C-H
M	C15 H24	4,450 →→	7	PART C-C
N	C15 H24	13,413 →→	3	PART C-C
O	C18 H28 O3	> 37,927 →	3	PART C-C

FIGURE 8. Summary of CHEMICS execution with 2D NMR data.

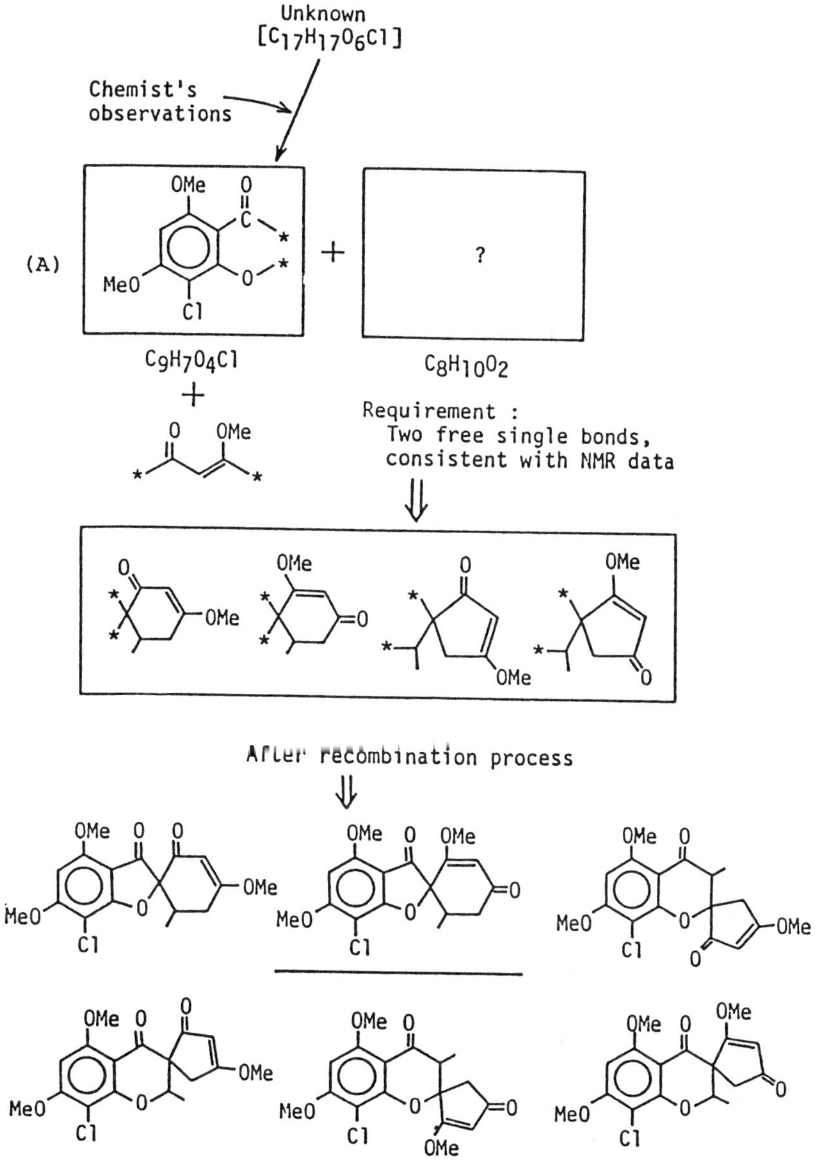

FIGURE 9
The conditions and results for elucidation of the counterpart and the candidates provided by connection of counterpartstructures with host (A).

known substructure, denoted as A, as the host part (Figure 9). If the composition of A, *i.e.,* $C_9H_7O_4Cl$, and the number of its single bonds, *i.e.,* two, are entered in the computer, calculation will be performed on the assumption that the remaining part (counterpart) has the composition of $C_8H_{10}O_2$ and two single bonds. Analysis of this compound by CHEMICS in terms of its molecular formula, ^{1}H -NMR and ^{13}C -NMR produces 65 components as components consistent with these data. However, of the 65, 16 components are not consistent with input data in consideration of constructing the counterpart, with the remaining 49 components being left for construction of the counterpart that is expressed as $C_8H_{10}O_2$. Thus, the operation, which is performed with reference to NMR data, generates four substructures as candidates for the counterpart, as shown in Figure 9. Finally, the four are connected with the host part (A) to generate six structures. The underlined structure correctly represents the structure of griseofulvin used as the unknown compound, as listed in Figure 9. Recently, it has been possible to utilize 2D NMR data to elucidate the counterpart structure.

The current CHEMICS has some optional analytical modules as described above. However, the most important aspect of CHEMICS is that the basic CHEMICS generates all possible structures consistent with input data without missing correct solutions and that all the optional modules mentioned so far are designed logically and utilized on this premise. In conclusion, it is clear that the current CHEMICS is a useful and powerful tool in structure elucidation problems.

REFERENCES

[1] Funatsu, K., Miyabayashi, N., Sasaki, S., *J. Chem. Info. Comput. Sci.*, 28, 19 (1988).

[2] Kudo, Y., Sasaki, S., *J.Chem.Doc.*, 14, 200 (1974)

[3] Sasaki, S., Abe, H., Hirota, Y., Ishida, Y., Kudo, Y., Ochiai, S., Saito, K., Yamasaki, T., *J. Chem. Inf. Comput. Sci.*, 18, 211 (1978)

[4] Fujiwara, I., Okuyama, T., Yamasaki, T., Abe, H., Sasaki, S., *Anal. Chim. Acta* 133, 527 (1981).

[5] Abe, H., Fujiwara, I., Nishimura, T., Okuyama, T., Kida, T., Sasaki, S., *Computer Enhanced Spectroscopy*, 1, 55 (1983).

[6] Funatsu, K., Del Carpio, C.A., Sasaki, S., *ibid.*, 3, 119 (1986).
Funatsu, K., Del Carpio, C.A., Sasaki, S., *ibid.*, 3, 133 (1986).
Funatsu, K., Del Carpio, C.A., Sasaki, S., Fresenius, Z., *Anal. Chem.*, 324, 750 (1986).

[7] Funatsu, K., Susuta, Y., Sasaki, S., *J. Chem. Info. Comput. Sci.*, 29, 6 (1989).

[8] Funatsu, K., Susuta, Y., Sasaki, S., *Anal. Chim. Acta* 220, 155 (1989)
[9] Funatsu, K., Katsumi, H., Sasaki, S., *Computer Enhanced Spectroscopy*, 3, 87 (1986).
[10] Funatsu, K., Susuta, Y., Sasaki, S., *Pure Appl. Chem.*, 61, 609 (1989)

EXTRACTING GENERIC KNOWLEDGE FROM SPECIFIC STRUCTURE/ SPECTRUM DATA BANKS. CASE OF A ^{13}C NMR DATA BANK

Michel Carabédian and Jacques-Emile Dubois
Institut de Topologie et de Dynamique des Systèmes
associé au CNRS, Université de Paris VII,
Paris, France

INTRODUCTION

In structural analysis, interpreting spectroscopic properties of molecules for their indentification is largely based on empirical knowledge. This latter is generally provided by modeling structural information (St) and spectral information (Sp) drawn from a more or less extensive data bank. We discuss here the evaluation of such models of knowledge and their relevance with regard to applications with the help of the ^{13}CNMR DARC PLURIDATA.$_{III}$ data bank ($^{13}CDP_{III}$, 16 000 structures, 195 000 $\delta^{13}C$) and of **ELCO** structural primitives (**E**nvironment that is **L**imited **C**oncentric and **O**rdered) from the EPIOS system.

GLOBAL DESCRIPTION OF RAW ST.SP INFORMATION

The advantage of the models studied is measured by their capacity to describe the reference population whose contents they formalize. To this end, a **global image** of the available raw information concretely represents the variability of the relationships implicitly managing this St.Sp information. This global image is obtained thanks to a **holograph** $H(\delta,E)$, linking each $\delta^{13}C$ value to its occurrence in the set reference spectra (Figure 1). Each occurrence of a $\delta^{13}C$ corresponds to an E environment of a ^{13}C nucleus in the reference structures.

The profile of this holograph globally characterizes the $^{13}CDP_{III}$ data bank and all its structures. It is taken as the reference to which representations taken from the SRS and MRS models described below are compared.

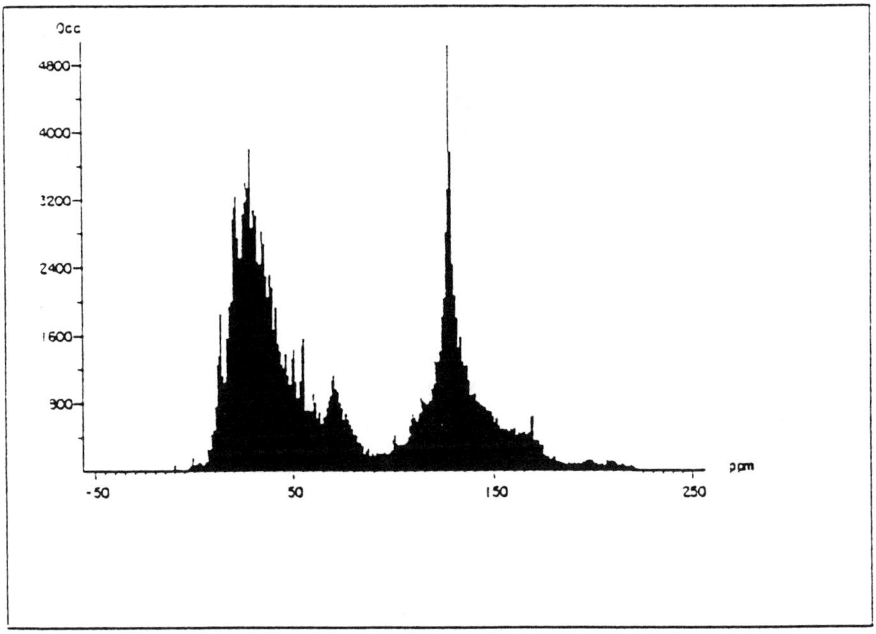

FIGURE 1

SIMPLE-RESONANCE SUBSPECTRA/SUBSTRUCTURE (SRS) MODEL

In ^{13}C NMR, relationships between structural and spectral information are classically elucidated by **Simple-Resonance Subspectra/Substructure (SRS)** rules. Substructures, freezing part of the active environment of a ^{13}C nucleus, are characterized by the variation range of the $\delta^{13}C$ behavior of the latter. The precision of this model is based exclusively on the specificity of the substructures characterized: the more specific the substructure, the more restricted is the variation interval of its central carbon.

Different types of $ELCO_i$, EPIOS structural primitives, are used to illustrate this influence of substructure specificity in the SRS model.

$ELCO_A$	$C_{Fo} - C_{A1}$
$ELCO_b$	$C_{Fo} - C_{A1}=$
$ELCO_B$	$C_{Fo} - C_{A1}=C$

The holographs $H(\Delta\delta, ELCO_i)$, represented in Figure 2, link each $\delta^{13}C$

value to the number of $ELCO_i$ whose $\Delta\delta^{13}C$ behavior is compatible with this value (*i.e.*, $\delta^{13}C \in \Delta\delta^{13}C$). With the $ELCO_A$ (Figure 2), the profile of the reference distribution $H(\delta,E)$ is greatly deformed, in particular by the shifting of the peaks (75 and 155 ppm instead of 30 and 130 ppm) and by the relative sinking of the first of them.

These deformations disappear with the $ELCO_b$ (Figure 2) which, despite their generic character, reveal the secondary peak ($\delta^{13}C$ 70 ppm) of the initial distribution. The description is again improved with the $ELCO_B$ (Figure 2). However, in this latter case the numerous primitives associated with each $\delta^{13}C$ ($\geq$800), increase the ambiguity of the modeled knowledge. This multiplication of primitives leads to an amplification of the combinatorial difficulties linked to their exploitation.

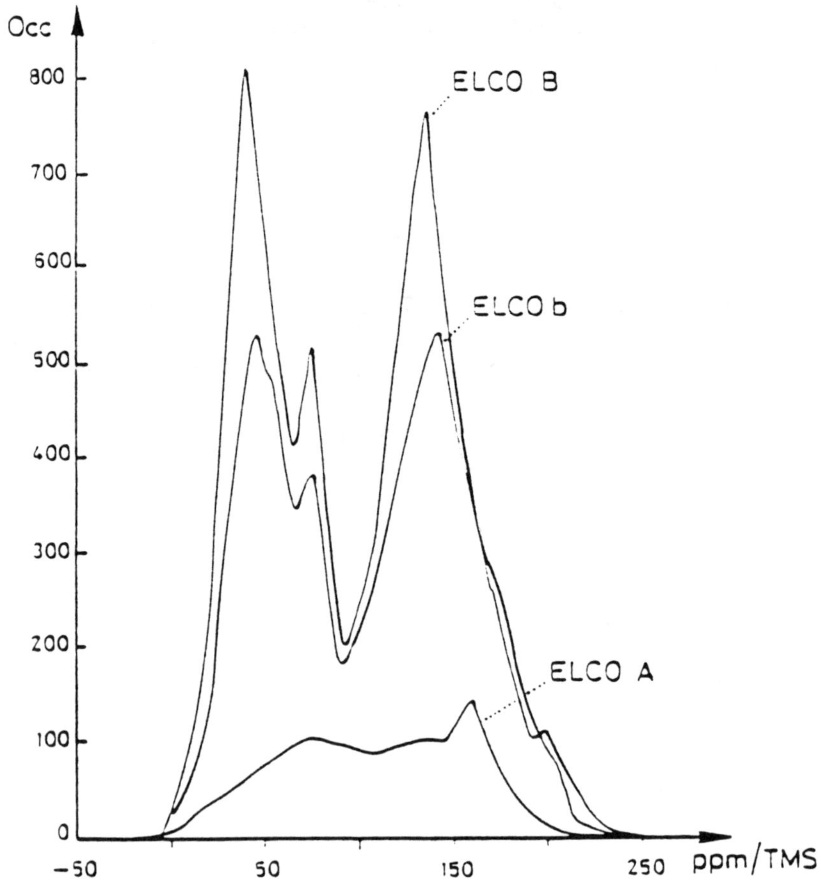

FIGURE 2

MULTI-RESONANCE SUBSPECTRA/SUBSTRUCTURE (MRS)

The Multi-Resonance Subspectra/Substructure (MRS) model avoids the linkage between its precision and substructure specificity. It relies on the use of $\delta^{13}C$ behavior of all the carbons of $ELCO_b$ primitives. Chemical shifts are no longer considered singly but in couples ($\delta^{13}C_{Fo}$, $\delta^{13}C_{Ai}$). They localized an $ELCO_b$ in a **multidimensional space** $\delta_{Fo} \times \delta_{Ai}$ each of whose four components is a **correlation plane**, $\delta_{Fo} \times \delta_{A1}$,.., $\delta_{Fo} \times \delta_{A4}$, assigned to the corresponding carbon couples (C_{Fo}, C_{A1}),.. ..,(C_{Fo}, C_{A4}) of the $ELCO_b$. The double viewpoint linked to the carbon couples (C_{Fo},C_{Ai}) extends perception of the environment of the $ELCO_b$ and organizes it according to the directions indicated by these couples. These directions are used to represent the holographs H($\Delta\delta_{Fo}$, $\Delta\delta_{Ai}$, $ELCO_b$) associating each chemical shift couple ($\delta^{13}C_{Fo}$, $\delta^{13}C_{Ai}$) of the correlation planes with the number of compatible $ELCO_b$ (*i.e.*, $\delta^{13}C_{Fo} \in \Delta\delta^{13}C_{Fo}$ and $\delta^{13}C_{Ai} \in \Delta\delta^{13}C_{Ai}$). Figure 3 shows the distribution of MRS relationships on the $\delta_{Fo} \times \delta_{Ai}$ level. The modeled knowledge is enriched by including this supplementary information, linking the $ELCO_b$ more closely to their structural environments.

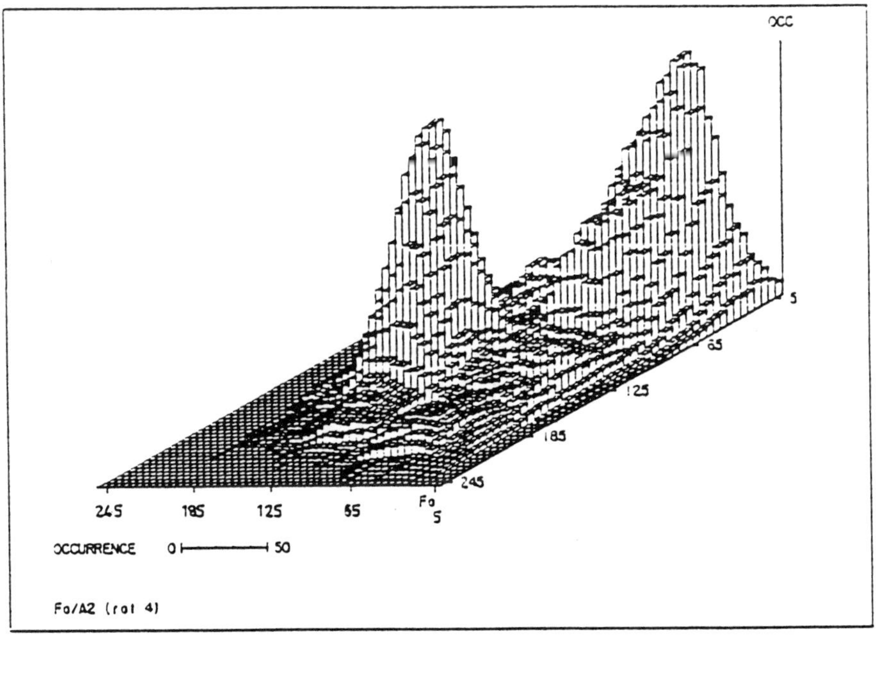

FIGURE 3

CONCLUSION

With the increasing power of computers, knowledge models can be more complex, and voluminous databases are managed by more intelligent DBMS. The **multidimensional MRS model** makes it possible to transcend the representation of knowledge in ^{13}C NMR by a more ambitious formalism than that of the classical SRS model. This knowledge is enriched with St and/or Sp information unknown to the SRS model. Extracting information from an NMR data bank with the MRS model and the use of holographs will greatly influence applications of computer aided molecular systems.

By defining a multidimensional space for knowledge representation, the way is opened for new strategies for exploiting it in these various applications.

MATERIALS PROPERTIES DATABASES

GLOBAL TRENDS IN MATERIALS DATA MANAGEMENT: REGIONAL OVERVIEW, WESTERN EUROPE

Keith W. Reynard
Wilkinson Consultancy Services
Stable Cottage, Broad Lane
Newdigate, Surrey RH5 5AT
United Kingdom

The activities in Western Europe have been dominated for several years by the CEC Materials Databank Demonstrator Programme, which ran from 1984 to 1989. By increasing awareness of what was happening and what is needed this program has had a major effect on the development of data banks in Europe. But there are other important developments and a better understanding of the problems that have be addressed as a result of the many national and international activities.

No one should ignore what goes on outside their region. Through the activities of CODATA, VAMAS and ASTM in addition to the well publicized work of the CEC the community of those active and in contact with each other on a regular basis is truly international. So the development from the US of the STN network and MPDN within it is as significant as the creation of a new initially local disk based system.

It is not only the large data banks that influence the market and the user. Small enterprising organizations are as important. They frequently provide a personal service in support of the data which a user now regards as an essential part of the value of the data service. The experience gained in building the small data bank and providing what the users require is itself of great value to larger organizations wishing to develop their own inhouse systems.

COMMISSION OF THE EUROPEAN COMMUNITIES

To a large extent the active individuals in the CEC have withdrawn to reflect on the past and to contemplate the future. They are developing their ideas for the next round whilst observing the activities of others. There is a gap between the end of the Demonstrator Programme and the beginning of whatever is to follow. That gap is certain to be twelve months and could be longer. It could be seen as bad planning, or as a beneficial respite.

The Demonstrator Programme came to a public end with a workshop held in Petten in December 1989. The proceedings and the conclusions drawn from the program and the workshop should soon be published by the European Commission. In retrospect it is clear that much has been learnt about the problems of providing access to a group of databases of disparate content and standard, in differing languages and serving different audiences. The exercise of hindsight, being the only certain human activity, also shows that were the program starting again now and not in 1984 much would be different. The political constraints would still be there. The choice of databases might well have been different had the development of the hardware been foreseen. These developments, particularly the explosion of the numbers of high speed desktop computers with hard disks with capacities between 40 and 300Mb, have changed for many the preferred choice of the means of presenting or conveying data from the vendor to the user. Better telecommunications, more international online services all have their effect on the expectations of users and on what the data bank managers should and do set out to supply to their users.

What did the Demonstrator Programme achieve? Very little that is tangible and that is still at the front of users minds, but a great deal that has contributed to the understanding of the problems that are yet to be solved. It stimulated the market and this after all is what DGXIII should be doing. Its most noticeable lack has been the omission of any work on the 'connections' required between data and application as opposed to data and user.

At the time of the first Petten Workshop in 1984 [1] I drew attention to the commercial success of the Physical Property Data Service (PPDS) managed by the Institution of Chemical Engineers in the UK. This provides a data service for the properties of pure substances and their mixtures. I drew attention to it because from its early days it set out to make it easy for the user to feed the data into design programs. Only now is this aspect being addressed by the materials data world. Admittedly the problems are more difficult because materials data modeling is so much harder and the user expects so much more from the provider of mechanical properties.

The other important aspect that has just begun to be understood properly is the process of 'material selection'. Again the present understanding results as much from the exploration of possibilities within the Demonstrator Programme as from any other source. However one should look back to the warnings from Waterman at the Schluchsee Workshop [2]. He suggested that material selection was only very rarely a blank check exercise and almost always an incremental process. The other realization that the process is not one of selection at all but a rejection process was an idea first applied to the materials world at the first ASTM Symposium on the Computerization of Materials Property Data in Philadelphia in 1987 [3]. In fact almost all so called selection processes are in reality processes of elimination.

The role of DGXIII of the CEC responsible for the Demonstrator Programme is 'the development of the market' not the development of the products. So DGXIII should not be taken to task for not doing what it should not have done. It succeeded in that many more engineers and materials scientists are aware of the problems and have been given cause and opportunity to discuss them. The work has also stimulated activity in the US and in Japan.

Where will it go next? The end of Programme review [4] sets out some but not all of the possibilities.

UNITED KINGDOM

The actions of the Department of Trade and Industry (DTI) or rather the implementation of the policies of successive Secretaries of State have been governed by two principles. The first is to avoid 'near market' activities and the second to stimulate the UK industry to take action on its own or in a European context.

This has meant that the scope for the direct support of the development of the materials database activity in the UK has been limited. The DTI decided that its most important role was in making industry, and especially the SME's, aware of what data, information and expertise was already available in the UK. This it has tried to do first by the PROMAT program of exhibitions and seminars and following that the Materials Matter Programme. For this latter some excellent video films were made that are both lively and technically informative. There is nevertheless some dissatisfaction with the result. A recent survey showed that one of the main reasons for the lack of use of new and advanced materials was lack of knowledge of cost, processability and performance. This came as no surprise to one employed in the dissemination of engineering design data for over fifteen years. The reasons for ignorance are many, ranging from wilful blindness, to obscure and unhelpful information sources and overselling of the virtues of new materials. The banner headline that greeted the surveys findings [5] suggested that awareness of new materials was worse now than before the DTI programs started. It could be argued that the nature of the questions asked led to this result. It could also be argued that now engineers in the UK are more aware of their ignorance and know where to go for answers when they need them. Knowledge, as Dr Johnson said, is as much about where to find information as actually having it.

The development of services providing a referral point for advice has been noticeable in the UK. The British Plastics Federation provides one such service answering over 20 000 enquiries a year. The DTI in collaboration with the Design Council has set up another, the Materials Information Centre, this already handles over 1000 a month. The World Metal Index based in the public library in Sheffield has an extensive resource on metals standards from all over the world and provides information to subscribers round the world. Many other research associations and centres also provide advice [6].

The most original work in the UK and in a stream of thought independent of all this is that of Ashby [7]. Taking very much the engineering designers' approach he has produced a series of 'maps' that aid the selection of materials not by single properties taken one or more at a time but by the engineering relationships of properties and the duty required of the component. These maps are still being developed and have recently been computerized.

What next? Perhaps the next stage of the Materials Matter activity will provide solutions for the delivery of information appropriate to present needs and technology.

FRANCE

A great deal of the activity in France [8] has been stimulated by CODATA France, the National Committee. Several very well attended and successful conferences have been held on databases and on composites. They have published a directory of French databases [9]. The work on the materials databases at CETIM has been partly funded from the tax on industry. There has of course been the very active participation in the Demonstrator

Programme and its workshops and seminars.

The unique feature of the French scene is the use of the Minitel system to promote the use of online services of all kinds but including material databases. This will be described in detail in the paper by Marx [10]. Due to its introduction millions of Frenchmen have no inhibitions about the use of online services, an achievement of enormous value and potential power.

COMITE EUROPEEN DE NORMALISATION

The approach of 1992 and its consequences for trade within the EEC has greatly increased the activity and size of the Comité Européen de Normalisation (CEN). Many standards dealing with products are required to be developed from existing national standards to reach the status of European Standards which will apply to the 12 countries of the European Community and the additional 6 of the European Free Trade Area (EFTA). For some subjects the pace is too quick and it seems very likely that some poor standards may result which will be worse than no standard at all. High on this list are designation systems for materials. Some comments on what is happening and the problems that may result are described in Reference 11.

Nevertheless the reduction in the number of standards from the multiplicity of national standards to the uniqueness of a European Standard is something from which all can benefit.

GERMANY

Many materials databases exist in Germany [12] and some were amongst the earliest publicly available examples. The newer ones have learned lessons from the pioneers and are now known and marketed throughout Europe. A particularly interesting example is the CAMPUS initiative. BASF, Bayer, Hoechst and Hüls decided to put together a database of agreed property values for a range of plastics which they all produced. By this means their customers could no longer accuse each one of them of telling a different story about the same material. This now exists on one disk and is being expanded as more companies join the project. A review of activities in Germany is provided in Reference 13.

OTHER EUROPEAN WORK

There is much fine work going on in many other countries. Some of it is well described in other papers in this conference and more can be found in the proceedings of other meetings [1-3, 14-16]. The motives of the

European Aluminium Federation in setting out to produce a database of the properties of the most common aluminium alloys are similar to those of the CAMPUS project. The work was described in Reference 17.

VAMAS

The Western European input into the Versailles Project on Advanced Materials and Standards is large. Projects on materials designations, materials data modeling, materials data exchange, data evaluation and the classification of advanced ceramics are in various stages of progress. The VAMAS Bulletin [18] provides an outline of what is happening with points of contact.

THE FUTURE

The matching of the inhouse data service [19], necessary to handle the data of high commercial value to its owner, and external services is causing more time and effort to be expended on the problems of data exchange. Increasingly the need to link data to design in a reliable way is revealing new problems. This topic will be addressed in the forthcoming CODATA/CEC conference due to take place at the Institute for Advanced Materials in Petten, The Netherlands in late 1991. A problem that is not the immediate one of the exchange format itself, but caused by its use, is the removal of the expert human interface that provides a check on the questions asked and the data transferred. Expertise and knowledge have yet to be built into the computerized stores of information sufficiently well.

What is also needed now is a study by someone with the most perfect crystal ball of the relationships that will develop in the next five to ten years between the various conveyors of information; the human expert, the hard copy, the floppy disc, the optical disc, and the online service; and the user.

The main danger that the user ignores at his peril is not that of the accuracy and reliability of the data themselves but the problems caused by the total but blind computer retrieval of the information in response to insufficiently precise, inaccurate or misleading instructions. When these data are then passed on blindly as in the linking of a data bank to a finite element program there are potential problems. To that end developments are to take place to provide front-end interfaces that will hopefully respond like an expert, providing checks and warnings of errors and ambiguities that could occur. How shall we capture corporate experience of in-service use of materials so that each generation of new engineers and scientists does not have to repeat the same painful learning experience?

BIBLIOGRAPHY

[1] *Factual Material Data Banks* Proceedings of a CEC Workshop held to provide input to the planning of the CEC Materials Demonstrator Programme. JRC Petten, The Netherlands, 14 - 16 November 1984, Editors H.Kröckel, K.W.Reynard, G.Steven

[2] *Materials Data Systems for Engineering* Proceedings of a CODATA Workshop. Schluchsee, The Black Forest, Federal Republic of Germany, 22 - 27 September 1985, Editors J.H.Westbrook, H.Behrens, G.Dathe, S.Iwata

[3] *Computerization and Networking of Materials and Databases* Proceedings of the 1st International Symposium sponsored by ASTM Committee E-49, Philadelphia, PA, USA, 2 - 4 November 1987, Editors J.S.Glazman and J.R.Rumble, Jr. ASTM STP 1017.

[4] *Summary Report on the Evaluation of the Materials Data-Bank Demonstrator Programme of the Commission of the European Communities*, MAT-EVA 1, prepared by N.Waterman for DGXIII, CEC, August 1990

[5] *Survey Reveals Decline in Materials Knowledge*, Eureka, July 1990, pp 4-8

[6] *UK Materials Information Sources*, 2nd edition, K.W.Reynard, The Design Council, Haymarket, London, to be published 1991

[7] *On the Engineering Properties of Materials*, M.F.Ashby, Acta Metallurgica, Vol.37, No. 5, pp1273-1293, 1989

[8] *Development and Coordination of Materials Data Banks in France*, B.Marx in Reference 15

[9] *Guide des Banques de Donnees Factuelles Françaises sur les Materiaux*, 1989, Editor F.Libmann, CODATA France DBMIST/MENJS, Paris, France, ISBN 2-907275-01-1

[10] *Access to Factual Materials Databases Through MINITEL*, B.Marx, 12th International CODATA Conference, Columbus, 1990

[11] *Materials Designation Systems, their Problems and Possible Solutions*, K.W.Reynard in Reference 15

[12] *Verzeichnis Deutschsprachiger Werstoff-Informationssysteme*, August 1990, Editor Dipl.- Ing. Annette Winzer, Fachinformationszentrum Werkstoffe e.V., Berlin, Germany

[13] *Cooperation - a Good Chance for Industry in Setting up Materials Data Banks*, A.Brandstätter, in Reference 15

[14] *Computerized Materials Data Systems* Proceedings of a CODATA Workshop devoted to the discussion of problems confronting their development. The Fairfield Glade, TN, USA, 7 - 11 November 1982, Editors J.H.Westbrook and J.R.Rumble, Jr

[15] *Computerization and Networking of Materials and Databases* Proceedings of the 2nd International Symposium sponsored by ASTM Committee E-49, Lake Buena Vista, FL, USA, 29 November - 1

December 1989, Editors J.S.Glazman and J.R.Rumble, Jr. To be published as an ASTM STP 1991

[16] *How to Introduce Computerized Factual Materials Information - A Small Country Point of View*, A.E.Valkonen, 12th International CODATA Conference, Columbus, 1990

[17] *Aluselect - Engineering Property Data for Aluminium Alloys*, R.Sandström and P.Schönholzer, in Reference 15

[18] *VAMAS Bulletin*, published in January and July each year, National Physical Laboratory, UK

[19] *Knowledge-Based Material Selection in Design*, R.J.Bamkin, B.J.Piearcey, Materials and Design, Vol. 11, No. 1, pp 25-29, February 1990

CURRENT ACTIVITY IN NORTH AMERICA ON NUMERICAL DATABASES ON MATERIALS PROPERTIES

J.H. Westbrook
Brookline Technology
5 Brookline Road
Ballston Spa, NY 12302, U.S.A.

CHARACTERIZATION OF MATERIALS DATABASES BUILT OR BUILDING

There are of the order of 100 known materials databases now existing in North America, roughly half of which can be said to contain properties of engineering materials, the others being concerned with scientific information on pure elements and compounds (crystal structures, thermodynamic data, nuclear data, phase diagrams, etc.)[1] The builders/vendors can be categorized as information vendors, government agencies, commercial publishers, universities, and not-for profit institutions. Professional societies for the most part, have not been very aggressive in computerizing their reference data. Information vendors make publicly available about half of the presently known databases even though they may not have been the original developers. Through seminar presentations and workshops, some 30 of the 100 are known to be private materials databases, built by industrial concerns for their own internal use. This group includes mostly major companies such as GE, General Dynamics, Dow, DuPont, McDonnell-Douglas, Martin-Marietta, and Lockheed; it is probable that unpublicized activities by many smaller companies remain unlisted and uncounted.

---

[1] Several directories listing numeric databases with brief descriptions may be found in the references shown in Appendix A. Representative subsets, specifically focussed on materials, are given in the proceedings of recent materials data workshops cited in Appendix B.

Materials databases can also be characterized by several parameters: by the source of the data entered, by the type of information included, by the intended use of the data, and by the available access mode. This kind of characterization is shown in Table 1 with a single example listed for each sub-type of characterization. Any particular database can, of course, be characterized by more than one parameter; for example, data on commodity materials may be taken from manufacturers' literature to construct a database on PC-floppy intended for use in materials selection. As might be expected, there are more databases extant of the sort in the hypothetical example just cited than is the case for evaluated data on properties of materials intended for designer use. The author is not aware of any database or system of databases which would serve the needs of a researcher wanting to "design" (*i.e.,* synthesize) a new material of desired characteristics from fundamental data on molecular structure, crystal structure, bond strength, electronic structure, microstructure, phase morphology, etc., although individual databases exist in certain of these sub-topical areas. With reference to access mode, it may be observed that many databases are available in multiple modes at the user's choice and that increasing use is being made of CD-ROM, especially for very large databases, *e.g.,* specifications, codes, and standards, where the need is for referral only, in a non-interactive mode.

NEEDS BEING SERVED

Twenty years ago or so when materials databases were first being built, the primary application objective was a relatively crude first cut at materials selection. Increasingly, as other aspects of engineering and manufacturing have become computerized, attention is being drawn to materials databases for materials optimization, component design, process optimization and materials synthesis as well as to databases on materials-related phenomenology, *e.g.,* corrosion, tribology and welding. Such developments have put new emphasis on data quality and reliability and comprehensiveness of coverage within the database or system of databases. In the U.S. these changing needs are reflected in the proceedings of the Intl. Conference on Data Engineering held biennially in Los Angeles since 1984, in the ASTM International Symposia of 1987 and 1989 [1,2], and in two focussed studies commissioned by National Institute of Standards and Technology that review data and database needs for high-tech materials [3] and for analytical instruments [4]. These more sophisticated applications have highlighted a number of problems with materials databases.

TABLE I

CATEGORIZATION OF DATABASE CHARACTERISTICS

Characteristic	Access Mode	Use	Type of Information	Data Source
	on-line	**materials selection**	**properties of commodity materials**	**handbook**
	EDEAC	METSEL/2	PLASPEC	MILHBK-5
	PC-floppy	**component design**	**material properties for design**	**test program**
	DIPPR	SPRING DESIGN	M-S COMPOSITES dbs[2]	STEELTUF
sub-types	**CD-ROM**	**materials design**	**specification referral**	**literature**
with	ASME	none	ASTM STANDARDS	MDF-1
examples[3]	B&PV CODE			
	mag tape	**process control**	**phenomenological data**	
	Cen-BASE	CUTDATA	ACTIS	
	MATERIALS			
	in-house only			
	WEAR DATA			

[2] constituents db, laminae db, laminate db

[3] further details of the databases listed may be found in Appendices A or B

PROBLEMS WITH MATERIALS DATABASES

Despite the large interest and activity in building and using materials databases, there remain many serious problems which to date have prevented their achieving their full potential in Computer-Aided Engineering. These problems include those of size, scope, reliability, access, data capture from print form, interfaces to application programs, and standardization. These will be discussed in turn.

Size and Scope - Most available databases are extremely restricted in size and scope, ranging from 10's of kbytes to a few Mbytes at most, and may be concerned with only a dozen or so materials to several hundred. In almost no instance does the user have access via a single database or system of databases to a truly comprehensive range of engineering materials and all their important engineering properties. By far most of the engineering materials databases extant concern mechanical properties of metallic materials, although there are a few on polymers and on composites. In addition, some few databases are narrowly focussed on such topics as environmental data, toxicology, materials stability, ferroelectric data, and dielectric behavior.

Reliability - Many of the databases now available include data of doubtful reliability and indeterminate origin. Several are admittedly no more than compilations of numbers from manufacturer's literature showing nominal or typical values of certain parameters. Considerable dissatisfaction has been expressed in this regard with reference to some of the larger PC and on-line materials databases offered commercially because their reliability is such as to limit their use to preliminary selection of candidate materials and in no way allows actual design calculations. Machine-readable versions of carefully evaluated data from NIST's Standard Reference Data Program are beginning to appear but are so far restricted to scientific data as opposed to engineering data. Other printed compilations of evaluated engineering data, *e.g.*, MPC and ASTM data publications, are only just now beginning to be computerized. In any event, all data in any computer file should be (but are rarely) fully characterized as to quality -- whatever that level may be. Furthermore, definitions of various quality levels need to be formulated and standardized.

Access and Access Mode - Knowing of the existence of a machine-readable database of interest does not guarantee that it is or can be accessible to prospective users. As mentioned earlier, about half the extant materials databases are not available to the general public because of national security issues, proprietarial concerns, or nuisance factors. Even if in principle these data were made available for sharing, technical barriers remain. Many of the private data files were developed in an engineering environment on VAX machines rather than on IBM, the *de facto* PC standard, or on Macintosh, attractive for its graphics capability and user-friendly features. Moreover, all use differing file structures, database management systems and terminologies.

Some databases are available in several modes, others in only a single mode. In general we do not yet have easy, automatic ways of up-loading or down-loading of databases in different modes nor does a given terminal or workstation accommodate a variety of tape drives, floppies of different sizes and storage densities, CD-ROM, etc.

Data Capture (*i.e.,* Computerization) - Low priority has thus far been accorded by governments, publishers and professional societies to the conversion of archived primary and reference data from the print form of pre-computer days to today's machine-readable form. This situation arises from both technical and economic difficulties. From a technical point-of-view, capture of a printed data exhibit (be it tabular or graphic) only as a raster-scanned "bit map" for the computer is only partially satisfactory as it does not allow selective editing, extraction of values or data manipulation. Furthermore, much of the needed metadata information from the exhibit is implicit, rather than explicit, lying in the structural logic, layout, type face, symbols, footnotes, unstated "standard conditions" etc. which are not necessarily included in the bit map approach to computerization. Sci-Tech Knowledge Systems has gone a long way toward solving these problems via an electronic template methodology applicable to both tables and graphs that have been described in a series of papers [5-8]. They have further developed software programs that can operate on a captured exhibit record to separate it into individual canonical work records which can be subsequently compiled into a searchable database. With the present state-of-the-art just described, conversion costs for printed data exhibits are of the order of $50 per exhibit. While such a figure may be acceptable for incorporation of a few critical exhibits into a computerized system, it clearly is uneconomic for the conversion *in toto* of a handbook or reference work that may contain thousands of tables and graphs. Yet, the possibility of a reduction in capture costs by a factor of 5 to 10 seems feasible, using automatic scanning and machine-recognition technologies, combined with the electronic template methodology already in hand.

Application Program Interfaces - Computer-Aided Engineering (CAE) now has at its disposal a broad variety of design and process optimization packages in such areas as beam design, fatigue life prediction, and electro-magnetic design or heat treatment of steel, machinability of metals and injection molding of plastics. Yet in all these cases, rather than for the programs to interface directly to a comprehensive database of relevant properties of a broad array of materials, the materials data requisite for the application of those programs must be input at the keyboard on an *ad hoc* basis. The reasons for this lack of integration of data and application programs are manifold: poor communication between the materials information community and the CAE community, inadequate breadth of scope of existing databases with regard to materials and properties, absence of information on the effects of key independent variables, and inadequate standardization in several areas as will next be discussed.

Standardization - There are enormous data and software standardization problems to be overcome before the most effective use can be made of material data via the computer, even with regard to data already in machine-readable form. These problems embrace materials and materials designations, terminology, test methods, test data reporting, database management systems, and the data structures themselves. In the US, ASTM, through its Committee E49 [9-11], is playing a leading role both in formulating standards which will promote uniformity and interchangability and in specifying minimal levels of acceptability of data. While E-49 initially focussed its attention on standards for describing engineering materials and data formats for engineering properties in computerized systems, the committee's work has recently been broadened to include standards for computer representation of chemical information on materials, such as nomenclature, structure, as well as analytical data. In both areas, engineering and chemical materials, the situation is now such that not only are separate individual databases unable to effectively interchange information and also require idiosyncratic user interfaces, but even those related and complementary databases, which have been connected into a so called network or information system, often suffer the same limitations [12].

ECONOMIC AND BUSINESS ISSUES

These matters have been reviewed in general terms by Rumble [13], but here are best discussed in reference to five particular systems, familiar to the author, and which are perhaps the most advanced business-wise in the materials data field:

Vendor	Database Product
ASM Int'l	MetSel/2 (Mat.DB)
Technical Database Services	Numerica
STN/CAS	MPD Network
Info Dex/J. Wiley	CenBASE/Materials 1990
Canadian Institute of Scientific and Technical Information	CAN/SND

MetSel/2 (Mat.DB) - This system is a PC-based system consisting of a database management program coupled with many sets of data on floppy disks [14]. A companion engineering graphics software package called EnPlot enables the user to plot data, save graphical displays and analyze graphs with non-linear curve-fitting techniques. Currently the MetSel/2 database is contained on over 50 360k floppy disks. Some alloy families, *e.g.*, titanium alloys are contained on one or two disks, others such as structural alloys may require 8 or 10. MetSel/2 has the potential to cover up to 40 properties for as many as 20 different tempers, environments, or temperatures; typically only 4-10 kbytes of data are stored for each material.

Initially most of the data were drawn selectively from the ASM Metals Handbook by ASM staff. More recently, materials producers have been invited to computerize their proprietary materials data in the MetSel/2 format. The resulting data disks are then distributed free to all users of the MetSel/2 system. Thus far, Inco, Cartech, Brush-Wellman, and Metallwerk Plansee have completed their databases. Still other organizations (*e.g.*, Battelle) are submitting data for MetSel/2 on a royalty basis. A future ASM program, under the general editorship of John Walter of GE R&D Center, consists of the compilation of a series of books on the Metallurgy, Structure and Properties of Industrial Alloys, emphasizing property data on individual alloys. These projects will be carried out by volunteer compilers and evaluators working under the direction of a topic editor and will result in both printed and machine-readable versions. Another future addition to MetSel/2 is a computerized edition of Woldman's Engineering Alloys.

The basic MetSel/2 program is sold at about $600, with the individual sets of data disks priced at about $300. The companion EnPlot graphics utility is about $400. ASM Int'l has more than 1000 users of MetSel/2 with about 10% overseas. It is claimed that the whole program is a profitable, self-supporting enterprise. This statement may be true on a current basis, but may overlook hidden subsidies and initial development costs. A third upgrade, called Mat.DB-3, reflecting broader materials coverage is now available at about the same price. Future plans call for networked and CD-ROM versions.

Numerica - This system is a cluster of databases and software packages in the chemical, chemical engineering, toxicology and environmental sciences areas [15]. Individual databases cover properties of specific chemical species and defined, multi-component mixtures and solutions. In contrast to MetSel/2 and MPD Network (to be described), the Numerica databases were largely developed by others, were not initially planned to work together and are only marketed by Technical Database Services. This limitation is partially overcome by inclusion of the free SYNDEX, a central synonym index file of chemical names in the Numerica cluster, the availability of the Hierarchical Tree Substructure Search System (TREE), and by the presence of several property estimation programs based on chemical structure and known properties of related species.

The currently offered products and services include both PC and on-line versions as well as some on magnetic tape. A basic subscription to Numerica is listed at $600, which includes SYNDEX and on-line access to 10 individual databases; usage fees are charged at $170/hour plus in many instances a $2.50 per hit charge. The products and services in the PC version range from $550 to $4000. Technical Database Services has been in business about 5 years, is independently owned and operated, and therefore is presumed to be profitable, without hidden subsidies. Few of the products they market were internally developed and individual arrangements have evidently been negotiated with the original developers in the majority of cases on a licensing or royalty basis.

MPD Network [16,17] - The National Materials Property Data Network, Inc. is a non-profit organization established in 1984 by the Materials Properties Council. It is supported by a group of over 60 corporate sponsors (a few overseas) who seek to create a network of on-line material property databases of high reliability. In mid-1987 the MPD Network became affiliated with the American Chemical Society's Chemical Abstracts Service (CAS) with the intent of providing access to MPD's databases on CAS's international scientific and technical information network, STN, with nodes in Columbus, Karlsruhe, and Tokyo. In addition, the CAS staff are working with the MPD staff on software enhancement, file design, data loading and marketing.

From the outset, MPD Network was conceived as a means of access to evaluated numeric data on material properties, contained in individual databases, but accessible by common interactive, user-friendly software and supported by common services such as unit conversion, thesauri, directories of other machine-readable data sources, etc. Its scope was intended to be comprehensive including metallic materials, composites, ceramics, polymers, electronic materials and welds and joints in all materials. Its property coverage was to be equally broad, covering mechanical properties, corrosion and electrochemical properties, physical properties, electrical and electronic properties, and applications and service experience.

The databases now on the network include:

MilHdbk 5	(design mechanical properties of metals)
ASMH	(properties of aerospace materials)
STEELTUF	(properties of pressure-vessel steels)
MARTUF	(properties of ship-building steels)
ALFRAC	(fracture toughness of aluminum alloys)
AAASD	(AA's Aluminum Standards and Data)
PLASPEC	(properties of commercial plastics)
MDF-1	(ASM's file of data from current literature)

To date, the Network has been accessible only by sponsoring companies and those contributing to building the Network and its supporting services. General public access will begin in 1990. No rate charges have yet been announced but several features of the charging schedule can be anticipated:

- deep discounts for corporate sponsors
- royalty payments to database contributors
- special arrangements for down-loading substantial subsets of the total set of files
- a charge structure which would include both on-line time and numbers of hits.

It is planned to continue to add other databases, other ancillary products and services, and continued updating, evaluation, and correction of individual data values

CenBase/Materials 1990 - This database [18] of more than 16 000 commercially available materials (thermoplastics, thermosets, elastomers, composites and metals) is derived entirely from the data sheets and other technical information supplied by about 200 manufacturers. A standardized data format is used in presenting up to 36 different physical properties as well as processing information, performance data, trade name, and supplier with address and phone number. All properties have been converted to the same notation and measurement units to facilitate comparisons. CenBASE is unique among commercial materials databases in two respects: first it is a joint venture between its developer, Info Dex, Inc. of Garden Grove, CA and an established publisher, John Wiley and Sons; second it is available in three different media - floppy disks, CD-ROM and print. The disk and CD-ROM versions are offered at about $1200 each, the 4-volume print set at about $600.

CAN/SND - CAN/SND is the Canadian Scientific Numeric Database Service which now allows access to six databases with a single phone call and in some instances with the potential for performing a variety of calculations.

The databases now available are all scientific in nature:

CRYSTDAT:	NBS Crystal Data Identification File
CRYSTIN:	Inorganic Crystal Structure Database
CRYSTMET:	NRCC Crystallographic Data File
CRYSTOR:	Cambridge Structural Database
FACT:	Facility for the Analysis of Chemical Thermodynamics
SPIR:	Search Program for Infrared Spectra

No information is available as to costs, numbers of users, or future plans for expanding the service. Other details may be found in the report of a recent Canadian Workshop [19], or are available from Dr. Gordon Wood in Ottawa, telephone (613) 993-3294.

CONCLUDING COMMENT

At present there is limited use of material property databases in the U.S. and Canada due to poor awareness of the availability of the existing databases and to the problems of narrow scope, indeterminate reliability, poor standardization, etc., discussed above under "Problems". The very high front-end costs of identifying data sources, of evaluating the data themselves, and of capturing printed data in machine-readable form have inhibited substantial projects in either the public, professional or private sectors. The modest involvement of the U.S. federal government, in contrast to the EEC and Japan, is also to be remarked. It has been confined thus far to some limited R&D and stimulative activities by NIST and to the building of special databases for the particular use of the mission agencies, rather than to any broad, coordinated national effort. Overall, the MPD Network with its breadth of vision, insistence on evaluated data, and array of user-friendly features in a harmonized, integrated network of compatible and complementary databases seems most likely of success. How soon their vision can be realized and whether the program will prove economic, only time will tell.

Finally, it may be remarked that databases, whether individual or a networked system thereof, are only an early step on the road to full electronic access to knowledge, a concept sometimes referred to as a knowledge system. In its ultimate development, such a system will incorporate not only databases with multi-media storage and output, but also enhanced and automated
interaction both with users and between system components as well as "expert systems" capabilities. This development will require that much more attention be paid to knowledge representation including: query parsing, semantic analysis of data files and exploitation of auxiliary terminological and directory files.

ACKNOWLEDGEMENT

The author is pleased to acknowledge the advice and assistance of Dr. W. Grattidge in the preparation of this paper. Portions of this paper were presented at the Concluding Workshop of the EEC Materials Database Demonstrator Programme, December 1989.

REFERENCES

[1] Glazman, J.S., and Rumble, J.R. Jr., eds., 1st Int'l. Symp., *Computerization and Networking of Materials Data Bases*, ASTM STP 1017, American Society for Testing and Materials, Philadelphia, PA 1989.

[2] Kaufman, J.G., and Glazman, J.S., eds., 2nd Int'l. Symp., *Computerization and Networking of Materials Databases*, ASTM STP xxxx, American Society for Testing and Materials, Philadelphia, PA 1990.

[3] "Data Needs for High-Tech Materials - A Report of a Meeting Held June 13, 1988," NDAB, National Academy Press 1989.

[4] "Automated Database Needs for the Computerized Instruments Industry-- A Report of a Meeting Held June 14, 1989," NDAB, National Academy Press 1989.

[5] Grattidge, W., Westbrook, J.H., Brown, C., and Novinger, W.B., "A Versatile Data Capture System for Archival Graphics and Text", from *Computer Handling and Dissemination of Data*, P.S. Glaeser, ed., Elsevier Science Publishers, B.V. (North Holland), CODATA 1987.

[6] Grattidge, W, "Capture of Published Materials Data", from 1st Int'l. Symp., *Computerization and Networking of Materials Data Bases*, ASTM STP 1017, J.S. Glazman, and J.R. Rumble, Jr., eds., American Society for Testing and Materials, Philadelphia, PA 1989, pp. 151-174.

[7] Grattidge, W., Lund, W.B., and Westbrook, J.H., "A Data Capture System for Printed Tabular Data", from Proc. 11th Int'l. CODATA Conf., Karlsruhe, FRG, *Scientific and Technical Data in a New Era*, P.S. Glaeser, ed., Hemisphere Press 1990.

[8] Westbrook, J.H. and Grattidge, W, "The Role of Metadata in the Design and Operation of a Materials Database" from 2nd Int'l. Symp., *Computerization and Networking of Materials Databases*, ASTM STP xxxx, J.G. Kaufman and J.S. Glazman, eds., American Society for Testing and Materials, Philadelphia, PA 1990.

[9] Kaufman, J.G., "Toward Standards for Computerizing Material Property Data - An Overview of the Activities of ASTM Committee E-49," from The Provision of Materials Property Data via Computerized Systems, A. Kozlov and E.F. Westrum, Jr., eds., *CODATA Bull.* 22(2) 1990, p 17.

[10] Rumble, J. Jr., "Standards for Materials Databases - ASTM Committee E-49", from 2nd Int'l. Symp., *Computerization and Networking of*

Materials Databases, ASTM STP xxxx, J.G. Kaufman and J.S. Glazman, American Society for Testing and Materials, Philadelphia, PA, 1990.

[11] Rumble, J. Jr., "Database Standards and Data Models - A Materials View and More" from Proc. 12th Int'l. CODATA Conf. Columbus, OH. 1990.

[12] Kaufman, J.G., "Issues in Networking Materials Databases," from Proc. 12th Int'l. CODATA Conf. Columbus, OH. 1990.

[13] Rumble, J.R. Jr., "Socioeconomic Barriers in Computerizing Materials Data," from 1st Int'l. Symp., *Computerization and Networking of Materials Data Bases*, ASTM STP 1017, J.S. Glazman and J.R. Rumble, Jr., eds., American Society for Testing and Materials, Philadelphia, PA, Society for Testing and Materials, Philadelphia, PA, 1989, pp. 216-226.

[14] Gall, T.L., Heller, M.E., and Wieda, W.A., "The Development of Mat.DB: A Computerized Materials Property Database System," from 2nd Int'l. Symp., *Computerization and Networking of Materials Databases*, ASTM STP xxxx, J.G. Kaufman and J.S. Glazman, eds., American Society for Testing and Materials, Philadelphia, PA, 1990.

[15] Green, M.R., "TDS/Numerica: Numeric Data in Chemistry and Engineering," from Proc. 12th Int'l. CODATA Conf. Columbus, OH. 1990.

[16] Kaufman, J.G., "The National Materials Property Data Network, Inc. - A Cooperative Approach to Reliable Performance Data," from 1st Int'l. Symp., *Computerization and Networking of Materials Data Bases*, ASTM STP 1017, J.S. Glazman, and J.R. Rumble, Jr., eds., American Society for Testing and Materials, Philadelphia, PA, 1989, pp. 55-62.

[17] Kaufman, J.G., "Online Access to Worldwide Sources of Materials Performance Data -The Materials Property Data (MPD) Network," from The Provision of Materials Property Data via Computerized Systems, A. Kozlov and E.F. Westrum, Jr., eds., *CODATA Bull.* 22 (2), 1990, p 7.

[18] Keblusek, M., "Technical Engineers Combine Desktop Publishing, Electronic Media for Large Databases," *PC Publishing*, March 1989, p22.

[19] Goyeche, S.M., "Workshop on Materials Property and Design Data Needs in Canada," ORTECH Intl., March 1989, 36pp.

APPENDIX A

Directories Including Materials Property Databases

Directory of Online Databases, Cuadra Associates, Santa Monica, Calif, (1985)

Williams, M.E., *Computer Readable Databases - A Directory and Data Sourcebook in Science, Technology & Medicine*, Elsevier (1989)

Data Base Directory, Knowledge Industry Publications/ASIS, White Plains, NY 750 pp. 1987

Rumble, J., Sauerwein, J., and Pennell, S., *Scientific and Technical Factual Databases for Energy Research and Development*, National Bureau of Standards, Report, March 1986.

Non-Bibliographic Data Banks in Science and Technology, S. Schwarz, D.G. Watson & Olov Alveldt, Eds., ICSU Press, distributed by UNIPUB, P.O.B. 1222, Ann Arbor, MI 48106 (1985)

EUSIDIC Database Guide 1983, (Learned Information Ltd., Oxford, England, 1983)

Hampel, V.E. et al., *An On-line Directory of Databases for Materials Properties*, UCRL-90276, Lawrence Livermore National Laboratory, May 1984.

Wawrousek, H., Westbrook, J.H., and Grattidge, W., "Data Sources of Mechanical and Physical Properties of Engineering Materials," *Physik Daten*, No. 30-1 (1989), Fachinformationszentrum - Karlsruhe, 1989, ~150 pp.

APPENDIX B

Materials Data Workshop Proceedings

Westbrook, J.H., and Rumble, J.R., eds., *Computerized Materials Data Systems*, Proceedings of the Materials Data Workshop, Fairfield Glade, TN, 1982, 133pp.

Rumble, J.R., and Westbrook, J.H., eds., *Computerizing Materials Data - A Workshop for the Nuclear Power Industry*, NBS SP 689, U.S. Government Printing Office, Washington, DC, January, 1985.

Krockel, H., Reynard, K., and Steven, G., eds., *Factual Material Data Banks*, CEC Workshop held at the Joint Research Center, Petten, The Netherlands, 14-16 November 1984, Office for Official Publications of the European Communities, Luxembourg, 1985.

Westbrook, J.H., Behrens, H., Dathe, G., and Iwata, S., eds., *Materials Data Systems for Engineering*, Proceedings of CODATA Workshop at Schluchsee, FRG, Fachinformationszentrum, Karlsruhe, (1986), 189pp.

Rumble, J.R. and Northrup, C.J.M. Jr., eds., *Computerized Materials Data - A Workshop for Ground Vehicle Engineering*, Society of Automotive Engineers, Warrendale, PA, 1986, 116pp.

Kaufman, J.G., and Prager, M. ed., *Materials Data for the Petrochemical Industry*, American Petroleum Institute, Washington, DC, (to be published)

Rumble, J.R., and Sibley, L., eds., "Towards a Tribology Data System," *NBS Spec. Publ. 737*, (1987), 132pp.

Westbrook J.H., and McCreight, L.R., eds., "Computerized Aerospace Materials Data," Proceedings of a June 1986 Workshop in El Segundo, CA, published by AIAA (1987), 201pp.

Siewart, T.A. and Jones, J.E., eds., "Computerization of Welding Information - A Workshop Report," *NBS Spec. Publ. 742*, (1988) 31pp.

Verink, E.D., Kolts, J., Rumble, J., and Ugiansky, G.M., "Corrosion Data Program Workshop Summary", *Materials Performance*, Vol 26, No. 4. April 1987, pp. 55-60.

Goyeche, S.M., "Workshop on Materials Property and Design Data Needs in Canada," *ORTECH Intl.*, March 1989, 36pp.

GLOBAL TRENDS IN MATERIALS DATA MANAGEMENT: REGIONAL OVERVIEW OF PRC

Xu Zhihong
Institute of Chemical Metallurgy (ICM)
Chinese Academy of Sciences (CAS)
Beijing, China

INTRODUCTION

The rapid development of computer technology provides a comprehensive chance for the development of a series of new material databases, and for the extension of developed databases also. The prominent feature of the past several year's activity is in the following two aspects: wide use of artificial intelligence (AI), combined with practical urgent needs; and extension of the application of database techniques into many new developing fields.

ACTIVE DATA ACTIVITIES

The following is a brief description of active data activities over the last 2-3 years.

1. **Materials database for aviation purposes.** In this database, nearly 8000 materials and four million data messages have been stored. A data compilation system has also been set up concurrently with the creation of the database. Most of the constituent members are obliged to constantly provide more accurate testing data. More than 230 specialists from different ministries participate, *e.g.,* Aviation, Metallurgy, Chemical Industry and the Chinese Academy of Sciences. It is aimed to answer inquiries searching and selecting materials; to draw the curve or curved surface (3D) as output for comparing properties etc. This work has been organized and done by the Data Center of Aviation Materials, in cooperation with a series of Institutions, *e.g.,* ICM, etc.

2. **Database of Basic Organic Compounds**. This has been a very active field in recent years; more than four types of databases have been released. The Tiantsin University's publications emphasis is on the collection of experimental data for the use of processing new prediction methods. The Dalian Institute's (DI) database is the PC-version mainly for education purposes. ICM's work is carried out on a VAX 780, and part of the work, *e.g.,* automatic functional group dissociation and analysis, has been transferred to a PC-version at the NIST in the USA (formerly NBS).

3. **Database of Inorganic Compounds**. This work is now carried out in China and also in the USA, through cooperation between ICM and NIST. The Inorganic Thermochemistry Database (ITDB) and Aqueous Thermodynamic Database (ATDB) will be released both in PC-version and VAX version in the near future. In addition, several versions, mainly for education, were also released in the past in China and a series of problems have been solved with these databases.

4. **Data Research Activities of CRAAMD**. The Chinese Research Association for Atomic and Molecular Data (CRAAMD) was established in the past two years. So far there have been ten institutions to join CRAAMD, and most of them are located in Beijing and Shanghai. There are four working groups: theoretical calculation; experimental measurement; compilation and evaluations; software for the entire group.

5. **Spectroscopic Databases**. In recent years a series of databases for detecting the basic properties of newly developed materials, *e.g.,* Mass Spectra Search System (MS) at the Institute of Chemistry (IC,CAS); C13 NMR Search System (CNMRSS) at the Institute of Applied Chemistry (IAC,CAS); IR-data Bank (IRDB) at the Institute of Organic Chemistry (IOC,CAS); Chromatography Data Bank at the Institute of Chemical Physics (ICP,CAS); X-ray Data Bank at Nankai University (NU); and the ESCA Spectrum Database has been set up and put into practical use at Beijing University and ICM. Three aspects of the work are being carried out: organizing the data collecting network; adding artificial intelligent program systems; and amalgamating them with instrumentation development.

6. **Databases in Some Specific fields**. A very distinct feature of database development in recent years has been to incorporate them to meet specific needs, *e.g.,* the database subordinated to the ECSS simulation system and developed by the Qingdao Institute of Chemical Engineering (QICE); the Material Database at Extreme Conditions, such as extreme low T, ultra high T, high pressure and other severe conditions developed by the joint work of 501 Institutes and ICM; the Toxicity Database for security developed by the

Institute of Environmental Chemistry, CAS; the Corrosion Databases for the special needs of building industrial plants developed by the Institute of Corrosion (ICR,CAS) Non-ferrous Alloy Database, and also the database of high temperature ceramics, the Rare Earth Database, including properties and resources, etc. It seems impossible to list all the databases here, and in the following paragraphs, I will emphasize AI development in the fields of data collection, evaluation, processing, prediction, and application.

AI DEVELOPMENT

The most attractive field is the development of knowledge based data systems and some expert systems for specific purposes. In the following, several examples will be given.

1. The first example is the AI technique used for the phase diagram database system. Usually, the experimental work on phase diagrams is tremendous, but the database work on phase diagrams is very difficult to carry out effectively. The key technique of extracting information is to develop a software package with the function of pattern recognition and a series of thermodynamic correlations, with which abundant messages can be drawn out from the huge amount of experimental phase diagram compilations. This method has been developed in ICM and Beijing Science and Technology Institute (BSTI), and will be released in the near future. In the meanwhile, a series of thermodynamic correlations and related programs have been linked so more messages can be obtained from the phase diagrams directly. Based on this technique, more and more phase diagram databases will be set up with no loss in data precision.

2. The second example is a system which automatically analyzes the functional group from the input chemical structure formula directly. Thereby, most of the physical and chemical properties can be deduced. A series of papers has been published on this. In order to save time programming many group contribution methods for many properties, a generalized analyzing method has been developed, which is based upon the graph theory and a series of AI techniques. With the aid of such an AI system the data generation and evaluation become easier and can be done by the chemical engineers or chemists directly. Further, the functional group theory has been improved by considering the space steo-structure factors, *i.e.,* incorporating functional group contribution and topology factors, characterizing the structure features.

3. The third example is to confront practical complicated systems. This means not only providing related data, but linking up to applied programs

to provide final answers to user's queries. A very instructive case is given in the following. There is a pyrite ore which contains small amounts of gold, silver, arsenic and sulfur compounds. The metallurgist intended to extract the Au, Ag but keep the As in the slag by using the pyro-extraction method. Before carrying out the experiment, we asked the help of the database of ITDB,IPES and also the related program system. Finally the most probable and best operating conditions for the pilot scale experimental research workers were ascertained.

4. Another example of an AI application is the development of the Inorganic Property Estimation System (IPES), by which a series of complicated problems can be confronted even for cases where there is no available data, for cases where there are some doubtful or suspicious data which may be detected and where recommended data with a reliable error range will be given. This system can be linked to other packages and databases to extend its fields of application and can also be used for critical data evaluation. It will be published in a "Computer Chemistry Monograph Series" (English) Vol. 1 with an attached software package. A block diagram is shown on the following page.

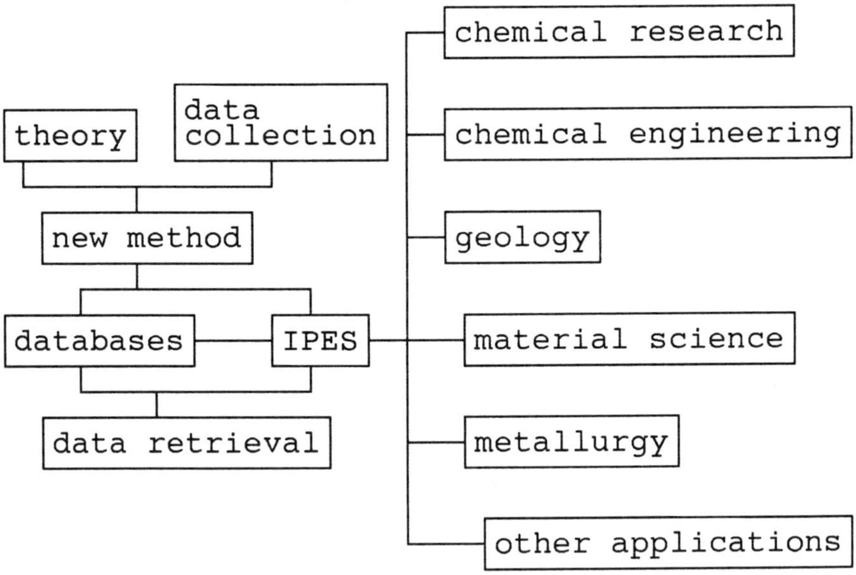

FIGURE 1. Schematic diagram of applications of IPES

5. The AI technique is widely used in the spectrum database and in directly-measured data analysis, *e.g.*, the IR-database system (IOC,CAS), NM13

database system (IAC,CAS), and the mass-spectrography database system (IC,CAS). Early this year, the Beijing University of Agriculture (BUA) finished work on a Near Infrared Diffuse Reflectance Spectroscopy Analysis (NIRDRSA), *i.e.,* using the Fourier transformation method to deal with the near infra-red spectrum of agricultural products, *e.g.,* the protein and also some contained trace elements. At present quite a few packages with AI functions have been developed for the extraction of useful messages from the direct spectroscopic measurement data by many institutions.

6. AI techniques now penetrate different fields of material work and, in many respects, it is difficult to list them all. According to the functions, they can be summarized into the following several aspects:

1). User oriented and facilitated interface
2). Data rules and prediction functions
3). Molecular and process synthesis
4). Group or fragment contribution and matching analysis
5). Topological representation of chemical compound
6). Graphic representation of chemical compounds and some special system
7). Pattern recognition for chemical processes and phase diagram
8). Factual database and knowledge base development using AI
9). Expert system for some specialized practical purposes
10). Fuzzy method applying to measurement data analysis

ACTIVITIES OF CHINESE CODATA COMMITTEE

There are many dispersed efforts in many institutions and universities in China, so there is an urgent need for the Chinese CODATA Committee to promote the exchange of messages among them, to create some channels to help Chinese scholars exchange their work with their counterparts abroad. The task groups in the fields of material and chemistry have done much to help, *e.g.,* to host the East Asian CODATA Conference in 1988 in China, to fund a few scholars to attend the CODATA International Conference, to help push several publications on computer applications in material sciences and chemistry. Furthermore, the project of setting up a network system in the Beijing academic circle will bring us a good chance of increasing cooperation in China and also abroad.

To my knowledge, the Chinese Scientific Publisher (CSP) will open a book store in New York in the near future, and a Computer Chemistry Monograph Series, sponsored by the Computer Chemistry Laboratory, CAS, will be distributed through this window in the USA and the West. This book series will not only cover material data activities, but also involve wider fields *e.g.*, QSAR, AI in computer chemistry, pattern recognition, simulation, etc.

Lastly, I would like to make an appeal to our international data society. Our limited budget brings some constraints to our database work, but the low cost of highly intelligent manpower is really a big resource for human beings, so I am sure it is worthy to encourage international cooperation in creating the new fields of data work in materials sciences, chemistry, chemical engineering, including AI and expert systems.

HOW TO INTRODUCE COMPUTERIZED FACTUAL MATERIALS INFORMATION: A SMALL COUNTRY POINT OF VIEW

Aki E. Valkonen
Helsinki University of Technology
Finland

1. INTRODUCTION

In most technical applications, materials and the associated information go hand in hand - the latter is needed to make proper use of the former possible. With the increase in both the number of different materials and the number of testing methods, the amount and the degree of complexity of the materials information available are bound to increase rapidly. These trends alone call for more efficient, *i.e.,* computerized, means of materials information management.

During the past twenty years, computerized materials reference data banks available through international information networks have developed into a necessity. At the same time, though, the introduction of computerized factual, *i.e.,* property, materials information has proved to be rather more difficult. The difficulties experienced are not of technical nature, only, but involve, *e.g.,* conceptual, cultural, and psychological elements as well [1,2,3].

Work is under way at least in the United States [4], in Europe [5], and in Japan [6] to develop commercially viable computerized factual materials information systems. As usual, it is the major industrialized countries that carry the torch; of the small industrialized countries only Sweden [7] seems to have shown a consistent effort in this area.

The purpose of this presentation is to elucidate the position of small industrialized countries in the area of computerized factual materials information using Finland as an example. The presentation draws from a recent pre-study [8] conducted by the author.

2. THE INSTITUTIONAL FRAMEWORK

By this time all industrialized countries have developed efficient national information services connected to well established international information networks. Obviously, most of the further developments also in the area of factual materials information are bound to occur
within this framework, especially in small countries.

2.1. The Small Country Case

The role of materials in any national economy can be illustrated by means of the simple "production line" model of Figure 1. A general observation from Figure 1 is that the way materials and the associated information are used affects the output of all national economies in a fundamental, yet complicated, manner. Therefore, not only materials but also the associated information possesses strategic value.

By definition, each small country typically produces no more than about one per cent of the world's new information. Thus small countries with their open economies are massive net importers of all kinds of information and exporters of industrial applications thereof, *i.e.,* products.

Small countries typically have few major corporations or strong industrial and professional associations. Because of this, there is a definite need for close cooperation between all these organizations and the governmental

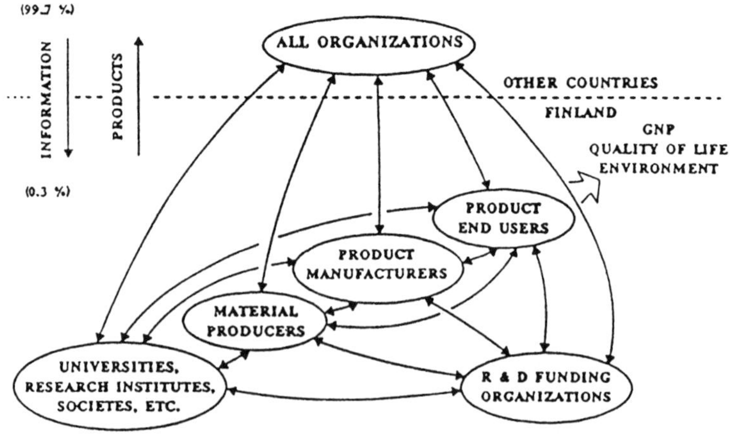

FIGURE 1. Materials in the Finnish economy.

funding bodies in the materials information area. In many cases, the availability of a single "national champion" showing enthusiasm and taking responsibility is a decisive force in small countries.

2.2. The Finnish Information Service Organization

The present Finnish information service organization involving both governmental and private elements is illustrated in Figure 2. The information end user typically first approaches a local service unit within his/her own company or at a (university) library. For most important professional areas, a number of national information service centers have been set up. For all technical areas, the Helsinki University of Technology Library serves as such a center. Another unit of comparable national importance is the Information Service of the Technical Research Center of Finland (VTT). The Council of Scientific Information (TINFO) is an advisory body involving representatives from all relevant interest groups.

2.3. Finland and the World Information Market

As shown in Figure 3, Finland is well connected to the world's online information networks. Furthermore, as shown by Figure 4, user activity is growing rapidly. One has to remember though that only about half of the total activity is directed towards international sources and that only a small fraction of it concerns materials information. Reference sources are responsible for most of the activity. In fact, only limited exploratory

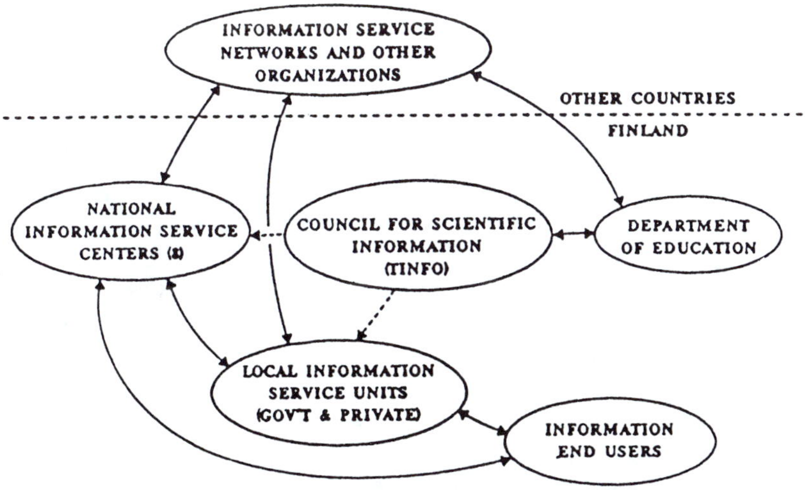

FIGURE 2. The Finnish information service organization.

attempts have been made to extract factual materials information from online data banks [9]. The same applies to the PC-based systems obtained from international vendors.

An interesting dichotomy can be seen in Finland's traditional approach to international cooperation in the information area. On the one hand, the Finnish information service specialists have adopted a very active role in many organizations that interest them, like UNESCO, IAEA, IFLA, FID, EUSIDIC, IATUL, etc. On the other hand, very little interest has been shown in the organizations most relevant to the materials community, *e.g.*, ASTM Committee E-49, CODATA, and VAMAS [10,11,12].

The same dichotomy appears in the Nordic scene. As illustrated by Figure 5, the organization is in place and active in developing an infrastructure for the Nordic information market. Yet attempts to initiate Nordic cooperation in the area of materials information have failed so far.

3. THE PRE-STUDY

In 1987, the concept of computerized factual materials information was still new to most in Finland. It was therefore necessary to adopt a comprehensive strategy for the pre-study and to base it on an analysis of the initial conditions in the country.

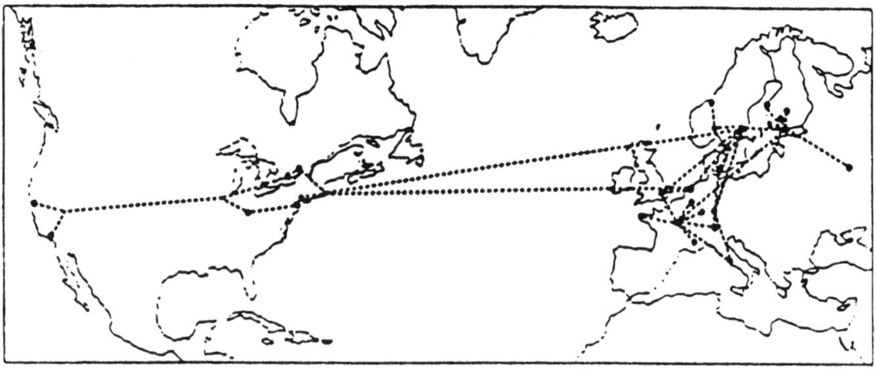

FIGURE 3
Finland's connections to the international online information networks.

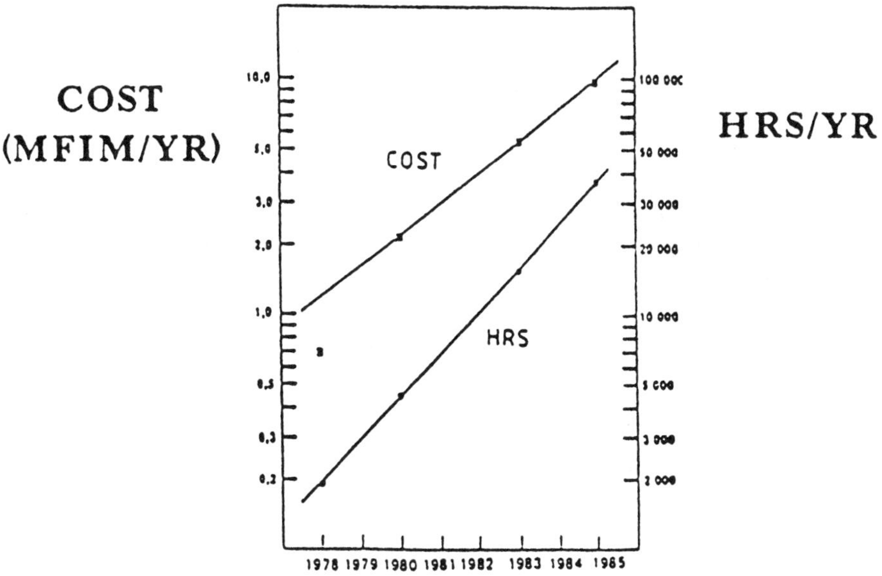

FIGURE 4
Development of the total online data bank user activity in Finland [9].

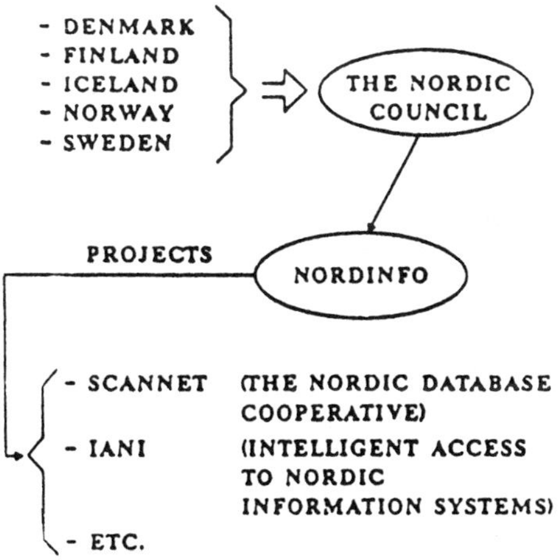

FIGURE 5
Structure of cooperation among Nordic countries in the information area.

3.1. Initial Conditions

The quality of the general information service infrastructure was found to be good in Finland. Therefore, activation of the materials and design communities as well as enhancement of the community interactions were chosen to be the focal points of the pre-study.

The Finnish materials community has a fairly sound record in producing hard copy sources of factual materials information. These are mostly booklets providing assistance for selection of structural materials. Because of this tradition, materials selection automatically became the first function to be examined in the pre-study. This, however, turned out to be too narrow of an approach and was later revised.

In 1987, the limited discussion concerning the role of computerized factual materials information was somewhat confused in Finland. The sources of confusion ranged from the basic concepts and terminology to the relationships between, *e.g.,* data banks and expert systems, to the needs of different user groups, if any. At that time, very few people had hands-on experience with either online or PC-based systems and these were not used in education. No Finnish materials producer provided their property data in electronically readable form. No national reference group existed in the area. Even with all these deficiencies Finland was no exception among the small industrialized countries, however. On the brighter side, limited efforts [13] were already being made to develop expert systems for the area of corrosion.

3.2. Objectives and Strategy

In a nutshell, the main objective of the pre-study was to provide a broad basis for the introduction of computerized factual materials information in Finland.

The strategy of the pre-study had six main components. These were to:

(i) Find out about the world situation by identifying key persons, programs, and systems. To accomplish this, 25 organizations in seven countries were visited.

(ii) Acquire a number of PC-based systems and use students to analyze them. The systems analyzed were MATEDS, METSEL2, PERITUS-ED, PLASCAMS, and SMI [14].

(iii) Perform conceptual analyses to provide a coherent basis for subsequent discussions.

(iv) Identify the options available to Finland and draft a national action plan.

(v) Present the findings in a national seminar for open discussion, including discussion of all Finnish projects.

(vi) Produce and distribute a comprehensive final report (in Finnish) and a summary report (in English). The present document serves the latter purpose.

The aim was to produce clear decisions, either positive or negative, to maximize the impact of the pre-study.

4. RESULTS FROM THE PRE-STUDY

Descriptions of the national and world situations, the results of the conceptual analyses, and the proposed action plan were used to solicit initial reactions in the seminar. In the following, brief descriptions of the latter three items are provided.

4.1. Conceptual Analyses

The analyses were focussed at the concepts of factual materials information and the related information systems.

4.1.1. Materials Information

The types of factual materials information considered here are data and knowledge. To be useful for any purpose, the individual data points of Figure 6a derived, *e.g.*, from experimental measurements must be supported by adequate background information, or metadata. Furthermore, the data points must be tied together in a credible manner to produce knowledge, Figure 6b, the only thing on which we can base our judgement. The relationships involved here may be quantitative or qualitative, and sometimes tacit.

The way people see and use materials information depends on their professional backgrounds as illustrated in Figure 6b. While most people recognize the operational role of measurements in producing parameter descriptions of the world, the natural leaning towards either the materials

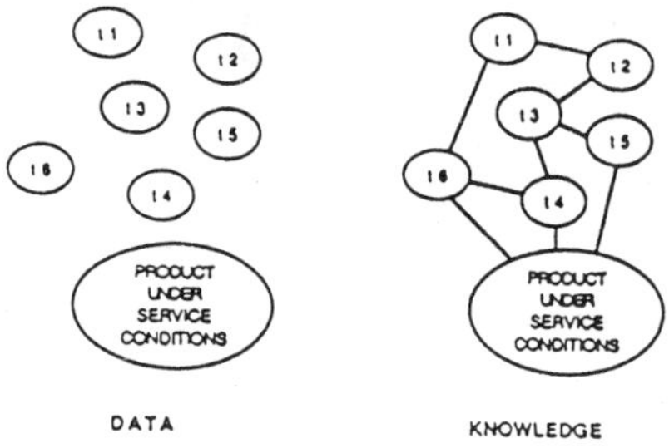

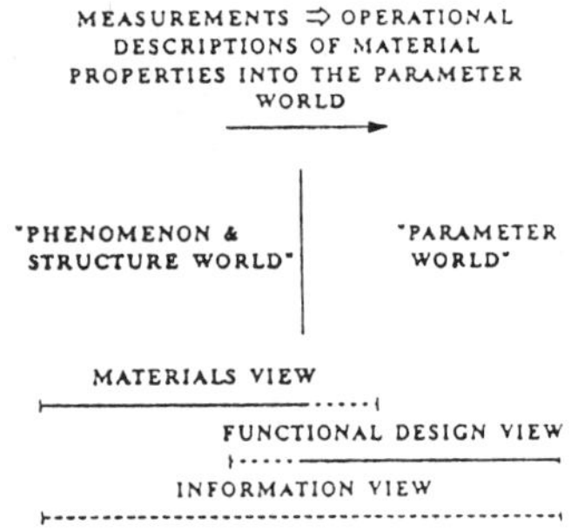

FIGURE 6
Materials information - data and knowledge (a); Interested parties and their views (b) [8].

view or the functional design view can be quite strong. The information specialists probably carry the most neutral view because of their detachment from the materials world.

The complexity of the materials information world together with the different needs of the end user groups gives rise to a large number of specialized materials information systems. Collaboration between the different interested parties is clearly required to produce a coherent outcome.

4.1.2. Materials Information Systems

The large number of different possible materials information systems possible often leads to considerable confusion in discussions. To help avoid this, the simplified hierarchical approach shown in Figure 7 was developed. The hierarchy accommodates both the general information/materials selection oriented materials view and the integration oriented design view at different levels of system sophistication. Levels 1 - 3 represent system types presently under development.

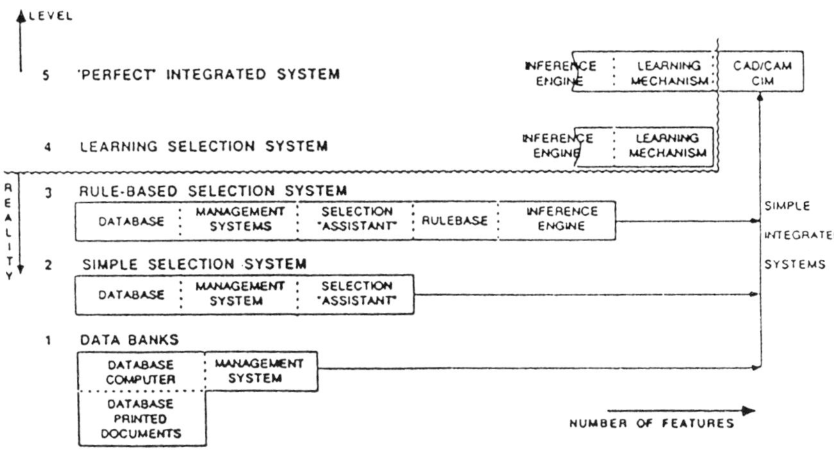

FIGURE 7. Materials information systems - a hierarchical approach [8].

A closer look at level 1 systems, data banks, is given in Figure 8. Recalling the online and PC options and recognizing the different types of materials property data available, a wide variety of different systems can be seen emerging from this simple classification. Some standards and/or guidelines ensuring, *e.g.*, compatibility, are clearly necessary.

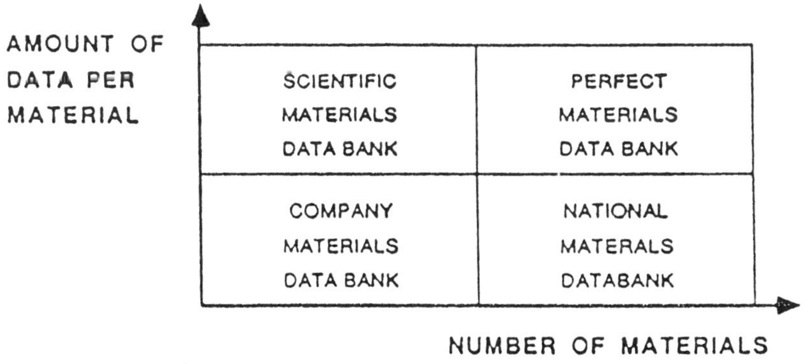

FIGURE 8. Materials data banks - a classification [8].

The possible benefits resulting from the use of computerized factual materials information systems are not presently well established. Therefore, careful cost/benefit analyses and end user evaluations will be needed in the future. Two proposed frameworks for such evaluations are shown in Figures 9a and 9b. The former framework represents an organization level approach and the latter represents an end user level approach.

4.2. Recommendations

The recommendations to be discussed relate broadly to national organization, domestic system development, international cooperation, and better use of materials information.

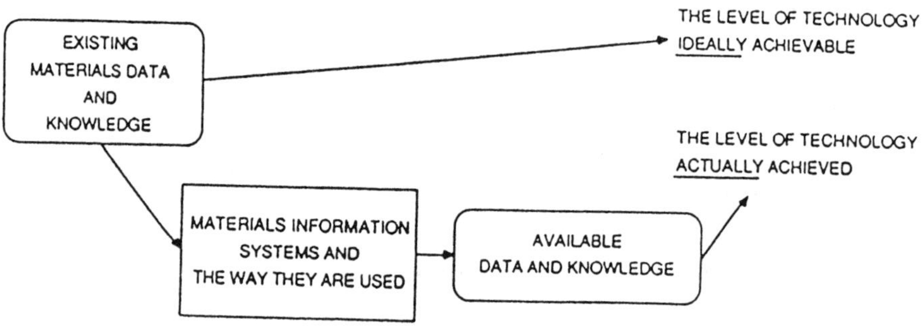

a.

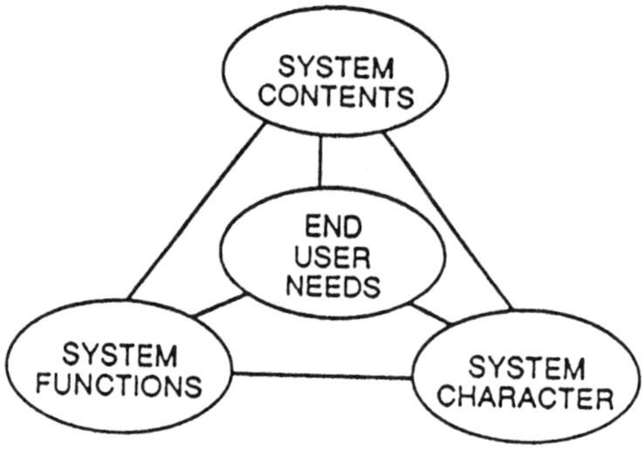

b.

FIGURE 9
Materials information systems - frameworks for evaluation at organization (a) and end user (b) levels [8]. In (a), "technology" may be replaced by any other variable as needed.

4.2.1. National Organization

The models of national organization to be considered include a national mailing address, a loose national reference group, and task groups for specific problems.

Of the existing organizations, the Council of Scientific Information (TINFO), Figure 2, and the Materials Board of the Finnish Metal, Engineering, and Electrotechnical Industries - FIMET are best positioned for the general tasks of coordination and promotion. If a national materials information group were to be established, then either the Helsinki University of Technology Library or the Information Service of the Technical Research Center of Finland (VTT) could serve as the host.

Whatever the future organizational developments will be, participation and interaction of all the interest groups should be secured.

4.2.2. Domestic System Development

When considering domestic system development projects one should abstain from reinventing the wheel. Following this rule, the development of a Finnish national materials data bank from scratch is not recommended. On the other hand, the Finnish materials producers are encouraged to provide their data in electronically readable form to their own customers and to any interested data bank operators. Development of different in-house systems, Figure 7, by Finnish engineering companies and research institutes is also recommended. Work of this kind helps develop the initial competency required for any advancement in the field and may also lead eventually to commercially feasible information products in some narrow areas.

4.2.3. International Cooperation

Participation in international cooperation is considered to be the most cost effective way to transfer the basics of factual materials information system culture to Finland. Both the actual systems work and matters of a more fundamental nature can be promoted in this manner.

In the systems area, the opportunities offered by the Swedish Materials Information (SMI) organization [7] should be seriously considered in Finland and in other Nordic countries as well. Through the resulting cooperation, the materials sector of the Nordic information market could be elevated with a reasonable effort to the general level discussed in section 2.3.

It is important to note that the work being done by international organizations, like the ASTM Committee E-49, CODATA, and VAMAS [10,11,12], affects the future of materials information not only directly but also indirectly, through materials and testing standards. Participation in the work of all these organizations is strongly recommended. This naturally requires commitments from at least one person and a funding organization. As a specific measure it is recommended that Finland become a member of CODATA.

4.2.4. Better Use of Materials Information

No one knows how efficiently materials information is being used in Finland. What can be said, though, is that better results can be achieved in the future only through improved education and organization of activities. Swift introduction of computerized materials information systems to the materials and design curricula at technical universities and institutes is an obvious priority in this area. Another might be the creation of a system for furnishing small-to-medium enterprises with up-to-date, versatile materials information and advice.

4.3. Short Term Reactions

About 80 people attended the working seminar held in May, 1988. As often happens with issues of an infrastructural nature, the audience's immediate reactions of the audience provided little guidance for the next steps. Rather, the qualitative reaction distribution (80% no opinion, 10% slightly curious, 5% positively curious, and 5% hostile) indicated the beginning of a long and slow process. This is the way it has reportedly happened in other countries, too.

5. STATUS REPORT

By the end of 1989, very little had been done in Finland to execute the action plan established in the pre-study. The national mailing address was established, however, and it is:

Mr. Harri Grohn
Federation of the Finnish Metal, Engineering, and
Electrotechnical Industries - FIMET
Unioninkatu 14, 00130 Helsinki, Finland
Tel. + 358 0 1923 421, Fax + 358 0 625 020

Other developments worth mentioning are that FIMET also became a member of the Swedish Materials Information (SMI), that another expert system project covering corrosion resistant coatings was initiated, and that wider use of the PC-based systems in education was accomplished. To some extent, the slow progress in Finland can be attributed to the lack of a "national champion" who would have actively pursued the plan of action.

6. SUMMARY

Introducing computerized factual materials information has not been easy anywhere, yet active system development is pursued in most major industrialized countries. In spite of their well developed information service infrastructures and strong dependence on imported information, many small industrialized countries have shown little active interest in participating in this work. To get things going in Finland, a one year pre-study of the options available was organized in 1987. A description of the background, goals, strategies, and results of the pre-study was provided, hoping that the experiences gained would be useful to other small countries as well. Solid background information, clear action plans, a long term commitment, and the need for "national champions" capable of initiating international cooperation were identified as some of the keys to success.

ACKNOWLEDGEMENTS

The pre-study was funded by the Finnish National Fund for Research and Development (SITRA) and the Helsinki University of Technology. This support and the helpful comments by Ms. Paivi Karjalainen-Roikonen and Dr. Norman Swindells are gratefully acknowledged.

REFERENCES

[1] *Computerized Materials Data Systems; the Proceedings of a Materials Data Workshop*. J. H. Westbrook & J. R. Rumble, Jr., Eds. Fairfield Glade, TN,1982, 133 p.

[2] Ostberg, G., A paradox in the Development of Computerized Materials Data Systems. *Materials & Design* 5(1984),15.

[3] Rumble, J. R., Jr., Socioeconomic Barriers in Computerizing Materials Data. *Computerization and Networking of Materials Data Bases*. ASTM STP 1017. J. S. Glazman & J. R. Rumble, Jr., Eds., American Society for Testing and Materials, Philadelphia, 1989, pp. 216-226.

[4] Kaufman, J.G., The National Materials Property Data Network, Inc. - A Cooperative National Approach to Reliable Performance Data. Ref. 3, pp. 55-62.

[5] Krockel, H. & Steven, G., European Activities Towards Integration and Harmonization of Materials Data Systems. Ref. 3, pp. 63-74.

[6] Nishijima, S., Monma, Y. & Kanao, M., Japanese Progress in Materials Data Bases. Ref. 3, pp. 80-91.

[7] Ullman, E. & Ryden, L., Development of a National Materials Data Base in Sweden. *Materials & Design* 8(1987)6.

[8] Valkonen, A.E., Computerized Materials Information Systems. *SITRA* A:90, Helsinki, 1989, 85 p. + App. (in Finnish)

[9] Lehti, M. & Eskola, P., User Activity of On-line Information Systems in Finland in 1985. Technical Research Center of Finland. Communication 673. Espoo, 1987, 76 p. (in Finnish)

[10] Hakkarainen, T., Carpen, L.I. & Hakkarainen, T., Microcomputer as Corrosion Expert - An Approach by Corrosion Specialists. *CORROSION 88 (NACE)*, Paper No.126.

[11] Kaufman, J.G., Standards for Computerized Materials Property Data - ASTM Committee E-49. Ref. 3, pp.7-22.

[12] Barrett, A.J., CODATA Activities on Materials Data. Ref. 3, pp.99-106.

[13] Reynard, K.W., VAMAS Activities on Materials Data Banks. Ref. 3, pp. 43-52.

[14] MATEDS, METSEL2, PERITUS-ED, PLASCAMS, and SMI are trademarks of SkanAluminium, ASM International, Matsel Systems, RAPRA Technology, and SMI, respectively.

GLOBAL TRENDS IN THE MANAGEMENT OF DATA ON MATERIALS - AN OVERVIEW

Anthony J. Barrett
Information Development International
P.O. Box 166
Chalfont St Giles, Bucks HP8 4JG
United Kingdom

INTRODUCTION

This paper is preceded by others each of which has given details of the trends, or developments, in the management of materials data in a particular geographical region. The purpose here is to look at the overall picture. It is also necessary to recall some of the origins of these developments for a worthwhile objective can only be reached if both the direction of a trend and its starting point are properly related. More than this, however, favourable trends need to persist; so the motivations behind some of them will be examined to discover whether they are sufficiently robust and how they may attract ongoing support.

MATERIALS DATA MANAGEMENT - THE HERITAGE

In the past the management of materials data within the walls of high tech companies, and in other restricted groups, may have been quite satisfactory to their privileged users. Looked at from the point of view of the more general materials user, however, the extent of the lack of proper management is, in hindsight, quite extraordinary. The following is a partial catalogue of data 'housekeeping' and management shortcomings which we are confronting in this final decade in relation to materials many of which have been in wide engineering use for the greater part of the century. In each case a reference to a recent paper is given which details what has to be done, or in some cases what is being done, by way of remedy.

----

* Chairman, CODATA Task Group on Materials Database Management.

Generally speaking:

* The materials used in engineering have yet to be identified and designated in an unambiguous way, [1].
* The results of tests which are made on engineering materials have yet to be reported in a reasonably common format, [2].
* The metadata, (without which no property data may be employed intelligently), have yet to be reported consistently and without fail, [3].
* The terminology in use very often lacks consistency in definition, abbreviation and symbolic notation, [2].
* Ways of indicating the quality of the data used for design and for other purposes have yet to be found, [2].
* Only recently, [4], has a start been made to list, in a comprehensive way, sources of data on the mechanical and physical properties of engineering materials.

Even before taking into account the additional requirements which the computerization of materials property data impose, the above catalogue could be extended considerably. A lay observer might well be tempted to ask 'how can the professional user of materials choose and use materials wisely in such an environment?'

The answer is that, for the most part, materials are only chosen and used wisely where there is a large body of empirical experience on which to base the choice or where there is a commercial or national interest to be served which makes it necessary, (even if not economically attractive), for companies and/or national bodies to create well managed compilations of data for restricted use. Major companies support the testing of materials and the recording of data to their own standards in their own design and procurement manuals, usually for company use only. Standards organizations provide limited ranges of data on relatively small sets of materials validated by expert committees for use only in very specific applications such as pressure vessel design. More extensive compilations of materials property data prepared to high standards include nationally certified data and databases such as those of the USSR's Research Centre on Materials Problems, (VNITSMV), [5]. Up to the present time these have not been conveniently available internationally because of language difficulties and because of the uncertainties involved in identifying materials equivalents in different designation systems.

Industry can not continue to thrive in such an environment. Gone are the days when engineering designers could cover the shortcomings of their knowledge by the profligate use of relatively cheap materials from secure sources of supply.

MOTIVATION FOR CHANGE

At the Local and National Level

The increase in the value placed on many materials and interest in an expanding range of new materials have placed high premiums on the selection and critical use of materials both for traditional and for new applications. This in turn affects the value placed upon what is known about materials and in particular upon the data relating to their physical performance.

The higher we go up the pyramid of specialization, the smaller is the market base which is available to support the high costs of providing data of known quality, [6]. So there have to be unusual pressures at work if effort and funds are to be expended on the provision of high quality property data on a company or even a national scale. Some of the best data compilations of this type have been made for materials applicable in high technology industries and have included only the materials originating in a single nation. A notable case in point are the data relating to the engineering properties of metallic materials used in aerospace. In the 1930's the United States was probably unique in having available for general use a comprehensive collection of mechanical strength, stiffness and related data for the materials used in its civil and military aircraft; these were the data in the ANC-5 Handbook, later to become Mil-Hbk 5, [7]. By contrast, in the United Kingdom, a comprehensive collection of validated data on metallic materials used in defence projects has been available for only the last 12 years, [8], although preparatory work for it started some 40 years ago.

At the Multinational Level - An Example and Some Lessons

Multinational interests can sometimes provide strong motivations for collaborative action in the management of technological matters which overcome local and national apathy. As noted in the previous paragraph, the USA has had a comprehensive collection of data on aerospace materials publicly available (for all practical purposes) for about 60 years. Other industrialized nations seem to have given attention to this need only within the last decade or so, if at all. Yet over thirty years ago there was sufficient economic and military motivation for the North Atlantic Treaty (NATO) nations to involve themselves in what was the first multinational programme to produce a compilation of high quality mechanical property and other data for engineering materials.

The NATO Advisory Group on Aerospace Research and Development (AGARD) Material Properties Handbook [9] provided data in four volumes for alloys of aluminium, magnesium, nickel and titanium and for steels produced in eight of the NATO countries. The scope of the data included chemical composition; physical properties; static strength; stiffness and fatigue properties; short time properties at, and recovered properties after, exposure to elevated temperature; properties under load and elevated temperature. The materials were identified clearly in terms of each nation's designation system. The format for the reporting of the data was common throughout and provided a model for some of the nations to use in developing their own internal standards for the reporting of numerical data and their accompanying metadata - though this last term was not in use at the time. Problems such as those relating to conversions between different systems of units and those related to the use of different notations and terminologies were recognized and practical, if by modern standards inelegant, ways of circumventing them were devised. The need to give an indication of data quality was also recognized and a three level statistical data basis coding was applied to all of the mechanical properties reported.

The first volume of the Handbook was issued in 1958. It was updated a number of times and was joined by three more volumes by 1966. It was used extensively and, for most of the nations involved, provided the only coherent source of data on their own materials which was available at that time and for some time following. A substantial amount of money was spent on setting up this unified data system and on developing the techniques for its management and production. However, the modest funding which was subsequently required to maintain and gradually improve the system could not be found. As the years went by the currency of the Handbook deteriorated and it fell, gradually and gracefully, into disuse.

A number of important lessons were learned during this project, both technical and managerial. These included the realization that the technical interests of multinational groups are generally more volatile than the interests of the individual nations within the group. It also became clear that those responsible for providing the funding for such projects may be impressed by attributes quite different to those which appeal to the intended user. In this last respect, for example, the handbook format was quite adequate, according to the working practices of the day, for the purpose of storing and retrieving high quality, numeric data. But to others it is just a book. Had it been necessary to invent some form of glamorous system in which to store the data, it might have appeared more attractive to its paymasters and support for the project might have continued longer. Its demise could be rationalized in a number of ways when it became clear that further support was not to be forthcoming.

A more important lesson was learned much later. Data systems and services which are provided by funding from a government purse may not need *selling* to earn their support - but they do need *marketing* to ensure that they shall flourish and survive.

MOTIVATION TO MAINTAIN CHANGE

With the emergence of new media for the storage, manipulation and communication of materials data there came a renewed interest in the setting up of high quality data collections and a rediscovery of the qualities needed in those collections - unambiguous designation, provision of metadata, and so on, as previously described. For the first time, however, many of these qualities were being sought not only for their intrinsic value but because the computerized media will not work properly, or even at all, if they are missing! Does this provide sufficient motivation to engage and maintain the extensive financial support that is needed?

COMPUTERIZED SYSTEMS - NEW INCENTIVES

Inconsistencies in materials data sets themselves and the lack of adequately defined metadata, and many other weaknesses in materials data compilations, have long been tolerated in passive storage media operated by human data users. Attempts to improve matters have had only limited success. But these shortcomings can not be tolerated at all when the storage medium is part of a costly system which when used, for example, in integrated computer aided engineering, will all but dispense completely with human intervention.

The time and costs involved in the electronic capture, storage, retrieval, manipulation and communication of materials data place a high premium on the quality of those data, upon the efficiency of their storage and retrieval and upon the necessity of sharing and interchanging them over a wide market. In turn, the opportunities which domestic and international data interchanges offer, in the spreading of costs and the increase of revenue, make other demands on management. Materials have to be uniquely identified, data have to be recorded consistently, terminology must be defined coherently, often in several languages, formats for the exchange of data must be standardized, and much more.

Why Computerize Materials Data?

Given that we are prepared to rectify severe deficiencies which we have tolerated for many years in the store of data on materials, and given that we are prepared to spend the money to tailor that store of data to suit the demands of storage and manipulation in a medium that is unforgiving of inconsistencies and irrationality, then there are no insuperable barriers to the setting up of effective, comprehensive, computerized materials data systems. A few such systems are already at an advanced stage of development, of course.

Because of the high capital and maintenance costs which are involved, the long term viability of these systems will depend upon the existence of a market populated with users who see sufficient benefits from using them. Such a market either already exists or has to be created but in either case the promoter of a system has to be able to sell it on the basis of responding to some preexisting need of offering some novel benefit at an acceptable unit price. Important steps have been taken to assess existing market needs in connection with the USA's Materials Data Network, [10], [11], [12], and the COMECON Standard Reference Data System has an ongoing procedure of consultation with the users of its materials and substances data banks. In the long term, however, creating and nurturing a market for computerized data systems will rely on materials database managers being able to specify actual benefits to commercial users. Specifying the attributes of their systems is not good enough and there is still some way to go before even those with a good deal of experience in the field can relate attributes and benefits in terms that are meaningful to data users, potential users, and those who sanction the expenditure of funds [13].

It is possible that the serving of preexisting markets and the creation of new ones will prove easier for well focused p.c. hosted databases relating to limited sets of materials, and for expert systems incorporating small materials databases (see below), than for large, comprehensive online systems.

Other Trends

One objective of materials database management is to assist the person simply wishing to retrieve materials data. At the other extreme is the requirement to interface materials data bank directly with automated engineering systems without any human intervention. Yet another is to support the expert system approach which couples the acquired and stored knowledge and experience of one or more human experts with a resource of high quality materials data. The purpose of these systems is to assist in such tasks as the reliable selection of materials, the application of materials information by relatively inexpert users or to speed the application of materials data by another expert. (This description of an expert system may not satisfy the purist, of course, but it is adequate for the purpose in hand).

Sustained, and at least modest, commercial success may be used as a criterion by which to judge the type of system which might be expected to persist and flourish. Three expert systems of the type described satisfy this criterion and may be cited to represent a number of successful developments of this type. PLASCAMS [14] assists the selection of plastics materials for specific applications, CUTDATA [15] relates the choice and specification of machine manufacturing processes and P-V DESIGNER [16] performs the design calculations for pressure vessels to BS 5500 and ASME VIII Codes. Although these systems perform very different analyses and syntheses, they have many features in common.

Each of them:

* Works in the personal computer environment.
* Is based upon a well tested body of expert knowledge.
* Incorporates an evaluated materials database.
* Is validated for a specific set of engineering tasks.
* Achieves a high level of presentational quality.
* Is subject to a mandatory updating routine.
* Offers swift access to technical help from expert staff.
* Has achieved some degree of international acceptance.
* Is supported by a long established organisation of unimpeachable integrity.

A similar list of basic attributes could be generated for any technological, databased system which has to be supported commercially in whole or in part. It is very easy to pay lip service to these attributes which are so obviously desirable. But achieving them in practice and presenting them in the market place requires management skills and experience which are as yet rare.

WHAT TRENDS WILL PERSIST?

For the remainder of this century social, political and economic factors are more likely to influence the activities of data managers than are new scientific and technical developments. Science and technology have been extensively patronized in all the industrial nations during the first nine decades and society is pressing for a payoff in the tenth. Some of the ways in which this pressure is being applied by society have been described in ref. [17].

One part of the industrialized world has organized itself on the basis of an economic system loosely described as 'market driven'. Several different interpretations of this term seem to exist and at one extreme it can mean 'consumer driven'. At another extreme it can mean that the market is driven, *i.e.,* that markets are created. Database managers in nations that may be thinking about regenerating their economies will need to be careful in understanding what such terms really mean. To be commercially successful, managers of materials databases - and all other technological databases for that matter - must respond to the consumer's perception of his own needs. But these managers must also understand that markets often have to be created for novel products and services; nowhere has this been more necessary, over the years, than in the successful promotion of high quality data and information systems.

Building up knowledge and experience in these matters will become an increasingly important activity for all materials database managers. It is a trend that should not upset those who see their job more from the scientific and technical viewpoint. Society's pressure for a return from its investment in science and technology should be seen as offering exciting and potentially fruitful prospects. This return will come only through the reliable understanding and application of knowledge and data. In turn, such application will be successful and economically viable in some relation to the relevance, and the efficient and effective use, of the stores of data which have been paid for in the past and to which only the database manager can provide the key.

Rearranged groupings of nations may shortly confront each other in strenuous economic competition. Our environment may deserve a better understanding of the data which relates to it than we are currently able to bring to bear. Our fellow men may demand a more professional service of explanation and advice than is provided at present by individual well trained experts who are, nonetheless, too often to be seen in undignified and confusing argument. The one underexploited resource that we have available to deal with these and many other social issues is knowledge and data which, like other resources, needs careful extraction and refinement [18]. Careful management of the data refinement process has always been needed and will be increasingly important as more and more data are stored electronically and become embedded in computer aided engineering systems. Because materials and substances, of all types, are fundamental to almost every aspect of human life, the successful development of materials database management techniques offers a particularly rich and rewarding occupation at the leading edge of information technology.

CONCLUSIONS

In conclusion some of the principal trends that have been identified will be summarized.

Preparations by standardization bodies and others to rectify long standing deficiencies in the data available for engineering materials are now underway. Data relevance and quality will be improved through the better management of materials designations, more complete and coherent reporting of test results and recording of metadata, more consistent statements of terminology, application of rational techniques for data refinement (evaluation and validation), proper recording of data quality parameters and recording of information on sources of data, and more. There is still a lot to be done to implement these improvements.

Steps are being taken which will reduce the reliance which has formerly had to be placed upon empirical experience or upon limited national and company compilations - where these have been available. To a large extent these processes are being aided by the need to produce computerized materials databases and the opportunities which have recently been created for multinational collaboration. These developments impose their own requirements for further change. In addition to cleaning up the resources of data by the management actions noted in the previous paragraph, the international computer environment demands the development of our management of language, units, data exchange formats and more.

A large part of the effort needed to develop materials data management is being supplied through what are, essentially, voluntary bodies. Notable in this respect at the multinational level are CODATA, ASTM Committee E-49, the COMECON Standard Reference Data System Working Group and the Versailles Project on Advanced Materials and Standards (VAMAS). However, voluntary effort alone will not suffice in the long term. Support will have to come increasingly from those who stand to benefit most from the rapid provision of reliable materials data in forms suitable for immediate use by humans or for use in automated engineering programs for materials selection, product design and manufacture.

Developing a market for engineering data requires a management expertise that is still rare. Where it exists in the materials data field it has produced some of the as yet relatively few systems which may be claimed to have sustained a modest commercial success over a reasonable period of time. These systems exhibit a number of common features which have been listed.

Large bodies of high quality materials data exist in nations which are currently debating the manners in which their economies shall be run in future; to some a 'market' economy seems to have its attractions. In this case the materials database manager needs to be aware that far more is required than an efficient and effective response to the 'consumer' or user of his services; it is often necessary to influence the creation of the market itself.

Materials are fundamental to almost every aspect of the life of any nation. Trends in the management of factual information and data on materials will continue to develop and must change in response to society's perception of what constitutes its well-being locally, nationally and globally.

REFERENCES

[1] Reynard, K.W., Materials Designation Systems, Proceedings of the Second International Symposium on Computerization of Materials Property Databases, ASTM STP 1106, Philadelphia, PA, 1990.

[2] Rumble, J., Standards for Materials Databases, ASTM Committee E49, Proceedings of the Second International Symposium on Computerization of Materials Property Databases, ASTM STP 1106, Philadelphia, PA, 1990.

[3 Westbrook, J.H., The Role of Metadata in the Design and Operation of a Materials Database, Proceedings of the Second International Symposium on Computerization of Materials Property Databases, ASTM STP 1106, Philadelphia, PA, 1990.

[4] Wawrousek, H., Westbrook, J.H., & Grattidge, W., Data Sources of Mechanical and Physical Properties of Engineering Materials. Physics Data No. 30-1, Fachinformationszentrum, Karlsruhe, 1989.

[5] Kozlov, A.D., Materials and Substance Data Banks in COMECON Countries and in the USSR in eds. Kozlov, A., and Westrum, E.F., The Provision of Materials Property Data via Computerized Systems, CODATA Bulletin Vol. 22, No. 2, Hemisphere Publishing Corporation, Washington, D.C., 1990.

[6] Krylov, V., Problems of Development of the Factual Data Bank "Timber" into an Automated Knowledge System, in eds. Kozlov, A. and Westrum, E.F., The Provision of Materials Property Data via Computerized Systems, CODATA Bulletin Vol. 22, No. 2, Hemisphere Publishing Corporation, Washington, D.C., 1990.

[7] Department of Defense, Military Standardization Handbook, Metallic

Materials and Elements, MIL-HDBK-5C, Department of Defense, Washington, DC.
[8] Ministry of Defense, Metallic Materials Data Handbook, Defence Standard 932, ESDU International, London.
[9] AGARD/NATO Material Properties Handbook: Vol.1 - Aluminium Alloys, Vol. 2 - Steels, Vol. 3 Magnesium, Nickel and Titanium Alloys, Vol. 4 - Heat Resisting Alloys, Advisory Group for Aerospace Research and Development, Paris, 1958, 1960, 1963, 1966.
[10] Rumble, J. and Westbrook, J.H., eds., Computerizing Materials Data - A Workshop for the Nuclear Power Industry, National Bureau of Standards Special Publication 689, Washington, D.C., January 1985.
[11] Rumble, J., Mitchell, M.R., and Northrup, R.T., eds., Computerized Materials Data - A Workshop for Ground Vehicle Engineering, Society of Automotive Engineers Report P-163, Warrendale, PA, August 1985.
[12] Westbrook, J.H. and McCreight, L.R., eds., Computerized Aerospace Materials Data -Proceedings of a Workshop, American Institute of Aeronautics and Astronautics Inc. New York, NY, 1987.
[13] Barrett, A.J., The Benefits and Economic Consequences of Materials Property Databases, Proceedings of the Second International Symposium on Computerization of Materials Property Databases, ASTM STP 1106, Philadelphia, PA, 1990.
[14] RAPRA, PLASCAMS Plastic Material Selector, Database and Software, Rubber and Plastics Research Association, Shawbury, UK, 1985 and later versions.
[15] METCUT, CUTDATA Machining Database and Software, Metcut Research Associates Inc. Cincinnati, OH, 1984 and later versions.
[16] ESDU, P-V DESIGNER, Pressure Vessel Design Database and Software, ESDU International, London, 1988 and later versions.
[17] Barrett, A.J., Social Implications of Data Quality, in Glaeser, P., ed., Proceedings of the 11th International CODATA Conference, Karlsruhe, 1988.
[18] Barrett, A.J., Refining Data Resources to Assist Technology Transfer, in 'Technology Transfer in Industrialized Countries', Sherman Gee ed., Sijthoff & Noordoff, Netherlands, 1979.

ISSUES IN NETWORKING MATERIALS DATABASES

J. G. Kaufman
The National Materials Property Data Network
Columbus, Ohio, U.S.A.

INTRODUCTION

Many of the key needs of materials scientists and engineers in improving access to materials information [1-3], most notably assistance in finding and accessing detailed, highly documented performance data from a wide variety of sources, can be met by the networking of materials databases. Most material scientists and engineers have or will soon have their own internal materials databases, whether on mainframes or micro-computers for larger organizations or on personal computer systems for smaller organizations and private consultants. Most work will be done on these internal systems. Periodically, the users of these systems will require additional information, and will prefer to access it directly electronically and download it to their own systems. By networking a variety of sources of related information, this type of transaction can be made simple and straightforward.

Several networks containing primarily scientific data and including a major focus on numeric materials data are in existence or some stage of development. These include the Materials Database Demonstrator Programme of the Commission of European Community [4], the Materials Property Data (MPD) Network [5], and STN International [6], the worldwide scientific and technical information Network. These are described below in terms of the technical hurdles to be dealt with in handling diverse materials databases.

It is beyond the scope of this paper to deal with communication networks, such as Sprintnet (formerly Telenet), Tymnet, Internet or Bitnet, or with general information networks such as Compuserve and Dialog. Internal organizational solutions in which different users and locations are networked in essentially closed systems also are not discussed in detail here. Instead the focus is on the technical issues in the networking of sources of numeric materials data, involving capability and ease of access, use and exchange of scientific information among interorganizational users.

THE TECHNICAL HURDLES

In discussing the technical hurdles, it is useful to be more specific about what is meant by networking in this discussion. For materials databases, it goes beyond the simple electronic connection and includes providing the ability to easily and reliably compare and exchange numeric data from the different databases, and ideally to search for and retrieve answer sets from many databases with common command languages and in concert.

One way of defining the technical hurdles is by noting the increasing levels of complexity that may have to be dealt with in networking multiple databases, starting with the simplest situation:

- Fully compatible databases at a single location

- Fully compatible databases at many different locations

- Relatively compatible but independent databases with mixed terminology

- Relatively incompatible databases with mixed terminology and different database management systems (DBMS)

Networking databases within single companies or organizations usually avoids of a number of these problems, because wholly compatible formats and terminology and a single DBMS can be mandated and controlled. Personal-computer and work-station environments tend to be of this type, and work well in many instances. The limitations of such systems arise when there is a need to add new data from other sources to these closed or limited systems, as is often the case. And the likely sources of such data may reside in a variety of locations and be stored within many different DBMSs. The commercial developments in networks, the CEC Demonstrator Programme and the MPD Network, both assume that users of many different types of systems will be seeking data and, therefore, that the networks must be flexible in providing access to their databases.

The stages of networking which can be dealt with in treating these problems while networking a number of materials databases include, in additive fashion:

- Networking databases on a single computer system at a single location in compatible format and DBMS;

- Linking geographically distributed but fully compatible databases with interactive software;

- Linking geographically distributed incompatible databases with "pass-through" communications;

- Creating new software to provide coordinated search of geographically distributed databases with different DBMS and terminology

Among the many issues to be dealt with in providing engineers and material scientists with direct access to machine-readable material property databases in any of the various electronic media available [7] are:

- Making the search and retrieval system very easy to use

- Dealing with the confusing terminology and nomenclature in the field

- Providing adequate flexibility in search strategies

- Displaying the data in clearly understood and logical groupings given the limitations of the media

- Providing adequate graphics capability for the user

- Providing ease of access and connection to the online system

- Assuring reasonable interface with PC and CD-ROM data systems including downloading capabilities, and

- Dealing with more than one database management system possibly more than one location, and

NETWORK SOLUTIONS

Given these various problems and partial or complete responses to the broad networking need, the basic elements to solutions are:

- A number of well-focused materials databases, assembled by experts in the respective fields, networked together for the benefit of users

- Access mode from geographically diverse sites
- A menu-driven interface to the networked system
- An interactive thesaurus/glossary system
- Standard formats for materials data
- Neutral data interchange formats

THE NETWORK INTERFACE

Materials database networks will be searched not only by experienced information specialists, but also by a broad new audience of engineers and scientists [7]. This end-user audience will include small engineering design companies and individual consultants as well as large organizations. In the case of numeric/factual databases, searches are often so specific that relying upon intermediate searchers, however knowledgeable, may require many iterations and still be largely unsatisfactory. Enabling the search to be performed by the user of the information improves the efficiency and cost effectiveness of the search.

Unlike trained professional information specialists, most engineers and material scientists spend only a portion of their time searching for material property data; the search and retrieval procedures must not be difficult to learn the first time or to recall upon returning to the system sometime later. They will not have the time to read ponderous manuals, learn complex command languages, and deal with cryptic response messages; all require a relearning process each time the system is used. Upon entering a data system, users expect to find a very easy-to-use interface, in which the steps are logical and largely intuitive or very smoothly guided. This may be dealt with by providing:

- Menu-driven search screens, arrayed in user-defined logic
- Search with the users language, avoiding the need for user knowledge of an array of specific commands to complete searches is avoided
- A variety of search paths, recognizing that different types of users (research, materials selection, design, quality assurance, etc) and different applications will require different queries, as discussed in greater detail below

- Incorporation of an extensive "metadata" system in the form of an interactive thesaurus and hierarchy, translating user queries to all other acceptable nomenclature and terminology, and responding quickly to clarify the meaning of names, terms and abbreviations. This must provide the common links across all sources linked by the network.

EASE OF ACCESS TO NETWORK OPERATIONS

As end-users begin to utilize online network systems, they will expect quick and easy access to the networks [7]. Unfortunately, that is not always their actual experience, as locating the correct telecommunications links to assure minimum cost connections, addressing or programming the local software to make the connection, and actually completing the link may be a very frustrating and discouraging process.

Network data systems hoping to attract many users from the engineering and material science communities will have to provide some preprogrammed software on an easy-to-install and personalized disks to minimize the problems and shorten the time involved in getting online. Still, the first logon will involve a little extra time, but in well-designed systems, follow-on accesses should be made quickly and routinely.

The cost of such online connections may also deter potential network users. However, by preparing well in advance and by choosing those systems in which charges are based upon actual data utilized (sometimes called value pricing) rather than time online, the feeling that the "clock is running" can be avoided, and search costs limited to useful information received. Both MPD Network and STN International utilize such value pricing, so searchers are not discouraged from taking their time to look carefully within the system for all useful data.

NETWORK SYSTEMS INTERFACE WITH PC AND CD-ROM SYSTEMS

Most users will maintain their own internal databases on some type of computerized system, whether it be a personal computer, a work station or a mainframe, and whether data storage is by tape, floppy disk or CD-ROM. Periodically, there will be a desire to update that internal system, ideally by going to a single data source like MPD Network, locating and accessing the required data, and downloading it into the internal database. Users will expect this to be a smooth and inexpensive process, not greatly hardware or software dependent.

By providing options for data transmission, *e.g.*, ASCII or DIF (a standard

"Data Interchange Format"), online systems may be responsive to much of this need, but considerable computer knowledge or experience may be required to make a smooth two-to-three step conversion. Ideally, data would be transferred between two systems operating on the same dbms, *e.g.,* ORACLE, a DBMS available at all levels. In most cases, however, at least one and likely two conversions will be needed, and that is not likely to change in the near future because of the absence of much progress in DBMS standardization among the engineering and material science community. Several groups, notably the Versailles Advanced Materials and Standards group and ASTM Committee E-49 on Computerization of Material Property Data, to develop a new neutral data interchange format for the exchange of data among databases by a recognized and consistent protocol particularly suited to complex numeric data. Once accepted and published, it should be adopted by all commercial operations in the field.

The principal operating mechanism for commercial network systems is clearly to offer the widest array of options available for the conversion of information for transfer to neutral formats. In this way, no constraints are imposed on the searchers and the greatest breadth of audience will be served.

CURRENT MAJOR NETWORK PROJECTS

Three illustrations of major materials information networking programs will be examined in the light of the points made earlier: a) the Materials Database Network Demonstrator Programme of the Commission of European Communities; b) the Materials Property Data (MPD) Network; and c) STN International.

The European Community Materials Data Network Demonstrator Programme [4] set out to develop a prototype system linking eleven independently developed numeric databases. The system developed to the point where users are provided with a common directory, and query within a menu-driven interface which database will contain the type of information desired. Once the key database is identified, access information is provided, but no direct connection is enabled and that is handled as a separate transaction.

Consideration is now being given to the next stage of development for the EC Programme. A next logical step might be to provide "pass-through" links to the individual databases, although much current opinion seems to favor provision of these particular databases in media other than common online access.

The MPD Network [5] is a service being developed by the National Materials Property Data Network, Inc. in cooperation with the American Chemical Society to provide improved access to worldwide sources of reliable numeric materials performance data. This step was taken in response to needs identified on an international scale by several groups including CODATA [3], the US National Institute of Standards and Technology (NIST; formerly, the Bureau of Standards) [2], and The Materials Properties Council (MPC, then called Metals Properties Council, 8). Two activities established a specific agenda for action on the subject: the Fairfield Glade Conference in 1982 [1], sponsored by the above groups, and the National Materials Advisory Board's study in 1983 [9].

There have been two major steps in the establishment of the MPD Network: first, the development of a research prototype network based upon SPIRES and the technology developed of the NBS/DOE/MPDN project [10] known as Materials Information for Science and Technology (MIST), and second, the building of the production MPD Network in MESSENGER software on STN International.

The operating philosophy of the MPD Network is to provide access to many worldwide sources of numeric materials data via a menu-driven interface supported by an interactive thesaurus and a data directory of other sources, as illustrated by the schematic in Figure 1. A common self-guiding command language is used to search all databases, and the searcher does not have to know in which database the answers are located in order to retrieve them. The issue of multiple locations is dealt with by the use of the STN International multiple host system.

Beginning in October of 1990, the first production offering of MPD Network will be made, encompassing about eight numeric materials databases in addition to the thesaurus and directory. A new software package will be available to help new online searchers deal with unfamiliar telecommunications procedures.

STN International [6] is the worldwide online scientific and technical information network operated jointly by American Chemical Society's Chemical Abstracts Service (CAS) in Columbus, Ohio; FIZ-Karlsruhe, a scientific and educational organization in Karlsruhe, FRG, and Japan Information Center of Science and Technology (JICST), in Tokyo, Japan. It was first established in 1983, and in earlier years concentrated mostly on bibliographic and chemical structure databases of interest to chemists and chemical engineers. More recently, there has been a much more intense focus on numeric data, primarily on the thermochemical and thermodynamic properties of substances.

In terms of the networking options discussed herein, STN International has dealt directly with the need to network different locations together through the establishment of its three service centers (nodes) on three continents.

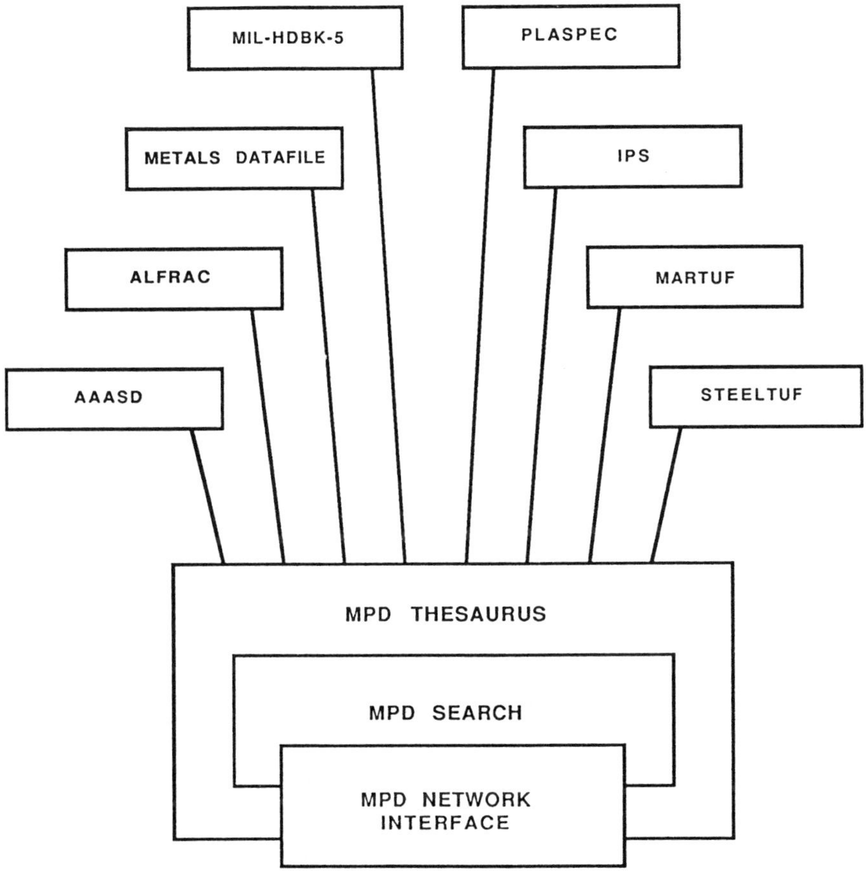

FIGURE 1. Schematic Plan of MPD Network of Materials Property Databases

A schematic representation of the STN International functional structure is shown in Figure 2. Users access STN and select from about 100 scientific technical databases; it is transparent to the user whether the database selected is hosted in the USA, Europe or Asia. Problems in dealing across the three service centers are minimized by utilizing the same software (MESSENGER) at all locations, and all databases are loaded in a common file structure.

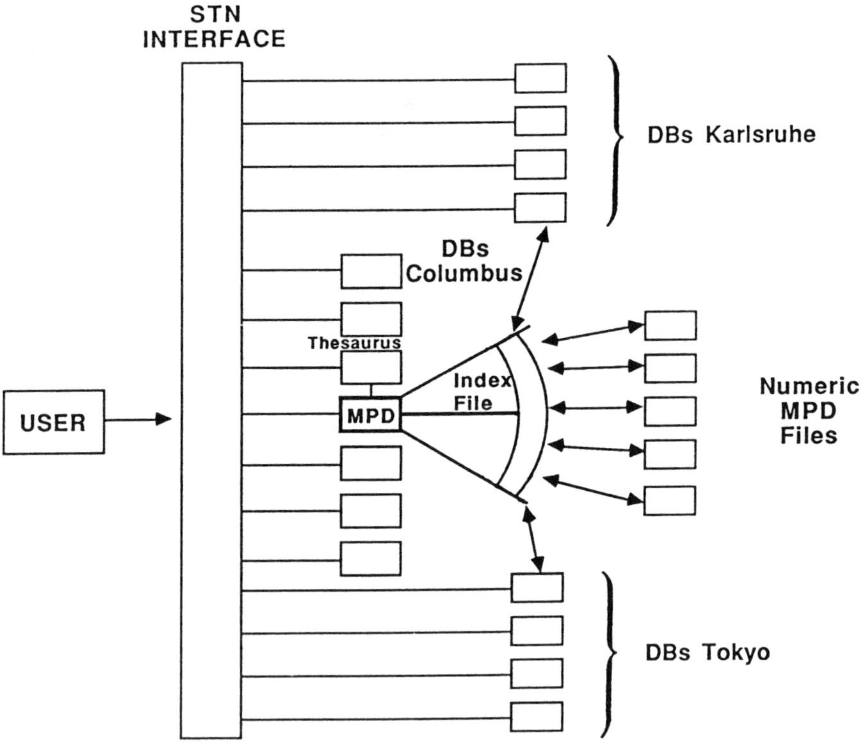

FIGURE 2 - Schematic of MPD Network on STN International

End-users problems with telecommunications and complex query formulation are addresses by STN International with a special software package known as STN EXPRESS. In addition to aiding access, it assists users in defining chemical structure queries before going online.

Until recently, databases on STN International have been searchable one at a time, though cross-over with queries from a common registry file of chemical substance information to other files is permitted. More recently, attention to joint searching of clusters of files is being developed, initially in a joint program with the MPD Network. STN International has incorporated a number of software capabilities directed especially at numeric data into the MESSENGER software, notably range searching, units conversion, tolerance setting, and table display.

THE FUTURE OF MATERIALS DATABASE NETWORKING

Relatively sophisticated networks of numeric scientific databases such as the MPD Network and STN International appear to be dealing adequately with the complexities of dealing with relatively diverse databases content, multiple locations and the simplification of user interactions by maintaining a common database management system across all nodes (service centers). Improving the ease of dealing with a larger number of nodes, as envisioned in the conceptual development of the MPD Network, might be a logical next extension of networking capability. There also will undoubtedly be substantial growth in the number of individual databases linked by these existing networks.

The major technical hurdle left untouched is the networking of materials databases with diverse database management systems. With the advent of standard data exchange formats, increasing the likelihood of predictable structure in incoming data from most sources, may make the last hurdle an unnecessary one. The significant expense to develop networking software able to deal with variable DBMSs may not be justified, in comparison with the task of preparing mapping programs to handle one or even a few standard formats in which incoming data would be provided.

The results is that the development of much more sophisticated materials database networks is relatively unlikely. As noted above, the addition of more nodes and many more databases may clearly be anticipated. However these advances plus the increased capability to deal with larger quantities of data on personal computer systems with new disk technologies makes major investments in totally new materials database networking technology relatively unnecessary.

SUMMARY

Networking of numeric materials databases presents several challenges in the design of systems attempting to deal with users' desires to access many sources simultaneously. Among the key elements are:

- Multiple but separate databases
- Mixed and inconsistent terminology
- Different locations
- Different database management systems

Thus far, those systems responding to these needs have had to compromise to some degree on some of these, and even the most completely developed, such as MPD Network on STN International, maintain a single search and retrieval software across all nodes of the system.

In materials data networks, as with individual databases, ease of use and consistency with user expectations are paramount in gaining acceptance by engineers and materials scientists. Among the key recommendations for systems most responsive to user expectations are: .nf

- User-oriented interface
- Interactive thesaurus
- Flexible search strategies
- Ease of telecommunications access
- Compatibility with PC, CD-ROM and other mainframe applications
- Ability to deal with multiple, distributed databases with a common command language
- Ability to deal with multiple database management systems via a standard neutral data interchange format

Advances in standard materials data interchange formats will make unlikely the expenditure of the necessary effort to develop networks capable of dealing across an undefined variety of database management systems.

REFERENCES

[1] *Computerized Materials Data Systems, Proceedings of the Fairfield Glade Conference*, J.H. Westbrook and J.R. Rumble, Editors, National Bureau of Standards, Gaithersburg, MD, 1983.

[2] Ambler, E., Engineering Property Data-A National Priority, *Standardization News*, ASTM, Philadelphia, August, 1985, pp. 46-50.

[3] *Materials Data for Engineering, Proceedings of a CODATA Workshop*, Schluchsee, FRG, J.H. Westbrook *et al*, Editors, FIZ-Karlsruhe, September, 1985.

[4] Kroeckel, H., and Steven, G., European Activities Towards the Integration and Harmonization of Materials Data Systems, *Proceedings of the First International Symposium on Computerization and Networking of Materials Property Data Bases*, J.S. Glazman and J.R. Rumble, Editors, ASTM STP 1017, Philadelphia, April, 1989, pp. 63-74.

[5] Kaufman, J.G., The National Materials Property Data Network: A Cooperative National Approach to Reliable Performance Data, *Proceedings of the First International Symposium on Computerization and Networking of Materials Data Bases*, J.S. Glazman and J.R. Rumble, Editors, ASTM STP 1017, Philadelphia, April, 1989, pp. 7-22.

[6] *Databases in Science and Technology - STN International*, The American Chemical Society, Chemical Abstracts Service, Columbus, 1989.

[7] Kaufman, J.G., Increasing Materials Data System Responsiveness to User Expectations, *Proceedings of the Second International Symposium on Computerization and Networking of Materials Data*, December, 1989, Orlando, Fla, ASTM STP 1106 (to be published).

[8] *An Online Materials Property Database*, Presented at the Winter Annual Meeting of ASME, MPC-20, J.A. Graham, Editor, ASME, New York, 1983.

[9] *Materials Data Management - Approaches to a Critical National Need*, National Materials Advisory Board (NMAB) Report No. 405, National Research Council, National Academy Press, Washington, September, 1983.

[10] Grattidge, W. *et al*, *Materials Information for Science and Technology*, NBS Special Technical Publication No. 726, National Bureau of Standards, Gaithersburg, MD, November, 1986.

STANDARDS FOR MATERIALS DATABASES: AN INTERNATIONAL CONCERN

N. Swindells and H. Kröckel
Commission of the European Communities
Institute for Advanced Materials
Joint Research Centre
Petten, The Netherlands

1. INTRODUCTION

Information is a commodity of central importance to any enterprise and particularly to manufacturing industry as the primary creator of wealth. Industries are both creators and consumers of information which will be distributed within a company, or industrial group or sector and value is added to the information by processing it and turning it into products. This information is in two forms: data, which are the numerical results of measurements, and knowledge, which is the understanding of the meaning of the items of data and of the relationships between them. Such information is an asset to the company which owns it since it has invested time, money and resources in acquiring it and it should recognise that this asset should be managed as carefully as all its more obvious assets in order to obtain a satisfactory return on its investment.

The availability and supply of information about engineering materials has come to be recognised as an important factor in industrial development only relatively recently and within the last five years the level of interest in this field has increased sharply and on a world-wide scale. The trade in materials products is a global one and it is becoming clear that the potential market for information on materials is also world-wide. Whenever a commodity is traded and subjected to operations which add value to it then standards are necessary so that all the participants in the process know what they are working with and what their obligations are. Materials information can be regarded as a commodity and therefore requires standards both to establish the conditions of its production and to accompany its subsequent storage, shipment and processing stages. These stages may take place within the same organisation but, for efficiency reasons, increasingly they take place in different organisations. These organisations may be in different countries with different working languages and national manufacturing practices. The availability of internationally standardised packet-switched telecommunications networks makes such interconnections a trivial matter. However, the ease of making the physical connections hides the fact that the **information** transferred by this means may be unintelligible to the receiver, particularly if the receiver is another computer program.

The need for international standards to facilitate the development of an international market in information is therefore well established and several workshops and reports [1] have called for such developments. The following sections attempt to analyse the implications of the international requirements in this subject, to show what progress has been made and to identify what still has to be achieved.

2. THE FLOW OF MATERIALS INFORMATION

A simplified model of the flow of materials information (data and knowledge) is shown in Figure 1. Each stage of this process in a company carries a cost which is only recovered from the profit when the product made by using the information is sold. Each stage therefore has to be optimised in relation to the circumstances. At each stage the information has to be stored in some form and the use of computer and communication technologies in materials research and engineering is causing a world-wide trend to computerize the flow and storage of the materials information which that engineering requires. This trend is marked by the intensive development and introduction of materials data and knowledge bases and of schemes for interfacing them to the systems with which they interact. Recently it has become more important to think of these interactions as being between machine and machine, involving diverse engineering software, instead of the interaction between machine and human, which has been the most common experience up until now.

Growing international experience of both public and private databases has shown that, for their proper function as components of the information flow, the optimization of a number of features is required in order to achieve this interaction. Important factors are:

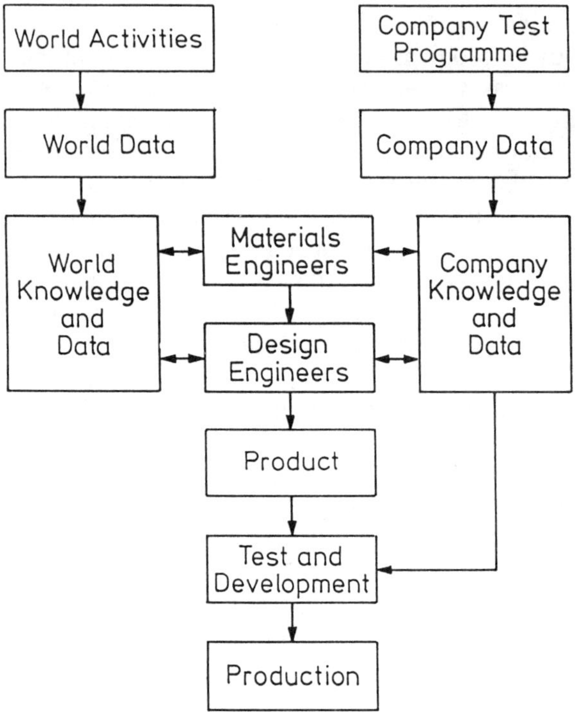

FIGURE 1 - Flow of materials information

- the data scope and relevance determined by the application;
- the data validity within that scope, arising from the origins of the data and its evaluation;
- the means of access to the data, which involves compatibility with other systems;
- the compatibility of the information to allow for automatic data interchange.

Optimization of the scope to a manageable size leads to databases of defined scope and design for a purpose which must be used in combination with others to cover wider needs. To provide a comprehensive data coverage a solution is sought in the linking of databases into integrated service networks. The development of such networks in the public domain is being attempted in both the USA and the European Community as well as in other regional groups and nation states. Inherent in the consequences of having to distribute information between different systems, because of its inhomogeneity, is the necessity to exchange information between heterogeneous collections of systems.

In addition to being exchangeable the data haveo be valid for the purpose, which establishes the need for some form of quality assurance for the information. The quality will be established by many factors stretching back to the quality of the origins but an important factor in this chain are the mathematical methods used to process the original, "raw" data and turn them into some other form suitable for a particular purpose, such as a specification or a design limit.

It is clear from Figure 1 that materials databases are part of a communication process and therefore the need for compatible access has several consequences. Multi-lingual terminology and standards to enable data exchange to take place between systems has come to be recognised as the central determining factor to enable the international market for information to develop.

3. THE ROLE OF STANDARDS

It is obvious that the various forms of interaction of materials data systems with each other and with a great variety of other systems in industrial, national and international environments require compatibility and interchangeability which can only be achieved by international standardization Developing standards for novel technology, which materials databases are, can be controversial. Standards should neither restrain development nor discourage innovation before a technology has reached maturity.

Materials data banks involve both post-maturity and pre-maturity standards. The post-maturity standards relate to some of the descriptions of materials, to the test procedures which generate property data and they control parts of the knowledge base with design codes and codes of practice. The pre-maturity standards attempt to address the areas of data, systems, operation, interfaces and interconnections between systems. Even the existing standards for materials and their test procedures need more stringent definitions for the designation and identification of materials and for the control over the recording of the results of standard tests.

Pre-mature standards for the structural and operational features of databases, such as system architecture, database organisation and user interfaces, should be avoided. Their task can be achieved at this stage of development by the definition of a "conceptual schema" and Codes of

Practice for functional requirements, such as the one which was developed by the Commission of the European Communities (CEC) and extended by CODATA [2].

4. PRE-STANDARDIZATION RESEARCH - THE ROLE OF VAMAS

To deal with the pre-maturity situation, which applies to most aspects of computerized materials information, it is necessary to proceed on the basis of an understanding of the problems which have been established by research. This is the role for which VAMAS was established: to stimulate and co-ordinate pre-standardisation research on advanced materials among the major industrialised nations, with the CEC representing the European Community (EC).

VAMAS Technical Working Area 10 (TWA 10), Materials Databanks, works on issues related to the developing standardization which will impact significantly on the building and use of computerised materials databases. This working area was established in 1985 in the form of a task group. The primary objectives are to:

- assess the role that standards can have in the computerized flow of materials information;
- identify needs, particular problem area and options for future standardisation activity;
- define, organise and coordinate pre-standardization research which addresses projects of international scope and transborder impact.

The objectives of TWA 10 are co-related with the activities of other international, national and regional institutions which are involved in the computerization of materials information and related enabling and standardizing activities, such as: CODATA, the CEC, ISO, ASTM, CEN (Comité Européen de Normalisation). TWA 10 endeavours to supplement and support the objectives and impact of these other organisations in the field of materials data systems where there is a benefit of a world-wide dimension.

The structure of the activities of the Technical Working Area 10 of VAMAS, concerned with materials databases, is shown in Figure 2, which attempts to summarise the outcomes of the first report. Two of the Projects undertaken, an inter-laboratory comparison of data evaluation methods and an inventory of materials designation systems, have either been concluded or are virtually complete and there are lessons from the results of these projects which have implications for the future.

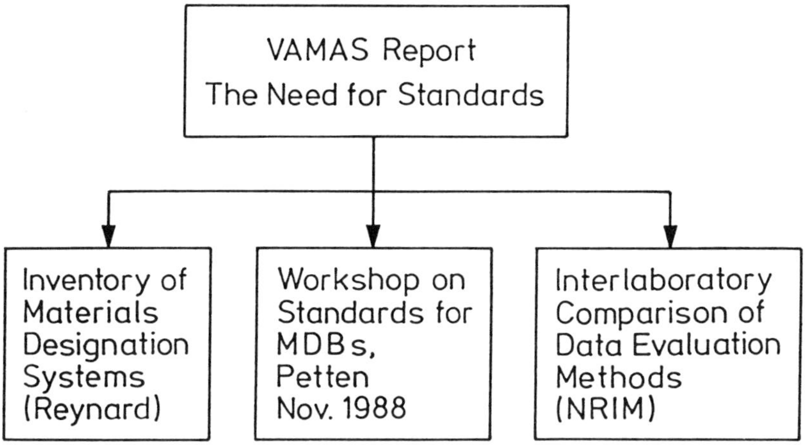

FIGURE 2
Structure of the activities of the Technical Working Area 10 of VAMAS

The comparison of data evaluation methods was concentrated on the methods used to refine or process data from tests on different aspects of creep and fatigue. In a round-robin exercise, participants were asked to use the most representative semi-empirical models which were also part of their numerical database system and apply the selected model to the same sets of data points circulated to all. The data sets included "well behaved" and "ill-natured" data for each kind of test.

The results for the creep data showed a large difference in computed curves at longer times from the application of commonly used models [3]. Only one method gave acceptable fit at 650 and 700 °C. The extrapolated stresses to cause rupture in 100 000 and 300 000 hours, which are typical values required to establish the allowable design stress for a high temperature application, showed remarkable differences depending on the data evaluation methods used.

The second area investigated, the designation systems for the labelling of materials in standards, is not yet complete. However, preliminary results [4] have shown that there is considerable potential for confusion and mis-identification arising from the use of similar or even identical labels for completely different materials when the world collection of information is considered. The study also showed that even the latest attempts to rationalise and standardise identifiers are failing to take into account the consequences of the international computerisation of materials information.

The general lesson from these two international investigations is that information handling and processing methods which may have been established with a local, or even national, consistency, do not have consistency on an international scale. They also show that the most basic of access procedures will fail to find valid information of relevance because the terminology is ambiguous and inadequate. If the development in the market for information on materials is to follow the growth of the international market in the materials products, which it must, then clearly the nature of that information is of concern to the international industrial, engineering and scientific communities.

This concern applies also to regional trading arrangements. It should be remembered that the EC is itself an international system of twelve sovereign Member States and nine working languages.

5. STEPS TO INTERNATIONAL STANDARDISATION

Standardisation at any level of organisation requires a number of conditions to be satisfied before effective progress can be achieved. These constitute a series of steps to achieving the goal of general international trade which have to be climbed and some of these steps and the way to overcome them can now be identified.

There must first be a clear financial benefit which would persuade diverse groups to pool their interests and contribute effort to achieve this common goal. The financial benefit from participating in the materials information market, in contrast to the market for chemical information, is currently too small to be a driving force. Progress through collaboration will therefore have to be as a consequence of an expression of hope, or be supported by central authorities at this stage. What is lacking is a financial model which expresses the costs currently borne by industry using existing practices which could be used as a basis for assessing the costs and benefits of the newer methods.

There are examples from some sectors where the financial incentives have been established. A recent workshop organised by VAMAS on designation systems for advanced engineering ceramics was such a case where the original motivation was the need to identify the ceramics with a high added value and separate them from the low value products such as furnace refractories. The collaboration of metal producing companies within the EC to reduce the number of specifications to which they have to manufacture material products is another example which has a clear financial justification. The general case has still to be made however.

Standardisation within the field of computerised materials information also needs the recognition of the requirements in the different parts of the field: at the information level, at the system level, at the interchange level, and at the access level.

At the information level, some definite progress on an international scale can be detected. The recent success to achieve a proposal for a model for the representation of a material for data exchange purposes in the STEP Programme of ISO should be of benefit for the development of systems. *Ad hoc* standards have been developed in some areas of materials by agreements to use common test procedures and methods of presenting data. In Europe, the European Aluminium Association of manufacturers has led the way in the metals field, which others groups will now have to follow. For engineering plastics the CAMPUS consortium of European manufactures has made considerable progress in attracting more collaborators to the original core of producers. The officers of ASTM Committee E-49 have repeatedly stated that they welcome international participation in the work of the Committee [5].

What is clear from the experience of the developments described above is that the *ad hoc* approaches, made on a regional or sectional basis and driven by strong financial forces, will make rapid progress while the truly international actions are probably too slow to have a strong influence on development at this stage. Therefore, ways have to be found for both speeding up the international developments and providing coordination between the various *ad hoc* activities in order to avoid conflict and duplication.

This is where there is a vital role for international organisations such as VAMAS and CODATA to play. Several actions of VAMAS have been described above. Within CODATA the Task Group on Database Management under the Chairmanship of Dr A. J. Barrett is active in the identification and analysis of issues which are relevant to the management and operation of systems. It was this Group which produced the guide to the building and operation of materials databases and is currently working on issues related to the benefits of using databases and also on the means for describing and specifying their size and functionality.

Within the EC further international programmes to follow the Materials Database Demonstrator Programme are under discussion which would build on the experience gained during that exercise. These programmes may also involve partnership with organisations from the European Free Trade Association (EFTA). Political and economic changes in Eastern Europe are increasing the opportunities for international programmes with members of COMECON, who are also members of CODATA.

There is still, however, widespread ignorance and misunderstanding within much of the engineering community about the issues involved in these developments and their economic importance. There is, therefore, a requirement for an educational process which is a necessary step to achieving wider participation and increasing the effectiveness of the contributing actions. The professional and scientific institutions in the materials field have a major role to play in this educational process and many of them are international in their membership and outlook. The Institute of Metals in the United Kingdom has recently created an official section of one of its major committees to enable the Institute to be able to develop policies for itself and to respond to national and international proposals for the computerisation of materials information. It will be able to inform its members and collect their response to important issues which will affect their working environment in the future.

6. CONCLUSIONS

Information on engineering materials has been identified as an important industrial resource only in relatively recent times and there is, therefore, a large degree of immaturity about the understanding of the issues involved and of the means for making progress on them.

The increasing recognition of the importance of the exchange of materials data between heterogeneous systems and software establishes the requirement for standardisation of terminology and the capability to deal with alternative formats.

The need for exchange and interchange of data also determines the need for the establishment of quality assurance procedures and validity criteria.

Probably the main needs are to generate a wider awareness, to increase the participation in international programmes to resolve these issues and to establish an international framework within which the supply of information in computerised form can develop alongside the international market in materials products.

At present, the economic strength of the materials sector of the information market is insufficient for it to support extensive actions on its own. While some progress has been made, further development will require the involvement of major industrial groups as well as national and regional central authorities but for this to occur the financial benefits from participation have to be established more clearly.

In addition, ways must be found for the coordination of these actions for the general international benefit. International organisations such as CODATA and VAMAS will have an increasingly important role to play in this task and the professional engineering institutes have a necessary function to educate their members and increase the numbers of experienced participants in the process.

7. REFERENCES

[1] Kröckel, H., Reynard, K.W., Rumble, J. (eds), "Factual Materials Databanks, the Need for Standards". *VAMAS report*, July 1987.

[2] Kaufman, J.G. (ed), Guide to Material Property Database Management, *CODATA Bulletin* no. 69 (Hemisphere Pub. Corp., Nov. 1988)

[3] Nishijima, S., Monma, Y., Kanazawa, K., National Research Institute for Metals, Tokyo, VAMAS report (to be published)

[4] Reynard, K.W., Wilkinson Consultancy Services, Broad Lane, Newdigate, Surrey RH5 5AT, England (private communication)

[5] Kaufman, J.G. *Proceedings of Second European Workshop on Materials Databases*, Petten, December 1989 (to be published)

DATABASE STANDARDS AND DATA MODELS - A MATERIALS VIEW AND MORE

John Rumble, Jr.
National Institute of Standards and Technology
Gaithersburg, MD, U.S.A.

INTRODUCTION

Databases containing material properties are asked many questions, such as:

> *"How do you find a material in a database and retrieve information about it?"*
>
> *"What data have been stored with test results?"*
>
> *"How can data be exchanged between databases?"*

The ease with which answers are developed determines how useful a database will be. In 1985 ASTM established Committee E49 on Computerized Material Property Data to help develop these answers by means of standard guidelines and practices that would facilitate and encourage materials database progress [1]. Today E49 is an active committee involving the worldwide community in its work and is in the process of finalizing many standards actions.

A second standards activity affecting materials databases is the ISO Standard for the Exchange of Product Data (STEP), an international effort aimed at facilitating transfer of computerized information about every engineering aspect of manufactured products [2]. The STEP Materials Committee has been developing a complete model of materials information that will support a variety of data exchange needs.

The purpose of this paper is to identify broad areas of standards concerns and information modeling as related to materials databases. The world of materials is extremely large and use of materials data even larger. Databases are being built for every type of materials, from wood to electronic materials, from concrete to pure chemicals. The technical approaches developed by E49 and ISO are by their very nature extensible beyond common structural engineering materials into the full realm of property data, that is, any collection of data related to properties of a substance. It is hoped that this paper will give guidance to work in these areas.

ASTM E49 WORK ON MATERIALS DESCRIPTION

Scientific and technical databases primarily deal with properties of materials, and the description of materials is fundamental to the storing and handling of computerized data in this area. The description of a material can be a very subtle matter with different description systems suitable for different applications. A purchasing agent wants to be able to specify enough information so the delivered product performs as planned. A researcher wants to have enough information to be able to reproduce someone else's research results. Materials specialists want to be able to refer to the material in a shorthand form to facilitate communication. Data publishers also want compact nomenclature to save space.

Each of these needs has two things in common: the need to be able to specify one particular material and the need to determine the equivalency of two materials so data sets generated separately can be combined.

The diversity of needs for description systems combined with the ease of changing minor aspects of an engineering material has led to a multiplicity of nomenclature systems. Every builder and user of materials databases must confront this problem which has led this topic to be an important target by ASTM Committee E49. Very early on, the committee realized that one could not choose between different systems for materials description since their use was by habit, by geographic location, and by need. Instead, the committee decided to develop a series of guidelines that would allow materials databases to handle as much of the complexity as desired, but to do so in a uniform way. The philosophy adopted consisted of several key elements.

a. Develop guidelines that would cover all the detail that anyone would report on a material

b. Specify a minimum set of information that *must* be reported to identify a material

c. Recognize some degree of hierarchy of materials description and allow determination of equivalency down to a specified level

d. Develop shorthand materials identification codes to facilitate brief or coded descriptions

A series of generic guidelines for the identification of different materials classes have been written and are being balloted by Committee E49 covering metals and alloys, ceramics, polymers, composites, and energetic materials. For these, seven primary types of information are specified, namely:

primary identifiers
specification
characterization
source
processing history
part detail
fabrication and service history

The generic guidelines have been developed in such a way that additional guidelines for specific materials may be developed. To date, such guidelines have been written for aluminum alloys, fibers, fillers and core materials for composites, and arc welds.

An additional feature is the support provided to determine materials equivalency which allows different data sets to be merged together. Materials equivalency can be at many levels, *e.g.*, ferrous alloys, steels, stainless steels, stainless steel 304, stainless steel 304 with a particular heat treatment and surface modification, etc. Various properties depend differently on the depth of classification, and having standard guidelines allows users to have flexibility in making comparisons.

ASTM E49 WORK ON RECORDING AND REPORTING DATA

Materials databases are being built that contain a wide variety of data such as test results, verification that materials meet specifications, and handbook data. Two questions must be addressed when adding data to a database.

"What information in addition to the 'property' value itself must be recorded to enhance the usability of a data value ?"

"What is the range of allowable information for a given data field ?"

Again, each materials database builder must answer these questions. Because users will want to take data from different databases and contrast and compare them, Committee E49 has developed standard guidelines for recording and reporting data. An important terminology point needs to be made here. By *data recording*, we mean the identification of fields of information that *SHOULD* be recorded with a property value. By *data reporting*, we mean the information that *MUST* be included as specified by a written procedure,r standard, or contract.

For testing of engineering materials for mechanical, corrosion, and tribological performance, as many as one hundred different fields of information can be recorded, covering details of the test specimens, the test procedure, actual measured results, derived and analyzed data, as well as environmental conditions. It is not intended that every field of information included in the recording formats will actually be used, but if the information is reported, the format will be defined.

Three different types of recording formats have been developed to date: For individual test methods, for combinations of similar test methods, *e.g.*, tensile tests, and for combinations of different tests in one area, *e.g.*, corrosion. Developing recording formats has not been as easy as hoped with major problems caused by subtle differences in the use of terminology or minor allowed variations in test procedures. For example, the results of composites tests depend significantly on humidity, both of the test environment and of the pretest sample handling. Translating those procedures into a finite number of data fields accurately takes time.

One type of recording format that has not been addressed by E49 is that of handbook or property data. In the materials area, results of many individual tests often are evaluated, validated, and combined together to give a unique value or range of values for a particular property. These can be called design values, minimum values, or nominal values depending on the review procedure, the data quality, and the application. A handbook or property value usually is a single number with a limited amount of supporting information, and is not directly traceable back to any individual test. As more and more handbooks are computerized, the need grows for recording formats for these types of data.

DATA QUALITY INDICATORS

Virtually every report on materials databases has emphasized the need for clear indicators of the quality of data in a database. Guidelines have been prepared by E49 for these as summarized in Table 1 that include major factors such as the reviewing body, the criteria for evaluation and validation, and the review procedure itself. The purpose of the indicators is not to be ultra critical of any particular data set, but rather to give users guidance as to the suitability of the data for an application. Clearly for critical applications, the need for quality is high, and when data are suspect, they must be verified. Use of these indicators should facilitate this process.

TABLE 1
Summary of Data Quality Indicators

Category	Examples
Data Source	Technical committee, producer
Class of Data	typical, design
Database Validation	yes or no
Validating Authority	
Completeness of Auxiliary Data	full, none
Test Procedures	standard
Security Status	unrestricted, classified

DATA EXCHANGE

A recent workshop [3] has identified four primary needs related to the exchange of computerized materials data, for commercial transactions, for support of computerized engineering, for direct exchange between databases, and for data entry into two or more databases.

Commercial Transactions

Materials data play an important role in commercial transactions. Data are often used to specify exactly what material is being purchased or shipped. Sometimes the material itself is involved; more often the primary focus is on a part or product, and the materials information is secondary. The computerization of these commercial transactions has been the subject of several standards activities, on the national level in the United States by ANSI Committee X12 and internationally as part of the EDIFACT standard [4].

Data Exchange between Materials Databases

In addition to the exchange of materials data in the context of larger data exchange activities, builders and users of materials themselves have some specialized data exchange needs. These relate to i) the need to exchange data, either individual records for comparison purposes or entire databases for concurrent use, between databases and ii) the need to create data entry files that can be used for several databases. At the Materials Data Interchange Workshop held at Rolls-Royce, Derby, England on September 14-15, 1989, a plan was outlined to test two pragmatic approaches for exchanging materials information under the auspices of Committee E49 and VAMAS. Preliminary tests are now underway.

Data Entry Exchange

Many groups now collect and enter data that eventually will be put into two or more databases, sometimes without any revision. Presently, there are no standards to facilitate this, and usually when a new database is loaded, special translation software must be developed, an expensive process. To support the reuse of data entry files of materials data, a well-defined neutral data entry format is needed. It is likely a subset of the neutral data exchange format discussed in the previous section can be identified to meet this need.

PRODUCT DATA STANDARDS - WHY?

A major international effort is developing standards to support exchange of data used in all phases of design, analysis, manufacture, test, and long-term support of *products*. Presently, each of these functions usually exists in a company as a separate island of computerized engineering, yet in the coming decade, passing data from one function to another will become commonplace.

The totality of the data which define the product for all applications over its expected life cycle is called "Product Data" and the standards work is called the "Standard for the Exchange of Product Model Data" (STEP) on the ISO level [2]. Product data include the geometry, topology, relationships, tolerances, attributes, materials, and features necessary to define completely a component part or an assembly of parts for the functions defined above.

The basic approach taken by STEP is that each computer-assisted engineering activity can be described by a formal information model that defines all the entities, their attributes, and their relationships. An entity is defined as an object, item, or thing about which information can be generated, stored, and exchanged. STEP has also defined a set of tools for the expression of that model. The tools include a modeling language [5], EXPRESS, a graphical representation of the model, called EXPRESS G (other graphical representations are also used), procedures for verifying conformance of the models, and tools to integrate related models together. The point of the model approach to data exchange is that physical implementation can be totally separated from the model by means of the formal language, thereby freeing the model developers from onerous details.

A wide variety of information models are under development including for drafting, geometry, finite element analysis, shape, and topology. One international ballot has been held and another is scheduled for 1991.

THE STEP MATERIALS INFORMATION MODEL

Because materials are integral to any manufactured product, STEP has a Materials Committee actively working with it. In 1989, the Materials Committee expanded its work and began a twofold approach to developing a materials model 1) to develop a general materials model that could cover a wide variety of engineering materials in a wide variety of engineering situations, and 2) to develop a more explicit model of information on polymeric composites that are analyzed using finite element methods.

This is not the forum to present the model in any great detail, especially as parts are dynamically progressing. However, the graphical representation in EXPRESS G will be briefly discussed to give the flavor of the elements of an information model.

A GENERAL MATERIALS MODEL

The materials model has three principal entities, as follows and as shown in Figure 1. The use of the underscore in the entity name is common in information modeling.

1. material
2. material-data-generation-environment
3. material-property

Each of the primary entities can be expanded further as is shown for the entity *material* in Figure 2 . Here there are three additional entities: processing-history, shape, and description-detail.

INFORMATION MODELING FOR OTHER SCIENTIFIC DATA

The use of standards and information models for scientific and engineering data is not limited to materials information. Every area of technical data

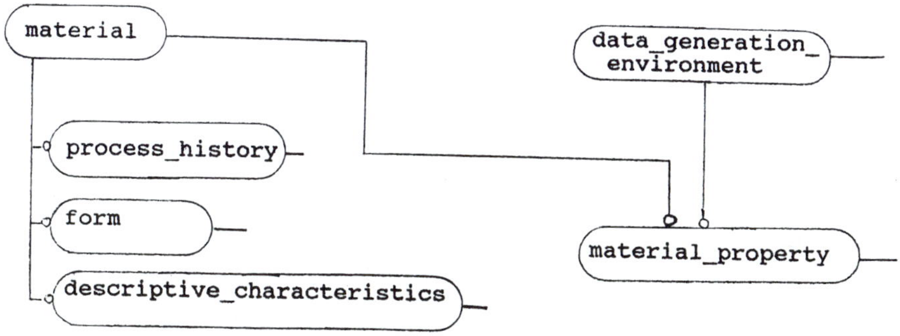

FIGURE 1
The overall STEP materials model consists of three primary entities (in ovals), **materials, data-generation-environment**, and **material-property**. Each of these can be further subdivided as shown by the entities under **material**. The small circles indicate direction.

can profit from these tools. Builders of technical databases that must describe substances, whether an engineering material, a chemical, a cell, or a bird, all need to have standard guidelines for describing the substance and recording pertinent data. It is expensive and even foolish to think that each builder must solve all the problems alone. Instead, consensus standards offer a way to reduce costs and arrive at good technical solutions.

The use of modern information modeling techniques for technical information is just starting. While it is tempting for the research scientist to insist that a good understanding of technical data exists, in fact, it does not. Formal information modeling tools are powerful and will bring new insights.

Already the work of ASTM Committee E49 has expanded to cover chemical information. Disciplines such as biology, geology, and others should be looking into forming their own groups.

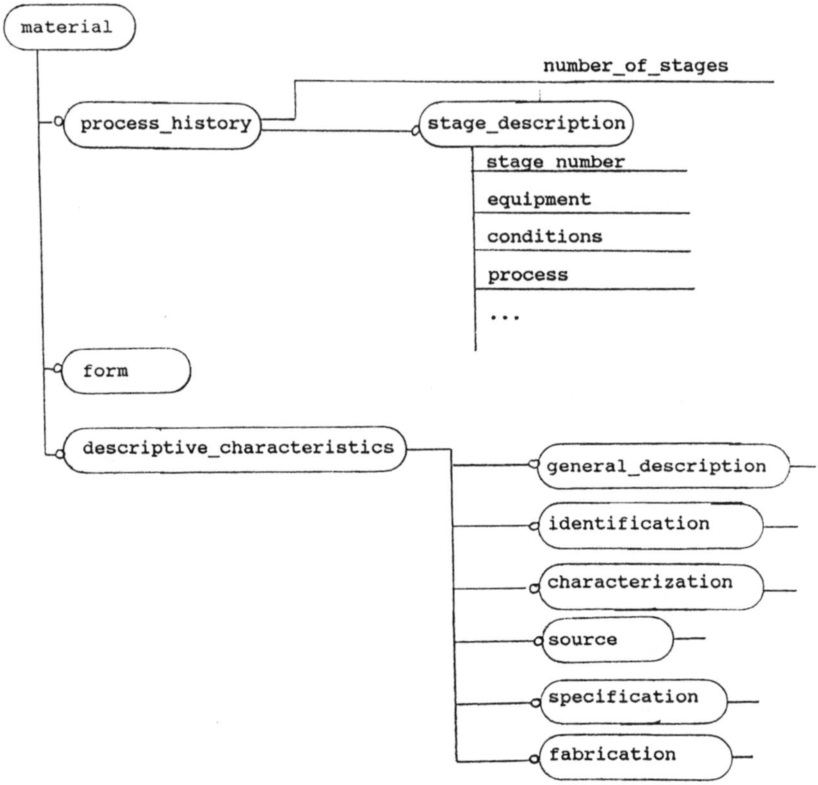

FIGURE 2

The STEP materials model goes into great detail. For example, the entity **process-history** has many attributes (as underlined) and other associated entities. Also, each subentity under **descriptive-characteristic** is expanded in detail.

REFERENCES

[1] J. G. Kaufman, "Standards for Computerized Materials Property Data - ASTM Committee E49," in *Computerization and Networking of Materials Databases*, J. Glazman and J. Rumble, Eds. (American Society for Testing and Materials, Philadelphia, PA, 1989).

[2] B. Smith, "External Representation of Product Definition Data" NISTIR89-4166 (U.S. Department of Commerce, National Institute of Standards and Technology, Gaithersburg, MD, 1989).

[3] J. Rumble, "Making Materials Database Standards International," *ASTM Standardization News*, 17, 32-36 (1989).
[4] "An Introduction to Electronic Data Interchange", ANSI ASCX-12 (American National Standards Institute, New York, NY, July 1987).

"Electronic Data Interchange for Administration, Commerce, and Trade (EDIFACT), ISO Draft Standard ISO/DIS 9735 (October 1987).
[5] "Information Modeling Language EXPRESS", Document Number N496 of ISO Committee TC184/SC4/WG1 (May 1990).

THE INFORMATION BASE SYSTEMS FOR MATERIALS RESEARCH

Yuzuru Fujiwara, Nobuo Ohbo, Hiroyuki Kitagawa
and Kazunori Yamaguchi
Institute of Electronics and Electronics
University of Tsukuba
Japan

INTRODUCTION

Computers and software have been used to support research and development of science and technology. Large accumulation of programs of numerical calculation, bibliographic and factual databases, and expert systems implemented in various fields are available and are used extensively.

One of the major problems in producing databases is manageability, especially identification of the entities unless small databases are concerned and provide access to data according to contents. Although both problems seem to be simple, it is not the case, because they are related with the meaning of data, which is one of the furthest goals of computers. Various data models have been proposed to improve capabilities of database management systems. For example, the relational model is very popular because it is easy to use and is theoretically well-founded. Many attempts are reported to extend the model *e.g.,* RM/T (the extended relational model) by Codd [1], ADT (abstracts data type) by Stonebraker [2], abstractions by Smith [3], and so on, and to overcome restrictions of a basic form of the relational model which requires that values are atomic and may not be structured. This means that data should be simple and that you may not input complicated data necessary for materials design. The network model is flexible and the hierarchical model has been used widely, while they have the same problems as those mentioned above. Object oriented DBS [4], the E-R model based DBS by P.P.S. Chen [5] etc. are also being developed but they are not appropriate for large scale information systems.

It is to be noted that the registry numbers and standard nomenclature cannot be the solution to these issues [7].

INFORMATION BASE SYSTEMS FOR MATERIALS RESEARCH

Non-linear optical materials information is taken as an example in a database called OPM-IBS (non-linear Optical Materials Information Base System) which contains bibliographic, spectral, graphic and text data of non-linear optical materials, and has been compiled for years. It has comprehensive data in this particular field and the contents are of high quality in the sense of critical evaluation as well as containing a sufficient quantity of information necessary for research and development [6].

In order to describe polymeric materials which are one of the major optical materials, it is necessary to include not only structures of repeating units but also other structural and nonstructural information, *i.e.,* explicit structural information contains that of repeating units, stereoregularity, irregular structures (*e.g.,* branches, chain ends, head-to-head addition of vinyl monomer, 1-2 or 3-4 addition in 1-4 addition of polyisoprene), degree of polymerization, and dispersion; implicit structural information contains that of production processes (*e.g.,* hydrogenated PIP/EPR), reactions (*e.g.,* chlorinated PE), starting monomer (*e.g.,* polyvinylalcohol from polyvinyl acetate); related structural information contains that of additives, catalysts and so on; and nonstructural information of the types of properties (*e.g.,* high density PE), processes (*e.g.,* high pressure polymerization), use (*e.g.,* engineering plastics) [6-11].

Although polymeric materials have many attributes to be described, all of them are not usually obtained. The lack of data is significant and materials cannot be fully specified. Moreover, it is not always required to know the value of every attribute, but the generic classes of materials are of concern. Sometimes, all of these attributes are not sufficient to describe compounds and yet further information is required such as isotope substitution, higher order structures due to mechanical or thermal treatment and so on.

On the contrary, minor differences between distinct values may be neglected from a practical point of view. In a word, polymeric materials are mixtures of many kinds of isomers and homologues, and the required specification depends on the view of users, where the corresponding sets of attributes are combinations of all attributes irrespective of the levels. Therefore, the constitution of key attributes must be dynamic and may not be unique. The main requirement for information-base systems of materials research and development is to contain comprehensive information and full fledged functions compatible with the human brain as shown in Figure 1.

Systems for material design have components of the analysis of requirements, the structure design, the design of process and composition, and the estimation and evaluation of candidate structures, which are the major part of optical material design. A particular example of a non-linear optical material information-base system is briefly sketched in Figure 2 to give a clear image of the material information-base system.

Requirement analysis may be performed automatically to some extent by preparing a thesaurus and a taxonomy of technical terms [10,12]. Therefore, the information-base system must be capable of giving an appropriate interpretation of requirements provided with a taxonomy ranging from a use level to a basic property level of materials. Moreover, the prepared structures of terms may not always give a complete analysis of requirements, and a supplementary interpretation should be given from the outside.

In this case, the system should be able to recognize the part it cannot interpret, then to show the part and request instructions to accept new concepts, resulting in reconstruction of the thesaurus. In other words, it is desired that the design engine have a learning mechanism.

1) **Structure design**. After those requirements are analyzed, a set of basic property descriptions is obtained. The first step of structure design is to give model structures of the target material which is adapted to these property descriptions. This is accomplished basically by searching correspondence between structures and properties (a kind of knowledge base) stored in the taxonomy.

However, it is clear that many logical conflicts could occur during reasoning steps if a simple deductive inference method were applied. In the actual process, materials researchers have to content themselves with adapting a starting model materials to a subset of descriptions, and to fit the remainder of the descriptions, in an effort to identify new descriptors where there are conflicts.

The second step of structure design is the optimization of the model structure through structural modification. As mentioned above, the model structure partly fulfills constraints, so it is necessary to change the substructures to accommodate other requirements. The governing principle for this optimization is usually "additive property". It is the assumption that properties of a whole structure can be considered as the sum of properties of constituent substructures, giving a guideline for structural modification.

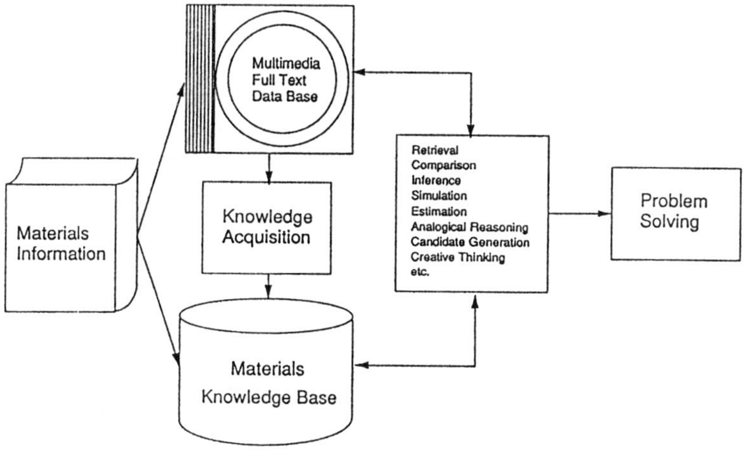

FIGURE 1. Materials Information Base System

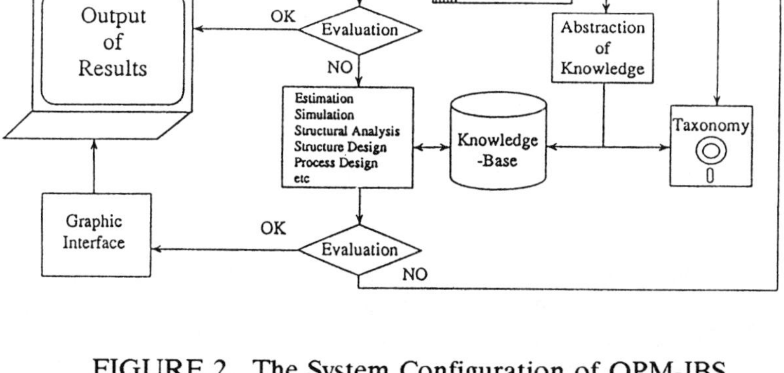

FIGURE 2. The System Configuration of OPM-IBS

While this estimation should be considered as a preliminary hypothesis to be tested by experiments, it should be noted that knowledge enables a researcher to estimate it. Therefore, it is necessary for the information-base system to provide a set of correspondences between properties and substructures so that it can give any combination of constituting units. This set of correspondences can be regarded as a kind of representation form of semantics about properties in terms of (sub)structures. Further, it is possible to combine the set with the thesaurus and the taxonomy of technical terms, so it may be considered as part of a representation scheme of semantics of expertise.

2) **Process and composition design.** There are various steps in process design and composition design, including combining materials, additional reagents, etc., and controlling their concentrations. It is necessary for R and D information-base systems to appropriately apply the knowledge to the given requirements, although this function requires semantic analysis and dynamic structurization of knowledge.

THE MODEL OF OPM - IBS SYSTEM AND DISCUSSIONS

OPM - IBS is based on the information model which is described as follows:

Let X = { x1, x2, ... xn } be a finite set of vertices,

$$H = (E1, E2, \dots Em), \qquad (1)$$

where Ei ≠ 0 (i= 1,2, ... m),

$$\bigcup_{i=1}^{m} Ei = X \qquad (2)$$

and xi may be a hypergraph itself *i.e.,* the model is a recursive labelled directed hypergraph.

The formal features of OPM - IBS are:
1) recursive representation of concepts,
2) objects can be entities, attributes, and links, and
3) meanings are carried by the information structure.

Since a huge quantity of data and knowledge is needed for a materials research information-base system, it is vital, in order to manage such a system, to introduce database management techniques. It seems promising to use a relational database for this purpose due to its logical clarity. However, relational databases have many constraints to integrate data and knowledge for materials design as mentioned above.

Those features of OPM - IBS are useful and practical, *e.g.,* storage of information is quite flexible and non-normal form data are allowed such as composite values, null values, multi media information and there are no actual constraints from data formats. Manageability is intensified to treat generic representation and is free from distinct entity presumption which is a serious constraint to identifiers of computer-readable-information in databases or in knowledge bases. Moreover, similarity access is realized by using powerful dynamic thesaurus and example-based taxonomy.

Most of the conventional database systems support only very simple data types such as integer, real number, string, etc., and lack functions which define new data types and manage them appropriately. Therefore, it is difficult for them to process data with diverse modalities and complexities such as compound names chemical graphs, tables, figures, time dependent values, etc.

In this respect, ADT-INGRES developed by Stonebraker et al. shows a direction which uses an abstract data type in a relational database context [2]. In ADT-INGRES, each individual column of a relation is regarded as ADTs (Abstract Data Types), and the implementation details are hidden from the level of application software. Operations are defined in terms of procedures written in programming language C which supports both database access and ADTs. In particular, it suggests that many of the problems concerning non-first normal form relation would be solved by using query command QUEL.ADTs. An object oriented database is more flexible as far as data formats and data via procedures are concerned . However, this approach causes serious problems of management of information especially identification and access.

The relationship between the logical view of the relational database and inference should be specified exactly in logical programming such as PROLOG. Logical schemas are very useful for deductive inference of the "if A then B", whereas it is not good at handling heuristic reasoning. Both types of inference are needed in material research systems, and a hybrid knowledge representation scheme is required to accommodate both of them and has been realized in the OPM - IBS.

It is known that frame-based knowledge representation is effective in the domain where the ratio of data to data descriptors is close to 1. This corresponds to the fact that taxonomy seems to match closely our intuition to structuralize the world. It also suggests enticing directions for processing inheritance, defaults, etc. While data for materials research range from that of the ratio 1:1 to that of the ratio 1:many, say three digits, it is important to data with a large ratio to have a thesaurus and a taxonomy.

CONCLUSION

A new information-base model is proposed for materials research and is called MIBS - SORITES (Materials Information Base Systems with Self Organizing Receptor Interconnections). The model can store, manage and manipulate composite information and can realize induction and learning capabilities to support scientists and engineers in the relevant fields.

ACKNOWLEDGEMENT

The authors appreciate the support by the Grant for Advancement of Science by the Ministry of Education and Culture (No.63880006 and No.024020547).

REFERENCE

[1] Codd, E.F., Extending the Database Relational Model to Capture More Meaning, *ACM TODS* 4(4) 1979.

[2] Stonebreaker, M., Rubenstein, B., and Guttman, A., Application of Abstract Data Types and Abstract Indices to CAD Data, *Proc. of Ann. Meeting Database Week*, San Jose, 1983, pp. 107-115.

[3] Smith, J.M., and Smith, D.C.P., Database Abstractions: Aggregation and Generalization, *ACM TODS* 2(2) 1977, pp. 105-133.

[4] Maier, D., Stein, J., Otis, A., and Purdy, A., Development of an Object Oriented DBMS, *Proc. ACM OOPSLA '86 Conference*, Portland, Oregon, 8, 1986.

[5] Chen, P.P.S., The Entity-Relationship Model--Toward a Unified View of Data, *ACM TODS* 1(1) 1976, pp. 9-36

[6] Fujiwara, Y., Nakayama, T., and Ohbo, N., Computer Aided Design System for Polymeric Materials, in *The Role of Data in Scientific Progress*. Codata-Eesevier, 1985, pp. 237-276.

[7] Fujiwara, Y., Ohbo, N., Databases and Knowledge Bases as Scientific Tools, *CODATA Bulletin* 64, 1986, pp. 23-27.

[8] Nishioka, A., Hatada, K., Fujiwara, Y., Polymer C13-NMR Database System with Bibliographic, Numerical, and Graphic Data, *Anal. Chem. Japan* 36(1), 1987, pp. 64-66.

[9] Fujiwara, Y., CAPDAS: Polymer Database on CD-ROM, *Information Management of Japan* 30(10), 1988, pp. 967-978.

[10] Fujiwara, Y., Lee, W.G., Ishikawa, Y., Nishioka, A., Hatada, K., and

Ohbo, N., A Dynamic Thesaurus for Intelligent Access to Research Databases, *Proc. the 44th FID Congress: Information-Knowledge-Evolution* 44(3), 1988, pp. 61-69.

[11] Fujiwara, Y., Murakami, H., Yamagishi, T., Ohbo, N., and Nakayama, T., A C13-NMR Databases System with Spectral Analysis and Estimation Functions for Polymer Research, *Japan and Germany Spectral Databases Workshop*, 1988.

[12] Fujiwara, Y., He, J., Chang, G., Ohbo, N., Kitawaga, H., and Yamaguchi, K., Self Organizing Information Base Systems for Materials Design, *Proc. of the 1th CAMSE*, Tokyo, August 1990.

MATERIALS DATA INTERCHANGE USING TABULAR FORMATS

Philip M. Sargent
Cambridge University Engineering Dept.
Cambridge, U.K.

MATERIALS DATA INTERCHANGE FORMATS

A simple data interchange format is presented below which is designed to offer the same facilities as dBase-III "flat-file" database files. The typical use envisaged is for taking tables of test data results produced by an automatic data acquisition system and hand-editing them so that they can be transferred to another organisation for storage or evaluation. The format is entirely at OSI level 7, "application" level, and relies on reliable end-to-end communication being set up by lower levels.

The exchange format here is purely syntactical. No fieldnames for materials or properties are defined as it is assumed that users will agree to refer to some independently collated thesaurus of technical terms. The only exceptions to this are a few "meta-fieldnames" describing catalogue structures. It is also demonstrated how to make the tabular format compatible with other data exchange standardization activities. The formats described here are more fully documented in a Cambridge University Engineering Department technical report [8].

Simplicity and User-Editing

The requirement to be simple for users to edit by hand has several implications. First, there must be no arbitrary "counts" such as numbers of records or lengths of strings to be typed in: it is awkward to have to re-edit a number at the beginning of the file whenever a spelling mistake is corrected near the end. The user should not have to make unnecessary decisions about the data which are not relevant to his own work, such as how long to allow for the length of text fields or the number of places of decimals required for numerics.

There should be no artificial and arbitrary limits on what can be typed so long as it obviously makes sense, this is an ideal but the proposed format goes further towards it than most. Software is quite capable of counting the number of fields, of distinguishing between strings and numbers, of measuring the length of the longest string and of recognising a wide variety of number formats; so it makes no sense to impose these tasks on the user.

dBase Files

The "dBase" file format is a *de facto* industry standard for the communication of database files between MS-DOS personal computers (PCs). Nearly all other database software products for PCs support translation to and from this format (*e.g.,* Borland's Reflex v2 and Paradox v3, Lotus' 1-2-3 v3, Quadbase's dQuery) and Ashton-Tate have published the specification [8]. The same file format is thus supported on more types of computers than will actually run the dBase program itself.

The format describes a single "flat-file", best thought of as a two-dimensional table of data where the columns are named (by "field-names") and the rows ("tuples") are not. There are a number of restrictions on the range of numbers permitted, the lengths of strings, the number of fields (columns) and the total size of any one file, but they are mostly not too onerous if they are handled by software, which they must be since the format is in binary and cannot be hand-edited.

CAMBRIDGE TABULAR DATA INTERCHANGE FORMAT

The plain-text translation of dBase datafiles is called the Cambridge Tabular Data Interchange Format (CTDIF). The actual format is best understood by first studying an example. In the following "file" the keywords are IMPLEMENTATION, NAME, FIELDLIST, ENDFIELDS, CTDIF-1, FIDTC-1. Strings are enclosed in double-quotes if they contain spaces or other separator characters, but need not be quoted otherwise. Only two datatypes are used: strings and numerics. Numerics are recognised whether they appear as integers or decimals, with or without an exponent. Separators can be spaces, linefeeds, tabs or commas in any mixture. Multiple separators are not significant.

```
CTDIF-1 0.1
implmentation "PMS dBase Converter v0.1 21-July-1989"
name NIMONICB updated 89/7/21
fieldlist "sample-no" weight length strength-MPa
elongation-to-fracture endfields
&&1-fred 3 5.0e-4 200.3 0.23
&&2BA 3.2 1e-3 205.2   0.235
"&&3Z ++" 3.333 1e-3 205.3   0.236
FIDTC-1
```

It can be seen that the data consists of a number of "tuples" (rows or records) where each tuple contains one value for each fieldname. The word "tuple" is used because the separators are not necessarily the spaces and linefeeds shown above which put one tuple on each row.

The IMPLEMENTATION string in the example describes the software that was used to prepare the datafile (it might be a person's name and a word-processor). The NAME field refers to the original name of the dBase file and the UPDATED field refers to the last date the data was edited or typed. The names of the fieldnames are listed between the keywords FIELDLIST and ENDFIELDS before the data itself appears.

Automatic Recognition of Types

The numeric and string types can be automatically recognised by the values that appear, so &&1-fred is clearly a string and 5.0e-4 is clearly a number, and this detection must look at all the values of a field before deciding which type it is. If the user requires strings which consist only of digits then they would have to be put in quotes, *e.g.*, "007". There is a slight danger that a single typing error such as O ("oh") for 0 ("zero") may cause an entire set of numbers to be classed as strings, but the translation software should be aware to this possibility and produce appropriate warning messages [8]. Thus the format is "strongly typed" but it does not require any type declarations (like the programming language ML but unlike Pascal).

Restrictions

We must apply a number of restrictions if we are to maintain free interconversion with dBase files. dBase does not permit NULL values for numeric (or date) fields. This lack of NULLs is a severe disadvantage for materials property data where absent values are very common. (Ways of providing this facility are described in the detailed format definition [8]).

Some of these restrictions are awkward and unpleasant, but rather than extend them immediately it makes sense to define a base format (this one) and a separate, upwardly compatible extended format which removes the restrictions. This is because there is a great deal to be gained by having a dBase- convertible format.

SGML AND CALS-CONFORMANT FORMATS

Any data, in any format, can be referred to from a Standard Generalised Markup Language (SGML) document by the name of the file in which it is stored [1]. This is true for images, vector drawings, recorded speech or music, anything. If there is a formatting program available which can produce printed output from such a data file, for example a translator that produced written music from a recording, then by referring to this program from within an SGML document it is possible to include the data so that they appear in the right place when the SGML document is printed. The tabular data format proposed here presents no problems when used in conjunction with SGML and thus it is also compatible with ODA and ODIF (Office Document Architecture and Office Document Interchange Format) by encoding the SGML using SDIF (SGML Document Interchange Format) [7].

CALS Conformancy

The American Department of Defense programme of Computer-Aided Acquisition and Logistic Support (CALS) currently does not specify a format to be used for tabular data. IGES (Initial Graphics Exchange Specification) formats are required for engineering drawings and vector graphics (later migrating to STEP (Standard for the Exchange of Product Data, ISO DP10303) as it becomes available), bitmap, raster and tiled-raster formats are defined for images, but only the very general military standard 1840A is defined for numeric data [5].

CALS uses SGML-format text documents to link together compound "documents" consisting of information recorded in any of the other formats using part of the facilities in SGML described above. Thus while CTDIF could be considered to be CALS- conformant purely because it can be used with SGML, this interpretation may not be accepted by other users of CALS standards and so conformance with MIL-STD-1840A must be considered. This military standard requires that files of data conforming to it be expressed in ASCII characters, CTDIF format can be reformatted in any layout without changing its meaning, so CTDIF files can be made conformant to MIL-STD- 1840A [8].

MULTI-TABULAR (RELATIONAL) FORMAT

There are many drawbacks of the simple, single tabular exchange format even without considering the restrictions imposed by dBase compatibility. These are:

- repeated data is repeated in the transmission
- single-point data requires a whole file to itself
- the available associativity is only very simple (see [9])

These can be alleviated by using multiple data files to describe the same set of data, a technique known as "normalisation". If all the data is sent (or stored) in a single table as defined above then it is "simply normalised" or "in 1st normal form", further normalisation removes redundancy without losing information. The principle involved is very simple: any one item of information should only be represented once. Howes [3] gives a "cookbook" approach and describes what to do in order to achieve better normalisation (and gives many examples) and Date [2] describes clearly and concisely why the method works. Ullman [11] gives formal mathematical proofs. A good bibliography and introduction to database techniques for materials information is given in the proceedings of the Schluchsee workshop [10].

Cambridge Multi-Tabular Format

The simplest extension to the simple tabular format is to add an extra definition file to a set of CTDIF-1 files encoded according to the simple tabular form. To distinguish this extension from the simple case, the format of the new definition file is called CTDIF-2 and contains a list of filenames which refer to simple CTDIF-1 files. A further step would be to add at the end of this definition file (before the CTDIF-2 terminator) the contents of all the simple files, complete with CTDIF-1 headers and terminators, rather than just their names. This has the advantage of neatness and conceptually provides precisely the same descriptive power. Here is an example of what the definition file might look like, note the descriptive comment on the 4th line:

```
CTDIF-2 0.1
implmentation "AMCENS Ctdif&&Z version 0.2 01/4/1989"
name RRNIM
"This is a whole bunch of stuff bought from RR"
filelist c:\NIMONICA.c-1 c:\rr\NIMONICB.c-1 d:\new\NIMONICC.c-
1 NIMONICD.c-1 NIMONICE.c-1 endfiles
FIDTC-2
```

Unfortunately in practice effective normalisation becomes increasingly difficult for the user as the associativity increases in complexity and there are many traps for the unwary [4], [3], [2].

EXTENDED FORMATS

The single-table and multiple-table CTDIF-1 and CTDIF-2 formats are files or collections of files which are dBase compatible but this will not always be adequate. The extended CTDIF+1 is, like CTDIF-1, a single-table format but most of the restrictions associated with dBase compatibility are removed.

The extensions to the single-table format can be carried through to collections of these tables as in the multi-tabular format CTDIF+2, this gives new freedoms but also new restrictions [9].

CODATA GUIDELINES

After the CODATA-sponsored Schluchsee meeting in 1985 an informal working group was established to devise a materials data interchange format and a set of guidelines produced. The format envisaged by CODATA must be capable of being understood by a scientist or engineer who is only a casual user of computers and must support the following facilities:

- numeric data with uncertainties
- graphs and their metadata
- tables and their metadata
- data functions (mathematical expressions)
- supporting text information
- arabic alphabets and extensions
- greek alphabet and common mathematical symbols as extended ASCII codes
- units.

But it should not attempt to support diagrams, pictures and the full-text of articles. In addition, the format itself should have the following properties:

- a route to future evolution without invalidating past versions
- easy recognition of a "unit" of data
- definition of new variables within the datafile
- easy identification of the beginning and end of the data
- identification of the sender
- identification of the intended recipient
- provision for naming a "unit" of data (a datafile)
- provision for the date and time of the request for the information

- location and delimiting of any "structural element" within a datafile

It can be seen that the Cambridge Multi-Tabular format CTDIF-2 handles most of these. The uncertainties of numerics and the specification of the structure of graphs can be modelled using multiple tables. This must be so since the full power of the relational model of data is available. The "definition of new variables" is the only defined behaviour for CTDIF: all fieldnames are declared but their meanings are not defined. Mathematical expressions can only be represented as strings, which is probably adequate.

Arabic and greek alphabets are independent of the definition of CTDIF. ISO has defined "octet" (byte) codes for several non-latin alphabets (including Japanese which requires 2-byte codes) and CTDIF could be used directly once translations of the keywords (such as FIELDNAMES) have been defined.

The greatest deficiency in the CTDIF formats from the CODATA point of view is not actually explicit in the CODATA guidelines, that is that there is no defined dictionary of fieldnames within CTDIF and that one must be separately agreed upon.

CONCLUSIONS

Simple tabular and multi-tabular (relational), dBase compatible and extended formats all have their uses and it is inevitable that if only one of these is adopted by a standards-making body, some user-communities would then develop others. It makes sense to forestall such a divergence of standards by designing a system where all types can coexist and where there are defined methods for transforming from one to the other. The work referred to in this paper defines Version 1.0 of CTDIF-1 and Version 1.0 of CTDIF-2 (dBase- compatible). It gives suggestions for the extended formats CTDIF+1 and CTDIF+2 but further thought is required to arrive at a sensible and workable set of extensions.

The systems described here, however, contain no mechanism to handle meanings or interpretation of terms. Therefore the CTDIF formats will only be useful to a data-sharing community if that community also defines a common fieldname- dictionary with definitions to ensure that meanings are also communicated as intended.

REFERENCES

[1] M. Bryan (1988) *SGML: An Author's Guide to the Standard Generalized*

Markup Language, Addison-Wesley Publ. Co. ISBN 0-201-17535-5

[2] C.J. Date, *An Introduction to Database Systems*, Fourth Edition, Vols I (1983) and II (1988), Addison-Wesley Publ. Co., Reading, Mass., USA, ISBN 0-201-14474-3.

[3] D.R. Howe (1985) *Data Analysis for Database Design*, Part 2: Normalisation and Part 3: Entity-Relationship Modelling, Edward Arnold Publ. Ltd. ISBN 0-7131-3481-X

[4] W. Kent, (1978) *Data and Reality: Basic Assumptions in Data Processing Reconsidered*, Elsevier North-Holland Inc., New York. ISBN 0-444--85187-9.

[5] MIL-STD-1840A Military Standard: Automated Interchange of Technical Information, 22 Dec.1987 + change notice 20 Dec.1988, American Dept. of Defence. Section 5.1.4.2 p19 and 5.1.4.9 p25.

[6] P.M. Sargent, (1988) *Materials Data Interchange for Component Manufacture*, Cambridge University Engineering Department UK, Technical Report CUED/C-MATLS/TR.147 Sept. 1988.

[7] P.M. Sargent, (1989) *Definition Study for the Establishment of Demonstrator Projects in Materials Data Interchange*, Contract No.320111 for CEC JRC Petten, June 1988.

[8] P.M. Sargent, (1989) *A Tabular Materials Data Interchange Format*, Cambridge University Engineering Department UK, Technical Report CUED/C-MATLS/TR.162 August 1989.

[9] P.M. Sargent, (1989) "Use of Abstraction in Creating Data Dictionaries for Materials Databanks", presented at ASTM Int. Symp. Computerization of Materials Data, Orlando, Nov.1989.

[10] J.H.Westbrook, H.Behrens, G.Dathe and S.Iwata (1986) Editors, *Material Data Systems for Engineering*, Proc. CODATA Workshop, Schluchsee, FRG, 1985. ISBN 3-88127-100-7.

[11] J.D. Ullman (1982) *Principles of Database Systems* 2nd Edition, Ch.7 on dependences and lossless decomposition, Pitman Publ. Ltd., London ISBN 0-914894-36-6

GMELIN HANDBOOK OF INORGANIC CHEMISTRY - RELATION OF PLANNED ELECTRONIC AND PRINTED VERSIONS AND FUTURE POLICY.

Ekkehard Fluck
Gmelin Institute for Inorganic Chemistry
of the Max Planck Society for the Advancement of Science
Frankfurt, Germany

INTRODUCTION: DEVELOPMENT OF CHEMICAL LITERATURE IN EUROPE

Allow me from the outset to review quickly the development of chemical journals in Europe. A considerable number of the earliest publications in the area of chemistry had their beginnings in Germany. In 1778 the first journal appeared: "Chemisches Journal für die Freunde der Naturlehre, Arzneygelahrtheit, Haushaltungskunst und Manufacturen" ("Chemical Journal for the Friends of Physics and Chemistry, Pharmacology, Household Skills, and Manufacturing"). The editor was Lorenz von Crell, who corresponded with many scientists in other countries, so that his journal contained contributions from France, England, and Sweden, in addition to those from Germany. Scheele, for example, published much of his original work in this journal. Besides this journal from Crell, who is seen today as the founder of chemical journalism, were a series of other publications. The pamphlet series, "Die neuesten Entdeckungen in der Chemie" ("The Newest Developments in Chemistry"), was among them; it appeared every six months. In its twelfth edition, von Crell justified the necessity of a new series, which would be published with greater frequency. His justification is as valid today as it was then. Namely: "After the establishment of my journals, the chemical notices, which I had collected for my readers, could be placed in their hands only once every six months, ... their praiseworthy curiosity for more knowledge was only later satisfied: Many perhaps used their efforts, time, and money in the meantime on such subjects, which they so often found previously treated, often still better: or they could perhaps finish their necessary work more easily, cheaper, and also even better ...".

How justifiable this concern still is today, is shown by estimates of costs to the German economy amounting up to 15 billion DM per year through unnoticed research results, even though they are published.

Shortly after von Crell's journal, the oldest chemical journal that is still published, "Annales de Chimie", appeared in France during the Revolution in 1789. It and others were edited by Lavoisier and Berthollet.

Up to 1841, Henry Carrington Bolton recorded 74 chemical journals in his "Catalogue of Scientific and Technical Periodicals 1665 - 1895", of which 38 were published in Germany, 8 each in France, England, and Italy, 5 in Holland, 3 in Belgium, 1 in Sweden, and 1 in Russia.

It is valid to this day that the use of journals in comparison to that of books is much more widely distributed in chemistry than in the other sciences.

THE GMELIN HANDBOOK OF INORGANIC CHEMISTRY

It is interesting that a long time ago, in spite of the relatively small number of journals, the necessity became recognized that the published knowledge therein has to be critically assessed and condensed, and organized according to substances. In 1817, the first edition of "Gmelins Handbuch der theoretischen Chemie" ("Gmelin's Handbook of Theoretical Chemistry") appeared as three volumes. Beginning with the fourth edition of 1842, an English translation was published by the Cavendish Society. With the beginning of the fifth edition, organic chemistry was published separately as the "Gmelins Handbuch der organischen Chemie" ("Gmelin's Handbook of Organic Chemistry") and later dealt with in an independent work, the "Beilstein Handbuch der Organischen Chemie" (the "Beilstein Handbook of Organic Chemistry").

The Gmelin Handbook is prepared by the Gmelin Institute of Inorganic Chemistry, which is part of the Max Planck Society of West Germany. The present Gmelin Handbook is already in its eighth edition. There are no plans for a ninth edition. Rather the eighth edition is considered as a framework to be continuously updated and expanded by additional volumes.

The format of this framework is provided by the Main Volumes - in general, one Main Volume for each element. To the Main Volume for each element are periodically added one or more Supplement Volumes. Of course, the Main Volumes and the Supplement Volumes are all parts of the single Gmelin Handbook.

The major topics covered in the volumes on an element are divided into chapters and further subdivided into sections and subsections. The data and concepts pertaining to this element and its compounds are organized and summarized within this framework. Thus, related information is compiled in the same place. It is this method of presenting information in context that allows the Gmelin Handbook to catalyze the reflection, the association of ideas, and perhaps, even the inspiration that make up the innovative thought process. Many a new idea has been prompted or stimulated by browsing through the Gmelin Handbook.

In addition, the researcher has publications available such as Chemical Abstracts and Current Abstracts in Chemistry. These publications and their associated computer-linked information services provide the chemist with current literature references and abstracts. They, however, operate within an abbreviated time frame. Indeed, in order to be up-to-date, they strive to make this time frame as short as possible. As a result the material they present is dispersed and highly diluted with respect to the question the individual chemist seeks to answer.

On the other hand, there are handbooks such as the Gmelin Handbook of Inorganic Chemistry that operate over a longer time frame. For the Gmelin Handbook, coverage begins with the literature closing date of the previous volume and extends up to shortly before publication date of the new volume.

The longer time frame allows Gmelin to compile enough material that has been published on an element or on a particular compound or group of compounds during a period of time, to give a complete picture of that element or compound. The information is critically evaluated, incorporated or discarded where appropriate, and correlated.

Let me at this point describe briefly the history of the Gmelin Handbook. The founder of The Gmelin Handbook, Leopold Gmelin, was born in 1788 in Tübingen. He became Professor of Chemistry at the University of Heidelberg. In 1817 - 1819 he published the first edition of his "Handbook of Theoretical Chemistry" in three volumes. They were designed to be used mainly by chemistry instructors in preparing their lectures.

The great success of the first edition of the Gmelin Handbook was brought about by three factors. The Handbook was much more comprehensive than any other chemical treatise of that era - it covered the entire field of chemistry. It was organized by subject matter, that is to say, by compounds. Leopold Gmelin put into practice the idea of compiling in one place all the facts pertaining to a particular compound - namely its preparation, its physical properties, and its chemical behavior. And just as is done today, the first edition substantiated each factual statement with a proper reference which unambiguously related all the reported data and concepts to the original literature. Furthermore, the scope and contents of the various chapters were varied according to the amount and type of information available.

Work on the seventh edition began in 1905. It was written by a group of scientists and served as a useful and important reference book when work was started on the current eighth edition of the Handbook in 1924.

Since 1945 the Gmelin Institute has been part of the Max Planck Society for the Advancement of Science. That in a nutshell is the 170-year history of the Gmelin Handbook.

What is the "Gmelin" of today, which elements and compounds are described, and how current is this description? To answer these questions, the Gmelin Institute has made the following material available:

1) the "Alphabetic Reference Chart" and
2) the "Complete Catalog".

The third and last way to find a specific compound in the Handbook is via the so-called "Formula Index". This thirty-volume index contains all defined elements, compounds, ions, and systems which had been described in the Gmelin Volumes appearing up to the end of 1987. The arrangement is alphabetical according to the element symbol, so that location of a specific element or compound is again simplified.

CHEMICAL LITERATURE AND PROGRESS OF SCIENCE

The invention by Johannes Gutenberg in 1440 of the printing process with single letters, that is, the invention of a technical process had made it possible for the first time, to make information accessible to a large group of people and to exchange scientific ideas over a large geographical area. Scientific work comes about in a steady, self-renewing process of recording, production, and dissemination of information:

1) recording, duplication, and transmission of new scientific results;
2) acceptance of the duplicated information in the scientific community;
3) assimilation of this information in accordance with scientific principles and subsequent production of new results, which are then distributed as new information, starting up the cycle again.

This portrayal makes clear why scientific productivity is closely coupled with the publication and distribution of knowledge by the medium of the printed word. If knowledge is distributed through the printed medium, then the findings and data can be checked and reproduced or falsified anywhere at any time. Information that was distributed by books and journals was of essential importance for scientific development in the centuries since Gutenberg's invention.

After the second World War, the expansion of scientific knowledge was made easier by another factor, namely the standardization of the utilized language; English became the lingua franca of science just as Latin was centuries ago.

The last two decades saw the beginning of a new period that was characterized by the unheard of expansion of scientific results and data and further by the almost simultaneous development of electronic technology in data processing. The background for the mass production of scientific information and data was the intensification of scientific activity around the world. The number of scientists engaged in research and development in the industrialized countries has doubled since 1965. The yield of research and development grew not only in relation to the national product but much more quickly.

With the rising literature flood, the storage problem for libraries became worse and worse. One first attempted a remedy or at least an allayment by centralizing the institutional libraries. Most colleges today have only one central library. This leads to a reduction in subscriptions of scientific journals, amounting to 60 % in Germany. Likewise, the circulation of scientific monographs has fallen 40 %. This development leads to an increase in costs of single copies, that is, it causes in the end that less information will be distributed for the same price. In addition one must also bear in mind that literature acquisition is linked with the high resulting costs of storage and preparation. This is a reason that more and more of the electronic media must be employed for literature storage. It has already led to scientific information being marketed in considerable quantity by this means. The first data banks in the field of chemistry consisted of bibliographical material and abstracts. The mentioned expansion of information concerns primarily the primary and tertiary literature. It will without a doubt no longer be possible to store in the primary literature all data determined by chemical investigations. They should find direct entrance into the data banks. In the future, the data bank can be in the position to return the detailed publication in full text, or preferably, the data will be processed and stored retrievably in a factual data bank.

The storage of facts in databases has unassessable advantages: only in this way can the large quantity of data, as exists today and which will assuredly grow in increasing quantity in the future, be space savingly archived and handled, and only factual databases make possible rapid access to the data.

In the future, the factual data banks will have their place next to the primary and secondary literature as the tertiary literature has always had up until now. However, they have incomparably larger possibilities than printed matter because they can be more complete, permit more rapid access of the data, and because they allow the data to be combined with each other and thus allow multidimensional formulations of questions. They, together with the primary and secondary literature will constitute a unified information system, in which primary and secondary literature will also be accessible on the computer screen in the course of time. This is already the case with the journals published by the American Chemical Society. Works such as the Gmelin Handbook can also be placed at one's disposal in full text on the computer screen, be it online or by CD-ROM. Based upon today's technical level, the entire Gmelin Handbook of Inorganic Chemistry of nearly 600 volumes can be stored on about four CD-ROM disks and could in principle exist on every laboratory bench.

Where one finds topics in the Gmelin Handbook, can already be obtained online with the help of the data bank GFI, which consists of the Gmelin Formula Index and the Complete Catalog of the Handbook and all significant information for the location of an article about a specific substance and specific facts contained in the printed Handbooks. GFI is accessible through STN International.

OUTLOOK TO THE GMELIN DATA BANK

The main features of the GMELIN data bank are the following. It will be a compound-oriented factual data bank with a fixed data structure containing information on purely inorganic compounds as well as organometallic and coordination compounds. The data are taken from the Gmelin Handbook of Inorganic Chemistry as far as possible, that is, they are evaluated data. The user can recognize this because in addition to the literature reference, the Gmelin reference will be given. Data, taken from literature which have not been treated as yet in the Handbook or which are extracted from the latest current literature, will be referenced to the corresponding literature source. The contents of the data pool are accessed through the data structure using a type of connection table format for covalent compounds and a Gmelin-own format for ionic compounds. The development of a special format for ionic structures was necessary in order to guarantee easy access to all available information on these materials. Besides compounds with integer indices there are those with index ranges or noninteger indices, isomorphous or diadoch compounds, intercalation and inclusion compounds, multicomponent systems of various types, alloys, doped materials, and so on. There will be, however, only one comprehensive data structure for facts on purely inorganic compounds and organometallic and coordination compounds with numerical and alphanumerical data and texts. The data are organized in information units and data fields. There will be 185 information units and 810 data fields. On a final level, this structure is composed of data records for the encoded substances. Data are recorded under headings such as:

1. Identification
2. General Information
3. Formation/Synthesis
4. Structure and Physical Properties
5. Properties of Multicomponent Systems
6. Electrochemistry
7. Chemical Behavior
8. Further Data
9. Bibliography

The structural and physical properties, *e.g.,* are subdivided:

4.1	Molecular Properties
4.2	Phase Transitions (one component)
4.3	Information about Condensed Phases
4.4	Mechanical Properties
4.5	Thermal Properties
4.6	Transport Phenomena

and further subdivided:

4.1.1	Molecular Shape and Symmetry
4.1.1.1	Information about Conformation, Bonding Models
4.1.1.2	General Information on Molecular Symmetries
4.1.1.3	Point Group
4.1.1.4	Internuclear Distances, Bond Angles, Dihedral Angles method of determination: 1,2,3... state of aggregation: 1,2,3...
4.1.2	Electronic States.....

These categories are forming information units in which the individual data fields are combined. One or more references are assigned to each information unit. A data field can belong to different types of classes dependent on its content and its use in subsequent queries.

The primary function of a substance-oriented numerical database is the arrangement of chemical knowledge about substances in such a way that is possible for a suitable retrieval system to find the information. A few sample applications are:

* Search for substances by way of proposed empirical formulas or fragments of formulas.

* Search for a specified structural formula or structural fragment.

* Search for substances possessing specific properties, for example, melting point, color, dipole moment.

* Search for the chemical behavior of substances, for example, reaction of a substance with one or more reactants, as well as reaction with general substance classes, for example, N-oxides, phosphorus heterocycles.

* Bibliographical search for authors and publication year.

* Search queries can be combined using logical operators such as AND, OR, NOT.

Although the development of this database is making good progress, the first online service will not be available before 1991. I may point out, however, that the Handbook and the Gmelin Online Data Base will independently continue to meet the information needs in chemistry.

GMELIN SATELLITE DATABASES

At present, the Gmelin Institute develops small databases which are dedicated to special subjects, such as ceramics, super conductors, topics in the field of material science, etc. They will be derived from the Gmelin Data Bank ("spin offs"). In addition, satellite databases will give more detailed information for special purposes. The Inorganic Crystal Structure Database (ICSD) can be considered to be one of those. It contains current information on more than 28 000 crystal structures of inorganic compounds, that is, compounds which do not contain C–C and/or C–H bonds, and which contain at least one of the nonmetallic elements, H, He, B, C, N, O,

F, Ne, Si, P, S, Cl, Ar, As, Se, Br, Kr, Te, I, Xe, At, or Rn. ICSD is, therefore, complementary to the databank of the Crystallographic Data Center (CSD) in Cambridge (UK) and to the Databank CRYSTMET for metallic phases, National Research Council in Canada. ICSD was originally created and produced by Profs. G. Bergerhoff (University of Bonn) and I.D. Brown (University of Hamilton, Ont.). Since 1 January 1989, it has been issued jointly by the Gmelin Institute and the Fachinformationszentrum (FIZ), Karlsruhe, in cooperation with the Institute of Inorganic Chemistry at the University Bonn.

Whereas the FIZ is responsible for the data input, the Gmelin Institute controls the quality of the information that is entered. The University of Bonn continues to share in the generation of descriptors, the development of the retrieval software, CRYSTIN, and various test programs of the project. The database ICSD may be accessed interactively via a telecommunications link to the host STN International at the Fachinformationszentrum Karlsruhe, with the retrieval system CRYSTIN. ICSD is also implemented at SERC (UK) and CISTI (Canada) using their own retrieval systems. It can be leased, along with the retrieval system CRYSTIN, from Fachinformationszentrum Karlsruhe for in-house use. The database is updated regularly. A CD-ROM version of ICSD is in preparation and will be available in 1990.

DETHERM: THERMOPHYSICAL PROPERTY DATA FOR THE OPTIMIZATION OF HEAT TRANSFER EQUIPMENT

David F. Ilten
DECHEMA
Frankfurt am Main
Federal Republic of Germany

INTRODUCTION

With the ever-increasing sensitivity of economic and pollution issues, the requirements for the performance of heat generation and heat transfer equipment are becoming continually more stringent. The "overall" methodologies and algorithms with LMTD values and correction factors traditionally used for the mathematical modelling of fired heaters, reformers, and heat exchangers are in many cases no longer adequate to meet these more rigorous specifications. Either overdesign will occur, which is wasteful of capital and materials, or underdesign will produce an exchanger which will operate at less than optimum conditions. This means waste of heat throughout the life of the unit. An approach that allows a much more satisfactory representation of the physical reality within these types of equipment and their functioning is the "stepwise" method [1,2]. In these methodologies the heat transfer or heat generation units are divided mathematically into a finite number of subunits, each one of which is treated individually and locally as a separate entity. The equations describing each local unit are solved individually and collectively with appropriate boundary conditions. This procedure is iterated until the desired convergence of the entire system is achieved. Certainly a more refined mathematical treatment of the simulation of these devices is of little value if the physical property data necessary for stepwise-calculations do not also have appropriate accuracy. Most important is that physical property data be available under the local conditions of composition, temperature and pressure actually attendant in each of the individual local units of the model employed. In general tables of values covering the complete range of temperature, pressure, and composition of the thermophysical and transport properties for the vapor and the condensed states of the pure components and complex mixtures utilized are necessary.

These requisite values of density, viscosity, enthalpy, thermal conductivity, heat capacity, surface tension and critical pressure are generated by the systems DETHERM-SDR, -SDC, -SDS and can be used in connection with such programs as SST (Heat Exchangers), FRNC-5 (Fired Heaters) or REFORMER for performing simulation calculations of high accuracy. These types of calculations are especially important if studies of fouling are undertaken.

RESULTS

The comparison of calculations carried out according to the averaging method with those calculated according to the stepwise method show that there are decided advantages to the stepwise method, assuming that adequate physical property data are available for all relevant values of temperature and pressure occurring. Also, a complete, detailed description of the various areas within the heat exchanger or the furnace or the tubes of the reformer can be achieved. This is important for determining eddy currents and studying the special effects which might occur within the piece of equipment.

Stepwise Shell and Tube Exchanger Simulation (SST) can improve the efficiency of heat transfer and monitor fouling in a plant and consequently reduce fuel consumption and flue gas emission from furnaces and boilers. Since FRNC-5 can improve the efficiency of fired heaters and boilers, the resulting optimized designs will release fewer flue gas tons with pollutants to the atmosphere. This is especially true for pollutants such as hydrocarbons, CO and sulfur compounds. This may not apply to NOX, because some waste heat recovery with FRNC-5 lowers flue gas temperature and thus increases NOX. However, if NH3 injection is used to lower NOX, the FRNC-5 program can be used to optimize the points of NH3 injection and thereby help to reduce NOX.

Those properties that are needed for the calculation are the following: density, viscosity, thermal conductivity, heat capacity, enthalpy, surface tension and liquid critical pressure. Viscosity and thermal conductivity have recently been treated in detail by Stephan and Heckenberger [4]. Especially correlations giving a functional representation of the variation of these transport properties with temperature, pressure and composition as well as diagrams of the results are presented. Only three methods can effectively describe viscosity over the entire fluid range: (1) The Method of Chung; (2)

The Method of Ely and Hanley; and (3) The Residual Viscosity Method. Some illustrative examples of the results of Stephan and Heckenberger demonstrating the dependencies of these properties on the variables temperature, pressure and composition are given.

The data for the liquid viscosity of water-ethanol mixtures demonstrate how greatly the viscosity can vary with temperature and composition. If the 80% composition line for ethanol is considered, the viscosity varies from roughly 6500 to 632 μPa.s as the temperature is increased from 275 to 350 K. Thus errors in the position of measuring the temperature can result in large errors in determination of the apparent local temperature. This in turn would lead to very great errors in the viscosity, which brings with it extreme errors in the heat transfer coefficient of the apparatus. Obviously this will influence the design of the heat exchanger. Assuming an error of 5 K is made in determining the temperature at 275 K (280 instead of 275 K is measured) then the viscosity is 5039.1 instead of 6487.0 μPa s, an error of 1447.9 or 22%. For 90% ethanol the percentage error is just as great: 3971.5 instead of 5115.5 μPa s, and error of 1144 μPa s or 22% as well. (cf. p. 318 in [4] and Figure 1). The thermal conductivity also varies greatly. At 275 K it assumes a value of 392.4 mW/K m for a concentration of 0.8 and 460.0 mW/K m for a mole fraction of 0.9 in ethanol at a pressure of 0.1 MPa (cf. p. 199 in [4] and Figure 2).

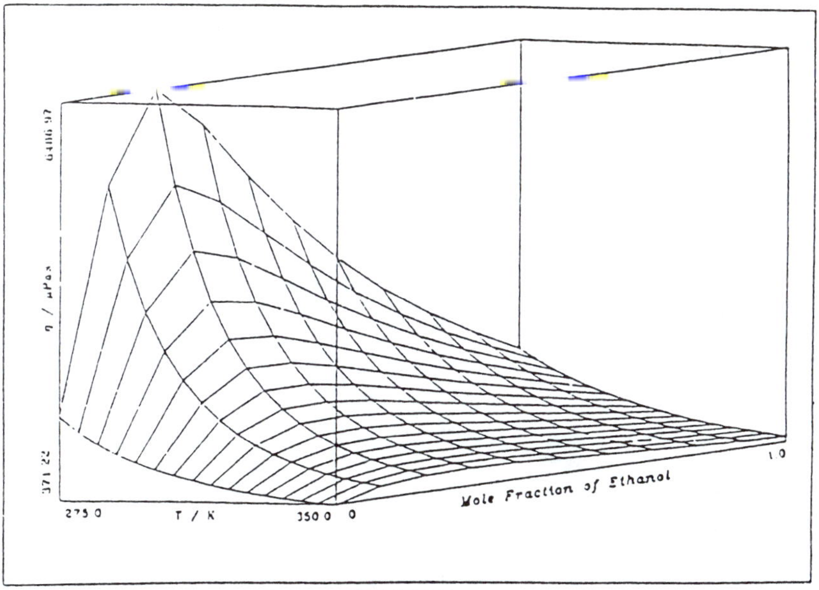

FIGURE 1
Liquid viscosity of water-ethanol mixtures at 0.1 MPa (linear axes)

This illustrates how essential accurate temperature and pressure values are to the stepwise method. In their treatment of the viscosity of liquids and gases Reid, Prausnitz and Poling recommend methods for correlating viscosities when no experimental data are available, estimating the effects of pressure on viscosity and estimating the viscosity of mixtures [5]. These have partially been incorporated into DETHERM. Future versions of the program will be oriented more toward modern interfaces and expert systems to aid the user in selecting the methods appropriate to the case at hand, depending upon the temperature, pressure and composition of the mixture being studied.

The following mixing rules were used in making the calculations presented here:

$$\lambda = [x_1\lambda_1^A + (1-x_1)\lambda_2^A]^{1/A} + x_1(1-x_1)B$$

(C21) (thermal conductivity)

$$\ln \eta = x_1 \ln \eta_1 + (1 - x_1)\ln \eta_2 + \ln\left\{1 + \frac{x_1(1 - x_1)}{A + B(1 - x_1)^2}\right\}$$

(C22) (viscosity)

with λ = thermal conductivity, η = viscosity, subscript 1, property of pure water, subscript 2, property of pure alcohol and x_1 = mole fraction of pure water; y_1 = viscosity of pure water; y_2 = viscosity of pure alcohol.

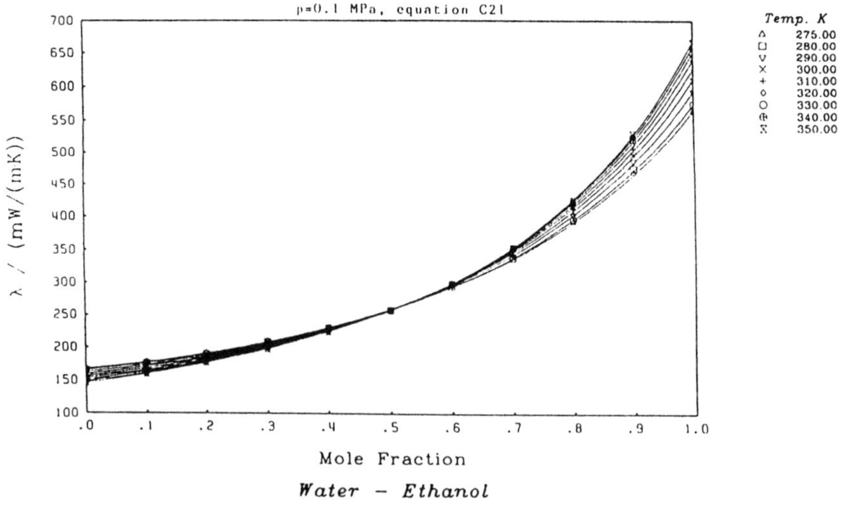

FIGURE 2

In a database such as DETHERM it can be assumed that there will be an improvement of data quality as a function of time. That is, the reliability of the data increases -- let us assume exponentially -- as a function of the time that has elapsed since they were entered into the database. A time constant can be defined, tau, analogous to a relaxation time which depends (roughly) upon the number of users and the intensity of the use of the data.

The more intensively the data are used the sooner and the more readily inaccuracies and inconsistencies can be discovered and corrected, whether these stem from the original literature or result from transfer of the data from one storage medium to another. This is, then, one of the specific advantages of a database that is used worldwide - the greater the number of users and the greater the variety of problems that are treated, the sooner inaccuracies will be discovered and the more reliable the database will become. This is also one of the great advantages of the worldwide cooperation among those producing and distributing databases. The greater the use and the critical analysis of the database certainly the more confidence one can have in using the values contained therein.

SUMMARY AND CONCLUSIONS

The more sensitive the mathematical simulation methods the greater is the required accuracy of the physical property data. Because the stepwise method yields results for the various regions of the furnaces and heat exchangers, where temperature, pressure and consequently the quality (% of fluid in the vapor state) vary, it is necessary to reliably know the physical property and especially the transport property and phase equilibrium (VLE) data to high accuracy as a function of temperature and pressure and composition. This applies to the vapor and liquid states as well. The density certainly varies as a function of the temperature and the pressure. As indicated in the diagrams shown, the viscosity and the thermal conductivities are strong functions of the density. Consequently these properties are also strongly dependent upon temperature and pressure. The stepwise method is inherently more accurate and capable of yielding a more detailed description of the geometry of the heat transfer equipment and of the internal flow condition and regimes as well [6-11].

It is of little avail, however, if adequate physical property data are not available. It is the purpose of DETHERM to provide these thermophysical property data under the conditions required - whether from the literature, through correlations or through estimation techniques, such as incremental methods. Then, with dual factors of increased mathematical simulation capability and adequate knowledge of the requisite thermophysical properties, the total simulation of the heat transfer system can be carried out to greater accuracy. This allows a significantly more reliable optimization of the equipment so that the desired improvements in economy and environmental protection can be achieved. Thus the more accurate stepwise simulation method brings advantages for the plant operator and for the environment and is a logical starting point for the design of new equipment and the improvement of existing installations.

BIBLIOGRAPHY

[1] Ilten, David F. *Proceedings, 3. UIT Conference*, June 1985, C.37. Simulating the Operation and Optimizing the Performance of Fired Heaters.

[2] Ilten, David F. *Proceedings of the Summer Simulation Conference (SCSC)*, Society for Computer Simulation. Studies in the Stepwise Simulation of Heat Transfer via Air Coolers. San Diego, p.313 (1986).

[3] Ilten, David F. and Eckermann, R. Physical Property Data Estimation Methods in DETHERM. *Proceedings Am. Inst. of Chem. Engineers National Meeting*, San Francisco, 1989, 41 K.

[4] Stephan K. and Heckenberger, T. *Chemistry Data Series*, Vol. X, Part I. Thermal Conductivity and Viscosity Data of Fluid Mixtures, Dechema, 1989.

[5] Reid, R.C., Prausnitz, J. and Poling, B. *The Properties of Gases and Liquids*. Fourth edition, McGraw-Hill, NY, 1987, p.388 ff.

[6] Kern, D.C., *Process Heat Transfer*. McGraw-Hill, Japan, 1965.

[7] PFR, *Handbook for Users of SST*, Los Angeles, 1987.

[8] PFR, *Handbook for the Users of FRNC-5*, Los Angeles, 1986.

[9] Humphreys and Glasgow, *Handbook for the Users of Heatex*, London, 1983.

[10] Mendonca, A.J.F., Nieto de Castro, C.A., Assael, M.J., Wakeham, W.A. The Economic Advantages of Accurate Transport Property Data for Heat Transfer Equipment. *Revista Portugesa de Quimica*, 23, 7 (1981), 7-11.

[11] Sieder, E.N. and G.E. Tate, *Ind. Eng. Chem.* 28, 1429-1436 (1936).

DIPPR IN ITS ELEVENTH YEAR

T. B. Selover
DIPPR Technical Director
3575 Traver Road
Shaker Heights, Ohio 44122
U.S.A.

The American Institute of Chemical Engineers created the Design Institute for Physical Property Data (DIPPR). Funded research work began in 1980. This paper presents the status of work in the eleventh year of operation. Activities of 12 projects will be discussed.

INTRODUCTION

In the early 1970's AIChE established the concept of Design Institutes. These are cooperative, industrially sponsored research efforts based on getting work done in an area of general interest at low cost to supporters. There are now 4 active AIChE groups. These are, with date of organization: Design Institute for Physical Property Data (DIPPR), 1978; Research Institute for Food Engineering (RIFE), 1984; Center for Chemical Process Safety (CCPS), 1985; and Center for Waste Reduction Technologies (CWRT), 1989. A fifth, Design Institute for Emergency Relief Systems (DIERS) has completed its work and established a user's group.

The subject of this paper, DIPPR, is now in its eleventh year of funded project work. A symposium honoring the completion of DIPPR's tenth year was held in San Francisco in November, 1989. There were 11 papers presented, along with an historical overview. The papers were published as an AIChE Symposium Series in 1990 [19].

At the 10th CODATA meeting in Ottawa, "A Status Report on DIPPR in its Seventh Year" was presented [l]. An update to that report follows.

ORGANIZATIONAL

Joining

An organization, consultant, or professor may join upon signing a legal agreement and paying dues. The annual dues structure is now set at $1500 for small and $3000 for large organizations. The level is determined by annual chemical sales and other pertinent business factors.

Membership

At the completion of 1989, there were 44 members from 6 countries. Included as members were 4 federal agencies (DOE, NIST, NSF, USDA) whose support is gratefully acknowledged.

The budget for 1989 projects was $628 100 with an anticipated 1990 budget of $708 000. Projects are funded on an annual basis subject to interest by sponsors. Project funding is in addition to dues.

Organization Structure

Project investigators report their results to a Technical Steering Committee headed by a chairman. The chairmen of each Steering Committee, along with chairmen of the Liaison, Dissemination, Membership/Public Relations Committees, report to the Technical Director. This group provides the technical leadership. The business and financial side is managed by an Administrative Committee. These two groups, representing the member companies, then are responsible to AIChE Council.

PROJECTS AND RESULTS

Data Compilation - Project 801

This is the largest project in terms of financial support and has been in existence for the entire eleven years. It is being conducted at The Pennsylvania State University, in the Chemical Engineering Department, under the direction of Professor Thomas Daubert. The 1990 funding level is $189 000.

The scope of Project 801 is the preparation of a set of self consistent, critically evaluated thermophysical property data for 1213 industrially important chemicals for public release by February 1991. This number will continue to increase in subsequent years.

The output of the project takes several different formats. The project sponsors receive semiannual update computer tapes with a complete listing of all chemical data, including reference data, revisions, and updates. This is called the Source File tape. The November 1990 tape will contain data on 1350 chemicals. There are several hundred thousand lines of source code on this tape. The information stored contains a section on identification, one on property constants, and one on temperature dependent properties. There are 26 constants and all sources are considered for judgment, regarding acceptance or rejection of that particular input. There are 13 temperature dependent properties. Each may have several different reference sources. All data are identified with quality code and reference source.

The data for 1117 chemicals have passed the DIPPR review committee and are available to the public. The format available to the public includes a loose-leaf handbook now called, *Physical and Thermodynamic Properties of Pure Chemicals: Data Compilation*. In August 1989, Hemisphere Publishing Corporation published tables [2] of 900 chemicals including updated, revised values for the first 346. The printed tables contain the property constants, equation coefficients, notes, references, and quality codes. Eventually, data on all chemicals will be available in this handbook format.

A Computer Dissemination Task Force was established, with its major responsibility the provision for public access to the computerized version of the DIPPR Source File. This has led to establishment of an Agreement with the Office of Standard Reference Data of the National Institute of Standards and Technology (NIST), to have them provide sale copies of the Source File tape containing the data retrieval software along with documentation. The tape is now available as part of the NIST Standard Reference Data program as Database 11 [3] and will run on IBM, VAX, HP, and PRIME computers. The current tape issued to the public contains 1117 chemicals. The next release to the public, in February 1991, will contain data on 1213 chemicals, and subsequent tapes will be issued in increments. Each tape will include corrections, updates, and data additions to chemicals in earlier issuances. An identical FORTRAN diskette version (not PC-DOS) for uploading onto a mainframe computer is also available from NIST at the same price.

An Educational Version of the Data Compilation for 100 common chemicals has been prepared by the project contractors for use as a teaching aid in classroom instruction. Full Source File and computation modes are included. The program is available through OSRD/NIST [3], as Database 11A.

The Task Force made arrangements with the STN International Division of Chemical Abstracts Service to provide on-line data access through a service bureau concept starting in June 1987 [4]. This arrangement currently provides access for individual users to data on the 1117 chemicals in the computer Source File.

Another function of the Task Force is the establishment of a set of guidelines for a personal computer version of the Data Compilation. This includes specifications for operation on the IBM PC/XT or /AT, or compatible computer. The programming language can be any widely accepted one such as ANSI FORTRAN 77, TURBO PASCAL, or C. The number of chemicals in the database will be equal to that in tape versions.

All 26 property constants and 13 temperature dependent properties, notes, and references are included. The Source File is not included. The program will provide pop-up windows, user callable interfaces, unit conversions, and calculation of temperature dependent properties. Technical Database Services [5] is a DIPPR-approved distributor of the PC program containing 1023 components at present.

Data Prediction Manual - Project 802

This project was in existence for the first ten years of DIPPR. It was carried out at The Pennsylvania State University Chemical Engineering Department under the direction of Professor Ronald Danner. Funding for 1989 was $110 000.

The scope of this project covered the preparation of the loose-leaf *Manual for Predicting Chemical Process Design Data* [6] which contains methods for predicting process design physical property data for pure component chemicals and their mixtures. It is to be comprehensive enough to cover polar and non-polar organics. The methods cover liquid and gas properties at low pressure and elevated pressure where corrections are necessary. In some chapters, aqueous mixtures are treated.

The manual contains 12 chapters. Each chapter is available now for purchase from AIChE [7]. Documentation reports on 10 of the 12 chapters, along with a phase equilibria special bibliography, are available now [7]. The prediction methods for properties of organometallics containing Si,B,Al will be included in a manual supplement.

Software for 10 of the chapters have been written in FORTRAN and will be available through a distributor as soon as the mechanism is worked out.

A linking program tying together all of the routines with an external pure component property database is also being developed. A monograph entitled *Thermodynamic Analysis of Vapor-Liquid Equilibria: Recommended Models and a Data Base Standard* has been developed. It covers three areas: database standard, vapor-liquid equilibrium models, and the computer programs. An interactive menu driven program on diskette will be included with the document. It will access the subroutines used for VLE model regression and predictions. This will become available to the public when complete. A description of the standard database was given by Danner [8].

Experimental VLE and PVT Data for Acetic Acid + H_20 - Project 804

This work was described in the Ottawa CODATA proceedings by Selover [1]. It is available in an AIChE Symposium Series volume [9].

Experimental Data on Mixtures - Project 805

Experimental work has been done at multiple sites in the U.S. and Europe by many contractors since 1980. The 1990 funding is comprised of $65 000, plus $35 000 as a National Science Foundation grant.

The scope of this project is the measurement of vapor-liquid equilibria on binary systems of interest to project supporters. An additional goal is to develop UNIFAC interaction parameters for functional groups not yet covered in the literature.

Through 1989, there have been 154 systems studied. The first 32 systems have been reported by Benson and Zudkevitch [9]. The second set of 39 systems was reported in August 1987 in an *AIChE Symposium Series* volume edited by Cline Black [10]. The third set of binaries was published in the same manner in the Fall of 1989 in a volume edited by Jones and Shih [11].

Aqueous Electrolyte Phase Equilibria - Project 811

This work has been completed and reported on in the Ottawa CODATA proceedings [1]. Results in the form of a book [12,7] and three NBS bibliographies [13,14,15] are available.

Pure Component Liquid Vapor Pressure -Project 821

The project Principal Investigator is Professor Thomas Daubert of The Pennsylvania State University's Chemical Engineering Department. The funding level for 1990 is $17 000. The project began in 1982.

The objective of this project is to measure vapor pressure from 10mm to the critical temperature on chemicals selected by project sponsors to fill gaps in the Data Compilation Project database and for supporters own interests.

In the first eight years of the project, 63 chemicals have been studied. Examples are: DEA, TEA, TEG, phenol, methacrylic acid, and MTBE. The results will be published in the *AIChE Symposium Series* upon release of the results by the Steering Committee. The results will also be added to the Data Compilation Project database. The first 22 chemicals are reported in [10]. The next set will be published in a 1990 *AIChE Symposium Series* volume and include the results of the 1985 through 1987 project years.

Pure Component Latent Heat of Vaporization and PVT Measurement - Project 832

Dr. Grant Wilson of Wiltec Research Co., Inc. in Provo, Utah was the project Principal Investigator. The work has been completed. The results were published in an *AIChE Symposium Series* volume [11] in the Fall of 1989 and added to the Data Compilation database.

The objective of this project was to measure latent heats and PVT data for associating organic acids which hydrogen bond and dimerize. Data are needed for phase equilibria and separation studies to compensate for non-ideal behavior. Measurements have been taken on 6 saturated and 3 unsaturated low molecular weight organic acids.

Critical Properties of Pure Organics - Project 851

The Principal Investigator is Professor Amyn Teja of the Georgia Institute of Technology's Chemical Engineering Department. Funding for 1990 is $22 000. The project began in 1985.

The objective of the project is to develop a technique for critical property measurement for thermally sensitive molecules, which in conventional apparatus would decompose or polymerize prior to reaching Tc. Two experimental methods have been used. In the earlier work, the sealed ampoule method produced values of critical temperature and density. In the more recent work, a low residence time flow apparatus has been used to obtain critical temperature and pressure.

The molecule types being studied include aldehydes, ethers, acids, glycols, alcohols, and hydrocarbons. Through 1989, there have been 63 molecules studied. The results will be published in an *AIChE Symposium Series* volume and added to the Data Compilation database. The first published set will come out in 1990, covering the initial three year's work.

Aqueous Electrolyte Solution Data Base - Project 861

The Principal Investigator on this project is Dr. David Neumann of the National Institute of Standards and Technology, Gaithersburg, MD. Evaluation of the contractor results is being completed during 1990. Funding has been $130 500 from DIPPR and $34 000 in grants from NIST over the project life.

The objective of the project is to produce a computational package to be used for the calculation of the activities and related thermodynamic properties for aqueous electrolyte solutions of 350 compounds as functions of temperature, pressure, and concentration. The software will contain a thermodynamic property database, programs for retrieving the data as well as referenced sources, algorithms for testing importance of complexing, and algorithms for estimating thermodynamic solution related properties. The results of this program will be available to the public at a future date as a PC product with documentation as well as a FORTRAN 77 package.

Determination of Pure Component Ideal Gas Heat of Formation - Project 871

This project began in 1987 with Dr. William Steele of the National Institute for Petroleum and Energy Research (NIPER) at Bartlesville, Oklahoma, as the Principal Investigator. The funding level in 1990 is $35 000 from DIPPR supporters, plus a $30 000 DOE grant. This project, now in its fourth year, will have studied 31 chemicals by the end of 1990.

The scope is the measurement of the enthalpy of combustion of chemicals selected by the project Steering Committee to use in a thermochemical cycle to determine the ideal gas heat of formation. The purpose is to evaluate the thermal sensitivity of hazardous chemicals. A second purpose is to fill gaps in the Benson group contribution method for estimating ideal gas heats of formation [16]. Methods for use of this are described in Chapter 11 of the Data Prediction Manual [6]. A computer program CHETAH (available from ASTM), which was developed by ASTM Committee E27.07 [17,18], also describes group additivity estimation procedures. The results of the first project year (9 chemicals) were published in an *AIChE Symposium Series* volume [11] in the Fall of 1989.

Polymer Solution Handbook - Project 881

This project, which began in 1988, has Professor Ronald Danner of The Pennsylvania State University's Chemical Engineering Department as its Principal Investigator. The funding level for 1990 is $92 000, including a $12 000 NIST grant. The objective of this four-year project is to develop a polymer solution handbook in hard copy and computerized versions. Progress in the first two years included:

(1) handbook contents and format;
(2) standardized data bank;
(3) data reduction procedures;
(4) predictive model development;
(5) handbook chapters and software for calculations to sponsors.

Mixture Property Data Base - Project 882

This project, in its third year, is being conducted under the direction of co-Principal Investigators Dr. Kenneth Marsh and Mr. Bruce Gammon at the Thermodynamics Research Center, Texas A&M University. The funding for 1990 is $61 000, including an $8 000 NIST grant. The objective of the project is to develop a computer searchable data file on evaluated experimental data for selected mixture properties.

The first two year's activities included:
(1) designing a mixture database to cover density, surface tension, critical properties (T_c, P_c), viscosity, thermal conductivity, diffusion coefficient, solubility;
(2) developing evaluation and correlation criteria;
(3) properties for alcohols plus water, alcohols plus hydrocarbons, organic acids plus water, and organic acids plus hydrocarbons.

TRC released 130 mixture tables to the sponsors for evaluation in late 1989.

Environmental, Safety, and Health Data Compilation - Project 901

This project developed out of the recognition of the need for a critically evaluated, internally consistent, computerized database covering the title properties for a select list of pure industrial chemicals with known hazards.

This project would be similar in structure to Project 801 on thermophysical properties of industrially important chemicals. It would satisfy the industry and regulatory agency needs for more accurate and complete property data.

Through a $20 000 grant generously provided by the U. S. Department of Agriculture, arrangements were made with the Syracuse Research Corporation to do a critical "up-front study". This would assist in defining the project's parameters such as properties, types of compounds, what is known (or not known), and who potential contractors might be. A Steering Committee Chairman has been appointed and work progresses on building project support. The intent is to select a contractor and begin work in 1990. A project budget of $150 000 has been set for the first year.

Environmental, Safety, and Health Data Prediction Manual - Project 902

The purpose of this proposed project is to develop, evaluate, and recommend procedures to predict parameters which are useful in determining environmental, safety, and health behavior of chemicals. There is a need for new and improved procedures for estimation methods, which are not now covered anywhere. This project would be the analog to Project 802, which developed a Data Prediction Manual for chemical properties of interest in process design work.

A Project Steering Committee Chairman has been selected, and work is progressing here, also, on developing sufficient support to begin with the contract work in 1990. A project budget of $75 000 has been set for the first year.

CONCLUSION

By meeting time in July 1990, DIPPR will be mid-way through its eleventh year of funded research. Budgeting for projects covering the eleven years totals $5 467 000. Through 1989, there have been six experimental and six data-oriented projects. Going into 1990, funding continued for four experimental and three data projects with anticipation that Projects 901 and 902 as data projects would start up.

The results of each of the six experimental projects are being published and added to the Data Compilation Project computer database. In this way, the computer data bank will serve as a repository for experimental data on both pure compounds and mixtures. The pure compound data will serve to fill gaps and correct old questionable data. The results are being published in paper copy, mainframe computer tape and diskette output, PC version on diskettes, and on-line access.

DIPPR's hopes are high for the start-up of the two new much needed environmental projects in 1990. Long range plans are being developed for a ceramics property database, a bioengineering database, as well as experimental work on mixture transport properties, fluid properties for absorption-refrigeration and advanced heat cycle engines.

REFERENCES

[1] Selover, T. B. and Buck, E. "A Status Report on DIPPR in its Seventh Year," *Computer Handling and Dissemination of Data*, P. S. Glaeser (ed.), Elsevier Science Publishers B. V. (North Holland), New York, NY, 1987, pp. 204-210.

[2] Daubert, T. E. and Danner, R. P., *Physical and Thermodynamic Properties of Pure Chemicals: Data Compilation*, Design Institute for Physical Property Data, Hemisphere Publishing Corp., 1989; 79 Madison Avenue, New York, NY 10016-7892.

[3] Office of Standard Reference Data, National Institute of Standards and Technology, Room A323-Physics Building, Gaithersburg, MD 20899.

[4] STN International, 2540 Olentangy River Road, P.O. Box 02228, Columbus, OH 43202.

[5] Technical Database Services, Inc., 10 Columbus Circle, New York, NY 10019.

[6] Danner, R. P. and Daubert, T. E. *Manual for Predicting Chemical Process Design Data*, Design Institute for Physical Property Data, American Institute of Chemical Engineers, New York, NY, 1983 (with supplements 1984, 1985, 1986, 1987).

[7] Publication Sales Department, American Institute of Chemical Engineers, 345 East 47th Street, New York, NY 10017.

[8] Danner, R. P. and Gess, M. A. "A Database Standard for the Evaluation of Vapor-Liquid Equilibrium Models," presented at the 4th CODATA Symposium on Critical Evaluation and Prediction of Phase Equilibria in Multicomponent Systems, September, 1989.

[9] Benson, M. S. and Zudkevitch, D. (eds.), "Experimental Results from the Design Institute for Physical Property Data I: Phase Equilibria," *AIChE Symposium Series*, **81** (244), 1985.

[10] Black, C. (ed.), "Experimental Results from the Design Institute for Physical Property Data: Phase Equilibria and Pure Component Properties," *AIChE Symposium Series*, **83** (256), 1987.

[11] Jones, D. K. and Shih, T. T. (eds.). "Experimental Results from the Design Institute for Physical Property Data: Phase Equilibria and Pure Component Properties. Part II," *AIChE Symposium Series*, **85** (271), 1989.

[12] Zemaitis, J. F., Clark, D. M., Rafal, M., and Scrivner, N. C. *Handbook of Aqueous Electrolyte Thermodynamics*, Design Institute for Physical Property Data, American Institute of Chemical Engineers, New York,

NY, 1986.

[13] Goldberg, R. N., "Compiled Thermodynamic Data Sources for Aqueous and Biochemical Systems: An Annotated Bibliography (1930-1983)," *NBS Special Publication 685*, U.S. Government Printing Office, Washington, DC, 1984.

[14] Goldberg, R.N. and Steckler, D.K. "A Bibliography of Sources of Thermodynamic Data for the Systems: CO_2+NH_3+H_2O, CO_2+H_2S+H_2O, H_2S+NH_3+H_2O, and CO_2+NH_3+H_2S+H_2O," *NBS Special Publication 699*, U.S. Government Printing Office, Washington, DC, 1985.

[15] Staples, B. R., Garvin, D., Smith-Magowan, D. et al, "Bibliographies of Industrial Interest: Thermodynamic Measurements on the Systems CO_2-H_2O, $CuCl_2$-H_2O, H_2SO_4-H_2O, NH_3-H_2O, $ZnCl_2$-H_2O, and H_3PO_4-H_2O," *NBS Special Publication 718*, U.S. Government Printing Office, Washington, DC, 1986.

[16] Benson, S. W., *Thermochemical Kinetics*, John Wiley and Sons, New York, NY, 1976.

[17] Seaton, W. H., Freedman, E. H., and Treweek, D. N. *CHETAH-4.4 The ASTM Chemical Thermodynamic and Energy Release Evaluation Program*, ASTM DS51A, American Society for Testing and Materials, Philadelphia, PA, 1990.

[18] Frurip, D. J., Freedman, E. H., and Hertel, G. R. "A New Release of the ASTM CHETAH Program for Hazard Evaluation: Versions for Mainframe and Personal Computers," *International Symposium on Runaway Reactions*, AIChE, New York, NY, 1989, p. 39; or *Plant/Operations Progress*, **8** (2), 100, (1989); **8** (4), 239, (1989).

[19] Selover, T.B. (ed), "Design Institute for Physical Property Data: Ten Years of Accomplishment," *AIChE Symposium Series*, **86** (275), 1990.

KNOWLEDGE BASED ORGANIC PHYSICAL PROPERTY DATA SYSTEM

Qian Dong, Zhihong Xu, Xinjiang Yan, Xiaoxia Li, and Li Guo
Institute of Chemical Metallurgy
Academia Sinica
P.O. Box 353
Beijing 100080
People's Republic of China

INTRODUCTION

Chemical engineering databases in various forms have been designed by experienced scientists and engineers at many organizations in the world. Some of these databases are: Physical Property Data Service (PPDS) [1], DIPPR Pure Component Data Compilation [2], and Engineering Chemistry Data Bases (ECDB) [3]. The authors have examined the chemical literature in databases, database developments and expert systems, studied related data activities, and heard the call for additional property data by scientists and engineers. Hence, it is obvious that a great need still exists for the development of a mature data system. Such a system should evolve from a systematic and continuous effort. In order to meet these requirements, much work must be done in areas such as accurate property prediction, data evaluation and in the linkage of databases to the application of artificial intelligence (AI).

The following sections of this paper provide the presentation of a newly built software product, KB-OPDS, covering its design principles, system architecture and software functions as well as artificial intelligence and graph theory application.

SYSTEM ARCHITECTURE

1. Design Principle

KB-OPDS is mainly designed to provide high quality data for the study and development of processes in chemical and petrochemical engineering, and to assist engineers in the selection of appropriate predictive methods. In addition, KB-OPDS offers detailed structural information for organic compounds in order to develop new predictive methods. The primary goals of this project are:

(a) to build a database consisting of a large number of chemical compounds and physical properties in order to meet the basic needs in chemical industry. The database should contain multiple retrieval schemes that facilitate data searching.

(b) to provide a data system to users with applicable and precise predictive methods when experimental data for chemical thermodynamic properties are not available. In general, due to their simplicity and practicality, group additive methods play an important role in the estimation of physical and chemical thermodynamic property. However, the methods demand that the users be able to analyze chemical structure and understand the relationship between property contribution and sub-structure elements. Therefore, generalized software for automatic analysis of functional groups suitable to diverse group additive methods is one of the essential components of KB-OPDS.

(c) to create a software package for organic structure information processing with a view toward improving group additive methods and other predictive methods. Although some group additive methods have wide applicability, their accuracy is sometimes limited because they only consider the contribution to a property from individual groups within a molecule, without regard for the effect of nearest or next-nearest neighbor interactions and stereo isomerism.

(d) to test and evaluate data either from the database or from other data sources in order to maintain good quality control of the database. This approach has difficulties not only because of the huge quantities of data but also because of limitations in computerized methods for data evaluation. A long range goal at ICM is to develop practical schemes for assessing the quality of models and data with the computer in order to increase the reliability of KB-OPDS.

2. Overall Structure of KB-OPDS

As shown in Figure 1, KB-OPDS is an effective integration of eight components: (1) a data bank, (2) a knowledge base, (3) a data management program, (4) a property prediction program, (5) a software package for automation of group additive methods, (6) a program dealing with organic structure processing, (7) a package for systematic qualification of data and models, (8) a menu-driven user interface.

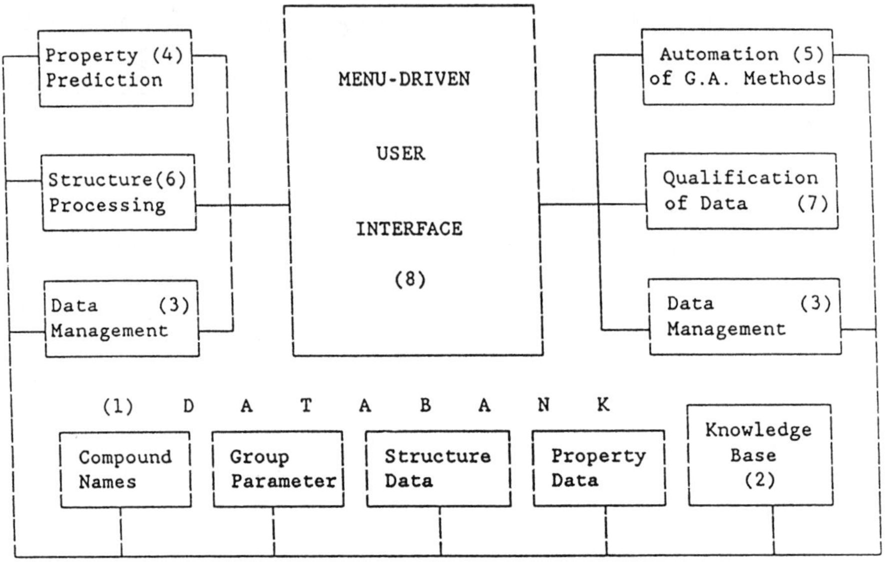

FIGURE 1. Outline of KB-OPDS

METHODOLOGIES USED FOR CREATING KB-OPDS

Knowledge Engineering Application

To begin with, the authors explored a great deal of literature reporting chemical and physical properties as well as the molecular structure of compounds. Then, the authors examined various predictive techniques, experimental data and consulted with many experts. Consequently, a great deal of specialized knowledge and experience was captured so that a knowledge base and an inference mechanism could be constructed.

A primary focus of the knowledge engineering application in KB-OPDS was the knowledge representation of molecular structures. All domain-specific knowledge (*e.g.*, compound structures, compound classification, principles of each group additive methods, etc.) were encoded in a knowledge base. A series of sets of alphanumeric symbols called "coding sets" were defined for the description of the domain-specific knowledge. Some of the coding sets devised for use in KB-OPDS for the manipulation of organic structural information are:

(a) The Organic Compound Coding Specially Designed for Chemical Engineering (OCSCE) is a chemical line notation for chemical engineers to communicate with the KB-OPDS system.

(b) A main group coding set describes groups, fragments and general molecular structure information.

(c) A standardized substructure coding set specifies groups and fragments for each group additive method.

(d) A structural information coding set represents the stereo structure effect of molecules.

(e) Another coding set is used for compound classification.

The inference mechanism is composed of hundreds of "IF THEN" rules and substructure matching strategies with alternative searching algorithms for cyclic and acyclic structures. The main function of the inference mechanism is to determine how the stored knowledge is to be used in parsing manipulation, group analysis and substructure matching.

The knowledge base and inference mechanism have permitted the full automation of the entire process of organic structure analysis. The analysis starts with the parsing of the OCSCE coded formula. The first step produces the main group codes. This is followed by a step which determines adjacency matrices for the molecule. The final step matches and generates the specified fragment codes for each group additive method.

Graph Theory Application

The nature of graph theory is such that it permits the study of the relationship between vertices and edges which constitute an object. As organic molecular structures are graphical objects in the above context, they can be studied and analyzed using graph-theoretical tools. Most chemical engineering data systems contain two parts: a database and a prediction program. The disadvantage of such systems is that they are unable to take full advantage of compound structural information. As a result, the system capabilities are limited in structure and substructure match, automatic analysis of functional groups, online parameter processing for group additive methods and the acquisition of stereo structural information. In order to enhance KB-OPDS, a program package for organic structure information processing is constructed on the basis of graph theory. The main function of the program is to analyze structure information identified from compounds with the aid of connection tables, adjacency matrices, distance matrices and color graphic matrices.

SUBSYSTEMS IN KB-OPDS

The eight components of the KB-OPDS system form five functional subsystems, which will be briefly described in the following sections. The source code of the KB-OPDS system is written in FORTRAN 77. It contains nearly six hundred subroutines with a total of approximately sixty thousand FORTRAN statements. The system operates on VAX 11/780 computers and the data management software adopted in the database is Rdb/VMS, which is commercially available on VAX 11/780 computers. The system is currently available from ICM.

1. Organic Physical Property Data Base (OPDB)[4]

OPDB is a collection of the following data sources -- REID [5], HTOC [6], DECHEMA[7], DIPPR [2], TDPC[8]. Six searching paths provided by the database enable users to locate certain compounds and their relevant property information from CAS registry number, compound name, formula, OCSCE structural code as well as characteristic code indicating compound characteristics, *i.e.,* toxicity, solubility, explosivity, flammability, etc. In addition, users may find other properties for some compounds by seeking those compounds for which the value of their properties ought to agree with a given range. There are 39 kinds of physical property data (Table I) and 21 items relating chemical characteristics for organic compounds available for the users of OPDB.

2. Physical Property Estimation Program (PPEP)[4]

Approximately 25 properties in 4 categories may be estimated in the PPEP program. The categories are: fundamental properties, thermal properties, thermodynamic properties, and transport properties. When selecting predictive techniques for PPEP, our concern is centered on the precision and applicability of the methods in the light of recommendation by the literature [10].

It is well known that a single predictive method is not applicable to all kinds of substances because of difference between polar and nonpolar substances. So, a method is first taken here to classify all compounds into four groups in accordance with their dipole moment value. A further step is to divide the predictive methods in PPEP into four classes based on their applicability toward the compounds with the different dipole moment value.

Table 1. Retrievable Data

Data	Items		
1.	boiling point	21.	flash point
2.	melting point	22.	flammability limit
3.	freezing point	23.	self-ignition temperature
4.	critical temperature	24.	refractive index
5.	critical pressure	25.	solubility parameter
6.	critical volume	26.	radius of gyration
7.	critical compressibility	27.	solid density
8.	acentric factor	28.	liquid density
9.	dipole moment	29.	saturated pressure
10.	standard heat of formation	30.	evaporation heat
11.	standard Gibb's energy	31.	solid heat capacity
12.	absolute entropy	32.	liquid heat capacity
13.	liquid density	33.	ideal gas heat capacity
14.	liquid molar volume	34.	second virial coefficient
15.	triple point temperature	35.	liquid viscosity
16.	triple point pressure	36.	vapor viscosity
17.	melting heat	37.	liquid thermal conductivity
18.	combustion heat	38.	vapor thermal conductivity
19.	Van der Waal's volume	39.	surface tension
20.	Van der Waal's area		

Two approaches are used in PPEP for helping engineers to have a better understanding of predictive methods involved in the system so as to appropriately use the methods for their specific problems. One of the approaches is to supply users with online help information concerning the application range, input data, average calculated deviation as well as references for each technique. In the second approach PPEP sets a flag code which tells the program to monitor the entire property calculation process and report error messages in detail.

3. Generalized Program of Automation of Group Additive Methods (GPAG)[4]

GPAG is a software package specifically designed to compute physical properties through various group additive methods. The system acts as follows: when it starts, users are only required to enter OCSCE coded formulas, GPAG is capable of automatically analyzing functional groups of molecules and extracting structure information from OCSCE coded formulas, and finally carrying out the property calculation. In addition, it has the ability to offer analyzed group codes, the number of groups and group parameters for the user's own program. The package currently involves 21 group additive methods that calculate 16 physical properties.

One of GPAG's unique features is the suitability of its methodologies for different kinds of group additive methods. GPAG covers the majority of group additive methods in the field of chemical thermodynamics. Since the principles of the group additive methods and organic structural information can be encoded by generalized representation methods, the system can be easily updated, with a minimum of programing, by the addition of a new group additive method, or the elimination an out-of-date method, or the modification of an existing method.

4. Organic Structure Information Processing (OSIP)[4]

Briefly, the principle of the OSIP program is, in the light of graph theory application in chemistry [9], capturing useful structural information from the compound structure for the KB-OPDS system. The program is equipped with the following four functions:

(a) to supply GPAG with stereo structure information of molecules such as cyclic or alicyclic, cis or trans, and a fragment connected to a chain or to a ring and so on.

(b) to suggest a numeric match scheme of colored distance matrix of molecules for quickly and accurately conducting a compound match in data retrieval.

(c) to advance a judging algorithm of the nearest similarity in adjacent connection for organic molecular similarity. This function tends to be a powerful tool for the property study, for example, when predicting the properties of an unknown substance by group additive method the contribution of unknown groups in the compound should be derived from those in the compounds with the most similar structure.

(d) to contain several topological indices, such as Wiener Distance Index, Randic Connectivity Index, Balaban Average Distance Sum Connectivity Index and Platt Index as well. Additionally, there is a property predictive method, combining topological indices with group additive methods, proposed by OSIP. In this method, the critical temperature, Tc, can be estimated without the need of the normal boiling point and the results derived can match well with other accurate methods for critical properties.

5. Systematic Qualification of Data and Models (SQDM)[4]

SQDM is an attempt to develop useful evaluation techniques in various ways under the support of KB-OPDS. It has provided the ability to improve the reliability of data and models in the KB-OPDS system. The three methods employed in SQDM are:

(a) Outlier checking according to the magnitude of a property. The concept behind this method is that a property value of a compound is generally within a definite range, and if the value deviates a great deal from its normal range, it is suspect.

(b) Qualification of data and methods based on the basic theories. An important way of checking data in SQDM is to use the basic theories in chemistry as a criterion, for example, "the vapor pressure of a saturated liquid at normal boiling point is 1 atm" may be taken as a criterion of data check.

(c) Cross checking data by comparing predicted data with experimental data. The predictive models of temperature dependent properties were systematically tested against experimental data at a number of temperature points and SQDM imitates what an expert may consider and propose for the expression of test results, which facilitates a vast amount of data testing for critical properties.

REFERENCES AND NOTES

[1] Edmonds, B. "PPDS - Physical Property Data Service," Thermodynamic Databases, *CODATA Bulletin*, 1985, No. 58, 6.

[2] Danner, R. P.; Daubert, T. E. "The DIPPR Data Compilation Project," Thermodynamic Databases, *CODATA Bulletin*, 1985, No.58, 14.

[3] Xu, Z; Wang, L. *Anal. Chim. Acta* 1988, 210, 115-121.

[4] Dong, Q. et al, "KB-OPDS," Research Report to the Chinese Academy of Sciences and the Ministry of Chemical Industry, China, (August, 1989), Available from the Institute of Chemical Metallurgy, Academia Sinica, P.O.Box 353, Beijing, China.

[5] Reid, R. C. et al. *The Properties of Gases and Liquids* 4th ed., McGraw-Hill Book Company, New York, (1987).

[6] Stephenson, R. M.; Malanowski, S. *Handbook of the Thermodynamics of Organic Compounds*, 1987.

[7] Simmrock, K. H.; Janowsky, R.; Ohnsorge, A. "Critical Data of Pure Substances (Ag - C7)", *Chemistry Data Series*, Vol. II, Part 1, Published by DECHEMA, 1986.

[8] Smith, B. D.; Srivastava, R. *Thermodynamic Data for Pure Compounds*, Parts A and B, 1986.

[9] King, R. B.; Rouvray, D. H. *Graph Theory and Topology in Chemistry*, The Netherlands, 1987.

DATABASES: INDISPENSABLE TOOLS FOR RESEARCH AND DEVELOPMENT

Dieter Rehm
Institut für Organische Chemie
Johann Wolfgang Goethe-Universität
Frankfurt am Main, Germany

1. COMPUTERS IN CHEMISTRY

Important areas to use computers in chemistry are

- Documentation and Information. Using up-to-date technology to make data of all types available to the scientific community for research and development is a preliminary condition for improving the quality of life for mankind.

- the development of new materials which will be added to or replace in part materials presently available in the human environment: "Chemistry as part of Material Sciences".

- the design of biologically active chemical compounds. This will lead to a better understanding of the processes of life and to the production of improved pharmaceuticals: "Chemistry as part of Life Sciences".

To indicate the position of our institute in these areas I want to mention some dates:

1979: Starting to use databases online for research.

1982: Introducing Chemical Information courses.

1986: Streamlining education of students to meet the challenge [1,2], "To think interdisciplinarily: to learn to recognize biological active chemical structures and to synthesize these by chemical or biological synthesis."

1987: Starting to build up an infrastructure connecting experimental methods of structure determination (X-ray analysis, NMR-spectroscopy) to central computer facilities including computer graphics to visualize and manipulate the three-dimensional structure of molecules, adding at the same time the possibility of performing energy minimizing calculations of molecular conformations using methods made available by computational chemistry as well as to implement in-house databases to retrieve data necessary for our research activities.

We believe that the points mentioned are necessary to do justice to our mission to educate young chemists in a way that they can cope with the imminent challenges to come in academia as well as in industry.

2. OUT-OF-HOUSE DATABASES

2.1 Primary Information

Due to a tradition of 160 years in chemical documentation we know that our knowledge in chemistry is based on 12.9 million documents (Figure 1) at the end of 1989; half a million new documents are added every year. Nobody knows how much additional material-not yet or never published-is available to parts of the scientific community only. In addition, chemists do need more and more data from literature outside the traditional chemical information sources, especially from the life sciences. Full text databases are definitely no substitute for printed information but can be additional, valuable access points for retrieving chemical data and concepts. One has to bear in mind that concepts often have a close connection to particular scientists and vanish with them.

2.2 Secondary Information

2.2.1 Citation Indexing

Citation indexing, introduced by Garfield in 1955 [3], is based on relationships of references given by publishing authors to earlier publications. In producing the *Science Citation Index* (SCI) at the Institute for Scientific Information (ISI) data entry errors may occur. However, we also know that scientists do not always honor the achievements obtained by others. They may be biased or really not know the facts! This is an important factor which

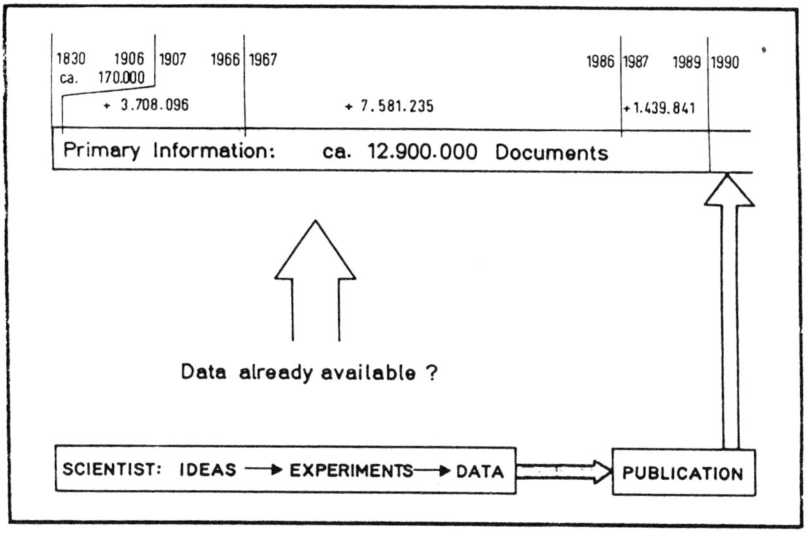

FIGURE 1

The Information Avalanche. Number of documents before 1907 originates from *Chemisches Zentralblatt*; all other statistics from *Chemical Abstracts Service* (CAS) publications (Equivalent patents excluded).

has to be taken into account when using the SCI. Improvement can only come from authors and some pressure by peer reviewers. The drawbacks have to be taken into account, for instance, when research sponsoring agencies want to elucidate the impact of a person or a corporation related research.

2.2.2 Abstracting and Indexing

Abstracting and indexing started in 1830 with the introduction of Chemisches Zentralblatt which lasted until 1969. Today Chemical Abstracts Service (CAS) [4] provides with its database, CA, access to chemical literature. We will have to have a closer look at what Maxwells' (MCC's) SCITECHINFORM (STI) can add to this from its cooperation with VINITI, the All Union Institute of Scientific and Technical Information of the Academy of Sciences of the USSR, when those databases go online [5]. The CA REGISTRY SYSTEM for chemical substances started in 1965. The quality of abstracting and indexing in CA and REGISTRY determines the real value of secondary information for chemists, and many human factors can influence the quality indeed:

- Keyboarding errors lead to wrong entries in data fields.
- Are all the papers in core chemistry journals really covered?
- Incomplete or wrong indexing due to limited thesauri or controlled vocabularies not up to date.
- Wrong stereochemical assignments of chemical compounds.

Improvement of secondary information [6] starts with the improvement of primary information. Authors should publish and editors, as well as peer reviewers, have to enforce:

- standardized bibliographic data, full first and middle names always in the same order; correct designation of the corporate sources, etc.
- titles and abstracts which really do contain information.
- no mixing of observation and interpretation.
- correct use of structural formulas including stereochemistry and CA Registry Numbers since structural formulas are the most valuable asset chemists have to structure chemical knowledge.

There are additional points. Perhaps peer reviewers should dedicate more time to their responsible and honorable task, to contribute to the improvement of primary information.

Since the abovementioned and additional conditions cannot be fully accomplished, abstractors and indexers have the obligation to comply with the high standards scientists expect. The latter should be aware that abstracting and indexing is scientific work just as is fundamental research. Feedback from authors to the producers of secondary information should be increased to improve the indexing in databases, provided the publishing scientist knows the valid rules of indexing and abstracting! The percentage of cooperating authors will be small and thus the responsibility of abstractors and indexers will increase!

At least 70 % of the documents published in chemistry can be retrieved using the CA and/or Registry databases. The latter allows structural as well as substructural searches in addition to multidimensional search profiles in CA. But databases older than 20 years increase the difficulties in retrieving the information needed [7]. Chemistry is a rapidly developing discipline. There is no way out. Complex queries have to be shifted from the bench chemist to the information specialist; his work should be recognized as part of the research done by a team of scientists!

One problem becomes crucial, to know about the existence of a document which may contain data needed does not mean one has immediate access to it. If it is not in a core journal the local library cannot provide the document. Document ordering online or by telefax and document delivery by telefax can be very fast and effective if one knows where to order. Yet these methods are still not routine in academia. Full text databases are available for core journals - which will be available in printed form anyway - and they are incomplete since graphics are missing in most cases. They are no remedy!

I have a dream -- which is technically feasible and could become real:

> *Would it not be wonderful to do conventional online searching and have simultaneously facsimile-type document delivery by high speed direct satellite communication?*

3 HANDBOOKS AND DATA COLLECTIONS

3.1 Handbooks: *Beilstein* and *Gmelin*

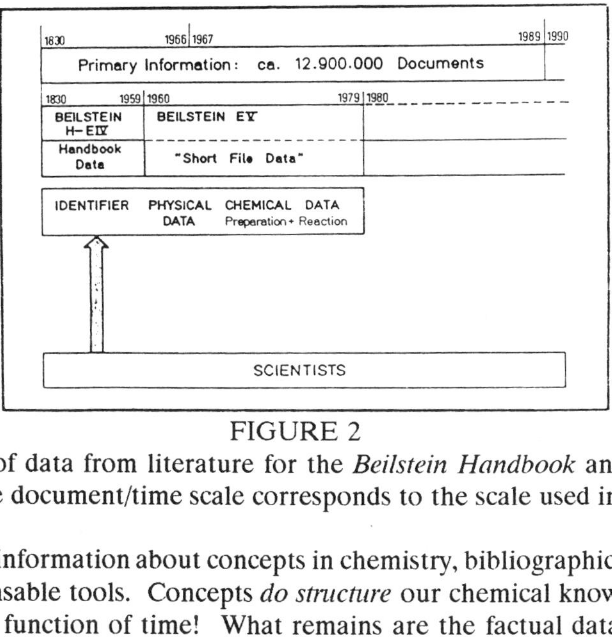

FIGURE 2

Extraction of data from literature for the *Beilstein Handbook* and *Beilstein Online*. The document/time scale corresponds to the scale used in Figure 1.

To retrieve information about concepts in chemistry, bibliographic databases are indispensable tools. Concepts *do structure* our chemical knowledge *and change* as a function of time! What remains are the factual data obtained by experiments. The natural ordering principle for data in chemistry is based on chemical compounds or, to be more precise, on structures of chemical compounds. From data available about the CA Registry and Beilstein one can estimate that by the end of 1990 at least 11.5 million chemical compounds will have been registered. Beilstein applies strict rules: one can be sure that a registered compound has been analyzed or synthesized at least once. Beilstein for organic and Gmelin for inorganic chemistry are by far the most comprehensive sources for validated data of chemical compounds since the data have been critically evaluated [8]. But Beilstein does not cover macro- and biomacromolecules and the greater part of the organometallic chemistry is with Gmelin; the latter is not yet available online to deliver factual data. Beilstein has now completed loading its database on several hosts. Figure 2 shows on a document/time scale what is offered: critically evaluated data are available up to 1959, the equivalence to what is printed in the *Beilstein Handbook*. Compounds can be identified by nomenclature, Beilstein Registry Number and - with limitations - by the CA Registry Number if already available, and by structural searches. The data fields include physical as well as chemical data. All information retrieved can be traced back to the primary literature. Not all fields contain displayable factual data but citations to original publications only. This is helpful since the availability of data is rarely included in CA. Data from the time range 1960 to 1979, that is the 5th Supplementary Series of the printed Handbook, have not yet been critically evaluated. Just by looking at the document/time scale in Figure 2 we realize that it will take years to convert the so-called "Short File Data" into evaluated "Handbook Data". Factual data from the literature since 1980 are urgently requested, a task which is in progress. There are other sources of data of the handbook type even available online but none are as comprehensive as Beilstein.

3.2 Data Collections

Data collections are available in selected areas of chemistry. Their existence is due to the need to have specific data from the current literature available in the laboratory. In this area we are crossing the borderline between out-of-house and in-house databases. These data collections are special since they are built up and used by specialists. There are, for example, data collections of:

- **Thermodynamic** and **Transport Properties** of pure substances and multicomponent systems. They may include calculation programs based on the laws of physics to deliver data for given conditions. These data are highly needed in technical chemistry.

- **Biological Data** with information about biological activities of compounds including especially toxicity.

- **Spectral Data** to assist the identification of substances. C^{13}NMR, infrared- and mass-spectroscopy data are the most prominent. In fact, there are knowledge databases for expert systems allowing simulation of spectra and similarity spectra searches to provide at least partial or even full structural information for an unknown substance. Databases and programs of this type are scattered around the world. You can buy pertinent data libraries along with your spectroscopic equipment. It is the object of a project sponsored by the German Bundesminister für Forschung und Technologie to build up a spectral data information system (SpecInfo, [9]) comprising as much evaluated data as possible in a unified information system comparable to the C^{13}NMR Data Retrieval System developed by BASF Ludwigshafen, available online on the Scientific Technical Network (STN).

- **Structural Data** containing three-dimensional structural information about molecules like the Cambridge Crystallographic Data File (CCDF) for organic molecules or the Brookhaven Data File for proteins (see below).

- **Chemical Reaction Data** to retrieve information on how transformations of chemical structures may be achieved (see below).

4. IN-HOUSE DATABASES AND COMPUTER APPLICATIONS

4.1 Laboratory Infrastructure [2,10]

Figure 3 outlines the infrastructure we implemented to assist the synthesis of bioactive substances. X-ray diffraction (limited to molecules up to medium molecular weight) and NMR-spectroscopy are available. In addition, in order to use the highly developed 2D-NMR methodology new 3D-NMR methods will be improved by C. Griesinger [11] and applied to biomacromolecules [12]. A separate database for structural information yielded by NMR-spectroscopy of biomolecules should be built up with worldwide cooperation. The dedicated computers of these experimental systems are interconnected to a DIGITAL EQUIPMENT VAX/VMS Local Area VAX Cluster (LAVC), and interactive graphical workstations: a PS390 system (Evans & Sutherland) and a CYBER910 (CDC). Nearly all the software packages available for Molecular Modeling and Molecular Dynamics for such a configuration are implemented [2]: Computational methods have been added to the experimental methods. E. Egert in our institute is going on to develop his MOMO Molecular Modeling System [13] which runs on VAXs as well as on MS-DOS high performance personal computers like the COMPAQ386/25 which is also part of our Local Area Network (LAN). The latter are also used to introduce our students to computational methods. Additional computer services are available to the members of our different research groups.

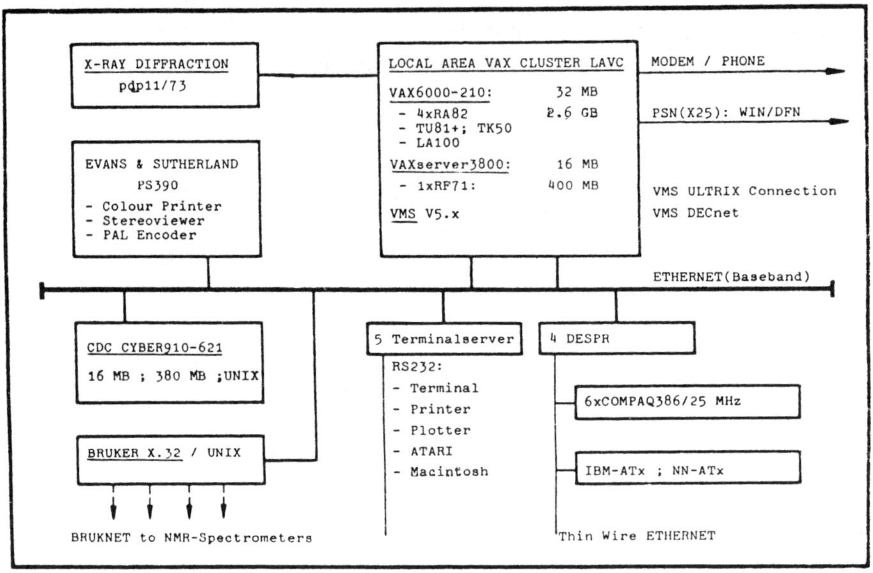

FIGURE 3
Outline of the components of the LAN in the Institute of Organic Chemistry, Frankfurt. Personal Computers (MS-DOS) are integrated via Digital Equipment's PSCSA software or as intelligent terminals connected to terminal servers.

4.2 The Outside Connection

One VAX is connected to a Packet Switched Network to make access possible to supercomputers for energy minimizing calculations of biomacromolecules, and to database hosts. Especially the databases available at STN within the Academic Programs of CAS, American Chemical Society (ACS) and FIZ Karlsruhe are used. In addition, searches in databases offered by DIALOG, ORBIT, BRS, DIMDI, FIZ TECHNIK, QUESTEL, ESA-IRS and DATA-STAR can be done. Searches are run by selected and trained PhD students. However, *every* student before earning his Diploma (M.S) has to absolve teaching units in Chemical Information [2]. These comprise classical and modern aspects and should help the young chemist to retrieve information from library holdings as well as to learn how to frame questions to be handled by online searches. Special emphasis is placed on developing a critical attitude towards answers retrieved from databases in general!

4.3 Reaction Databases

The first database available dealing with chemical reactions is Chemical Reaction Documentation Service (CRDS), produced by DERWENT and offered by System Development Corporation, today MCC's Orbit Search Service. The contents of this database include Theilheimer's printed equivalent [14] and material from the *J. Synth. Meth.* (JSM). CRDS was already available online before interaction with a database in the Language of Chemistry: Structural Formulas, was feasible. In addition, this material today is available as datafiles for in-house systems.

DATA COLLECTIONS: REACTION DATABASES

Out-of-House:	CRDS	*DERWENT*	*(ORBIT)*
	CASREACT	*CAS*	*(STN)*
	BEILSTEIN	*BEILSTEIN*	*(STN; DIALOG)*
In-House:	SYNLIB	*Distributed Chem.Graphics*	
	- Current / Contributed		
	ORAC	*ORAC Ltd./MCC*	
	- THEILHEIMER	*(1946 - 80)*	
	- Current / Contributed		
	REACCS	*Molecular Design/MCC*	
	- THEILHEIMER	*(1946 - 80)*	
	- JSM	*(1980 - 88)*	
	- ORGSYN	*(1921 - 87)*	
	- Current / Contributed		
	- CHIRAS	*(1975 - 88)*	
	- METALYSIS	*(1974 - 89)*	
	- CCR	*(1986 - 89)*	(By ISI)

FIGURE 4
Data Collections: Reaction Databases. Database, Producer, and Hosts for Out-of-House; Retrieval System, Producer and Datafiles with literature time ranges covered for In-House Systems are given.

The field of reaction databases is a difficult one. A chemist is interested in getting a precise prescription for transforming a partial structure of a molecule into a target structure and complications arising from the presence of other partial structures in the starting material have to be taken into account. At least he wants a hint of how it could eventually be done by analogy. He wants the reaction conditions displayed together with feedback to the literature. He is *definitely not* interested in retrieving all references to documents where the same reaction has been used. But the latter is the character of CAS's CASREACT database [15] and, to quote Heller [16], "it is easy to be swamped away with the volume of this database". BEILSTEIN in its present form is not what I consider to be a reaction database; it can, however, provide information how to prepare a certain compound.

The in-house systems better meet the demands of a bench chemist. At present, three major reaction retrieval systems, differing in their search capabilities, are available [16-20] (Figure 4). Two of those belong to MCC [19,20]. The data files are in part identical. For current literature there is no danger today of retrieving too much duplicate information [18]. CURRENT CHEMICAL REACTION (CCR) is equivalent to ISI's printed product using MOLECULAR DESIGN's retrieval system. Actually a chemist should use - if he has the appropriate infrastructure - these systems and data files in parallel. Another reaction database of the same type will join this collection: FIZ CHEMIE in Berlin will offer a computerized version of its printed ChemInform [21], a project sponsored by the "German Bundesminister für Forschung und Technologie". To make more use of the evaluated ChemInform data these will be available in formats compatible with some of the retrieval systems already in existence.

In my opinion this is the future-oriented concept. Building reaction databases is expensive. How a reaction or a sequence of reactions is dealt with is highly subject to the point of view the abstractor takes. To obtain the optimum, the development of standard formats to transfer information between different retrieval systems [22] should be enforced. It is imperative to establish a minimum set of standard rules on how to document reactions. What we need is information about new and improved reactions and not what may be found in a textbook. Selection by specialists and cooperation is necessary.

4.4 Structural Information and Computational Methods

G. Quinkert and his coworkers [23] in our institute are synthesizing medium-sized natural substances showing biological activity. A typical target molecule is (+)-Aspicilin, a macrolide. Aspicilin is an 18-membered cyclic molecule. It is interesting from the synthetic point of view. Structural data of Aspicilin and its precursors derived from X-ray diffraction and/or structural data as a result of molecular modeling calculations based on the principles of molecular mechanics can be compared. The ultimate goal is to elucidate principles which determine the stereocontrol of key reactions in synthesis. If stereocontrol can be perfectly realized the target compound is formed without its enatiomer as a byproduct. Analysis of the geometry of specific partial structures of molecules, whose structural data are available in CCDF, with the help of statistical methods available support reaction models; computer time needed even for these relatively small molecules is reduced since the calculations of conformations having low potential energy can then be based on constraints which are justified by experimental data. The CCDF can be considered to be a database of small structures determined experimentally which can be used to build up larger molecules reducing computational uncertainties. Cyclosporin A and Didemnin have been looked at by a combination of X-ray analysis, NMR-spectroscopy, as well as by molecular dynamics calculations [24].

4.5 Structural Information and Biomacromolecules

Structural data of proteins are available in the Brookhaven Protein Data File. These biomacromolecules can be visualized in real time. Their superstructure can be analyzed looking for instance for helices or beta-sheets. The structural data are starting points to perform calculations on derivatives or to simulate substrate-receptor interactions. We have also implemented databases in-house with sequence information of DNA and proteins. J. Engels and his coworkers [25, 26] make use of these when designing new synthetic genes in DNA recombination techniques. This is also an area where we have to expect an avalanche of data. Yet some of these data are wrong because of errors in extracting the data from the literature.

5. CONCLUSION

"DATA FOR DISCOVERY". Yes, they are necessary! We do need databases as part of an infrastructure for future-oriented research and development. It is the obligation of scientists to contribute to our scientific knowledge data of all kinds. Responsibility for the quality of data starts with the responsibility for what is published. The interdependence of bench scientists and those producing databases and data collections will increase and both have to share the responsibility for quality by eliminating human factors whenever possible. Hosts offering information produced by others and having no responsibility for the quality of data, I consider also to be part of the information infrastructure and thus members of the scientific community. Provided they agree with this point of view their activities cannot always be profit-oriented.

ACKNOWLEDGEMENT

The interdisciplinary concept of student education and research in our institute has been initiated by my colleague G. Quinkert (chemical synthesis of bioactive compounds, especially macrolides). Other colleagues involved are E. Egert (since April 1989: X-ray diffraction; development of molecular modeling software), J. Engels (biological syntheses of biomacromolecules; Interleukin-2), C. Griesinger (since January 1990: 2D- and 3D-NMR methods; proteins and peptides), H. Kessler (until March 1990: NMR; molecular dynamics; peptides). The realization of the infrastructure necessary has been made possible particularly with a generous grant (1986-1992) from the "German Bundesminister für Forschung und Technologie".

LITERATURE

[1] G. Quinkert: "Gezielte Synthese Bioaktiv Wirkstoffe, Forschungs-und Lehrkonzeption der Frankfurter Organischen Chemie", Lecture, Industrie- und Handelskammer Frankfurt am Main, Jan.12 th, 1988.

[2] D. Rehm: "Computeranwendungen in der Chemie", Mitteilungsblatt der Fachgruppe CHEMIE - INFORMATION - COMPUTER der GDCh (17), 1990, 9-19 (ISSN 0178-4927) and literature mentioned there in connection with "Frankfurter Model".

[3] E. Garfield: "Citation Indexes for Sciences", *Science* 122 (1955) 108-111.

[4] See: Citations retrieved by an online search in CA, Section 20.

[5] K. Maxwell: "Maxwell Communication Corporation (MCC) and American Chemical Society (ACS): Friend or Foes?", INFOBASE'90: Contribution to the Special Symposium: "The Future of Electronic Information Services in Chemistry"; Frankfurt, May 16th,1990.

[6] D. Rehm: "Zur Verbesserung der Qualitaet der Sekundaerinformation", in: Tagungsbericht zur 2. Vortragstagung der Fachgruppe CHEMIE-INFORMATION der GDCh, Frankfurt am Main 1985, 4-19 (ISBN 3-924763-02-X).

[7] S.K. Hudnut: "Considerations in Searching Databases Spanning 20 Years", in: *Proceedings of the 12th IOLIM London 1988*, 459-465.

[8] R. Luckenbach, R. Ecker, J. Sunkel: "The Critical Screening and Assesment of Scientific Results without Loss of Information -- Possible or Not?", *Angew. Chem.*, Int. Ed. Engl. 20 (1981) 841-849; *Angew. Chem.* 93 (1981) 876-885. Comment: This publication has not been covered by CAS!

[9] J.M. Czermak: "A Policy for Science and Technical Information in Chemistry", in: *Proceedings of the Montreux International Chemical Information Conference 1989*, 13-18 (ISBN 3-540-51804-5).

[10] D. Rehm: "Chemie-Information: Anwendungen jenseits traditioneller

Datenbasen", in: *Tagungsbericht zu 10.* Fruehjahrstagung der Online-Benutzergruppe der DGD, Frankfurt 1988, 93-116.
[11] C. Griesinger, O.W. Sorensen, R.R. Ernst: "A Practical Approach to Threedimensional NMR Spectroscopy", *Magn. Reson.* 73 (1987) 574-579; see also: *J. Am. Chem. Soc.* 109 (1987) 7227-7228; *Magn. Reson.* 84 (1989) 14-63.
[12] H. Oschkinat, C. Griesinger, P.J. Kraulis, O.W. Sorensen, R.R. Ernst, A.M. Gronenborn, G.M. Clore: "Three dimensional NMR Spectroscopy of a Protein in Solution", *Nature* 332 (1988) 374-376.
[13] H. Beck, E. Egert: "MOMO - A New Molecular Modeling Program", in: *Computational Methods in Chemical Design*, Tagung Schloss Elmau 1988, 103; H. Beck: "MOMO - Ein Beitrag zur Weiterentwicklung des Molecular Modeling", Dissertation, Goettingen 1989.
[14] W. Theilheimer (ed.): *Synthetic Methods of Organic Chemistry*, S. Karger, Basel.
[15] R.C. Dana: "Where do they all come from? Appropriate Coverage of the Literature for a Chemical Reaction Database", in: *Proceedings of the 13th IOLIM London 1989*, 129-138.
[16] S.R. Heller: "A Survey of Reaction Databases", in: *Proceedings of the 13th IOLIM London 1989*, 119-127; E. Zass, S. Mueller, *Chimia* 40 (1986) 38-50.
[17] R.E. Buntrock: "Chemical Reaction Searching: CASREACT and REACCS", *Database* 12 (1988) 124-127.
[18] J.H. Borkent, F. Oukes, J.H. Nordijk: "Chemical Reaction Searching Compared in REACCS, SYNLIB, and ORAC", *J. Chem. Inf. Comp. Sci.* 28 (1988) 148-150.
[19] G.A. Hopkinson: "Recent Development in Reaction Searching", in: *Proceedings of the 13th IOLIM London 1989*, 139-145; P. Johnson, *Chem. Brit.* 1985 59-67.
[20] A.J. Kos, G. Grethe: "Reaktionsdatenbanken - Werkzeuge fuer den Synthese-Chemiker", *Nachr. Chem. Tech. Lab.* 35 (1987) 586-594; J.E Mills et al.: "REACCS in the Chemical Development Environment", *J. Chem. Inf. Comp. Sci.* 28 (1988) 153-163.
[21] J. Gasteiger, C. Weiske: "ChemInform - An Integrated Information System on Chemical Reactions", in: *Proceedings of the 13th IOLIM London 1989*, 147-154.
[22] J.M. Barnard: "Draft Specification for Revised Version of the Standard Molecular Data (SMD) Format", *J. Chem. Inf. Comp. Sci.* 30 (1990) 81-96.
[23] G. Quinkert et al.: "Synthese des Flechtenmacrolids (+)-Aspicilin mit Photolactonisierung als Schluesselreaktion", *Helv. Chim. Acta* 71 (1988) 1719-1794; M. Eichhorn, Dissertation, Frankfurt 1990; U. Doeller, Dissertation, Frankfurt 1990, F. Kueber, Frankfurt, priv. comm..

[24] J. Lautz, H. Kessler, R. Kaptein, W.F. van Gunsteren: "Molecular Dynamics Simulation of Cyclosporin A: The Crystal Structure and Dynamic Modeling of a Structure in apolar Solution based on NMR Data", *J. Comput.-Aided Mol. Des.* 1 (1987) 219-241; H. Kesssler et al.: "Conformational Analysis of Didemnins. A multidisciplinary Approach by means of X-Ray, NMR, Molecular Dynamics, and Molecular Mechanics Techniques", *Helv. Chim. Acta* 72 (1989) 530-555.

[25] J.W. Engels, E. Uhlmann: "Gene Synthesis", *Angew. Chem.*, Int. Ed. Eng. 28 (1989) 716-734; *Angew. Chem.* 101 (1989) 733-752.

[26] T. Beckers, H.J. Hauser, D. Huesken, J.W. Engels: "Expression and Characterization of a Des-methionine Mutant Interleukin-2 Receptor (TAC Protein) with Interleukin-2 Binding", *J. Biol. Chem.* 263 (1988) 8359-8365.

CHEMICAL DATA USED IN PROCESS CONTROL: INDUSTRIAL NEEDS

Marcelle Gaune-Escard
I.U.S.T.I./S.E.T.T. UA 1168 C.N.R.S.
Université de Provence, Centre de St Jérôme
13397 Marseille Cédex 13, France

INTRODUCTION

The general question has been, and is, the thrust of many articles and conferences that attempt to define the problems and stress the industrial needs for data.

First of all, the first problem is communication since even the word "data" may have a different meaning for a scientist and an engineer; this is of the same nature as the distinction between fundamental and applied research. Data are input parameters required by the design engineer. Therefore data have first to be available and then to be reliable. The effect of inaccurate data of thermodynamic properties of materials on the design and operation of different units of chemical processing can be considerable and a number of papers have been written detailing design problems (and in some cases failures) resulting from inaccurate data.

During the last years, many advances were made in the field of data banks all over the world and most thermochemical data banks are now integrated information systems able to compute properties and phase equilibria for pure substances and their mixtures in the state at user-specified conditions.

But the needs of thermodynamic data of technological interest are also, in a real sense, unpredictable. Thus, with the exception of those very few substances whose utility is broad and long term, the probability is quite small that a need will exist at any given time for some particular substance or mixture chosen at random. On the other hand, at any particular time, the probability is quite large that a need exists for thermodynamic data of some kind for some substance and that this need was not previously known.

In this context, there is really a need of data oriented towards a particular application. This requires the expertise of a scientist and the information can be experimental measurements, smoothed or correlated measurements, or the results of a prediction procedure. There is nothing short-term in this approach. Furthermore, the scientist will find that solving the industrial need might well lead to greater insight into materials behavior and suggest future research directions.

Examples of application will be given in the field of high temperature melts.

It is no secret that industry in the main is still reluctant to contemplate processes based either on electrolysis or on the use of molten salts.

ELECTROWINNING IN MOLTEN SALTS

Molten salts electrolysis has been widely used in producing and/or refining a considerable number of elements in quantities ranging from pilot-plant to very large scale commercial production. A list of these elements would include lithium, sodium, beryllium, magnesium, calcium, aluminum, titanium, hafnium and fluorine.

Capitalizing on the wealth of experience built up over decades, industrial companies, like PECHINEY, are now putting their know-how to profitable use in related areas, namely:

- electrowinning of the rare earth metals, reactive metals, refractory metals and very pure Group IVB and VB metals;

- electrorefining in molten salts (*e.g.*, sequential refining employing more than one electrolyte);

- electrolytic recycling of metal scrap and waste.

Electrolytic elaboration of metals from melts, involves a compromise between several parameters to be optimized.

Electrolysis has many advantages over conventional pyrometallurgical processes employing metallic reducing agents (C, Si, ..):

- it is selective since potential, electrode overvoltages and valency state (complexing) of the electrolyte can be adjusted.

- it allows elements either very electropositive or very electronegative to be obtained

- it is a quasi-continuous process and can be easily automated.

These advantages outweigh some drawbacks such as high capital and operation costs related to energy use (electricity), limitation of productivity by current density.

As a result, the design and engineering of an electrolytic process raises a number of technological challenges for the cell itself but also for the electrolyte and the salt to be electrolyzed:

ELECTROLYTE	SALT
• Phase diagram	• solubility
• stability/hygroscopy	• stability/hygroscopy
• vapor pressure	• vapor pressure
• complexing ability	etc...
• viscosity	
• conductivity	
etc...	

Thermodynamic properties play an important role and the choice of a suitable molten salt solvent is directly related to the operation temperature and also to the "average valency" of the electrolytic bath. For the elaboration of niobium, for instance, from $NbCl_5$ (m.p. 478 K, b.p. 520 K) the choice of a chloride melt as a solvent induces appreciable losses by evaporation (eutectic chloride mixtures generally melt at temperatures higher than 650 K). The problem is therefore to find a suitable solvent including anionic species, like F^-, corresponding to a higher stability of the niobium species in the melt.

Another example is the production of rare earth metals. Neodymium, for instance, is used for the fabrication of magnets; alloys of neodymium can be obtained either by reduction with calcium or by electrolysis. In the electrolytic process a compromise had to be found between the following features:

- in molten chloride baths, a poor current efficiency is obtained because of the two coexisting valence states (II and III). Adding fluorides to the bath results in a stabilization of the III valence but also induces formation of neodymium oxychlorides and related operating problems.

- in molten fluoride melts, electrolysis of NdF_3 is easier but costs are higher ; electrolysis of oxides would not pose any problem of anodic reaction but is not promoted by the low solubility.

Nevertheless a compromise has been found and a process successfully developed [1] : a derivative of the industrial product, hydrated neodymium carbonate, is dissolved and electrolyzed in a mixture of molten fluorides at 900 °C.

Refining of elements is also an important application in the molten salt area, *e.g.*, aluminum electrorefining by the "3-layer" Gadeau process which is a sequential refining employing more than one electrolyte [2]. This process uses chloride/fluoride melts, which involve lower energy consumption than required for fluoride-only melts and of adjustable complexing ability with respect to the impurities to be removed.

In the above examples, data are needed on the thermodynamics of neodymium halide-based melts.

- Experimental thermochemical investigations conducted by high temperature calorimetry, differential enthalpic analysis, differential scanning calorimetry can provide information on phase equilibria in the melt.

- From a theoretical point of view, suitable modeling of these melts involving complex species, should be developed. The classical models used so far for the most simple molten salts mixtures are not suitable; the melts involved here are not simple since they involve i) ions with different valency, ii) ionic and non-ionic components and iii) several components.

HAZARDOUS WASTE DISPOSAL AND MOLTEN SALTS

The disposal of hazardous wastes is receiving increasing attention. A novel molten salt process has been developed [3] for different kinds of wastes :

- organic waste (polyethylene, PVC, organic muds and emulsions, benzenic and phenolic by-products)
- inorganic waste (asbestos, glass wool or glass fibers, mineral muds)
- mixed waste (organic + mineral waste, organic + metallic waste)

The methods used so far for waste disposal are incineration and fusion which enable efficient volume reduction but also include some drawbacks such as:

- in incineration, sorting of heterogeneous wastes according to different energetic features (PCI), considerable capital investment into stack gas cleaning equipment, ...
- in fusion, very high operation temperatures (1700 °C for asbestos) involving high capital and operation costs, uneasy ash removal, ...

The present molten salt process offers several advantages :

- very efficient heat transfer
- retention of noxious contaminants in the melt
- melting and retention of ash by the melt
- efficient destruction of hazardous chemicals.

The waste is introduced as a pulverized solid into the high temperature melt.

The composition of the silica-based melt is adjusted according the category of the waste to be treated.

The nature of the waste to be treated also resulted in three different versions of the process including (organic and mixed waste) or not (inorganic waste) pyrolysis and gasification under oxidizing atmosphere.

Data were needed to solve this problem and research was performed on the solubility of waste in several high temperature melts in order to evidence a suitable solvent.

REFERENCES

[1] Pechiney - French Patent FR 2 494 725.
[2] R. Sevin, *J. four électrique & indus. chim.*, 1964, 8, 79.

THERMODYNAMIC AND TRANSPORT PROPERTIES OF GASES FOR COMPUTER AIDED ENGINEERING

Ludwig Silberring
Silberring Engineering Ltd.
Zurich, Switzerland.

INTRODUCTION

The available information on properties of gases is ample, but still far from complete. Most of it has been generated in the pre-computer era and presented in a form which is inconvenient for the latter. An adequately universal and reliable method of calculation of the properties of real gas mixtures does not exist.

The well known virial equation of state allows us to calculate the thermodynamic properties of real gases and their mixtures in a wide range of parameters without arbitrary assumptions. But the existing knowledge on the virial coefficients and their temperature derivatives is still unsatisfactory, especially for interactions among different molecules and in particular beyond the ranges covered by the bulk of experimental data. The author has developed a new temperature function allowing us to fill these gaps, at least with probable information. Some characteristics of data that are important for a wide and successful application in CAE have also been reviewed.

A program system, based on the above considerations, returns the PVT data, the properties derived therefrom and the transport properties either in the form of a set of selected tables or in function of selected sets of particular parameters. It already covers 57 substances, but others can be added as soon as a minimum of reliable information about it is found or generated. Output is available either on the computer screen or to a disk file or from the computer RAM for further treatment in user's application programs.

The author is indebted to Prof. Dr. Hans H. Günthard of the Swiss Federal Institute of Technology for his valuable advice and for the review of this paper.

OBJECTIVES AND LIMITATIONS

Data for CAE should cover wide ranges of substances, their mixtures, phases and parameters in order to be useful for an unpredictable variety of application programs. All mathematic functions invented so far by humankind do not, however, succeed in describing the complex properties of matter in a sufficiently general, manageable and precise way.

If little or nothing is known within the desirable ranges of substances or parameters, then at least probable and thermodynamically consistent extrapolations must be estimated. It should be kept in mind that the possibility to check and, if necessary, complete the intermediate results of calculations is often restricted if not entirely lost during application of CAE.

Data for CAE shall be available not only in the traditional form of printed tables, but also as tables displayed on a computer screen. In both cases the user must be free to select the requested kind of tables, the substances to be included in any particular set, the preferred units, the parameter limits and steps, as well as such details as the output mode and format. In addition, data for CAE must also be available as a function of any consistent set of input parameters. In the latter case, aside from the possibilities of keyboard input and the already mentioned possibilities of output, an exchange of information between the data calculation software and any kind of user's application software must be possible via the computer RAM in order to allow integration of the former software into the latter.

Data for CAE must be applicable to the calculations of the chemical equilibria and of the thermal effects of chemical reactions. This should be possible without needing to refer to any separate sets of information. Hence such data must refer to a common energy and entropy level, valid for all substances and all their modifications.

Not only various isomers, but also isotopes and such hyperfine structure variants as ortho and para modification of hydrogen and its isotopes should be preferably considered as distinct substances, at least whenever such substances are characterized by significant differences of properties.

Data for CAE should be represented as far as practical by analytical formulae, which should be as uniform as possible in order to restrict both the necessary storage space and the necessary amount of the program code and hence to keep the calculation speed high.

It is easier to formulate the above conditions than to fulfill them. At least some of them are conflicting and an optimum compromise must be sought in this respect. This article describes a basis for a computer program system which can deliver data of real gases and their mixtures according to these criteria, at least within significant ranges of parameters. Beyond such ranges a similarly general treatment is not possible; specific formulations or data banks, beyond the scope of the following text, must then be consulted.

The said program system delivers data tables which include the compressibility factor, the fugacity coefficient, the isobaric heat capacity, enthalpy, entropy, viscosity, thermal conductivity and the Prandtl number of any real gas among those available on files and/or of any mixture of such gases as a function of pressure and temperature. The program returns also the fugacity coefficient of each individual gas in the mixture. The second virial coefficient and its temperature derivatives up to the second order are also returned as a function of temperature, if requested.

Another variant of the program system returns all parameters listed above as a function of any pair selected from five of them (pressure, temperature, volume, enthalpy, entropy) or as a function of any one of them if output is requested in the dew point or the resublimation point.

RELATION WITH EXISTING DATA COMPILATIONS

Thermodynamic properties of dilute gases, usually called ideal gases, the molecules of which are composed of not too many atoms, have been very precisely estimated during the last decades by statistical calculations based on quantum mechanics. The application of these methods becomes, however, difficult with the growing size and complexity of the molecules. Beyond some point calorimetric data might be better than those obtained by said calculations.

Many sets of tables of properties of gases are available, but only a few of them are based on a careful scrutiny of the huge amount of individual reports on theoretical or experimental research. An extensive program of investigation of properties of hydrocarbons was started in the U.S.A. in the 1940s as the API-44 Project. This activity is continued now by the Thermodynamics Research Center (TRC) of the Texas A&M University in College Station. It also covers a number of non-hydrocarbons.

The most complete investigations of the thermodynamic properties of inorganic substances, which also includes some light hydrocarbons, were also initiated in the U.S.A. in the 1950s as a response to the requirements of space technology. The results of the associated activity have been known since 1964 as the "JANAF Thermochemical Tables" incorporated into the National Standard Reference Data System (NSRDS).

The TRC and JANAF tables are restricted to pure substances and deliver their thermodynamic properties in selected standard states. The TRC tables also include other data for most substances. The third edition of the JANAF Thermochemical Tables (1985) includes real gas properties of water at three selected pressures. NSRDS periodically publishes research reports on properties of individual substances, including properties of real gases.

TRC and NSRDS data sets represent valuable sources for computer aided engineering. Most of these data are, however, available only in tabulated form, whereby the format of the tables from both these sources is not identical. Such data need to be further manipulated prior to their use in process calculation programs. The recent availability of some of these data on computer-readable media facilitates but does not remove the necessity of the said manipulations. These data have been extensively but not exclusively used as the basis for the program system referred to in this paper. The main objective of the latter is, however, an extension of the available information to the properties of real gas mixtures. For the sake of consistency, the same calculation methods must be used for individual gases since each of them represents a limit case of any mixture containing it.

At this opportunity some modifications, described below, have been applied to the NSRDS and/or TRC and/or IUPAC conventions.

ISOTOPES AND HYPERFINE STRUCTURE VARIANTS

Most data tables, including those of NSRDS, refer to so called natural mixture of isotopes, in spite of the fact that the ratio of isotopes in materials of different origin is not constant, even if such materials have not been influenced by human actions. As already postulated, it is useful for some applications to consider each isotope as a distinct substance. For other applications the differences in properties based on any of the above conventions remain insignificant.

The same is valid for the already mentioned hyperfine structure variants of hydrogen and its isotopes. The properties of any mixture of ortho and para species of hydrogen, deuterium or tritium can easily be derived from the properties of the corresponding pure components, whereas the inverse procedure is impossible without additional information.

ENERGY REFERENCE LEVEL

The very old custom of referring energy data to an arbitrary level of 25 °C has been retained in the NSRDS system. The following modifications have been considered as useful, in particular if data are destined only for gases, as it is the case in the present paper:

* The gas phase at (any) unit fugacity is always considered as the standard reference state.
* Absolute zero temperature represents the energy reference level for every gas.
* The heat of formation of every gas is specified at the above selected energy reference level and is equal to the negative value of the energy, necessary to dissociate the molecules into free atoms in their ground state.

The first of the above conditions eliminates the necessity of deriving the properties of gases from the properties of other phases. The second one facilitates the presentation of data in tabular or graphical form and shortens the sequence of calculations necessary to determine any energy related data at any conditions. Finally the last of the above selections allows us to include in the energy of formation all information about the formation of different molecules from identical atoms, such as the ortho and para modifications of hydrogen and its isotopes.

STORING THE DATA AND SPACING THE ENTRIES

Thermodynamic properties in standard state can be calculated by the formulae of statistical mechanics whenever they are requested. For this purpose it is adequate to store only a moderate number of constants. A certain variety of formulae, however, must be applied to different kinds of molecules. Furthermore, it is sometimes necessary to combine several hundred terms corresponding to various combinations of quantum numbers in order to obtain data for a single temperature value. This could lead to excessive computing time. Finally, many data originate from calorimetric measurements and are available only in table form, which cannot be easily fitted into analytical formulae. The same can be concluded about data on the transport properties of dilute gases, which originate from a variety of sources.

It follows that data in the standard reference state destined for CAE must be also stored in table form. The spacing of the temperature entries in the low temperature range must, however, be narrowed in comparison to the constant spacing of 100K adopted by the NSRDS tables. Otherwise it would be difficult to retain the high precision of these data for intermediate temperatures, even if sophisticated interpolation methods were applied.

REAL GAS CORRECTIONS

Most real gas corrections rise with rising gas density, but depend also on other parameters. Density must be restricted for the application of any formulae which cannot cover the whole single phase fluid properties, since there is no distinct limit between the liquid and gaseous phase at supercritical temperature.

The laws of thermodynamics allow us to derive all thermodynamic properties of real gases and their mixtures from a relationship between any set of three independent parameters. Usually, the relationship between pressure, temperature, and volume (PVT data) is determined by a combination of molecular theories and experimental information and other derivations follow therefrom. This is, however, not the only possible nor necessarily the best way. Theoretical or experimental investigation of other parameters may contribute to our knowledge in this field.

The apparently modest task of determining the relationship between the three parameters is less simple than it looks at first glance.

One set of problems is associated with the amount of information still needed. For gas mixtures not only the global parameters of a mixture are usually sought, but also some properties of each individual gas in the mixture are often requested. Assuming that PVT data are used as a basis for the calculation of all other properties, knowledge of the partial volume of every component as a function of pressure and temperature besides the global PVT relationship for each composition of each mixture is necessary. To date, only a few mixtures have been more or less adequately investigated in view of providing an approach to the above amount of knowledge.

Another set of problems is associated with the discrepancies between the ranges of parameters within which information might be requested, and those within which it is available. Industrial processes often operate far beyond the parameter ranges adequately covered by laboratory experiments.

Still another set of problems is associated with the discrepancy between the sought and possible precision and completeness of the experimental data. The thermodynamic relationships use not only the values of the functions, but also their partial derivatives up to the second order. Even slight tolerances in the former can lead to large errors in the latter.

Great efforts have been made towards description of the PVT data of real gases by analytical functions or by equations of state since the first well known endeavor by Van der Waals. Most of them attempt to include in their range critical properties in order to derive their constants from the law of corresponding states. Others use a significant number of constants, the variable sets of which are defined for a more or less restricted number of substances. The properties of real gases cannot be represented within the precision of the experimental data by any one of these equations. Their weakest point is associated with the lack of adequately founded rules for the combination of the said constants for gas mixtures. Available computer software often offers some variety of equations of state and gives to the user the possibility and the pain of an ambiguous choice between them.

Data for many individual gases have been extensively investigated in specific research papers. At least the recent ones include sets of analytical formulae, which allow us to calculate everything. These formulae are often similar in type but seldom identical for different substances. Most of them are based on the Leiden type of virial equation of state.

The said formulae include a significant number of substance specific coefficients and are valid within the limits of parameters selected for each individual research paper. In most cases they deliver high quality data within these limits, but usually cannot be applied for extrapolations beyond this. To date there is no way to derive similar quality data for real gas mixtures from such formulae.

Selected properties of particular gas mixtures have been investigated in a number of particular research papers. They cover usually restricted categories of substances within narrow ranges of parameters. They are useful for checking general purpose relationships, but cannot replace them.

The already mentioned virial equation is founded in statistical thermodynamics. Its subsequent virial coefficients are associated with interactions among pairs of molecules, their triplets, and so on. The same equation is valid for gas mixtures. The virial coefficients can be derived for this purpose without arbitrary assumptions from the corresponding coefficients of the individual gases, from those characterizing the interactions among pairs, triplets and so on of different molecules (hereafter called interaction virials) and from the molar composition of a mixture. The properties of a mixture of any composition could therefore be precisely described up to high densities in any temperature range, provided all above virial coefficients were known for the entire requested temperature range. They are not.

Some information is available on the second interaction virials for some pairs of different molecules. However, only a small part of these data allows us to estimate the necessary temperature derivatives with reasonable tolerance.

Few mixtures have been investigated with great precision and their PVT data have been fitted into a virial equation of state using up to five virial coefficients. In the case of binary mixtures, the interaction virials for pairs of different molecules can be deduced therefrom. The available information is, however, inadequate to do so also for higher interaction virials. Data on mixtures of more than two components, unless available for a set of different compositions, can be used only for checking otherwise estimated interactions.

Two conclusions follow from the above. Firstly, for a wide range of substances and temperatures, the available information does not allow us to deduce any reasonable data beyond the range of validity of the virial equation truncated after the second coefficient. Secondly, less rigorous methods must be accepted to find out the interaction virials necessary not only for the calculation of the second virial coefficient of any mixture but also for the calculation of the fugacities of gas components in each mixture.

As the law of corresponding states holds for each component of a mixture, it is reasonable to expect that it holds also for the interactions in pairs of different molecules in such a mixture. However, even in this case, hypotheses must be made in order to find out the relevant critical temperature and volume. Such hypotheses are available, but some of them are still far from being adequately verified.

The virial equation of state, truncated after the second coefficient, has been used for the program system described in this paper. Precise real gas correction can be obtained in this way in a wide temperature range and at least up to moderate densities. A comparison of the data calculated by the virial equation of state, truncated after the second coefficient, with high quality data of a number of individual gases and of some well investigated gas mixtures leads to a conclusion that the above density limit depends heavily on the temperature. Two corresponding ranges of parameters are shown in Figure 1. Within the first of them, data originating from the truncated virial equation are almost as precise as they are known, whereas higher tolerances must be accepted in the second one.

An upper temperature limit does not appear in these considerations. Similarly the density limits could apparently continue to rise with a rising

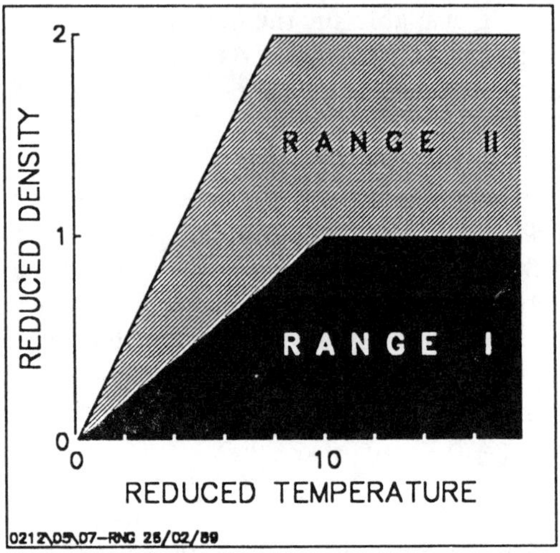

FIGURE 1. Ranges of parameters covered by the program system.

temperature. Real gas properties at high temperatures are, however, not adequately known. For this reason an upper density limit is suggested for each of the above ranges.

Figure 2 shows both above ranges in a temperature-entropy diagram of argon. The ranges in which data can be calculated by the virial equation can

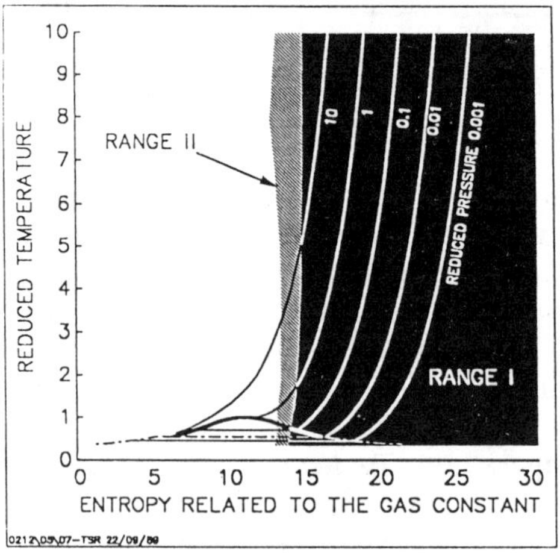

FIGURE 2

Ranges of parameters covered by the program system in a typical temperature-entropy diagram. The thick solid line shows the liquid-vapor equilibrium, the dash-dot line corresponds to the solid limits.

extend beyond the phase boundary limit into the metastable region of a subcooled vapor and, in this way, data can be estimated even in such conditions. But the minimum compressibility factor must be restricted to do this, in addition to the previously described density limits. Figure 2 is based on the assumption, that the compressibility factor must be not less than twice its critical value.

All limits described above and the associated typical tolerances of the output data are summarized in Table 1.

TABLE 1. Limits of parameter ranges and associated typical tolerances of the output data

	First set of limits		Second set of limits	
Limits of parameter ranges (whichever is less)				
Maximum reduced density	1		2	
Maximum ration between the reduced density and the reduced temperature	0.10		0.25	
Minimum ration between the compressibility factor and its critical value	2		2	
Typical tolerances of the output data	ave.	max.	ave.	max.
compressibility factor	0.005	0.03	0.03	0.14
Enthalpy above 0 K related to the gas constant and temperature	0.012	0.07	0.05	0.30
Entropy related to the gas constant	0.010	0.05	0.05	0.30
Free enthalpy above 0 K related to the gas constant and the temperature	0.003	0.02	0.02	0.09

THE TEMPERATURE FUNCTION FOR THE SECOND VIRIAL COEFFICIENT

The available knowledge about the intermolecular forces between molecules and the available computing power are insufficient for a sufficiently precise theoretical scrutiny of the relationship between the second virial coefficient and temperature. Empirical functions are, therefore, used in most cases for an approximation of this relationship, whereby the constants appearing in such functions are fitted to yield optimum agreement with experimental information. The latter is, however, available only within a more or less restricted temperature range which seldom covers the actual needs of science and technology. The weak point of the said empirical functions is associated with the incertitude of their values and, in particular, the values of their temperature derivatives near and beyond both ends of the temperature range covered by adequate experimental evidence.

Some properties of the sought functions and their temperature derivatives, at least up to the second order, are experimentally proven, at least for some gases, and are listed below. Unless and until the opposite is demonstrated, it can be assumed that these properties remain valid for all gases.

1. One only extreme value; a maximum or a minimum for the derivatives of even or odd order respectively.

2. Monotonic shape on both sides of the said extreme values.

3. An approach to a limit value (positive for the function and zero for all its temperature derivatives) with rising temperature.

The known equations of state and the known analytical approximations of the second virial coefficient as a function of temperature cannot fulfill simultaneously all above conditions. The following function can:

$$B/V_c = \sum_{z=0}^{\infty} A_z \exp(-K_z T/T_c) \qquad (1)$$

whereby B designates the second virial coefficient, V_c the critical volume, T and T_c respectively the temperature and its critical value. A_z and K_z are constants; $K_o = 0$ and all remaining values of K_z are terms of a geometric progression with a common ratio of 2, *i.e.*, for all $z > 0$.

$$K_z = 2^{(z-1)} K_1 \qquad (2)$$

and whereby for all $z > 1$ the following relationships hold for the constants A_z:

$$\frac{A_{z+3}/A_{z+2}}{A_{z+2}/A_{z+1}} = \frac{A_{z+2}/A_{z+1}}{A_{z+1}/A_z} \qquad (3)$$

The constant C: *WPDA* represents the high temperature limit of the second virial coefficient (related to the critical volume). In addition to this value there are four independent constants A_z, namely A_1 to A_4 and one independent constant K_1. Everything else follows from the relationships (2) and (3). Altogether there are six independent constants for description of the second virial coefficient of each substance.

The function (1) can be successfully applied to represent the experimental data within the precision of their knowledge for a number of substances investigated so far by the author of this article. In addition, the conditions 1° to 3° formulated above can be fulfilled in temperature ranges extrapolated towards both low and high values for at least six temperature derivatives of the second virial coefficient.

The constants A_z and K_1 can be estimated by fitting experimental information into the function (1), whenever adequate and reliable information is available for each particular substance. Otherwise, Pitzer's extension of the law of corresponding states can be applied.

A few examples of comparison of the second virial coefficient and its temperature derivatives calculated by (1) for some substances with data from various sources are shown in Figures 3 to 5. The temperature derivatives of these coefficients appear usually in thermodynamic relations as product of themselves and temperature in a power equal to the order of the derivative. The following designations are, therefore, useful for shortening the symbols:

$$B' = TdB/dT \qquad (4)$$

$$B'' = T^2 d^2 B/dt^2 \qquad (5)$$

A double logarithmic scale has been selected in most cases for the graphic presentation in order to obtain useful diagrams for wide temperature ranges. The virial coefficient and its temperature derivatives are, however, equal to zero at some temperature values. To avoid the associated problem of the logarithmic scale, the following functions of the n—th derivatives of B have been used for the ordinates:

for even values of *n*

$$f(B,n) = -\ln(1-B^{(n)}/V_c) \qquad (6)$$

for odd values of *n*

$$f(B,n) = \ln(1+B^{(n)}/V_c) \tag{7}$$

The function (1) has been selected for calculation of real gas properties by the program system outlined in this paper. Space allowed for this article does not permit a more in-depth discussion. Results of its application are, however, available from the program system which prints the second virial coefficient and its two temperature derivatives whenever requested.

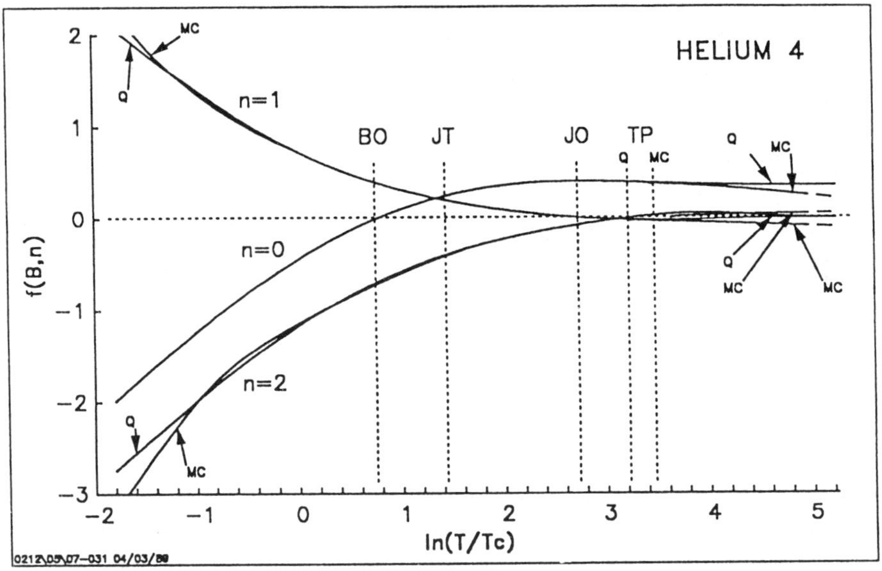

Figure 3
Second virial coefficient of helium 4 and its temperature derivatives. Comparison of data (Q) by function (1) with values MC, (dashed line if extrapolated) calculated by the equation of R. D. McCarty, J. Phys. Chem. Ref. Data, 2, 923, (1973). BO, JT, JO and TP designate respectively the Boyle temperature, the Joule-Thomson effect inversion temperature, the Joule effect inversion temperature (both latter at low pressure limit) and the turning point of the second virial coefficient, all for the function (Q).

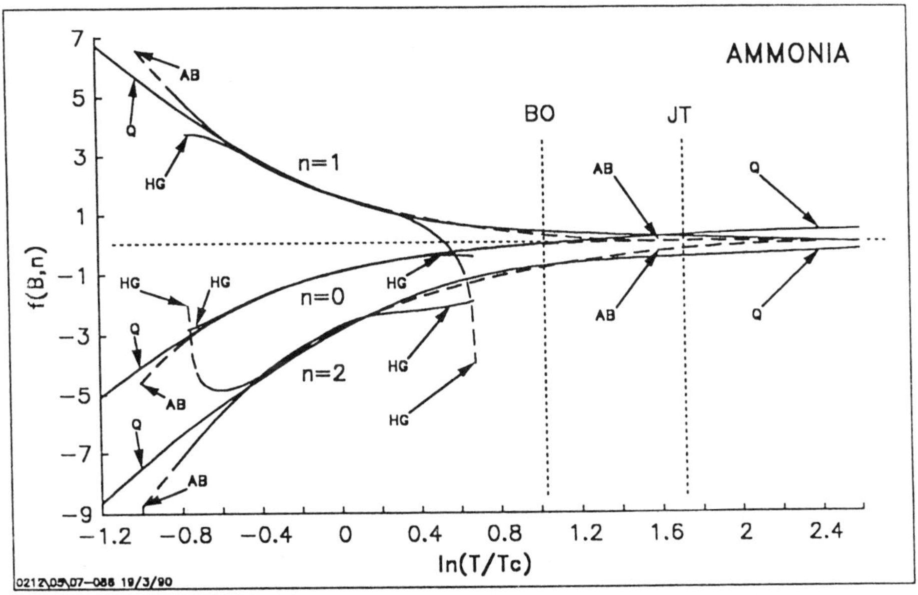

FIGURE 4
Second virial coefficient of ammonia and its temperature derivatives. Comparison of data (Q) by function (1) with values according to formulations (HG) of L. Haar and J. S. Gallagher, J. Phys. Chem. Ref. Data, 7, 635 (1978) and (AB) of J. Ahrendts and H. D. Baehr, VDI-Forschungsheft 596 (1979). BO, and JT designate respectively the Boyle temperature and the Joule-Thomson effect inversion temperature (the latter at low pressure limit), both for the function (Q).

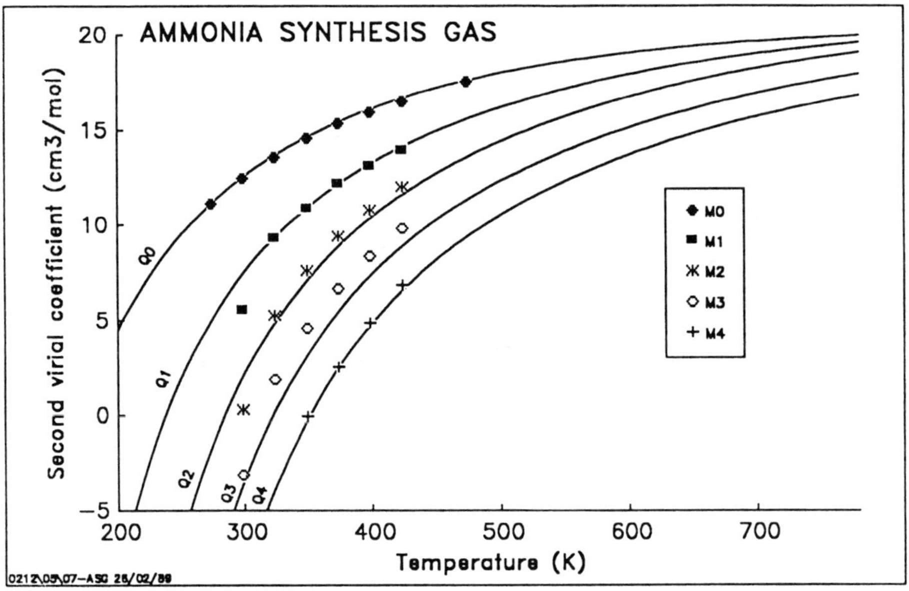

FIGURE 5

Second virial coefficient of ammonia synthesis gas with various mole fractions of ammonia. Comparison of data (lines Q0 through Q4) calculated by (1) with experimental data (point sets M0 through M4) of A. Michels and al., Appl. sci. Res. AI, 258 (1949) AI, 378 (1949), A3, 1 (1953), A4, 180 (1954). The mole fractions of components in the mixtures are as follows:

Data set	0	1	2	3	4
H2	0.75	0.665	0.601	0.5856	0.586
N2	0.25	0.264	0.276	0.2388	0.196
NH3	0	0.071	0.123	0.1756	0.218

THERM: THERMODYNAMIC PROPERTY ESTIMATION FOR GAS PHASE RADICALS and MOLECULES

Edward R. Ritter and Joseph W. Bozzelli
New Jersey Institute of Technology
Chemical Engineering and Chemistry Dept.
Newark, NJ. 07102, U.S.A.

INTRODUCTION

Benson's group estimation technique is an accurate method for the estimation of ideal gas phase heat capacities, heats of formation, and entropies of molecules. This technique is thoroughly discussed in Benson's text **Thermochemical Kinetics** [1] as well as other sources. [2,3,4,6] This method assumes that the properties for a chemical substance are the sum of the contributions from each group or polyvalent atom (central atom) in that molecule. It is referred to as a second order estimation technique since next- nearest-neighbor corrections, and to some extent, chemical structure are accounted for. Estimation based upon chemical bond contributions alone are known as first order estimation techniques, while those based upon atomic contributions alone are referred to as zero order techniques [7]. The second order estimates are naturally more accurate than lower order techniques, however, more information about the molecule is required. Several other estimation techniques based upon group contribution principles are presented in Reid, Prausnitz, and Sherwood [4]. This method, however, has become the most widely accepted due, in part, to its ease of use and relative accuracy when compared with other techniques.

Group contributions were derived by Benson and co-workers [2] and various other researchers [6,8,9,10,11,12,13,14,15] by breaking similar molecules with known thermodynamic properties into their constituent groups and then performing multivariable linear regression to find group contributions which gave the best fit to available experimental property data.

To use Benson's method, one must become familiar with the notation used to describe the groups. For example if we consider chlorobenzene (C_6H_5Cl)

we say that it has one C_B-(Cl) group and five C_B-(H) groups. C_B-(Cl) refers to a carbon atom in a benzene ring which is attached to a Cl atom, while C_B-(H) refers to a carbon atom in a benzene ring which is attached to an H atom. THERM identifies C_B-(Cl) as CB/CL and C_B-(H) as CB/H. For a second example consider propane (C_3H_8). This molecule contains two C-(H_3)(C) groups for the two terminal methyls, and one C-(H_2)(C_2) for the center CH_2 group. THERM identifies C-(H_3)(C) as C/C/H3, with C--(H_2)(C_2) identified as C/C2/H2. We feel alphabetical order is preferred for simplicity in remembering the order of atoms in the group id. In addition to the group id's, various corrections for symmetry, optical isomers, ring structure, steric effects must be included where necessary.

OTHER COMPUTER IMPLEMENTATIONS OF BENSON'S METHOD:

Benson's method has been programmed by others [16,17,18]. The most notable implementation of this estimation technique on computer is the code called CHETAH [16,17] which is distributed by ASTM. This program has been in use since 1974. Its primary purpose is to predict chemical reactivity hazards. Many publications are available which demonstrate its usefulness [7].

THERM was not designed to compete with or replace CHETAH. It was written to automate several tasks which are routine and important to high temperature reaction modeling studies. There are several important differences between THERM and CHETAH. THERM estimates properties between 300 and 5000 K while CHETAH estimates are valid from 300 - 1500 K, a range less suitable for combustion studies. THERM generates thermodynamic property functions in the NASA format but does not address hazard assessment. Properties for both radicals and molecules can be estimated using THERM, while CHETAH is used for stable molecules only.

The method for calculation of radical species is similar for H_f to that implemented by Muller, Scacchi, and Come [18], but was developed independently.

SOURCE OF GROUP CONTRIBUTION DATA:

Group data for molecules containing C, O, N, S, and halogen atoms were obtained from Benson [1,2,3] ; Reid, et al. [4] ; Stein and Fahr [12] ; Cohen [6] ; and Patel, Ritter, and Bozzelli [13]. Radical group contributions were derived from Benson [1] , McMillen and Golden [19] , Griller [20] and Lossing. [21,22] Bond dissociation increments [14] were derived from Tsang [23] , Slagle and Gutman [24,25] , McMillian and Golden [19]. Ring corrections for C, O, N, and S containing rings were obtained by Patel, Ritter, and Bozzelli [13].

EXAMPLES OF THE THERM PROGRAM:

In Table I, ΔH_f^o for 27 assorted species are compared with literature values obtained from various sources as noted. In most cases, estimates agree within 2.5 kJ mol^{-1}. Deviations range from 0.0 kJ mol^{-1} for chloroethane (C_2H_5Cl) to 15 kJ mol^{-1} for pyrene ($C_{16}H_{10}$).

PHENOL

PHENOXY

The structures for phenol and phenoxy radical are shown above. ΔH_f^o(298 K) for phenol (C_6H_6O) is estimated as -93.30 kJ mol^{-1}; while Burcat [26] gives -96.36 kJ mol^{-1}. Seven group contributions are considered for phenol. Phenol is comprised of 5 CB/H groups [CB-(H)], one CB/O group [CB-(O)], and one O/CB/H group [O-(H)(C)]. Groups in brackets refer to names appearing in Benson [1], while those with slashes are the equivalent group name identified by THERM. Figure 1 is a sample of the documentation generated when estimating a species. Elemental formula (C_6H_5OH), $C_{p\infty}$ (limiting high temperature heat capacity), symmetry number and optical isomer corrections (if any) for entropy, and the number of rotors in the molecule (if any) are also recorded.

Properties for radicals may be estimated two different ways. One may estimate thermodynamic properties directly with radical group contributions as described in Benson [1]. A second method applies a bond dissociation (BD) increment to stable molecules reflecting loss of an H atom from that species. We prefer this method, especially when estimating resonantly stabilized radicals.

The bond dissociation (BD) groups we have developed incorporate the following:

- accurate bond energies (Central Atom - Hydrogen Atom Bonds) for the specific class of compounds.
- entropy corrections for electron spin
- Entropy and heat capacity corrections for changes in rotational barrier for the rotors connected to radical centers ([1] tables A.18 - A.20)

TABLE 1. $H_f^o(g)$ [kJ mol^{-1}]

formula	species	calc	exp	deviation	ref
C5H6	cyclopentadiene	135.56	133.64	1.92	32
C7H8	toluene	49.41	50.17	-0.75	"
C8H8	styrene	147.36	147.70	-0.33	"
C8H10	ethyl benzene	29.08	29.92	-O.84	"
C9H8	indene	169.12	163.51	5.61	"
C9H10	indan	61.67	60.33	1.34	"
C9H12	n-propyl benzene	8.74	7.91	0.84	"
C9H12	i-propyl benzene	2.64	4.02	-1.38	"
C10H8	azulene	313.47	307.52	5.94	"
C10H8	naphthalene	150.62	150.83	-0.21	"
C12H10	acenaphthane	153.34	156.48	-3.14	"
C14H10	anthracene	218.40	230.96	-12.55	"
C14H10	phenanthrene	209.20	207.19	2.01	"
C16H10	fluoranthene	286.14	291.96	-5.82	"
C16H10	pyrene	230.96	215.85	15.10	"
C18H12	triphenylene	258.57	265.27	-6.69	"
C2H60	dimethyl ether	-181.59	-184.05	2.47	"
C6H7N	aniline	87.03	86.86	0.17	"
C2H5Cl	chloroethane	-111.71	-111.71	0.00	"
C6H5Cl	chlorobenzene	53.14	51.84	1.30	"
C6H5F	fluorobenzene	-110.04	-116.57	6.53	"
C6H5I	iodobenzene	163.18	162.55	0.63	"
C7H8	toluene	49.41	50.00	-0.59	"
C6H60	phenol	-93.30	-96.36	3.05	26
C6H50	phenoxy radical	50.63	47.70	2.93	"
C12H10	biphenyl	179.58	182.13	-2.55	"

```
SPECIES
PHENOL      <----------------- species name
     Thermo estimation for molecule
PHENOL                                        C6H5OH <------- elemental formula
UNITS: KJ
GROUPS  3
Gr# - GROUP ID -      Quantity
   1 - O/CB/H            - 1      <------------------- groups considered
   2 - CB/O              - 1
   3 - CB/H              - 5
   Hf    S    Cp 300  400     500     600     800     1000    1500
 -93.30  314.52 102.09 133.47 160.33  181.29  211.79  232.46    .00   high temperature
        CPINF =  307.60  <-------------------------------------------- limiting heat capacity
NROTORS:  1  <--------------------------- number of rotors
SYMMETRY      2  <--------------------------- symmetry number
 CREATION DATE:  1/23/89
 ENDSPECIES

  SPECIES
 PHENOXY        <---------------- radical's name
Thermo estimation for radical
 PHENOXY                                         C6H5O
 RADICAL BASED UPON PARENT PHENOL <---- radical calculated from this parent
        molecule
    PARENT FORMULA                        C6H5OH
PARENT SYMMETRY           2
 UNITS: KJ
 GROUPS  4
 Gr# - GROUP ID  -          Quantity
    1 - O/CB/H            - 1
    2 - CB/O              - 1
    3 - CB/H              - 5
    4 - PHENOXY           - 1      <--------- bond dissociation group (BD group)
    Hf     S      Cp 300  400    500     600     800    1000    1500
   50.63  303.64  96.32 125.02 149.75  169.12  197.40  216.52    .00
         CPINF =  282.66
 SYMMETRY      2
R ln(2) has been added to S to account   <-------- correction to entropy for electron spin
        for unpaired electron
 BOND  361.92  <------------------ bond dissociation energy shown in kJ mol-1
  CREATION DATE:  1/23/89
  ENDSPECIES
```

FIGURE 1

BD groups are based on specific bond energies, and differences in heat capacities and entropy for specific classes of molecules, where the thermodynamic properties of the radicals and parent molecules are accurately known. The BD Groups have one additional advantage over those of the radical groups developed by Benson [1] in that only one BD Group is needed for a given radical. In the Benson scheme a radical group is needed for each central atom radical, in addition to a group for each central atom group attached to the radical center. This represents a much larger data set for the radical species thermo.

Documentation for phenoxy radical, which was estimated in this way, is shown in Figure 1. Additional notes which are recorded for radicals include bond dissociation energy (298 K) for loss of hydrogen atom from the parent molecule, entropy correction for a free electron, and the name of the parent molecule. $\Delta H_f(298)$ for phenoxy is estimated as 50.62 kJ mol^{-1} while Burcat [26] gives ΔH_f equal to 47.7 kJ mol^{-1} a difference of only 2.9 kJ mol^{-1} as shown in Table I.

Modified NASA format polynomial coefficients are generated by THERM for use by such computer codes as CHEMKIN. Polynomial coefficients are valid over the temperature range from 300 - 5000 K. The major difference in our modified NASA format is that the number of rotors in the species are recorded. The NASA format includes the species name, creation date/reference, elemental composition, phase, lower and upper temperature limits for the polynomial, and the break point temperature (T_{mid}). Fourteen coefficients follow. The first seven coefficients are used to calculate properties at temperatures above T_{mid}, while the second seven coefficients apply to temperatures below T_{mid} (as described by Kee [31] and Burcat [26]). The break point temperature (T_{mid}) is located at a point of tangency between the two polynomials. T_{mid} is determined by matching C_p, H^o_f, and S^o to 0.005 % ; while dC_p/dT, dH_f/dT, and dS/dT are matched within an absolute tolerance of 0.005. Solving for a point of tangency between two polynomials differs from the method cited by Kee, *et. al.* [31]

Thermo property tables can be generated from the polynomials. These tables contain species name, $\Delta H_f(298)$, $\Delta S(298)$, and C_p at 300 - 1500 K. In addition, creation date, elemental composition, phase (g) and number of rotors are recorded. An extended table to 5000 K can also be generated. Units for tables can either be in kcal mol^{-1} for ΔH_f and cal mol^{-1} K for ΔS and C_p or kJ mol^{-1} for ΔH_f and J mol^{-1} K for ΔS and C_p.

In Figure 1, C_p (1500K) for Phenol is listed as 0.0 since no contribution was available at this temperature for one of the groups. However, the temperature range for C_p data can be extended by THERM to 5000 K by using available low temperature C_p data (300 - 1000 K). This is done by projecting an asymptote to the high temperature limiting heat capacity ($C_{p\infty}$). To do this we use an harmonic oscillator equation (HOE) derived from statistical mechanics to describe vibrational contributions to C_p [33]. Two fourth order polynomials which overlap by 500 K are then determined by linear regression of data estimated with this HOE equation. A point of tangency

(T_{mid}) is determined between the polynomials using a line search method. Alternatively, extrapolations can be performed using either an exponential function or the Wilhoit polynomials [33]. All three of these extrapolation methods are included in the THERM package.

Heat capacity estimates determined in this fashion are compared with literature data in Figure 2 for dimethyl ether, phenol, and biphenyl. It should be emphasized that the solid lines are generated from group additivity values alone, while symbols (literature values) result from rigorous calculations requiring frequency data for all vibrational modes in addition to contributions from all restricted rotors in the particular species. We obtain excellent agreement with typical maximum errors less than 1.5%. Literature data for this comparison are obtained from Stull [30] for dimethyl ether and from Burcat [26] for biphenyl and phenol. Heat capacity estimates for other species agree similarly when compared to available literature data.

One of the powerful features of this computer program is the automatic recalculation procedure. Once one records an estimate with THERM in the format shown in Figure 1, polynomials and tables can be recalculated automatically to reflect changes or improvements made to the group contribution database. This is necessary since new data continue to become available which allow improved estimates of bond dissociation energies, radical increments and groups which themselves are only estimates. This allows a thermodynamic database to become flexible accepting new data in addition to allowing users to examine the effects of uncertainties in bond energies and group values on conclusions drawn from modeling.

In addition to calculating data from group additivity, data may be entered interactively from literature sources allowing the required polynomials to be generated for literature data as well. Automatic recalculation does not effect literature data, or any species where auto-recalculation has been disabled.

THERM contains a chemical reaction interpreter for calculation of thermodynamic property changes of reaction as functions of temperature. One may calculate thermodynamic property changes for a desired reaction or an entire CHEMKIN input file. The thermodynamic properties which are calculated are ΔU_r {ΔE_r}, ΔH_r, ΔS_r, ΔG_r, equilibrium constant (K_c) and A_f/A_r: ratio of forward to reverse Arrhenius A factors. All species appearing in a reaction must be defined in the database. Property changes are estimated as a function of temperature over a range specified by the user. This is useful for kineticists wishing to check thermodynamic and kinetic consistency of reaction mechanisms being developed. An example is shown in Table II for the overall reaction of vinyl chloride with hydrogen. This reaction is shown to be exothermic by about 63 kJ mol^{-1} with an equilibrium constant favoring the products ethane and HCl. Shown in this table are the reactants, products and thermodynamic properties of each at 298 K. A list which contains the ΔH_r, ΔU_r (ΔE_r), ΔS_r, equilibrium constant K_c, and ΔG_r tabulated between 300 - 2000 K follows.

Table 2. Thermodynamic Analysis for Reaction

Rx	C2H3CL	+ H2	= C2H4	+ HCL
Hf (KJ/mol)	23.012	.000	52.300	-92.048
S (J/mol K)	174.473	130.541	218.823	186.606

dHr (kJ/mol) (298K) =	-62.76	dHr avg (298., 1500. K) =	-65.76
dU (dE) (kJ/mol) (") =	-62.76	dUr avg (298., 1500. K) =	-65.76
dSr (J/mol K) (") =	100.42	dSr avg (298., 1500. K) =	94.75
dGr (kJ/mol) (") =	-92.70	dGr avg (298., 1500. K) =	-150.95
Kc (") =	1.745E+16	Kc avg (298., 1500. K) =	5.898E+08

T (K)	dH(KJ/mol)	dU(KJ/mol)	dS(J/mol K)	Kc	dG(KJ/mol)
300.00	-6.278E+01	-6.278E+01	1.004E+02	1.493E+16	-9.288E+01
400.00	-6.388E+01	-6.388E+01	9.720E+01	2.630E+13	-1.028E+02
500.00	-6.501E+01	-6.501E+01	9.466E+01	5.466E+11	-1.123E+02
600.00	-6.609E+01	-6.609E+01	9.270E+01	3.950E+10	-1.217E+02
800.00	-6.777E+01	-6.777E+01	9.025E+01	1.381E+09	-1.400E+02
1000.00	-6.871E+01	-6.871E+01	8.919E+01	1.773E+08	-1.579E+02
1200.00	-6.900E+01	-6.900E+01	8.892E+01	4.455E+07	-1.757E+02
1500.00	-6.876E+01	-6.876E+01	8.909E+01	1.119E+07	-2.024E+02
2000.00	-6.757E+01	-6.757E+01	8.977E+01	2.846E+06	-2.471E+02

CONCLUSIONS

We have developed a computer code which can be used to enter, estimate, and edit thermodynamic properties for gas phase molecules and radicals. Some important aspects of this program are heat capacity extrapolation to 5000 K, thermo property polynomial determination, and calculation of thermodynamic property changes for reaction. Prediction/estimates typically compare favorably with available literature data.

Interested parties are encouraged to contact the authors for details on receiving a complementary copy of this program in addition to user documentation. The program is available in an executable format only.

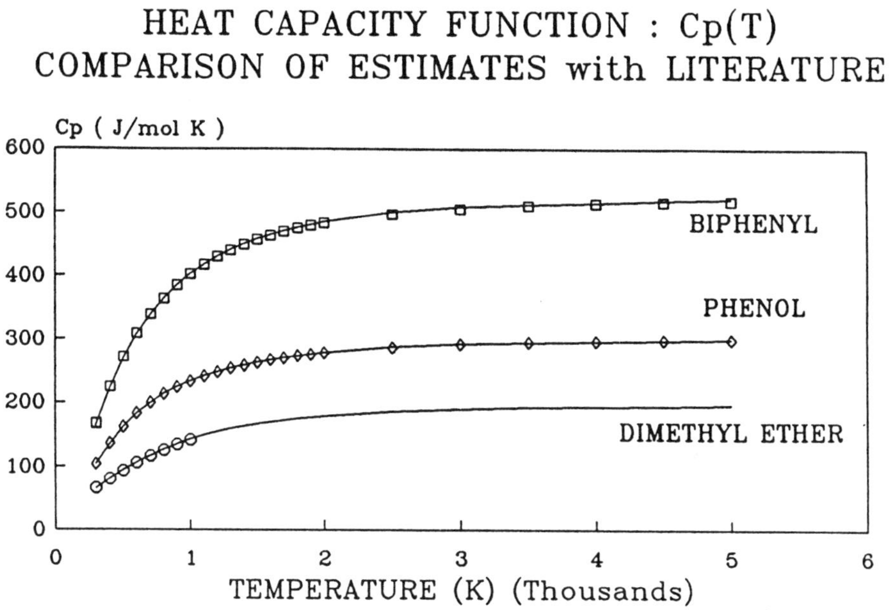

FIGURE 2

Symbols are literature C_p data while solid lines are estimates from the THERM computer code.

REFERENCES

[1] Benson, S., Thermochemical Kinetics, John Wiley and Sons, New York (1976).

[2] Benson, S.W. and J.H. Buss, J. Chem. Phys.,29,546 (1958).

[3] Benson, S.W., F. R. Cruickshank, D. M. Golden, G. R. Haugen, H. E. O'Neal, A. S. Rogers, R. Shaw, and R. Walsh, Chem. Rev., 69, 279 (1969).

[4] Reid, R.C., J. M. Prausnitz, and T. K. Sherwood, Properties of Gases and Liquids, McGraw Hill BookCo, New York (1977).

[5] Kee, R.J., Miller, J.A., Jefferson, T. H., Sanida Report # SAND80-80-03, 1980.

(6] Cohen, N., Aerospace Report No. ATR-88(7073)-2, Aerospace Corporation, El Segundo, California (1988).

[7] Hoffmann, J. M. and D. C. Maser, eds., ACS Symposium Series 274 : Chemical Hazard Process Review, American Chemical Society, Washington, D.C. 1985.
[8] Stein, S. E., D. M. Golden, and S. W. Benson, J. Phys. Chem., 81, 4, 1977.
[9] Shaw, R., D. M. Golden, S. W. Benson, J. Phys. Chem, 81, 18, 1977.
[10] Stein, S. E., D. M. Golden, and S. W. Benson, J Phys Chem., 81, 4, 1977.
[11] Eigenmann, H. K., D. M. Golden, and S. W. Benson, J Phys. Chem, 77, 13, 1973.
[12] Stein, S.E. and Fahr, A., J. Phys. Chem. 1985, 89, 3714.
[13] Patel, S., E. R. Ritter, and J. W. Bozzelli, manuscript in preparation, 1989
[14] This work.
[15] Domalski, E. S. and E. D. Hearing, J. Phys. Chem. Ref. Data, 17, 4, 1988.
[16] Freedman, E. and W. H. Seaton, USA Ballistic Research Laboratories Memorandum Report No. 2320, Aberdeen Proving Ground, Maryland, 1973.
[17] Frurip, D. J., E. Freedman, and G. R. Hertel, Proceedings of the Int. Symp. on Runaway Reactions, Cambridge, Mass. 1989.
[18] Muller, C., G. Scacchi, and G. M. Come, AICHE 77th Annual Meeting, San Francisco, 1984.
[19] McMillian, D. F. and Golden, D. M., Ann. Rev. Phys. Chem. 1982, 33,493.
[20] Griller, D. and Castelhano, A.L., J. Am. Chem. Soc., 1982, 104, 3655.
[21] Griller, D. and Lossing, F. P., J. Am. Chem. Soc., 1981, 103, 1586.
[22] Holmes, J.L., Lossing, F. P.., and Maccoll, A., preprint submitted to J. Am. Chem. Soc., 1988.
[23] Tsang, W., J. Am. Chem. Soc., 1985, 107, 2872.
[24] Slagle, I. and Gutman, D., J. Am. Chem. Soc., 1988, 110, 3084.
[25] Slagle, I. and Gutman, D., J. Am. Chem. Soc., 1988, 110, 3092.
[26] Burcat, A., Zeleznik, F.J., and McBride, B.J., NASA Technical Memorandum # 83800, 1985.
[27] Hanson, R. J. and K. H. Haskell, Sandia National Laboratories Report, SAND77-0552, 1978.
[28] Hanson, R. J. and K. H. Haskell, Sandia National Laboratories Report, SAND78-1290, 1979.
[29] McBride, B. J. and S. Gordon, NASA Technical Memo: NASA TN-D-4097, 1967.
[30] Stull, D.R., Westrum, E.F.Jr., and Sinke, G.C., THE CHEMICAL THERMO-DYNAMICS OF ORGANIC COMPOUNDS, Robert E. Krieger Publishing Company, Malibar, Florida (1987).

[31] Kee, R.J., Rupley, F.M., and Miller, J.A., Sandia National Laboratories Report, SAND87-8215, 1987.

[32] Cox, J.D., Pilcher, G., Thermochemistry of Organic and Organometalic Compounds, Academic Press, New York, 1970.

[33] Ritter, E.R., Doctoral Dissertation, NJIT 1989.

DATABASES IN THE BIOLOGICAL SCIENCES

COMPUTATIONAL MOLECULAR BIOLOGY

Dr. Arthur M. Lesk
Medical Research Council - Laboratory of Molecular Biology
University Postgraduate School
Cambridge, United Kingdom

Computational molecular biology has become a mature field of science. It attained this state as a result of the growth of the amount of data available about protein and DNA sequences and structures, of the growth in detail and profundity of our understanding of the mechanisms of the processes of life, and in the ability of computational methods to offer genuine help in interpreting and suggesting experiments. Many active and constructive dialogues are now taking place between investigators determining gene sequences and those who are able to analyze them to identify unknown proteins and to attempt to interpret their function. Other dialogues are occurring between investigators whose primary interest is in the area of sequence analysis and those who are determining and studying three dimensional structures of proteins and nucleic acids.

As a result of this rapid growth, CODATA (the Committee on Data for Science and Technology of the International Council of Scientific Unions) established a Task Group on the Coordination of Protein Sequence Data Banks, of which Prof. B. Keil of the Institut Pasteur was Chairman until his retirement; the office is now held by Prof. A. Tsugita of the Science University of Tokyo. Other members of the group represent many countries, and many disciplines within the general area of computational molecular biology. It has been our privilege to study and observe the flow of scientific research beyond the bounds of our individual research interests. Our goal has been to do what we can to remove any impediment to the channelling of the tremendous vigor of this field into the most productive directions possible.

We have identified the following questions as those that we can address, in order to serve the field best:

- What data are available?
- What calculations are done?
- How can one gain access to the data and to the necessary programs?
- In view of the growing integration of studies of structures with studies of sequences, how can one best bridge the gulf between the one-dimensional and the three-dimensional?

Here I can only briefly summarize some of the most salient points:

- The data banks of protein and nucleic acid sequences and structures have become essential research tools in many areas of life sciences.

- The growth of sequence information will in the very near future saturate the current means of collection and distribution. Increases in the current types of resources--that is, buying more computers and hiring more people--will be unable to keep up.

- When the growth of the data banks is examined in this light, it is obvious that a pressing need exists for the computational methods to keep up with the rapidly expanding body of sequence and structural data. Advances are likely to include (1) the invention of new algorithms and data structures, (2) the development of more powerful and general techniques for storage and organization of databases and information retrieval systems, (3) the applications of supercomputers, (4) the development of special-purpose hardware, and (5) the greater integration of world-wide scientific intercommunications and data exchange, over computer networks.

- Major DNA sequencing projects now contemplated, including the sequencing of the entire human and rice genomes, will provide quantities of data vast even on the scale of the current information explosion. The scientific harvest of these results can be extracted from the data only by equally ambitious developments in computational methods of identification and analysis of gene sequences and the mechanisms of their translation and regulation.

- It is no more than realistic to suggest that it is not and will not be possible in a foreseeable future to extract more than a very small fraction of the protein structural information stored in the genetic sequences by experimental techniques alone. Nor will it soon be possible to achieve a completely *a priori* prediction of the function and three-dimensional structure of proteins from amino acid sequences alone, at a level comparable with the detail of an X-ray structure determination.

It follows that what we must do is to clarify the rules governing the three-dimensional folding of amino acid chains by computational methods based on the information available in the data banks of known sequences and structures. It is now generally recognized that investigations based on sequences alone often fall short of success because they deal with structure only indirectly. Conversely, already some of the most important and challenging questions in contemporary research arise where sequence and structural studies intersect.

If there is to be one general conclusion, it is that the integration of investigations of sequence and structure will continue to grow, and that appropriate computational methods must be developed, distributed and described, to support the evolution of the field in this direction. The large repertoire of algorithms and software already in use in investigations of the three-dimensional structures of proteins and nucleic acids must be coordinated with the sequence databases and software.

SEQUENCE DATABANKS: TOWARDS A DE FACTO NETWORK

W.C. Barker and D.G. George
National Biomedical Research Foundation
Washington, D.C., U.S.A.

The sequence databanks contain representations of the structures of biological macromolecules. These molecules are linear polymers composed of small covalently linked chemical units, nucleotides in the case of DNA and RNA and amino acids in the case of proteins. There are 20 common types of amino acids and they are symbolized by standard one-letter abbreviations. Similarly, the nucleotides that compose DNA and RNA also have standard one-letter abbreviations. With these notation systems, the basic structure of a protein or nucleic acid can be represented in a computer databank by a string of letters called the sequence or primary structure of the protein or nucleic acid. An entry in a sequence databank typically also contains text information that identifies the molecule and its biological source, cites the primary literature, and notes functional characteristics and structural features of the molecule.

One of the most common uses of a sequence databank is to compare new sequence data with that already in the databank. This has two purposes: to verify that the sequence really is new and to discover if it is similar, in whole or in part, to any known sequence. Such similarity can serve to direct further research into the structure and function of a molecule by suggesting testable hypotheses based on the structural similarity. Having found some similar sequences, the textual information becomes important in order to learn more about them and to direct the investigation to the original literature. Aligning a new sequence with similar sequences can allow inference of comparative information that cannot be derived from a single sequence. For example, the evolution of organisms can be inferred from protein or nucleic acid sequences. One can also identify patterns and signals in the sequences and use these in the examination of new sequences.

Moreover, the use of alignments of related sequences can significantly improve predictions of the three-dimensional structures of the proteins.

Ideally a sequence databank will be comprehensive, complete, correct, and well organized (preferably nonredundant). These ideals are easier to attain when the quantity of data is limited. The data can be collected, organized, and maintained by a small group of scientists who use the data for their own research [1]. They have the expertise to evaluate the data and are highly motivated to keep the database up to date and error-free. Moreover, such databanks can be funded out of one investigator's research funds. What happens, however, when the quantity of data being generated overwhelms the capacities (and budget) of a small research group? This, in fact, is the situation that developed during the 1980's with the sequence databanks. There are a number of strategies for coping with this situation [2]. Generally they involve either sacrificing validation, annotation, and organization in favor of completeness or dividing the effort (and the cost). In practice, both strategies have been followed by the sequence databanks, although cutting back on validation and annotation is regarded as a temporary measure until a fully functional network of collaborating scientists can be established. Such a network may include volunteers to locate data in journals that they routinely read, researchers who submit data directly, curators who help to maintain quality and consistency in particular areas covered by the databank, and collaborating centers for collecting and distributing the data.

Thus, perhaps the single most important achievement of the CODATA Task Group on Coordination of Protein Sequence Data Banks [3] was catalyzing the formation of the international collaboration for the Protein Sequence Database [4]. This collaboration, called PIR-International, consists of three centers that collect and annotate the data and distribute the database: the Protein Identification Resource (PIR) directed by Dr. Winona C. Barker at the National Biomedical Research Foundation in Washington, the International Protein Information Database in Japan (JIPID) headed by Professor Akira Tsugita at the Science University of Tokyo, and the Martinsried Institute for Protein Sequences (MIPS) directed by Dr. H. Werner Mewes at the Max Planck Institute for Biochemistry in West Germany. These centers also engage in other projects, both cooperatively and independently, including software development and support, training of users, computational support for individual researchers and genome sequencing projects, and development of related databases. Coincidentally, the major nucleic acid databanks are also organized into three centers in the same geographical areas (GenBank in the United States [5], the European Molecular Biology Laboratory's Nucleotide Data Library [6], and the DNA

Data Bank of Japan) and cooperative efforts have been established between the protein and nucleic acid database centers in each geographical area. The two networks have much in common, including an overlap of a large fraction of their users. In consideration of this overlap and to stimulate closer interactions between these groups, the CODATA Task Group was reconstituted, in 1989, as the Task Group on Biological Macromolecules [7]. Its annual meetings provide a forum for establishing and maintaining a "de facto" network among the protein and nucleic acid sequence databanks and a number of related databases. At these meetings, database creators, noncommercial distributors, and users discuss their common problems, compare their individual approaches, and consider ways to enhance accessibility to users. The Task Group has also encouraged the formation of new databases devoted to carbohydrate structure, NMR investigation of protein structure, and protein sequence variants.

The network model is appropriate for biological databanks because it reflects the organization of biological knowledge. Scientists tend to be knowledgeable not only in their own narrow areas but also in areas that are adjacent or closely related. Moreover, it is critical in a scientific analysis to evaluate all evidence concerning the topic under investigation. Therefore, scientists need access to databases in related fields, as well as in their own fields, and to other broadly useful information. Although in a specific field it is desirable for a databank to be very complete, up to date, and detailed, these factors are less important when databanks outside of the field are consulted. In this case other factors such as accessibility, ease of information retrieval, cross-connections to other databases, and breadth of coverage may be more important. These, in fact, are the advantages offered by large, centralized databanks -- everything is in one place, the format is uniform, and access is widely available (at least in the developed countries). The large number of users provides economic incentive for wide distribution, often within established channels such as libraries or online database services. The goal of a network of collaborating database centers is to provide the advantages of both small specialized databanks and large comprehensive databanks.

Another advantage of a network of collaborating centers in that each center can be supported independently. Producers and users of the data can be found in every country. It may be easier to obtain local support for local efforts than to find a single governmental agency, philanthropy, or commercial enterprise that is willing to invest the millions of dollars that would be necessary to support a centralized databank covering a wide area of biological knowledge.

However, there are enormous challenges to making an international network model effective for a large scale databank. Each collaborating center must have adequate financing not only for its own work but also to support the coordination of efforts with the other centers. Conditions of financial support will be different for each center because of national differences in funding mechanisms, laws, and customs. Attitudes toward the concept of an international effort may vary and the integrity of the network will be endangered if political considerations (or any other problems) disrupt funding to one of the centers.

In order to make available a complete collection in the face of an already existing backlog of data, the sequence databanks must make data public before they are evaluated. Therefore, they must not only coordinate initial data entry but also subsequent upgrading, comparing, merging, and organizing in order to avoid duplication of effort. Effective coordination between geographically distant groups is a challenge that is made feasible only by international electronic communication. Unfortunately, the requirement for high-tech communication may limit the participation of some segments of the scientific community. Achieving good coordination will be time-consuming and may require interpersonal, diplomatic, and managerial skills that are beyond the training and experience of most scientists. The Protein Sequence Database also must coordinate with related databanks, particularly the nucleic acid sequence and protein structure databanks, but also others, such as gene mapping databanks, taxonomic databases, databanks of protein function and properties, and so forth. Major goals of these interactions are to establish cross-referencing systems between the databanks and to encourage the use of standard nomenclature and more uniform terminology.

In spite of the challenges and difficulties, it is necessary for biological databanks to continue to form networks and to promote standardization. It cannot be overemphasized that support from the scientific community is critical for the survival of the individual databanks that are attempting to form and maintain broader networks. Moreover, scientists must lobby for the continued existence of the networks as well as for the individual data centers. The advantages of the network must be brought to the attention of funding agencies and institutional and governmental bureaucracies. CODATA has several important roles in encouraging networking among biological databanks: it fosters international and interdisciplinary communication and cooperation in a nonpolitical atmosphere; it supports enhancement of and wide access to nomenclature standards; and it influences scientists, scientific organizations and unions, and governments and funding agencies to support the emerging databank networks.

ACKNOWLEDGMENTS

The preparation of this manuscript was supported by NIH grant LM05206. We thank Dr. Lois T. Hunt for helpful criticism and Angela Murakami for technical assistance.

REFERENCES

[1] Lide, D.R., Jr., Critical data for critical needs, *Science* 212, 1981, pp. 1343-1349.

[2] Barker, W.C., George, D.G., and Hunt, L.T., More about less or less about more? The choices facing biological information resources, in Stobaugh, R.E. (ed.), *Frontiers of Chemistry: Volume 1 Biotechnology*, pp. 35-51. Chemical Abstracts Service, Columbus, Ohio, 1989.

[3] Keil, B., Databases in molecular biology: a CODATA task group at work, *Protein Seq. Data Anal.* 1, 1987, pp. 123-126.

[4] Barker, W.C., George, D.G., and Hunt, L.T., Protein sequence database, *Adv. Enzymol.* 183, 1990, pp. 31-49.

[5] Burks, C. et al., GenBank: current status and future directions, *Adv. Enzymol.* 183, 1990, pp. 3-22.

[6] Kahn, P. and Cameron, G., EMBL Data Library, *Adv. Enzymol.* 183, 1990, pp. 23-31.

[7] Keil, B., Cooperation between databases and scientific community, *Adv. Enzymol.* 183, 1990, pp. 50-60.

MOLECULAR-GENETICS DATABASE AND SOFTWARE DEVELOPMENT IN THE SOVIET UNION: THE PROBLEM OF DATABASE INTEGRATION

A.A. Alexandrov
Institute of Molecular Genetics
Russian Academy of Sciences
Moscow, Russia

I would like to present herewith the results of work carried out jointly in the scientific-technical bioinformatics program "Geninform" of the Soviet Union and several Comecon countries.

The main topics of this program are the following:

1. The development of new methods of biopolymers structures analysis for the identification of its biological functions.
2. The creation of new data banks and in the future the creation of an integrated data bank on molecular genetics, joining different levels information from molecular to physiological nature.
3. The creation of software for biopolymers structure analysis, including the analysis of three dimensional structures.
4. The creation of expert systems of biopolymers structures analysis on the basis of developed data banks, programs and by use of artificial intelligence technology.
5. The creation of mathematical model of molecular-genetics structures and processes.
6. The development of means for integration different programs on the basis of expert system technology and in the future creating an integrated system of molecular-genetics information analysis.
7. The development of teaching systems and organization of teaching of molecular-biologist users.

In our country we use primarily IBM-PC compatible computers and we have developed all necessary programs for analysis of molecular-genetics information. Now we have designed the database management systems for the main molecular-biology database and several complexes of programs for biopolymers structures analysis.

Now I would like to describe in more detail the situation about the database creation.

I would like to give you some brief information about new databases developed in our country. The most developed of them is the database of enzymes and metabolic pathways.

Enzymes, biological catalysts of protein nature, lie at the basis of the vital activity of all living beings. Information on enzymes and their related complex catalytic systems, metabolic pathways, is of extreme interest to a very broad range of investigators in biology, medicine, biotechnology, agriculture and ecology. This information is necessary in synthesizing new pharmacological agents for man and animals and various pesticides for agriculture and forestry, and in developing a variety of new biotechnological processes in the microbiological and food industries.

Under Prof. Selkov at the Institute of Biophysics USSR AS the data bank of Enzymes and Metabolic Pathwaysn, accumulating this rich information, was developed.

The database has a format allowing representation of all complex information in a computer-readable form.

At present, the bank contains about 4000 entries and it is forseen that the information will increase by about 2000 entries/year.

The next database being created at Novosibirsk Institute of Molecular Biology of Ministry of Medical and Microbiological Industry is accumulating biological and medical properties of peptides and proteins. It is structurally close to the database mentioned above. It is of great significance both for pharmacology and medicine since peptides are well known to be the medicine of the future.

To provide the experimental works on gene engineering and creating new genomes producentes for biotechnology at the Institute of Molecular Genetics USSR AS the database of the gene engineering vectors was created. It contains the information about the sequences' functional features and restrictional maps of different vectors and biological properties of their hosts.

The special DBMS and the set of programs provide the searching possibilities and can imitate all the gene engineering operations for constructing the necessary vectors.

At present, we are designing the expert system allowing users to automatically construct the vectors with the necessary properties.

The next system was developed for studying the functional features of biopolymers sequences. This system includes the database of the functional signals searching models, the set of programs realizing different searching algorithms and necessary parameters. These systems are oriented for user biologists unfamiliar with computer techniques.

So let me touch on some general problems of database development.

We want our database to contain much more information that will be available for computer analysis. At the same time it is necessary for biologist users to have opportunities to work with information from different databases.

These demands determine the main trends in database development.

The first trend is database differentiation. The development of different databases with different information contents and special formats make it possible to enter the maximum of formalized information.

The second trend is the database integration. To ensure the complex use of different databases we are going to develop a molecular biology integrated database; not only at the physical level of integration but the development of biological links between the objects and processes described in the different databases. Thus, we have already designed the format for the joint databases of nucleic and proteins sequences and their functional signals.

But now we have realized that formalized databases concern only specific aspects of molecular-biological information. We have discovered this while developing an integrated database on the well studied molecular biological object - one of the smallest bacteriophage organisms, T4.

Many times we have changed the formats of several databases on different properties of this object for example genetics, structure, biochemistry, etc. but in vain - the main part of the important information appeared in commentaries, but not in formalized fields.

Then we used quite a new approach to the problem, as we believe.

We rejected any formalization and created a database on encyclopedia principles. It consists of short referats describing the key notions, connecting to one another by means of contexts notes. In can be called structurized reviews. It can include the tree-like structures and pictures. Different parts of such system are easily joined together by means of context notes, supplementing each other.

As far as it is known the encyclopedia principle isn't quite new - it has been used since the creation of Bible.

But we believe such an encyclopedia system is fitting for computer technology including key words lists control and realizing different service functions and is of great effectiveness for the keeping and generalization of knowledge.

We think the integrated database must include the encyclopedia system by means of which different formalized databases and other systems such as mathematical models will be joined together.

Schematically it should look like the following diagram:

Integrated data bank on human molecular genetics

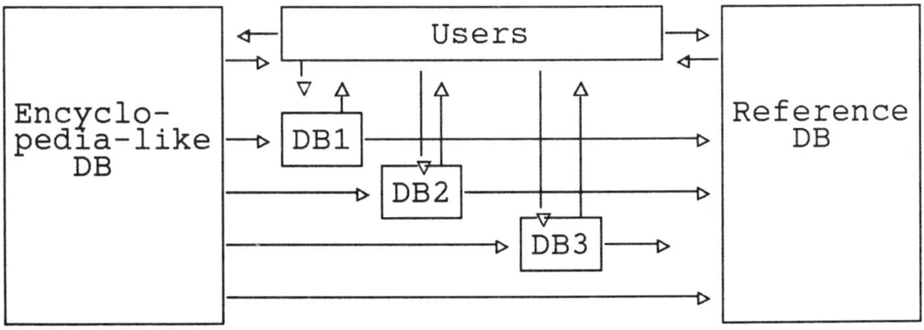

FIGURE 1

Supposed scheme of integrated data bank on human molecular genetic; DB1 - DB3, factographic data banks: nucleotides and proteins sequences, functional signal, genes and genetic markers, enzymes and metabolic pathways, hereditary diseases.

It seems to me at first that it is not necessary for all these databases to work as one joined system.

They can be autonomous, but it is necessary to ensure easy passing to users from one system to another and adjusting key notions lists. Later on the system is sure to be ruled by a general DBMS.

In the not too far future, under the state human genome project, we are going to work out the integrated database of human molecular genetics.

I think it would be very fruitful to arrange the international cooperation in these actions and especially in the creation of the International Computer Encyclopedia on Molecular Biology.

PHARMACOLOGICAL DATA BANKS, VALIDATION TECHNICS

C. Mercier and J.-E. Dubois
Institut de Topologie et de Dynamique des Systèmes
Université de Paris VII, C.N.R.S.
Paris, France

INTRODUCTION

The volume of scientific data in pharmacology, their diversity (structural, physicochemical, quantum, biochemical, biological, clinical data...) as well as their complex interpretation, points out the importance of creating homogeneous systems to exploit them. To retain this data potential, the information is stored in banks and managed by means of Data Base Management Systems. However, if these systems offer fast and simple access to the information, they do not make it possible to detect some less evident characteristics such as the interdependence between diverse parameters or the data coherence (redundancy, measurement errors). The search for such information is necessary to rationally develop a data bank and is particularly important in biology and pharmacology to plan experiments which are often expensive, difficult, imprecise and badly standardized. The diverse multivariate analysis methods--regression, factorial analysis, cluster analysis, classification methods--constitute a way to tackle such complex problems.

In the field of Computer Aided Drug Design, we have developed a dynamic method for creating and exploring pharmacological data banks in order to rationalize the planning of experiments. The method uses a homogeneous system for Computer Aided Management and Analysis of Pharmacological data, known as CAMAP [1].

CAMAP SYSTEM

The CAMAP system, set up in the context of the DARC structural language [2], integrates a specific management software and two data treatment systems for multivariate analysis and Structure-Activity correlation search methods, known as ANALDONE [1] and CALPHI [3] respectively. These are connected to a pharmacological data bank, organized around the concept of molecular graph, the support of all information, so as to provide a logical organization of the pragmatic and heuristic data of the field studied. The complete system comprises a powerful graphic device for handling structural and biological data as well as the results of the treatments concerning them. It facilitates exchanges between the disciplines concerned and the interpretation of the relationships between experimental data, which play a particularly important role in the design of further research and the up-dating of data banks.

EXPLORING AND VALIDATING PHARMACOLOGICAL DATA

This step aims to optimize the quality of biological tests. The coherence of pharmacological data and their interdependence are assessed by multiple factorial analysis methods. Regularities or outliers make it possible to estimate the reliability of biological tests and to estimate which tests are the most representative of the activity sought. It is intended to assist the planning of pharmacological experiments at minimal cost.

Pharmacological information essentially comprises qualitative data as symptoms observed on animals and quantitative data as toxicity tests or specific activity tests measured on diverse animal species or isolated organs.

QUALITATIVE DATA

Physiological and behaviour symptoms are generally numerous and the relationships between the observations are often complex. Moreover, the measurements are neither precise nor reliable, since they are qualitative and have a subjective character. Indeed, if some physiological parameters, such as respiratory or cardiac frequencies, can be rigourously measured while others, such as salivation or pupil expansion, approximately estimated, the situation is much more complex for behaviour symptoms, such as aggressivity or analgesic activity, whose scale of variation is completely dependent on the experimenter. A simplified representation of these measurements and of their relationships is thus essential to control the consistency of the data.

In anticholinergic research, the "atropinic" syndrome is considered by the pharmacologists as a specific and non-ambiguous profile of central anticholinergic activity on the dog. This behavioural profile is characterized by the simultaneous presence of four central symptoms when the specific symptom "pousse au mur" is present, and is eventually associated with three peripheral symptoms (Trouiller, Lecolier et Leblanc, unpublished results).

Pharmacological interest in this syndrome prompts us to verify the coherence of its profile and, eventually to specify it by means of other symptoms present in the anticholinergic database. We used Multiple Correspondence Analysis to detect the interdependence between the 91 modalities of the 25 symptoms (each symptom is evaluated on a scale including two, four or seven modalities) associated with the 154 compounds tested for central activity. The poor results obtained (inertia%: 1st axis 6%, 2nd axis 4%, 3rd axis 4%), suggest a relative independence of the characters. Representation of the symptoms in the space generated by the three first factorial axes (Figure 1) confirms it: we note an independence of the toxic and central symptoms and a partial dependence of the "atropinic" syndrome with two of the three peripheral symptoms; we discover a lack of dependence between this syndrome and the four central symptoms which are theoretically associated with it.

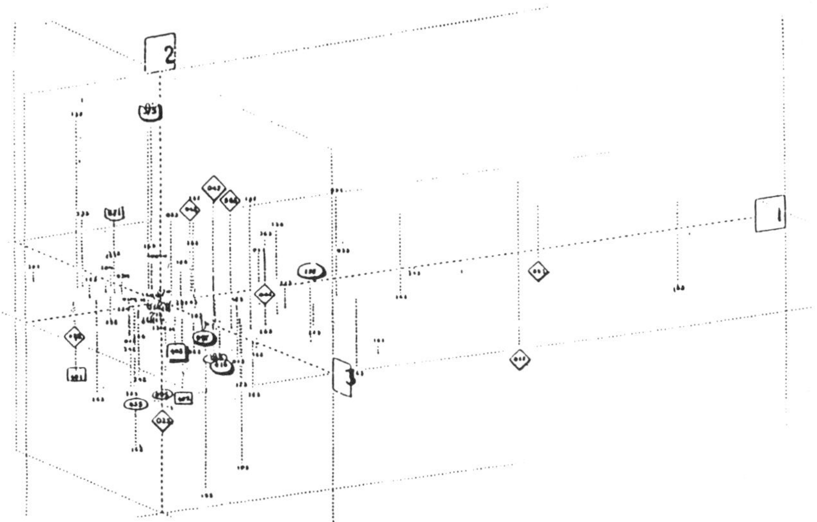

FIGURE 1. Distribution of system modalities by MCA

☐ "Atropinic" syndrome modalities
◇ central, ⬭ peripheral, toxic symptom modalities

This surprising result led us to check the symptoms of the compounds with an active "atropinic" syndrome. None of the compounds selected had simultaneously the four central symptoms. Moreover, one of these symptoms was never present. By analyzing the laboratory reports with the pharmacologists, we discovered that the central symptoms were not systematically reported and that the "atropinic" syndrome codification was ambiguous. This study led to the definition of a new codification protocol with the pharmacologists and made possible a rational up-dating of the behavioural data observed on the dog of the "anticholinergic" bank.

QUANTITATIVE DATA

Specific activity tests are often measured on several animal species. The methods used to explore these quantitative data are essentially multiple regression analysis and Principle Component analysis.

The discovery of a significant correlation between central anticholinergic activity tests on the dog and the rat led to a minimal cost experimentation planning [4].

Simultaneously, retesting certain compounds, which appear to behave abnormally, led the pharmacologists to specify the profile of the test on the dog and to obtain reliable measurements. Compounds to be retested have a difference between the calculated and observed values three times greater than the experimental average deviation. The compounds detected with a particular behaviour and retested further were then found to be in the correlation cluster. This shows the importance of detecting these singular points to plan experiments.

In the search for molecules with an optimal profile including two activity tests and an undesirable side effect, two tests were selected as the most significant by Principle Component Analysis of the five available ones respectively determined on the mouse, the rat, the dog and on an isolated organ [1]. Again in this study, retesting the outliers led to reliable data.

REFERENCES

[1] Mercier, C., Paillasseur, J.-L., Dubois, J.-E., Trouiller, G., Desnoyer, B.; "Système d'aide à la décision en pharmacologie. Application aux anticholinergiques par analyse multivariée des données d'activité." *Eur. J. Med. Chem.*, 1989, *24*, 111-121.

[2] Dubois, J.-E.; in *Computer Representation and Manipulation of Chemical Information*, Wipke, W.T., Heller, S.R., Fellmann, R.J., Hyde, E. (eds.), Wiley New York, 1974, Chapter 10, 239-264.

[3] Mercier, C., Fabart, V., Sobel, Y., Dubois, J.-E.; "Modeling alcohol metabolism with the DARC/CALPHI system." *J. Med. Chem.*, 1991, *34*, 934-942.

[4] Mercier, C., Trouiller, G., Dubois, J.-E.; "DARC Computer Aided Design System in Anticholinergic Research." *Quant. Struct.-Act. Rel.*, 1990, *9*, 88-93.

THE CARCINOGENICITY INFORMATION DATABASE OF ENVIRONMENTAL SUBSTANCES (CIDES)

Mildred Green
Technical Database Services, Inc.
New York, NY 10019, U.S.A.

At TDS, we have developed a database called CIDES, the Carcinogenicity Database of Environmental Substances. CIDES summarizes the results of a wide variety of cancer-related studies involving approximately 1000 chemicals. In addition, chemical property data is provided relating to the transfer and persistence of each chemical in the environment. The data elements are organized to present a rapid and comprehensive view of the literature in the field. Our goal is to combine in one database sufficient information to provide researchers from various health- related disciplines with a tool for evaluating the potential for human risk associated with each substance included.

In building CIDES, we have extracted approximately 40 000 records from over 5300 references. Our greatest effort has been to evaluate the literature in six categories of studies related to carcinogenicity and mutagenicity: human epidemiology, whole animal carcinogenesis, transformations in mammalian cell lines and in mammalian tissues and cells, bacterial tests, and other assays (Table 1). Both positive and negative results are included in all categories. The file structure for the database is sufficiently flexible to encompass a variety of studies involving the different species, test systems and end points which typically occur within each CIDES category.

Carcinogenesis in humans has been reported for relatively few substances and the information available is of uneven quality. The determination of carcinogenicity is based more often on experiments in rodents, although tests involving other mammals are not uncommon. In whole-animal studies, the end point measured is the rate of tumor production in one or more organs. As each experiment runs for the life-span of tens if not hundreds of animals, the budget may be as high as $1-4 million for a period of two years or more. The investment that is required dictates that relatively few chemicals can be tested in whole animals. Much cancer-relevant information is obtained from short-term assays which measure chromosome damage in mammalian tissues and cell systems or mutagenesis in nonmammalian species, especially bacteria.

Table 1. Screen summarizing the available studies for a single substance

(C) TDS, 1990

------------------SUMMARY OF ALL CIDES CATEGORIES------------------

50-00-0
FORMALDEHYDE

Cat#	Name	Wt	# Studies	# + Studies	% + Studies
1	Whole Animal Carcinogenesis	35	5	4	80.0
2	Mammalian Cell Lines	20	38	32	84.2
3	Mammalian Tissue or Cells	20	32	6	18.8
4	Bacterial Tests	15	23	12	52.2
5	Miscellaneous Tests	10	14	14	100.0
6	Human Carcinogenesis	100	13	6	46.2
	Total		125	74	

CR/W: 66/100 Human CR/W: 46/100

Select Categories (#) separated by a comma, or (A)ll and press Return ...

Since no single test is currently accepted as fully adequate for predictive purposes, results from a battery of tests would generally be more persuasive if all tests gave consistent results. In practice, a series of tests involving different biological systems may give different, perhaps even conflicting predictions for some chemicals. It is even possible that the same test run in different laboratories under slightly different conditions might give different results. A unique feature in CIDES is the Carcinogenicity Ratio (CR), an objective procedure for evaluating the results from a variety of different cancer-related tests found in the literature. The CR is calculated each time a table summarizing the studies available for a given CIDES substance is displayed.

The CR is a pair of numbers which is indicative of a substance's potential for carcinogenesis: the Carcinogenicity Ratio (CR) and the Weight of the Evidence (W). The CR provides an overall figure of the percent positive studies across all categories, and W reflects the number of categories and the extent of the testing which have contributed to the calculation. Generally, if the CR and the W are greater than 50, one would conclude that the substance is likely to be a human carcinogen. For Category 6, the Human CR is equal to the percent of the total number of studies which are positive and W is always 100 if there are more than 5 studies. For Categories 1-5, the CR = 100 (CI/W), where CR is the product of the sums of the percent positive studies (Pi) multiplied by the weighting factors for each category (Ki). To determine W, the Ki is summed for each category in which data are available. If the number of studies (N) in a category falls below a minimum of 5, the Ki used in calculating the Weight of the Evidence (W) is modified as follows Ki = (N/5)Ki. The CR is designed to aid in the evaluation of potentially carcinogenic substances by providing an objective rating based on test findings.

Since our objective was to create a resource which would be useful to scientists with differing needs and backgrounds - environmental chemists, toxicologists, health and safety officers, pharmaceutical scientists, information specialists and others - we have developed a synonym file for the substances contained in the database. Included are CAS Registry Numbers and as many systematic, common and trade names as we could locate. The CIDES synonym file has been incorporated into Syndex, the synonym index of the **Numerica** online system of TDS. By consulting Syndex, the online user can locate other sources of information throughout the **Numerica** system which pertain to the chemicals included in CIDES. TDS has also provided a menu-driven interface which can make CIDES easy to search, even for those who may not have training or experience in database searching. The users manual fully documents the online search system.

Once a chemical has been identified to the system, the user may retrieve its physical properties: *e.g.*, the solubility, vapor pressure biodegradation rate and many other factors which relate to the environmental transport and fate of substances. We have attempted to compile experimental measurements for all properties, however, for many chemicals, this information is not available. On the assumption that estimates are preferable to blank fields, we have utilized accepted models to predict properties from structure or from other parameters. Estimates are flagged to alert the user to the higher uncertainty in the value.

For each substance, the carcinogenicity data are summarized in a table listing the number of experimental studies in CIDES and, when available, the number of human epidemiological studies. The software we have developed utilizes this information in calculating the CR. From Table 1 it is apparent that were the data from human studies not available the CR would have indicated the potential carcinogenicity of this chemical. The organization of the summary table also provides information which can be used to help select data for retrieval (Table 2).

Table 2. Search Options for CIDES Categories 1- 6

Category	Search Options
1. Whole animal carcinogenesis	a. species
	b. tumor type
	c. tumor site
	d. route of exposure
2. Mammalian cell lines	a. cell line
	b. name of test
3. Mammalian tissues on cells	a. species
	b. cell/organ
	c. name of test
4. Bacterial tests	a. name of test
5. Other assays	none
6. Human carcinogenesis	a. tumor type
	b. tumor site
	c. route of exposure

Table 3. Selection terms for the four search options in Category 1 (Whole Animal Carcinogenesis)

(C) TDS, 1990

----------- CIDES Category 1 ------- WHOLE ANIMAL CARCINOGENESIS------------------------

1. Selection terms for Species: CHICKEN; CHINESE HAMSTER; DOG; GUINEA PIG; MONKEY; MOUSE; RABBIT; RAT; SYRIAN HAMSTER; ALL OTHER;

2. Selection terms for Tumor Type: MALIGNANT; BENIGN;

3. Selection terms for Tumor Site: BONE; BONE MARROW; CENTRAL NERVOUS SYSTEM; ESOPHAGUS; INTESTINE; KIDNEY; LIVER; LUNG; LYMPHATIC SYSTEM; MAMMARY

   GLAND; NASAL CAVITY; OVARY; PANCREAS; PERITONEAL CAVITY; SKIN; TESTIS; THYROID;

   UTERUS; ALL OTHER;

4. Selection terms for Route of Exposure: DIET; GASTRIC INTUBATION; IMPLANTATION; INHALATION; INTRAPERITONEAL INJECTION; INTRATRACHEAL INSTILLATION;

   ORAL; SUBCUTANEOUS; TOPICAL; ALL OTHER;

Press Return to continue ...

The user may limit a search to specific types of studies by selecting parameters for the many search options that are available within the categories (Table 3). Once the information that corresponds to the search terms has been defined, individual studies may be displayed for sequential browsing on a monitor or all available studies may be downloaded locally to hard disk. Table 4 provides an example of the data and the screen format for a study retrieved from Category 1.

Table 4. A sample study from Category 1 showing the effect of formaldehyde on tumor promotion

(C) TDS, 1990

----------- CIDES Category 1 ------- WHOLE ANIMAL CARCINOGENESIS------------------------

CASRN:50-00-0 Study #:1 # Records:15
SELLAKUMAR, A R; SNYDER, C A ET AL 1985
TOXICOLOGY AND APPLIED PHARMACOLOGY, V 81, P 401
Sec Ref:

SPRAGUE-DAWLEY RAT
Exposed:100 # Control:99
Sex:M Route:INHALATION Leng Exposure:624 DAY

Rec	Dose	TS	TT	Yield/Exp	Yield/Con	Call	ST
1	15 PPM	6	35	13/100	0/99	+	N
2	15 PPM	6		45/100	0/99	+	N
3	15 PPM	6	4	1/100	0/99	-	N
4	15 PPM	6	38	1/100	0/99	-	N
5	15 PPM	6	44	1/100	0/99	-	N
6	15 PPM	6	35	11/100	0/99	+	N
7	15 PPM	6		27/100	0/99	+	N

Select Record (#) for rest of record, or (C)ontinue with list
and press Return ...1

Study #:1 Record #: 1
Tumor Site (TS):NASAL CAVITY
Tumor Type (TT):PAPILLOMA

Age Start:9 WK Elapsed Time:624 DAY P-Value:<.05

Vehicle:AIR Freq Exp:5X/WK

Dose Comment:AGENT WAS PREMIXED WITH 10 PPM OF HYDROGEN CHLORIDE. RATS WERE EXPOSED FOR LIFE.

Sec Treat:

Comment:AVERAGE LATENCY PERIOD WAS 603-645 DAYS.

Press Return for Table of Results ...

TDS is providing users with online access to CIDES through the **Numerica** cluster of databases and software systems. The carcinogenicity data, qualified through the inclusion of physical properties, provides information for assessing the risk of human exposure to substances in the natural and occupational environment. Another application of CIDES is the study of the potency of carcinogens through the dose-response data that are provided. In addition, we anticipate that CIDES will also become a resource for modelling structure-activity and other relationships between chemicals and cancer. Through the dissemination of CIDES, TDS hopes to challenge the user to identify additional applications and to request new and improved information. Ultimately, the data coverage should extend to all substances identified as known or potential carcinogens.

ACKNOWLEDGEMENT

Supported in part by the National Institutes of Health (NIEHS) and by New York State Science & Technology Foundation.

LANGUAL: AN AUTOMATED METHOD FOR DESCRIBING, CAPTURING AND RETRIEVING DATA ABOUT FOOD

Thomas C. Hendricks
Center for Food Safety and Applied Nutrition
U.S. Food and Drug Administration
200 C Street, S.W.
Washington, D.C. 20204, U.S.A.

LanguaL, which stands for "Langue des aLiments or language of food", is an automated method for describing, capturing and retrieving data about food. It has been developed by the Center for Food Safety and Applied Nutrition (CFSAN) of the U.S. Food and Drug Administration (FDA) over the last fifteen years as an ongoing cooperative effort of specialists in food technology, information science and nutrition.

LanguaL is based on the concept that:

* Any food (or food product) can be systematically described by a combination of characteristics
* These characteristics can be categorized into viewpoints and coded for computer processing
* The resulting viewpoint/characteristic codes can be used to retrieve data about the food from external databases.

This paper will describe LanguaL in some detail. It will then present an in-depth example of how LanguaL can be applied. Finally, it will review LanguaL's use internationally and postulate its acceptance as a world-wide standard.

HOW IS FOOD DESCRIBED?

One can systematically describe any food or food product using carefully selected points of view, in order to categorize its:

* Food group
* Origin
* Physical attributes
* Processing
* Packaging
* Dietary uses
* Miscellaneous characteristics.

Each viewpoint is called a "factor." There are at present thirteen (13) factors in LanguaL. The characteristics related to them are called "factor terms". TABLE I presents each factor by category together with a brief description (where appropriate) and examples of factor terms.

Table 1

FOOD GROUP		
A. Product Type	Derived from a combination of consumption, functional and manufacturing characteristics	Dairy product, poultry/poultry product, beverage, gravy or sauce, sweetener
ORIGIN		
B1. Food Source	Species of plant or animal, of chemical food source	Cattle, abalone, wheat carob bean, garlic
B2. Part of Plant or Animal		Leaf, fruit, skeletal meat, organ meat
PHYSICAL ATTRIBUTES		
C. Physical State, Shape or Form		Liquid, semiliquid, solid whole natural shape, divided into pieces
PROCESSING		
D1. Extent of Heat Treatment		Fully cooked, partially cooked, uncooked, raw

Table 1 (cont)

D2. Cooking Method	Cooked by dry or moist heat; cooked with fat; cooked by microwave	Sauteed, baked or roasted, griddled, toasted, popped, deep-fried
D3. Treatment Applied	Additional processing steps, including adding, substituting, or removing components	Enriched, sweetened, egg added, fat or oil added, fat removed, decaffeinated
D4. Preservation Method	Primary preservation method	Dehydrated or dried, frozen, preserved by adding chemicals
	PACKAGING	
E1. Packing Medium		Packed in broth, packed in gelatin, packed in gravy or sauce
E2. Container or Wrapping	Container material, form, and possibly other characteristics	Paperboard tray with wrapper, plastic boil-in-bag, glass container, aluminum lid, plastic lining
E3. Food Contact Surface	The surface(s) with which the food is in contact	Ceramic, cork, paperboard, glass, metal, plastic
	DIETARY USES	
F. Consumer Group/ Dietary Use	Human or animal; special dietary characteristics	Human food low fat, human food sodium-free, human food very low sodium, human food reduced calorie
	MISCELLANEOUS CHARACTERISTICS	
Z. Adjunct Characteristics of Food	Additional miscellaneous descriptors	Pink fish flesh, shoulder (meat cut), choice (grade), edible sausage casing, mold rind, dry mix

As an example, consider the commercial food product "Corn Flakes" (see Figure 1). Its Product Type factor term, which identifies the food group it belongs to based on common consumption, functional or manufacturing characteristics, is "Breakfast cereal." The Food Source factor term, which identifies the individual plant or animal from which the food product (or its major ingredient) is derived, would be "Field corn." The Part of Plant or Animal factor term, which describes the anatomical part of the plant or animal from which the food product (or its major ingredient) is derived, is "Seed or kernel, skin removed, germ removed (endosperm)." Its Physical State, Shape or Form factor term, which distinguishes between liquids and solids and further describes solids in terms of shape or form, is "Whole, shape achieved by forming, thickness less than 0.3 cm." The Extent of Heat Treatment factor term, which is used to broadly characterize a food product based on the amount of heat applied, is "Fully cooked." The Cooking Method factor term, which identifies the way food products are cooked, reheated or warmed, is "Not applicable" because heat treatment is inherent in the process of making Corn Flakes. The Treatment Applied factor term, which is used to describe components added or subtracted as well as processes involved in producing the food product and can have multiple values, includes:

* Sucrose added
* Flavoring or spice extract or concentrate added
* Vitamin added
* Iron added
* Flaked
* Water removed

The Preservation Method factor term, which identifies the primary method for preventing or retarding microbial or enzymatic spoilage of a food product, is "Dehydrated or dried." The Packing Medium factor term, which describes the medium in which the food is packed for preservation, handling and/or palatability, is "No packing medium used" in this example. The Container or Wrapping factor term, which identifies the material comprising the main container as well as any liners, lids or ends, is "Paperboard container with paper liner." The Food Contact Surface factor term, which identifies the specific container materials in direct contact with the food product and can have multiple values, includes:

* Wax
* Paperboard or paper.

HOW IS FOOD DESCRIBED?

Each viewpoint is called a FACTOR.
The characteristics related to it are called FACTOR TERMS.

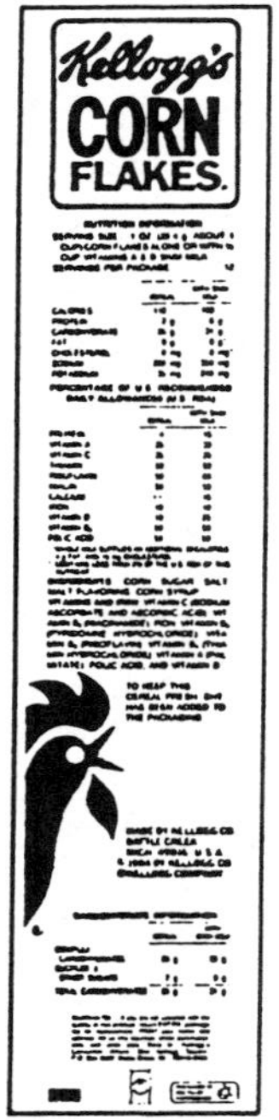

Consider the food product CORN FLAKES:

FACTOR	FACTOR TERM
PRODUCT TYPE	Breakfast cereal
FOOD SOURCE	Field corn
PART OF PLANT OR ANIMAL	Seed or kernel, skin removed, germ removed (endosperm)
PHYSICAL STATE, SHAPE OR FORM	Whole, shape achieved by forming, thickness <0.3 cm.
EXTENT OF HEAT TREATMENT	Fully cooked
COOKING METHOD	Cooking method not applicable
TREATMENT APPLIED	Sucrose added; flavoring or spice extract or concentrate added; vitamin added; iron added; flaked; water removed.
PRESERVATION METHOD	Dehydrated or dried
PACKING MEDIUM	No packing medium used
CONTAINER OR WRAPPING	Paperboard container with paper liner
FOOD CONTACT SURFACE	Wax; paperboard or paper
CONSUMER GROUP/DIETARY USE	Human food, no age specification, regular diet
ADJUNCT CHARACTERISTICS OF FOOD	None

FIGURE 1

The Consumer Group/Dietary Use factor term, which specifies who uses the food product, is "Human food, no age specification, regular diet." The Adjunct Characteristics of Food factor term, which allows for miscellaneous descriptions, does not have any value for Corn Flakes.

As another example, consider the homemade food product "Breaded Fried Chicken." Figure 2 displays its factors and factor terms. As can be seen from these examples, virtually any food or food product can be categorized and characterized in this systematic fashion.

HOW ARE FACTOR TERMS IDENTIFIED?

In order to facilitate computer processing, each factor term is assigned an alphanumeric code identifying the factor and the unique characteristic (*e.g.*, A258 = Product Type "Breakfast cereal," A273 = Product Type "Poultry or poultry product"). Figures 3 and 4 show this coding schema for the Corn Flakes and Fried Chicken examples described above.

HOW IS INFORMATION STORED?

A computer record contains the food (product) name and assigned factor term codes, as well as product identification codes (*e.g.*, Universal Product Code or UPC) for accessing external databases.

Figures 5 and 6 depict these data for the Corn Flakes and Fried Chicken examples described above.

Thus, if the Corn Flakes record were selected as part of a search, it would "point" the user to additional information in the following databases:

* FDA SIREN (Scientific Information Retrieval and Exchange Network, FDA/CFSAN)
* FDA Total Diet (Total Diet Study, FDA/CFSAN)
* USDA Nutrient Data Base (Handbook #8). (Nutrient Data Base for Standard Reference, U.S. Department of Agriculture (USDA))

as well as any other references (*e.g.*, UPC where applicable). The Fried Chicken record would have similar "pointers" to additional data. This means that a wide variety of food composition and food consumption databases can be referenced by a single LanguaL search, using their existing coding schemes without change. Concomitantly, there is no need to know the codes or structure of the databases being simultaneously searched by LanguaL.

HOW IS FOOD DESCRIBED?

Consider the food product
HOMEMADE BREADED
FRIED CHICKEN:

FACTOR	FACTOR TERM
PRODUCT TYPE	Poultry or poultry product
FOOD SOURCE	Chicken
PART OF PLANT OR ANIMAL	Skeletal meat part, with bone, with skin
PHYSICAL STATE, SHAPE OR FORM	Whole, natural shape
EXTENT OF HEAT TREATMENT	Fully cooked
COOKING METHOD	Cooked with added fat
TREATMENT APPLIED	Fat or oil coated; Grain added; Breaded, batter-coated
PRESERVATION METHOD	No preservation method used
PACKING MEDIUM	No packing medium used
CONTAINER OR WRAPPING	No container or wrapping used
FOOD CONTACT SURFACE	No food contact surface present
CONSUMER GROUP/DIETARY USE	Human food, no age specification, regular diet
ADJUNCT CHARACTERISTICS OF FOOD	Meat color, mixture

FIGURE 2

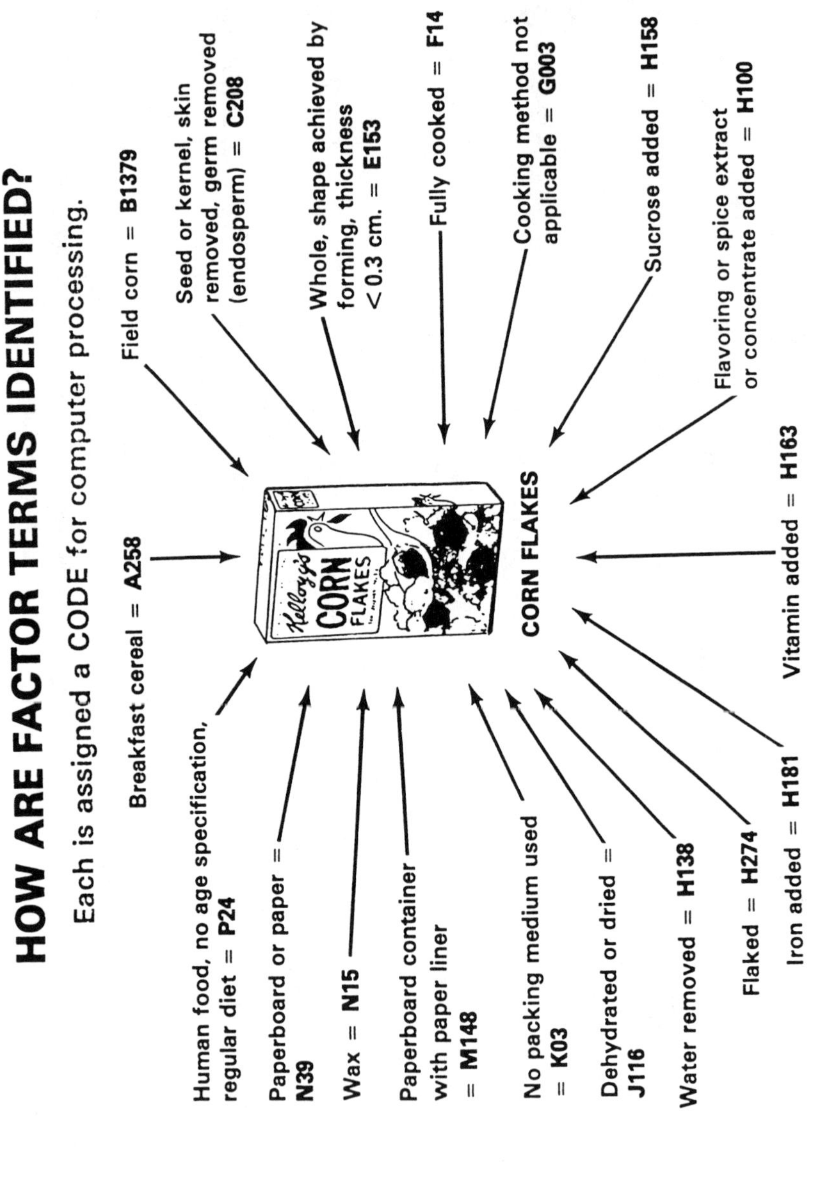
HOW ARE FACTOR TERMS IDENTIFIED?
Each is assigned a CODE for computer processing.
Breakfast cereal = A258
Field corn = B1379
Seed or kernel, skin removed, germ removed (endosperm) = C208
Whole, shape achieved by forming, thickness < 0.3 cm. = E153
Fully cooked = F14
Cooking method not applicable = G003
Sucrose added = H158
Flavoring or spice extract or concentrate added = H100
Vitamin added = H163
Iron added = H181
Flaked = H274
Water removed = H138
Dehydrated or dried = J116
No packing medium used = K03
Paperboard container with paper liner = M148
Wax = N15
Paperboard or paper = N39
Human food, no age specification, regular diet = P24
Kellogg's CORN FLAKES
CORN FLAKES

FIGURE 3

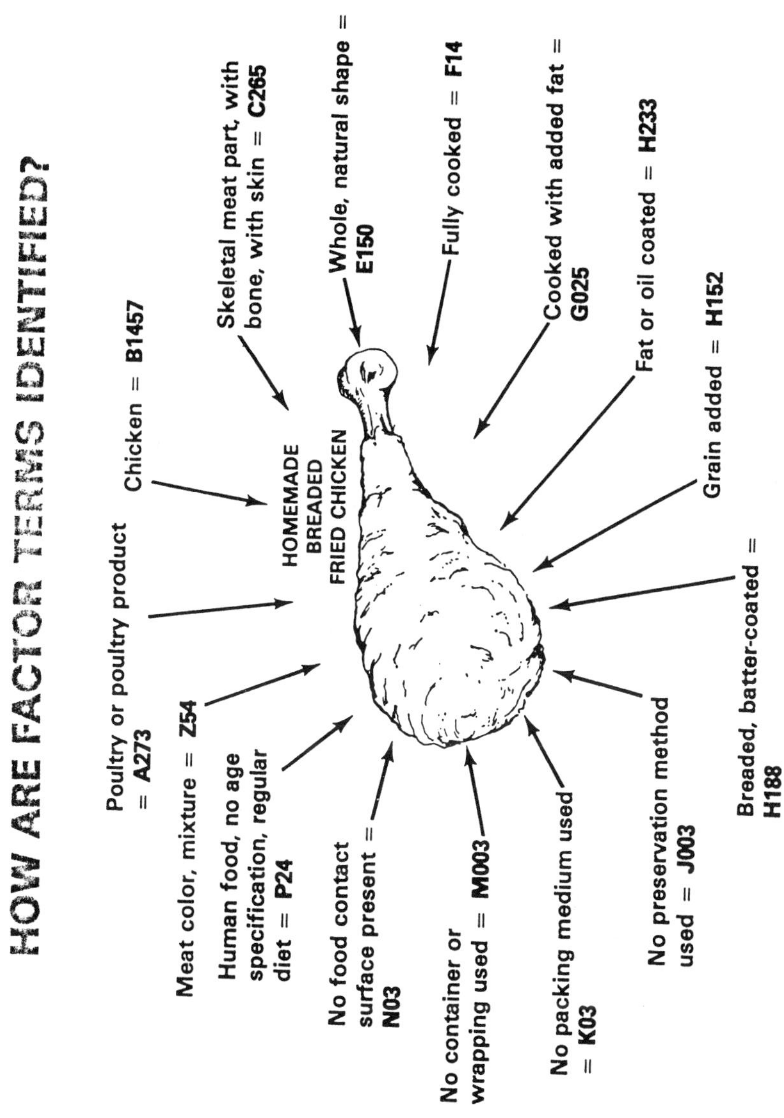
HOW ARE FACTOR TERMS IDENTIFIED?
HOMEMADE BREADED FRIED CHICKEN
Poultry or poultry product = **A273**
Chicken = **B1457**
Skeletal meat part, with bone, with skin = **C265**
Whole, natural shape = **E150**
Fully cooked = **F14**
Cooked with added fat = **G025**
Fat or oil coated = **H233**
Grain added = **H152**
Breaded, batter-coated = **H188**
No preservation method used = **J003**
No packing medium used = **K03**
No container or wrapping used = **M003**
No food contact surface present = **N03**
Human food, no age specification, regular diet = **P24**
Meat color, mixture = **Z54**

FIGURE 4

HOW IS INFORMATION STORED?
A computer record contains the food (product) name and assigned factor codes, as well as product identification codes for accessing external data bases(s).
CORN FLAKES
A258.B1379.C208.E153.F14.G003.
H100.H138.H158.H163.H181.H274.
J116.K03.M148.N15.N39.P24
F2904 (FDA SIREN)
TDS071 (FDA TOTAL DIET)
08020 (USDA HANDBOOK #8)
UPC381100 (ANY OTHER REFERENCE)
Langual

FIGURE 5

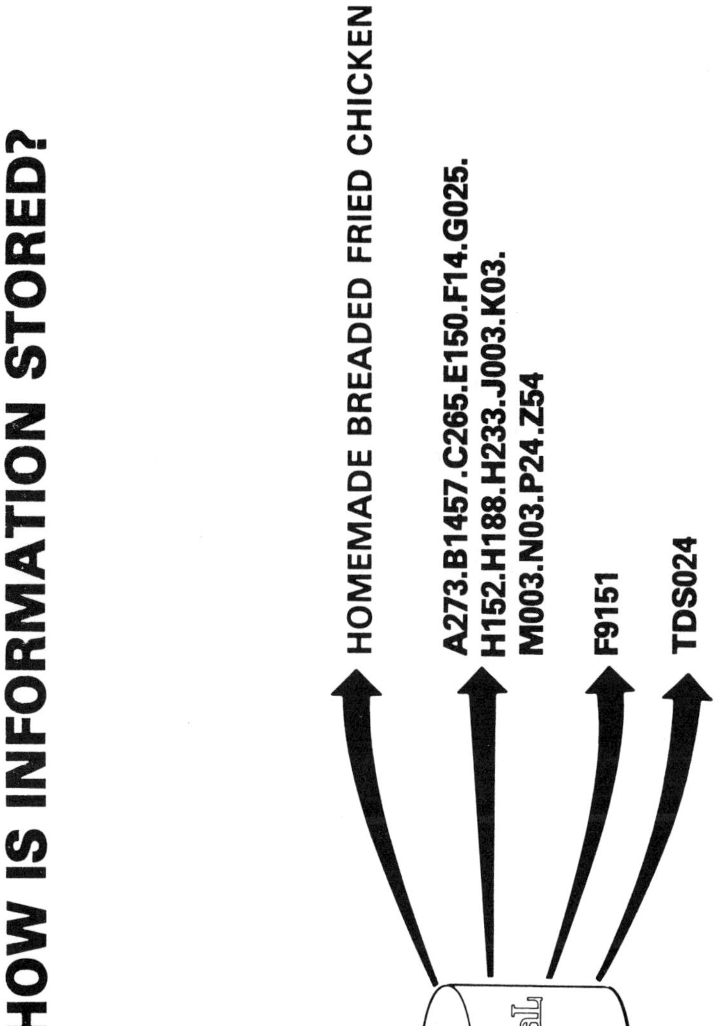
HOW IS INFORMATION STORED?
HOMEMADE BREADED FRIED CHICKEN
A273.B1457.C265.E150.F14.G025.
H152.H188.H233.J003.K03.
M003.N03.P24.Z54
F9151
TDS024
LanguaL

FIGURE 6

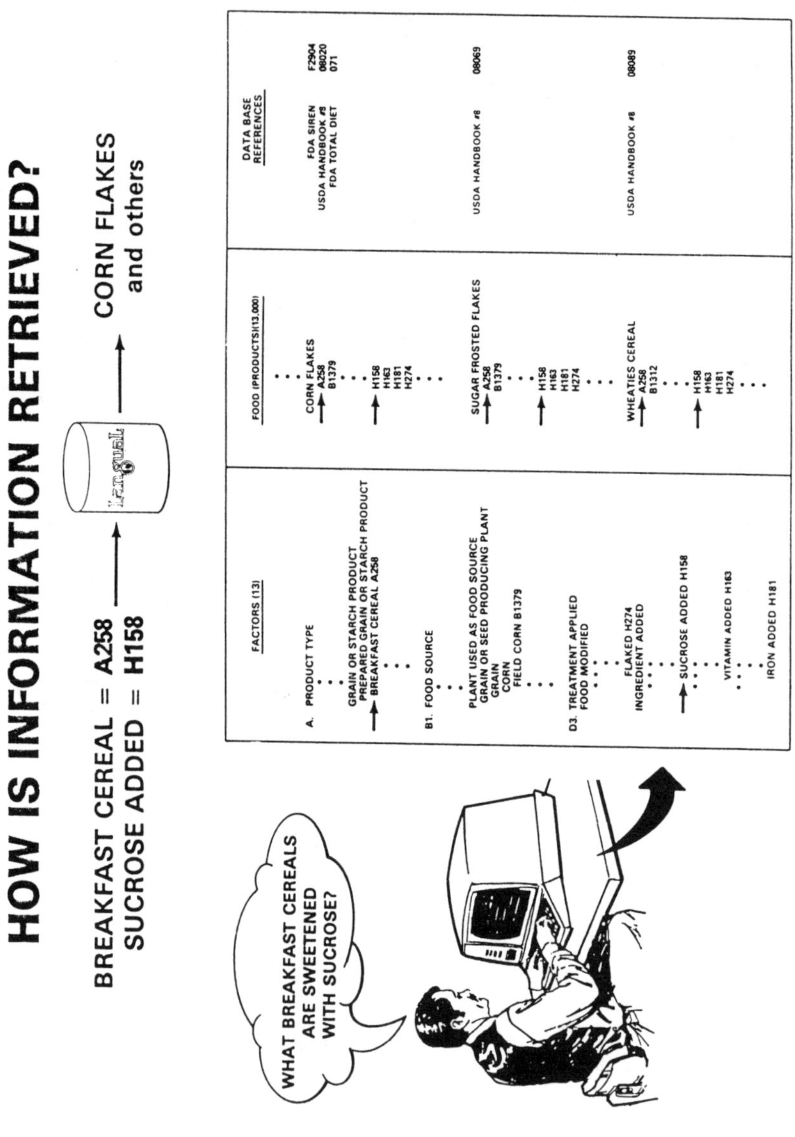
HOW IS INFORMATION RETRIEVED?
BREAKFAST CEREAL = A258
SUCROSE ADDED = H158
CORN FLAKES
and others
WHAT BREAKFAST CEREALS ARE SWEETENED WITH SUCROSE?
FACTORS (13)
A. PRODUCT TYPE
GRAIN OR STARCH PRODUCT
PREPARED GRAIN OR STARCH PRODUCT
BREAKFAST CEREAL A258
B1. FOOD SOURCE
PLANT USED AS FOOD SOURCE
GRAIN OR SEED PRODUCING PLANT
GRAIN
CORN
FIELD CORN B1379
D3. TREATMENT APPLIED
FOOD MODIFIED
FLAKED H274
INGREDIENT ADDED
SUCROSE ADDED H158
VITAMIN ADDED H163
IRON ADDED H181
FOOD (PRODUCTS)(13,000)
CORN FLAKES
A258
B1379
H158
H163
H181
H274
SUGAR FROSTED FLAKES
A258
B1379
H158
H163
H181
H274
WHEATIES CEREAL
A258
B1312
H158
H163
H181
H274
DATA BASE REFERENCES
FDA SIREN F2904
USDA HANDBOOK #8 08020
FDA TOTAL DIET 071
USDA HANDBOOK #8 08069
USDA HANDBOOK #8 08089

FIGURE 7

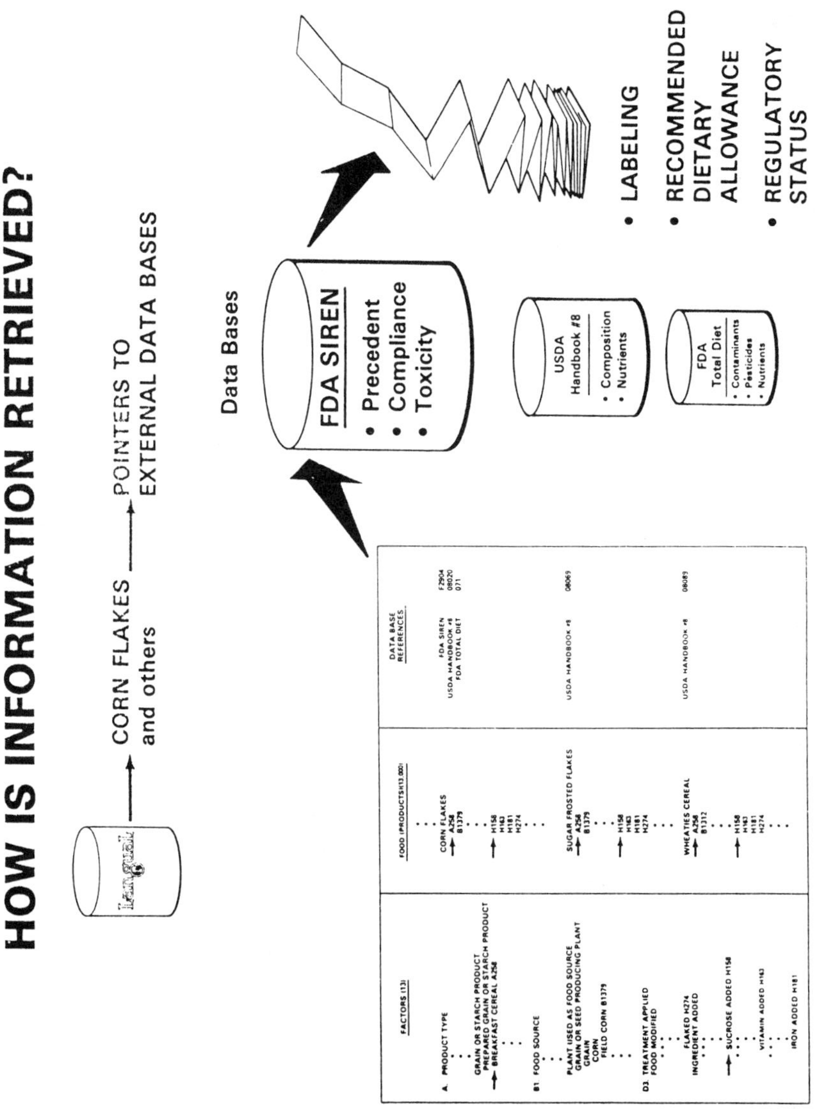
HOW IS INFORMATION RETRIEVED?
CORN FLAKES and others
POINTERS TO EXTERNAL DATA BASES
Data Bases
FDA SIREN
• Precedent
• Compliance
• Toxicity
USDA Handbook #8
• Composition
• Nutrients
FDA Total Diet
• Contaminants
• Pesticides
• Nutrients
• LABELING
• RECOMMENDED DIETARY ALLOWANCE
• REGULATORY STATUS

FIGURE 8

HOW IS INFORMATION RETRIEVED?

In general, a LanguaL search is conducted to answer a specific question. The records selected as a result of this search contain pointers to outside databases. These databases may then be accessed (using the pointers) to obtain very detailed information related to the original query.

For example, consider the question: "What Breakfast Cereals are Sweetened with Sucrose"? By conducting a boolean search of all the coded foods for those whose LanguaL Product Type factor is "Breakfast cereal" (A258) *and* whose Treatment Applied factor (multiple occurrence) includes "Sucrose added," a number of food (product) records will be selected, including the Corn Flakes example described above. Figures 7 and 8 depict this process. Each selected record contains at least one pointer to an external database where additional information related to the original query can be obtained. Perhaps data about regulatory (compliance) activities related to sucrose sweetened breakfast cereal from FDA's SIREN database might be of interest. On the other hand, food composition and nutrient data for sucrose sweetened breakfast cereals from USDA's Nutrient Data Base (Handbook #8) could be obtained. Moreover, information on residues from contaminants and pesticides as well as additional nutritional data could be readily accessed in FDA's Total Diet Study database. Thus, this one LanguaL query would turn up a wealth of information about sucrose sweetened breakfast cereals. Such information would be difficult (if not impossible) to obtain in any other way.

WHERE DOES THIS LEAD?

LanguaL can facilitate direct links to many different food consumption and analytical databases as well as bibliographic files, worldwide. In addition to the FDA and USDA linkages discussed above, LanguaL is also being used by the National Cancer Institute (NCI) in its studies of diet's relationship to cancer incidence. Furthermore, Langual is being applied on an international level, with government agencies in Denmark, France and the United Kingdom using it for their endeavors.

At FDA/CFSAN a conscientious effort is being made to expand the number and variety of outside databases accessible using LanguaL. For example, work is underway to incorporate all 1987-88 USDA Nationwide Food Consumption Survey (NFCS) foods, thus providing a valuable link to up-to-date food consumption data for the U.S. Also, foods and food products whose standards are specified by Title 21 (Food and Drugs) of the Code of Federal Regulations (CFR) will be coded. This will allow access to any database with CFR food references.

In addition, all Codex Alimentarius food standards (analogous to CFR standards discussed above) will be coded so that any database with Codex references can be easily accessed. This should prove useful in international trade. With the advent of the European Economic Community (EEC) in the early 1990's, there will be a need for standardized food descriptions as an adjunct to "harmonized" tariff schedules. LanguaL could prove very useful in satisfying this need. In fact, it may provide the only effective way for linking with databases from the Eastern Bloc nations as they become a force in international commerce. With more widespread use, LanguaL could well become an international standard.

A HISTORY OF DATA RECORDING, ANALYSIS, AND DISSEMINATION

J. H. Westbrook
Brookline Technology
Ballston Spa, NY, U.S.A.

INTRODUCTION

The community of scientists and engineers that constitute CODATA are chartered to improve the collection, organization, analysis and dissemination of data in virtually every field of science and technology. Caught up in our concerns with mastering the huge volumes of data currently pouring out from our laboratories and observational instruments, we too readily forget that we are part of a tradition that goes back many thousands of years.

Though their recording techniques were crude and often cumbersome, and their analytical methods primitive, our ancient predecessors were motivated in their data activities by the same forces that impel us today:

- curiosity to understand the natural world
- the desire to pass that understanding to succeeding generations
- self aggrandizement (both economic and "quality of life")
- power (political, military, and religious)

A common thread running through man's responses to all these motivating forces is the goal of ensuring (or at least, improving) the predictability of events. The predictability of events important to man range from the weather (when will the floods come?) to geography (can a record be made showing how to get there from here?), to physico-chemical processes (what recipe should be followed to obtain a desired result?). A few examples to be given subsequently in this paper will illustrate this theme in a variety of fields.

Another common thread to be seen in data activities in nearly every field of science is the enormous impact of data compilations. Such aggregations of quantitative information are important for many advantages and opportunities:

- convenience of access
- condensation and homogenization of raw data
- formats tailored for the application
- perception of patterns
- detection of errors
- definition of gaps and inconsistencies
- basis for formulating and testing theories

They thus provide both the spring-board for new advances in science and the basis for ready application of that which was known. It is, therefore, not surprising that the collection of astronomical data by Ptolemy remained a key reference for a millennium, that the first organized pharmacopoeia was still judged worthy of printing for the first time 1400 years after Dioscorides wrote it, and that the systematic arrangement of the elements by their atomic weights by Mendeleev over 100 years ago continues to yield fresh insights in chemistry, metallurgy, and physics.

DATA REPRESENTATION

Number Systems. The earliest forms of data representation were marks on a stick or bone to indicate scores or tallies*. Marshack [1] has analyzed artifacts dated to the Magdelenian period in the ice age, about 25 000-30 000 BC and concludes that the markings are scientific records not mere decorations. One such record, on an antler baton from the Le Placard site in France, has been strongly correlated with a lunar phasing as shown in Figure 1. Similar markings on artifacts of the Ishango people of Zaire (9000-6500 BC) have received the same sort of interpretation.

Large numbers obviously require a more powerful and sophisticated numeration system than simple slash marks. The Egyptians used a decimal numerations system as early as 3000 BC. Throughout the world, number systems based on man's 10 fingers were most common, but bases of 5 and 20 also appeared. The next step was the adoption of special symbols for numbers greater than 4 or 5 as shown in the comparison [2] of numerical symbols in Figure 2. The Babylonians (~2000 BC) contributed the enormously valuable place-value notation scheme. Theirs was based on a sexagesimal system, and clumsy using only two symbols, one representing

----

* From the Anglo-Saxon, *sceren* = to cut and the French *tailler* = to cut, respectively.

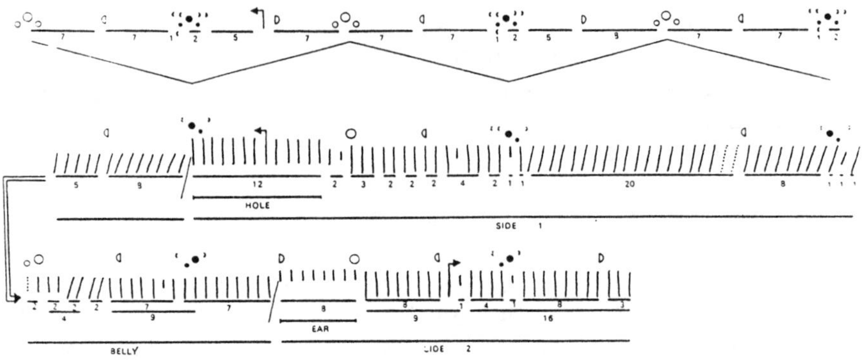

FIGURE 1
Markings on the Le Placard baton from the Magdelenian III period. Microscopic examination shows the engraved marks to have been made by at least 25 different points, thus arguing against their having been made at the same time. When the markings on the three sides of the baton are laid sequentially against a lunar model, an extremely close correlation is obtained extending just over four months.

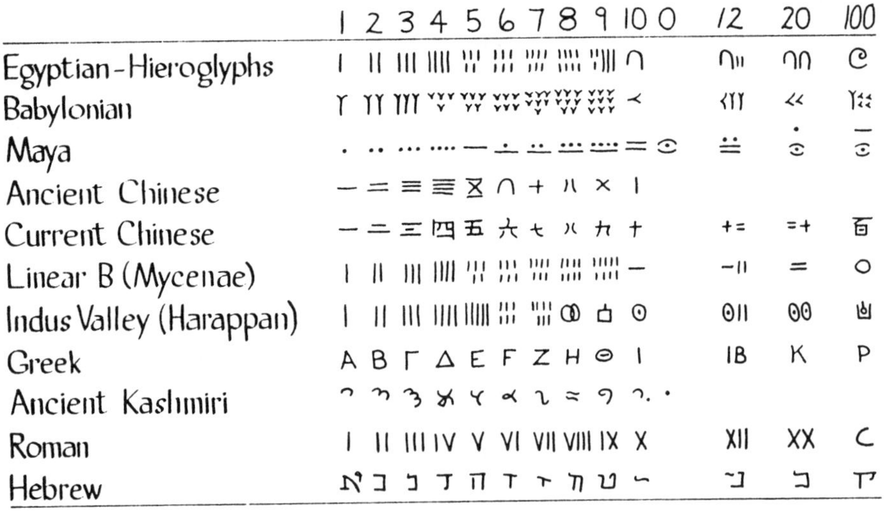

FIGURE 2
Comparison of numeric symbols from several ancient cultures.

1 or 60^n and the other 10 or 10×60^n; hence the notation was often ambiguous. Their other difficulty was not having a functional zero*. This final piece of the numeration story, introduction of the zero (at first a dot, later opened to a closed loop), came from the Hindus, perhaps as early as 500 AD, but the earliest extant document containing a zero is dated 595 AD. The Indian numerals were gradually transformed by the Muslims, and the so-called Arabic numerals reached the West via the Islamic civilization in the tenth century, principally through an arithmetic book by the Persian, al-Khwarazmi, which also gave to English the words "algorithm" (after the author's name) and "cipher" (Arabic for zero).

Lists, Tables, Maps and Graphs. With means for writing both words and numbers in hand, new ways of representing scientific understanding evolved. The Sumerians (3500-2000 BC) developed a so-called "science of lists" which reflected their tendency to classify all experimental or observational data. While many of these word lists refer to ordinary articles of human life and experience, those in the exact sciences treated, catalogued, and classified animals, plants and minerals. Tables, regular rectilinear arrays of numbers, were introduced by the Babylonians to present in a concise format the results of certain mathematical calculations: tables of multiplication, squares, cubes, roots and reciprocals. The Egyptians prepared numerous astronomical tables of star culminations and star risings. The Arabs also make extensive astronomical compilations in tabular form, called *zijes***.

Records of spatial relationships of objects, which we now call maps, extend back very far in time. Stone carvings of some of the most prominent constellations, those of Ursa Major, Ursa Minor, and the Pleiades, were made in the Megalithic age. The first known geographic map on bone (20 000-10 000 BC) has been found near Mezherich in the USSR. By 2300 BC, Sargon of Akkhad was using maps for taxation purposes.

The last major form of data representation, the graph, was a much later development. A single example has been found [4] of a time series graph, a 10th century plot of the inclinations of the planets as a function of

----

* The Maya also invented a place-value notation but based on 20 rather than 60; it also lacked a functional zero.

** The word *zij* came into Arabic from Sanskrit via Pahlavi. Its original meaning was "straight lines," connected with the linear furrows of a plowed field, and was transferred to connote the tabular format because of the lines used to array the data [3].

time and is illustrated in Figure 3. The plot must be regarded as an anachronism, for nothing else like it appeared for centuries. Descartes (1596-1650) was apparently the first to conceive the advantages of a graphical representation of the spatial location of an entity (reputedly by noticing how the location of a fly in the 3-dimensional space of a room could be described by a coordinate system). From this it was a short step to a full generalization of graphical representation of any function or data set and a fruitful linking of the previously separate branches of mathematics: geometry and algebra. The general use, however, of cartesian plots, bar graphs, and pie charts did not commence until the 18th century; the leading graphic innovators in this period were William Playfair, an English political economist, and J. H. Lambert, a Swiss-German scientist/mathematician [5].

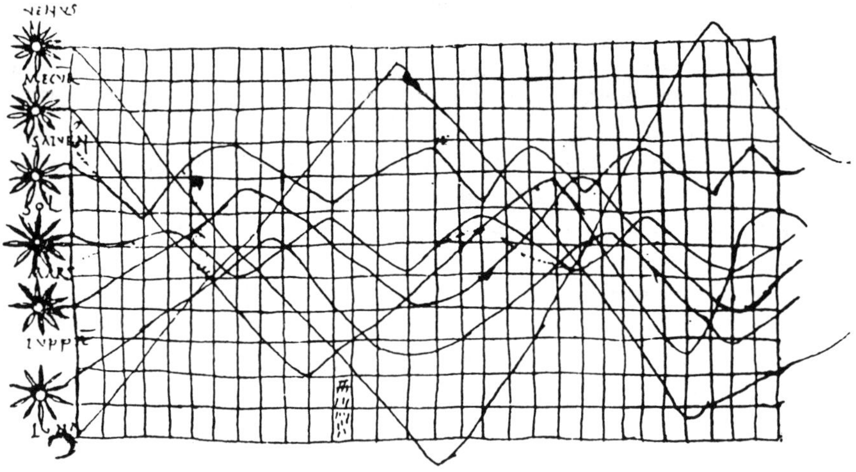

FIGURE 3

Inclination of the planetary orbits as a function of time from a monastic textbook of the 10th century.

DATA ACTIVITIES IN FOUR FIELDS

Summaries of some of the landmark advances in data recording and compilation in four technical fields, astronomy, the life sciences, geography, and technology, are listed in Tables I-IV. Essays, even books, could be, and have been, written about each item listed in these tables. Here, we are confined to a few illustrative remarks.

Astronomy. The earliest efforts in gathering and recording astronomical data were simply descriptive, noting the changing phases of the moon, the changing times and places through the year of sunrise and sunset, the arrangement and apparent motion of the constellations, and the anomalous movement of the morning and evening "stars" and other planets*. As the number of quantitative records increased, the time period extended over which observations were made, and the precision of observations improved, the astonishing mathematical regularity of the universe became apparent. This led in time to the predictability of anomalies such as eclipses and the detection of subtleties in the heavenly motions. By the fourth century, Seleucid astronomers in Babylonia had compiled an emphemeris for the planet Saturn, tabulating numbers which could predict the apparently wandering motion of that planet against the background of the "fixed stars." In succeeding centuries the completeness and precision of emphemerides and star catalogs steadily improved.

Hipparchus of Rhodes, greatest of the Greek astronomers, observed in 134 BC a new star in the constellation Scorpio, for which he could find no prior record. Unable to decide whether it was really new or simply not recognized because of the fragmentary and unsystematic records of the past, he determined to remove this ambiguity for succeeding astronomers by compiling an organized catalog of the location and brightness of over 1000 stars. He also is usually credited with the discovery of the precession of the

----

* Much that was learned was undoubtedly not recorded. The increasing specialization accompanying the advance of science, and the shift in knowledge from the common man to the specialists have influenced data recording in a back-handed way. Thus Brown [6] remarks, "Astronomy, for instance, was probably a part of every man's knowledge, even in very ancient civilization, a heritage passed down either by word of mouth or in the writings of the priests. Therefore, the known facts regarding the heavens were no more worthy of special note than the rising of the sun or the fact that the desert was full of sand."

equinoxes, that is the fact that the sun in its annual motion takes very slightly longer to return to its original position in the zodiac than it does to return to the equator from one Spring to the next. This discovery is particularly remarkable since the annual displacement is only about 50 seconds of arc, far less than the limit of accuracy of visual observations. Thus the discovery was based, not on successive annual observations by an individual astronomer, but only by comparison of contemporary observations with those recorded by others a century or more earlier*.

Life Sciences. At first, when the fragmentary knowledge of anatomy, physiology and disease could only be transmitted orally, medical prognosis was limited, indeed. With the rise of urban civilizations, sufficient concentration of population occurred that doctors could compare cases, organize the gathering and production of medicinal plants, confer with their colleagues and begin to record their observations. The famous Edwin Smith Egyptian papyrus on surgery and external medicine is a seventeenth century BC copy of a work of about 1000 years earlier. It is often regarded as the first scientific book in the sense that it is a record of facts and observations which then lead to inductively determined conclusions.

Dioscorides of Anazorbos (Cilicia), an army doctor of the first century AD, produced a five-section treatise, *Materia Medica*, the major portion of which was botany. In this book he names each of 600 plants, states the various other names by which it was known, describes it, explains its medical uses, and provides an identifying illustration [8]. The work was immensely popular, was translated from the original Greek to Latin, then to Arabic, and ultimately to many of the European languages. As remarked earlier, Dioscorides' *Materia Medica* was after 1400 years still considered so important that a printed edition was issued in the fifteenth century. An illustration from a Latin translation of a thirteenth century Arabic manuscript is shown in Figure 4.

Carl Linnaeus, Swedish naturalist, at age 28, published in 1735 his *Systems of Nature* a complete, systematic taxonomy of botany, zoology, and mineralogy. His scheme for the later did not survive, but his classification principles for plants and animals, as well as his binomial system of

---

* de Santillana and von Dechend [7] suggest that a qualitative knowledge of the procession may even extend back before recorded history by being introduced into mythological tales passed on by word of mouth from generation to generation.

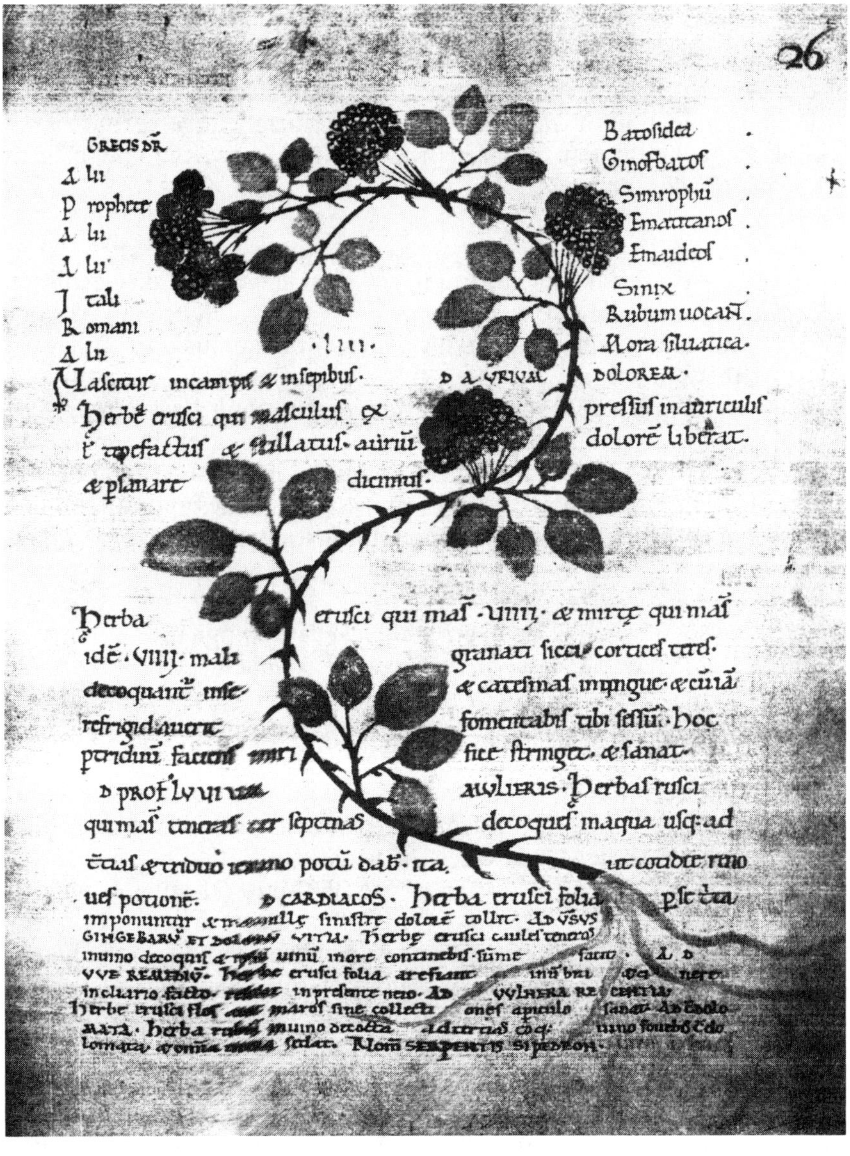

FIGURE 4

A page from Dioscorides' "Materia Medica", translated from Greek to Arabic and then to Latin for use in medieval Europe.

terminology (genera and species) are used to this day. By the time his most important work, the *Species Plantarum*, was published in 1753, he had classified more than 18 000 plants, many of which he had collected himself and identified for the first time. This achievement is an excellent illustration of the fact that organizational breakthroughs in science are possible only with the conjunction of a great mind and a critically large corpus of data. It is also noteworthy that Linnaeus was the first to use the symbols ♂ and ♀ for "male" and "female."

Geography. As a means for recording geographic data and displaying such information intelligibly, the map has no equal. Hence a history of geographical data becomes essentially a history of map making. It has been said that there are three requisite skills for map making: a capability for close observation, an aptitude for drawing, and ingenuity in the representation of complex information. With reference to the latter, the map maker must contend with devising satisfactory 2-dimensional representations of the spherical Earth, choosing a scale or combination of scales appropriate to his subject, and inventing a means for representing topographical or phenomenological data.

Of all of the significant events in geographical data compilation summarized in Table III, that most deserving of further comment is Ptolemy's *Geographia*. Ptolemy was a Graeco-Egyptian working in Alexandria, site of the most outstanding library and data center of his day. It has been said of the *Geographia* that "few books have exerted a more profound and stimulating influence on the progress of civilization" [9]. In this work, an example of which appears in Figure 5, Ptolemy introduced a number of innovations which persist today: he standardized the map's orientation,north at the top, east to the right. He divided each of the 360° into 60 minutes and each minute into 60 seconds. He recognized that maps drawn with various sphere-to-plane projections can only give an approximation on the plane of the true relative sizes and shapes of regions on the actual spherical surface, and that any choice among them is necessarily a compromise. He emphasized the importance of data evaluation and outlined techniques for its implementation. The gazetteer accompanying the text and maps of the *Geographia* locates 8000 (!) places by their latitude and longitude. He insisted on astronomical determination of these quantities wherever possible, in preference to deriving place locations from traveler's tales. Ptolemy has been criticized for not being wholly original and for publishing a work rife with errors [10]. Yet for almost 1500 years no one else did better. Would that any of us today will match this achievement!

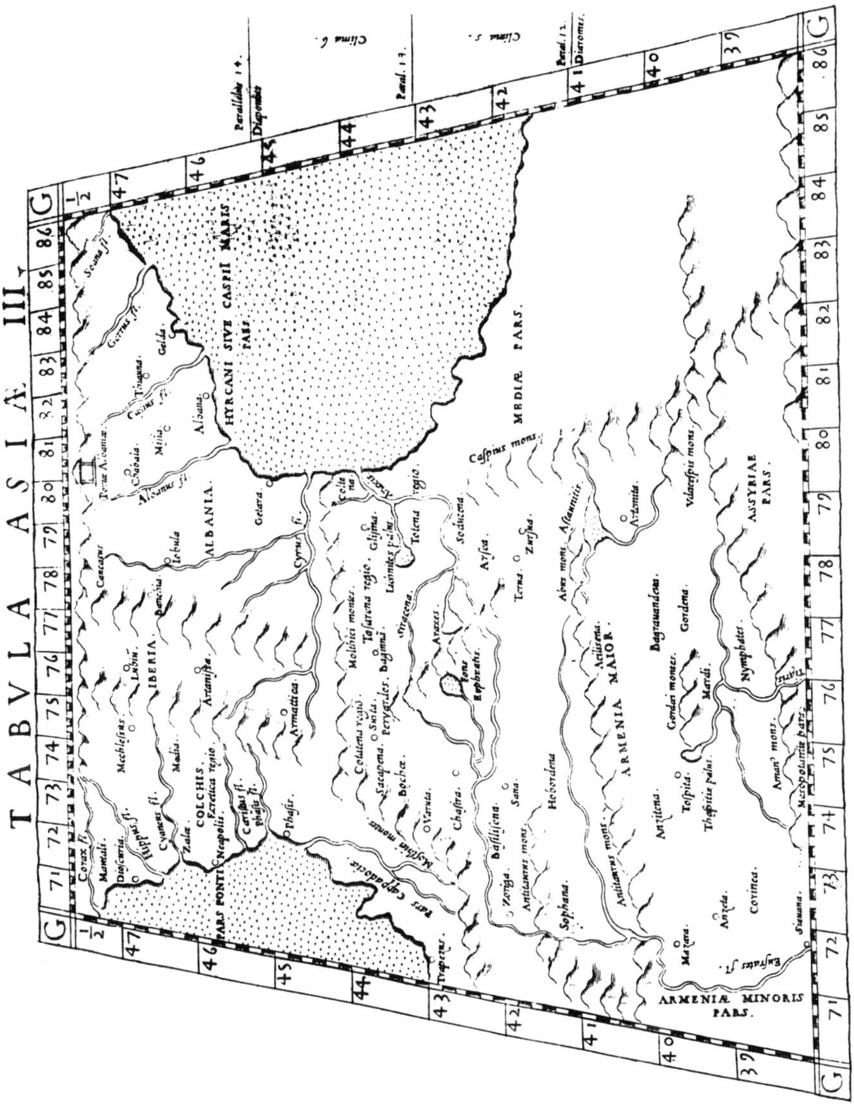

FIGURE 5
An example of one of Ptolemy's maps, Asia III, showing the region of the Caucasus between the Black and Caspian Seas, northern Iran, and eastern Turkey. Ptolemy's conical projection is used. From Gastaldo (after Munster) in the 1561 edition by Vincenzo Valgrisi of Venice.

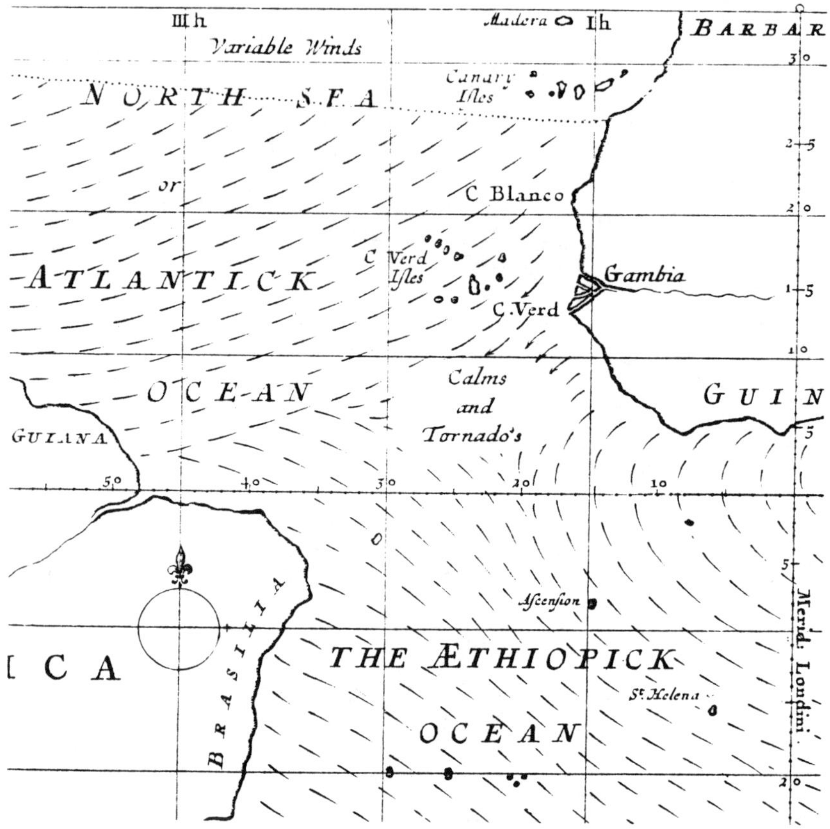

FIGURE 6
One of the first data maps: a part of Edmund Halley's chart of the trade winds and monsoons on a world map. The sharp end of each "little stroak" points to the direction from whence the wind comes. E. Halley, *Phil. Trans.*, **183** (1686) 153-168.

From the earliest times maps were recognized as a compact record of such valuable information (military, economic, or political) that access to them must be restricted and the maps themselves carefully guarded. Ironically, a large fraction of old maps has disappeared expressly because they were heavily used,often at sea or in the field, rather than in a library or chart--room. Others were intentionally destroyed because they were regarded as ephemeral documents to be replaced as soon as new ones with more complete or more accurate information became available. In later years, survival was aided by the development of the bound atlas or collection of maps. This concept was first implemented in 1570 by Ortelius [11], who was also responsible for early adoption of many other aspects of good practice in data compilation. He chose a standard format, sought international collaboration, cataloged the authorities whose work he had consulted or copied, was not ashamed to publish errata, and specifically invited criticism and suggestions for improvement of later editions,all of which we emulate today.

Technology. Even when freed from the elements of magic and religion, technological records, as compared to scientific records, were infrequently imbued with the quantitative notations and relationships we now refer to as data. There were reasons for this. One was simply the difficulty of describing, explicitly and quantitatively, processes and products which were complicated in the extreme and poorly understood even when reliably reproducible. Secondly, mastery of the mysteries of a craft was an economic asset to be jealously guarded and passed to one's descendants or selected apprentices only through oral tradition and "on-the-job" training. Even the few early records of technological data we have are more in the nature of notes for adepts than of instructions for novices.

An important early class of technological works are the compendia of recipes in various fields, examples of which are noted in Table IV. Another, appearing again in a variety of fields, are tables of numbers for engineers and other practical men, characterized by a two-level hierarchy. In the first level are tables of observation of two or more related quantities. When from these it was possible to deduce an empirical or theoretical formula for the topic at hand, then the formula could be used to create tables of execution for the easier application. An early example of the latter is the range tables for firearms which first appear from the end of the fifteenth century. By the eighteenth century, representation of mathematical understanding of engineering design and natural phenomena in tabular and formulaic form began to be recorded in engineering texts, particularly by the French, the leading engineers of that era. Examples may be cited for bridges (Gautier 1716), earthworks and other constructions (Belidor 1729), structural mechanics (Girard 1789), and canals (Chezy 1750). In America one of the first engineering handbooks published was the *Brewers and Tanners Handbook* (1813). Early application of steam power was sheer empiricism, but in the mid nineteenth century the work of the Frenchman, Regnault, compiling data on the properties of steam, extended and improved by Thomson and Rankine in the UK, finally put this field on a sound basis with the necessary data in convenient tabulated form. In another field of great commercial importance, Bowditch, American self-taught mathematician and navigator, revised an earlier work by the Englishman Moore which he found fraught with errors in text, tables, and charts. He later, at age 29, produced *The New American Practical Navigator*, published in 1802. This work was a complete handbook of navigation and became an instant success as it was, in accuracy, pedagogy and style, the best in the English language. Bowditch continued to improve it through the 10 editions appearing during his lifetime, and it is in print even today as a publication of the US Hydrographic Office [12]!

DATA RECORDING AND DISSEMINATION

Recording Materials. A wide variety of materials have been used from early times for the recording of data: stone, wood, bone, ivory, silk, clay, papyrus, and parchment among others. These presented a variety of combinations of features such as ease of preparation, ease of recording, durability, convenience in handling and storing, cost, etc. An example of a cuneiform record, formed by indenting a wedge-shaped stylus on a clay tablet, is shown in Figure 7. Before this is dismissed as merely an interesting, curious, and cumbersome artifact, it is well to reflect on several facts. First, for over half the time that man has known how to write, clay was the predominant recording material! Secondly, cuneiform [13], one of the earliest means of preserving information in a written record, was adapted to at least fifteen different languages, and continued to be used actively for more than 3000 years, rivalled in this respect only by Chinese ideographs. Finally, the tablet of Figure 7, more than 4200 years old, is just as readable today as when it was incised. Will any of our present day laboratory notebooks and floppy disks match that record? It is very doubtful!

Wood and later stone structures as in Stonehenge and other megalithic works were arranged, not simply as monuments or ceremonial affairs, but to fix the orientation of the rising, setting, and conjunction of various heavenly bodies. A new computer analysis of an ancient Irish tomb (~3100 BC, more than 1000 years prior to Stonehenge) has shown it to be aligned with the mid-winter sunrise [14].

Two unusual recording devices may also be mentioned. The quipu of the Incas used knots in an assemblage of diversely colored cords, whose spatial relationships, type and position of knot and length of cord conveyed such information as census data, inventories, and military and work force rosters. The so-called stick charts of the early Polynesians, one of which is illustrated in Figure 8, are another remarkable record type [15]. Such charts are made from lengths of palm fiber, tied together with threads of coconut fiber to form an irregular lattice. Shells representing islands are tied to certain intersections. These charts are not to be looked upon as true scalar representations of the dispositions of islands scattered in the ocean, but

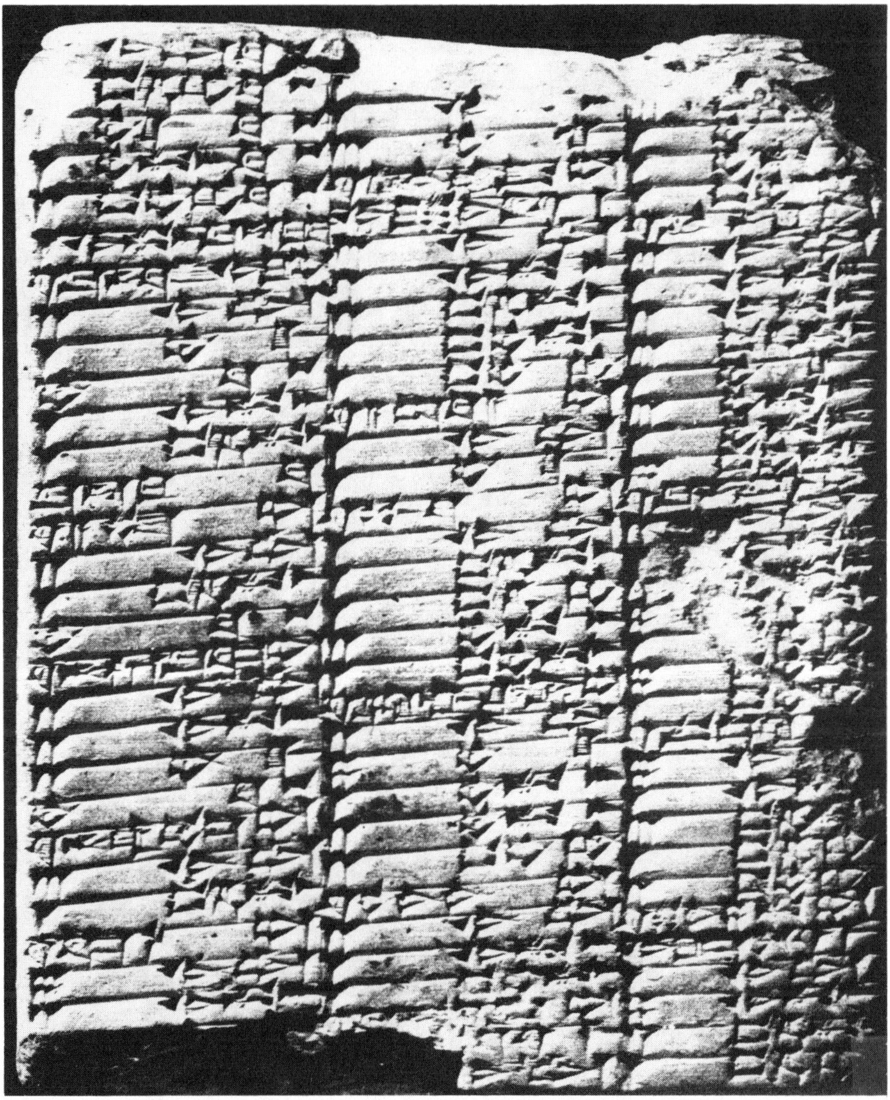

FIGURE 7
A clay tablet inscribed with cuneiform writing from ~2000 BC.

rather a record of the directions of prevailing wave crests and the refractions of these crests as affected by the presence of islands. Successful navigation across thousands of miles of open ocean was then achieved by using these "maps" to maintain an appropriate angle between the crest pattern and the axis of the boat.

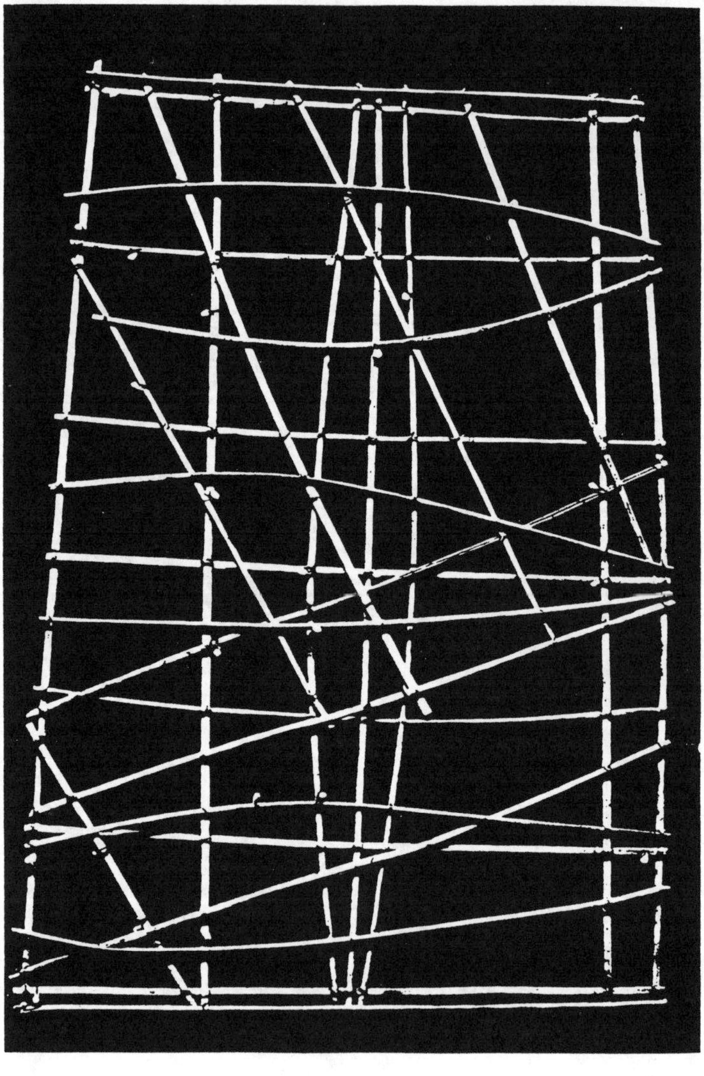

FIGURE 8
A stick chart used by the Marshall Islanders for oceanic navigation.

The two most common recording materials of the modern age, paper and magnetic particles, also have interesting histories*. The invention of paper is commonly ascribed to Tsai Lun, a eunuch in the service of the Emperor in the Eastern Han Dynasty in China about 105 AD. More recently, however, the date has been pushed back another 100-150 years to the Western Han Dynasty. The early Chinese papers were made from mulberry bark, hemp, and other vegetable fibers, and finally from linen rags. The Arabs learned of the Chinese invention of paper in the eighth century and brought it to the Western world where its manufacture commenced in Spain and Italy in the thirteenth century.

The idea of using magnetic particles to store information is much more recent, but far older than many people would credit [16]. A man named Oberlin Smith proposed the recording of electrical information by magnetized particles in a magazine article in 1888. The first reduction to practice of magnetic recording was by the Danish engineer, Poulsen, about the turn of the century, but his system, using a steel wire, was never widely adopted. The first version of the modern magnetic tape is based on the 1927 patent of J. A. O'Neill for his process of drying a liquid suspension of magnetic particles on the surface of a paper strip. Early applications of magnetic tape recording were for voice messages and music reproduction. In 1950 the US government bought the first magnetic recorder intended for capture of scientific data.

Printing [17]. Written communications before the advent of printing, whether political proclamations, religious works, technical recipe books, or compilations of scientific data, were few in number, expensive (because they had to be copied by hand by skilled people), readily lost or destroyed, and not widely circulated. All that was radically changed by the printing process. Indeed, Ziman [10] has remarked that "Modern science arose shortly after .... printing; ....this may have been no accident....the communication system needed in the scientific community could not have been provided by a less powerful technique."

The invention of printing is usually attributed to Johann Gutenberg in the mid-fifteenth century and is largely thought of in terms of the introduction

----

* Even a capsule history of photography would take us too far afield, but it is interesting to note that astronomical photographic records were being made (1850), less than twenty years following the achievement of the first true photograph by Niepce and Daguerre.

of a means of casting and assembling movable type. In fact, what Gutenberg did was to perfect an entire technological system: the type, the ink, the paper, and the press, each of which had to be specially developed and adapted for his purpose (see Figure 9). The result was no less than a revolution! The first dated book from Gutenberg's Mainz press came in 1457. Within 23 years there were presses in 100 towns, all across Europe; within 50 years eight million books had been printed!

FIGURE 9
A sixteenth century print shop showing the various operations: type-setting, proofing, inking plates, and printing.

Among the consequences of printing we may cite:

- freedom from copyist's errors
- increased availability of information
- preservative power (works once composed not readily lost to the world
- communication networks with feedback
- improved data compilation (better organized for storage and retrieval)
- accurate illustrations
- standardization of documents with respect to format, orthography, and spelling
- acceleration of the rate of intellectual developments

Some of the first printed works in the West of scientific interest [19] included:

1472 Aristotle's *Physics*
1473 Avicenna's *Canon of Medicine*
1474 Regiomontanus' *Ephermerides Astronomicae*
1477 Ptolemy's *Geographia*
1483 *Alphonsine Tables* (compiled by al-Zarkali (1029-87)
1483 Theophrastus' *De causis planatorum* and *De historia plantorum*
1485 Schoffer's *Hortus Sanitalis* (a pharmaceutical handbook)
1490-1598
over 600 (!) editions of Galen translated and printed
1491 von Megensberg's *Book of Nature*
1496 epitome of Ptolemy's *Almagest* from a twelfth century Arab edition

Notwithstanding the above, it has now become established that Gutenberg was in fact anticipated by the Chinese and Koreans by several hundred years. The Chinese had practiced printing and stamping on cloth and paper using carved wood blocks or engraved stone seals for centuries before the first extant block-printed book, the *Diamond Sutra*, appeared in 836 AD. The first printing of a book on a scientific subject came in the mid ninth century, the Hsuan Chieh Lu or *Mysterious Antidotorum*. It summarized the life and work of a famous alchemist, Lui Hung, and was published in an edition of several thousand copies! Needham [20] recognizes Pi Sheng, a Chinese chemical and metallurgical artisan as the inventor of movable type printing ~1045. Pi Sheng apparently worked with characters formed from clay, then baked and mounted in resin plates for printing. Still later, building on experience with woodblock printing imported from China, Koreans of the Koryo era (1230's) invented separately cast, movable *metal* type [21]. As with Gutenberg, they found that successful printing required special ink, special paper, and special means (bronze trays in this case) to hold the type aligned while printing. The first Korean book printed with movable type was a work of religious ritual. By the Yi dynasty, with many improvements in the printing process*, several astronomical books were printed during King Sejong's reign (1419-1450).

Computational Devices. Perhaps the earliest computational device known is that shown in Figure 10, the abacus**, whose origins are unclear. It had

---

* A task force of people assigned to this project were expert astronomical instrument makers.

** From the Hebrew *abaq* for dust.

three forms: a board covered with dust on which marks could be readily made; a board with loose stones* that could be arranged in rows of grooves corresponding to units, tens, hundreds, etc., and a frame in which counters could be strung on wires. The abacus was known to both the Greeks and Romans as well as the Chinese who may have learned of it from Roman merchants trading along the old silk road.

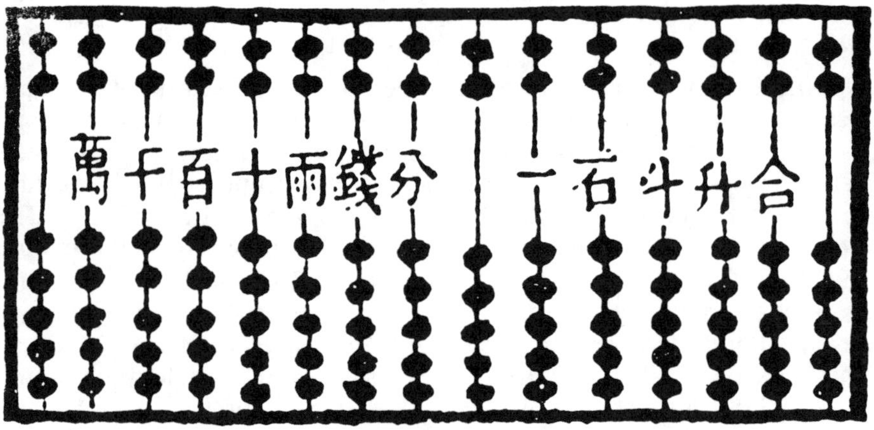

FIGURE 10

An early printed picture (China ca. 1590) of the abacus, the first mechanical calculator. The counters were moved along the wires toward the center of the rack (where the Chinese characters appear in the illustration) to form a number. The counters in the two upper tiers have the value of five; those in the lower tiers have the value of one. This particular abacus can represent number up to 1×10^{15}.

Following the discovery of stereographic projection on a plane (Appolonius, third century B.C.), it became possible to construct the famous astronomical instrument and calculator, the astrolabe, an example of which is shown in Figure 11. It consists of series of flat, engraved plates with a common mounting that represent the projection of the circles of the tropics, the

* The Latin *calculus* for stone led to calculate and to calculus.

ecliptic, etc., as well as the positions of the stars, on the plane of the equator. By utilizing a few simple sightings, rotation of the metal discs can therefore demonstrate, without calculation, the position of the sun among the stars, the hours of rising and setting of the sun and stars, the time, the meridian altitude of a star, etc., or conversely, from these data,the latitude of the observer could be computed. This Greek invention was perfected by the Arabs and introduced to Europe by Gerbert in the tenth century. A somewhat related invention is the antikythera mechanism, a Greek calendar computer of ~80 BC, researched by Price [22], which employed a very sophisticated train of gears (including a differential gear!) to give the correct mean periodic rotations of the sun, moon and five planets and displayed the calendrical results using pointer readings on a digital dial.

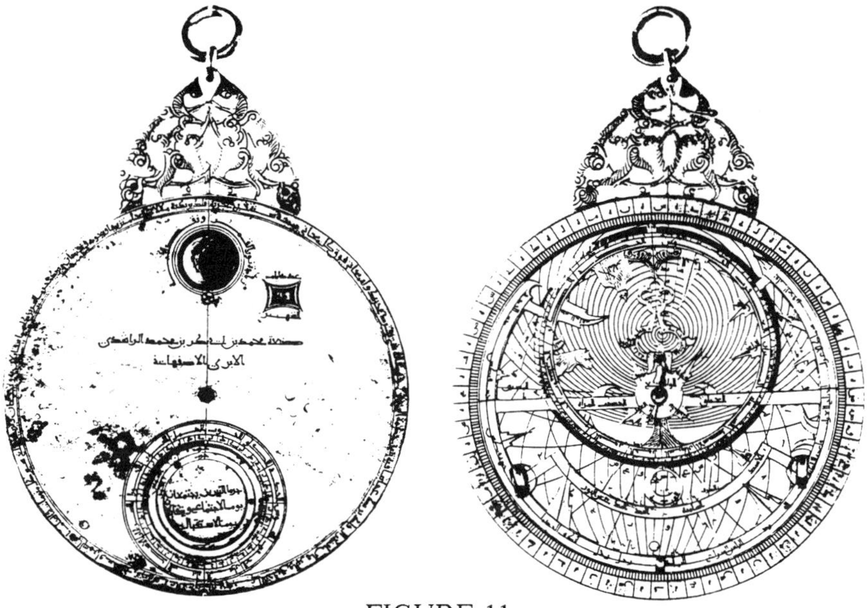

FIGURE 11
An Arabic astrolabe (back-left and front-right) used to convert star sightings to date and hour. Readings were obtained from windows in the discs as at left, or from the circumferential scales as at right.

A kind of mechanized abacus was devised by Blaise Pascal at age 19 in 1642 to help his father, a receiver of taxes, add up his accounts. The counters of the abacus were replaced by gear teeth and the fingers of the calculator with a mechanical clutch device (which he called a *sautoir*) for carrying forward tens, hundreds, etc., as they were built up during the operation of the machine. Leibniz' contribution in the years 1671-94 was the "stepped reckoner" which converted the simple adding machine to one which could multiply and divide.

Napier's invention of logarithms (1614) led to analog devices based on them: Grunter's "line of numbers" (1620) and Oughtred's rule (1621), and finally to the slide rule in the form we know, a graduated slide moving through a fixed stock containing other logarithmic scales, introduced by Robert Bissaker in 1645.

The origins of the modern computer go back to Jacquard, a French silk weaver, who in 1800 perfected an earlier idea of Vaucanson to automate the pattern-generating aspect of the weaving process by incorporating the necessary instructions on a series of punched cards. Charles Babbage, an Englishman, proposed a general purpose calculation device based on this principle which he called an "analytical engine." Babbage's machine was never built, but Herman Hollerith, an engineer attached to the health statistics division of the U.S. census, designed one based on punched cards and used it to complete the 1890 census at twice the speed of the previous decennial census and at a considerable saving in money (see Figure 12). Other extensions of the mechanized analog calculator included Vanevar Bush's 1925 Differential Analyzer and Aiken's Harvard Mark I computer, later commercialized by IBM as the Automatic Sequence Controlled Calculator of 1944, still using Jacquard's punched cards. Electronic calculators, based on binary arithmetic going back to Leibniz, began to be conceived and developed in the 1930's and 1940's for specialized applications by such men as Wynn-Williams in England, Couffignal in France, and Atanasoff in the U.S. The first general purpose electronic computer was the U.S. Army's ENIAC (Electronic Numerical Integrator and Computer), built in 1946 by Eckert and Mauchly at the University of Pennsylvania. In 1960 the first tables using an electronic computer for calculation were compiled for the properties of steam at the National Engineering Laboratory at Glasgow.

CONCLUDING COMMENTS

This brief essay has attempted to outline a general history of data recording, analysis, and dissemination, and, in so doing, to inspire others in the CODATA community to dig more deeply into the foundations of their individual fields. It is hoped that the review has also been informative in illustrating four general observations:

- **that the ancients had exactly the same motivations and goals for their data activities as we do today**

(They would fully understand and support our space program and the project for the mapping of the human genome, although they would be astounded by our technological and computational capabilities.)

- **that significant contributions in data recording and handling have been made by many different peoples of the world, widely separated in time and space**

(an interesting example of bi-national collaboration [23] using data from over 700 years of records is illustrated in Figure 13.)

- **that new technology, both for data recording and for calculation, has had a tremendous impact in the data field.**

(For recording materials, reflect on the consequences of the transition from clay to paper, from manuscript to print, from print to magnetic tape and disks; the next transition 3-d optical storage [24] may be expected to have an equally great effect.) For calculational devices, only 2000 years separate the abacus from today's supercomputer, yet consider the difference in the speed and complexity of the calculations that can be performed and the volume of data handled*.

- **that in any field of science, new insights,even on old topics or phenomena,can be revealed by:**

  - **more data**
  - **better data**
  - **improved analysis**
  - **longer time frame**

(As a final example, both of the value of ancient records per se and of the extended time frame, Pang et al. [26] have used computer analysis of Chinese records of time and place of sunrise eclipses dating back to 1876 BC to determine that the Earth's rotation rate (the length of the day) was then 70 milliseconds shorter than now!)

---

* Oryx Energy Co. [25] estimates that in petroleum prospecting a 3-d seismic survey of a three square-mile block in the Gulf of Mexico involves 134×10^9 pieces of data, requiring three months of supercomputer time to digest.

FIGURE 12
The machine devised by Herman Hollerith using punched cards to compile data for the 1890 U.S. federal census.

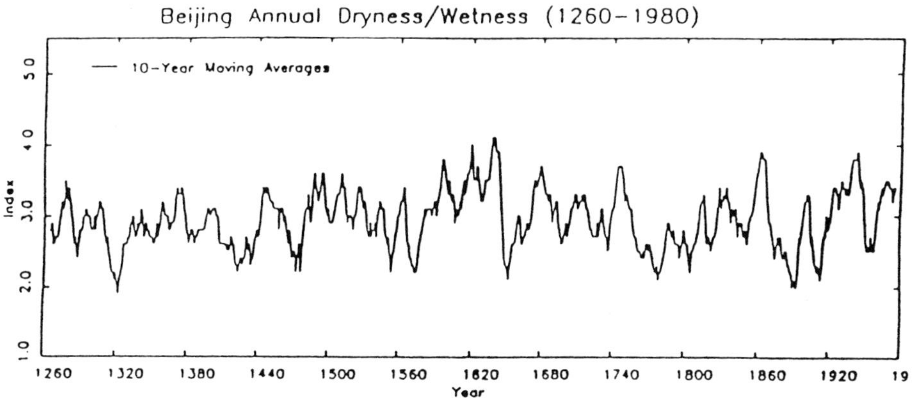

FIGURE 13
A 700 year time series for annual precipitation compiled by combining instrumental data for the past century with proxy historical records dating back to the 13th century. Analogous plots have been prepared of July mean temperature and the Fall harvest.

REFERENCES

[1] Marshak, A., *The Roots of Civilization: The Cognitive Beginnings of Man's First Art, Symbol, and Notation,* McGraw-Hill, New York (1972).

[2] Delmonte, J., *Origins of Materials and Processes,* Technomic Publishing Co., Lancaster, PA (1985) 388 pp.

[3] Nasr, S.H., *Islamic Science: An Illustrated Study,* World of Islam Festival Publ. Co. (1976) 273 pp.

[4] Funkhouser, H.G., "A Note on a Tenth Century Graph," *Osiris* **1** (1936) 260-262.

[5] Tilling, L., "Early Experimental Graphs," *British J. History of Science,* **8** (1975) 192-213.

[6] Brown, L.A., *The Story of Maps,* Bonanza Books, New York (1949) p. 5.

[7] de Santillana, G. and von Dechend, H., *Hamlet's Mill,* Gambit Press, Boston (1968).

[8] Riddle, J.M., *Dioscorides on Pharmacy and Medicine*, U. Texas Press (1985) 298 pp.

[9] Brown, L.A. *op. cit.* p. 74.

[10] Newton, R.R., *The Crime of Claudius Ptolemy*, Johns Hopkins U. Press, (1977) 411 pp.

[11] Koeman, C., *The History of Abraham Ortelius and his Theatrum Orbis Terrarum*, Sequoia, Lausanne, (1964) 64 pp.
[12] Struik, D.J., *Yankee Science in the Making,* Little, Brown and Co., Boston (1948) p. 72.
[13] Walker, C.B.F., *Reading the Past: Cuneiform*, U. Calif. Press/British Museum, (1987) 64 pp.
[14] Ray, T.P., "The Winter Solstice Phenomenon at New Grange, Ireland: Accident or Design?," *Nature,* **337** (1989) 343-5.
[15] Davenport, W., *Marshall Islands Navigational Charts*, Imago Mundi, **15** (1960) 19-26.
[16] Anderson, K.J., "Magnetic Recording Materials," *Materials Research Society Bulletin* (March 1990) 88-89.
[17] Eisenstein, E., *The Printing Press as an Agent of Change*, Cambridge University Press (1980) 852 pp.
[18] Ziman, J.M., *Public Knowledge: An Essay Concerning the Social Dimension of Science*, Cambridge University Press (1968).
[19] Klebs, A.C., "Incunabula scientifica et medica," *Osiris*, 4 (1938), 1-359.
[20] Needham, J., *Science and Civilization in China*, vol. V, Part 3, p. 187. Cambridge University Press (1976).
[21] Jeon, S-w., *Science and Technology in Korea: Traditional Instruments and Techniques*, MIT Press, Cambridge, MA (1974) 383 pp.
[22] Price, D. deS., "Gears from the Greeks: The Antikythera Mechanism, A Calendar Computer from ca. 80 BC," *Trans. Amer. Phil. Soc.*, New Series 64, part 7 (1974) 70 pp.
[23] Koomanoff, F.A., Ye Duzheng, Zhao Jianping, Riches, M.R., Wang, W-C, and Tao Shiyan, "The United States Department of Energy and the People's Republic of China's Chinese Academy of Sciences Joint Research on the Greenhouse Effect," *Bull. Amer. Meteorological Soc.* 69 (1988) 1301.
[24] Parthenopoulos, D.A. and Rentzepis, P.M., "Three-Dimensional Optical Storage Memory," *Science* 245 (1989) 843-45.
[25] Dubashi, J., "Images and Imaginations," *Financial World* (24 July 1990) 58.
[26] Pang, K.D., Yau, K., Chou, H-H, and Wolff, R., "Computer Analysis of Some Ancient Chinese Sunrise Eclipse Records to Determine the Earth's Rotation Rate," *Vistas in Astronomy*, 31 (1988) 833-847.

TABLE I. Significant Events in Data Recording and Compilation

ASTRONOMY

Era	Event
25-30 000 BC	tallies of lunar records made in Europe
4228 BC	Egyptian calendar of 365 days, oldest fixed date known
1876 BC	Chinese record of a solar eclipse
1800-1750 BC	star catalog and planetary records in Babylonia under Hammurabi
1450-1400 BC	Stonehenge in England
600 BC	Thales of Miletus (now Turkey) predicts a solar eclipse
150 BC	Hipparchos of Rhodes creates star catalog of > 1000 stars
150 AD	Ptolemy in Alexandria writes *Megale syntaxis mathematike,* called by the Arabs the *Almagest*
300-309 AD	Chen Zhuo combines star maps of: Shih Shen Gan De 300 to 291 BC Wu Xien
28BC-1638 AD	continuous records of sunspots by Chinese
1007	ibn Yunis of Cairo, Hakemite tables, compilation of 200 years of stellar observations
1029-1087	al Zarkali, of Spain, edits *Toledan Zij* (tables of planetary and stellar positions)
1247	Suzhou planisphere stelae, 1500 stars
1394-1449	Ulugh Beg, grandson of Tamerlane, Mongol ruler and astronomer in Samarkand, compiles first substantial star catalog since Ptolemy
1515	Albrecht Durer's woodcut planispheres published in Nuremberg, the first printed, astronomical maps in the West
1588	G.P. Galuci in Italy produces *Theatrum Mundi et Temporis,* the first printed star atlas with coordinates
1627	Rudolphine tables by Kepler, more accurate than any before because based on T. Brahe's meticulous observations and Kepler's theory

TABLE II. Significant Events in Data Recording and Compilation

LIFE SCIENCES

Era (Century)	Event
2200 BC	Sumerian Science of Lists, *e.g.,* zoology, botany
17th BC	Egyptian Smith papyrus • surgery and external medicine • oldest scientific document
4th BC	Greek classifications of living things • Aristotle (animals) • Theophrastus (plants)
1st AD	Chinese Pharmacopoeia • 300 plants • 36 minerals
40-49 AD	Dioscorides' *Materia Medica* • 600 plants • 1000 drugs
180-190 AD	Galen's compilation of all medical knowledge
6th	*Yogasataka*, Indian medical compendium, still consulted today in Sri Lanka
800	Rhazes' *Liber continens,* medical encyclopedia
1000-1009	Avicenna's *Canon of Medicine* in 5 vols.
1135-1204	Maimonides' *Discourse on Poisons and Antidotes....,* 1800 drugs
1410-1419	Rinio's *Liber de simplicibus* describes and illustrates 400 plants with medicinal uses
1543	Vesalius, *De Humani Corporis Fabrica*
1596	Li Shi-Chen's *Great Pharmacopoeia*, (Pen Tshao Kang Mu)* 1074 plants 443 animals and >8000 medical uses for them 217 minerals
1735	Linnaeus' *System of Nature*

* This and other Chinese records of medicinal plants, going back 3000 years, are being entered into a computerized database (See Item 3P-2, Scientific Program and Abstracts for 12th Int'l CODATA Conference, Columbus, Ohio, 1990.)

TABLE III. Significant Events in Data Recording and Compilation

GEOGRAPHY

Era (Century)	Event
20-10 000 BC	first known map on bone, Mezherich, USSR
3800 BC	oldest known map from civilized world (Babylonia)
500 BC	Babylonian world map
227 BC	Chinese maps drawn on silk
20-39 AD	Strabo's 8 vol. *Geography*
100 AD	Chang Heng, Chinese astronomer, introduces the square grip to mapping used to indicate scale, as a referencing system, or to alter scale
150 AD	Ptolemy's Geographia
6th	Li Tao-Yuan's *Shui Ching Chu,* a description and mapping of >1000 Chinese rivers
11th	al Biruni, Persian mathematician and physicist, *Determination of the Coordinates of Cities*
1155	first printed map in China
12th	al-Idrisi, Arab at court of Roger II of Sicily, foremost geographer of Middle Ages
13th	portolanos or pelagic sailing charts which require an accompanying data book of distances and compass bearings
1459	Fra Mauro's World Map, 6 feet in diameter, incorporates both facts (Marco Polo's travel reports) and speculation (kingdom of Prester John)
1570	A. Ortelius, first modern atlas
thematic or data maps	
1585	Teixeira - isarithms of magnetic declination
1688	Halley - trade winds
1817	von Humboldt - isotherms
1820	Brandes - synoptic maps of meterological data

TABLE IV. Significant Events in Data Recording and Compilation

TECHNOLOGY

Era (Century)	Event
17th BC	Assyrian tablets on glass-making
15th BC	Chinese bone inscriptions on brewing of beer
7th BC	library of Asur-bani-pal of Assyria tables of formulae for making solders, pigments, glasses, and alloys
180-189 AD	Egyptian alchemical writings
8th	Lucca manuscript, *Compositions variae*
8th	*Dan Jing Nei Fu Liuhuang Fa,* by Sun Simiao (formula for gunpowder)
9th	*Mappae Clavicula** (a little key to the world of medieval techniques)
1110-1140	Theophilus, *On Diverse Arts** by Roger of Helmarshausen
	Hieronymus Brunschwygk
1500	*Small Book* (distillation and
1512	*Big Book* chemical practice)
1520	*Probierbuchlein** (little book of assays)
1540	V. Biringuccio, *De la pirotechnica,**
1540	Rosetti, *Plictho de L'arte de Tentore** (on dyeing)
1556	G. Agricola's *De Re Metallica** on mining, mineralogy, and metallurgy. A how-to-do-it book in the finest tradition, supported with many illustrations
1550	Piccolpasso, *Three Books of the Potter's Art*
1580	B. Palissy, handbook for making glazed pottery
1612	Neri, handbook of glass-making

* modern translations of these works, together with annotations and commentary, have recently been published.

SOURCES FOR ILLUSTRATIONS

Figure 1 Marshack, Ref. [1]
Figure 2 Delmonte, Ref. [2]
Figure 3 Tufte, E.R., *The Visual Display of Quantitative Information*, Graphic Press, Cheshire, C5T (1983), p. 28.
Figure 4 Burke, J., *The Day the Universe Changed*, Little, Brown and Co. (1985), p. 43.
Figure 5 from the author's personal collection
Figure 6 Tufte, *op. cit.*, p. 23.
Figure 7 Posner, E., *Archives in the Ancient World*, Harvard University Press, Cambridge, MA (1972), p. 17.
Figure 8 Bagrow, L., *History of Cartography*, R.A. Skelton, (ed), Harvard University Press, Cambridge, MA (1966), Plate IV.
Figure 9 Burke, J. *op. cit.*, p. 105.
Figure 10 de Bono, E. (ed), *Eureka! - An Illustrated History of Inventions from the Wheel to the Computer*, Holt, Rinehart, and Winston, New York (1974), p. 204.
Figure 11 Burke, J. *op. cit.*, p. 37.
Figure 12 Burke, J. *op. cit.*, p. 113.
Figure 13 Koomanoff, F.A. *et al.*, Ref. [23].

GENERAL BIBLIOGRAPHY

Bagrow, L., *History of Cartography,* R. A. Skelton, (ed.), Harvard University Press, Cambridge, MA (1966), 312 pp.

Bernal, J. D., *Science in History,* 4 vols., C. A. Walls & Co., London (1969), 1330 pp.

Cipolla, C. M. and Birdsall, D., *The Technology of Man - A Visual History,* Holt, Rinehart, and Winston, New York (1980).

Clagett, M., *History of Science,* U. Wisconsin Press, Milwaukee, WI (1969).

Daumas, M. (ed.), *A History of Technology and Invention,* 2 vols., Crown Publishers, New York (1969).

Forbes, R. J., *A History of Science and Technology,* Penguin Books, Baltimore, MD (1963).

Gille, B., *The History of Techniques,* 2 vols., Gordon and Breach, Montreux, Switzerland (1986), 1410 pp.

Hellemans, A. and Bunch, B., *The Timetables of Science,* Simon and Schuster, New York (1988), 656 pp.

Kranzberg, M. and Pursell, C. W. (eds.), *Technology in Western Civilization,* vol. 1, Oxford U. Press (1967).

Mason, S. M., *A History of Science,* Collier Books, New York (1962), 638 pp.

Michel, H., *Scientific Instruments in Art and History,* Viking Press, New York (1967), 208 pp.

Nasr, S. H., *Science and Civilization in Islam,* New American Library, New York (1970).

Needham, J. W. (ed.), *Science and Civilization in China,* vols. 1-6, Cambridge University Press (1954-70).

Neugebauer, O., *The Exact Sciences in Antiquity,* Dover, New York (1969).

Ronan, C., *Lost Discoveries,* Weathervane Books, New York (1976), 125 pp.

Sarton, G., *Introduction to the History of Science,* 3 vols., Williams and Winston, Baltimore, MD (1927-48).

Sarton, G., *A History of Science:* vol. 1, *Ancient Science in the Gold Age of Greece* (1952), 646 pp; vol. 2, *Hellenistic Science and Culture in the Last Three Centuries BC* (1959), 554 pp., W. W. Norton, New York.

Semler, E. G., *Engineering Heritage,* 2 vols., Heinmann Educational Books, Ltd., London (1966).

Singer, C., Holmyard, E. J., and Hall, A. R., *A History of Technology,* 5 vols., Oxford University press (1954-58).

Taton, R. (ed.), *History of Science,* 4 vols., Basic Books, New York (1963).

Wallis, H. M. and Robinson, A. H. (eds), *Cartographical Innovations,* Map Collectors Publications, London (1987), 353 pp.

PERSPECTIVES ON CODATA

Edgar F. Westrum, Jr.
(Former Secretary General of CODATA)
University of Michigan
Ann Arbor, Michigan USA

INTRODUCTION

We have learned from Jack Westbrook's interesting historical presentation of data over the centuries that data has been with us for a long time.

But an organization to cope with data problems is one of much more recent origin less than 25 years old. Launched under ICSU (International Council of Scientific Unions) at the Bombay, India, ICSU General Assembly in 1966 with much help by USA's Professor Harrison Brown, it took root with the collaboration of Professor F. D. Rossini and Dr. Guy Waddington, and soon grew into a healthy flourishing young Scientific Committee of ICSU and began at once to make waves. (Guy Waddington by the way is, to the best of my knowledge, the only individual to be made a co-opted member of CODATA. That should give you a firm impression of the great respect people had for his contributions.)

In its formative years, it was concerned only about data in the core sciences physics and chemistry. After the LeCreusot (1972) General Assembly its charter was broadened to cover many other sciences and its scope gradually broadened to include many other scientific disciplines. In particular, the expansion involved the geological and biological sciences and thus space and time dependent data as well as observational data that could not be repeated as in laboratory experiments. With the increased endeavor its representation by Union and National scientists expanded to cope with its now broadened mission.

As a rough estimate. CODATA has had about 5MS income since its inception. This has gone mainly into payment of two or three staff salaries and the travel and lodging expenses of carefully selected small Task Groups of scientists to achieve defined objectives. The initiatory Headquarter's Office was under the direction of Dr. Guy Waddington as Director. The international office for CODATA was subsequently moved to Frankfort, F.R.G. (1968) as the Central Office and later to the Hotel Noaille (together with ICSU) in Paris (1973) as the CODATA Secretariat which is still very functional today. The Executive Secretary, Mme. Phyllis Glaeser, has served CODATA since the Secretariat has been in Paris.

But the scientific talent and time contributed by the officers, the General Assembly, the Executive Committees, and the Task Group and Commission members is a priceless asset and the secret of CODATA's impact.

But what has CODATA done over this period? "Is the game really worth the candle?"

It's a fair question and it deserves a reasoned response. So, let me try to give at least a partial response (as there are severe constraints on time) at this session.

CODATA'S SCIENTIFIC ENDEAVORS

CODATA's scientific clout is largely in its Task Groups. To get a better appreciation of the work of CODATA we need to look more closely at some of the Task Groups in the following array.

CODATA'S TASK GROUPS

Task Groups

Fundamental Constants
Chemical Thermodynamic Tables
Geothermodynamic Data
Multisatellite Thematic Mapping
Computer Graphics and Artificial Intelligence

Biological Task Groups

Biological Macromolecules
Hybridoma Data Bank
Microbial Strain Data Network
Systematic Nomenclature for Foods in Numerical Data Banks
Protein Sequence Database

Other Task Groups

CODATA Referral Database
Critically Evaluated Phase Equilibrium Data
Data Sources in East-Asian Countries
Materials Database Management

A few terse comments may help to put them in perspective even though many titles are rather self-explanatory. The Fundamental Constants Task Group periodically (typically six to eight years) makes assessments of the magnitude and reliability of values of important physical science values. These are now disseminated by many standardizing laboratories around the world in preference to determining their own values.

The Chemical Thermodynamics Table group has devised procedures for creating compilations of thermochemical and thermophysical quantities and developed procedures to establish catalogs of literature data and the computer procedures to permit crtical evaluation and the eventual updating of the tables. In addition, a hard bound volume of the carefully established "Key Values of Thermodynamic Data" which are intended to serve without modification for periods of about a decade. These constitute 298.15 K entropies and enthalpies of individual substances. In addition a sample prototype table was prepared for calcium compounds, alloys, and solutions. Complimentary copies (ca. 250) enabled the solicitation of comments and approval on the proposed establishment of formats and presentations to ensure their maximum utility for the scientific community. But the book is proving to be a beste seller in its own right. Soon it will be joined by a similar volume emphasizing the main values for iron compounds.

The Geothermodynamic Data tables are similar but they encompass larger ranges of pressures and temperatures, as well as emphasis on solid solutions and molten magmas, etc.

The CODATA Referral Database is a bibliographic database on fields selected for their importance to developing countries. The database is continually being increased in magnitude, in the number of records as well as simply keeping it current.

A very active group is the Materials Database Management Task Group. Their concern is primarily with industrially important data.

CODATA Commissions (two are noted below) are concerned with generic problems or in the supervision of Task Groups in certain areas.

The CODATA Working Groups are appointed by the Executive Committee on an interim basis. Their ultimate establishment as a Task Group is provided in cases of need for additional activity by the subsequent General Assembly.

Codata Commissions

Commission on Industrial Data
Commission on Terminology and Nomenclature in Biology

CODATA WORKING GROUPS

One of the earliest Task Groups (actually the second one), founded in 1968 in Washington, D.C., by Professor M. Kotani was entitled Accessibility and Dissemination of Data (ADD). This Task Group provided the impetus for much of CODATA's work in the first sixteen years of its existence (1968--1984).

Many training courses on data handling were offered in this era. Some were quite modest and elementary in dealing with data handling; others were highly specialized.

In the United States and elsewhere courses in the statistical treatment of data were promulgated. Their absence today unfortunately does not permit the assumption that there is no longer a need for such education.

Not all of CODATA endeavors have been a roaring success. Establishment of a World Data Referral Center in 1985 was abandoned by the Executive Committee about half of them argued that the time for such an endeavor had expired while the other half argued that the time was not yet ripe for such an endeavor.

Dramatic successes, however, were:

- Training Courses on Data, Tsukuba Science City, Japan, in 1980
- Symposium on Man-Machine Communication for Scientific Data Freiburg, F.R.G. Handling, Freiburg, F.R.G., July 1973
- Task Group on Computer Use (Computer Handling Data), 1967-1984

The above Symposium under the Chairmanship of Dr. Norman Jones was noteworthy for bringing together a diverse collection of computer experts and for the success of devising a special booklet to facilitate getting the large group of participants well acquainted with each other in so short a time.

The Symposium was under the auspices of the Computer Use Task Group, the very first of CODATA's Task Groups to get under way.

Despite the importance of the digital computer for data management, for about the next four years, CODATA did not have a Task Group dealing specifically with computer applications.

Nonetheless, since its creation almost 25 years ago, CODATA has carried out a program to improve the quality, reliability, and accessibility of numerical data in all fields of science and technology. Much of this endeavor has centered on the use of computer technology for the storage, management, and dissemination of scientific data. Thus CODATA has promoted the use of common formats and interchange standards for all groups compiling certain specific types of data. In other cases CODATA has served as an umbrella to allow organizations in different countries to pool their data in a central data bank. More generally, CODATA has endeavored to spread information about new and useful data management techniques to scientists in all disciplines and all countries.

The dynamic nature of science and technology leads to changes in both the demands for data management and the techniques available for meeting these demands. Some of these changes result from the sheer amount of data which must be managed in programs such as mapping the human genome or monitoring environmental changes with remote sensing satellites. Other problems are presented by the need to integrate data of many different types in attacking such challenges as global warming. Finally, as data become more voluminous and more complex, we face a major task in representing the data in graphical and other forms which can be grasped by the human mind.

Recognizing this new set of challenges, CODATA has established a Task Group on Artificial Intelligence and Computer Graphics (AIGRA) under the Chairmanship of Prof. J. E. Dubois. This group is charged with exploring new global handling and interpretation of data as knowledge potential tools in conjunction with the use of new techniques currently being developed in computer science that may help to solve these data management problems faced by scientists and engineers. Their initial endeavor in 1989, a workshop on "New Perspectives in Scientific Complex Data Managaement," will appear later in 1990 as CODATA Bulletin 22-(4).

CODATA'S INTERNATIONAL CONFERENCES

Another aspect of CODATA's impact on data is through the biennial

CODATA International Conferences. These have provided a multi-disciplinary forum at which scientists from many disciplines could meet and profit by data developments in other branches of science.

Codata International Conferences

1968	Arnoldshain, F.R.G.
1970	St. Andrews (Scotland), U.K.
1972	LeCreusot, France
1974	Tsakhcadsor, U.S.S.R.
1976	Boulder (CO), U.S.A.
1978	Santa Flavia, Italy
1980	Kyoto, Japan
1982	Jachranka, Poland
1984	Jerusalem, Israel
1986	Ottawa, Canada
1988	Karlsruhe, F.R.G.
1990	Columbus (OH), U.S.A.
1992	[Beijing, China]

CODATA PUBLICATIONS

Since a limited number of people can participate in the Symposia, the Conference, and the International CODATA Conferences, the publication of Newsletters, brochures, Special Reports, Bulletins, and Conference Proceedings is important to provide access to the developments made by CODATA by a wider audience. Such communication is as important even within the CODATA family as it is for other scientists.

INFORMATION TECHNOLOGY

CODATA provides a focus and a forum for information specialists and those either full time or part time dedicated to critical evaluation and data handling. Recent comments like that of R. L. Scheier are relevant:

> *...Information technology isn't a war-horse that can be ridden to glory...."It's just a tool and an increasingly common and inexpensive one at that. The real power comes from the way people analyze information, make decisions and work together to produce products. That's the war-horse information systems specialists should be learning to ride."*

Robert L. Scheier
Editorial, PC Week

ADMINISTRATIVE STRUCTURE

Because so many of you are here for the first time in a CODATA Conference/meeting, a brief comment on the administrative structure of CODATA may be in order. There are essentially four types of CODATA Membership:

Codata Membership

•National Members
•Union Members
•Co-opted Members
- -
•Supporting Organizations

At the outset there were 6 National and 10 Union Members. Now there are 20 of each representing a tripling and doubling of numbers. Today there are about 5 organizations (largely ICSU bodies) as Co-opted Members and about 27 Supporting Members.

CODATA does not have individual members.

Administrative Structure

General Assembly: Delegates, Officers, and Guests
Executive Committee: Officers and Members
Secretariat: Staff

The General Assembly is CODATA's prime governing body and involves about 50-60 participants. It meets usually in conjunction with the CODATA Conference. The Executive Committee about a dozen scientists provides interim decision making, and the Officers and postal ballots provide a final tier of action between the General Assemblies.

CONCLUDING SCIENTIFIC POSTSCRIPT

CODATA has provided a very cost effective development in information technology and in the management and handling of data. Not only has it provided a forum for discussions of data problems but it has prepared a record of the rapidly changing state of the art and, in particular, the increasing role of the computer in data management. For a more detailed summary consult the classified lists of CODATA Bulletins (about 82), increasing at the rate of 4 (ca. 500 pages per annum); of Newsletters (about 54); of Proceedings (about 12); of Books and Monographs (about 14), as well as brochures, and journal articles in the literature.

CODATA PERSPECTIVES FOR THE 1990'S

David R. Lide
Immediate Past-President of CODATA
Office of Standard Reference Data
National Institute of Standards and Technology
P.O. Box 3752
Gaithersburg, MD 20885, U.S.A.

CODATA was started in 1966 by several far-sighted scientists who recognized that the management of scientific data could no longer be left to the *ad hoc* efforts of a few dedicated individuals. At that time it was evident that the rapid expansion of scientific research which had occurred since the end of World War II was leading to a corresponding expansion in the amount of data generated. Not only were there more scientists doing research, but new automated instrumentation made it possible for a single individual to produce data at a far higher rate than had hitherto been possible. If this investment in research was to be fully utilized, better mechanisms were needed to evaluate, store, retrieve, and disseminate the data. Organizations were, in fact, being established to carry out these functions, and an international umbrella which would encourage and coordinate such efforts seemed desirable. This was the driving force for creating CODATA.

Now, 24 years later, the rate of generation of scientific data has reached a level much higher than the founders of CODATA probably anticipated. But more than that, it is unlikely that the first leaders of CODATA ever envisioned the great ethical and legal debates which would arise over data - debates over which scientists should be given access to basic data, law suits against professional societies, and concern that distribution of biomedical data might infringe the rights of individuals. The world has certainly changed.

Although it was created by ICSU as a multidisciplinary scientific committee, the initial focus of CODATA was clearly on the physical sciences. This is not surprising, considering that the founders were all physicists, chemists, and engineers. At the first CODATA Conference, held in Germany in 1968, the program dealt exclusively with physical and chemical data. Of the 94 attendees, there were two geologists and one biologist. Even in 1976, when the CODATA Conference was held in Boulder, Colorado, there were 10 sessions devoted to physics, chemistry, and engineering and only three each to the biosciences and geosciences. The program committee for the 1976 conference, had one astronomer and one biologist to represent areas outside the physical sciences.

The 1990 Conference is much more evenly balanced from a disciplinary standpoint. Furthermore, with its strong emphasis on data aspects of global change and several sessions dealing with generic techniques relevant to all types of scientific data, the conference program demonstrates that CODATA has progressed toward the goal of addressing the full range of disciplinary concerns of ICSU.

So where should CODATA be heading in the 1990's? My thoughts are purely personal, but I throw them out for whatever use they may be for those who will lead CODATA in the next decade.

First, I feel CODATA should continue the types of activities which have been productive up to now. This includes, in particular, projects aimed at coordinating the work of groups in different countries which are building databases of a specific kind. We have made a real impact through coordinating multinational efforts in fields such as thermodynamic properties, protein sequence databases, and fundamental physical constants. Other areas will undoubtably appear where data centers or institutes express a need for an international umbrella organization which will help to avoid duplication of effort and develop standards to promote compatibility and exchange of data. CODATA should be alert to such needs and should be prepared to accept a leadership role.

The educational role of CODATA has been recognized from the beginning. A large number of workshops and tutorial publications have helped promulgate new techniques for data handling and analysis which are applicable to different scientific disciplines. My personal view is that CODATA should do more in this area. It is questionable whether CODATA can really influence research at the cutting edge of information technology. Our resources are small, and there are many other driving forces which are much more powerful. However, CODATA can certainly help to spread the results of such research to working scientists who must deal with large amounts of data in their own fields. A number of papers at this conference have emphasized that the advances in computer technology in the 1990's promise to be even greater than the changes we saw in the 1980's. When advances occur at such a rapid rate, it is not easy for the average scientist to keep up with them, or even to recognize which ones might be useful to him. Computer scientists, like other professionals, develop their own jargon which is often hard for the rest of us to fathom. CODATA can perform a real service by interpreting these advances in information technology so that biologists, chemists, physicists, and geoscientists can capitalize on them. Several mechanisms for achieving this suggest themselves, such as monographs on data management, review articles in disciplinary journals, and joint workshops with ICSU Unions or other disciplinary bodies. We have used these mechanisms in the past, but much more can be done.

There is another area where CODATA has done very little but where I feel it should be able to serve a useful role. This is the area of ethical, legal, and policy issues. When we held our strategic planning meeting at La Gaillarde in 1983, I do not recall this topic coming up in the discussion. Today, it is hard to escape it, and we even find the subject covered in the popular press. Proposed databases in the biological and social sciences raise ethical issues which are hotly debated. Both legal and ethical issues arise regarding access to data when proprietary commercial concerns are involved. And the protection of intellectual property in an age where one command on the computer can copy megabytes of data in a few seconds is a very sensitive issue. I believe these questions are much too important to be left to the lawyers and politicians, who tend to be abysmally ignorant of the way scientific information exchange really works. CODATA can do an important service to science by helping to clarify these complex and sensitive issues.

Finally, it is clear that the International Geosphere-Biosphere Program will be a top priority in the 1990's. Going beyond the ICSU, global change is becoming a crucial political issue throughout the world. I hardly need to belabor the point that data management will receive much attention in these programs. The problem for CODATA is to define a clear role for itself in the IGBP. The Officers and Executive Committee have spent many hours discussing this subject over the last four years, and I feel some frustration over the fact that we have not yet been able to focus on the proper CODATA role. However, the sessions on global change at this Conference have been extremely helpful, and I feel we are making progress. If I had to list the one topic which is most crucial to CODATA in the 1990's, it would be our role in data aspects of the global change program.

In conclusion, we see that CODATA has undergone significant changes since its founding 24 years ago. Some of the functions envisioned by its early leaders no longer seem so important. However, new challenges have arisen which vindicate their judgement that ICSU should have a standing committee to deal with data questions spanning all scientific disciplines. To paraphrase Voltaire, if CODATA did not exist today, we would have to invent it. I see many challenges and opportunities in the 1990's and I am confident that CODATA will meet them.

PERSPECTIVES AND FUTURE DIRECTIONS FROM CODATA '90

Margaret E. Courain, Ph.D.
Rutgers University
New Brunswick, NJ, U.S.A.

INTRODUCTION

The idea for the final CODATA '90 session came from the Scientific Program Committee meeting in Paris in February 1989. Edgar Westrum and Phyllis Glaeser were recounting the achievements of CODATA from its founding in 1966. They were most impressive. The enthusiasm of that meeting endured the passage of time and evolved into a session in which Jack Westbrook took a retrospective look at the history of data recording, analysis, and dissemination before CODATA. Edgar Westrum provided a factual perspective on the role that CODATA has played in the past 25 years as an organization set up by ICSU to address the global data problems of science and technology.

I presented the final paper as Scientific Program Chairman seeking to find Future Directions from CODATA '90 in a picture story of the conference and the balanced perspective which was contributed by the entire Scientific Program Committee as they commented on the six themes of the conference: Prediction of Global Change, Spatial Databases, Materials Data Systems, Expert Systems and Other Knowledge Tools, Trends in Integration of Information Across Biology, and Impact of New Technology on Data Handling.

PERSPECTIVE ON CODATA '90 FROM THE PROGRAM CHAIRMAN'S CHAIR

CODATA is a reflection of our world. Since 1988, it has opened up dramatically. New bridges between countries and disciplines have been built.

CODATA is now a critical catalyst not only for physical and chemical *reactions*, but scientific and technological *interactions*.

The plans of CODATA '88 have become the large database demonstrations of CODATA '90.

Speed of Progress: An initiative started at the last international CODATA Conference in Karlsruhe has accomplished so much so rapidly that it became the subject of a well received Plenary Session this morning (Day 4). I (Marjorie Courain) am speaking of the *Commission on Terminology and Nomenclature of Biology: Goals and Activities* by Lois Blaine.

In order to gain a balanced Perspective on CODATA '90, the final Program Committee meeting was held on the last day of the conference. Each of the members contributed one paragraph to the following summation:

The Day 1 Theme was Global Change: The quality of all the presentations was outstanding, from our **Keynote Speaker, Dr. Kenneth Wilson** speaking on *Future Directions of Science and Large Scale Computing* to the Countries' Poster Session at the end of the day.

The Global Change Day was a milestone for CODATA. It reflected the power of a multidisciplinary attack on the problem and the need for long term data sets from all parts of the world. The volume and diversity of data is perhaps new to CODATA. It brought people with new-to-CODATA disciplinary foci.

All country delegates were asked to present a poster of Global Change activities in their country. Dr. Thomas Malone chaired the Poster Round Table and Cynthia Carter served as Rapporteur. It was a good start for discussions with data representatives from all countries, and those with experience in those countries. Both Tom Malone and Peter Thacher stressed that much of the interaction between the geosphere and biosphere occurs in the vast geographic areas and large human populations of the lesser developed counties. The ultimate challenge is to understand and manage the interactions between economic growth and productivity of food, goods, and services, and health maintenance that require energy sources as well as waste management, which cannot be reasonably achieved without an understanding of the causes and effects of what we have come to call global change.

This provided a valuable contribution, a mechanism for discussion and sharing of thoughts on what the CODATA program on IGBP ought to consider. It showed the range of data programs from remote-sensing data that develops geographic mapping technique (*e.g.*, Israel's poster) to ecological and health data aspects (Hungary). It also showed that there remains a need to put our efforts into bringing the biological and ecological sciences more fruitfully into the IGBP, a task that will be a major challenge in terms of CODATA's role in IGBP.

Spatial Data was the theme of Day 2: Significant thrust in various disciplines. 2-D and 3-D representations of data fundamental to analysis of large data volumes. Plenary (Day 2) on Arctic by Doug Posson gave a good example by both talk and presentation of a whole new way of presenting data applicable to many disciplines.

Error Propagation and tracking common to many disciplines. It was a theme that ran through a number of the talks. Dealing with levels of the resulting uncertainty is a topic that came up and should be considered in the future.

Human factors: in design, building, and later, integration of disparate databases are often forgotten in execution leading to compounding of mistakes. They have an impact on overall quality of data. We have powerful systems now, but we should remember that powerful systems can compound mistakes.

In addition to Global Change as a major new topic for CODATA, sessions on the other themes of the Conference also had strong cross-disciplinary attendance.

Three significant trends in Biology were well covered: the human genome project, interaction between databases, and nomenclature and terminology.

At CODATA '90, the original charge always given to any ICSU committee to be inter- and cross-disciplinary is truly being achieved and pervaded the sessions and the CODATA activities.

Our Poster Sessions were patterned after CODATA '86 in Ottawa with chairmen and round-table discussions.

A PICTURE STORY OF THE CONFERENCE

Unfortunately, it is not possible to reprint the slides of my picture story of the Conference so I shall briefly list the captions here as I presented them, let people search their visual memories and hope that the slides shall one day be reprinted elsewhere. Some of the captions helped to fill in a bit of a story line.

1. Getting Ready for the Conference Breakfast in the Regency Club of the Hyatt on Sunday morning, July 15. Note how relaxed everyone is: D. Lide, S. Levasseur, P. Glaeser, C. Carter, and M. Courain.

2. **Registration Area** never looked like this again for the whole week, as more than 300 people registered for one of the largest CODATA conferences ever.

3. **The CODATA Secretariat Office** was just down the hall. It included the local arrangements, functions, volunteers, PCs, and a constantly used xerox machine. Everyone had some reason to go there at least once during the conference.

4. **The Opening Session** included welcome from the local arrangements chairman (G. Platau), the president of Downtown Columbus, Inc. (E. Armentrout), the Executive Director of Ohio's Thomas Edison Program (C. Coburn), our president (D. Lide), and scientific program chairman (M. Courain), who introduced our keynote speaker, Dr. Kenneth G. Wilson.

5. **Our Keynote Speaker, Dr. Kenneth Wilson** speaking on *Future Directions of Science and Large Scale Computing* challenged us to look back and ahead 400 years. Questions and response from the audience ran the session into overtime and got our conference off to an exciting start.

6. **Our Day 1 Speakers** allowed us to use a photo opportunity to record all of them who were participating in the Global Change sessions.

7. **Coffee Break** after the keynote session just outside the ballroom provided attendees with a chance to talk a little more with Dr. Wilson.

8. **Opening of the Exhibits** was on Monday afternoon.

9. **Database Demonstrations** were held on Tuesday and Wednesday afternoons, most of them complementing the presentations in the sessions.

10. **Day 2 Plenary Speaker, Dr. Douglas Posson** speaking on *Geographic Information Systems: the Arctic, a Sensitive Subset of the Globe* illustrated his talk with an on-line system demonstration which kept his audience involved even during the coffee break that followed.

11. **Our Day 2 Speakers** included many from materials data systems, expert systems and other knowledge tools.

12. **The Columbus Museum of Art** was open on Tuesday evening for us to enjoy its impressive collection of art and to be their guest at an evening long reception, during which we met the wives and husbands of the attendees. M. Courain with Gerard and Mrs. Platau and another member of CAS.

13. At the same reception, M. Courain with G. Rosenblatt (USNC) and L. Gurvich (U.S.S.R.).

14. **Day 3 Plenary Speaker, Dr. Charles Cantor** is included in this slide of the Day 3 speakers. His talk on *Human Genome Sequencing: Technical, Legal, and Ethical Issues* gave added emphasis to the inclusion of both the biosciences as well as the geosciences within CODATA.

15. **The Secretariat Office** continued to be as busy as the meeting rooms, as they prepared copies of all invited papers for Scientific Program Committee review before publication in the **Data for Discovery** Volume of Proceedings of the Conference.

16. **Pre-Banquet Entertainment** at our reception in the Galbraeth Pavilion set the mood for an evening of relaxation and enjoyment.

17. **A CODATA Non-binding Banquet Resolution** was offered by Bill Begell on the CODATA semidimensionless parameter.

18. **Day 4 Plenary Speaker, Ms. Lois Blaine** is included in the slide of Day 4 speakers. She discussed the impressive progress of the CODATA Commission on the Terminology and Nomenclature of Biology established just two years ago.

19. **Luncheon Meeting of the CODATA '90 Scientific Program Committee** included a discussion of their views on the conference. Members shown in the photo are Drs. D. Abir, A. Tsugita, and M. Krichevsky.

AUTHOR INDEX